LA GRANGE PUBLIC LIBRARY

3 1:

MW01015033

LA GRANGE
PUBLIC LIBRARY

10 West Cossitt Avenue
La Grange, IL 60525
lagrangelibrary.org   708.215.3200

Gloria Swanson

ALSO BY STEPHEN MICHAEL SHEARER

Beautiful: The Life of Hedy Lamarr

Patricia Neal: An Unquiet Life

LA GRANGE PUBLIC LIBRARY
10 WEST COSSITT
LA GRANGE, ILLINOIS 60525

Gloria Swanson

THE ULTIMATE STAR

Stephen Michael Shearer

WITHDRAWN

Thomas Dunne Books

St. Martin's Press  New York

AUG 2013

An appendix to *Gloria Swanson: The Ultimate Star,* detailing her film, television, radio, and stage career, can be downloaded from the author's Web site, www.smsmybooks.com.

Frontispiece: Gloria Swanson photographed by Edward Steichen, 1924

THOMAS DUNNE BOOKS.
An imprint of St. Martin's Press.

GLORIA SWANSON. Copyright © 2013 by Stephen Michael Shearer.
Foreword copyright © 2013 by Jeanine Basinger. All rights reserved.
Printed in the United States of America. For information, address
St. Martin's Press, 175 Fifth Avenue, New York, N.Y. 10010.

www.thomasdunnebooks.com

www.stmartins.com

Library of Congress Cataloging-in-Publication Data

Shearer, Stephen Michael, 1951–
    Gloria Swanson : the ultimate star / Stephen Michael Shearer.
        pages   cm
    ISBN 978-1-250-00155-9 (hardcover)
    ISBN 978-1-250-01366-8 (e-book)
    1. Swanson, Gloria.   2. Motion picture actors and actresses—United States—Biography.
I. Title.
    PN2287.S9S53 2013
    791.4302'8092—dc23
    [B]   2013003731

St. Martin's Press books may be purchased for educational, business, or promotional use. For information on bulk purchases, please contact Macmillan Corporate and Premium Sales Department at 1-800-221-7945 extension 5442 or write specialmarkets@macmillan.com.

First Edition: September 2013

10   9   8   7   6   5   4   3   2   1

791.4302
SWA

This book is for my mother,

Billie Melba Sypult Turner

(February 12, 1925–January 26, 2013),

and is dedicated to those who

treasure and understand the importance of motion pictures—

its history, its stars, its need for perpetuation—

and to all

"those wonderful people out there in the dark."

Contents

CONTENTS

[I] wish you [a] long [journey], full of adventure, full of knowledge . . .

Better [you] take many years . . . [so that you] are old [when] you reach the island, wealthy with all that you have gained on the way . . .

[And] wise as you have become, with so much experience, you will understand what it means . . .

> *Ithaca*, 1911
> Literal translation from the Greek
> Constantine P. Cavafy

Love has no other desire but to fulfill itself.

> On Love
> From *The Prophet*, 1923
> Kahlil Gibran

Foreword

BY JEANINE BASINGER

Gloria Swanson might have been tiny (only 4'11" tall), but as we all know, she was also *big*. (It was the movies that got small.) How big *was* Swanson? It's hard to believe. She was actress, producer, businesswoman, fashion designer, writer, nutritionist, self-publicist, pioneer health food advocate, wife to six husbands, mother of three, grandmother of seven, and yes, of course, a world-famous silent movie star, one of the few who continued her fame into the sound era. Although today most people know her only as Norma Desmond, the tragic has-been from *Sunset Boulevard* (1950), Swanson's life and career were nothing short of spectacular.

Swanson is much more than Norma Desmond, even though Desmond was enough for any one career. DeMille called Gloria Swanson "the movie star of all movie stars" when she decided to embrace an extravagant off-screen lifestyle in the 1920s. She was celebrated as "the second woman in Hollywood to make a million [Mary Pickford would have been the first], but the first to spend it." Swanson lived it up. She was ahead of her time in understanding that "movie star" was itself a role, one to be lived off screen as well as on. She was scandalous, flamboyant, quotable, unpredictable, and fans couldn't get enough of her. What makes Swanson so terribly interesting, however, is that she was also practical, hardworking, ambitious, and ultimately a survivor.

Some movie stars have sensational careers, but dull lives. Some have sensational lives, but dull careers. With Swanson, nothing is dull. Her personal life
plays like a crazy movie plot (those six husbands are the least of it). Her filmography is a Who's Who list of Hollywood royalty with co-stars and collabora-
tors such as Charlie Chaplin, Rudolph Valentino, Cecil B. DeMille, Erich Von
Stroheim, Mack Sennett, et al. Her movies are rich and varied. There are
at least three on-screen Swansons: slapstick comedienne, glamorous fashion
plate, and serious actress. I love all three, and have a favorite movie moment
for each one. In the 1925 comedy *Stage Struck*, Swanson, a natural clown, plays
a waitress in a pancake house. She juggles trays, flips cakes, falls down, gets
kicked in the pants, but hits her high note when she puts on a boxer's outfit to
climb in the ring (billed as "Kid Sock 'Em") to knock out her rival, Gertrude
Astor. (Those who think Lucille Ball was the only beautiful woman who could
do physical comedy should see Swanson in *Stage Struck*.) In her fashion roles,
on the other hand, Swanson was the ultimate 1920s symbol of the sophisticated, soignée modern American woman.

She might have been short in height, but she could still swan around
loaded with fur, jewels, fifty-foot trains, high headdresses, and peacock
feathers. My favorite is Swanson's bathtub scene in *Male and Female* (1919).
Everything stops dead while she disrobes, immerses in bubbles, and then
showers in rose petals. Even without any clothes on, Swanson was a fashion-
ista. I love her comedy and her baubles, but I probably love her best when
she's a serious actress. As the title character in *Sadie Thompson* (1928), she
uses her eloquent and expressive face when Sadie repents for her life as a
prostitute. Swanson plays it slowly, removing all her natural vibrant energy,
letting life leak out of her, body and soul. She collapses into herself, deflating
from a sexy hotcha honey down into a remorseful little mouse . . . right before a viewer's eyes.

How can a woman like this be more or less forgotten today, reduced to one
latter-day performance, no matter how great it might have been? Although
Swanson wrote her autobiography (a bestseller) in 1980, there's not been a
single full-length book written about her in the three decades since. It's high
time someone told Swanson's story from a fresh, objective point of view, using
the now-available materials in the Harry Ransom Center in Austin, Texas. As

a young woman, Swanson promised, "I have decided that when I am a star, I will be every inch and every moment the star!" She more than lived up to that promise, and there's nobody better than Stephen Michael Shearer to tell us in every detail how she did it, both on and off the screen.

Gloria Swanson

Introduction

Long before Hollywood made stars,
there were stars who made Hollywood.
—*A&E Biography*, "The Greatest Star," July 29, 1997

During the golden age of silent motion pictures, the 1920s, Gloria Swanson was the biggest film star in the world. By 1925 her pictures such as *Male and Female, Beyond the Rocks, Her Gilded Cage, Bluebeard's Eighth Wife, The Humming Bird, A Society Scandal,* and *Manhandled,* all for Famous Players–Lasky/Paramount, had made millions. Swanson's face was immediately recognizable around the world, and fans and foes alike could not get enough of her. Through her own forceful determination, choice scripts, important directors, and extraordinary good luck, Swanson embodied what it was to be a movie star, living big in films as well as in real life. Her every move drew attention, men desired her, and women emulated her fashions and style.

In retrospect, Swanson has emerged as one of Hollywood's very first film icons. Where Charlie Chaplin, the "Little Tramp," made us laugh, Lillian Gish, the eternal virgin, brought us tears, Pearl White gave us thrills, Theda Bara sent temperatures rising, Douglas Fairbanks and William S. Hart were our heroes, and Mary Pickford was America's Sweetheart, a somewhat homely, gauche, and uneducated girl from Illinois named Gloria Swanson became the screen's very first glamour queen.

"To the movie audiences of the twenties, Gloria Swanson was the embodiment of the American dream of beauty, wealth, and sophistication," wrote one author. "Petite, chic, her teeth dazzling white, her coiffure flawless and gleaming like patent leather, she was the queen of Hollywood. Her appeal to men was obvious, yet women, too, were attracted. As they watched her sweep through luxurious settings in sumptuous costumes, she reflected their daydreams. This was what it was like to be rich and beautiful. They studied every detail and imitated what they could . . . [She] exerted an attraction that went beyond commonplace physical beauty. There were more beautiful women in the movies, but none possessed her silken grace and regal self-assurance."[1]

Gloria knew at an early age what she wanted to be. When she became a star in the 1920s, an era marked by opulence and poverty, glamour and drabness— an age when our culture was healing from the horrors of World War I, racing with the excitement of opportunity and prosperity—Hollywood was evolving. The stars of the '20s believed their careers would last forever, yet many did not survive the decade as the silent film gave way to the "talkies."

"Gloria always knew what was right for Gloria," said one of her contemporaries. "She always made the right decisions; films, men, marriages, business. She always knew when to push it away and say she had had enough. Gloria was always independent. And she always survived."[2] "Gloria did more than represent all that to her movie audiences," recalled silent film actress Colleen Moore. "She represented it to everybody in Hollywood as well. And when you add to her glamour a very good mind, a sparkling wit, a talent for conversation, and a childlike quality of mischief and laughter, you get a combination that is devastating."[3]

Movie magazines perpetuated the myth of these film gods. "We were the romance and the royalty of the U.S. We were the fairy tales come true," Gloria once said.[4] Actress Doris Kenyon told a writer, "Gloria showed the rest of us how to be movie stars. We had to learn. She was born one."[5] "We've never had a star that twinkled brighter than Gloria," wrote columnist Hedda Hopper in 1950.[6] Film director Cecil B. DeMille deemed, "When you put them all together and add them up, Gloria Swanson was the movie star of all movie stars."[7]

Film historian Richard Koszarski has noted that Swanson's movie career did not display a "conventional arc of achievement," but rather a "series of plateaus."[8] Beginning in films in 1914, Gloria rose from the ranks of extras to become a leading lady in less than five years, moving over to Mack Sennett's studio for a series of short comedies, and eventually landing a feature contract with the old Triangle Company. Discovered by DeMille and signed to Famous Players–Lasky, which became Paramount, Gloria glistened in one opulent and sophisticated marital sex drama after another, decked out in tons of jewels, yards of satins, and hundreds of furs and feathers.

"It must be admitted that few, if any, of Gloria's films were exactly works of art," wrote another film historian. "They were too flamboyant, too determined to be 'sock' attractions . . . Gloria's acting, often stirringly dramatic and sometimes surprisingly tender, was prone to theatrics and mannerisms of gesture and expression."[9] And indeed, her silent films followed a successful formula. Sadly, today many are lost. Those that survive are surprisingly vital and captivating.

Silent motion picture acting was different from today's. "In those days we used to have to figure out what we were going to do to portray a thought," Gloria said in 1975. "It might be good in the dialogue, but dialogue wouldn't show on the screen. The more you could show how you felt by the movements of your body or the things that you did the better actor you were."[10] Because movies were silent, with the musical accompaniment supplied in movie houses ranging from rickety single pianos or small combos to full symphonic orchestras, film acting by necessity had to be expressed physically. Swanson's later performances were often highly mannered because her style of acting had been honed and polished in the silent era.

Swanson has two stars on the Hollywood Walk of Fame—one for her achievements in films and one for her work in television. After her film popularity waned, she became a pioneer in the new medium of television in the late 1940s. Surprisingly, her television work was not only prolific but often very good. By necessity she had to tone down her acting for the intimate small screen. Some of Swanson's best work can be found scattered among the few dramatic television programs in which she starred.

Yet, even as her silent films have faded from memory, viewers are still mesmerized by Swanson's brilliant 1950 comeback in *Sunset Boulevard,* the one motion picture she will forever be associated with and remembered for. Whenever *Sunset Boulevard* is mentioned, one wants to quote. The script by Billy Wilder, Charles Brackett, and D. M. Marshman Jr. is timeless, and more apropos as the years fly by:

JOE GILLIS (William Holden): Wait a minute—haven't I seen you before? I know your face.

NORMA DESMOND (Gloria Swanson): Get out! Or shall I call my
   servant?
GILLIS: You're Norma Desmond. You used to be in silent pictures—you
   used to be big.
DESMOND: I *am* big. It's the pictures that got small.

There was indeed a great deal of Gloria Swanson in the character of Norma Desmond. She lived opulently, spending every dime she ever earned. She enjoyed an important silent movie career; as Desmond's servant and former director Max, portrayed by Swanson's former director Erich von Stroheim, proudly proclaims, "Madame is the greatest star of them all." Desmond owned the most gloriously gaudy and elaborate of Hollywood mansions (Swanson's at her peak came complete with an army of servants); she was chauffered about Hollywood in the most expensive limousines, dressed in couturier fashions, expensively bejeweled, and elegantly coiffed. She was a star. Her commands were etched in stone, and people trembled at her disapproval. There the similarities cease.

Gloria did not live in the past, and she was not unbalanced. But she was difficult, and she was completely narcissistic, void of sincere modesty. Her self-absorption, which doomed her marriages, equally distanced her from her children during crucial periods of their lives. Her younger daughter, Michelle Farmer Amon, once commented, "I wasn't really close to my mother; in fact I was terrified of her . . . We had what you might call a love-hate relationship. Her idea of having a lot of children was fine, but I question whether she should have confined us with a nanny and not seen us. Maybe she should have sacrificed a bit of her life to care for us. It was, however, another era and in those days people did not kiss and cuddle their children. She would sort of kiss the air around my head."[11] Years before, Michelle stated sadly, "Being Gloria Swanson's daughter has not been simple."[12]

However, granddaughter Brooke Anderson Young recalled that later in life Gloria had mellowed considerably. Never openly reflective, Swanson still possessed the star quality and the allure that captivated millions of fans. Said Brooke, "Her commanding presence was that of a lady, always dressed in hats, a scarf, or a turban, and gloves. Her porcelain skin and red, always red, lipstick were an exquisite combination with her deep blue eyes, adorned with inch-long false eyelashes, and teeth that glowed with what my mother often said, 'an extra layer of enamel.' She laughed frequently and enjoyed life to the fullest, never a gossip, never one to reminisce. She lived in the present, full of spiritual quest and gratitude for whatever the day would bring."[13]

After her film career ended with the advent of the talkies—she had produced the last handful of her pictures—Gloria sought other avenues to express her energies and talent. She took to the stage, she became a patent industry chief, she took up fashion design, and she wrote society and fashion-tip newspaper columns. She even worked in the travel industry. And she was a pioneer in television.

During her last decades, Gloria was adamant about proper nutrition and diet. Her radical views were expressed openly, sometimes unexpectedly, and always with complete conviction. She had, after all, used her own body as a shrine to healthy living, curing her own illnesses and strongly influencing those who came into contact with her ideas of proper care. "During the time I knew her and especially when I first met her, she was attacked, lampooned, [and] mocked for her views on health," said actor Dirk Benedict, star of television's *Battlestar Galactica* and *The A-Team*. "It is hard to communicate how different the times were. Curing her ovarian cancer with diet just amused the hell out of the Establishment . . . medicine, Hollywood, talk show hosts, everyone. She was way, way ahead of her time and would NOT bend nor be quiet about it . . . You don't meet too many people in your lifetime, famous and otherwise, who have the courage to live and defend their personal convictions, no matter what the consequences."[14]

"She was incredibly feminine in appearance, but she had a masculine mind," said her daughter Michelle. "She had a dominating personality. She wanted to do all the jobs [on the set]—the lighting, camerawork, everything. She made sure what she said was the law."[15] The petite Swanson's need to dominate was also one of her major flaws. She possessed a determination and conviction of self-worth that threatened the masculinity of her husbands, lovers, and male associates. At the same time she was well aware of the power of her sensuality and sexuality, and used these attributes to seduce her conquests.

There is no doubt that Gloria loved herself; her own children and grandchildren remembered many loving things about her, but cuddles, her presence, and kisses were not among those memories. Of all her six husbands she was fond of only one—husband number three, Henri de la Falaise. By her own admission, the only man she ever really loved was her father. (Others would say she only loved her mother.) Her legions of paramours more or less served their purposes for whatever amount of time she allotted them. Yet from all of them—Mickey Neilan, Joel McCrea, Joseph Kennedy, Herbert Marshall, Gustave Schirmer, Lewis Bredin, and the rest—it was always *romance* Swanson was seeking. She never found in a man the love she felt for herself.

Gloria carefully selected moments of her work and life to include in her autobiography, a book she herself did not actually pen but authorized. In the process she created her own history. One writer noted in regard to her affair with Joseph P. Kennedy, for instance, "Swanson's autobiography is exceedingly well written (thanks in part to ghostwriters, including Wayne Lawson and William Dufty) and it has been taken verbatim . . . ever since. Yet when her accounts are compared with newspapers of the day, other witnesses, or most convincingly her own papers, events are occasionally out of order and her actions are slanted to position herself as an otherwise intelligent person overwhelmed by Kennedy's strength and sincerity. However, she doesn't create events out of whole cloth and that is what makes her account . . . so intriguing."[16]

Gloria Swanson was so much more than just Norma Desmond. She was a unique woman who managed to create a remarkable career in motion pictures in an era when most women were resigned to marriage, children, and housework. She was a woman who explored uncharted ground in Hollywood, which transformed her into a star. Gloria was always keen on looking ahead, scouting untraveled fields to conquer, and searching endlessly for new ideas and adventures. Her own ego forbade her limitations. She saw no boundaries.

"Never say never," Swanson once said, "for if you live long enough, chances are you will not be able to abide by its restrictions. Never is a long, undependable time, and life is too full of rich possibilities to have restrictions placed upon it."[17] During the course of her eighty-four years, Gloria Swanson created in our culture what it was to be a star. To the public she was a film idol. To other great stars of her own day, she was their ideal, the ultimate star.

1

Chicago

"When I was a little girl, I used to dream day dreams all day long," Gloria Swanson once told her secretary. "I dreamed of having all the pretty things that every girl wants. I dreamed of finding happiness in love. The only difference between the average girl and myself was that I set about making my dreams come true."[1]

Gloria always lived by her own beliefs. She once stated quite emphatically, "I feel sure that unborn babies pick their parents."[2] She never believed anything was accidental. By that same reasoning, babies probably also pick where they are born. For Gloria, it was in Chicago, Illinois.

The 1890 U.S. Census reported the nation's Swedish population to be over 800,000 (causing a major concern in Sweden, as its national population had begun to dwindle). Most Swedish immigrants were young and unmarried Lutherans. Primarily they were farmers. Yet some settled in urban communities such as Chicago's "Swede Town," adopting new trades to earn enough money to eventually buy farms. In 1900, Chicago could boast of being the world's fifth-largest city, a large percentage of its population being of German, Irish, Swedish, and Polish decent. By 1910, the city supported 407 movie houses, twice more per capita than New York City.

Whereas Swedish immigration was fueled by economic opportunity, Polish

immigration was ignited by cultural suppression, brought on by an age of in-
dustrialization, turning many peasant Polish farmers into migrant workers. By
1900, Chicago and its suburbs were home to one of the largest Polish American
communities in the country. One could not walk down a city block without
hearing Polish spoken.

Into this melting pot was born Gloria Swanson. Her Swedish-Lutheran
paternal grandfather was Jons (Americanized to James or John) Peter Swanson, a shoemaker born in November 1849 in Vastina (Småland), Sweden.[3] Jons
and his wife Johanna (nee Schoberg) had immigrated to Chicago with John's
younger brother Carl Albert. The family resided in Chicago's 11th District on
West Elizabeth Street. Jons and Johanna would have a total of thirteen children, according to Gloria, including her aunt May and two uncles, Charles and
Jonathan.

Joseph Theodore, the oldest of their sons, was born in Chicago in November
1874. He met Adelaide M. Klanowski, born July 15, 1878, in the summer of 1897.[4]
Adelaide, called Addie, was the daughter of saloonkeeper and shoemaker Herman Klanowski, born in Prussia in 1849, and his wife Bertha May (one of another
thirteen children), who was born in Baden-Baden, Germany, in 1856.

Gloria's great-grandfather May came to America in 1852. His house on
LaSalle Street burned to the ground during the Great Chicago Fire of 1871, and
the family lost everything. After their marriage in the 1880s Herman and Bertha resided on Clark Street with Bertha's sister Clara. The family later moved to
213 Ashland Avenue around the turn of the century. Herman and Bertha had
two sons, Edward, born January 1873, and Herman Jr., born in 1877. After granddaughter Gloria was born, Bertha divorced Herman Klanowski and remarried
a pleasant fellow named Mr. Lew, by whom she had a daughter named Lola.

Joseph T. Swanson was a handsome, lean, and restless man with blue eyes. He
had once worked for a local politician, but found politics not his métier. He became a civilian clerk attached to the Army Transport Service. (Later, after serving
in Europe during the Great War, he was given the rank of captain.) On January 4,
1898, in Milwaukee, Wisconsin, Joseph Swanson married Addie Klanowski.

Addie was not well educated. And because she was a bit of a romantic, she
chose marriage over life as a Polish working girl, which usually meant toiling
in restaurants, laundries, or the garment district. Joseph and Addie moved to
a two-story wooden frame house located at 150 Seminary Avenue in Chicago

soon after their marriage.[5] On the first Monday of Holy Week, March 27, 1899, their only child, a girl, was born.[6] The attending physician was thirty-four-year-old Dr. Willis D. Storer, who three years earlier had delivered in Los Angeles the future film dance director Busby Berkeley. The Swansons christened their daughter Gloria May Josephine Swanson. Even as an infant, Baby Gloria was fashionably adorned.

Addie was quite a seamstress, and to distract attention from what she felt were Gloria's large ears, she fashioned huge bows for her hair and large hats for her to wear. She always saw that her daughter was dressed in clean and fancy dresses, usually with large collars. Despite Bertha's stern warning that Addie spoiled the child, she willfully did just that, and Joseph reluctantly allowed his wife her way.

"She never dressed the way the other girls dressed," Gloria's second daughter, Michelle, would recall in an interview. "She always had something particular. She told me that when she was a child her mother would make something special for her."[7] Though she was a pretty young girl with an olive complexion and almond-shaped blue eyes—perhaps her most attractive feature—Gloria also was her worst critic. "How I hated my teeth," she remarked years later. "They were so big and square that I always kept my mouth covered with my hand when I smiled."[8] A modest remark, and selectively true.

When Gloria entered grade school she was determined not to pay attention in class, much to the consternation of her second-grade teacher, Bertha L. Wernecke. She would spend her time drawing pictures of herself, her parents, and her pets.[9] Addie took her child's doodlings as God-given talent, and, according to Gloria, enrolled her in classes at the Chicago Art Institute at an early age.

While attending the Art Institute, she wrote, she once peeked into an art class where a half-clad male model was posing. Sex, which was never discussed in front of her, held a deep and insatiable fascination. She expounded on this some years later. "I hated being a child," she told a movie magazine writer. "I wanted terribly to be grown-up. I was never interested in things of childhood. I felt always that I was simply marking time through an intolerably dull and monotonous prelude to something real, something mysterious and poignant . . . No doubt sex and marriage and the having of children were the hidden, half-guessed at things that so intrigued me."[10]

There exist pictures of little Gloria playing with her dolls. However, as Gloria

Swanson, movie star, she would distance herself from her childhood normalcy. "I never played with dolls," she claimed. "I had as a child no maternal complex. I seldom played with other children. I preferred my own company or the company of adults from whom I might, at some unexpected moment, catch a glimpse of the mystery I continually felt them to know."[11]

In 1907 Joseph was transferred to the Key West Barracks in Florida. Addie and Gloria remained in Chicago until the late spring. The importance of her father in Gloria's early life and his influence on her emotional development cannot be overestimated. Her feelings for men as an adult would be governed by her longings for security and guidance from the man she most desired in her life. "My father was the greatest single influence in my life during the years when my mind was plastic, when it was in the formative state," she related in the 1920s. "But for him I might have been a stenographer or a clerk in a department store . . . It was his philosophy in my up-bringing more than anything else which gave me the wisdom, the ability and the strength to take advantage of the opportunities which, later in life, came my way."[12] Her own elder daughter confirmed Joseph's impact on his only child. "She had a keen mind and curious mind," Gloria Daly stated. "She always said her father instilled that in her—to search out the answers for a lot of things."[13]

Addie and Gloria joined Joseph in the spring of 1908. He met them at the Tampa Bay Hotel in Tampa, and the family spent the day sightseeing. At the Key West Army Base, they soon settled into their new house, which stood on stilts and had a large veranda.

Gloria loved Florida because of the sunshine and the feel of the tropics. She also discovered she liked to sing. Attending a Protestant church, she was asked by her Sunday school teacher to warble a solo at a service. Imitating Addie's singing voice, eight-year-old Gloria somehow got through "The Rosary." With that and the encouragement of a local actress named Venice Hayes, she sang again in a show staged at the Odd Fellows Hall, on Caroline Street. She chose "As the World Rolls On," sans accompaniment, as no one was available to play the piano. Amateur night in the Keys for sure, but she felt like a star, soaking up the attention.

On October 11, 1909, a major hurricane hit the Keys. The women and children on the base had been evacuated, Addie and Gloria departing by boat to New York. They then traveled by train to Chicago, where their hurricane survival story made Gloria popular among the other children. At the beginning of the summer Addie and Gloria rejoined Joseph in Key West.

In 1910 Joseph was restationed, and the family moved to San Juan, Puerto Rico. They would live there until 1913, with Addie and Gloria taking a boat to and from Florida and a train back and forth from New York or Florida to Chicago for visits. Gloria's education would suffer.

"I was in 16 different grammar schools," Gloria recalled. "Then I'd be whisked away, because my father was in the Army and I was an Army brat. I'd spend six months of the year in Chicago with my mother and grandmother, and six months in tropical countries with my father. I was always being put forward a grade, put backward a grade—on a treadmill. I don't think I learned *one* solid substantial thing in school."[14]

During their times together Joseph spoke intelligently to his only child, not imitating childish "baby talk" as did Addie. In Puerto Rico of a warm and heavily scented evening, when the heavenly Southern Cross was on display, the balmy trade winds wafting the air, Joseph would tell Gloria the names of stars and explain the conundrum of infinity. Gloria longed to explore the unknown, and these moments with her father she never forgot.

Gloria wore her hair long in pigtails or full down her back, sometimes with bangs, always with a large hat or with a bow atop her head. Pictures taken on board ship and in San Juan with other army children show her leading a pet goat and holding a blond doll. Gloria felt very special indeed. "I was an Army brat," she once remarked. "I hung around adults a lot but was shy with children my own age."[15]

Gloria's first acting role was in a public school production of *The American Girl*, in which she also sang a song backed by a chorus of other girls. A young beau sent her flowers, and her father posted a star on her dressing room door with her name on it—"Gloria Swanson," not Glory as everyone called her—which bolstered her importance. Thirteen-year-old Gloria knew she was good, and decided then and there on the stage of the San Juan Opera House to become an opera diva.

Gloria had been enrolled in private school in San Juan but convinced her parents to allow her to attend public school so she could perform in plays. She was also possibly motivated by the opportunity to be around boys. She had recently received a letter from young, blond Carlton Swiggett from New York, whom she had met while he was vacationing in Puerto Rico. She was determined to be his girlfriend.

As she approached puberty Gloria was very aware of her burgeoning sexuality. "Looking back on my life," she related in an unedited recording in 1955, "what I tried to do was to find satisfaction for my physical as well as the mental . . . And this was a very difficult thing to do . . . and my father was probably the person that I was in love with . . . I can remember when I was quite young, maybe thirteen or fourteen years old, the awakening pertaining to—sex. I can remember he smelled good to me and I already associate—because I have the nose of a rabbit—I always associate this sense of smell with people that I like . . . Also I looked up to him because there was nothing that I wanted to know that he didn't seem to be able to answer."[16]

Through her father Gloria met Medora Grimes, a year older than she, from Staten Island, New York, whose wealthy family Joseph had shown around Puerto Rico. Before Medora sailed back to New York, Gloria promised to visit her. Her self-assurance knew no boundaries. "I was enormously self-confident," she later told a journalist. "I always expected to be invited to everything and to be the center of things when I was invited. If a play was given, in school, at a club, in any gathering I was confident that I would be asked to be the star performer. I was the invincible and central factor of the universe, I thought."[17]

In 1913 Joseph was stationed at Governors Island off Manhattan, and Gloria and her mother moved back to Chicago to live with Grandma Lew. Gloria was reluctantly enrolled into eighth grade at Chicago's Lincoln School. Though she was never very good at disciplined study, on June 26, 1914, she graduated, effectively ending her formal education. She was fifteen years old.

2

Essanay

The week after her graduation, Gloria's Aunt Ingrid (Inga) Johnson asked her if she would like to visit Chicago's Essanay movie studio, located at 1333–45 West Argyle Street. Inga, fascinated with motion pictures, knew Essanay Studio's co-owner, George Kirke Spoor.

Gloria picked out one of her new outfits stitched by Addie. In her autobiography, she would often bend the facts, change them radically, or conveniently forget them altogether. But with fashions, especially *her* fashions, she seemed to never forget a detail: an Irene Castle–styled black-and-white checkered ensemble, a slit up the skirt front, with a green waistcoat, and a black cutaway jacket, she would later recall.[1] She also wore a little Knox felt hat as well.

On the day of the visit, Inga and Gloria trolleyed to Argyle Street, where they were met at the entrance of Essanay by a young fellow who would guide them through the studio. They witnessed first a highly volatile slapstick routine being filmed under intensely bright, hot lights in a huge basement area. Much to Gloria's disgust they saw a large man dressed as a maid being pummeled by a dozen sweaty men and women in a roughhouse sequence.

Taken upstairs to watch a wedding scene in progress for another film, Gloria found the proceedings more to her liking. Essanay's stars at that time included the screen's most romantic leading man, Francis X. Bushman, the beautiful Beverly Bayne, actresses Gerda Holmes and Ruth Stonehouse, and the handsome actors Bryant Washburn and Richard Travers, names now long forgotten.

Among the comedians Essanay employed for their slapstick comedies so popular at the time was cross-eyed Ben Turpin. The fellow dressed in drag in the basement was Wallace Beery.

According to Gloria, a casting director, Mr. Babile, approached her and asked for her name and address, stating that the studio was always interested in new faces. She was sure she had been noticed because of what she was wearing. The following day she was asked to report to the studio at one o'clock that afternoon, and to wear the same outfit.

Assured she would not have to do slapstick, Gloria returned to Argyle Street. She was then shuffled upstairs to where the same twenty-some actors were gathered in a continuation of the wedding scene from the day before. She was instructed to rush up to the bride, Gerda Holmes, and hand her a bouquet of flowers and smile until Holmes looked at the bridegroom, Richard Travers. The sequence took but a few minutes.[2] For that day she was paid $3.25, a fortune for doing nothing, or so she thought.

Gloria and her aunt spent the following day shopping at the department store Marshall Field's. When they returned home, Addie told her she had missed a call from the people at Essanay who had wanted to use her that day in the same outfit for a continuation of the wedding scene, a "portrait" sequence, to be filmed outside a church. (The picture was *At the End of a Perfect Day,* released on January 26, 1915.) Within a few days Essanay called again, and she was now used as a dress extra—meaning she supplied her own wardrobe—in a café sequence in another film (*The Song of the Soul,* released on October 2, 1914).[3]

Gloria liked the pay and agreed to do another bit in a party scene in yet another picture. On the arm of an older man, she was required to smile and shake hands with the host and hostess (*The Devil's Signature,* which was released September 11, 1914). The director, Harry McRae Webster, had also helmed the Holmes-Travers picture. According to Gloria, Webster was furious with her for not appearing for "the portrait scene" in the wedding film, and he berated her in front of strangers. With that she decided she would not continue work in photoplays. She had made $9.75 all told at Essanay. As far as she was concerned that was enough for her expenses for her planned trip to New York, and good riddance to motion pictures. Later, she defiantly wrote in her memoirs she wanted to become an opera singer.[4]

Despite Gloria's frequent denial that she ever wanted to be in movies,

Francis X. Bushman, in a recent biography, recalled a different scenario. "I was going into the office one morning when I saw this girl sitting on a railing," he recounted. "She was small, had a little piquant nose, and couldn't have been more than fourteen. Far too young and far too pretty to be hanging around such a den of wolves. I told her to get away from there; that she was just a kid and should be in school. But she came back again and again. Finally I told her that if I caught her there one more time I'd tell her mother. When I didn't see her the next day I felt I had done my good deed."[5]

Gloria took the train to New York and was met at Grand Central Terminal by Joseph, who then showed her the city. Visiting Medora Grimes at her large stone home, Gloria had her first glimpse of true opulence. The Grimeses threw a party the following week where Gloria was imperiously introduced to guests as the Cuban princess, the Spanish princess, or the Puerto Rican princess and was most self-conscious throughout the evening.

While Gloria was visiting New York, Addie notified her that Essanay was offering her a standard contract of $13.25 a week, or $20.00 if she worked on Saturdays. Her parents had quarreled a great deal about money over the years. Now she could earn nearly as much as her army captain father. Besides, Joseph was faced with possibly being transferred yet again, this time to Manila in the Philippines. Gloria could not fathom returning to school, only to transfer so far away. Her mind was set.

She shared her plans with her father. She would sign with Essanay, and with the money she earned she would continue classes at the Chicago Art Institute, to study privately and possibly become a singer. Joseph knew it was useless to try to change her mind. In turn, Gloria relied on her father's judgments. She wrote, "'Take your time, Glory,' Daddy said. 'Remember life is ninety-five percent anticipation and only five percent realization.'"[6] Back in Chicago, Gloria and Addie moved out of Grandma Lew's home and took an apartment of their own. And Gloria signed the Essanay contract.

The first film studio in Chicago, Essanay Studios was formed in 1907 by thirty-four-year-old Illinois-born George K. Spoor and his partner, twenty-seven-year-old film actor Gilbert M. "Broncho Billy" Anderson (born Max Aronson in Little Rock, Arkansas, in 1880). Together they created the name of their company from their initials, S and A. "The MGM of the Silents," as Essanay was later called, was initially located on North Wells Street in two brick buildings that are now the home of St. Augustine College, and later moved to Argyle Street. In 1913, a West Coast sister studio was constructed in Niles, California.

"Like most early film studios of the period," wrote one film historian, "the company was a fly-by-night operation. The cavernous warehouse was packed to the gills with a collection of broken-down props—old clothes, rusted cars, headless mannequins—and its small staff, a troupe of loud and often foul-mouthed former stage actors, puttered around the studio building sets, mending costumes, performing stunts before the camera, playing practical jokes on each other. Cameramen operated crude, hand-cranked machines, and due to poor indoor lighting, all filming had to be done outside. When the sky turned cloudy, the actors sullenly waited around the studio for the next sunny day."[7]

For ten brief years, by which time the motion picture industry had moved west, Spoor ran the Chicago studio and Anderson the California-based operation.[8] Together they produced a long and highly successful run of westerns and comedies, totaling nearly two thousand pictures, including fifteen hundred short and feature films made in Chicago and five hundred short pictures filmed in California. The Chicago Essanay also produced a successful series of romantic dramas starring screen lovers Beverly Bayne and Francis X. Bushman, who in 1925 would secure lasting screen immortality as Messala in MGM's epic *Ben-Hur: A Tale of the Christ*.

Also under contract at Essanay was a less than successful slapstick comic, the crude and burly actor named Wallace Beery, who appeared in short comedies, nearly thirty in all, as the large and homely maid named Sweedie, which turned minimal profits. Aside from Ben Turpin, there were no other major comic stars at the Chicago-based studio until 1914. "The 'Essanay gang' was eclectic, to say the least," wrote one biographer. "Actor Wallace Beery, a noisy drunk, chased starlets around the lot, Francis X. Bushman came to work in a lavender limousine, and the cross-eyed Ben Turpin was so homely and clumsy that it was comic."[9]

In early December 1914, the slightly built (5'3") Charles Spencer Chaplin, a former English music hall comedian, stepped off the train in Chicago with Gilbert M. Anderson. Anderson had wooed the comic away from California (and tempting offers from Universal Studios) after Chaplin's yearlong stay with Mack Sennett's Keystone Studios, where he starred or was featured at $100 a week in nearly three dozen short and feature comedies. Taking up residency in the Brewster Apartments on Diversey Parkway in Chicago, Chaplin had yet to hit his stride with his immortal persona the "Little Tramp," which he had visually introduced in Sennett's *Kid Auto Races at Venice* that very year. It would take him his tenure at Essanay, at $1,250 a week, with a $10,000 bonus for signing, to realize his enduring role.

In 1911, Louella O. Parsons, a $9-a-week employee in the syndication department of the *Chicago Tribune* who wrote short stories at night, was hired by Essanay as its chief scenario editor. Louella "sorted through the scripts that came to the studio"—not scripts as we think of them now, but brief plot summaries, most of them submitted by amateur movie buffs—"found some promising ones, and sent twenty-five-dollar checks to the lucky writers whose works would be made into films," wrote her biographer. "On her desk sat a row of boxes with the names of Essanay's directors, and Louella dropped the new scripts into the boxes randomly. 'Directors might yell and moan over my choice of story, but when they were handed a play by me, they didn't have any other court of appeal,' she recalled."[10]

Spoor was livid at the salary and contract Anderson had offered in order to acquire Chaplin. An efficiency man, Homer Boushey, was hired. He and Parsons clashed from the start. Boushey thought she was overpaid and financially irresponsible for spending up to $75 for a single screenplay. The studio decided to phase out Parsons's position and employ professional screenwriters. Eventually in 1915 Parsons priced herself right out of a job.

Gloria joined the ranks of contract extras, a fact she would long attempt to minimize and forget. Among those extras were her future leading man Rod La Rocque and the underaged Virginia Bowker, who shared a dressing room with her until Virginia was physically forced by her father to leave Essanay. Her second roomie was Agnes Eyre Henkel (later Ayres). Next door to the girls was star Beverly Bayne's dressing room.

Before he married her, Francis X. Bushman, then already wed and the father of five, would frequent Bayne's dressing room, which was against studio rules. Gloria and her roommates would tingle with excitement during those visits. Bushman was quite the peacock. He wore a massive amethyst ring, and in his lavender limo he had a small spotlight set to illuminate his magnificent profile for his adoring female admirers. Shortly before Gloria left Essanay, Bushman passed her in wardrobe and casually placed his hand on her exposed knee. She reacted by slapping him firmly on his celebrated face. Not one word passed between them.

Gloria received her first billing for a bit part in the Bushman-Bayne Ruritanian romance *The Ambition of the Baron* (released January 15, 1915). Then she and Virginia Bowker portrayed snobbish young girls attending a dressy affair in Wally Beery's *Sweedie Goes to College* (released February 8, 1915), directed by E. Mason "Lightning" Hopper. The film's plot told of the big and homely maid Sweedie assuming a position at a college girls' dormitory with numerous slapstick encounters. "I penciled on dramatic eyebrows and we wore our best clothes," Gloria recalled.[11] Beery helped Gloria and Virginia with their characters, suggesting they "believe" he was really a female and, to show how superior they felt, never look at Sweedie above the wrists as "she" waited on them and mugged, thus allowing the audience to feel smarter and more sympathetic to his character. "Remember, it's the maids just off the boat who go to pictures. Society folks don't," Beery said.

Gloria would later write that much of her time at Essanay was spent changing costumes and waiting in the basement to be called for the next scene. The director was the only one allowed a script, she said, and he would usually be the only one who knew what the scene was about.[12]

In his first film for Essanay, Chaplin was allowed near autonomy. He declined the original script offered him by Parsons and chose to improvise his way through the production. Chaplin, who always had a sharp eye for young girls, spotted Gloria at the studio and decided to test her for his leading lady.

Chaplin would spend an unsuccessful morning with the young girl, going through tried and true slapstick routines such as kicking each other in the pants, bumping into objects, and falling about. (Gloria wrote he made her laugh, though pictures made on the set that morning show a determined Chaplin and a very solemn Gloria.) Unfortunately, she could not handle spontaneous physical comedy, finding it unfunny. And she made little effort to conceal her displeasure. Try as he might, with his gentle voice and patient demeanor, Chaplin could not get a natural performance from her. And he did not see a future in comedy for this girl. The following day she was told that Mr. Chaplin believed she didn't have what it took to be in his picture."[13] Gloria was originally supposed to drop her purse, bend over, and receive a kick in the seat. She found this appalling and told Chaplin she she wouldn't do it—"I think it's vulgar anyway."[14]

Wrote Chaplin in his autobiography, "After I had had several interviews, one applicant seemed a possibility, a rather pretty young girl whom the company had just signed up. But oh, God! I could not get a reaction out of her. She was so unsatisfactory that I gave up and dismissed her."[15] Chaplin would candidly admit in later years, "She reminded me of myself. So I [didn't] want her to play in my films."[16] Physically it was true—they both had small bodies and large heads.

Until the day she died, the serious-minded Gloria Swanson fiercely denied she was ever in a Chaplin film. However, along with Agnes Ayres, Gloria can be seen in Chaplin's *His New Job* (released February 1, 1915) in the first part of the comedy as a stenographer typing at a desk with her hair piled atop her head. She then shared a brief sequence with Chaplin and disappeared for the remainder of the film. A satirical look at the movie industry, *His New Job* has Charlie (Chaplin) applying for a job at the Lockstone Film Studio (a take on Keystone). He stands in for the leading man, causing all sorts of mayhem, until the actor arrives and Charlie is fired.

His New Job is possibly the only glimpse of Gloria at Essanay still in existence; sadly, most of the Essanay films are lost. *His New Job* races along at a frantic pace, utilizing the new moving-camera effect—the camera actually moved as it filmed the action—so successfully executed in the classic 1914 Italian feature film *Cabiria*. In *His New Job* Chaplin is near his prime, humorously inserting moments of slapstick throughout, giving a strong foretaste of his genius to come. The critics raved. "It is absolutely necessary to laugh at Chaplin," wrote the *Chicago Tribune*.[17]

Gloria and Virginia Bowker would spend hours playing their ukuleles between scenes. With another new girlfriend, June Walker, and sometimes with Rod La Rocque, Gloria would lunch down the street at Sternberg's on the corner of Argyle and Broadway, where one could get a soda (or a beer) and a meatball for a nickel. Chaplin once treated Gloria to a soda at the Green Mill Gardens, known for its beautiful outdoor sunken gardens, on Broadway at Lawrence Avenue.

Gloria continued to be cast in bits, such as a maid in the society drama *The Misjudged Mrs. Hartley* (released January 15, 1915), with Bryant Washburn and Ruth Stonehouse. She finally landed a leading role in *The Fable of Elvira and Farina and the Meal Ticket*, written by George Ade (released February 3, 1915).

The story tells of Farina's father, the Meal Ticket (Rapley Holmes), becoming

rich and his wife Elvira (Lillian Drew) and her daughter Farina (Gloria) becoming uppity, traveling to Europe, and returning with pseudo-sophisticated
airs. Gloria recalled that she was informed she would be visible throughout the
film, and believing she was the star, she felt she would need many new changes
of outfits. When the director told the cast the plot of the story, Gloria knew it
would not be a "refined" epic, but another run-of-the-mill Essanay picture.[18] It
was supposed to be a comedy, but Gloria did not find it so.

More suited to her personality, insisted Gloria, were sophisticated dramas.
As a vamp, she somewhat amateurishly impersonated her way through *The
Romance of an American Duchess* (released June 8, 1915), in which she seduces
thirty-year-old Richard Travers away from Ruth Stonehouse. Gloria thought
naïvely that all she had to do to express sophistication and maturity was to put
her hair up and smoke endless cigarettes.[19] In the silly storyline, Gloria portrays an adventuress hired to break up the marriage of the Duke de Longtour
and an American heiress. The duke then befriends the adventuress, who tells
him of the plot, and all ends well.

There was a dramatic scene in the picture that required Gloria to cry. The
director asked if she needed help with her tears, and she assured him she
would produce them on cue. Gloria wrote in her memoirs that when the director called for action she performed before the camera in a highly emotional
state, impressing the cast and crew with her dramatics. Leaving the set to return to her dressing room, Gloria passed veteran character actress Helen Dunbar, who told her she would someday become a fine actress. Gloria's reply was
simple: "Yes, I know. I'm going to be very famous."[20]

Regarding *The Romance of an American Duchess*, film historian DeWitt
Bodeen wrote, "This was the film in which the future Swanson of glamorous
authority and potent star-chemistry first manifested itself, however elemen-
tary the incarnation. In some scenes she glows from the screen so incandescent that she almost throws the rather trivial little romantic drama
off-balance."[21]

Before he became a major film star in his own right, Wallace Beery was a
brawny, hard-living lout, unpolished and rough around the edges, a young
man who was strangely, sensuously attractive to young girls. He drove a swank,
sporty Stutz Bearcat to the studio every day and parked it next to Bushman's
lavender limo. Beery *was* somewhat handsome, looking a bit like the young

Melvyn Douglas, but without an educated vocabulary or much culture. Beery also possessed an animalistic manly and muscular body, and he harbored a no-nonsense approach to sex. He was exactly what the impressionable Gloria Swanson was looking for. According to her, Beery was quite a catch.

Every girl at the studio wanted Beery to give her a ride in his car after work. He had been a race car driver, or so he said. He once asked to drop Gloria off at her house. She accepted, with an attitude, feigning complete indifference to him. After several more after-work drives home, he asked her if she would like to see his digs. She agreed. As expected, once inside Wally made a pass, and Gloria, so she wrote, calmly turned around and walked out the door. He drove her home in silence.

Within weeks Gloria was starring (as "Gloria Mae") opposite Beery in *The Broken Pledge* (released June 17, 1915), a non-Sweedie film written by Parsons (though largely improvised) about three young women who vow never to wed and to remain independently liberated, a bit of an advanced idea for the era. Gloria wrote that after the interrupted pass episode she avoided Wally after 6:00 P.M., choosing rides with a chap who owned a Stanley Steamer. But Wally's Stutz Bearcat still fascinated, and his aggressive pursuit of her still caused her heart to race. The two soon began seeing each other regularly.

In late May 1915, after filming *The Broken Pledge,* a series of muddled events transpired that would change Gloria's life dramatically. Wally was accused by the irate parents of an underage minor at the studio of inappropriate behavior, which resulted in a check of birthdate records of all the young girls at Essanay. Gloria's job was saved as she was now sixteen, but Wally disappeared from the studio. At the same time, Gloria's father advised Addie and his daughter he was about to be transferred to Manila. Then Gloria received a postcard from Wally posted from Niles, California. He was at the western Essanay Studio to complete his contract. In her autobiography Swanson conveniently did not disclose what Wally wrote her or why.

Gloria's grandfather Klanowski had died, leaving Addie and her sister an inheritance large enough for Addie and Gloria to make a trip to California for a proper vacation before continuing on to the Philippines. Exactly what Gloria did between May 1915 and January 1916 when she departed for California remains clouded. When she left Essanay in Chicago, the studio's Mr. Babile wrote down the name of Mack Sennett and told Gloria she should look him up once she arrived out west. Then Gloria wrote Beery, this after the scandalous affair at the studio, to ask him if he knew a place she and her mother could stay once they reached Los Angeles.

Gloria's story remains suspicious. With the headway she was making in her career, it seems strange she would give it all up to move to Manila and to return to school. That seems implausible. The truth may be this—at that time she had her mind focused on working in California and her heart set on capturing Beery. Whether she agreed with her or not, Addie, who was unhappy in her own marriage, simply went along with her headstrong daughter's decisions.

Whatever the actual reasons for her departure from Chicago, in California Gloria's life would change forever.

3

Sennett

Wallace Fitzgerald Beery was born in Kansas City, Missouri, on April 1, 1885. His father, Noah W., was a police officer who earned $80 a month. Wally, as he was called by his mother Margaret, was the youngest of three brothers; William and Noah came before him. Rebellious and rambunctious as a youth, Wally ran away from home at the age of sixteen and joined the Ringling Bros. Circus as an assistant elephant trainer earning $3.50 a week. Two years later, in 1903, after being mauled by a leopard, Beery headed to New York, where he performed on the stage, landing work as a chorus boy along with his brother Noah for impresario Henry W. Savage. "But there was no lace on my cuffs," Beery boasted.[1] At over six feet in height, and weighing 190 pounds, Wally indeed cut quite a figure with the ladies.

Beery's big break came when he stepped in for Raymond Hitchcock (who himself suddenly had to skip town because of a morals charge involving a minor) in *The Yankee Tourist* in 1907, making Wally the toast of Broadway, though he never earned more than $70 a week. By 1912 he was broke, left stranded in Chicago after the closing of the play *The Balkan Princess*.

Wally was noticed in that production by film director Harry McRae Webster, however, and signed with Essanay Film Studio for $75 a week. In late July 1914, during the making of *Sweedie's Skate* (released September 21, 1914), he eyed the fifteen-year-old Gloria Swanson. As he would later recall, "I liked the looks of this Swanson girl. She was a darned sweet kid, modest as could be and pretty."[2]

To protect their interest after the morals charge, Essanay's Spoor and Anderson had sent Beery to the safety of the California studio, but the move proved a disaster. Soon Beery, so said the press, signed with a Japanese film company to make pictures overseas. Beery reneged on that and eventually contracted with the Universal Film Manufacturing Company, which had recently begun operation in the San Fernando Valley, near the Cahuenga Pass. There Beery directed and acted in a handful of unsuccessful film comedies, all released in 1916. (One of the pictures, *Sweedie the Janitor,* revived his film character.)

When Wally sent the postcard to Gloria that fall of 1915, that's all it took. She eagerly pursued the tall and tanned actor, who, with a beaming smile on his face, was waiting at the Santa Fe Depot in downtown Los Angeles to meet her and Addie in January of 1916.

According to Francis X. Bushman's memories of young Gloria, possibly there was another reason she pursued Wally west: "She was *in.* . . . She made it. Right away Wally Beery—the biggest wolf in the place—got to her and, before long, he *had* to marry her. Get the point?"[3]

Gloria's story of her and Wally's early relationship was somewhat more bucolic. In California before her arrival, Wally remarked to a friend who was looking at the autographed photo Gloria had given him, "She's a nice kid . . . but I don't know what I'll do with a wife. She's coming through, with her mother, and I'll marry her, I guess. She's a nice girl, all right."[4]

Gloria and her mother arrived in California, their intent obvious. Gloria and Wally were going to wed. She wrote in her memoirs that Wally had found a place for her and her mother to live, a two-room upper-floor apartment in a two-story building on Cahuenga Boulevard, then a tree-lined street. Wally then was rooming with his brother Noah in Niles.

Hollywood in 1916 was still a small agricultural community, surrounded by acres of oil derricks, fields of neatly planted lima beans, and in some areas pastures of carnations and poppies, the air heavy with the sweet scent of eucalyptus and orange groves. Walnut trees lined the railroad tracks.

The town of Hollywood, named in 1887, was incorporated in 1903. The first film studio in the Southern California area was the Selig Polyscope Company, which was built in 1909 in Edendale.[5] The first feature-length western shot in Hollywood was *The Squaw Man,* released in February 1914 by the Jesse L.

Lasky Feature Play Company, which was located at the corner of Selma and Vine Streets. The picture's directors were Oscar Apfel and Cecil B. DeMille.

The country's film industry, especially that part based in the Los Angeles area, flourished in the late 1910s. Most pictures were still made on the fly. Since there were no schools of motion picture study, they were often crudely filmed and acted. Most of the film players in California were neither highly educated nor stage trained. It was a hit-or-miss type of industry.

About the early days of filming in California, veteran director King Vidor recalled in 1980, "The whole idea of Hollywood in those days was very temporal, very precarious, with a feeling of uncertainty in the air . . . The making of motion pictures had not yet established itself as an industry, or an art form, to any recognizable degree. There was no feeling of lasting existence about it. Everything had an air of expendability."[6] In the 1920s, though, studios would become film factories, latching onto proven formulas and developing talent to fill the growing need for pictures as movie theaters sprang up all across the country.

Addie wasted little time with her newfound freedom in California and started seeing a wealthy fellow named Matthew Burns. Gloria herself was optimistic about her own future. According to her memoirs, Wally pleaded with her to follow up on the introduction to Sennett, and she decided to do so—but not before she became Mrs. Wallace Beery. Though she wrote she married Beery long after she began with Sennett, in fact they wed before she signed her Keystone contract.

According to Gloria the two courted for several months (actually it was less than two), with Wally driving up weekends from Niles Canyon across the San Bernardino Mountains in his car, taking her fishing at Big Bear Lake, and warbling romantic tunes to her (he had a beautiful singing voice). "The primitive side of Gloria which so often flashes out in her pictures," wrote longtime newspaper writer Adela Rogers St. Johns, "yielded to Beery's immense strength and dominating masculinity."[7] "We had lots of fun together," Gloria would remember.[8] The two were married at the Pasadena City Courthouse on her seventeenth birthday, March 27, 1916. Addie was the delighted witness.

According to Gloria, on their wedding night Wally raped her. Possibly he liked rough sex and was none too gentle with the romantically inclined young girl. At any rate, she wrote he hurt her and made her bleed. Damning everyone who had allowed her those girlhood romantic notions, especially Wally, she concluded that very night that it "was a man's world."[9] The next morning she left Wally and returned with her mother by train to Los Angeles. She told Wally she would stay with Addie just long enough so that Wally and Noah could bring their parents to California. Then she would return to him. Gloria's stay with Addie would be brief. "My mother and I could always look out the same window without ever seeing the same thing," she stated in later years.[10]

Within a week Gloria was on the Keystone lot, having taken the trolley to Edendale, dressed in her finest. She wrote she went alone, but Wally actually accompanied her. Arriving at the Keystone Studio, she was recognized by Frank Hase, a family friend she knew years before in Key West, and was introduced to an assistant production manager, thirty-seven-year-old Hampton Del Ruth (older brother of director Roy Del Ruth), who quickly escorted her into Sennett's office.

In Edendale (now part of Echo Park), the industrious Canadian-born former film comic and Biograph director Mack Sennett had created the Keystone Studios in 1912 when he purchased the Bison Studio located at 1712 Alessandro Street (now Glendale Boulevard). The studio's main building, still standing today, was the first totally enclosed film stage and studio in the world.

Noted for his slapstick shorts, which featured car chases, pratfalls, custard pie fights, and frenetic physical humor, Sennett created a magical world of comedy. His pictures with the Keystone Kops, the Sennett Bathing Beauties, Charlie Chaplin, Mabel Normand, Mack Swain, Louise Fazenda, Chester Conklin, Roscoe "Fatty" Arbuckle, and Ford Sterling had become internationally popular. In 1915, along with D. W. Griffith and Thomas Ince, Sennett helped create the Triangle Company, which released feature-length films as well as the Keystone product.

"Contrary to myth," wrote Keystone historian Simon Louvish, "Keystone movies were, by 1915, extensively scripted, the synopses and treatments running to about seven or eight pages, though the later scripts for a two-reeler could run to as many as seventeen pages . . . Directors and actors were left to sort out their little bits of comedy 'biz' on the set, but the scenes and movements of the characters were blocked in."[11]

The late screenwriter Alan Selwyn recalled shortly before his death in 2002 one of his many casting-couch stories involving Sennett, stating "Mack Sennett's door and fly were always open. No girl even got on the lot if she hadn't first been on his casting couch. Among the ones who didn't walk away (and there were probably hundreds of them) were Gloria Swanson, Mabel Normand, Norma Talmadge and her sister Natalie."[12] According to Sennett's version, repeated in the press several times, his meeting with Gloria took place at night.

Sennett spotted Gloria standing by his window, in the company of a tall, burly man who remained waiting outside. While interviewing her, Sennett glanced out his window and watched the fellow shuffling his feet, scanning the sky, and just killing time. "She said her name was Gloria, that she had worked for Essanay in Chicago, and that she was ambitious," he later wrote. "She had a cute nose and beautiful eyes . . . I went overboard. 'Gloria, I think you have a good chance to succeed in this business if you're willing to work hard and learn, and start from scratch.'"[13] He asked her to appear the following morning ready for work at eight o'clock, and then she left with the man who had been waiting outside for her.

"Well I come to the studio the next morning and look around for the young dame and she don't show up," Sennett continued (more in his own voice) in a 1926 interview, "and I think to myself . . . that's a devil of a note . . . and I inquire around to see if anybody's seen her, because I knew she'd get on in pictures . . . Well she don't show up till 11 o'clock, and then she's smilin' up [to me] and I says: 'Where you been?' An' she answers smilin': 'Well, you see Mister Sennett—after you gave me the job last night I went and got married. [Pointing to Wally, she continued] That's my husband.'"[14] Gloria's version of her first meeting with the self-professed "King of Comedy" reads a bit differently than his, of course, with Sennett being rude to her, criticizing her outfit, and telling her to show up the following Thursday.

Whatever the circumstances, Gloria signed a six-month Keystone contract on May 29, 1916, for $65 a week ending November 28, with an option clause increasing her salary to $75 a week beginning May 28, 1917. Living several hours away from his wife, Wally insisted she move in with his parents in the small, two-story house he and his brother Noah had found on Alvarado Street in Edendale, "so tiny that you couldn't help seeing Wally's spare shoes under the bed," wrote Gloria's future secretary Dorothy B. Daniels.[15] The arrangement was insufferable. Beery's mother and father expressed complete indifference to their young daughter-in-law. When Wally came to live with them, his and Gloria's nights were passionate, their days argumentative. "Under all the joking and clowning and backslapping and flirting," she later wrote, "he was a desperate gypsy . . . At thirty he was a bachelor who had never quite succeeded anywhere at anything."[16]

Gloria was soon cast in *Sunshine* (released May 6, 1916), which featured the Sennett Bathing Beauties. Previewed in late April at the Woodley Theater in Los Angeles, *Sunshine* was a box-office hit. Gloria would always deny she was an official Sennett Bathing Beauty, but she did pose in swimsuits with the other girls, and she certainly left "behind enough evidence to fuel the legacy."[17] Her feigned disgust and her later claim that she hated slapstick and could not swim held, quite literally, little water.

Gloria was assigned a dressing room with Mary Thurman and Maude Wayne. Actress Marie Prevost, one of the perennial Sennett Bathing Beauties, commented on Gloria some years later. "She was more intelligent and essentially dignified," said Prevost, "and except for Phyllis Haver and myself, she kept her distance. Not that I blamed her. Those Sennett Bathing Girls were a dumb lot for the most part."[18]

Proving her screen viability in her first Sennett short, Gloria was next paired with the slightly built comedian Bobby Vernon in the first of a series of nine light romances they would make together, the brainchild of Hampton Del Ruth. Two years older than Gloria, Bobby Vernon stood only 5'3". When the two were paired in casting, Sennett was pleased. He then wisely told Gloria to remove her heavy makeup and act her age. Their first comedy was *A Dash of Courage* (released May 7, 1916), about a young woman who turns a criminal in to the police.

On a one-picture basis, Sennett also cast Wally as the Police Chief in this delightful little film directed by Charles Parrott (later known as Charley Chase). *A Dash of Courage* was more a Wallace Beery film than a Bobby-Gloria romance. There are criminals, there are chases, and there are pratfalls. It was a modest beginning, though according to Swanson's memoirs, after the film's release, she was immediately given a raise to $100 a week.

Wrote Clarence Badger, then a Sennett screenwriter, "Bobby had a wonderful inborn sense of comedy. Gloria was radiant. She sparkled with ideas. Wally the same . . . Following the finish of our picture . . . he [Sennett] rushed into my office shouting: 'It's a bear, Badger, a bear.' Which sounded like a pun, badger-bear. As he continued: 'That Swanson dame's sure got it—swell. That Beery bird, too—great. And Vernon—what a revelation! We'll team the three of them—sure-fire box office. And so began the series of Keystone comedies I made with Gloria Swanson."[19]

Continuing with the silliness, Gloria and Bobby were cast in *Hearts and Sparks* (released June 4, 1916), which was much the same, again directed by Parrott, with a screenplay by Roy Del Ruth. Audiences found the Vernon-Swanson teaming delightful, and the series took off. Gloria recalled that these days at Sennett were the first time she enjoyed working in pictures, and that she learned a great deal about acting from making these little comedies. Though she found physical humor below her dignity, she did have fun working with Bobby Vernon. On the studio lot, he never failed to treat her as his very own steady. The Vernon-Swanson unit was a comfortable and easy company.

Much of the action of the Vernon-Swanson films was improvised in a studio bungalow. Gloria never worried about how she looked or how her hair was styled. She would fondly recall the days when the sun was up, the crew racing madly to a location to film, and then, when the sky would cloud up, rushing back to the studio to practice new stunts.[20]

The popularity of the Vernon-Swanson romantic comedies was far-reaching. One nine year-old girl in Cherryville, Kansas, the future actress Louise Brooks, "was especially enthralled by Gloria Swanson—the most exciting new face of the year."[21]

Keystone premiered a Swanson-Vernon comedy every month. *A Social Cub* (released July 26, 1916), directed by Clarence Badger, was the next. Filmed in early June, this outing has Gloria choosing between Bobby and the older Reggie Morris. Trifling nonsense. Wrote one commentator about these comedies: "Swanson came on icy and reserved, off-screen as well as on, for those who did not know her well, and this blended—or rather contrasted—well with Bobby's more ebullient, outgoing, sparkling personality. Both being diminutive added to the 'cute' effect. With Swanson shy and coy but not exactly unresponsive, and little Bobby darting around her like an excited puppy-dog, the chemistry coming from the screen was one audiences found irresistible."[22]

The following month Sennett released *The Danger Girl* (August 25, 1916), a prime example of sight gags and improvisational storytelling. In private Wally had been teaching Gloria how to drive, and she liked speed. Watching her race recklessly onto the Sennett lot, Charles Parrott had an idea for the film. Bobby jilts his girlfriend (Myrtle Lind) for the "Danger Girl" (Helen Bray), who has all the men chasing her. Gloria and her brother show up on the scene, and after much confusion, numerous chases, and complicated physical situations, everything is sorted out, and Gloria and Bobby are united at fade-out.

Filmed in late July and early August 1916, *The Danger Girl* is one of less than a handful of Gloria's Keystone pictures still in existence. Gloria's vibrancy and daring skill are apparent. In most of the Vernon-Swanson romances she is dressed femininely fashionable. She is petite and lovely, her face and eyes emotionally expressive. In her first scene driving a roadster, filmed in the gardens behind the Beverly Hills Hotel, she races by Helen Bray on horseback and actually knocks the actress's horse over.

According to historical sources, *Love on Skates* was the shooting title of *The Danger Girl*. Their next film, however, was officially titled *Love on Skates* and has Gloria and Bobby meeting at a skating rink. It was released in September 1916 and was another typical Vernon-Swanson romance, but this time with an emphasis on thrills and Bobby taking control of the dangerous stunts, including an auto chase with Bobby at the wheel. Charles Parrott recalled that Gloria was "frightened to death of Bobby Vernon's reckless stunt ideas" but, exhibiting courage, went along with them. "Bobby always had more essential courage and drive—and imagination—than I did in these wild, actionful sequences," she recalled in 1925. "I preferred the romantic scenes to those, but I went along—ruefully."[23]

Gloria and Bobby's next picture, *Haystacks and Steeples* (released October 1, 1916), again under the direction of Clarence Badger, was more of the same, but this time with an emphasis on romance. Gloria's aunt wants her to marry a supposedly wealthy playboy (Reggie Morris), but she instead falls for country bumpkin Bobby. In the finale she is fashionably dressed and photographed in a stunning wedding gown, surrounded by Sennett Beauty bridesmaids.

"I remember one day watching her in a wedding scene," wrote gossip writer Harry Carr. "Something had gone wrong with the lights and Gloria, the bride, had to wait and wait. She was sulky and cross. I stood there watching her with

Mack Sennett. I remember he turned to me and said: 'That girl is going to be one of the greatest artistes the screen has ever known.'"[24] Some saw the budding actress as temperamental and petulant. But those who created the film industry saw something else. Gloria herself soon realized her performance depended on the technicians and the director, and that if she was going to continue in the movie business she would need to be good.[25]

For their next picture, *The Nick of Time Baby,* Gloria and Bobby were teamed with Sennett's Great Dane Teddy, a canine star who was then as popular in pictures as Rin-Tin-Tin. In this rural comedy, Bobby is a chorus boy who inherits a fortune from his uncle. He is in love with the blacksmith's daughter (Gloria). A rival (Earle Rodney) also wants her and plans to deprive Bobby of his fortune by hiring a couple to abandon their baby and threaten Bobby's legitimate claim to the money. The baby, it is assumed, is now the heir. Its parents return and the infant disappears. Teddy helps find the baby, and Bobby wins Gloria at the end.[26]

The Nick of Time Baby, released shortly before Christmas 1916, was a huge hit (billed as "#1 of the Sennett Super-Keystone Comedies" and "The First Special Keystone Comedy De Luxe—A sensation everywhere, and guaranteed to cause more laughs and excitement than any comedy ever produced").[27] Teddy was billed as "The Greatest Dog Performer on Earth."[28] Grace Kingsley of the *Los Angeles Times* commented, "One of the stunts Teddy does in 'Nick-of-Time-Baby' is rescue a babe from drowning, carry it home, put it to bed, get the bottle and insert the business end of the same in the baby's mouth. Some dog!"[29]

Mack Sennett brought Wallace Beery into his fold on October 30, 1916, as a director and actor for $50 a week with options rising to $100 by January 30, 1917. Living with Wally's parents in the small cottage down the street from the Sennett Studio, next to the studio garage (where actors never failed to dent their cars driving in and out), Wally and Gloria continued to live as man and wife. In short order Wally started claiming Gloria's paycheck along with his own each payday.

Wally bought a robin's-egg-blue car to match an outfit Gloria owned. On the sides of the car he painted WALLY AND GLORY. To surprise her he drove it to the Ambassador Hotel, where she was gossiping with girlfriends. When she saw it, Gloria swooned and complimented Wally on his taste. With her friends watching, Gloria lounged back in the backseat and casually told Wally, "Home, James." "To the shocked delight of Gloria's pals," wrote one pair of Hollywood historians, "Wally lurched around, bodily yanked his dainty wife out of the back seat into the front, and bellowed, 'Don't ever give me that 'Home, James' stuff!' "[30]

About Wally, Gloria would comment that he spent lavishly on women, cars, and clothes, living from payday to payday, childishly borrowing money and making deals that never materialized.[31] Often he would physically abuse and hit her. "They weren't particularly nice people, the two of them," recalled Minta Durfee, Fatty Arbuckle's first wife. "He was very gruff and drank most of the time and he was foul-mouthed. And she thought she was better than anyone else. She used to say to Mack that she was an actress, not a slapstick type like Mabel Normand . . . but I do feel sorry for her, the way Beery treated her, always pushing her around in front of everyone." Durfee added, "She lost her first child because of that: one day he was so rough, he slapped her so hard she fell down a flight of stairs."[32]

Shortly after the filming of *The Nick of Time Baby,* Gloria wrote, she discovered she was pregnant. Possibly having a baby right now as her career was building was not in the plans, or she simply did not want Wally's child. According to her memoirs, Wally feigned happiness at his pending fatherhood, took her to dinner to celebrate, and advised her to keep working until she began to show.

Within days, she wrote, Gloria awoke feeling ill. Wally dashed to a drugstore and obtained some pills. Gloria relates her mother-in-law coldly watching her down a handful of the medicine before she became sick and blacked out. When she came to in a doctor's office, she was told she had miscarried. She dressed and left, changing trolleys twice on her way back to Alvarado Street, where she packed her bags. Leaving on foot and taking the remaining pills with her, she stopped by a drugstore and asked the pharmacist what they were for, explaining that a friend had said they would be good for cramps and morning sickness. He told her the pills induced natural abortion. Distraught and holding back tears, she left Wally and caught a trolley to her mother's apartment. So she wrote in her book. Perhaps, though, it was not that simple.

Wally's temper got him in trouble with Sennett more than once, and

Sennett would eventually fire him in October 1917. Already, though, Gloria's growing confidence was leading her to look elsewhere for work. She was tired of being a comedienne, and her attitude was beginning to show at the studio.

4

Triangle

Whatever discord Wally and Gloria may have had did not stop Sennett from casting them together in yet another Vernon-Swanson comedy, *Teddy at the Throttle* (released in April 1917). Gloria had not worked for Sennett in six months. The plot of *Teddy at the Throttle* was self-explanatory. The lovers Bobby Knight (Vernon), an heir, and Gloria Dawn (Swanson), are threatened by Gloria's lustful guardian Henry Black (Wallace Beery). Gloria rebuffs his advances and he ties her to a railroad track. She blows a whistle to summon her wonder dog Teddy. In the nick of time Teddy warns the oncoming train to stop. Teddy then chases Black up a tree and drags him back to justice. Good dog! Fade out!

"Sennett . . . seemed to see her as just another comedy asset in the barn," wrote one Keystone biographer about Gloria. "He kept teaming her with Teddy, the studio dog . . . reputed to be a 'one-take dog . . . He did his bit and [would] then curl up in a corner, oblivious to all the other frenzied thespians."[1]

The "tie her to the railroad track" sequence appeared time and again in Sennett's pictures—1915's *An Innocent Villain,* for example: "Our stars had to get run over by trains, leap from bridges, and risk their necks for laughs," Sennett said.[2] During this one, Wally was a little too forceful and rough, according to Gloria. She asked director Badger specifically not to rehearse her too long with him. Their contempt for each other off and on the screen was very real. Though she did not file divorce papers on Wally until late in 1917, they would separate in June of that year.

Discouraged and miserable, Gloria complained in earnest to Mack Sennett. She felt slapstick "was a world of falling planks and banana peels and wet paint and sticky wads of gum, of funny-looking fat men with painted mustaches blowing foam off beer at each other, of stern battle-axes wielding rolling pins and wearing curlers in their hair, and of cute giggly hoydens getting teased, tickled, and chased."[3]

Though she boasted she once had saved Wally's career by talking Sennett into hiring him back after one of his periodic firings, Gloria was at the same time sabotaging her own. After one quarrel in early 1917, when Sennett refused her a pay raise, she walked off the lot and traipsed over to Universal to appear in *Baseball Madness*, a one-reel wonder released on May 8, 1917. A comedy short about a baseball hero's exploits on and off the diamond, it was directed by and starred Billy Mason. Gloria had little to do other than look pretty.

However, she still had to fulfill her Keystone contract, and by May she was back on the lot, rushed into another Vernon-Swanson comedy, *Dangers of a Bride* (released June 22, 1917). Co-directed by Badger and Vernon, this picture has Bobby once again in pursuit of Gloria, who in the film was chic and nicely dressed. However, *Dangers of a Bride* just did not jell. Badger withdrew it from circulation and made drastic changes, and the two directors blamed each other for its eventual failure. Gloria blamed everybody. Also released in the fall of 1917 was *Whose Baby?*, again directed by Clarence Badger. It, too, was not a success.

At Keystone plans were in the works for one more attempt to resurrect the Vernon-Swanson chemistry, this time in an elaborate costume picture with the lovers and Teddy the Wonder Dog. Entitled *The Sultan's Wife* (with title cards reading *Caught in a Harem*, its shooting title) and again directed by Badger, the picture featured a bevy of none too talented and arguably not too pretty Sennett Bathing Beauties, in sequences rivaling those by DeMille, at the sultan's (actually a rajah's) palace.

Bobby and his girlfriend Gloria become entangled inside a rajah's palace in India and escape by calling for Teddy to save them. Gloria looks quite fetching in a stylish contemporary white suit and sailor jacket, and absolutely stunning in a chiffon-and-strung-beads costume in the harem sequences. The film is sheer nonsense, quickly paced, tightly edited, and quite fun. Released on September 30, 1917, *The Sultan's Wife* was moderately successful, and was the last teaming of Gloria and Bobby Vernon.

As early as June 1917 Sennett began dissolving his association with Triangle. He eventually sold the Keystone name and took complete control over his own studio, selling out many of his players' contracts to other studios. Regrouping his company under the banner of "Mack Sennett Comedies," he let Bobby Vernon go to Triangle because he had asked for a raise. But Sennett kept Gloria, and told her he thought he could make another Mabel Normand out of her. Infuriated, Swanson replied she did not want to be another anybody.[4] She was determined to be a dramatic actress and to make serious films.

Wrote one Hollywood historian, "Hollywood was one of the most class-conscious enclaves in the country for the simple reason it had none."[5] To break free of Sennett, Gloria acquired a manager-agent named Milton K. Young, who, on September 19, 1917, sent him a letter:

> Dear Sir: Mrs. Gloria Swanson requests me to advise you that she will discontinue her services with the Keystone Film Company. Yours very truly, Milton K. Young.[6]

There was one picture left for Gloria under her Sennett contract, however, and it proved her point. *The Pullman Bride,* released November 4, 1917, starred Gloria opposite the fat forty-one-year-old comic Mack Swain, lecherous villain Chester Conklin, and the Sennett Bathing Beauties in their skimpiest attire in a beach romp that held all the slapstick shtick that so appalled Gloria's sensibilities.

Gloria detested the assignment. She was humiliated by "having one's skirts lifted and dodging bricks. That wasn't my idea of true stardom, however much attention it might get."[7] Always quick to complain, she said, "I did my comedies like Duse might have done them. I guess I was one of the first deadpan comedians. I was funny because I didn't try to be funny. The more serious I got, the funnier the scene became. And I hated it all; I loathed *Pullman Bride* because it was the first time Mr. Sennett had put me in low comedy."[8] At the end of the filming, Sennett tore her contract in two.

Though Gloria had left Wally, she would not be divorced from him for some time. Through a lawyer friend of Addie's she learned that Wally did not want to give her a divorce. She soon realized that by having quit films, the only work she had ever had, she was now straddled by her limited education, and her future did not look promising.[9] Connecting with Clarence Badger and Bobby Vernon over at Triangle, Gloria was told they liked their new studio, where they were turning out one short picture after another. Badger invited Gloria to Triangle and offered her a role in a short film he was beginning.[10]

Spying an expensive bottle-green suit with a squirrel collar in a store window and knowing she could not afford it, Gloria bought it anyway.[11] She then caught three trolleys to the Triangle Studios in Culver City. While waiting to see Badger, she was noticed by film director Jack Conway, who handed her the script of *Smoke,* based on a *Saturday Evening Post* short story. Gloria had never held an actual script in her hands before, but she liked the role Conway penciled in for her to read, that of a vamp who seduces a man away from another woman. In the film she would have to manage a couple of dangerous stunts. Conway had been impressed with her in *The Danger Girl,* her fearless character showing spunk and determination. *Smoke* was exactly what she was looking for. Within thirty minutes she agreed to sign with Triangle at a salary that would nearly match what she had been earning at Sennett's Keystone.

The Triangle Film Corporation had been founded by the Aitken brothers, Harry and Roy, in the summer of 1915, after Harry had made a fortune on the roadshow presentation of D. W. Griffith's *The Birth of a Nation* (1915). Together they had envisioned it as a prestige releasing company for the films of Mack Sennett, D. W. Griffith, and Thomas Ince. By joining forces with these prominent directors, Triangle became a major studio in Culver City featuring such stars as Lillian and Dorothy Gish, Mary Pickford, Roscoe "Fatty" Arbuckle, and Douglas Fairbanks. But in 1916 Triangle's first production had been Griffith's mammoth *Intolerance,* which nearly bankrupted the fledgling company. Payrolls were missed, cash was tight, and the studio's stars began leaving in droves.

By 1917 Triangle was suffering from too much expansion and had lost its three big producers, including Sennett, that summer. The head of Triangle was now H. O. Davis, a former newspaper editor and publisher, who successfully produced feature-length pictures with limited budgets.

What Triangle did not have in production values for its studio-based programmers it made up for in new stars and quality directors. Director Jack Conway was exactly what Gloria needed at this point of her career. Born in Minnesota, the thirty-year-old, self-educated Conway was currently separated from his wife Viola Barry.[12] He spoke of film as an art form to the impressionable

Gloria and enthusiastically educated her on fashion and hairstyles. When *Smoke* began production in the fall of 1917, Gloria was transported into an atmosphere of elegance and refinement. She had never known such an intelligent, refined, and attractive man as Conway. "Finding she had a crush on Conway, Gloria proceeded to learn all she could about the director, down to the type of cologne he wore."[13]

In *Smoke*, Gloria portrayed Patricia Reynolds, a recklessly loose woman moving about in society who saves her crippled friend Jim Wheeler (Edward Peil Jr.) from drowning. She falls in love with him and is redeemed from her wicked ways. Gloria was allowed to select her own wardrobe, and Conway was very careful to photograph her flatteringly. And Gloria registered a remarkable impact on film. Her part was substantially expanded, and the studio started a dedicated promotion campaign for their new star.

When *Smoke,* now retitled *You Can't Believe Everything,* wrapped, Conway invited Gloria to the latest popular meeting place of the stars, the elegant Alexandria Hotel, which featured a marvelous marbled lobby. Picking her up in his chauffeured limousine, Conway informed her of the buildup Triangle planned for her. She had impressed Conway by doing her own stunts in the film, including a dive off the fifteen-foot-high Wilmington dock at the port of Los Angeles into deep, dark waters for a night scene, which she did *before* she told the director she could not swim. Gloria was now to receive star billing. However, Triangle chose to hold back *You Can't Believe Everything* and rush into filming a couple more films starring Gloria before releasing it. Triangle, said Conway, was willing to give her anything she wanted.

What she wanted was a new, larger apartment for her and her mother. She also wanted a Kissel coupe, and she told Conway she wanted a divorce from Wally, who was dragging his feet because the war allowed men of draft age who were married to remain exempt. Wally was in his early thirties, and Conway figured that once Beery was deferred later that year he would agree. After dinner and dancing, Conway delivered Gloria back to her mother's apartment and gently kissed her good night.

Now earning $100 a week, within days Gloria had moved with her mother from Addie's tiny apartment on St. Francis Court to Court Corinne, a group of small bungalows occupied primarily by single young actresses. Gloria also was given the Kissel coupe she wanted. She made friends with Sylvia Joslin and out-of-work actress Beatrice La Plante. La Plante then introduced her to another out-of-work actor named John Gilbert, who became a friend.

The idea of silent film acting being merely a series of exaggerated poses coupled with grimacing facial expressions was a fallacy, as Jack Conway explained to Gloria. She would later write that to act in silent films one had to express emotions at the start of the line and retain something at the end of that line so as to allow the title cards to fill in the content. One had to perform almost unnaturally in a scene so as to make it natural on the screen, delaying and controlling reactions. Once that was learned, it then had to be ignored so as not to let the camera record one's thinking about it.[14]

Gloria took that into consideration as she was groomed to take her place as a promising new star on the Triangle roster. She would be given the same buildup afforded the Gish sisters and Alma Rubens. Gloria dreamed of becoming as big a film star as Mary Pickford. As the industry boomed and the stars gained public popularity, Hollywood became the center of a glittering nightlife.

During the early 1910s entertaining in Los Angeles was largely confined to the home. Baron Long's Vernon Country Club, which introduced jazz to the cinema colony, would attract a large following by the late teens. It was there Gloria met for the first time a $35-a-week taxi dancer named Rudolph Valentino, who had come to town in 1917. At the epicenter of film star gatherings were the Hollywood Hotel, a sprawling old wooden structure where its proprietress Miss Hershey supervised the Thursday night social dance, and the Alexandria Hotel, which opened in 1906. "It was where the snobs dined and had their fancy parties," Gloria once commented.[15] Socializing at night was as vital an effort as working at the studio during the day.

For her second Triangle picture, *Society for Sale*, Gloria's director was the twenty-five-year-old Frank Borzage.[16] The film told a silly yarn about a London mannequin (a fashion model), Phyllis Clyne (Gloria), who pays a titled English blue blood, Bill (William Desmond), to pass her off in society as his fiancée, and the inevitable happens when they fall in love. Romantic mush.

Released on April 21, 1918, as the first of Gloria's eight Triangle features, *Society for Sale* was panned by *Variety*: "This film, as a whole, is disappointing, because the story lacks the punch and there is no entertainment in watching a crowd of men and women carry on aimless dialog, drink tea, play cards, or saunter snail-like through reel after reel with nothing of a thrilling or diverting nature being climaxed."[17] Yet at Los Angeles's Riviera Theater *Society for Sale* proved a banner attraction during its initial run.

Triangle's resident fashion designer was Peggy Hamilton. Hamilton "had an eye for line, a vision for color and a genius for knowing what women should wear," wrote Adela Rogers St. Johns in 1923. "Peggy saw Gloria, then a restless, unstable, unsettled personality and, with that sure instinct of hers—that Parisian training, perceived something of the Gloria to come, the butterfly still hidden in the chrysalis."[18] Hamilton would prove to be one of her first fashion mentors.

In *Society for Sale* Gloria was photographed lovingly (by cinematographer Pliny Horne) in numerous close-ups. She did not get along well with the rest of the cast, however, especially with the stalwart William Desmond, who resented that he was handed his role "in support" of the studio's newest buildup. She did not work well with Borzage during the quick filming either. Gloria knew the story was dated and weak.[19] She longed for Jack Conway. For her next picture she got him.

Rushed into production was *Her Decision,* released on May 12, 1918. In this film Phyllis Dunbar (Gloria) is a stenographer who works for middle-aged Martin Rankin (J. Barney Sherry). To obtain money for her unfortunate sister Inah (Ann Forrest), Phyllis marries Martin, making a decision to learn to love him.

Featuring exquisite photography by Elgin Lessley, *Her Decision* proved a modest success when it opened at the Alhambra Theater in Los Angeles. "Jack Conway in directing the picture has given it a number of touches that will appeal to the feminine, and has developed a feature that should fill program requirement," said "Ibog" in *Variety.*[20] One reviewer wrote, "Little Gloria Swanson is a sweet little thing, and she is certainly highlighted here to her best advantage, but they just have to do better by her."[21] Another critic praised the film: "Wonderful stage settings, delightful dances, and a wondrous ensemble of crowds are featured in this production."[22] (One wonders what picture he saw.)

Director Jack Conway hated this assignment and told Gloria he was leaving the studio. Future director Henry "Nick" Grinde was a script clerk at Triangle then and remembered the set of *Her Decision* during a particularly tense moment. "I went out on the set which was the old Stage 1 . . . And there was Jack Conway, who was directing Gloria Swanson and J. Barney Sherry, swear-

ing and throwing his hat at a property man." When Conway asked the property man where a pocketbook was for the scene, the fellow replied, "I dunno,
I'm no mind reader." To which Conway replied, "Well, you're certainly no
property man either."[23]

Conway told Gloria no one at the studio besides the two of them had any
class. He then signed with Metro, where he hit his stride. As Triangle was starting to promote its output as "Clean Pictures for Clean People," in a last-moment
bid to keep going, Gloria had to have wondered where her romantic dramas
would fit in.

Shortly before her next film, *Station Content,* began filming Gloria was approached by Oscar Goodstadt, casting director for Famous Players–Lasky. He
represented director Cecil B. DeMille, who had inquired about her availability
for a picture, *Till I Come Back to You.* With stars in her eyes, Gloria met with
DeMille and told him she had no written contract with Triangle and would be
free to work for him.[25] When she told Triangle she would now be working for
DeMille, within days Triangle lawyers presented the case to an impartial arbitra-
tor at the Motion Picture Association. DeMille and Famous Players–Lasky were
then informed that although Gloria had no written contract, she had accepted a
raise. Forced to sign a legal contract, Gloria was now bound to Triangle.

The plot of *Station Content,* directed by Arthur Hoyt, dealt with Kitty
Manning (Gloria) leaving her husband Jim (Lee Hill), a railroad telegrapher,
after their child dies. She is forced to overnight at a small train station similar
to the one she and Jim had run. Seeing how happy the station operator and his
wife are, Kitty has second thoughts. When the operator becomes suddenly ill,
Kitty offers to assume responsibility for the station. A storm comes up, and
lightning destroys the trestle. Kitty, realizing the next train will be derailed,
jumps onto a railroad cycle to stop it.

Drama, adventure, and romance all rolled up in five reels, *Station Content*
was Gloria's third, and some say worst, Triangle picture, released on June 16,
1918, and opening in Los Angeles at the Riviera Theater. One critic wrote, "The
lure of the city for the small-town girl is graphically pictured . . . Gloria Swanson will be remembered for her superb . . . characterization . . . This time [she]
is seen as a Triangle star in her own right, and in a vehicle that gives her plenty
of opportunities for emotional acting."[26] Voiced one trade journal, "Swanson
and her cast under Arthur Hoyt's direction labor mightily to make something

meaningful of this soppy mishmash but are defeated by a scenario that makes no real sense."[27]

Gloria's career suffered after Conway's departure. It was temporarily reprieved with the release of *You Can't Believe Everything* (June 23), the week after the premiere of *Station Content*. Triangle had invested a great deal of money in advertising the picture, featuring Gloria in numerous newspaper fashion spreads, and *You Can't Believe Everything* picked up some fairly good notices. About Gloria, one critic commented, "A charming actress and a burgeoning star, who shows she has deserved better material than Sennett gave her."[28] The *Moving Picture World* found her "likable and lovable" with a "fetching figure."[29]

Wrote the reviewer in *Variety*, "The complete improbability and many inconsistencies of the plot are forgotten by the cleverness of the several fine actors, the fine direction and general excellence of production. They are quite a fearful lot, these people, and it is consoling that in no real 'smart' set—at least not many—or in any other set, are their counterpoints to be found. Gloria Swanson makes of Patricia a dashing, fearless, yet appealing young woman."[30]

What appeared promising now became banal, as Gloria was thrown back into projects with little to recommend them. In *Everywoman's Husband* (released July 7, 1918), she portrayed Edith Emerson, who per her mother's (Lillian Langdon) advice keeps her husband Frank (Joe King) on a tight and critical leash. He has an affair. Edith reforms, and Frank leaves his mistress to return to his loving wife.

The critics came down hard on this celluloid misfire, directed by Gilbert P. Hamilton. *Variety* sighed that the picture was "the same old triangle, husband, wife, and sympathetic woman friend," saving its one favored comment for last, "Gloria Swanson and Joe King look and act like the average bride and groom, and Lillian Langdon as the mother-in-law is capital."[31]

Gloria did not like director Hamilton at first, as she was used to Jack Conway. She treated him badly when *Everywoman's Husband* commenced filming. However, she soon realized that he was working through his contract, just as she was, as Triangle churned out one bad picture after another. In time the two became good friends.[32]

As World War I raged on in Europe, like all the other film studios, Triangle began a series of patriotic, anti-German melodramas. Gloria's last three pictures of her contract emphasized this trend. In the first, *Shifting Sands*, Marcia Gray

(Gloria) is a struggling artist who is mistakenly sent to prison when her rent collector Henry Von Holtz (Harvey Clark) accuses her of robbery. Years pass, and
Marcia marries John Stanford (Joe King). The rent collector, now a German spy
using the name Sir George Denby, comes to stay with Marcia and John, who
works with the Intelligence Department. Marcia does not recognize Von Holtz at
first. But when she does, his plans are foiled.

Variety noted, "Triangle has a picture of good average . . . with a plot perhaps
a little more original than some, and not more improbable than many. One is
called upon nowadays to imagine, believe and take for granted so much on the
screen it sometimes becomes difficult to distinguish the abnormal from the dull-
as-ditchwater . . . It does not require extraordinary histrionic gifts to depict the
conventional 'wronged girl,' but Miss Swanson gets all she can out of the part."[33]

Shifting Sands was directed by the eccentric Englishman Albert Parker,
who was sympathetic to Gloria's personality and feelings about this kind of
poor material. However, Shifting Sands was sumptuously produced, and she
looked radiant. Though editing and title cards were weak, the film was entertaining, showing off Gloria's remarkable dramatic potential. Parker captivated
her personally, and the two began a quiet romance. Making a picture a month,
she was eager for her contract to end, though she later related that when she
and Parker made Secret Code they thoroughly enjoyed the experience.[34]

The plot of Secret Code is ridiculous. The story by Adela Rogers St. Johns, a
former reporter for the San Francisco Examiner, told of Sally Carter (Gloria),
who marries Senator John Rand (J. Barney Sherry). He finds that with the out-
break of war, he must devote all his time to work. Lola Walling (Rhy Alexander)
is a spy for the Kaiser and portrays herself as a confidante to the senator. She
leads John into believing his wife is sending messages to the Kaiser concealed in
the stitching of the mufflers she crochets. However, there is another explanation
for Sally's sewing.

St. Johns remembered meeting Swanson for the first time and having as low
an opinion of Gloria as Gloria did of her script. "Gloria Swanson was an igno-
rant, awkward, sloppy kid from the outposts of Chicago," wrote St. Johns. "Then
she was a slow-minded, narrow, bewildered girl soaked to the bone with the
deepest inferiority complex any human being ever owned . . . Sullen, shy, terribly
pathetic . . . Her clothes were impossible. You have no idea really. Everything
was wrong. Her underclothes bunched in the most unexpected places.

"Her hair was none too tidily dressed in a sort of mop at the back of her neck . . . After one look at her, I—being concerned with the success of my story—proceeded to have internal convulsions. She was awful. Short and inclined to be dumpy. A strange face, dominated by sullen, gray-green eyes, with a long nose tilted upward and a defiant mouth whose upper lip seemed too short to cover big, strong, white teeth. Her sweater caught in bewildering scallops over her hips and the heels of her slightly worn white pumps were badly run down. Her sailor hat kept a precarious perch under her heavy, red-brown hair. When she spoke, which was seldom, her voice had a harsh, uncultivated note."[35] A none too appealing image.

When *Secret Code* opened on September 8, 1918, at Loew's New York Theater, *Photoplay* said the two stars, J. Barney Sherry and Gloria, made the picture "decidedly better."[36] Another reviewer called *Secret Code* "one of the most regrettable cinematic offerings of the season."[37] Yet another acknowledged it "a weird and oppressive mélange of Washington intrigue, Swanson agonizing and overwrought mugging by a bevy of actors who knew they had a bad scenario on their hands and thought too much hamming might disguise too little sense all-round. It doesn't work."[38] Neither did Gloria's next one.

E. Mason Hopper, the same "Lightning" Hopper who had worked at Essanay, took the reins of *Wife or Country*, mercifully the last of her patriotic anti-German trilogy. *Wife or Country* tells of German spy Gretchen Barker (Gretchen Lederer), who has married and reformed alcoholic Dale Barker (Harry Mestayer). Barker later falls for his attractive stenographer, Sylvia Hamilton (Gloria), who loves him but leaves her job because he is married, and goes to work for Dr. Meyer Stahl (Jack Richardson), who is the head of a German spy ring. When Sylvia discovers this she gives authorities a list of Stahl's accomplices, not realizing Gretchen is on the list. Barker must decide between his wife and his country.

Shot in ten days, *Wife or Country* (released December 19, 1918) was rushed through production by Hopper, who used the same crude directorial techniques he had mastered at Essanay. Critics were tired of these spy ring epics at any rate; as one wrote, "Of spy pictures apparently there is no end, and this one . . . is just another."[39] Said another, "The question now is whether or not the public will continue to want stories with that 'spy' stuff. If they do, then this one will pass with the rest."[40]

Wife or Country tanked at the box office. Armistice had been called in November 1918, the month prior to its release. On November 26, Gloria's mother, who had acquired her divorce around that time from Joseph Swanson, married Matthew Burns.[41] Burns, a wealthy, short man who "smelled of cough drops"[42] and had ginger-colored hair and a mustache, had been courting Addie for some time. Gloria could not see what her mother, who blushed and giggled at the drop of his name, could possibly see in the man. After they wed, Addie and Burns took in Gloria's grandmother Bertha to live with them.

Gloria was making respectable money now and purchased an expensively furnished house on Harper Avenue that had once belonged to stage actor Tyrone Power Sr. She brought along Bea La Plante, who had become her unofficial secretary-companion, to live with her. On December 13, 1918, Gloria and Wallace Beery's divorce was final. He had won the decree on the grounds that she had deserted him. She wrote him, "I don't want you to cry. Please don't coax me and don't run around and make a fool of yourself."[43] Wally simply dismissed their marriage with, "She wanted the fancy life—to put on airs and all that."[44] In later years he caustically commented, "I was too young for her."[45]

Triangle was facing bankruptcy. The day after "Lightning" Hopper bellowed his last "Perfect! Cut!", effectively ending production of *Wife or Country*, Triangle studio manager Ollie Sellers stopped by Gloria's home to announce the studio would close its doors in two months.[46] He told her that Harry Aitken was willing to terminate her contract immediately. DeMille had called the studio repeatedly wanting her to replace his current leading lady in what probably was *Old Wives for New,* then set to begin shooting in March 1918. Sellers offered to call Oscar Goodstadt on Gloria's telephone to arrange a meeting with DeMille that very day. This done, he then drove her to Famous Players–Lasky, located at Sunset and Vine.

Working for Cecil B. DeMille and his Artcraft Pictures, produced by Famous Players–Lasky and released through Paramount, meant Gloria had arrived. DeMille had watched her progress in pictures for some time.

He wrote in his autobiography, "I saw authority, as well as beauty, in Gloria Swanson when first I noticed her simply leaning against a door in a Mack Sennett comedy. Gloria was, of course, very young then, but I saw a future that she could have in pictures if her career was properly handled . . . I never told her, until after her first few successes under my direction, why I was handling her career in a certain way; but she was intelligent enough to know and patient enough to wait. I kept her, so to speak, under wraps designed by Alphretta [Alpharetta] Hoffman and later Mitchell Leisen, and worn in settings of Wilfred Buckland's best creation."[47]

On December 20, 1918, Gloria signed a four-page contract with the Famous Players–Lasky Corporation, agreeing to commence work for the studio on January 1, 1919, continuing until January 1, 1921, beginning at a salary of $150 a week, with increments building up to $350 in her second year. That was to be followed with another two-year option, her salary to peak at $550 a week. The document was then signed by Gloria and DeMille.

"She was so excited she didn't know what to do," commented Adela Rogers St. Johns about Gloria at the time. "And she said, 'The thing in my life I've always wanted the most is a beautiful, elegant automobile painted orchid-color.' And I said, 'Gloria, you can't have an automobile painted orchid-color.'

"'Yes I can, and what's more I'm going to.' And right then, Miss Gloria Swanson set the fact that she did not do what other people did, she was to do something that made other people do what Gloria Swanson did."[48]

Gloria was now stepping into the world to which she felt entitled—a world of glamour and class, a make-believe world where she would be treated respectably. At the same time, along with Mary Pickford and Douglas Fairbanks, Gloria Swanson was creating the star system.

5

DeMille

By 1919 Cecil Blount DeMille had become one of the most important directors in Hollywood. Born in Ashfield, Massachusetts, on August 12, 1881, he was the second son of Henry Churchill de Mille, a lay Episcopal minister, who taught at Columbia University, and Matilda Beatrice Samuel. Cecil's religious upbringing was to become influential in his later career. His older brother William C. was an important stage playwright and early film director as well.[1] Agnes de Mille, William's daughter, became a noted Broadway stage choreographer (*Oklahoma!, Carousel, Brigadoon*). Cecil made his stage debut as an actor in 1900, later working as a stage director and playwright with producer Jesse L. Lasky. In 1913 he joined Lasky and his brother-in-law Samuel Goldfish (later Goldwyn) in California to produce film versions of popular plays. Their first was *The Squaw Man* in 1914.

An immense success, *The Squaw Man* solidified DeMille's motion picture career. Within two years he was the director general of the newly formed Famous Players–Lasky Corporation, created the summer of 1916 when Lasky's Feature Play Company merged with Adolph Zukor's Famous Players Films Company. Recognized as one of the most bankable film directors in the industry, DeMille made a series of highly acclaimed pictures starring the likes of Mary Pickford (in *The Little American* with Wallace Beery in 1917), Metropolitan Opera coloratura soprano Geraldine Farrar, Victor Moore, Mae Murray, and the virile Wallace Reid.

At the end of the decade, DeMille began filming a trilogy of modern sex dramas dealing with errant husbands and wives. The first, *Old Wives for New* (released May 20, 1918), starred Elliott Dexter. The second was *Don't Change Your Husband* (released January 26, 1919), and the third was *Why Change Your Wife?* (released May 2, 1920). These socio-sexual dramas were possibly, as one DeMille biographer put it, " 'the wish-dreams of the twenties'; subjectively, they had coincided with Cecil in real life playing out of his own sexual fantasies."[2]

Filming on *Don't Change Your Husband* began on October 12, 1918, before Gloria had signed her contract. In fact, her first scene was photographed on November 7, the week of the "False Armistice" shortly before the close of World War I. Gloria recalled her first day stepping onto the DeMille lot. DeMille never began shooting until after ten in the morning, and she was amazed to find real flowers on the set. She then was told she would be wearing real jewels and expensive gowns made of exquisite fabrics designed by DeMille's costumer Alpharetta Hoffman.

After being shown her dressing room, with its mirrored wall and vanity, she was introduced to her diminutive African American maid Hattie Wilson Tabourne (who was later responsible for Famous Players–Lasky's noted hairpiece stylings of the 1920s). Gloria was then allowed to spend as much time as necessary on the set to familiarize herself with the trappings. DeMille then entered "like Caesar" with his retinue, which included screenwriter Jeanie Macpherson and assistant directors Sam Wood and Cullen Tate.[3] Also present was DeMille's Filipino boy, who instinctively caught the boss's jacket when he shed it and shoved a chair under DeMille when he sat.

Gloria recalled the moment: "Mr. DeMille beamed when he saw me. He came over . . . and led me to the set . . . In a voice not much louder than a whisper he said we would begin with a simple scene . . . would start shooting as soon as I was ready."[4] Gloria was allowed to do her own makeup and pick her own jewelry. DeMille even provided a violinist to lend his actors proper mood for each scene.

Gloria would later write that DeMille would run the previous day's rushes during lunch hour so that actors could catch their mistakes and perfect their portrayals. She soon was able to view herself with a semblance of objectivity, securing gestures and repeating expressions which only enhanced her performances in following pictures.[5]

Don't Change Your Husband tells the story of James Denby Porter (Elliott Dexter), a businessman who neglects his wife Leila (Gloria), himself, and his appearance. His habits are annoying. He drops ashes when smoking cigars, he wears scruffy shoes, he snores, he dunks toast in his morning coffee, and he eats raw onions. Leila tires of him after he forgets their anniversary. She divorces James and marries playboy Schuyler Van Sutphen (Lew Cody). She soon realizes he is taking her for her jewels and has a cutie on the side, Toddles Thomas (DeMille's real-life mistress, the terribly untalented Julia Faye). James changes his ways, improves his appearance, and reclaims Leila.

Now that she was a dramatic leading lady in quality motion pictures, Gloria changed her look. For this she entrusted her appearance to makeup and glamour stylist Max Factor. It was Factor who used makeup several shades darker than Gloria had used before and customized her eye shadow for maximum effect. Her hair was altered even more dramatically. She was known for her full, frizzy shoulder-length bob in her comedies, but Factor now gave Gloria a strong and severe shorter cut, which was augmented by Hattie's inventive hairpieces.

With World War I ending, new values were replacing the old. "The old social order, rigid, exclusive, aristocratic, was breaking up," wrote social historian Benjamin B. Hampton. "There was an intense curiosity about wealth, about the manner of the life of the rich, about the things that money can buy, clothes, houses, decorations, cars, and a thousand and one appurtenances of modern American life."[6]

Noted film historian Jeanine Basinger commented on Gloria's persona upon the release of *Don't Change Your Husband,* "DeMille . . . found the Swanson definition . . . He turned her into a symbol of a particularly new kind of American woman; sophisticated, soignee, and definitely not a virgin. Although young, this woman was married, so she already knew about the birds and the bees. She was rich, magnificently and luxuriously dressed, with jewelry to knock 'em dead in Peoria. She was not to be found sitting home by the fireside; she was out in the world, ready for something to happen, riding in fast cars, shopping, dancing, smoking, doing pretty much whatever she felt."[7]

Don't Change Your Husband wrapped on November 19, 1918, and cost $73,922.14. Gloria made a huge impact on audiences of 1919 when the picture was released in February. Film historian DeWitt Bodeen wrote, "The roles she performed in [DeMille's] opulent problem dramas were always sympathetic ones. She was the wife, never the other woman . . . and always extravagantly gowned . . . The DeMille-Swanson films . . . educated a countless number of feminine moviegoers . . . [and] stirred the hearts and minds of women all over the world."[8] In this picture Gloria was gowned in over two dozen costumes, including the three "If I Were King" dream sequence fantasy outfits. Whether sporting frothy day dresses or swanky off-the-shoulder evening gowns (complete with peacock or ostrich feather fans), Swanson was stunning to behold.

The reviews for *Don't Change Your Husband* were superb. DeMille's gamble on casting Gloria paid off. "Cecil B. DeMille's latest Artcraft release . . . bears the hallmark of a high-class picture," said one critic. "Gloria Swanson's Leila Porter is convincing and she reads into the characterization of the wife a gentle personality which reaches the hearts of everyone. She earns the sympathy of her audience, but not by any attempt at 'wishy-washy' heroics."[9] Mae Tinee of the *Chicago Daily Tribune* wrote, "Gloria Swanson is a pretty and clever actress with distinctive style in dress and coiffure. She is most effective."[10] And *Motion Picture* magazine was delighted with her: "We do not hesitate to proclaim Gloria Swanson one of the distinctive acquisitions of the silent play, not only pictorially, but dramatically."[11]

Gloria would later compare working for DeMille to playing in the children's area of an exclusive department store.[12] *Don't Change Your Husband* was the first DeMille picture to be packaged with an aggressive and costly ad and publicity campaign. For months the industry trades heralded and exploited it in multipage articles and promotions, and the film was largely successful because of that. As the second of DeMille's trilogy, *Don't Change Your Husband* was an improvement over *Old Wives for New,* and it grossed $292,394.10. On January 21, 1919, Gloria signed a new contract with Famous Players–Lasky giving her a raise of $50 a week.

Now she was invited to parties where, as a Sennett contract player, she would never have been seen before. Gloria's face and name were featured in beauty endorsements for Ingram's Milkwood Cream, Hermo "Hair-Lustr," and Maybell Laboratories of Chicago cosmetic ads promoting "Lash-Brow-Ine," all of which successfully launched her into the world of glamour. She still purchased her favorite perfume from the Sam Kress drugstore at Hollywood and Cahuenga Pass, but she no longer bought her clothes off the rack. Now the studio lent her couture gowns for her public appearances. Her personal life took a turn for the better as well.

One evening Elliott Dexter and his wife actress Marie Doro invited Gloria to the Ship's Café, where she was introduced to eccentric Pasadena socialite Richard "Craney" Gartz, the heir to the Crane Plumbing fortune. Though Gartz was worth millions, he was a socialist radical well versed in Marxist literature. Correctly categorized as a pretentious, shallow, overtly critical snob, he was nevertheless also extremely attractive, cultivated, and a fine dancer. Gloria was drawn to him immediately. The two became lovers.

Gartz introduced Gloria to the world of great writers, such as George Bernard Shaw and Henrik Ibsen, and to the great minds of Sigmund Freud and Karl Marx. Gloria relished the education. Ever the romantic, she wanted to marry, but unfortunately Gartz just was not the marrying type. When Craney visited her on the set of her next picture and snidely criticized DeMille, she ceased their affair. (By the end of 1919 Gartz had fled the country because of a "red scare," resulting in vigilante activities against leftists and threats of federal imprisonment.)

Gloria's next DeMille picture was *For Better, For Worse.* Based on a play by Edgar Selwyn, with a scenario by Jeanie Macpherson and an adaptation by William C. deMille, the story told of two rivals, Dr. Edward "Ned" Meade (Elliott Dexter) and Richard Burton (Tom Forman), who vie for the hand of Sylvia Norcross (Gloria). Torn between the two, Sylvia eventually marries Dr. Meade when Burton finds love with Betty Hoyt (Wanda Hawley).

Turgidly dramatic, *For Better, For Worse,* filmed between January 27 and March 24, 1919, comes complete with a flashback sequence, with Gloria portraying, unnecessarily, three women in history who stood by their men. DeMille always enjoyed these flourishes, and Gloria found them romantic and inspirational. Some viewers found them ridiculous and silly. This time even the critics weren't fooled by the melodramatic goings-on. Said *Variety,* "It is a most unsatisfactory tale and the conclusion cannot be anything but distasteful, whichever way it breaks . . . Gloria Swanson . . . plays Sylvia with no sincerity but a lot of make-up on her eyes and lips that photograph too darkly . . . 'For Better, For Worse,' is like one of those Broadway shows you see and enjoy at the time, but do not recommend to inquiring friends."[13]

When the picture premiered in New York on April 27, 1919, the *New York*

Times wrote, "Some of the scenes are eloquent. They do not need subtitles or explanations of any kind. They speak for themselves."[14] However, one Chicago critic called the end result "over-produced, over-emotional, over-reverential hogwash."[15] *For Better, For Worse,* handsomely photographed by the legendary James Wong Howe, was DeMille's most expensive production since *The Woman God Forgot* in 1917, costing $111,260.93 and grossing back $256,072.97. It possibly can be forgiven its failures in light of the next DeMille-Swanson production, *Male and Female.*

Loosely based on Sir James M. Barrie's play *The Admirable Crichton,* with an adaptation by Jeanie Macpherson, DeMille's *Male and Female* tells of Lady Mary Lasenby (Gloria), the daughter of Lord Loam (Theodore Roberts), who is engaged to Lord Brockelhurst (Robert Cain) though not in love with him, and of the highly educated William Crichton, the Loam butler (Thomas Meighan), who is adored by Tweeny the scullery maid (Lila Lee). On an outing aboard Loam's yacht, the pampered socialites are shipwrecked on a deserted island. Crichton, realizing their peril, takes over command of the castaways. Lady Mary comes to respect him and falls in love with her former servant when he rescues her from a leopard (on a deserted island). After he tells her a tale of ancient Babylon, they plan to wed. When all are rescued, however, they revert back to their class positions.

DeMille originally planned to film in Honolulu after production work at the studio was completed. Instead locations were utilized at the Iverson Ranch, in Chatsworth, the Channel Islands National Park (the Santa Cruz Islands), and Santa Catalina Island off the coast of Southern California. Elliott Dexter, on the treadmill in every DeMille production, it seemed, was the first choice for Crichton. But he suffered a nervous breakdown shortly before filming commenced, and the rugged Thomas Meighan stepped in, fresh from his breakthrough role in *The Miracle Man* with Lon Chaney. (Gloria had been considered for the role of "Rose" in that film.)

Crichton's reading of William Ernest Henley's poem "When I Was a King of Babylon" set in motion the spectacular (and totally non-Barrie) Babylon flashback, which featured Bebe Daniels as the king's favorite. In the sequence, Gloria, wearing an impressive beaded pearl and sequined lamé gown with a long train (made of batik) and an immense bejeweled white peacock-feathered headdress, and tottering on wooden high-heel clogs "in the shape of Babylonian bulls standing on their forelegs with wings that came up the sides of Gloria's feet" to give her stature (a costume designed by Mitchell Leisen),[16] is sacrificed in the lion's den—one of the film's two most memorable sequences.

This was the last scene photographed for the picture. Gloria had watched Thomas Meighan carry a live (and highly drugged) leopard on his shoulder in a previous sequence. She in turn courageously told DeMille she wanted to re-create Gabriel Max's famous 1908 painting *The Lion's Bride,* with her character entering a lion's den, and then a tableau of her death. A drained swimming pool was used for the "vision" sequence, in which the King of Babylon (Meighan) sentences his bride to the lions for not forsaking her Christianity. (Christians in Babylon?)

Apparently DeMille had second thoughts before filming and decided to ax the scene, believing it too dangerous. Gloria insisted they continue. Before it was filmed with "the sacred lions of Ishtar," she was asked if she was menstruating. She said no, and the lion tamers, pistols in hand, took their positions. As she began her entrance in the scene, the tension on the set was palpable. She somewhat humorously later wrote that the greatest risk of injury to her was the sheer weight of her costume.[17]

Gloria recalled feeling the lion's paw on her bare back and hearing it breathe on her body. Listening to the snap of the lion tamer's whip and hearing the cranking of the camera recording the moment, Gloria remembered her body tingling with excitement and fear. When the lion roared his heated breath seemed to caress her body.[18] The next sequence shows her lying on her stomach, a lion beside her, his paw on her body. Gloria loved to exaggerate her fearlessness.

DeMille was delighted with Gloria's spunk and bravery and would forever after call her "Young Fellow" as a sign of his approval and acceptance of her as an artist. At the end of the shoot, the "Old Man," as he was fondly called, sat her on his knee and gave her a gold mesh purse with a square sapphire in the center as a gift for her bravery.

In *Male and Female* Gloria also made history by simulating taking a bath in the nude, a scene carefully filmed and revealing nothing, in a sunken tub. DeMille spent days attempting to convince Swanson to do the scene, and for the first time ever he placed armed guards around the set to prevent outsiders from watching. Another total "non-Barrie" moment.

When told the title of his work had been changed, James M. Barrie remarked, "Capital. Wish I'd thought of it myself."[19] One ponders what Barrie's thoughts were regarding the fanciful addition of the tub scene. Popularized and exploited by DeMille, a bathing sequence was integrated into nearly every film he made thereafter, most famously in Claudette Colbert's asses'-milk bath in *The Sign of the Cross* (Paramount, 1932).

For *Male and Female,* in the scene with Gloria and the two maids, one the ubiquitous Julia Faye, DeMille told Gloria to take her time and smell and relish the rosewater Faye pours over her. In DeMille's estimation, the bathing scene was an art unto itself. "The bath became a mystical shrine dedicated to the gods," said one DeMille biography, "and the art of bathing was shown as a ceremony rather than merely a sanitary duty. Undressing was not just the removing of clothes, but a progressive revelation of entrancing beauty, a study of diminishing draperies."[20]

In *Male and Female,* the special effects for the shipwreck sequence were created by Fred Waller, the man who would later invent Cinerama. Third assistant cameraman was James Wong Howe. The editor of the picture was Anne Bauchens. A stellar cast of artists. "DeMille's films were the stuff of fantasy," said another historian. "But they were also instructive, providing lavish and intimate details of how the upper class lived."[21] In his boudoir epics, the audiences were shown gorgeous clothes, champagne suppers, and fine jewels. And DeMille's props were real. The moviegoer might not know that a couture gown cost $7,000, but the actress wearing it would.

Production concluded on July 30, 1919, and immediately *Male and Female* was given the Famous Players–Lasky mighty publicity exploitation. It had a lot to recommend it. Sheet music dedicated to Swanson and entitled "Gloria" (lyrics by Fifi-Tot Seymour and music by M. K. Jerome) was published by the Waterson, Berlin and Snyder Co., New York, and did brisk business.

Costuming was of the utmost importance in all of DeMille's pictures. "I want clothes that will make people gasp when they see them," DeMille had dictated to his costume designers. "I don't want to see any clothes anybody could possibly buy in a store."[22] DeMille brought artist-designer Paul Iribe from Paris to assist in designing the sets and some of the costumes for *Male and Female.* For the Babylonian sequence, Mitchell Leisen was in his element. Other costumes for the picture were created by Clare West. Gloria wore nearly a dozen costumes in the picture; for the shipwreck sequence, she tread water in a $3,000 gown made of gold point, with strands of bugle beads and sequins, which nearly drowned her, accessorized with a scarf banded with sable.

Rumors circulated soon after the release of *Don't Change Your Husband* that Gloria and DeMille were having an affair, a not too difficult conclusion to draw. DeMille's wife Constance reacted as she always did when such gossip began to fester; she invited young Gloria to their home to squash the talk. Gloria was always attracted to older men, protective "daddy"-types, who would provide for and discipline her. DeMille was no exception. However, the great director was shrewd enough not to become involved.

DeMille's daughter Cecilia related an incident her father confided to her: "Gloria and Cecil were watching rushes of *Male and Female* together. Gloria really had a crush on him and she just got up—in the midst of it and in the flickering light from the film—and sat on his lap and put her arms around him. He said [to Cecilia], 'I sat there, I never moved. I never put her back in her seat or expressed any emotion. I kept my hands to myself. I think it was the hardest thing I ever did.' And I asked him, 'Why did you do it?' and he said, 'I had a star who was in love with me. I could pull more out of her in a day if we remained friends. If we became lovers I would have lost some of my control.'"[23] Instead DeMille stuck to his devoted mistresses, Julia Faye, screenwriter Jeanie Macpherson, and secretary Gladys Rosson.

One of the biggest box-office hits of 1919, and considered by many as one of the greatest American silent pictures shot between 1912 and 1920, *Male and Female* cost $168,619. By the end of 1919, in just one month, it had grossed $1,256,226.19.[24] When it premiered on November 23, critics were generous in their praise. *Motion Picture* magazine swooned, "[DeMille] paints with a lavish brush. The sensuous loveliness of his pictures is remembered long after other pallid photoplays are long forgotten. Here Gloria Swanson, indeed a beautifully modeled subject, is the chief mummer for his lavishness. Such glittering costumes of gold, soft furs, rare pearls and shimmering silks!"[25] Lavishness had its benefits.

When the picture opened at the Rivoli Theater in New York, the *New York Times* said, "It is not Barrie. It is not English. It is a typically American movie romance . . . Lavishly staged, skillfully directed, adequately acted, with a good story well told, it is a remarkable film."[26] The *Chicago Daily News* found the

film "exceedingly gorgeous—and exceedingly long . . . And despite the gor-
geousness, methinks the tail is too long for the peacock."[27] Said DeMille's friend
Charles Chaplin somewhat caustically years later, "After *Male and Female*,
DeMille's work never went beyond the chemise and the boudoir."[28]

Photoplay wrote, "It is a typical DeMille production—audacious, glitter-
ing, intriguing, superlatively elegant, and quite without heart. It reminds me
of one of our great California flowers, glowing with all the colors of the rainbow and devoid of fragrance."[29] One astute film historian commented, "Sir
James Barrie must have been shaken to his Scottish core when he saw what
DeMille had wrought from his play."[30] When *Male and Female* opened in Los
Angeles at Grauman's Rialto, "Fred" in *Variety* caught DeMille's eroticism:
"Gloria Swanson . . . appears to advantage in both the London and the desert[ed]
island scenes, looking beautiful at all times, especially as she slips into the
sunken bath."[31]

Thomas Meighan was praised for his work as Crichton. Extremely popular at
the time, the forty-year-old actor was handsomely masculine, though his acting
consisted mainly of a series of scowls and slow-moving, stiff-armed gestures of
dismissal. Interestingly, many moviegoers were impressed with Gloria's enuncia-
tion, though they could not hear her voice. Her lips were easy to read as she
repeated her silent lines.

Joseph Swanson had returned from the war and was stationed at Fort
MacArthur, outside Los Angeles. He had served in France and was nervous
and melancholy, suffering the emotional effects of battle. Gloria allowed him
to stay for several months at a time with her at her home on Wilcox Avenue.
She had not seen him since 1914, and their reunion was cordial, though she
wrote in her book she was leery of his drinking. Her housemate Bea suggested
his subdued behavior and sullen attitude might be caused by narcotics, though
there were no physical indications of any abuse.

For her fourth DeMille picture, Gloria was cast as Beth Gordon, again
opposite Thomas Meighan, as her husband Robert, in *Why Change Your Wife?*,
an answer film to *Don't Change Your Husband*, with a screenplay by Sada
Cowan and Olga Printzlau. The film began production on September 2, 1919. It
tells the common story of the Gordons who have been married for some years
and find their life together unraveling. Beth has become dowdy and aspires for
finer things in life, while Robert prefers simpler pleasures. Beth nags him about

everything. Robert leaves her and has a dalliance with and then marries "Mai-son Chic" lingerie model Sally Clark (Bebe Daniels). He meets Beth again on a train to New York. After he suffers a concussion, Robert is taken to Beth's home, and she calls Sally. When she arrives at Beth's flat, the two women bat-tle. In the end, Beth wins Robert back, and Sally settles for alimony.

William C. deMille had planned to direct this film and star Elliott Dexter. But when Dexter dropped out because of illness, brother Cecil took over. Clare West designed costumes and gowns for *Why Change Your Wife?*, assisted by Mitchell Leisen, who created absurdly preposterous swimming outfits for the pool extravaganza at the hotel. "Gloria . . . [was] expected to wear a different gown in every scene and each more lavish than the previous one," wrote one Hollywood costume historian. "In retrospect the clothes worn by the DeMille stars look bizarre but producers didn't care about realism and DeMille's rec-ipe for success was sex, sets, and costumes."[32]

Gloria wore another dozen costumes in the picture, ranging from dowdy to strangely futuristic. Bebe Daniels was dressed fashionably as well, and in one scene at the dress shop, Julia Faye, wearing a ridiculous-appearing, loud-checkered, knee-length, fringed bathing suit, dark stockings, and shoes, spouts the foolish title-carded line, "When a girl can wear a bathing suit like this, it's her duty to do so."

Filming completed on October 22, 1919, at a cost of $129,349.31. An ex-tremely entertaining film to watch even today, *Why Change Your Wife?* offers a remarkably appealing performance by Gloria. Even at her most nagging, one sympathizes with her character. "Although a notably plump and absurdly over-dressed Swanson looks ten years older than her actual age . . . ," wrote the late Gavin Lambert, "in this Jazz Age drama, for contemporary moviegoers she represented an ideal, the chic and sophisticated young American woman."[33]

Why Change Your Wife? was a sensation, earning back over $1 million world-wide ($759,228 in the United States and $250,000 in Europe).[34] When released at Grauman's Million Dollar Theater in downtown Los Angeles on May 2, 1920, after weeks of preview screenings, *Why Change Your Wife?* broke all attendance records.

Motion Picture magazine proclaimed the ninety-minute film a call for domesticity and found DeMille's stars appealing: "Gloria Swanson is certainly his finest bit of clay. She reflects his messages better than any mirror . . . [and]

Tom Meighan is more handsome than ever."[35] Burns Mantle in *Photoplay* wrote, "[DeMille] spills the spice box into *Why Change Your Wife?* And the result is a rare concoction—the most gorgeously sensual film of the month; in decoration the most costly, in physical allure the most fascinating, in effect the most immoral."[36]

Why Change Your Wife? proved to be the best and most popular of the DeMille social dramas. After its release, other film producers "turned their studios into fashion shops, and the screen was flooded with imitations of the DeMille discovery. Wise wives, foolish wives, clever and stupid wives, any kind of wives, were portrayed in every variety of domestic situation that gave an opportunity for display of wealth, money-getting and money-spending, smart clothes, and romance."[37]

Gloria bought into the opulence her screen persona offered her. For *Theatre Magazine,* she stated, "All my salary goes for clothes and furniture. I buy much more expensive clothes than I should; much more expensive than I ever did before. And I am always buying chairs and pictures and things for my home. I used to be quite satisfied with the simpler things in garments and house furnishings. Where I will finish I don't know—probably in the poor house. Unless some one takes me in charge and curbs my wild extravagance I shall become a State charge."[38]

Around this time, Adela Rogers St. Johns recalled an incident that became Hollywood folklore. Gloria had become the DeMille Mannequin—dressing in private and public as her film heroines, she was often garbed in totally impractical costumes burdened with strings of beads, clusters of feathers, dangling bejeweled baubles and fringe, and long dragging trains. Sadly, too, she had grandly assumed airs of pretentious sophistication. Once at a huge ball at the Ambassador Hotel, she arrived draped in black and rhinestones. "Her hair was dressed a la Medusa," wrote St. Johns. "Suffering the agonies of inferiority, as all eyes were upon her, she had no escape but to freeze into the role she knew best and stay there."[39]

At one point that evening, no-nonsense actress Mae Busch, standing next to Gloria, smiled graciously. "And Gloria gave her a regal DeMille bow," St. Johns continued. "Naturally. She was in the part and didn't know how to get out of it." Leveling a cold eye at Gloria, Busch lit into her, telling her exactly what kind of idiot she was making out of herself. "You can't fool Mamie Busch.

I know you're not the Czarina. I knew you when—" Busch barked. The room was quiet as the two silently stared at each other. Gloria then stepped up to Busch, extended her hand and sweetly smiled at the older actress and said, "I'm sorry you took it that way, Mae. I'm awfully glad to see you. I just had on my company manners."[40]

During the filming of *Why Change Your Wife?* Gloria treated her father and Bea to dinner at the Alexandria Hotel. From across the room Gloria was sent a card from a Herbert K. Somborn, president of Equity Pictures Corporation. She invited the sandy-haired Somborn over to the table. Introducing himself, he offered Gloria greetings from actress Clara Kimball Young and asked if she would have dinner with him at Ms. Young's home. Herbert was a banker from New York, intimately involved in Young's finances and career. Gloria agreed, and after a drink, the two bid each other good evening. Herbert was impressed with her, and the next morning sent her a bouquet of chrysanthemums in a straw basket lined with moss. The following Sunday they dined with Clara Kimball Young.[41]

Gloria learned the actress's latest film, *The Eyes of Youth,* was distributed by Equity Pictures. It had been directed by Albert Parker and featured Gloria's young friend Rudolph Valentino, whom she would often go horseback riding with in the Hollywood hills on Sundays, her only day off. "I was already a star, and he and I would look down at that little place down there called Hollywood," she recalled in 1978, "and he had dreams. He wasn't a star in those days. His reputation was *dreadful.* He was called a gigolo. What did that mean? It meant that he danced with people and then he got paid for it. So I didn't think that was horrible. He had very good manners. He was a gentleman. He was nice and kind."[42]

Young lived in one of those large, expensively furnished mansions in Pasadena. Bedecked in jewels, she carried herself as a woman with extreme confidence. That evening the two actresses talked film. Young knew how to promote and package herself as a viable film commodity. Gloria was very impressed with the older woman's business acumen and paid heed to her advice.

Later, when Somborn drove her home, he kissed Gloria good night, and the two soon began seeing each other. Even though he was nearly twenty years her senior, Herbert "kissed well, without any awkwardness or detachment," Gloria would later write, indicating to her that he did not wish to waste time with preliminary foreplay, yet promising her romantic and dedicated romance for years to come.[43]

On November 1, 1919, Grace Kingsley of the *Los Angeles Times* announced their engagement.

6

Famous Players–Lasky

Certainly there were reasons why Gloria Swanson picked Herbert K. Somborn for her second husband. First and foremost, she was determined to chart her own career. After talking to Clara Kimball Young, Gloria reevaluated her position with Famous Players–Lasky. Somborn was a successful businessman and knew the intricacies of the film industry. Professing financial security, physical desire, and love for her, he would surely be beneficial to Gloria in maneuvering the studio hierarchy as well.

Famous Players–Lasky had promised Gloria a vacation, a trip to New York, upon completion of *Male and Female.* Instead, DeMille immediately rushed her into another picture. Scheduled to head east in late October, she was called back for retakes on *Why Change Your Wife?* She now planned to leave for New York and stay a month. It was then announced her next picture for DeMille, set to begin in early December, was to be a biblical spectacle, the prodigal son parable *The Wanderer,* based on Maurice V. Samuels's 1917 play.[1] Repeatedly, Gloria's desire for time off was halted by the studio. After meeting Herbert K. Somborn, she firmed up plans of her own.

Herbert Klee Somborn was born in Philadelphia on November 26, 1880, to Morris and Rose Somborn. Of Jewish descent, the 5'8", blue-eyed Somborn was the nephew of New York financier S. W. Straus. Herbert was known as a pioneer film producer, and later distributor. He had made a fortune and name for himself by the time he was thirty-five years old. At the time he met Gloria, he was residing at the Alexandria Hotel and was considered one of the wealthiest men in Pasadena.

Famous Players–Lasky and DeMille were not happy about Gloria's engagement. Her drawing power was acknowledged by Grace Kingsley, who wrote, "[She] is one of the most talented of film stars, and, it is said, her popularity since she joined the DeMille forces exceeds even that of many a star appearing with her company. She has, as a matter of fact, been a sort of a fad with young women all over the country, so far as her striking little mannerisms and her particular manner of dressing is [sic] concerned, and this is true among the sophisticated fans of the big towns equally with those of the small—a striking tribute to Miss Swanson's fascination."[2]

An elaborate wedding was planned in December upon completion of retakes on *Why Change Your Wife?* On Saturday, November 8, 1919, Somborn took Gloria to dinner and ordered champagne. As they toasted their coming marriage, Somborn's friend and colleague film director Marshall "Mickey" Neilan approached their table. According to Gloria, he asked her for a dance, and on the floor the twenty-nine-year-old Neilan told her that even though she was marrying his pal Herbert, someday she would marry him. (Gloria would frequently portray herself as a bewitching Lorelei, able to captivate a man at first sight.) Returning to her table, she did not mention the conversation to Herbert.

Herbert had received telegrams from his partners Pat Powers and Joe Schnitzer out east, requesting he return as soon as possible. Gloria was free until after the New Year, when she was scheduled to start DeMille's *Something to Think About,* his *Wanderer* now abandoned. The couple booked a wedding suite at the Alexandria Hotel, and on Saturday, December 20, 1919, they were quietly married. Officiating was Herbert's friend Judge Charles H. Crawford, who later was loosely associated with an organized crime syndicate in Los Angeles known as the City Hall Gang. (Crawford was allegedly the role model for numerous Raymond Chandler villains.)

Wedding congratulations poured in from leaders in the industry as well as Gloria's father, now stationed in San Antonio, Texas. During the days that followed, the papers wrote that Gloria and Herbert were honeymooning in San Francisco. They were actually holed up at the Alexandria for several days, Herbert giving her expensive presents and she loving the adoration as she enjoyed the first "vacation" she had had in years. Gloria found Herbert to be considerate, generous, and romantic.[3] But problems were brewing in New York.

Powerful producer Lewis J. Selznick, president of Clara Kimball Young's film company and father of David O. Selznick, in an aggressive effort to take over distribution of Equity Pictures, was threatening to sue theater owners if they showed *The Eyes of Youth,* starring Young. Young's director and current lover, Harry Garson, was now over budget and making a shambles of her current photoplay. Equity Pictures was on the verge of financial failure. Herbert had to return to New York; he asked Gloria if he might review her contract before he left. Upon doing so he made some keen observations about her arrangement with DeMille and Famous Players–Lasky.

Herbert explained that over the past three weeks of December both her bosses, Jesse Lasky and Adolph Zukor, had been battling with exhibitors who were attempting to gain control over the distribution of their product. Exhibitors had gathered at the Alexandria Hotel (perhaps explaining Somborn's presence) to plan a $40 million merger and sign a five-year contract with every theater owner in the country to stop the takeover. That was why small independent companies like Equity were facing failure, and why Douglas Fairbanks, Mary Pickford, D. W. Griffith, and Charles Chaplin were merging together to create their own releasing company. Gloria's career was skyrocketing—her name now appeared in Paramount advertising above Thomas Meighan and Cecil B. DeMille. She was a big star.

So what had she done wrong? By signing her original 1918 contract, and in January 1919 accepting $50 more a week (Lasky had coerced DeMille to flatter her into doing so), she had given Famous Players–Lasky (Paramount) the right to use her name to secure block bookings of their films by selling four Swanson pictures a year to any individual theater contingent on the owner buying thirty-five other films sight unseen. For that Gloria was paid "nothing," as Herbert explained. (Clara Kimball Young, for example, received $25,000 a picture, plus a percentage of the gross.)

Herbert was furious. "We've got to get you out of the hands of the Eastern European Jews," he stated.[4] Somborn arranged a conversation with film producer Harry Cohn in the dining room of the Alexandria, telling him they were seeking to break Gloria's contract and have her star in a film with director Mickey Neilan with money supplied by financier Pat Powers. Did Cohn know a good lawyer? The trap was set.

Herbert then left for New York on the Overland Limited on January 11, 1920, to consult with his attorneys about Gloria's contract. Perhaps because she was a bit frightened of facing DeMille when production started up on *Something to Think About,* or possibly to ensure Herbert would secure her future while he was in New York, Gloria bombarded her new husband with telegrams on his rail journey eastbound. Her first one read:

> I AM MAD WHY DIDN'T YOU MAKE ME GET UP I DON'T KNOW
> WHAT TO DO GOING FOR A RIDE AS SOON AS I HAVE MY LONE-
> SOME BREAKFAST BE SURE TO WRITE EVERY DAY AND YOU
> MUST TELEPHONE TOO ALL MY LOVE DADDY DEAR[5]

More telegrams followed until Herbert returned on January 21.

Production commenced on *Something to Think About* on January 20. It was a decided change of pace for Gloria, whom the public had come to recognize as a sleek and beautiful glamour queen. In the film she was now to enact a common blacksmith's daughter ("the flower of the forge"). Gloria was out of her element. With another plodding screenplay by Jeanie Macpherson, the story tells of a wealthy crippled art student named David Markley (Elliott Dexter) who falls in love with Ruth (Gloria), daughter of the village blacksmith, Luke Anderson (Theodore Roberts). Ruth runs off with Jim Dirk (Monte Blue). Angered, Luke begs God to never let him see his daughter again and is blinded by sparks. Jim dies, and after Ruth gives birth to their son, Danny (Mickey Moore), she returns home, and David falls in love with her all over again.

Completed on March 30, *Something to Think About* was a true DeMille moral tale. Somehow during its telling Gloria is given fancy duds to parade about in during the second half of the picture. Clare West created these costumes, which ranged from simple and dreary to stunningly yet elegantly silly.

During the filming, Gloria was presented with unpaid bills from the Alexandria Hotel, a desk drawer full, including the tab for a necklace Herbert had bought her. He could not explain any of it away. She quickly became disillusioned about Herbert, realizing perhaps that he was relying on her income to sustain their lifestyle.[6] She paid off the bills, and the couple took a modest apartment at Yucca and Wilcox.

As production wrapped on *Something to Think About,* Gloria discovered she was pregnant. This created a bit of problem as DeMille wanted to continue the DeMille-Swanson juggernaut. The powers at Famous Players–Lasky felt motherhood would diminish her box office. Gloria weighed her options. If she kept the baby, at least her husband would be held financially responsible, and she did want a child. But telling her boss Jesse L. Lasky was going to be difficult. When she did, he advised her that the timing was bad; the studio had invested too much in her for her to take time off. "Nobody but God can dictate whether I'm going to have a baby," she allegedly told him.[7] Then, when she confessed Herbert had read her contract and suggested it would be invalid after January 1, 1921, because of its inequity in the studio's favor, the mogul became furious.

For a month after the completion of *Something to Think About* Gloria continued to receive her weekly studio check. When she was later called back to Lasky's office, he proudly told her the studio was going to make her a star. Paramount was going to give her the big buildup and indulge her with the star treatment, more money, a deluge of press, and reverential treatment. "Being a star meant having a private bungalow on the set like Mary Pickford's and around-the-clock maids and studio cars and trips to Europe," Gloria surmised in her memoirs.[8] Yet she also wrote she begged *not* to become a star yet, because she wanted to continue working with DeMille, but Lasky advised her Adolph Zukor and DeMille both thought it was the appropriate time to make the change. The facts were obvious. She had become too big a star to be directed by one director at Paramount.[9]

DeMille, no doubt with orders from Paramount's top office, comforted Gloria. He later wrote, "The public, not I, made Gloria Swanson a star. Exhibitors began to demand that she be given star treatment."[10] "I wanted to stay with Mr. DeMille," she later humbly recalled. "Everybody thought I was out of my mind. But DeMille told me I had to leave him, I had to go and be a star on my own because, he said, 'You're a star and I'm a star, and we can't put all our eggs in one basket.' I said, 'But Mr. DeMille, if I leave you I won't have this and I won't have that, and I know they'll economize on something else . . .' He said, 'No, young fellow, it will be all right. You go ahead."[11] One wonders if Jeanie Macpherson wrote this dialogue.

It was, however, a two-way street. Gloria knew she had the studio at her mercy as long as she remained pregnant and continued her threats of leaving on January 1, 1921, encouraged by Herbert. "Swanson had talent and personality," wrote one DeMille biographer. "She might very well have become a star under any circumstances. 'I do things under the guise of Gloria Swanson that me, Gloria, doesn't want to do but I do because it's expected of me,' Swanson explained. 'I use her most of the time to support me. She's been a tool.' "[12] Also, by choosing to have her baby, she broke with tradition by not keeping her pending motherhood a secret.

On July 11, 1920, the *New York Times* reported that Gloria Swanson, "Cecil B. DeMille's most married and unmarried heroine," had signed a new five-year contract with Famous Players–Lasky Corporation, which would elevate her to stardom in "photoplays selected and supervised (though not directed) by Mr. DeMille."[13] Gloria and Lasky handled the negotiations, deliberately excluding Herbert from the deal. Her new salary was $2,500 per week, escalating to $3,500 by the end of 1921. Paramount would have the option to renew her for $6,000 a week the fourth year and $7,000 the fifth. She would make four pictures a year. "I have decided that when I become a star," Gloria triumphantly announced, "I will be every inch and every moment a star! Everybody from the studio gateman to the highest executive will know it."[14]

At 7 A.M. on Thursday, October 7, 1920, Gloria gave birth to her first, and Herbert's only, child, a girl delivered by Dr. R. L. Byron. She named her Gloria. It was a difficult birth, and the physician had to use forceps. Gloria was given chloroform, and after coming to, she was handed her baby daughter. Gloria wrote, "The first thing she did was to reach for my breast, and the ecstasy overwhelmed me."[15] A week after giving birth, she was visited by DeMille, who brought her a baby necklace of tiny pearls with a diamond clasp. His actual purpose for the call was to ask her to make one more picture with him as director. She agreed without telling Herbert.

When *Something to Think About* premiered in New York at the Criterion Theater at Forty-Fourth and Broadway, on October 17, the critics were somewhat baffled. Ads raved: "You Can't Afford to Miss This One" and "A Picture with a Soul!" *The New York Times* found, "Mr. DeMille is a maker of motion pictures. Whether they mean anything or not—and many of them do—they are works of cinematographic skill . . . Praise and blame for the authorship of this story must go to Jeanie Macpherson."[16] The *Los Angeles Times* wrote, "Mr. DeMille has given the screen a drama which will live in the minds and hearts of the spectators as a story full of thought. Gloria Swanson establishes a new adage—that while clothes may make the woman they have nothing whatever to do with making the actress."[17] The picture made money, costing $169,330 and grossing $901,848.51 in the United States alone.

Gloria's new film with DeMille was *The Affairs of Anatol,* formerly titled *Five Kisses,* based on a cycle of ten short plays by Arthur Schnitzler. Changing Schnitzler's plays considerably, Jeanie Macpherson, with a generous assist by screenwriters Beulah Marie Dix, Lorna Moon, and Elmer Harris, created a convoluted screenplay that satisfied the director.

DeMille lost many of his stock players after this film. *Anatol* became a farewell of sorts for his leading ladies Gloria, Bebe Daniels, Wanda Hawley, and Agnes Ayres. DeMille was not happy with the assignment, not understanding Schnitzler's psychological subplots, nor was he pleased to have his stars leaving him. For the stellar role of Anatol, DeMille selected the tragically doomed Wallace Reid. "Wallace was the number-one box-office star, the King," recalled actor Conrad Nagel. "And he was one of the most charming, most lovable, wonderful guys I've ever known. There wasn't the slightest bit of conceit in him. He took himself seriously. No ego there at all. But perhaps he was overwhelmed."[18]

The handsome William Wallace Reid was born in St. Louis in 1891. Incredibly attractive and athletic, Reid started in movies in 1910 and married actress Dorothy Davenport in 1913. He became Paramount's biggest male star, later dubbed "The Screen's Most Perfect Lover" by none other than romance novelist Elinor Glyn. In 1919, while filming *The Valley of the Giants,* Reid suffered head and lower vertebrae injuries in a train wreck. To enable the actor to complete the picture and ease his pain, a doctor injected him with morphine. Reid continued taking morphine orally, long past the time he should have stopped. He sadly became an addict. For a while, despite the ravages of the disease, Wally continued handing in fine film performances.

By the time of *The Affairs of Anatol,* Reid's dependency was making inroads on his work. Gloria would later write that Wallace Reid made her feel uneasy and uncomfortable, though she never saw him use drugs.[19]

The Affairs of Anatol tells a tale of wealthy Manhattan socialite Anatol de Witt Spencer (Reid) and his beautiful wife Vivian (Gloria), who are out on the town with his friend Max Runyon (Elliott Dexter). Anatol complains to Max that he finds there is too much "honey" in his honeymoon. And thus begins for Anatol an episodic journey to find romance on a spiritual and altruistic level. Through four separate episodes of near-infidelity, Anatol, smitten with his purpose, is equally disillusioned by its reality. Along the way he is enticed by a former girlfriend, Emilie Dixon (Wanda Hawley), has a flirtation with a farmer's wife, Annie Elliott (Agnes Ayres), and is thwarted in a rendezvous with vamp Satan Synne (Bebe Daniels). (A fifth episode with Dorothy Cummings was deleted.)

Art decorator Wilfred Buckland was also leaving DeMille's auspices to work with director Allan Dwan's new independent production unit. DeMille then assigned French designer Paul Iribe, one of the founders of the art deco movement in the United States (he had also designed costumes for *Male and Female*), to create the startling interior sets for *Anatol,* undeniably conceiving the most attractive of all DeMille's silent films. Iribe also designed costumes for *Anatol* with Clare West.

Photography was shared by Alvin Wyckoff and Karl Struss. With hand-colored title cards, and beautiful pink, purple, red, and blue tints, *The Affairs of Anatol* was a lushly produced and richly crafted picture. It cost $176,508.08.

Gloria had not lost much weight after the birth of her baby. During a fitting, screenwriter Jeanie Macpherson, a frustrated actress, made a biting remark about Gloria's weight to her in front of others. Gloria told DeMille about the comment, and he advised her, "As a star you have to learn to hear what you want to hear, ignore what you have to ignore. You have to learn to take the cream and leave the milk."[20] Gloria never forgot DeMille's advice; it helped her explain away her critics.

Upon completion of *Anatol,* on January 25, after only a brief rest, Gloria was rushed into the first picture of her new contract. Even before *Something to Think About* was released Jesse Lasky, in an effort to "elevate" the screen, announced that the "veddy Brr-itish" and very eccentric fifty-six-year-old Elinor

Glyn had been commissioned by Paramount to write a screenplay for Gloria. Glyn was the younger sister of Lucy Wallace, Lady Duff-Gordon, a *Titanic* survivor, who under the professional name of Lucile became the first internationally recognized British couturier.[21] Beginning in 1900 Elinor, or Madame Glyn, as she preferred to be addressed, produced over forty romance novels, including *Beyond the Rocks* (1906) and *Three Weeks* (1907), which producer Samuel Goldwyn had optioned. Not to be outdone, Lasky contracted Glyn's services and thought up the title *The Great Moment*. All Madame Glyn needed to do was write the story.

Bridging the literary gap between turn-of-the-century Victorianism and new ideals, in her romances Glyn best symbolized, with fanciful idealization and innocence, modern acceptance of friendship, acquaintances, and sex partnership between men and women. "Had the war, the vote, short skirts, and a supposition of equality banished romance?" asked historian Marjorie Rosen. "Elinor Glyn thought so. What the world needed now, she felt, was great love, noble and aristocratic. She tapped a hidden vein and came up with pure gold."[22] Thus, upon her arrival into Hollywood, movies entered a period of Ruritanian romance. Before Elinor Glyn, writers had not played a major role in films. Her domination in Hollywood during the 1920s was unequivocal.

Sailing into New York aboard the liner *Mauretania* in the autumn of 1920, Glyn was met at the foot of the gangplank by Lasky himself. "Flaming red hair, green eyes, powder-white face, dripping with leopard skins, she looked more like one of her own heroines than an authoress," wrote Jesse Lasky Jr.[23] In California, Madame Glyn glided into Lasky's studio office draped in a leopard-print gown and glittering with $250,000 worth of diamonds, ready to take him, Paramount, and Hollywood by storm. She settled into the Hollywood Hotel, catered to by her maid Blinky and dressmaker Miss Morgan, who created the fashion concoctions Madame dreamed up for herself to wear. Decorating her two-room suite with Oriental rugs, Persian divans, Buddhas, crystal balls, gongs, and a large tiger skin rug, Madame Glyn became her best publicist, hosting Sunday afternoon teas dressed in pastel Persian pajamas (designed by her sister Lucile) and reciting poetry while sprawled out on a purple pillow on her fur rug.

The plot of *The Great Moment* is typical Glyn nonsense. Diplomat Lord

Edward Pelham (Alec B. Francis) fears his child Nadine (Gloria), who has been raised exclusively in their English country house, will become like her wild Russian gypsy mother Nada (also Gloria in flashback in a dual role). On a visit to Nevada, Nadine encounters engineer Bayard Delavel (Milton Sills), who saves her life after she is bitten by a poisonous snake. Nadine is reunited with her father in Washington, D.C., and agrees to marry millionaire Howard Hopper (Arthur Stuart Hull). But the night of their engagement ball, she is reunited with her lover Delavel.

Sam Wood, who had dealt in selling land before becoming an assistant director for DeMille, was assigned to direct *The Great Moment*. He was unenthusiastic about the project, and Gloria wasn't happy with Wood, either, stating, "He was all right, but he was a real estate dealer at heart."[24] Still, Wood directed eight Swanson pictures in a row.

The Great Moment is a lost film. The crucial sequence in the picture, obviously "the great moment," is Glyn at her most self-expressive erotic. According to Charlie Chaplin, whose own recollections were somewhat clouded by the time he wrote his 1966 memoirs, Gloria's character "goes horseback riding alone, and, being interested in botany, gets off her horse to inspect a rare flower. As she bends over it, a deadly viper strikes and bites her right on the bosom." When she screams in pain and fear, the man she truly loves, Delavel, appears.

"Suddenly he picks her up, tears at her shirtwaist, and bares her gleaming white shoulders, then turns her away from the vulgar glare of the camera, bends over her and with his mouth extracts the poison, spitting it out as he does so. As a result of this successful operation she marries him."[25] Madame Glyn had originally written the action to take place on a leopard-skin rug, but during production no description of the sequence was making sense. Written in Wood's copy of the scenario was the instruction "Rather than describe the scene, Madame Glyn will personally enact it on the set."[26]

Glyn was not impressed with Gloria at first. Wrote Jesse Lasky Jr., "When she couldn't prevail upon my father to remove Gloria Swanson as the leading lady she attempted to remold the already famous star into the sort of heroine she felt her script required."[27] Upon meeting Gloria, Glyn magnanimously pronounced, "Extraordinary . . . your proportions are perfect . . . Egyptian; anyone can see that . . . ."[28] "Gloria Swanson has the look of a huntress. That is the secret of her fascination," Glyn informed Adela Rogers St. Johns.[29]

Gloria would recall Madame Glyn as carrying herself with rigid British dignity. Describing her appearance, Gloria said that she was the first woman she had ever met who wore false eyelashes. Blind as a bat, Glyn's vanity forbade she ever wear eyeglasses. She thus had to take small baby steps as she navigated across a room so as not to trip. Her massive white teeth were prominently set off by flaming red hair wrapped about her head like a turban, and she wore excessive amounts of perfume. She was indeed something unlike Hollywood had ever known. Her declarations of proper behavior were to be heeded.[30] Glyn actually coached Gloria on proper etiquette, "something that took Miss Swanson many a year to live down," wrote film historians Richard Griffith and Arthur Mayer.[31]

Hollywood, still searching for its own cultural definition, loved her and unashamedly paid homage to this vainglorious maven. "If Hollywood hadn't existed, Elinor Glyn would have had to invent it," Anita Loos once wrote.[32] She was invited everywhere in town. At an exclusive dinner party at Samuel Goldwyn's home to celebrate the completion of Charlie Chaplin's *The Kid,* Madame Glyn, upon nervously meeting the comic, said, "You don't look as funny as I expected."

"Neither do you," Chaplin replied.[33]

Given carte blanche, and even a brief cameo in *The Affairs of Anatol* (as a bridge player at the hypnotism party), Madame Glyn was feted as royalty. She maintained a strict and irksome control over her screenplays, supervising every detail of the productions. She even had contractual prerogative over the choice of a leading man. For *The Great Moment,* she chose Paramount's latest male sex god, Rudolph Valentino. He had just made a huge impact at Metro with *The Four Horsemen of the Apocalypse.* Valentino was unfortunately unavailable. So she settled for Milton Sills, whom she suddenly proclaimed had "It," that indefinable star power. Filming began on *The Great Moment* in late January.

Because of her reluctance to allow him to take over her career, coupled with his dependency on her income, Gloria and Herbert had begun to argue frequently. He advised they take a suite at the new Ambassador Hotel, so he could keep up appearances. When they received the first month's bill, Gloria was shocked. During her pregnancy she had made friends with Violet "Peggy" Urson, a Christian Science practitioner and wife of Frank Urson, one of Mickey Neilan's assistant directors. Peggy suggested they take a bungalow at the Hollywood Hotel, which they did.

The Great Moment wrapped in May, and on the fifth Gloria and the baby moved to a little inn at Silver Lake. Within days Gloria heard that Herbert had moved out of their bungalow. When he was taken to the Westlake Hospital for a minor operation, she visited him, and in the presence of director Harry Garson announced her plans for divorce. "I must have my career. Nothing can interfere," she stated.[34]

During the filming of *The Great Moment,* Gloria and Madame Glyn were quite close. "She went everywhere and passed her fearsome verdicts on everything," Gloria said. "'This is glamorous' she would say. 'That is hideous' she would say, as she baby-stepped through this or that dining room or garden party. People moved aside for her as if she were a sorceress on fire or a giant sting ray. After Herbert moved out of my life, Elinor got in the habit of taking me with her on her social rounds . . . going places with Elinor was never dull."[35]

When *The Great Moment* opened at New York's Rivoli Theater the week of July 25, the *New York Times* critic wrote, "The 'moment' is not particularly 'great,' even by comparison with the many lesser moments that make up the hour or more that the story runs—or walks . . . So many incredible things happen, and the action is imbedded in such an artificial setting, that the story creates no illusion. Neither Miss Glyn nor Sam Wood . . . has been able to conceal the obvious effort of the piece to be sensational. And it doesn't succeed in being sensational, either." He also observed Gloria was "an actress imminently capable in some roles, [but] does not fit into her part . . . [and] never seems the wild young thing she is supposed to be."[36]

When the picture opened at Grauman's Rialto in Los Angeles in mid-August, Edwin Schallert, drama critic for the *Los Angeles Times,* declared it "a highly entertaining photoplay. You'll enjoy it . . . Gloria Swanson's gowns are both new, numerous and gorgeous, and she wears them with such an air of languid loveliness."[37] Gloria's several costumes in the film were indeed stunning; one gown sported a four-foot pearl and ermine train.

After the tremendous buildup Paramount had invested in publicizing her maiden starring vehicle, and the subsequent tepid reception critics and audiences gave *The Great Moment,* Gloria was indeed fortunate that DeMille's *The Affairs of Anatol* was held back and released in September.

7

Paramount

As filming of *Under the Lash,* Gloria's next project, commenced shooting in the summer of 1921, Paramount realized *The Great Moment* was going to be a wash and decided to patch the "fifth kiss" segment of *The Affairs of Anatol,* which had cost the studio $44,127 to film, together with additional deleted sequences and pad them out to create a completely new feature film starring Gloria and Wallace Reid. Possibly in hopes the public would not be the wiser, the studio entitled the pastiche *Don't Tell Everything.* Title cards would create a new plot.

Under the Lash, based on the Claude and Alice Askew novel and 1906 play *The Shulamite,* starred Gloria as Deborah Krillet, the wife of a religious zealot, South African Boer farmer Simeon Krillet (Russell Simpson). He threatens to beat her after he catches her reading Shakespeare's *Romeo and Juliet.* Deborah falls in love with married land overseer Robert Waring (Mahlon Hamilton). Robert shoots Simeon when he threatens Deborah, and Deborah grants Simeon's property and money over to his sister. Robert and Deborah are united by fade-out. The screenplay for *Under the Lash* was dark, dated, and gloomy.

The film was a deliberate departure for Gloria, and she wore no fancy gowns or jewels. It was directed by the gentle and kindly Sam Wood, who included a then-astounding storm sequence featuring trees being "struck" by lightning (exploded by technicians).

On Wednesday, August 17, Matthew P. Burns, Addie's second husband, died suddenly at the age of forty-nine, at their home at 926 Edgemont Avenue. He had successfully owned and operated the Harvard Shoe Stores Company and the System Shoe Stores. Burns was buried in the Hollywood Cemetery. He left no children. His widow was the next of kin, besides a brother and two sisters.

Burns's $100,000 estate bequeathed $500 to each of his siblings and one nephew, and $2,000 to his bookkeeper. The balance was left to Addie. In early October, the family contested the will, claiming Burns was not of sound mind and had actually suffered a nervous breakdown the year before, when the will was made out. They also contended the marriage was possibly not valid and accused Addie of paying a Mr. and Mrs. Frank Hayes $100 to introduce her to Burns. Gloria's name was brought into the proceedings when the siblings insinuated that Burns had all along been in love with her. They said she had seduced him, then, reminding Burns she was married, suggested he should marry her mother. The whole mess would drag on in court for years.

Meanwhile, Paramount, after a long delay, premiered *The Affairs of Anatol* on Sunday, September 11, in New York at the Rialto and Rivoli theaters. Ads heralded, "All Star Cast!! The Roster Reads Like a Who's Who!" "THINK WHAT IT MEANS TO SEE ALL THESE CELEBRITIES AND YOUR FAVORITE IN THIS BIG PHOTOPLAY," and "People Have Been Talking About It for a Year In Advance! They'll Be Talking About It for Ten Years After Seeing It!"[1] Adolph Zukor boasted *The Affairs of Anatol* "was undoubtedly the best thing we have ever done with the greatest cast ever assembled for one picture."[2]

The *New York Times* led the reviews. "Here is Mr. DeMille at his best. Whether or not you like it is another matter . . . Mr. DeMille, it appears, must be ornate and artificial at all times, and his style is not suited, therefore, to stories of real people and serious import . . . Gloria Swanson is decorative."[3]

Other critics were unimpressed. One British reviewer, G. R. Doyle, moaned that *The Affairs of Anatol* was the worst film he had ever seen.[4] Robert E. Sherwood, writing for *Life* on September 18, chimed in with "Should be enormously popular, especially with those who think Schnitzler is a cheese."[5] The September issue of *Motion Picture Classic* magazine crucified the film: "Nothing left of Schnitzler but the title. The subtle craftsmanship, the sentimental melancholy and the humorous cynicism have given way to crudity and even clumsy vulgarity. We look upon 'The Affairs of Anatol' as the worst massacre since Custer's forces were wiped out by the redskins. The silken DeMille is certainly running riot."[6]

Viewed today in all its pristine restored splendor, with color tints, hand-colored title cards, and a brief early two-tone Technicolor sequence (of the nude Satan Synne), *The Affairs of Anatol* is stunning to behold, startling to watch, yet difficult to take seriously. Wally Reid looks great in tuxedos, and Gloria is gorgeous in nearly a dozen different costumes. Historically important, it was a DeMille-Super Production, the first motion picture with a deliberately all-star cast.[7] When all was said and done, *The Affairs of Anatol* grossed $1,191,789.19.

Scott Eyman in his biography of DeMille accurately sets these social sex dramas into contemporary perspective, giving DeMille credit for "showcasing the new woman that made her appearance after World War I. No longer did a wife need to be devoted solely to family and community; now she could be interested in clothes, in sexual experimentation, in using a man for whatever she could get."[8] With Gloria as the leading female exponent of these pictures, the public assumed she was in person the same character she portrayed on the screen. She had made DeMille and Paramount millions at the box office, and DeMille and the public made Gloria a star.

Under the Lash crept onto the big screens on October 16, 1921, with very little ballyhoo. Lasky knew he had a turkey. Audiences were expecting to see their Gloria decked out in glamorous gowns and furs. They were sadly disappointed. Word of mouth spread quickly, and the verdict was a unanimous thumbs-down. Nothing could save *Under the Lash,* and it became the first starring film of Gloria's to lose money at the box office.

Variety reviewer "Fred" waxed clever: "Sam Wood . . . should be taken to task . . . Miss Swanson is equally to blame, for she has been in pictures long enough to know her profile does not screen to advantage, and therefore she should avoid any close-ups or semi-close-up shots with herself in that position. Incidentally, that mourning costume Miss Swanson as Deborah managed to have right after her husband's death, even though she was in the midst of the South African veldt, would seem to indicate that she expected the bewhiskered Simeon to be bumped off at any minute."[9] When *Under the Lash* opened at Grauman's Million Dollar Theater, the critic in the *Moving Picture World* only noticed Gloria's costumes: "She isn't exactly the type to be found on a Boer farm and she wears a frock in the last scene that is entirely out of character."[10]

The September 1921 issue of *Photoplay* announced Herbert was staying at the Los Angeles Athletic Club, while Gloria and their baby lived at the Beverly Hills Hollywood Hotel. One columnist stated the cause of their separation was due to temperamental incompatibility and quoted Gloria: "Madame Glyn does not believe in marriage for artists, since she claims that 'marriage is good and art is good, but they do not appear to assimilate perfection.' Her theory is that great artists must not be bound within the narrow walls of domesticity."[11]

Paramount released *Don't Tell Everything* on November 13. It had a fleshed-out plot fashioned by Albert Shelby Le Vino, from a story by Lorna Moon (the same of Anatol and his "fifth kiss.") A story line was developed with added players and a couple of additional scenes of Wallace Reid, Gloria, Elliott Dexter, and Dorothy Cummings filmed within a week's duration. It was quite simple to change the characters' names, and switch the existing scenes around to fit the needs of the new scenario; this was a silent film, after all.

The new plot told of Marian Westover (Gloria), who is loved by both wealthy Cullen Dale (Reid), who wants to marry her, and his best friend, Harvey Gilroy (Dexter), who longs for her in silence. Cullen and Marian marry, but she is jealous of his former girlfriends, especially Jessica Ramsey (Cummings), who invites them to a mountain lodge. When a storm prevents Cullen from coming home one night, Marian enlists the help of Harvey to find him.

Surprisingly, the picture turned out quite nicely, and it pleased audiences. Possibly it was because Gloria wore additional fashions that had been created for her for *The Affairs of Anatol*. Director Sam Wood was a bit embarrassed about taking over concepts created by DeMille. He did cast his daughter, billed as Baby Gloria Wood (later stage and screen actress K. T. Stevens), in the picture as Cullen's niece. One critic allowed, "It's all standard fare, what we've come to expect from Swanson-Dexter-Reid, but they make this somewhat warmed-over situational stew entertaining."[12]

While on the town with Madame Glyn, Gloria encountered director Mickey Neilan at the Leather Pump Room at the Ambassador. As she and Neilan danced, he reminded her of the evening when she and Herbert had announced their engagement. When they returned to the table and Neilan bid adieu, Madame Glyn, lighting one of her Benson & Hedges cigarettes, looked askance at Gloria and advised her, "*But . . . my . . . dear,* nab him."[13] With Madame Glyn's approbation, she tried her best.

California-born Marshall Ambrose Neilan, known as "Mickey," was born April 11, 1891. At an early age he worked as an actor to support his widowed mother. Starting in pictures in 1912 for Kalem Studios in Santa Monica, Neilan became a director within a year, and in 1915 was one of the founders of the Motion Picture Directors Association, along with William Desmond Taylor, Allan Dwan, and DeMille. Hired by Mary Pickford Films in 1916, he directed "America's Sweetheart" in some of her classic silent features released by Artcraft, including *Rebecca of Sunnybrook Farm* (1917), *Amaryllis of Clothesline Alley* (1918), and *Daddy-Long-Legs* (1919).

Starting in 1920, Neilan ran his own motion picture production company. He had married actress Gertrude Bambrick in 1913. When he started pursuing Gloria in 1921, his divorce was not yet final. Still, Mickey could make Gloria laugh. He talked of music, film, and art, and she was smitten. Truly a Renaissance man, he even composed the haunting theme "Wonderful One" especially for Gloria. Published in 1922 by Leo Feist as a "Waltz Song" (strangely dedicated "To Julie"), it was given words by Theodora Morse (aka Dorothy Terris) and, with music fleshed out by Paul Whiteman and Ferde Grofé, was recorded by Whiteman on RCA Victor the following year. "Wonderful One" became the couple's love song.

Marshall Neilan "had a great talent, and the films he made had an unbeatable combination of humor, heart, and box office," wrote actress Colleen Moore in her memoirs. "He drank too much and too often, and when he had too much to drink he could be sharp-tongued and mean. Yet for all his wisecracks he was a kind, warm hearted person . . . He was a charming, crazy, obstinate Irishman who lived a full and exciting life—a complex man and a maddening one sometimes, but never a dull one."[14] Neilan had many romances throughout his marriage, one in particular with Ziegfeld Follies beauty Peggy Hopkins Joyce, who married often and always quite well. "The big romance in Mickey's own life was more than big," continued Moore. "It was spectacular . . . At the time Mickey was engaged to Blanche Sweet . . . [who] was displaced by a woman who didn't just represent glamour. She invented the word."[15]

Mickey encouraged Gloria to spread her wings: "Get away from Hollywood for a while. Go somewhere where they won't always remember that you used to be an extra girl. You need more self-confidence. You need a little ego. Go to

Europe first. Get some real clothes. Come back to New York and let the Big Town show you things. You'll be a knockout there."[16]

Neilan had won Gloria's heart. He was not the first man with whom she had an affair. Before her marriage to Herbert Somborn, and during their separation, she was rumored to have been involved with most of her leading men, the exceptions being Wallace Reid, Rudolph Valentino, and Elliott Dexter. But Neilan was different. Gloria wrote that Mickey always knew where the best times and best alcohol in Hollywood could be had.[17] She found her lover enchanting.

In good spirits when she began her next picture in the fall of 1921, Gloria was again directed by Sam Wood, whom she was learning to appreciate, in *Her Husband's Trademark*. With a story by Clara Beranger and scenario by Lorna Moon, *Her Husband's Trademark* told of Lois Miller (Gloria), who is wooed by both ambitious engineer Allan Franklin (Richard Wayne) and James Berkeley (Stuart Holmes), who longs to be wealthy. Berkeley wins Lois's hand, and they marry. Though he never becomes as rich as he would like, he keeps Lois as a "trophy" wife, his "trademark." Allan and Lois realize they love each other, and she scorns James when he shows indifference. In Mexico bandits try to kidnap Lois, and James is killed. Allan rescues Lois, and they flee across the border back into the United States.

Jesse Lasky, still smarting after the debacle of *Under the Lash*, vowed Gloria would never be seen on the screen again in anything but fabulous costumes. For her new picture he saw that she was coiffed and gowned in over twenty different Ethel Chaffin costumes (including a fur coat made of twelve black and ten black-and-white Australian opossum pelts) and six "very lavish creations and two striking negligees."[18] When production ended on *Her Husband's Trademark*, Gloria was quickly assigned *Beyond the Rocks*, which had an extravagant story by the outré Madame Glyn. Her co-star was Rudolph Valentino.

Motion pictures had from their inception long been considered a form of "art," and thus exempt from censorship under the protection of the Constitution. This freedom, which film producers frequently abused, had sometimes taken on rather seamy and exploitative overtones. In 1915 the Supreme Court ruled motion pictures were product and not art, and thus not protected by free speech. Church groups and grassroots conservatives were grumbling rather forcefully by 1921, when a major scandal hit the press and the nation reeled from the fall of one of its most beloved and revered comedians, Roscoe "Fatty" Arbuckle. On Labor Day weekend, Arbuckle, suffering from burns to his buttocks from an on-the-set accident, along with actor-director Lowell Sherman and cameraman Fred Fischbach, threw a drunken bash in suite 1220 of the St. Francis Hotel in San Francisco. One of the partygoers, bit-part movie actress Virginia Rappe, became violently ill and within a few days died.

Rappe's death was placed squarely in Arbuckle's lap, so to speak, when he was arrested on September 10 and charged with murder by rape. It was alleged the starlet had been ruptured internally, because of Arbuckle's sizable girth and weight, or possibly by the insertion of a soda bottle. The none-too-virtuous Rappe's death was actually caused by her low tolerance to bootleg alcohol, coupled with complications to her reproductive organs due to several botched abortions. However, Arbuckle faced the wrath of the courts in three separate trials, though he was eventually acquitted.

But the damage was done, and Arbuckle was finished in pictures, his films banned and his once loyal public turned against him. He became persona non grata in Tinseltown and was vilified by morally outraged women's clubs like the National Council of Catholic Women, various youth movements such as the Boys Club of America, and church organizations, all of which screamed for film censorship. Filmmakers in Hollywood began to listen. For years each individual state, via its own censorship board, would edit and censor a picture to meet its requirements. This cost the industry over $2 million a year in spliced and damaged films. It was time a cover-all action was set in place.

By the early 1920s the federal government and thirty-six states were threatening to enact severe penalties against the Hollywood studios. The Catholic Legion of Decency complained to the recently organized Bank of America and Italy, which helped finance the motion picture companies. The bank was headed by the very Catholic Amadeo Giannini, who agreed to rescind further financing to the movie studios unless an organized censorship system was established and its rules adhered to. Enter newly appointed postmaster general of the United States under President Warren G. Harding, forty-one-year-old William "Will" H. Hays.

Approached by film moguls Lewis J. Selznick and Saul Rogers on December 8, 1921, Hays resigned as postmaster general on January 14, 1922, and became the president of the Motion Picture Producers and Distributors of

America (MPPDA) beginning in March at a salary of $100,000 a year. Silent film actor Conrad Nagel recalled that the studio heads secured "Will Hays, the greatest politician of that era, and they organized the Hays Office. Hays went to work, brought the censorship offices together, and said, 'Tell us what you object to, and we will try and cut it out of the source.' That was the code's primary function. The producers signed up. Hays was their czar. What his office said went . . . Hays saved the motion picture industry."[19]

When he arrived in Los Angeles in July 1922, Hays was afforded a hero's welcome, complete with a parade down bunting-lined streets with flags flying, and a huge all-star turnout at a banquet at the Ambassador Hotel in his honor. Everyone in Hollywood was there to honor the man chosen to save them from their vices.[20] Hays's position as the industry "spokesman" there to "clean up pictures" in the wake of the Arbuckle trials was basically a publicity ploy to placate the growing moral concern of the moviegoing public. With great fanfare, censorship rules were drawn up—no nudity, no immoral conduct, etc. Those dictates were then promptly put away and ignored, until a national calamity, the Great Depression, brought about a revision of the code in 1934. Gloria's film career was little affected by all this as *Beyond the Rocks* geared up to lens.

Gloria was now the second-most-popular female box-office attraction in the country after Mary Pickford. After years of professional struggle, Rudolph Valentino, born Rodulphus Petrus Philibertus Raphael (sometimes listed as Rodolfo Pietro Filiberto Raffaele) Guglielmi in Castellaneta, Italy, in 1895, was now a huge box-office star. Metro scenarist June Mathis saw something in the 5'10", 156-pound former dancer and "gigolo" and championed him. Perhaps it was talent; perhaps it was something else. In any event, Valentino made a huge impression in *The Four Horsemen of the Apocalypse,* released in March of 1921 (Wallace Beery was also in the film). Valentino then became the Sheik, co-starring in the film of that title with Gloria's friend Agnes Ayres, for Famous Players–Lasky. It became a sensation and catapulted Valentino into superstardom. Elinor Glyn pronounced he possessed the elusive "It" that she periodically and magnanimously bestowed upon her chosen few throughout the decade.

Signing a contract with Famous Players–Lasky in November, Valentino was paid $1,250 a week. Rudy, as he was affectionately known, married in 1919 one of Russian actress Alla Nazimova's protégés, actress Jean Acker. However, the marriage was never consummated. Acker was a lesbian and unceremoniously turned Rudy out on their wedding night. They would not divorce until 1923. By then he was heavily embroiled in a romance with the former socialite Nata-cha Rambova (real name Winifred Hudnut), who it was rumored also shared a lesbian relationship with Nazimova.

Elinor Glyn fashioned a screenplay based on her novel *Beyond the Rocks,* which literary critics of the day had found "depraved and unsavory."[21] (*The New York Times* panned the novel in 1906: "The whole moral atmosphere of the book is of a decidedly unwholesome and vitiated character.")[22] Director Sam Wood, attempting to emulate DeMille, included rescues, romance, adventure, glamorous clothes, and the popular "vision" flashback scenes, which only heightened the film's drawing power.

The story told of young Theodora Fitzgerald (Gloria), who is saved from drowning by Lord Hector Bracondale (Rudolph Valentino). Yet she marries the rich and elderly Josiah Brown (Robert Bolder) to please her father, Captain Dominic Fitzgerald (Alec B. Francis). Theodora and Hector meet numerous times before they realize they love each other, and in the end, through a letter switch, they are finally united.

Filming began in late 1921 and ended five weeks later, with some scenes shot off the coast of Catalina Island. The cast and crew initially enjoyed the location shoot. Gloria and Valentino were still friends. (He had once gifted her with a monogrammed silver-tipped riding crop on her birthday.) The two would dance the tango, and have late-night pillow fights in the halls of their Catalina hotel. Elinor Glyn, who saw *herself* portraying her heroines, got along with Valentino fabulously. In Hollywood he would take Madame out dancing.

One of the rules in the Hays censorship bylaws was the duration of a screen kiss, which could not last for more than ten feet of celluloid. Thus the kissing scenes in *Beyond the Rocks* were filmed twice, recalled Swanson—one short kiss for the American audiences, and then a long and lingering one for the European markets. "Poor Rudy could hardly get his nostrils flaring before the American version was over," Swanson wrote.[23] For a love scene on a couch, Wood had a small orchestra playing passionate music off the set, as Madame Glyn recited her words from her novel to Gloria and Rudy. All very silly, yet very typical of the silent film era.

Madame Glyn insisted on designing some of the costumes and arranging the sets to suit herself. She would argue heatedly with director Wood. "They never heard of powdered footmen [servants with powdered real hair], and I had to argue with the head property man about it . . . He wanted them to wear wigs!!!" she wrote. Madame Glyn, with all her self-important portentous pontifications, would in private belittle Gloria. Writing her elderly mother in England, she remarked, "It is a pity Miss Swanson is such a marionette and so common but the public adore her. She has a 'sex charm' which attracts men— you will loathe her in the part."[24]

In Hollywood, tension on the set multiplied with the inclusion of Natacha Rambova into the mix. Though she offhandedly called *Beyond the Rocks* "costume-drama trash" and pronounced the picture "completely unworthy of Valentino" Rambova nonetheless was paid $700 a week as one of the film's costume designers.[25] Jesse Lasky was immediately besieged by complaints from the director and technicians regarding Rambova's imperious control over Valentino. Natacha designed his "vision" costumes in the film, and his eighteenth-century waistcoats emphasized her distinct touch of combining modern with historical. "The stinginess of Lasky's production budget," wrote her biographer, "its cheap sets and costumes, became the more apparent in contrast to Valentino's striking wardrobe."[26]

Rudy was enamored with the woman (they were "engaged," though he was still married at the time), and during the filming he sided with Natacha in her rampages of self-delusion and importance. Gloria surprised Rudy when she grew distant. Soon enough he was arguing with Sam Wood and following not his direction but Natacha's. Rambova criticized the players for overacting at Rudy's expense and belittled cinematographer Alvin Gilks, accusing him of not photographing Valentino at his best. She continually told Gloria how fortunate she was to be working with the great Valentino, although Gloria herself later remarked, "And they call this dago the World's Greatest Lover? I'd prefer to call him the World's Biggest Wanker!"[27]

Once when Gloria failed to hit her mark in a particular scene with Rudy, Rambova rudely spat at her feet. Things came to a complete halt on the set, and without a word Gloria and the crew walked off. Lasky was promptly summoned down to the set and made a plea to the cast and crew on Valentino's behalf to remain calm. At the end of the filming both Gloria and Wood told Valentino to his face they would never work with him again.

Beyond the Rocks completed production in early February. Gloria was diplomatic in her comments, rhapsodizing over the experience of making the picture. "I think I enjoyed [it] in the making more than any other picture I have been in . . . I like Mme. Glyn very much, like her stories," Gloria swooned. "Then, besides, I felt absolutely at home in the part: and working with Mr. Valentino was a pleasure—he is charming, and a perfect technician."[28]

Gloria's contract guaranteed her exclusive billing over the title of *Beyond the Rocks.* Jesse Lasky advised her he wanted to feature Valentino's name above the title as well. "It's all right if you want to put his name above the title below mine, Mr. Lasky," she replied. "But if I allow you to do that, I think you should have the studio send me on a trip to Europe at the studio's expense."[29] With that she and Mickey covertly planned a rendezvous in Paris. If found out by the Hays board, she could be publicly condemned and face losing her contract. She was fully aware of the consequences. Gloria knew she was skating on thin ice.[30] Keeping secrets was part of the game.

On the heels of the Arbuckle case, on February 1 film director William Desmond Taylor was discovered murdered in his home. His death would reveal alleged scandalous love affairs with actresses Mary Miles Minter and Mabel Normand, plus homosexual sex, drugs, infidelity, assumed identities, and occult leanings. Hollywood was reeling with scandal. "When everything came out in the papers," Gloria recalled about the Taylor murder, "I knew better than to ask."[31]

On February 19, *Her Husband's Trademark* opened. *Photoplay* found the picture "a thoroughly entertaining film. It's pure hokum, but you can't help liking it—*and* Gloria."[32] One Chicago critic was more to the point: "Swanson's forced to mannequinize as much as attitudinize, and acting *per se* has nothing to do with her display, but how she makes you pay attention!"[33]

Gloria started her next picture, *Her Gilded Cage,* in the spring of 1922. Based on the play *The Love Dreams* by Elmer Harris and Anne Nichols, and again directed by Sam Wood, the story told of Suzanne Ornoff (Gloria), the daughter of an impoverished aristocratic family, who agrees to become the musical entertainer "Fleur d'Amour, the favorite of King Ferdinand" in the press in order to help her uncle and her invalid sister Jacqueline (Anne Cornwall). The ruse is successful, and she takes her act to New York, where her lover Arnold Pell (David Powell), an American artist, becomes confused as to Suzanne's true character. Eventually he sees her for who she really is. Much ado about nothing.

The picture displayed Gloria wearing a large amount of tantalizing clothing and feathered headgear, and the whole thing was completed after four weeks on June 5. Gloria announced to the press during the first week of filming that she was taking a two-month vacation, her first to Europe, when the picture was completed. This was news to Paramount, although she later wrote that she and Lasky had agreed upon it prior to her signing off on Valentino's billing in *Beyond the Rocks*. Infuriated, and obviously a bit confused, and disavowing any promises to Gloria, Lasky wired Adolph Zukor at his New York office at 485 Fifth Avenue on March 14:

AM VERY DISTURBED OVER RUMOR THAT SWANSON . . .
IS SAILING FOR EUROPE SOON AS THIS PICTURE IS FINISHED . . .
SHE HAS NEVER MENTIONED MATTER TO ME OR STUDIO
MANAGEMENT STOP . . . WEEKLY COST OF SWANSON UNIT IS
FOUR THOUSAND DOLLARS INCLUDING DIRECTOR SCENARIO
WRITER AND STAFF AND IT WAS FOR THIS REASON I PERSIS-
TENTLY REFUSED [TO] ALLOW HER VACATION AT OUR EX-
PENSE . . . IF GLORIA LEAVES ON VACATION UNDER SALARY
I FORESEE ENDLESS TROUBLE WITH OUR OTHER ARTISTS[34]

Zukor's reply was quick in coming, in a night letter dated March 15 to Lasky at 6284 Selma Avenue:

Very much surprised Swanson led you to believe I made her promise of trip to Europe. She arrived in San Francisco without my knowledge and during all the time I saw her there as well as in Los Angeles she kept harping on European trip . . . She however jokingly remarked my agreeing to have Valentino featured I am sure will get you more out of the picture than what a trip to Europe will cost and under the circumstances I take it for granted that I am going . . . I assure you there was no agreement or promise on my part to her.[35]

Gloria told the press she and Peggy Urson, who now acted as her secretary and handled all of her affairs, were booked on the White Star liner *Homeric,* set to sail from New York on Sunday, April 16. Before leaving by rail from Los

Angeles on April 8, Gloria was visited by Lasky, who asked if, when her contract came up for renewal in January, she would agree to make five instead of
four pictures a year. She told Lasky she would think about it. Obviously she
was testing her position with Paramount and so far succeeding in her plans.
Lasky also agreed to pay Gloria $2,500 a week during her vacation.

After arriving in New York on Thursday, April 13, and checking into the
Plaza Hotel, Gloria and Peggy enjoyed a two-day shopping spree. Then, shortly
before boarding the *Homeric,* Gloria visited Lasky, who had come to New York
to present her with a new contract, at his Manhattan office. When she looked
over the document, she found it was vague in specifying the number of films
she was scheduled to make annually. She told Lasky she would read it and
would let him know if she would re-sign before she embarked for Europe. As
she left his office, she was buttonholed by Louella Parsons, now working for
William Randolph Hearst's syndicated papers. After telling the columnist that
she would miss her baby daughter so terribly for two months (little Gloria was
left in Herbert's capable care), and that she and Peggy intended to shop in
Paris, Gloria quickly launched into her schedule. What she failed to mention to
Parsons, to Lasky, and most certainly to her husband was that Peggy was a
"beard." Gloria's true intent in going to Europe was, of course, to meet up with
her lover Mickey in Paris.

While in New York Gloria filmed a brief conversation with Thomas Meighan
for experimental sound film pioneer Lee de Forest at his Phonofilm facility
located at the General Talking Pictures Corp. on Forty-Second Street. On board
the *Homeric* before sailing, Gloria was interviewed and photographed by the
press. Summoning a messenger, at the last moment before the gangplank was
raised, she sent a letter to Lasky reminding him of her August 12, 1920, contract, and its conditions, which he could renew before January 1, 1921, or not.[36]

In London her contract was delivered, signed by Lasky, guaranteeing her
three more years beginning on January 1 at $5,000 a week, double her current
salary, and ending at $7,000. Lasky had given up trying to squeeze a fifth pic-
ture out of her. (A copy was also delivered to Gloria in Paris and Berlin—Lasky
not wanting his star to be tempted by any other studio.)

Upon arrival in England the women were given deluxe treatment everywhere they went. Paramount had arranged press interviews, and Gloria was
recognized in every European city she visited thereafter. While at Claridge's in

London, the Crillon in Paris, and the Adlon in Berlin, Gloria took in the sights. However, in London she received terrible press. "The general attitude of Miss Gloria Swanson, and particularly that of Mrs. Frank Urson, has completely upset the London newspaper men," began a Paramount interoffice memo. Gloria had been asked by the studio to attend the Kinema Ball at the Hotel Cecil, and she had not replied. Prominent newsmen gathered at Waterloo Station to meet her on Sunday, April 23, and "were told that Miss Swanson was too tired to be interviewed but they might talk to her as she walked to a taxi!"[37]

On Monday she refused any interviews, after having invited over thirty newspapermen to a tea on Tuesday. She canceled at noon, then changed her mind half an hour later, and then declined to talk about her pictures before abruptly leaving with Peggy "without dismissing her guests or wishing them good day." Peggy informed the studio that Mr. Zukor had expressed that Gloria do no publicity and that "she was to have complete rest." Arrogantly, Urson then declared to newsmen, "Publicity didn't mean a thing to Miss Swanson."[38]

Gloria's war with Paramount had begun in earnest. She would reflect many years later, "I always had to be left alone to do things my way . . . I don't want to be told what's right or what's going to be best for me."[39] With her new status as a major Paramount film star, Gloria was experiencing a euphoria that she found empowering and intoxicating.

In Paris she shopped at the finest couturiers on the Continent—at the "palace" of Lanvin and at Poiret, Panquin, and Worth, all of which featured the latest fashions with raised hemlines that exposed the knees. When Mickey arrived in Paris, he showed Gloria the Louvre and Versailles, and, under the romantic spell of the City of Lights, the two enjoyed a passionate romance. For six weeks in Paris Gloria was in love, infatuated with the city and the wealth of luxuries she was experiencing. Paris made her come alive. With Mickey by her side, Gloria felt she was experiencing the honeymoon she never had with either Wally Beery or Herbert.[40] The fact that she was still legally married and the mother of an infant daughter back in California did not distract her in the least.

Neilan was quite a drinker, and when drunk he could become difficult. In Paris his boozing went unabated. One evening when he arrived late for a dinner with Gloria, after he had been at a watering hole with film studio head Roy Aitken, the couple had their first major row. The argument turned ugly, with

Mickey threatening suicide and Gloria ordering him to leave her and marry actress Blanche Sweet, to whom he had become engaged now that his divorce was final. At some point the two began to laugh at their drama, made passionate love, and then went nightclubbing in Montmartre for the rest of the evening. According to actress Colleen Moore, during that famous fight, Gloria knocked Mickey over the head with a champagne bottle; as he recalled later, "Only Gloria would use a magnum—and filled, at that."[41]

The scenario repeated itself the following evening. Two days later Mickey left for London. Gloria discovered that though she loved Neilan, and she enjoyed making love with him, she simply could not tolerate his behavior. His drinking led to constant arguments. She realized the honeymoon was over. (An apocryphal story has it that she sent Mickey a telegram in London, where he sojourned briefly before returning to New York, attempting to end the relationship by wiring her impetuous lover: FORGET ABOUT ME. His reply was succinct: FORGOTTEN.)

Again bad press plagued Gloria in Paris when she told one reporter, "I have come to Europe temporarily to escape Hollywood," because "the people in Hollywood spy on each other."[42] (By the time she got back to the States she had a lot of explaining to do.) When she and Peggy returned to England from Paris, a box from Cartier's awaited her in their hotel suite. It was from Mickey. Gloria assumed it was a peace offering. Opening it, she discovered a display of simple garden rocks and a card that read, "This is the load you have taken off my mind."[43] Gloria burst out laughing, knowing it was useless to resist him. The two women then took the boat train to Southampton and boarded the *Mauretania* on May 27 for their return voyage.

In New York, Gloria checked into the Plaza Hotel. Mickey met up with her hours later. In yet another confrontation, Neilan told her he wanted to direct her in films, he thought Sam Wood was ruining her film career, and he wanted to marry her. According to Gloria, she told Mickey the only way she would marry him was if he married Blanche first, and stayed married until her divorce was final with Herbert. This time he listened to her. (Possibly she saved face by inventing this story.)

Gloria, Mickey, and Peggy Urson boarded the westbound train to Chicago, arriving in the Windy City the same day as Blanche Sweet's eastbound train from Los Angeles. (In Chicago, Gloria was asked by cub newspaper reporter

Arthur Sheekman, future husband of actress Gloria Stuart, "Who are your favorite authors, Miss Swanson?" To which Swanson replied ever so grandly, "Zane Grey and Sigmund 'Frood' [mispronouncing Freud]."[44] That very afternoon, June 7, Marshall Neilan and Blanche Sweet wed. Gloria arrived quietly back in Los Angeles on Sunday, June 11.

8

Stardom

The eighty-minute *Beyond the Rocks* opened to mixed reviews yet did tremendous business in Los Angeles at Grauman's Rialto Theater on April 30, 1922. Ads declared: "Everything about [the film] is expensive—gowns, jewels, houses, restaurants, all designed to make people gasp."[1] Grace Kingsley of the *Los Angeles Times* noted, "Valentino's vogue, Elinor's Eros, Gloria's gowns—that's the blessed triumvirate which seems to be entirely failure proof... 'Beyond the Rocks' will not, I fear, be beyond the rhetorical rocks of the critics. The story is commonplace, and might have been written by any Trotty Two-Shoes of the scenario department. On the other hand, it is without the special Glyn tang; it's a de-nogged eggnog. Rudy Valentino kisses with the meter on... Gloria Swanson does good work and suffers in about 500 beautiful gowns."[2]

The picture opened in New York on May 7 at the Rivoli Theater at Times Square with a Buster Keaton comedy. The *New York Times* was casual in its assessment: "Gloria Swanson can wear clothes. So can Rodolph [*sic*] Valentino... [The climax of the story] is reached through a series of incredible incidents, and if the leading characters do little else but wear clothes, and if, also, much of the action takes place on apparently artificial mountains and before what seem to be painted back drops, can the result be called an interesting photoplay? Not by those who want a little character and a little truth in their entertainment, anyhow. If you get through the photoplay, however, you will be rewarded, for after it comes the latest Buster Keaton comedy, 'The Paleface.'"[3]

Beautifully restored today, *Beyond the Rocks* is most impressive. The performances of Swanson and Valentino, despite the difficulties on the set, are intriguing to watch. Rarely does one have the opportunity to witness such stylized and unique film icons from that era performing together. The mandatory flashback sequence, the "Arch of Psych" pantomime, clumsily placed in the film with the stars in eighteenth-century costume, is jarringly silly and totally irrelevant, and the scenario itself sloppily and fantastically written. And strangely, both Swanson and Valentino seem to misinterpret their characters. Instead of portraying Theodora as innocent and pure, Gloria enacts her as a coquette, and Valentino plays Bracondale as a young lothario experiencing his first romantic crush instead of as a wise and cynical man of the world.

Despite these glaring contradictions, the intriguingly disparate performances of the two stars, as well as that of Robert Bolder as the martyred husband, save *Beyond the Rocks* from banality even today. "When I look at a picture like *Beyond the Rocks*," wrote acclaimed director Martin Scorsese, "I marvel at the sheer beauty and sophistication of silent cinema."[4] *Beyond the Rocks* remains a milestone for its pairing of two of the greatest silent screen stars of the era.

Once back in Hollywood Gloria began *The Impossible Mrs. Bellew*, an appropriate title for the petulant and willful star. Lance Bellew (Robert Cain) ignores his wife Betty (Gloria) for the affection of Naomi Templeton (June Elvidge). He becomes jealous when Betty is seen with his friend Jerry Woodruff (Richard Wayne), whom he shoots in anger. Because of her love for their son Michael (Mickey Moore), Betty does not contest Lance's divorce accusations in court, and Michael is taken away from her. In Europe she befriends author John Helstan (Conrad Nagel), whose father, Rev. D. Helstan (Herbert Standing), asks her to give his son up. Lance and his aunt Agatha (Gertrude Astor) have a change of heart and take Michael to France to see his mother. John learns the truth about Betty and forgives her. It's the Swanson unit and formula film at work again.

That summer, Gloria's "escaping Hollywood" remark made in Paris caught up with her. Through her press agent, H. L. Reichenbach, she told the *New York Morning Telegraph*, "I never gave out any sort of an interview in Paris much less one attacking Hollywood. Why, rather than detesting the place I love it so much that I am making plans now to build a new home here . . . I went overseas for vacation, a rest, not an 'escape.' I travelled incognito in France and not until the very last days was I known there as Gloria Swanson. Therefore, it is doubly a mystery to me how I could have been coupled with such false dispatch."[5] So much folderol. Gloria may have been able to circumvent criticism for this incident, but in July she was dragged through the mire of her mother Addie's scandal.

On July 10 the first round of the Matthew P. Burns family lawsuit, filed by attorney T. C. Ridgeway on November 26, 1919, was heard in the Probate Court of Judge James C. Rives. Proceedings lasted throughout the month, and Gloria's name was mentioned in the papers frequently. Judge Rives threw out all testimony of conspiracy involving Addie and Gloria and advised the jury that their decision rested solely on the question of the shoe merchant's sanity. On July 19, a jury of ten women and two men ruled Burns was indeed not of sound mind when his will was executed. Rives granted Addie the rights to the $25,000 Edgemont Road house and an insurance policy but only half of the estate ($50,000). Addie's attorneys pledged an appeal, which was denied on October 19.

Gloria's latest picture, *Her Gilded Cage,* opened on August 5, and the public flocked to see her in one marvelous getup after another. For the most part the critics were stumped. Said *Photoplay,* "There is really little to this but the decorative presence of Gloria Swanson. The photoplay is an orchid growing out of a tin can."[6] When the picture played in Los Angeles in September at Grauman's Rialto Theater, one critic commented, "The advertising had convinced me that it was going to be—oh, very wicked. It wasn't; it was, on the contrary, almost painfully the reverse."[7]

"With her bad posture, her Illinois twang, her gamin toughness, the movie magazines posed her as the smartest dressed woman in Hollywood, and she loved it," wrote film historians Richard Griffith and Arthur Mayer.[8] Considered Hollywood's leading authority on fashion, Gloria herself was none too reticent in voicing her personal opinions on dress and the American woman. In a lengthy article for the *Los Angeles Times* in late August, she told columnist Grace Wilcox about her experiences visiting the leading couturier houses of Paris, explaining why she had spent $10,000 on fashions on her recent trip. (In 1922 it would take the average shopgirl about eight years to earn that much money!) "Any woman who thinks she can save money by buying her fall and winter wardrobe in Paris is doomed to disappointment," she sighed.[9]

The Impossible Mrs. Bellew completed production in late August, and immediately Gloria began *My American Wife*. In it, Kentuckian Natalie Chester (Gloria) meets Argentinian Manuel La Tessa (Antonio Moreno) at a horse race. They marry. At a party Pedro De Grossa (Gino Corrado) insults Natalie, and Manuel challenges him to a duel. Pedro leaves the country. Manuel accepts a position with his country's government, his American bride by his side.

Antonio Moreno would later state that Gloria did not much care for him, and during their scenes together she would mutter "decidedly disconcerting quips between kisses."[10] She agreed with her friend Aileen Pringle, who was also in the picture, about Moreno: "Obviously he never had an idea above his waist."[11] At the same time, Gloria was presented with competition at Paramount.

In September 1922 German film star Pola Negri arrived in Hollywood. Born Barbara Apolonia Chalupiec in Lipno, Poland, on December 31, 1897 (or 1894), the darkly exotic Negri had made quite a sensation in Europe in 1918 when she starred in the German UFA film *Dei Augen der Mumie Ma (The Eyes of the Mummy)*, directed at her insistence by Ernst Lubitsch. By 1922 Negri had appeared in such international UFA masterpieces as *Carmen (Gypsy Blood)*, again in 1918 with Lubitsch, the spectacle *Madame Dubarry (Passion)* in 1919, and *Sumurun (One Arabian Night)* and *Sappho (Mad Love)*, both in 1920. Primarily because of the American success of *Passion*, Negri contracted with Famous Players–Lasky for $5,000 a week, announcing her commitment on July 6, 1922.

Arriving in New York on board the liner *Majestic* on September 12, Pola was coached by fellow passenger Mabel Normand to say no to everything Paramount offered her; that way she could secure the same star position she enjoyed in Europe. Pola had already married and divorced Count Eugeniusz Dambski, and her imperial personage was not assumed. She was the first of the great European stars to come to America to make films. The following year *Motion Picture* magazine noted that Negri "walked into Hollywood with the hauteur of an empress" and that she possessed what few others in Tinseltown had—"power."[12] The sultry, heavy-lidded Pola was referred to as a "magnificent wildcat" and "a tiger woman."[13] Gloria now had a rival. Famous Players–Lasky welcomed the challenge.

Gloria hated the whole atmosphere of competition, and she was becoming increasingly difficult. In his autobiography, Adolph Zukor wrote, "On the set Queen Gloria could be temperamental, refusing to make scenes over, criticizing her wardrobe, the scenery, or her dressing room quarters. But finally someone would say, 'Look, Gloria, we've got to get the work done,' and she would come down to earth. The little Chicago west side girl was never far below the glamorous surface."[14] Still, Gloria was willful.

The Impossible Mrs. Bellew premiered at New York's Rivoli Theater on October 22, 1922. By now Gloria's films were formulated, "an elaborate tease,"[15] and usually followed the same theme. Her character is an innocent victim accused of being immoral. In the end she is found to be a good woman, and her tormentors are chastised for pointing accusing fingers toward poor Gloria's character.

Photoplay editor James R. Quirk, always quick to champion Gloria in print, felt the Swanson unit was slackening in their search for strong vehicles for their star. His magazine reflected his feelings about *The Impossible Mrs. Bellew*: "Again Gloria Swanson in dire emotional difficulties and bizarre frocks . . . Not much of a story but, if you like Gloria, this one will have optical interest."[16] *Variety* critic "Rush" wrote, "The only thing about it that is high class is the fine clothes worn by Miss Swanson, and even the clothes are expensive rather than fine . . . It belongs in a neighborhood theatre and not on Broadway . . . The production department has spread itself on a picture that isn't worth the trouble."[17]

Fans couldn't have cared less. They came in droves to see their idol Gloria dressed to the nines, and they wanted what she had. Conrad Nagel recalled that during the filming of *The Impossible Mrs. Bellew* a vial of perfume was needed as a distinctive prop in a scene. "So the prop man bought a little black bottle, very oddly shaped, of a perfume called 'Christmas Night,'" he recalled. "Nobody had ever heard of this expensive perfume. After the picture came out they sold a million bottles. A million bottles of that perfume; 'Christmas Night' was *the* thing."[18]

By the end of the year she had completed *Prodigal Daughters,* begun in late November. Here she portrayed a "flaming youth," Elinor "Swifty" Forbes; she and her sister Marjory (Vera Reynolds) are the daughters of wealthy locomotive owner J. D. (Theodore Roberts) and Mrs. Forbes (Louise Dresser). The girls choose to leave home and live the life of bohemians, smoking and drinking with youthful abandon in Greenwich Village.

Just before the Christmas holidays of 1922, *My American Wife* premiered in New York at the Rivoli Theater. Wrote "Fred" in *Variety*, "An altogether interesting feature production . . . For picturesque values there is nothing left to be desired ... Miss Swanson, however, does not seem to register as effectively in this production as she has in the past. In several scenes her style of hair dressing seemed to distract from her face, and in the early outdoor scenes lines and shadows in her face marred her beauty. [Antonio] Moreno was splendid."[19] However, *Photoplay* lamented the picture had "a weak story fizzed up by the personalities of Gloria Swanson and Antonio Moreno."[20]

In Los Angeles *My American Wife* opened on January 26, 1923, at the spectacular new 4,400-seat Grauman's Metropolitan Theater, "the Show Place of the World" located at Sixth Street and Hill. Estimated crowds of between 20,000 and 30,000 waited outside on the street to catch a glimpse of their favorite stars as they arrived that evening.

Despite Mickey's marriage to Blanche Sweet, Gloria and he had resumed their affair. Neilan was literally living with her and little Gloria by then, and encouraging Gloria, now that her salary had doubled, to purchase a new home. She advised Peggy Urson to obtain the twenty-two-room King Gillette mansion in Beverly Hills, an Italian Renaissance palazzo complete with an enormous black marble bath (one of five) with a golden tub. Located at 904 North Crescent Drive, the mansion was built by King Camp Gillette, of the razors fortune, for his sister, and it had enchanted Gloria since her days at Sennett. Its current owner, Jesse Speidel of Wheeling, West Virginia, was asking $105,000 plus an additional $45,000 for the furnishings.[21] Since most of her money was tied up in real estate, Mickey lent Gloria the down payment of $18,000.

After hiring a maid, butler, and cook, Gloria settled into her new home, one of the largest in Hollywood, with little Gloria and a Russian wolfhound named Ivan. The mansion boasted one of the first elevators in a private home in town. Gloria's magnificent inlaid kidney-shaped boudoir desk stood in one corner of her reception room, which was draped in peacock silk. Her breakfast room was in cream and gold, and the living and dining rooms were filled with paintings and tapestries. Her 1,000-square-foot terrace overlooked meticulously groomed green lawns studded with palm and acacia trees. *Photoplay* magazine called the estate "gorgeousness beyond other grounds."[22] So proud of her new home was Gloria, she allowed some of *Prodigal Daughters* to be lensed there.

Silent screen actress Colleen Moore recalled Gloria's twenty-fourth birthday party in 1923, which Mickey threw for her at the mansion. He had built her a new basement projection room and had a truckload of American Beauty roses dumped on her half-acre front lawn that day. A veritable "Who's Who" of Hollywood royalty arrived at Gloria's home for the evening's celebration. She appeared after cocktails standing at the top of the stairs breathtakingly gowned in a red ruffled dress, "looking like a painting by Velázques." The room went quiet, with all eyes on her, as she descended the stairs smiling and greeting each guest with an apology. Mickey stood nearby "enchanted, his adoration of her plain to see, an electric wave passing between them that could be felt by everybody present."[23]

Around this same time, Gloria chose to adopt a baby so little Gloria would have a playmate and not remain an only child, as she herself had been.[24] Sonny Smith, born in Oakland, California, on October 31, 1922, was the son of twenty-five-year-old mail carrier Harry Iver Jones of San Francisco and twenty-six-year-old Mary Agnes Daly, who were not married. Sonny was placed in a foundling home run by the Children's Home Society and settled in Gloria's care on March 13, 1923. She was given a six-month probationary period before adoption proceedings would be considered. The boy's name was changed to Joseph Patrick Swanson, after Gloria's father, who continued to come in and out of her life. The family would forever call the boy "Brother." "Growing up I was very protective of him," his sister Gloria would say many years later. "He and I were very, very close."[25]

Gloria and Herbert Somborn had separated on March 15, 1921. She assumed her divorce would be granted on a technicality—a case of Herbert's desertion by leaving their home. After their separation, she had enthusiastically engaged in numerous adulterous affairs, including the one with Mickey. Before Herbert knew of the affair, however, Neilan had hired him to make a national tour promoting his most recent picture, thus ensuring that Mickey and Gloria would be able to rendezvous undisturbed. "[He] had Somborn telephone him every evening at eight California time from whatever city he was in that day," wrote Hedda Hopper. "When Somborn hung up, Neilan would have the operator check back to verify where the call had originated."[26]

Gloria was floored in February 1923 when Somborn prepared a divorce action against her, charging adultery with over a dozen different men, ranging from Sam Wood, Jesse Lasky, Adolph Zukor, and Cecil B. DeMille, who were all presumably innocent, to Mickey Neilan, who was pay dirt. Gloria had underestimated Herbert's ultimate motivation and tenacity. She had flagrantly enjoyed brief affairs with many of her leading men, including the very married Thomas Meighan. Herbert was suing her to the tune of $150,000 and was threatening to fight her for custody of little Gloria.

Gloria, set to begin a new picture, was unaware of the consequences at first. Cecil B. DeMille was not. While actively campaigning against censorship, he was fully aware of every immoral act transpiring in Hollywood. Gloria's behavior particularly worried him. On January 18, 1923, Wallace Reid had died, and his addiction was now common knowledge. With the William Desmond Taylor murder still unsolved, and the Arbuckle sex scandal fresh in the public mind, the film industry was under heavy scrutiny. Gloria Swanson was one of the most admired and prominent of film personages. Thus DeMille, his dedication to his studio and to his industry unfaltering, was quick to act.

On February 14, he determinedly wired Jesse Lasky:

> HAVE HAD A LONG TALK WITH IMPORTANT ATTORNEY REPRE-
> SENTING HUSBAND OF STAR IN PRODUCTION 273 SCANDALOUS
> PUBLICITY BOMB WILL EXPLODE WITHIN WEEK OR TEN DAYS
> RECENT ACTION IN EUROPE WITH DIRECTOR OF STELLA
> MARIS [Neilan directed *Stella Maris* in 1918]. WILL RECEIVE FULL
> PUBLICITY . . . HAVE OBTAINED PERMISSION FROM INTER-
> ESTED PARTY TO TELL YOU LADY HERSELF DOES NOT KNOW
> STORM IS ABOUT TO BREAK . . . [WILL] ENDEAVOR TO MAKE
> SOME SETTLEMENT AS MATTER WILL PROBABLY REOPEN
> ATTACKS ON WHOLE INDUSTRY STOP HAVE LITTLE HOPE
> HOWEVER OF BEING ABLE TO AFFECT ANY COMPROMISE
> AS REVENGE PLAYS IMPORTANT PART[27]

Three days later DeMille asked Lasky to ask Will Hays to wire him a warning he could present to Gloria.

Gloria was soon advised of Herbert's planned suit. The following day, she met with DeMille, who handed her a devastating telegram from Will Hays, which informed DeMille that if the whole affair was made public, Gloria would, without a doubt, be permanently barred from the screen.[28]

Immediately, Paramount representatives scoured the country seeking affidavits from hotels to verify Gloria and Neilan had *not* stayed together there.

They accomplished little. DeMille then began negotiating a settlement with Herbert. Because he had advised Gloria on her 1920 contract with Famous Players–Lasky, Somborn demanded 10 percent of all of her earnings from that date forward, which equaled about $120,000 over the term of her still-valid contract. DeMille kept Lasky updated by wire of his negotiations. The talks took weeks. Believing Somborn would take less for a cash settlement, DeMille wired Lasky on March 6 that the following evening the matter would be final, and that Herbert would settle for $25,000, plus an additional $10,000, if the matter could be considered closed in time to begin shooting *Bluebeard's Eighth Wife* that Thursday.[29]

Gloria was advised of the negotiations and spoke with her father, who told her for the sake of the children to settle. She acquiesced. She did not have the money, so she accepted a loan from the studio. She also reluctantly agreed to do "some extra pictures."[30] On March 16, DeMille asked for $35,000 for her from Paramount in exchange for an additional picture. With Lasky's check in hand, Gloria then wrote one out to Herbert. The financial matter settled, the divorce then proceeded.

On March 22 Gloria signed an addendum to her existing contract that added an additional picture at a weekly rate of $7,000, less $431.03 garnishment, beginning March 28 until the loan amount was paid back. Also, the fourth clause of the document stated definitely that if "at any time in the future, through no fault of the Third Party [the studio] and/or without its connivance and consent, First Party [Gloria] shall be charged with adulterous conduct or immoral relations with men other than her husband, and such charges or any of them are published in the public press, the waiver herein contained shall be null and void and of no force or effect."[31] That meant if she was not more careful (or discreet), she would be fired. The document was signed by Gloria Swanson Somborn, Herbert Somborn, and Jesse L. Lasky.

After the completion of *Bluebeard's Eighth Wife*, Gloria confronted Hays at a function and asked him about the telegram he sent to DeMille. Hays adamantly denied he had sent a telegram and said he was unaware of its existence. She bought his excuse but did not approach DeMille about the conversation. She did talk with Lasky, who said he had no other recourse but to have DeMille advise her of the severe ramifications of the suit and force her to sign the document. Forever after she never trusted either her former mentor or Lasky and

Famous Players. The documents prove otherwise—Hays was a good liar, and "Lasky took the fall."[32]

Gloria then was forced to allow Herbert to file suit against her, which he did on March 28 in Superior Court, charging her with desertion, the same accusation Wallace Beery had used in his divorce action. Default was entered on April 17 in the second suit for divorce by Herbert, and the case headed for trial. A divorce was then granted to him on the grounds of desertion on September 19, 1923, by Judge Burks. The judge, concerned over the future welfare of baby Gloria, decreed that Somborn establish a trust fund for the child, to which he agreed. Gloria, represented by her attorney Milton Cohen in court, was not present at the ruling.

Assigned twenty-four-year-old former *Hollywood News* reporter Jimmy Fidler as her new press agent, Gloria reluctantly agreed to his planned campaign for damage control. She had fired her previous five press agents because, typical of her ego, she felt she was her best advocate. Jumping at the chance to represent the nation's top star, Fidler later recalled his thoughts on his assignment. "The truth hit me like a bolt of lightning," he recalled. "I was making it too hot for the studios [as a newspaper reporter] and they couldn't get rid of me legally so they wooed me away from the *News* and into a job where they knew I'd be fired. I was learning about Hollywood—the hard way!"[33] (Fidler left Gloria shortly thereafter, yet the two remained lifelong friends. He then created his own agency, which lasted until the Crash of 1929, and later became a celebrity columnist for the New York *Daily News* and the *Los Angeles Times*.)

In April *Prodigal Daughters* opened to largely bland reviews but unsurprisingly huge box office. "I have enjoyed my part in the making of 'Prodigal Daughters' because it serves as a mirror to our girls which will benefit them in no small way," Gloria imperiously advised fans in January.[34] Opening in Los Angeles at Grauman's Metropolitan Theater, *Prodigal Daughters* was a pleasant enough change of pace, although Gloria really didn't symbolize flaming youth. Sid Grauman himself led off the congratulations in his ads. "Miss Gloria Swanson: In 'Prodigal Daughters' you have made your far greatest picture."[35]

Variety reviewer "Rush" said it all: "The picture presents an unfortunate handling of Gloria Swanson which injures it in many ways. The fan public has been long accustomed to seeing Miss Swanson in a certain type of heroine, a woman of sophistication and the wearer of the last word in modes. This time they have made her a giddy flapper, and the result is a disappointment. The fatal thing about the effort is that the star loses the interest of startling dresses. In trying to make her a butterfly young thing they have adapted her frocks to the character, and generally the whole affair is off the key. Miss Swanson doesn't look herself, and from the way she plays she must have felt out of her element."[36]

Poet Carl Sandburg, today not known as a movie critic, wrote of Gloria in *Prodigal Daughters* in one of his rare published reviews: "In the role of 'Swiftie' Forbes, Miss Swanson, as usual, assumes the character of a woman who understands her own fascinating powers over men, and is always doing things dashing, reckless, full of pep, pepper and pepperino. Anyone doubting Miss Swanson is loaded to the guards and filled with tip, Tabasco sauce and hot chili beans may be convinced otherwise in witnessing her in this performance."[37]

Bluebeard's Eighth Wife, Gloria's next opus, based on the hit 1921 Broadway play, which starred Ina Claire, was purchased specifically for her. The clever plot told of Mona de Briac (Gloria), the beautiful daughter of an impoverished French nobleman, Marquis de Briac (Paul Weigel), who is forced into marriage to a wealthy American, John Brandon (Huntley Gordon), who loves her. He has been married seven times before. Mona is so incensed about John's previous marriages that she tries to force him into divorce by not consummating their marriage, by feigning infidelity, and by demanding large amounts of money from him.

For the picture Gloria sported a new, shorter hairstyle, a bobbed creation, shingled up the back. Filming concluded in early May. It was the last of the Sam Wood–Gloria Swanson unit pictures. "Each one was worse than the last," she later commented, the major difference being a new leading man and the number of gowns she wore.[38]

Disgusted with having been manipulated by DeMille and the studio, Gloria determinedly threw herself into her affair with Mickey. It was not smooth sailing. The couple fought incessantly, arguing usually over his drinking and lack of commitment. One evening at a private party held at her home, a drunken Neilan and an equally inebriated actor, Norman Kerry, began to fight. When they attempted to continue the argument outside, she locked them both in a closet to pound each other out of fear that her relationship with the married Neilan would make the papers.

Meanwhile Paramount was encouraging a publicity-driven feud between

Gloria and Pola Negri that was nothing more than that—publicity. Both actresses had their own devoted followings, and both women played the same type of enchantress. However, they hardly knew each other, and the gimmicks that the studio dreamed up to tantalize their fans were borderline infantile. Pola always thought Gloria went along with the studio hype, and felt that was unfortunate. Gloria always maintained that it was Pola who incited the so-called feud.

Perhaps it all began with the legend of the cats. The studio had fans believing that Gloria feared felines and Pola adored them. Stories made the rounds of stray cats vanishing from the studio lots throughout the day, then reappearing the following morning, depending on Gloria's and Pola's shooting schedules. "*Me* afraid of cats?" Gloria told the press. "Didn't I let the King of Beasts rest a paw on my bare back in *Male and Female*? Really, they'll have to do better!"[39] She then had distributed a series of publicity pictures of her holding a kitten.

Mickey encouraged Gloria to consider filming in New York, telling her, "Hollywood is nothing but sunshine, and eventually that fries the brains."[40] Mickey's drinking was making unfortunate inroads on his faltering career. In the past year he had directed four unsuccessful films, all for the Goldwyn Corporation. He was currently helming *The Rendezvous* with Conrad Nagel and Richard Travers in Hollywood and thus could not accompany Gloria to New York when the time came.

After she completed *Bluebeard's Eighth Wife*, Gloria found she required a minor operation as a result of little Gloria's difficult birth three years before. Pushing the envelope, she told Jesse Lasky she not only preferred her hospital stay be in New York, she also insisted on making pictures at Paramount's East Coast studio in Queens, New York, with either director Allan Dwan or Mickey Neilan.

Dwan had recently advised Mickey of a Broadway play, *Zaza*, which he thought would make a perfect film vehicle for Gloria. At first she was hesitant about the script, telling Mickey she couldn't do it. Working with her on the screenplay, he eventually got her excited about it, and she took it to Lasky. Because she had just dodged a bullet with her recent divorce action, he agreed to her demands, and a new Allan Dwan–Gloria Swanson unit was set up at the Astoria Studio on Long Island.

"What I'd like," Gloria told the press, "is a variety of parts. My hope is to make not more than four pictures a year. Let one of them be a clothes horse

picture if the public insists upon it, but then let the second one show me in ging-
ham or in rags and without a startling head dress. The third I'd like to have an
intensely emotional role, preferably without a happy ending, and the fourth a
light period play with a large leaven of comedy. The trouble is . . . that when
one proves a box office value in a certain kind of role one is kept doing just that
kind of thing until there is real peril of becoming stale. I have been dressed up
so much that I feel like wearing a mother hubbard by way of contrast."[41]

Leaving baby Gloria and "Brother" Joseph at her mansion in the care of
their nanny, Gloria placed her cars, which included a Pierce Arrow and a Hudson, into storage and asked her father, now stationed at Fort MacArthur, California, to keep an eye on her home. In the first week of May she departed by
train—in a private car—for New York, where she would star in some of her
greatest film triumphs.

9

New York

Arriving in Manhattan, Gloria took up temporary residence at the Gladstone Hotel, 114–122 East Fifty-Second Street, dining her first evening with Allan Dwan.[1] Dwan, a respected and gifted director, so disliked Hollywood it was said Paramount built the East Coast Studio in Astoria just for him. Born April 3, 1885, Dwan started in pictures in 1908 in La Mesa, Arizona. Before his death ninety-six years later he would proudly state that by his own estimation he had made over 1,850 films, including numerous one-reelers.

Dwan had directed Douglas Fairbanks in Hollywood in the successful *Robin Hood* (United Artists, 1922) and was one of the inventors of the moving dolly shot (in Paramount's *David Harum* in 1915). Recently divorced, the Canadian-born Dwan was a cultured and educated man who had been a scriptwriter at Essanay Studios before moving over to Triangle. He had given young Mickey Neilan his first break in pictures. Gloria took to Dwan immediately, and it was Dwan who later stated Gloria had the body of a woman and the brain of a man. Dwan also found her an apartment at 950 Park Avenue to sublet while making her first picture. It had been owned by stage actor Richard Bennett, father of actresses Constance, Barbara, and Joan Bennett.

Production was set to begin on *Zaza* at the end of the month. Gloria liked *Zaza*, whose plot was simple. Zaza (Gloria) is a Parisian music hall soubrette who falls in love with French diplomat Bernard Dufresne (H. B. Warner), who she thinks is unmarried. He proposes to her, but her jealous colleague Florianne

(Mary Thurman) tells her Dufresne is married and the father of a young daughter (Helen Mack). Zaza breaks off her affair with him. Years pass, and Zaza meets up with Dufresne after his wife has died, and the two are reunited.[2]

"That was the first one I did with Gloria Swanson," said Allan Dwan to his biographer, director Peter Bogdanovich. "She was out here working for Paramount and they kind of had a grudge against her for some reason and weren't handling her well. And I was having a problem with them myself . . . Now, Mickey Neilan was interested in Gloria and he asked me to get her out of this bad environment too, so I brought her over and put her in a story I'd chosen called *Zaza*. My agreement with the studio was that if I met the budget I'd receive a bonus on each picture, so of course I was interested in keeping the budget down, and did. Gloria worked well—*Zaza* was a smash hit—and that was the start of the new Swanson."[3]

Based on the 1904 French play *Zaza*, a boulevard drama by François Berton and Charles Simon, the story had been filmed three times before. Dwan's 1923 version was beautifully mounted and photographed by the gifted Harold Rosson, who would comment about filming Gloria, "I had the great pleasure of photographing [a number] of her pictures [three total], and if she had not been agreeable to the results that she could see, I probably would not have worked with her. I do believe that the reason I photographed her on so many occasions was that the director who worked with her, Allan Dwan [whom Rosson also found to be a "charming man, great director"], had a very happy arrangement of working with me."[4]

The Astoria Studio was located on Long Island in Queens on thirteen acres made accessible over the East River after the building of the Fifty-Ninth Street Bridge in 1909 and the introduction of the elevated subway in 1917. It opened its doors on September 20, 1920. Compared to the Famous Players–Lasky operations on the West Coast, and a third studio in Islington, England, the Astoria-based company was considered the jewel of the triumvirate. The California studio was better suited for outdoor and action pictures, while the East Coast studio was perfect for anything with a European flavor. "Astoria's output was in fact diverse, ranging from stage comedies and performers . . . to melodramas that exploited New York locations," wrote film historian Matthew Bernstein.[5]

With executive offices at 250 West Fifty-seventh Street in Manhattan, Paramount employed some of the best directors on the East Coast—Dwan, Sidney

Olcott, and even D. W. Griffith, who had run into some difficult times in California. Among the roster of film stars employed at "the Big House," as the Astoria Studio was affectionately called by old-timers, were Richard Barthelmess, Billie Burke, May McAvoy, Elsie Ferguson, Thomas Meighan, Rod La Rocque, Adolphe Menjou, W. C. Fields, and William Powell. In 1924 Rudolph Valentino filmed *Monsieur Beaucaire* and *The Sainted Devil* on the lot.

There was, and still is, an exciting vitality to living and working in New York. Gloria would later recall the Astoria Studio as a place of innovation, burgeoning with creative spirit and inhabited by an artistic ensemble of Hollywood castoffs and rebels.[6]

For *Zaza,* Dwan saw to it that the sets would rival anything seen in Hollywood. A Parisian café was constructed and took up the main stage at the studio. Location shooting for Zaza's country retreat was done on the estate of W. W. Buhrman and at an 1828 gristmill and country store in Douglastown (now Ally Pond Park). H.M.K. Smith was the studio's resident designer and selected most of the gowns and costumes used by the other players, but it was Norman Norell who designed and created Gloria's costumes.

In the film Gloria played a soubrette, a curly-haired chorus girl, a role she would repeat in spirit four years later in *Fine Manners.* She always said *Zaza* was "the fastest, easiest, most enjoyable picture I had ever made."[7] In those days, according to various sources, the script was not always adhered to, and often anyone with a clever idea or a piece of business that might help a scene was allowed to volunteer it to the director. Experimentation was done on the spot, and a fight sequence between Zaza (Gloria) and Florianne (Mary Thurman) was completed in a single take because Gloria had only one copy of the dress for the sequence.

When shooting scenes, inspiration emanated from the on-set musicians hired to create moods for the stars. On *Zaza,* French music was de rigueur. And for Gloria's more important scenes, her two favorite pieces, "Avalon" and "Mon Homme," were used as well as selections from French operas and comedies.

The summer of 1923 was an extremely hot one in New York, before the days of commonplace air-conditioning. During filming under the klieg lights, temperatures soared. Dwan had huge blocks of ice placed on either side of the set and strategically located electric fans to blow over them to keep the actors cool and the production going.

From mid-June until December 20, Gloria rented what had been Norma Talmadge's two-and-one-half story frame mansion on Little Neck Bay in Bayside. Talmadge had thrown lavish parties and expansive barbeques there, and her sister Natalie wed silent film comic Buster Keaton on the property. Gloria's landlord was now film producer Joseph M. Schenck, Talmadge's husband. She paid $2,000 upon signing the lease and an additional $2,000 on August 15, plus her utilities. (Rudolph Valentino leased the property directly across from her when he came out east the following year. Future New York City mayor Fiorello Henry La Guardia lived right down the street.)

On August 5 *Bluebeard's Eighth Wife* opened at New York's 1,960-seat Rialto Theater and was another box-office triumph for Gloria. *The New York Times* said the entertainment "was not only an amusing picture, but one which is ably directed and beautifully staged. It gives Gloria Swanson plenty of opportunity to roll her long-lashed eyes and to wear expensive creations . . . Miss Swanson is to be congratulated on the vehicle chosen for her on this occasion."[8] With its stunning shots of "California's Eden," Monterey, the picture proved a rollicking success, bringing in over $18,000 the first week at the Rialto alone. Later the *Times* added, "[*Bluebeard's Eighth Wife*] is one of the best farces ever put to the screen."[9]

Photoplay voted Gloria's "the Best Performance of the Month," calling the film "nothing risqué, nothing gained . . . one of Gloria Swanson's best pictures."[10] Due to the newly enforced censorship rules, Swanson's version was considerably tame, though she was magnificently gowned and coiffed and displayed much more glamour than Claudette Colbert in her 1938 remake for Paramount opposite Gary Cooper (directed by Ernst Lubitsch, with a screenplay by Charles Brackett and Billy Wilder). *Bluebeard's Eighth Wife* is possibly one of the finest of Gloria's silent films. It sparkles with energy, and she never looked more attractive and enticing. One enthusiastic reviewer agreed: "Gloria Swanson, more entrancingly beautiful, more bewitchingly gowned, more distinctively and delightfully Swanson than ever . . . 'Bluebeard's Eighth Wife' is unquestionably Gloria Swanson's best picture."[11]

With shooting completed on *Zaza*, Gloria had to face her health issues. Since little Gloria's birth a cyst had grown on the tissue between Gloria's vagina and rectum, and surgery was imminent. Shortly before noon on Friday, August 10, accompanied by her East Coast secretary Jane West, Gloria was driven to the private hospital of Dr. Samuel G. Gant at 691 Lexington Avenue.

That afternoon at three o'clock an operation was performed to remove the growth. When she came to, Gloria was advised that though the cyst had been removed, she now had a hole in the tissue. It could be treated with drugs or further surgery. When she asked why it just couldn't be allowed to heal by itself, she was told it was an internal hole and would be prone to infection.

The press had been alerted to Gloria's mysterious illness, though accurate details were lacking. *The New York Times* reported that she had been rushed to the hospital on August 8 complaining of intestinal pain and was immediately rushed into surgery. According to the *Times,* the doctor announced she had suffered a breakdown due to overwork and would remain in the hospital another three weeks before transferring to the Westchester Biltmore Country Club in Rye for convalescence. The truth was quite different.

Within days Gloria checked out of the hospital and retreated to her Bayside home, had her maid purchase several medicine droppers and a large bottle of sterilized saltwater, and sent for her children, who arrived by train a week later. For three weeks, she wrote, she lay on her terrace, with pillows behind her back, her legs propped up and spread wide apart like scissors to allow the sun to heal the wound, and every ten minutes she applied sterilized saltwater. Within days, with no fever arising and the pain rapidly subsiding, she knew the treatment was working. When she checked back with her physician, according to her memoirs, he pronounced her cured and like new.

By the end of the summer Gloria was ready to begin her next picture, *The Humming Bird,* to be directed by Sidney Olcott.[12] The story takes place in France, and tells of Toinette (Gloria), called "the Humming Bird," the Apache (meaning "hoodlum" and pronounced "A-*pahsh*") leader of a band of thieves in the Montmartre district of Paris. American news reporter Randall Carey (Edmund Burns, who played the minister in *Male and Female*) is recruited to locate the Humming Bird. When he does, he falls in love with Toinette. The Great War breaks out, Randall volunteers for the service, and Toinette encourages her gang to defend France.

Gloria had petitioned for a good script so she could remain in New York and was awarded with one when she met screenwriter Forrest Halsey, who adapted *The Humming Bird* from a play by Maude Fulton. The screenplay gave Gloria the challenge she was looking for, a chance to perform and develop a character without the accoutrements of high fashion and glamour. At the same time she also had her sights set on landing the lead in *Peter Pan* for the studio's planned version of the perennially popular James M. Barrie play. By performing in *The Humming Bird* she expected to impress executives with her appearance in men's clothing.

Settling into New York, Gloria also took a string of three suites at the Gladstone Apartments, one for her, one for the children, nannies, and secretary, and one to entertain. In Los Angeles, Gloria's mother was unfortunately in the news again when she and her secretary Wanna La Plante were held up while being driven by chauffeur A. E. Hayward to her home at 926 North Edgemont. Two bandits took $2,000 worth of cash and jewels and relieved Hayward of his watch. One of the suspects brought in for questioning was Howard E. Watt, Addie's new fiancé. The investigation was still ongoing when later that month Addie won a partial victory in a contest of her late husband's will.

As that drama played itself out, on November 19, $750 was awarded to Denshiro Nishimoto (who had sued for $36,200) against Addie and Watt for the accidental death of Nishimoto's nine-year-old son, who had been killed by a car driven by Watt and owned by Addie. Then on November 27 Watt filed a $50,000 unjust arrest and imprisonment suit against Addie and three other persons in regard to the robbery. Two days later he was arrested again at the County Hospital bedside of eighteen-year-old Paula Gale claiming to be *her* fiancé after securing a marriage license from her. Clearly the man was unstable. Watt was soon placed behind bars. All this unsavory business was quickly hushed, and Gloria never referred to it in her autobiography. Except for a tax lien of $321.63 leveled against her in June 1925, Addie kept a fairly low profile from then on.

In New York *Zaza* premiered at the Rivoli Theater on September 16. Critics were none too keen on the picture. *The New York Times* said, "It cannot be truthfully said that Miss Swanson makes a good, or even credible, Zaza. She seems real neither in her sin nor in her expiation—nor, one imagines, in the eventual happiness and benefit of clergy that the finish promises but does not reveal... Yesterday afternoon's audiences did not seem to take the picture seriously."[13]

When it opened at Grauman's Metropolitan in Los Angeles, Edwin Schallert said, "*Zaza* presents a typical instance, in that, while Gloria began by being somebody utterly unusual and to a high degree interesting, she became before the end of the production just Gloria Swanson, parading in tinseled gowns in front of glittering sets."[14] Her version of *Zaza* would have been much better without the censor's cuts. *Zaza,* too, was remade in 1938, directed by George Cukor with, once again, Claudette Colbert, and co-starring Herbert Marshall.

The iconic Louise Brooks later wrote in an unpublished essay on Swanson, "When I was 12, I gave up dolls and fell in love with Gloria Swanson . . . Her dark hair and blue eyes, her nippy nose, her darling little feet—she was a thousand times lovelier than a bunch of dolls that all looked alike anyhow . . . She was mine. And when she started changing in her movies, I didn't like it a bit. It was gradual, but by the time I saw *Zaza* in 1924, she was another person. Her face was all makeup . . . Her eyes . . . seemed to have lost all their shadowy softness. And when she looked straight out of them, her eyes looked like the light behind them had gone out."[15] Something *was* changing in Gloria; a certain hardening and maturity in her appearance were settling in. However, *Zaza* still proved a box-office hit.

Filming of *The Humming Bird* continued along the same course as *Zaza,* and director and star got along famously. Scenes of trench battle were filmed at North Beach, now the site of LaGuardia Airport, and old Fort Schuyler was used as the St. Lazare Prison. Gloria, pleased to do a character role without the benefit of elaborate costumes, threw herself into her part. For a fight sequence with Edmund Burns and the gendarmes, rehearsals were mandatory. Even so, under the bright klieg lights, Burns accidently cuffed the jaw of the other actor in the scene. At the same time, Gloria was called upon to kick a knife out of the hand of one of the gendarmes, an effort that took three shots to accomplish.

On October 1 Captain Joseph T. Swanson died suddenly of a heart attack at the age of fifty-two at Fort MacArthur, California, where he was based as a field clerk in the Quartermaster's Corps of the U.S. Army. Gloria, midway through the filming of *The Humming Bird,* was notified of her father's wish to be buried in Chicago. On October 4 Captain Swanson was accorded full military honors in formal services held at Fort MacArthur. The body was then sent by rail to Chicago accompanied by Captain E. D. Russ, post quartermaster, per Gloria's instructions. She left New York with Jane West on October 6 and arrived in Chicago two days later.

"Daddy was the most complicated figure in my life," Gloria wrote years later.[16] (She did not mention her father left behind a lady friend, Virginia

Nightengale, whom Gloria would keep in contact with for several years.) She would, until the day she died, often call her latest lover "Daddy," but to show that little-girl vulnerability publicly or to her bosses would have been taboo.

On November 14, while completing *The Humming Bird*, Gloria was stricken with a case of "klieg eyes," a burning of the retina caused by the bright intensity of the powerful studio lights. She was required to rest at her Park Avenue apartment for several days. While lying in the dark Gloria attended to business by sending a letter on November 15 to Adolph Zukor regarding Pola Negri's forthcoming film *Shadows of Paris*, which was similar in theme to *The Humming Bird*. After the Great War, anything and everything to do with France was au courant; suddenly it seemed every play, every novel, every motion picture had a French locale, title, or character. In the letter she acknowledged Zukor's confirmation that *her* picture would be released on January 24, 1924, and Negri's opus would follow on February 11.[17] When the time came, *The New York Times* would write about the "feud," "For our part we can readily imagine that Pola Negri will be far more imaginative in such a production than the petite favorite Gloria Swanson."[18] That must have galled Gloria. In any case, she came out the victor in this battle, handing in a vivid performance in a blockbuster film that far out distanced Pola's.

That November, her affair with Mickey waning, Gloria began seeing tall, mustachioed social gadfly LeRoy "Sport" Pierpont Ward, brother of Sylvia Joslin, her old friend from the Court Corinne days. Ten years older than Gloria, Sport Ward came from Middletown, Connecticut, and was a 1911 graduate of Cornell University, where he had majored in architecture and was elected the school's head cheerleader. He was also a member of Phi Gamma Delta fraternity.

Ward was known everywhere in New York society. He knew the best spots to be seen, was a close friend of young state senator Jimmy Walker, and was on a first-name basis with everyone who was anyone. Taking Gloria under his wing, Sport Ward introduced her to theater and classical music. She watched Jeanne Eagels in *Rain*, Alfred Lunt and Lynn Fontanne in *The Guardsman*, Eddie Cantor in *Kid Boots*, her old friend from the Essanay days June Walker, now a huge Broadway star, in *The Nervous Wreck* and *The Glass Slipper*, and Eleonara Duse in *The Lady from the Sea* at the Metropolitan Opera House.

Gloria heard violinist Jascha Heifetz at Carnegie Hall and became familiar with opera legends Galli-Curci, Rosa Ponselle, and Maria Jeritza. Ward took her to watch Babe Ruth and the New York Yankees and to catch a tennis match with Bill Tilden, and she was introduced to novelist James Hilton. Ward took her to "21" and the Colony to dine, and they would journey up to Harlem to listen to jazz. Reflecting on the New York of the 1920s, Gloria reminisced in later life, "There was an excitement about everything . . . You had beautiful restaurants and lovely ladies dressed for the occasion, not looking like they were going to a gym."[19]

By the end of 1923 Gloria was a sophisticated young woman. Noting her at the premiere of DeMille's first *The Ten Commandments,* writer Helen Klumph wrote in the *Los Angeles Times,* "She no longer comes upon one's sight like a crash of cymbals. She is more like an insinuating melody. She has more poise, more dignity, and infinitely greater charm than the less cosmopolitan Gloria who came here months ago."[20] At the end of the year Jesse Lasky announced that Gloria's next picture, to begin immediately, would be called *She Who Laughs Last.* It was based on the Alfred Sutro play *The Laughing Lady,* which had starred Ethel Barrymore.

Professionally Gloria was nearing the peak of her popularity, receiving over ten thousand fan letters a week. In January 1924 she asked Sport to locate a home for her in the country. A friend of his found a sprawling twenty-five-acre estate owned by Marie de Palkowska featuring a twelve-room colonial farmhouse with green-stained shingles atop Kitchawan Hill with views of up to fifty miles, in Croton-on-Hudson, forty miles north of the city. Gloria bought the property that June through her broker George Howe.

Production began in early January on *She Who Laughs Last,* now called *A Society Scandal.* As directed by Allan Dwan, the story told of young Major Hector Colbert (Allan Simpson), who sues his beautiful wife Marjorie (Gloria), heiress to the De Peyster millions, after Harrison Peters (Ricardo Cortez) maliciously compromises her in her boudoir at the Schuyler-Burr mansion. Hector's lawyer, Daniel Farr (Rod La Rocque), believes Marjorie to be innocent but secures the divorce for his client, ruining Marjorie's reputation in the process. Marjorie plots to get even with Farr but confesses her plans to him when she realizes she loves him.

For her leading men, Gloria had two strong contenders. The first was Ricardo Cortez, a former boxer who had once worked on Wall Street. The twenty-three-year-old actor had entered pictures during the "Latin Lover" phase popularized by Valentino. After *A Society Scandal* was completed, Gloria briefly enjoyed his company. Cortez later would be known as the only actor in Hollywood ever to receive billing over Greta Garbo, in her American film debut in *The Torrent* (MGM, 1926).

Gloria's other leading man was Rod La Rocque, whom she professed not to have known before *A Society Scandal* (though they had met in Chicago nearly ten years earlier). Soon he became her lover. Stating he was the most beautiful man she had ever known, she fell in love with the tall, handsome La Rocque, and the two were quickly an item. She later recalled that their affair was "hectic . . . We had lovers' quarrels all the time."[21] Within a week after they started seeing each other, La Rocque proposed marriage to her. Suddenly Sport Ward vanished from her list of beaus. He had served his purpose.

Again head over heels in romance, if not exactly love, with her handsome leading man, Gloria wrote, "He was physically beautiful and had a brilliant mind . . . I wanted to be with him every minute."[22] She was prepared to marry him, but La Rocque could not reconcile her exhaustive "romantic" past. Nor did he care for her surrounding herself with other young, strappingly good-looking men, many of whom were, so she insisted, just platonic pals. Realizing their affair was fleeting, the two opted to become just friends.[23]

Filming began on *A Society Scandal* with scenes shot in the ballroom of the Ritz Hotel with 250 dress extras.[24] Once again Gloria was a fashion mannequin, decked out in fourteen extravagant gowns and a handful of elaborately designed headgear.

On January 13 *The Humming Bird* opened in New York at the Rivoli Theater to positive reviews. "This is a particularly engrossing picture," raved *The New York Times*. "At the very beginning one is struck by the artistic lighting effects, when figures faintly relieved from the silhouette form are shown in a sequence. Soon afterward one sees Gloria Swanson in the role of the Apache . . . [She] is quick as a fly, and her facial expressions are quite fitting to the type she plays . . . It is one of the best pictures of Paris and Apaches we have ever seen, and one in which there is not an uninteresting moment."[25] "Fred" of *Variety* was in agreement. "A picture you won't be able to get away from," he wrote. "It is the best thing Gloria Swanson has done up to date, and the best part of it is that in this production she puts over a role without a lot of clothes. Just Gloria Swanson, and Sidney Olcott has made her act . . . Olcott has a touch here and there that is going to get anyone, and, what is more, he has rescued Gloria Swanson from a clothes horse."[26]

An after-premiere party was held for Gloria at the Astoria Studio. It was also a sort of housewarming for the new dressing room bungalow built specifically for her, with a walnut secretary, red and purple damask settees, a grand piano with pictures of her children on top, and a pencil sketch she made, a "crazy watercolor of herself her friends tease her about."[27] Complete with wheels to make it mobile, the bungalow was surrounded by small trees and a gravel walk. Over a hundred celebrities, including Richard Dix, Marion Davies, and Gloria's close friend Lois Wilson, attended the affair.

The overflow were served and entertained in the garden erected around the small abode. Everybody took home movies of everybody else. Wrote Helen Klumph for the *Los Angeles Times,* "In [*The Humming Bird*] Miss Swanson gives a magnetic performance of the little gamin in boy's clothes . . . There is no longer any doubt about Gloria's ability to act . . . When I left the Rivoli Theater I was convinced Gloria Swanson was a clever player. When I left the party of hers a few hours later . . . I decided that genius was the word."[28]

A huge success in California as well, *The Humming Bird* was held over more than four weeks at most theaters where it played. It earned over $1 million for Paramount worldwide.

Gloria and Dwan were decidedly a winning duo as well, and for her next picture, *Manhandled,* the studio insisted they deliver glamour, although the title of the film became the subject of one of the Hays Office's censorship issues. Based upon Arthur Stringer's *Saturday Evening Post* short story of the same name and developed by screenwriter Frank Tuttle, the plot was about a simple Manhattan shopgirl.

On March 9 *A Society Scandal* premiered at New York's Rivoli Theater. The *New York Times* was glad to see Gloria back in high fashion: "This week . . . [Gloria] blazes forth in her full sartorial glory and makes up for any deficiency of splendor in a previous effort . . . Clothes seem to inspire Miss Swanson and she performs with marked ability in this picture . . . But there are certain close-ups, in which Miss Swanson appears almost matronly, to which too much time is given."[29] *Photoplay* liked the picture: "Gloria Swanson is growing in stature as an actress by leaps and bounds. She has developed a power of facial expression and breadth of gesture that are strikingly effective."[30]

The following month, when the film opened in Los Angeles at Grauman's Metropolitan Theater (along with the comedy short *Reno or Bust* with Bobby Vernon), Edwin Schallert wrote, "Gloria Swanson used to languish in pictures . . . But somehow this one seems to be an exception . . . After 'The Humming Bird,' though, it strikes me as a come down."[31]

At the Astoria Studio production had begun on *Manhandled*. Its story is charming. Tessa McGuire (Gloria) is a basement clerk at Thorndyke's Department Store. She commutes by subway every day to her job in Manhattan. Her boyfriend Jimmy "Babe" Hogan (Tom Moore) forgets a date he has planned with her one evening. When her friend Pinkie Moran (Lilyan Tashman) invites her to a party at the studio of Robert Brandt (Ian Keith), she becomes a hit through her impersonations. Arno Riccardi (a young Frank Morgan, who would portray the Wizard of Oz in 1939) offers Tessa a job at his store, a style emporium, impersonating a Russian countess. (Gloria gleefully based her send-up of the countess on Pola Negri.) Jimmy, in the meantime, becomes successful with his automobile carburetor invention. When Jimmy finds Tessa bedecked in gowns and jewels, he accuses her of being "manhandled." She tells him the truth, she is only pretending, and he forgives her when he realizes that Tessa loves only him.

While maintaining her staff and mansion in California, Gloria continued to entertain lavishly at her Gladstone Hotel suite, leaving her children safe and secure upstate at the Croton-on-Hudson estate under the care of their nanny, nurse, and household staff. She had also purchased a large set of small rooms, servants' quarters, and utility rooms atop the Park Chambers Hotel at Sixth Avenue and Fifty-Eighth Street and was having Sport Ward redesign the space into a penthouse for her. It would take over a year. Living extravagantly had become her style.

When Famous Players–Lasky bought the film rights to the successful Frederick Lonsdale Broadway play *Aren't We All,* Gloria's name was mentioned for the feminine lead. She did not do the film. Instead she was hoping for the lead in Paramount's forthcoming production of *Peter Pan*. Her work in *The Humming Bird* had impressed producers, and her name was seriously bantered about for the role of Peter. "There is no telling what Gloria may prove that she can do," wrote the *Los Angeles Times*.[32]

Gloria made a dramatic transformation in appearance between *A Society Scandal* and *Manhandled*. Her hair was bobbed, her eyebrows plucked, and her mouth altered by makeup. To prepare for the role of a salesgirl, she actually donned a disguise and horn-rimmed glasses and worked two days at the five-and-ten counter at Gimbel's. The other salesgirls did not recognize her and talked openly about actress Gloria Swanson, calling her a "sappy blonde."[33] Her leading man in *Manhandled* was forty-one-year-old actor Tom Moore, older brother of Owen Moore, Mary Pickford's first husband. At this juncture in Swanson's career, older leading men were cast opposite her to give her a more youthful appearance. Though he was a fine performer, Moore was a bit long in the tooth to portray a youthful inventor. Also in the cast was dancer Ann Pennington, a Ziegfeld Follies star.

There are several typical Dwan touches in the comedy-drama *Manhandled*: the expansive party sequence peopled with artists, sculptors, literary types, intelligent folks of prestige; false accusations by the heroes; overhead camera shots and staging through windows and doors; the use of inventions. Dwan had utilized a real courtroom for a scene in *A Society Scandal*; the *Manhandled* subway sequence was shot in the busy morning hours of the New York system.

Then there was the famous drawing room episode with Gloria impersonating Beatrice Lillie and Charlie Chaplin. Gloria frequently told how she was just clowning about the set between takes when she picked up a bowler hat and an umbrella and regaled the crew with an improvised impersonation of Chaplin. Dwan was so enchanted with her remarkable parody, so she said, that he incorporated the bit in the film. "I did it again in *Sunset Boulevard* but it was better when I did it in *Manhandled* because my face was rounder [then]," Swanson later commented. "I was too thin to look like him when I was in *Sunset Boulevard*"[34] *Manhandled* became one of her most appealing pictures.

When it completed production on April 8, Gloria began a Ruritanian romance, *Her Love Story* (originally titled *A Woman of Fire*), which commenced shooting the first week in May. Based on the story "Her Majesty, the Queen" by

Mary Roberts Rinehart, it told of Balkan Princess Marie of Viatavia (Gloria), who falls in love with the Captain of the King's Guard, Rudi Kavor (Ian Keith). Marie's father the Archduke (George Fawcett) promises her hand to the king (Echlin Gayer) of a neighboring country. Marie and Rudi are married by a Gypsy, and the Duke banishes Rudi from the country. Rudi eventually returns to help Marie and claim their child from the palace. They then settle in another country. Romantic stuff at best, but handled and performed very earnestly. Early scenes with Ian Keith and Gloria were shot at Douglastown, Long Island. The company then moved on to Kensico, New York, for other exterior shots.

Gloria by her own account was upset with Jesse Lasky for not officially offering her the plum role of the season in *Peter Pan*.[35] By her reckoning, she had starred in DeMille's *Male and Female,* based on Sir James M. Barrie's *The Admirable Crichton,* and so she felt it was more than logical she be cast as "the boy who never grew up" in Barrie's *Peter Pan*. She even had photographs made of her as Peter to impress the Paramount executives. They did not.

Screenwriter Forrest Halsey, the first openly gay man Gloria ever knew, then advocated she travel to England and talk to Sir James himself, so she could remind him that more people saw *Male and Female* than would ever see *The Admirable Crichton* and that she had already played in boy's clothing in *The Humming Bird*. Halsey also suggested, Gloria wrote, that she journey to France to try to obtain the film rights to *Madame Sans-Gêne,* a play by Emile Moreau and Victorien Sardou. When he told Gloria the plot of *Madame Sans-Gêne,* she immediately loved the story and felt it should be filmed in France, instead of Astoria or Hollywood.

Gloria had planned another European jaunt shortly after the filming of *Manhandled* and was scheduled to depart with Jane West on Saturday, April 12. She summoned Addie to come out east, and then, leaving the children with their nanny, staff, and grandmother, embarked for Europe.

10

Europe

American photographer Edward Steichen frequented Gloria's Gladstone Hotel suite in 1923. By the next year the forty-five-year-old photographer had several important portrait studies published by Condé Nast. Shortly before embarking for Europe, Gloria was photographed by Steichen to publicize *Her Love Story* in *Vanity Fair,* and the last resulting portrait—that of her full face behind a cover of dark lace, her eyes staring straight ahead—has become an iconic symbol of the 1920s, one of the first of a new genre of art, the celebrity photograph.

"The day I made the picture," Steichen wrote, ". . . Gloria Swanson and I had had a long session with many changes of costume and different lighting effects. At the end of the session, I took a piece of black lace veil and hung it in front of her face. She recognized the idea at once. Her eyes dilated, and her look was that of a leopardess lurking behind leafy shrubbery, watching her prey. You don't have to explain things to a dynamic and intelligent personality like Miss Swanson. Her mind works swiftly and intuitively."[1]

Boarding the *Homeric* with Jane West on June 2, Gloria was determined to meet Sir James M. Barrie as soon as she set foot in England. It did not happen. When the women arrived in London and checked into Claridge's, according to Gloria's account, within days the British newspapers announced actress Betty Bronson had been personally selected by Sir James himself to star in *Peter Pan.*[2] Still . . . "I met Barrie in London," Gloria inaccurately told the press. "But we only talked about books and things. I'm not the type for Peter at all. Barrie said he was going to write a play especially for me, though."[3] Swanson was a pro when it came to subterfuge and self-promotion.

According to her book, Gloria then set her sights on acquiring the Moreau-Sardou play, *Madame Sans-Gêne.* At the Hotel Plaza Athenée in Paris she engaged in discussion with André Daven, a young producer/director/actor and cinema critic for the French publication *Bonsoir,* who had requested an interview.[4] Daven would later produce the *Revue Negre* at the Théâtre des Champs-Elysées in 1925, which took Paris by storm and made an international celebrity out of Josephine Baker. Rudolph Valentino acknowledged the twenty-four-year-old Daven as the "one great love" of his life in his unpublished memoirs and secured him a small role for $60 a week in *Monsieur Beaucaire,* filmed at the Astoria Studio.[5]

Gloria said she then contacted Adolphe Osso, Paramount chief in Europe, who told her the French would never sell the film rights to a foreign company (Germany's UFA Studio had tried repeatedly and been denied), and that the French government would not allow filming on actual locations such as the Palace de Fontainebleau and the Château de Malmaison because they were all now historical monuments.

Described as a historical romance (it was more romance than historical), the play *Madame Sans-Gêne,* based on a real-life heroine who disguised herself as a man during the Revolution and actually participated in several of Napoleon's campaigns, was first performed at the Vaudeville Theater in Paris on October 27, 1893, starring the legendary French actress Réjane. Other performances were staged in London and in New York, as well as a popular French revival in 1900. Twice the play was converted into opera. Filmed versions included a French short in 1900, a 1909 Danish version, and a full-length 1911 French feature that starred Mme. Réjane with Edmond Duquesne as Napoleon.[6]

Contrary to Gloria's boast, according to an October 1914 newspaper account, William H. Wiley of New York had been assigned the American rights to sell, transfer, and stage *Madame Sans-Gêne* around January 28, 1898, for $1.00. When the play had opened at the Broadway Theater in New York in January 1895, it starred Kathryn Kidder. Under her married name, Kathryn Kidder Anspacher, she then optioned the film rights of the play for $1,500 in March 1922 for actress

Reine Davies, sister of Marion Davies. In fact, a company letter from Adolph Zukor to Jesse L. Lasky, dated April 10, 1923, stated that *Madame Sans-Gêne* had been acquired as a vehicle for Pola Negri. (Gloria at the same time was assigned *Zaza*.) On April 11, 1923, Kathryn Kidder Anspacher sold the property to Famous Players–Lasky for $19,500.[7]

According to Gloria's memoirs, it took a delicately worded article by Daven in *Bonsoir* to convince the French to acquiesce. She remarked that Daven's article was magnificently written and tactfully diplomatic, claiming it made Paramount, and in particular Adolph Zukor and Jesse Lasky, a forerunner in cultural diplomacy. Daven was then inundated with admiring letters from politicians and artists alike when the article was published, forcing Hollywood to buckle within days. As usual, Gloria suggested this triumph was her own.[8]

After agreeing to make one more picture at the Astoria Studio before the October start date of *Madame Sans-Gêne*, Gloria and Jane embarked on a heroic shopping spree, purchasing all they could "for the children" before boarding the *Leviathan* in Cherbourg on July 15 with a newly acquired English sheepdog.[9]

On board the crossing were violinist Jascha Heifetz and Mary Pickford and her husband Douglas Fairbanks. During the voyage Mary told Gloria that she, too, had campaigned for the role of Peter Pan, and Lasky had even offered her the part if she would star in two additional pictures for the studio. Gloria told her that Lasky wouldn't even discuss it with her. (With a sly smile, Mary confided to Gloria that the actress who had *really* thought she would play Peter Pan all along was Lillian Gish.)

Both Doug and Mary suggested Gloria join up with United Artists, the production company they had founded with D. W. Griffith and Charlie Chaplin in 1919 that gave each of them creative control and 20 percent of the profits from their total film output. By 1924, Griffith had dropped out, Joseph Schenck had been hired as the company's president (he was the president of Art Cinema and also on the board of Giannini's Bank of America, which lent the money to Art Cinema to finance the UA product), and his wife Norma Talmadge, her sister Constance, and their younger sister Natalie's husband, comedian Buster Keaton, were now part of the organization. They told Gloria that the other members would approve her joining them, as their total box-office draw could be possibly in the millions.

Arriving in New York at nine o'clock the evening of July 22, over five hundred people greeted and shook hands with Pickford and Fairbanks, the biggest stars of the day, upon returning from a successful tour of Russia. Almost lost in the shuffle were the maharajah and maharanee of Jind, the Duchess of Richelieu, fifty American athletes who had participated in the recent Olympics in France, Heifetz, and Gloria.[10]

Gloria then rushed into *Wages of Virtue,* which had a six-week shooting schedule. Cast opposite her was twenty-three-year-old Ben Lyon, who had just completed *Lily of the Dust* with Pola Negri. (Lyon would achieve screen immortality in 1930 in Howard Hughes's UA air epic *Hell's Angels,* and then he would marry actress Bebe Daniels.) Gloria took one look at the strapping, six-foot-tall tall Lyon and liked what she saw. The two became, briefly, lovers.

The story of *Wages of Virtue,* by Forrest Halsey, based on the play by Percival Christopher Wren, told of a romance in Algiers, with elements of *Under Two Flags* and a bit of *The Sheik* thrown in for good measure. Traveling-show strongman Luigi (Ivan Linow) saves Carmelita (Gloria) from drowning, and she joins him on the road. After he kills his assistant Giuseppe (Armand Cortes) in a jealous rage, the two flee to Algiers, and Luigi enlists in the French Foreign Legion. Carmelita becomes the proprietress of a café and a favorite of the American Legion regiment and then meets Marvin (Ben Lyon). At first remaining loyal to Luigi out of gratitude, Carmelita stabs him after she learns that he plans to marry Madame La Cantiniere (Adrienne D'Ambricourt). Luigi has Marvin framed before he dies. The Legionnaires rectify the problem, and Carmelita and Marvin are united.

Manhandled opened at New York's Rivoli Theater on July 27. *The New York Times* raved, "Miss Swanson proves her versatility as a film actress, this time as a clever comedienne. Her efforts are greatly assisted by the able and restrained direction of Allan Dwan . . . Miss Swanson was clever in 'The Humming Bird,' but she is, if anything, more pleasing in 'Manhandled' . . . This is one of the few films which we have heard draw spontaneous applause from the audience, even before the last fade-out."[11]

Today, four of Gloria's eight films with Allan Dwan are lost. If they were of the quality of *Manhandled,* they are sorely missed. *Manhandled* is delightfully charming, in no small part because of her animated performance. She is in constant motion, and one cannot take one's eyes off her. The production itself is well mounted, the lighting and editing economically stylized. Her send-ups of Pola Negri, Beatrice Lillie, and Chaplin are enchanting. Peter Bogdanovich recognized this and noted in his book on Dwan, "Filmed with great authenticity on actual locations, the picture has an ingratiating and bubbly charm that is irresistible."[12]

Louise Brooks wrote of Gloria in *Manhandled* in an unpublished profile. "Not that she wasn't beautiful in stunning costumes and just as exciting flying about, kicking and fighting and getting away with it . . . [But] all the delicate seriousness of her Sennett days had been replaced in her comedy scenes by self-approval. At the end of [*Manhandled*] I wanted to give her some dog candy, so much like a charming little black poodle she had been, going through her tricks."[13]

After shooting was completed, Gloria agreed that her next picture after *Madame Sans-Gêne* would be an adaptation of Coningsby Dawson's *The Coast of Folly,* and Allan Dwan took off for Europe in November to scout location exteriors on the Riviera.

Her Love Story premiered August 31 in Los Angeles at Grauman's Metropolitan Theater. Edwin Schallert of the *Los Angeles Times* wrote that it was "still another Gloria Swanson! . . . It is not a production that is convincing or real . . . Gloria does much to relieve the very heavy murky plot with the illumination of her presence. In a few scenes she carries acting to the extremity of overacting, but had the situations been really convincing, this might not have been so obvious."[14] Still, there were those who found the whole frothy affair to their liking. "Our Gloria can surely do no wrong," wrote one enchanted journalist in his review. "She has never been more regal, more compelling, more authoritatively charming, more radiant."[15]

Her Love Story might have tickled the fringe of some reviewers' frocks, but the genre of Ruritanian romances was dying out. When the film opened at the Rivoli Theater in New York on October 5, "Fred" in *Variety* wrote, "It seems hardly probable that Broadway will want it or that the Main Street folks will go wild about it. There is one thing, however, in the picture's favor, and that is the coupling of the name Gloria Swanson with the title of the picture . . . Gloria Swanson is delightful as the young princess and magnificent as the queen. The one scene alone, where she is being torn from her son, is worth sitting through the picture."[16] *The New York Times* commented, "Gloria Swanson blossoms out this week . . . [She] knows her New York, and therefore the idea of playing a wealthy woman or a shopgirl is natural to her . . . Her acting in this new picture is therefore not up to her usual standard . . . In a number of scenes of this current photoplay Miss Swanson's thoughts appear to be wandering."[17]

Wages of Virtue wrapped in late August, and Gloria directed her sights on the much bigger project now at hand, the filming of *Madame Sans-Gêne* in France. Paramount was investing $700,000 into the lavish production. It was the first major American-French film production, and Swanson was one of the first Hollywood stars to work abroad.

On Wednesday, September 3, 1924, accompanied by Jane West, her mother Addie, three-year-old Gloria Jr., infant Joseph, a governess, and her maid Ethel, Gloria boarded the Cunard liner *Berengaria*. Also on board were Forrest Halsey and "a pale young man" whom he declared was his "assistant."[18]

The suite Gloria secured had its own private tiled veranda overlooking the sea, a private dining room for entertaining, and a luxurious boudoir. It had just been occupied by the Prince of Wales, traveling with Lord Louis Mountbatten and his wife, and vacated the day before. Gloria would be making $7,000 a week as of January 1, and she could well afford the luxury.

Upon arriving in Paris, Gloria and her retinue checked into the Hotel de Crillon, and almost immediately preproduction publicity began. The following evening, dressed in a stylish white gown, and carrying a simple long-stemmed red rose (she would latch onto carnations in later years), she paraded for two hours beside Daven, who acted as interpreter, in the ballroom of the Crillon at a special reception to introduce the American star to the Parisians. She would write in her memoirs how all the elegant men, wearing their medals and decorations, and all the elegantly dressed women surrounded her, wanting to talk to her, to touch her, all the while her head spinning in the wafting aroma of expensive perfume.[19]

The story of *Madame Sans-Gêne* tells of the proprietress of a Paris laundry, Catherine Hubscher (Gloria), known as Madame Sans-Gêne, "Madame Devil-May-Care." Her clients include a young lieutenant Napoleon Bonaparte (Jean Lorette), for whom she swipes fine clothing from her wealthy customers. During the French Revolution she meets Sergeant Le Febvre (Charles de Rochefort), and they wed. Catherine follows her husband into the field of war and joins him in battle. After the Revolution, Napoleon (now older and played by Emile

Drain) becomes emperor of France, and his wife Marie Louise (Suzanne Bianchetti) empress. His Le Febvre becomes the Duke of Danzig.

As the Duchess of Danzig, Catherine insults Bonaparte's sisters with her crude behavior. The sisters plan to embarrass and ruin Catherine at a large reception at Compiègne, but Catherine surprises everyone with her elegant manners and grace. Then, taunted by court whispers, she lashes out, calling them all Revolution-made nobodies. Napoleon demands Le Febvre divorce Catherine. In private, Catherine reminds the emperor of their early days when she loved him, of his unpaid bills, and of her devoted service to him and France during the Revolution. Napoleon rescinds his command.

All the players in the picture besides Gloria were French, with the exception of the British actor Warwick Ward, who portrayed Count de Neipperg. Actor Charles de Rochefort was already familiar to American audiences as Ramses in DeMille's *The Ten Commandments.* One new discovery was Arlette Marchal, who so impressed Gloria that she brought the young French actress to Hollywood. They would remain lifelong friends.

The design of the some three thousand period costumes for the picture was assigned to René Hubert at the suggestion of the director, Léonce Perret, one of the early pioneers of French cinema.[20]

Filming would be intense and difficult as there would be two versions of *Madame Sans-Gêne,* one for American audiences and one for foreign markets. The picture's cinematography was handled by George Webber, who had lensed Gloria's last two films and whom she insisted upon. Photography of Napoleon's three residences required production to start immediately, on October 3, before winter set in. Many scenes were shot at the Palace de Compiègne. It had survived the Revolution and was the residence of the imperial family. (It was there, too, that Napoleon met Marie Louise.) The Château de Malmaison was allowed to be used as a location for the first time by the French Fine Arts Ministry, but only with the guarantee the picture would be directed by a Frenchman. At the Château de Fontainebleau the company was able to film inside eighteen rooms, including one in which the inlaid wooden floor contained over thirty-six different kinds of wood; the company and crew were required to wear slippers so as not to mar it.

Some minimal shooting was conducted at Compiègne in Napoleon's own library; his coat of arms–marked leather-bound books and actual quill pen and blotting paper, which he had used for signing treaties, were used in the film. For Madame Sans-Gêne's presentation to Napoleon, the Salle Henri II in Fontainebleau also appeared for the first time on celluloid.[21] Suzanne Bianchetti, as the empress, actually awoke in the film in the same bed used by Marie Louise, Marie de Medicis, Maria Theresa, and Josephine. The five-foot-diameter globe photographed in the film was Napoleon's very own, and it still retained his paint-smudged fingerprints.

In *Beyond the Rocks,* Elinor Glyn had scripted a brief dream sequence about a little lady-in-waiting to the Queen of France who was so bewitching, yet reserved, that she was "the despair of all the gallants of the Court." Gloria awkwardly pretended to be nobility opposite the equally stilted Valentino, using only her imagination to see her through. Now that dream was about to become a reality. Because of the language barrier, she asked Daven to find someone to act as translator, escort, and runner for her. Sometime in early October, Halsey and Daven introduced Gloria to Henri, the Marquis de la Falaise de la Coudraye, known simply as "Hank," an impoverished French nobleman whose ancestry was documented as far back as 1190[22] and who ran a small insurance business. (His true name was James Henri Le Bailly de la Falaise, Marquis de La Coudraye.) Born February 11, 1898, in Saint Cyr-l'Ecole, France, the handsome, 5'10", blue-eyed, dark-haired Henri, fluent enough in English to be witty, was assigned as her interpreter.

Henri had fought in the Great War, enlisting at the age of seventeen. After serving in the Somme offensive in 1916 and suffering wounds in his leg after transferring to the tank division in 1917, he was awarded the Croix de Guerre and two citations. In 1919, Henri squired American movie actress Pearl White, who was opening a casino and hotel in Biarritz, around Paris. He then was seen frequently about the Continent with the famous stage entertainers the Dolly Sisters, Roszika (Rosie) and Janszieka (Jenny), White's close friends. Apparently Henri was undecided on which one he liked better. Lillian Gish would gush admiringly later in Hollywood that in her eyes Henri was "a real war hero. In his bathing-suit he presents a graphic picture of what modern warfare does to a man—he is so cut-and-shot and covered with scars."[23]

Gloria insisted upon moving out of her hotel, telling Henri she wanted a private home where she and her entourage could reside in privacy. Pointing out a particularly lovely *hotel particulier,* a private mansion, on the Place des Etats-

Unis, she asked if it could be had for rental. Henri knew the owner, the Marquis de Brantes, who fortuitously was leaving the Continent for the winter. He agreed to lease the luxuriously appointed house, complete with twenty-three servants, to her. Gloria's personal suite occupied four rooms designed in a futuristic, cubist style.

Gloria's children adored Henri, who was now her lover, and would favor him over all of Swanson's husbands. As little Gloria would recall later, "He was our favorite . . . He never interfered with us. Others would interfere in that they would make suggestions as to how we should be brought up or something. But he was a lovely person."[24]

Gloria's favorite expression became "Vous n'avez qu'à demander au Marquis de la Falaise de la Coudraye."[25] ("You ask the Marquis de la Falaise de la Coudraye.") Soon she and Henri were spending long afternoons lunching at the Château Madrid and enjoying their nights in Montmartre. On October 27, the *Los Angeles Times* reported of the affair, "All Paris is watching the manner in which the Marquis de Falaise, a true Parisian blueblood, is angling for the heart and hand of Gloria Swanson . . . Whether Gloria is taking the Marquis seriously is something only she can answer. But it is obvious the Marquis is very much in love with Gloria. Gloria is living like a queen. New dresses, gowns, jewels, and what-nots are purchased almost daily."[26]

René Hubert's costumes for Gloria in *Madame Sans-Gêne* were stunning. One in particular featured an ermine mantle with an estimated value of 75,000 francs. Gloria purchased a great deal of her personal wardrobe from some of the best couture houses in Paris, including some startling modern frocks executed by Sonia Delaunay (known for her cubist patchwork designs) at the recently opened Maison Delaunay. "[Gloria] once showed me clothes she had made in Paris during the twenties," said designer Noel Taylor. "They were built up from the inside because she was so small."[27]

Photoplay reported Gloria spent in 1924 $5,000 on purses, $25,000 on furs, $10,000 on lingerie, $9,600 on silk stockings, $6,000 on perfume, $50,000 on gowns, and $500,000 on jewels, including a 5.1 carat rectangular diamond ring.[28] (With a presale value of $140,000, it was auctioned at Christie's Jewels Department in Paris in May 2011.) Once, to avoid reporters trailing her in Paris, she ducked into Cartier, stepping out ten minutes later with a pair of gem-encrusted crystal bracelets valued at $20,000.

Besides spending lavishly on clothes and accessories, Gloria threw costly costume balls in her rented palace, handing out party favors and gifts from Cartier. With Henri by her side, bedecked in spats, suede gloves, and a silver monogrammed walking stick, she also learned about social charm and manipulation, all the while picking the "best" friends and the "best" wine and throwing the "grandest" parties. "He knew French snobbery and decorum and protocol down to the minutest detail," she said about Henri, "and he never allowed me to miss a beat."[29] When Allan Dwan and his assistant director Richard Rosson arrived in Paris, he had already been notified of Gloria's extravagant spending and ostentatious living. Sure enough, Gloria, dressed in gold satin, her chauffeur garbed in a sky-blue uniform, arrived at the train station to fetch Dwan and Rosson in a leopard-skin-upholstered, block-long sky-blue Mercedes.

Back in the States, *Wages of Virtue* opened to disappointing reviews in Los Angeles the same week as Pola Negri's successful *Forbidden Paradise* with Rod La Rocque. Edwin Schallert was perplexed: "Where is the Gloria Swanson of 'The Humming Bird' and 'Manhandled'? Or is 'Wages of Virtue' a sample of what her forthcoming pictures are to be like? I hope not. Because if 'Madame Sans-Gene,' her next production, resembles it . . . I'll look for other entertainment."[30]

In New York, where *Wages of Virtue* opened on Sunday, November 23, the same day as Valentino's *A Sainted Devil,* it was a tremendous success, with standing-room-only audiences, and police called to hold back the crowds. Gloria's performance was heralded, and Mordaunt Hall, in one of his first film reviews for *The New York Times,* stated, "Miss Swanson is particularly good where she pretends to have fallen down a flight of steps in a faint . . . She then takes her audience into her confidence by winking at them when Marvin is not looking."[31]

Acerbic *Los Angeles Times* columnist Harry Carr was never a great fan of Gloria's, but he did pen a rather accurate picture of her work, while still taking a swipe. "The more I see of Gloria the more am I impressed with the fact that the screen has never known another like her. It isn't that she is a great actress. I have never seen but two great actresses. One was Duse, and the other wasn't Gloria."[32]

While filming *Madame Sans-Gêne* in November, Gloria traveled to Brussels by deluxe express with Henri, Jane West, Madeleine Guitty, Halsey, and his ever-present "assistant" for an event at the U.S. Embassy and a film festival in her honor. On the last night of their stay, after Halsey and his "assistant" had a loud, embarrassingly bitchy lovers' quarrel and retired from the bar to their hotel suite, Gloria and Henri lingered and talked over drinks. She told Henri she soon would be making $1,000 a day, even on Sundays. "I am sorry I have nothing to offer you, Gloria," he told her.

"Such as?" she asked.

"Money. I have none . . . I am sorry."[33]

Gloria realized Henri was the only man she desired at that moment. He was tall, dark, handsome, cultured, connected, and titled. As they entered the elevator to take them to their floor, she took Henri's hand. He walked her to her suite. Then, once back in Paris, Henri proposed to Gloria officially in her drawing room.

Gloria took Daven into her confidence. As do many women, she often befriended gay men, attracted by their male beauty, wit, and sometimes honesty. Like herself, they shared her sexual passion for men. Homosexuals also offered her culture and escape with little threat of physical intimacy. One such man was Daven, whose uncanny resemblance to Valentino landed him into the narcissistic idol's bedroom. Gloria and Daven were seen together constantly. When *Madame Sans-Gêne* completed filming in early December, Gloria focused on her future.

Gloria fancifully wrote in her memoirs that the only thing she desired in life then was to become the Marquise de la Falaise de la Coudraye and to live in Paris.[34] By her own account she would always remember December 1924 as the happiest month of her life. By her own account, she knew she was spending foolishly, but she rationalized that she had never had so much fun doing so.[35] Gloria Swanson in love was a force of nature. Then, in the middle of December, she discovered she was pregnant. The ramifications of this were threatening.

In her autobiography, Gloria went to great lengths to explain her subsequent actions. She wrote that because she was still married to Herbert Somborn, the dreaded morals clause in her contract would come into play; she feared her career would be destroyed, and she was waiting for her divorce papers to be sent to her, which would take until the middle of January. This is simply untrue. Her divorce from Herbert had been finalized in September 1923 and widely published in the newspapers at that time. So why the subterfuge?

Possibly Gloria and Henri did not want a baby. She was, after all, one of the most recognizable stars in the world, and another pregnancy would jeopardize her future film commitments. And she was making a great deal of money. Famous Players–Lasky had heard in late 1924 that she was considering signing with United Artists to produce her own pictures. In January she was offered a renegotiation of her contract at more than double the amount, jumping from $7,000 to $15,000 a week. Perhaps she was unsure about marriage to a titled, albeit impoverished, nobleman. Whatever the true cause of her actions, Gloria chose to have an abortion at this critical stage of her career, and, at least according to her memoirs, she did not tell Henri. (Gloria admitted to her last husband she had had three abortions, one shortly after her split from Herbert.)[36]

Coldly combining business with her personal drama, Gloria wrote in her memoirs of her fears of forfeiting her studio contract and relinquishing her position as one of the world's highest paid film stars, and thus she would possibly lose Henri, who had become accustomed to living the same lifestyle as she.[37] Calculating perhaps, but realistic. She wrote that she confided in Daven and set about her plan. Daven arranged for an operation. Gloria, so she wrote, was horrified when she learned that Henri had set their wedding date for Wednesday, January 28—the day before her scheduled abortion.

This makes interesting drama and passable suspense, but it is not credible. Never one to take actual responsibility for her own needless actions, Gloria inevitably embellished the truth, endowed herself with great courage, and became the heroine of the drama. In this particular case, her tale of the reasons for the abortion grates against the saga as documented at that time.[38]

The facts are that Gloria and Henri were wed at the *mairie* of the Sixteenth Arrondissement (a Paris borough hall) shortly after noon on January 28, 1925. The bride wore a simple beige suit with a large purple orchid pinned to her bosom, a black hat, and flesh-colored stockings with "openwork" shoes. Henri wore a full-dress suit. For her witness, she chose Hallet Johnson, first secretary of the U.S. Embassy, and standing up for Henri was Baron Robert D'Aiguy. Present at the ceremony were André Daven, M. Léonce and Mme. Perret, René Hubert, the mayor's wife, newspaper correspondent Basil Woon, and Henri's brother Alain. Gloria's mother and the children were not there when Henri slipped a platinum circlet of diamonds on her finger and the long-bearded mayor of Passy pronounced them wed.

Gloria then called her mother at their hotel with the news. Addie was furious that she had not been notified beforehand, but she joined the party at the Plaza Athenée Hotel, where a wedding brunch was held. Addie was cold and petulant at the reception, vowing to take the first steamer back to New York, which she did. That afternoon Gloria saw her dressmakers.

"We are going to California for our honeymoon, where we can take a long rest," Gloria advised the waiting press as Henri smoked a cigarette from an eighteen-inch-long amber cigarette holder, a gift from his bride. "I am going back to Fontainebleau tomorrow and I won't get another breathing spell until we sail. I am happy beyond words."[39] Between nervous puffs on a cigarette of her own while Henri talked about his plans *not* to enter the movies, Gloria called her chauffeur to bring their limousine around for the shopping tour she had planned. Forrest Halsey, back in Hollywood, gleefully told the press, "I might be considered as the father of the romance. When they got married they sent me a cable saying, 'Your children have done it.'"[40]

On January 30, Gloria, now Mme. La Marquise de la Falaise et de la Coudraye, informed the press she was keeping her husband as her interpreter. "I do not like the rough language some American film directors use and I cannot understand what the Frenchmen say, so I need Henri to explain things to me and translate instructions to them . . . [Henri] probably will go into the automobile business in the United States, as he is greatly interested in machines."[41]

Henry Wales reported in the *Los Angeles Times* that Gloria's mother had declined interviews and callers, refusing to give any statements, "as her daughter gave her strict orders that no more publicity be given the marriage, except that she gives out herself."[42] In the ensuing events in her memoirs, Gloria presents herself as a helpless female. In fact she was meticulously directing her own destiny. *She* was in control. When asked by the press how it felt to be a real marchioness, she grandly replied, "Rank isn't everything."[43]

By all accounts Gloria and Henri were joyously happy, having booked to sail to America on board the liner *Berengaria* on February 18. What they could not know was that Gloria was about to face a very real crisis, one that nearly cost her her life.

11

La Grande Illusion

Gloria wrote that she had the abortion the day after her wedding. André Daven took her to an elegant apartment building where the doctor had his offices. It was all over by lunchtime. That morning René Hubert had escorted Addie by train to Cherbourg to return to America, and Jane West was left to care for the children in Paris. Once she returned to the hotel, Gloria wrote, she had André take Henri to the Ritz for lunch, while she rested. The following morning she awoke with a high fever and agonizing pain. Taking only hot tea, her temperature escalated. After three days she was finally rushed to a hospital and diagnosed with a tetanus infection. Several times, she wrote, she attempted to tell her husband what she had done. She didn't.

Hospital records no longer exist, but contemporary news reports confirmed Gloria was indeed suffering from an infection. The press was told at the time Gloria was "in bed" and did not "intend to get up." She grew worse as the third night progressed, and at two o'clock in the morning she was rushed by ambulance to the private hospital Villa Moliere in Auteuil suffering from peritonitis. There, said the press, she underwent an emergency operation, waking up afterward hemorrhaging.[1]

According to a statement made by her physicians, Gloria had undergone an operation two years before and had taken a recent fall from a horse while filming *Madame Sans-Gêne* at Fontainbleau that caused "grave internal trouble which resulted in last night's sudden relapse and the operation."[2] Her surgeon informed the press she would have died within two hours had he not operated. What caused the infection and the bleeding, either a botched abortion or a previous operation aggravated by a fall, will probably never be known for certain.

On February 20 Gloria's fever shot up to 103, and she was now showing signs of septic poisoning. In the days before antibiotics this development was ominous.

Three days later her condition turned even graver, and she had to undergo another operation for peritonitis, with a blood transfusion scheduled to follow. Adolph Zukor, in Cannes, received a cable from his secretary that Gloria had died; the next day the treasurer of the company, his relative Eugene Zukor, denied the report to the studio chief and the press after receiving encouraging news from Major Charles H. Bell, studio manager in Paris.

By February 25 the papers reported a major improvement. Gloria had had another transfusion and was now feeling better and taking food. The reports in America were awash with the story, and some wondered if Paramount stock would be in any way affected should the star die. The following day, little Gloria and "Brother" arrived aboard the liner *France* in New York, accompanied by a nurse and their governess. They were not told of their mother's illness. Addie and the children were then transported to the farm in Croton-on-Hudson.

By the end of February Gloria's recovery was progressing well. She and Henri took a month to recuperate on the Riviera before returning to America. Her hair had been shaved during her illness, and she was not receiving guests. Throughout the day she wrote letters to friends or sketched while she regained her strength.

It is telling that in her memoirs, in the midst of her account of the abortion and its aftermath, Gloria coolly commented, "In addition to everything else, California would be *so* dull after Paris that spring." She continued, "The new word for 1925 was 'chic,' which everybody repeated constantly but nobody could define." Gloria goes on in the same paragraph to talk about the couturiers who had raised skirt hems above the knees, and of the artists Van Dongen and Vertes, of cubism, and the exposition of *arts decoratifs*, which was soon to open, and Antoine, *"the* coiffeur" who introduced the new short hairstyle for spring. She wrote she wished to remain in that atmosphere of flowers, fashion, and culture always.[3] There seemed to be no regrets.

Warner Bros., "believing her the greatest box-office attraction now appearing in pictures,"[4] had made a firm offer in February to obtain Gloria's services for $17,000 a week if she would sign with them, which prompted Famous Players–Lasky now to counteroffer with $17,500 a week, according to the *New York Times*. In March the *Chicago Tribune* announced Paramount had made an offer to Gloria for a two-year contract at $250,000 a picture, with a minimum of four pictures a year. She told the press she would decide when she returned to America.

In early March it was reported that the Gloria-Lasky contract still was unsigned. According to her attorney, Gloria still might be "grabbed away from Famous Players–Lasky by a rival producer."[5] The London *Sunday Express* headlined on its front page that she had signed a 500-pound-a-day, 182,000-pound-a-year contract (approximately $21,227.00 then; by today's rate $287,000 U.S.).

Through a series of coded telegrams, there was another "potentially explosive alliance" in the works—between Gloria and DeMille, now producing his own films for DeMille Pictures Corporation. Mickey Neilan had approached DeMille to suggest they form a separate combine where he and DeMille would direct one picture each with Swanson, with other directors filming a couple of pictures or more with her a year. As Gloria was equally interested in making films of quality and sustenance, her attorney advised them that if they could equal Paramount's offer for a new contract, she would sign with them. Despite DeMille's enthusiasm and agreement to match any figure necessary the deal never materialized.[6]

On the new passport she was hastily issued through the American Embassy on March 17, 1925, Gloria's name was changed from Gloria Swanson Somborn to Gloria Swanson de la Falaise. The following day she and Henri boarded the liner *Paris* in Le Havre en route to New York, telling the press, "We will be back in France in a year's time."[7]

While still at sea, Adolph Zukor sent Gloria the following cablegram:

WOULD SUGGEST AN INTERVIEW ON YOUR ARRIVAL AT PIER . . .
MY ASSOCIATES AND I PLAN TO GIVE YOU A BIG PUBLIC
RECEPTION BUT . . . WOULD PREFER TO GIVE A LITTLE
LATER TO GIVE US AMPLE TIME TO INVITE A VERY
REPRESENTATIVE GATHERING INCLUDING PRESS[8]

Zukor was probably unaware his message would not sit well with Gloria. Any attempt to delay her triumphant moment, her arrival back into her native land after her near-death experience, was unthinkable.

When the *Paris* docked in New York on the evening of March 24, the press surrounded Gloria and Henri on deck and bombarded them with questions: What did Henri think of American women? What did he think of the New York skyline? (Which, he answered, he could not see because they were crowding around him and blocking his view.) Gloria wore an outfit she had designed while recuperating, a skirt of dyed ermine, with a jumper-length woven coat. She also flashed a large ruby solitaire. It was her engagement ring. She told the press in reference to the couple's romance, "It just happened. How does any one know how it happens? If you've been in love you understand."[9]

Staying in New York briefly, before they retreated to Croton-on-Hudson the first week in April, Gloria and Henri attended a Broadway performance of *Rose Marie*. "They were delayed outside the theater by a tremendous throng of people massed there to see them," reported one writer. "When they came inside after the curtain had risen, the performance on stage halted, the houselights came up, and the entire audience gave the famous couple a standing ovation."[10]

In New York Gloria showed off her marquis in style. On April 14, she was "officially" welcomed home by Paramount at a dinner-dance held at the Park Lane Hotel in her honor. Some eight hundred guests attended. When she and Henri entered the ballroom, they were greeted by spontaneous applause and a standing ovation as the orchestra struck up "The Marseillaise."

At the Colony Club soon after, they drank illegal champagne. When he uncorked a fresh bottle, accidentally splashing the bare back of the beautiful actress Constance Bennett, Henri humbly apologized. Henri was stunned when the witty young blonde laughingly retorted, "Think nothing of it, Marquis! I never complain about bathing in champagne!"[11] It would not be his last encounter with the flirtatious Miss Bennett.

Paramount went out of its way to promote *Madame Sans-Gêne,* spending a great deal of money while garnering reams of publicity. To accommodate the crowds for its premiere at the Rivoli Theater, a gala opening at $5 a ticket was planned for April 17. Ringers were hired to shout outside the theater, "Vive la Republique! Vive Gloria! Vive M. Zukor et M. Lasky."[12] The Rivoli, as well as other buildings on both sides of Broadway from Forty-Ninth to Fifty-Ninth

Streets, flew giant American Stars and Stripes and French tricolor buntings and streamers for the event. French "soldiers" were posted outside two sentry boxes at the theater, its whole facade covered with Gloria's name in lights, the largest example seen up to that time in New York. Onlookers were held at bay by uniformed police. It was a spectacular opening. Invitations had been sent to French diplomats in Washington, D.C., and to New York consulate officials. Inside the theater, after the strains of "The Marseillaise" faded, the orchestra struck up music compiled by Forrest Halsey.

After a brief stage show of performers in eighteenth-century costumes, the film began. *Life* magazine said, "Finally, as a sort of afterthought, the projection machines started whirring, and 'Mme. Sans-Gene' was revealed upon the cold, dispassionate surface of the screen. It proved to be a thoroughly dull picture, and indicated that all the loud-mouthed exploitation in the world cannot atone for the absence of drama."[13] Most of the New York papers raved about the opening, but unfortunately reviews of the film were decidedly mixed.

Mordaunt Hall of *The New York Times* seemed more impressed with the spectacle of Gloria and her marquis than the picture itself. "Aside from Miss Swanson's performance and possibly that of the roles of Napoleon and La Rousette, the characterization that is obtainable on the stage is lacking in the picture. Somehow the players are pleasant but rather flat. The idea of having the titles in English without a tinge of French is unsatisfactory in several stretches. When Madame Sans-Gene, as the vivandiere, marches through the streets with the troops Gloria Swanson appears to be only certain of one word in the national anthem, and that is 'Marchons!' In other scenes it is plain that Madame Sans-Gene is speaking English."[14]

The picture itself, after all the ballyhoo, proved anticlimactic. Nevertheless, *Madame Sans-Gêne* was a tremendous box-office success, breaking house records at the Rivoli, grossing $41,300 its first week. After Paramount excised thirty minutes from the picture, they were able to add an extra showing every day.

After the launch, on Saturday, April 18, 1925, Gloria and Henri boarded a train to Chicago, where they joined 125 Famous Players–Lasky officials on April 21 on a luxuriously appointed special eleven-car train section headed for the annual Paramount convention to be held in Hollywood. Gloria and her maid were the only women on board. Wiring ahead, she advised Paramount,

"Am arriving Monday with Marquis. Arrange ovation."[15] Interviewed in the Windy City, Gloria, stylishly dressed in Lanvin, with a green satin blouse, a green straw cloche hat, and a large green emerald next to her wedding ring and holding a tan leather purse, gave an interview to the papers.

She was asked about her children. On May 6, 1925, Joseph Patrick Swanson would legally become her son. About showing her husband New York, Gloria waxed poetic. "Why, I never had so much fun as when I took Henry up to the top of the Woolworth Building. After that we went into the Grand Central Station to see the sights. Yes, we even bought postcards."[16]

When the train pulled into the Santa Fe Station in San Bernardino in the early morning hours of April 24, half the town's population was there to greet them, pelting the train cars with flowers. Schoolchildren were given bouquets to give to Paramount distribution executives, and a five-minute tribute was arranged. At the end of the ceremony, carloads of San Bernardino society folk drove to Los Angeles for the premiere of *Madame Sans-Gêne* that evening at Grauman's Million Dollar Theater.

Arriving at the Los Angeles train depot around noon, Gloria noticed hundreds of people on the platform gathered to greet her and Henri, including the United Artists contingency—Pickford, Fairbanks, Chaplin, Griffith, Norma Talmadge, and her husband Joseph Schenck. Paramount also made sure DeMille and Valentino were present. Gloria was dumbfounded. Leaning heavily on Henri's arm, dressed in a light colored, spring ensemble, she was heard to moan inside the car, "Oh, good Lord."[17]

A high platform had been erected for speakers to begin their official welcome. Two brass bands were on hand, as well as the mayor of Los Angeles, George E. Cryer. Henri led Gloria to her limousine as the crowd threw showers of roses. Newswoman Louella Parsons rode in the car with them as the parade wound through downtown Los Angeles and ended at Paramount, where again they were mobbed. Gloria, standing in the open car, loudly proclaimed to her adoring subjects, "I am so happy to be home, I can't tell you."[18]

Hedda Hopper, who seemed to participate in everything outside the Creation, wrote of Gloria's triumphant return to Hollywood, "I was here and saw her reception after 'Sans Gene' in Hollywood. I was on Vine Street. The whole street was roped off from Sunset to Selma. In the middle of the street they'd built a huge platform—ten feet high. On it was a brass band. Banners from one end of the street to the other stretched out like fresh laundry on a line of streamers reading 'Welcome Home, Gloria.'

"The public schools had been let out for the day. The sidewalks were roped off. Thousands of school children lined the block with their parents behind them . . . Flowers, roses, all kinds of flowers, any flower that was blooming on a stalk was cut off and put in garbage pails—bright new shining garbage pails— because a bucket wasn't big enough to hold them. And as Gloria's car slowly rounded the corner from Sunset Blvd. and came into Vine, the band struck up, the school children pelted her with flowers (nearly put her eyes out) and all pandemonium broke loose. It took her about ten minutes to go from the corner to the gate half a block up the street. It was an emotion orgy."[19]

Fashion designer Edith Head recalled that Paramount shut down for the whole day so its employees could join in the revelry. When the parade reached the studio, the executives were lined up to kiss Gloria's hand, as employees threw more flowers at the magical couple.

After settling into the Crescent Drive mansion that afternoon, Gloria and Henri rested before the West Coast premiere, which promised to be the most spectacular opening Hollywood would see for some time. On Friday evening, April 24, at Grauman's Million Dollar Theater, Gloria, simply gowned in clinging silver lamé, wearing no jewels but her wedding ring and the decoration, the Palmes Académiques, given to her by the French government, on the arm of her marquis, in white tie and tails and sporting his Croix de Guerre, stepped from a limo, followed by Addie, dressed to the hilt for her first film premiere. The crowds, cordoned off to the sides as the party was ushered into the theater, went wild with enthusiasm at their first glimpse of Gloria. (Among the many stars present were Mickey Neilan and Blanche Sweet, Wallace Beery, Norma Shearer, Raoul Walsh, Adolph Zukor, Jesse Lasky, and Constance Bennett.)

When Gloria and Henri reached the main door into the theater, she recalled that as they entered the darkened theater, the lights burst upon them, the orchestra struck up "Home, Sweet Home," the audience gasped, and then it broke into thunderous applause.[20] The effusive Adela Rogers St. Johns noted, "I saw men standing on their seats, waving their arms, other women tearing off their orchids and flinging them into the aisle for Gloria Swanson to walk on— and I saw Mack Sennett frankly wiping the tears from his proud face."[21]

Wrote actress Colleen Moore, "The theater was jammed with the young and the beautiful, all in glittering attire. Just before the lights dimmed, the orchestra struck up "La Marseillaise." A spotlight was turned to the rear of the theater. There was Gloria in a shimmering white gown coming down the aisle on the arm of her handsome, titled husband. They looked like the king and queen of some mythical Balkan kingdom."[22] Gloria was magnanimously seated between Cecil B. DeMille and Mack Sennett, her early mentors. As soon as the picture began, she, Henri, and Addie were ushered out the side entrance to avoid hysteria after the showing.

Gloria dramatically begins her memoirs with the opening night of *Madame Sans-Gêne* in Hollywood, one of the most memorable and triumphant nights of her young life. After passionately summarizing her and Henri's affair and the abortion, she ends her prologue with this conversation: Once inside the limo parked in the alley of the theater, on the long drive back to her home on Crescent Drive, Addie noticed Gloria was exceptionally quiet. She asked her why she was not overjoyed on this, the most spectacular night of her life. "It should have happened when I'm fifty," Gloria wrote she replied. "I'm only twenty-six. What's left? How can I top it?"[23] Now that she had reached the mountaintop, she had to go down the other side.

Wisdom comes with age. It is doubtful those thoughts even entered Gloria's mind that evening; however, she truly may have looked back on the whole remarkable experience that way. In 1925 her tremendous plans and her colossal ego far surpassed any thoughts of moderation, appreciation, and reflection. She was in major contract negotiations, and held a unique position within the industry that would allow her to make millions of dollars as her own producer. She was also self-assured enough to think she had learned as much as any studio head or film mogul, if not more. Gloria's ambitions in 1925 knew no bounds.[24]

In early May production began on the last four films under Gloria's existing Paramount contract. The first picture was *The Coast of Folly*, directed by Allan Dwan, with a poor screenplay by Forrest Halsey. Rod La Rocque was originally set to play opposite her, but a new Paramount find, Anthony Jewitt, was given the part. Originally set for the French Riviera, location shooting was then switched to Miami, Florida, and then to the beach of San Diego's fabulous Hotel del Coronado. *The Coast of Folly* told of Nadine Gathaway (Gloria) leaving her priggish husband and disappearing for twenty years. When he dies, his entire fortune is left to their daughter Joyce (Gloria again) on the condition she avoid scandal. Joyce becomes involved with Larry Fay (Jewitt), whose wife Constance (Dorothy Cummings) sues for alienation of affection. Nadine, now the Countess de Tauro, hears about the scandal in Paris. She returns to the States determined to aid her daughter. In the end Constance drops the suit, and Larry and Joyce are united.

The filming of the beach scenes was more or less supervised by Gloria. Boasted set designer Hans Dreier, "She knows all about interiors. Her sense of artistic effects is amazing. In the general atmosphere of a drawing, the distribution of furniture and its style, the hanging of paintings and the type of decoration, she offers suggestions that are invaluable." She even assisted Halsey with the screenplay. Said Halsey, "She keeps in touch with every phase of the production. When it is finished it is truly a Gloria Swanson picture."[25]

"When I'm creating a character, it's quite possible I will steal from life," she informed a journalist. "In one particular instance I was playing two parts—a mother and her daughter. The daughter was a very athletic type, and the mother was a foolish woman who didn't want her husband to know that she had a grown child. She was trying to be young. So I copied her clothes from Fannie Ward, a famous woman in those days who'd had plastic surgery, had jewelry and chiffon to cover her neck, and things like this. Then I took the walk of Elinor Glyn, who was quite blind but too vain to wear glasses, so she was a little uneasy on her feet."[26]

Now settled in California, Gloria and Henri entertained at Crescent Drive on a prodigious scale. They enjoyed extravagant shopping sprees, driving about town in her luxurious real-leopard-upholstered Lanci, while luxury auto designer Raymond Dietrich was at work creating a new vehicle for them. In New York, extensive renovations were made on her home at Croton-on-Hudson, as the family planned on spending the following summer there. Gloria had her secretary place dinner invitations by telephone with the formidable command, "Madame la Marquise de la Falaise de la Coudraye would like you to dine with her."[27]

Gloria and Henri would often invite from seventy-five to a hundred people to dinner, handing out solid gold compacts to the ladies and solid gold cigarette cases to the gentlemen as favors. Liveried butlers seated the guests, tremendously impressing them as they had only seen such opulence "in the movies." Gloria had also developed a grand habit of standing in one spot, insisting her guests approach her and pay homage. Champagne would flow all night.

Gloria would later recall the parties they would have. "But they weren't stuffy affairs. Everyone knew each other and we had fun. I remember once I had a ju-jitsu exhibition after dinner. Ronald Colman and Dick Barthelmess insisted on trying it, and they threw each other all around the living room."[28] Young Lita Grey, dating Charlie Chaplin at the time, recalled meeting Gloria at one soiree. "Here was Gloria Swanson, radiant yet vaguely haughty, a star who appeared just a trifle too aware of being one," Lita recalled.[29]

"When I go to the theater I am pointed out as Gloria Swanson and stared at," she complained to a journalist. "Knowing that this will happen, I must prepare as best I can for the battery of eyes, a far more critical battery, I might say, than the cameras. If I were to affect simple things, people would be disappointed and perhaps steer clear of my pictures . . . When I used to appear in the De Mille [*sic*] productions, everything was done to make them look perfect. Time and energy and labor were expended like water. Now I am a star, working on a program schedule, holding up the heavy end of each picture. Do you realize that when you are a star the success of the picture depends upon you? . . . I can't say that it's a bed of roses, the star's life."[30]

Gloria would always defend her extravagant lifestyle, rationalizing in 1965, "The public wanted us to live like kings and queens. So we did . . . And why not? We were in love with life. We were making more money than we ever dreamed existed and there was no reason to believe it would ever stop."[31] She later reflected, "It would be impossible nowadays, but then I had 11 servants. You had to have that many to keep up such a place. There would be a governess for my children, gardeners, cooks, butlers, upstairs maids and downstairs maids."[32]

"After her marriage," said film producer Joe Pasternak, who was an assistant director during the filming of *Stage Struck* at the Astoria Studio, "Gloria became very conscious of her rights and privileges." She now advised her film crews she was no longer to be addressed by her first name or as "Miss Swanson," as they had been doing. "People like the operating cameramen had a terrible time. They had been saying things like, 'Hey Gloria, would you move over just a bit to the left? That's it honey, stand right there.' Now they had to change to: 'Would the Marquise be kind enough, please, to move slightly to the left?'"[33]

In later life Gloria was wise enough to see her pretensions, writing in 1980,

"I had become as bad as all the other people in Hollywood when I went to parties; I forgot everybody who wasn't above the title as soon as I shook his or her hand and thanked him or her for the kind remarks about my pictures."[34] But at the time, she lived like a queen and she expected to be treated like one. Future film producer A. C. Lyles, then recently hired by Paramount as an office boy, recalled watching Gloria make an entrance into the studio when *The Coast of Folly* was shooting. As her chauffeured limousine pulled up, girls hired for the specific purpose tossed rose petals in front of her to walk upon.

Then there was the ongoing feud between Gloria and Pola Negri. Because films at the time were without sound, sets for different productions could be built side by side. Pola insisted on soft, emotional music by small orchestras to create the proper mood while she was filming, and the sets on either side of hers were requested to keep completely silent during her peak emotional scenes. ("Pola is nutty as a bed-bug," William Randolph Hearst once told Marion Davies.[35]) Legend has it that while Negri was in the midst of emoting during a breathtakingly quiet, dramatic climax (possibly in *Flower of Night*), next door on Gloria's set of *The Coast of Folly* a brass band, hired for the day, struck up a rousing military march. Director Allan Dwan had arranged the incident, but Negri always suspected it was at Gloria's instigation.

Negri recalled in her memoirs a particular function the studio had requested she and Gloria attend. She wrote that because Gloria was jealous of her relationship with Charlie Chaplin, she dictated she would not make an entrance until after Pola. Interpreting that to mean Gloria felt she was a more important star, Pola sent the studio chiefs the same directive. Both women sat in their dressing rooms as the evening progressed, each refusing to make her entrance before the other.

Finally, Negri, wearing a magnificent silver-threaded French brocade designer gown, took the high road and made her appearance first, to a burst of applause. She was then seated next to Adolph Zukor. "Gloria is an excellent show-woman and she bided her time until just the right moment, when all the excitement caused by my appearance had died away," Pola modestly wrote. "Unfortunately, communication between us had become so strained that we had not checked on our gowns. Her entrance was ruined when she appeared in *exactly* the same gown I was wearing. The designer had neglected to tell either of us that the other had bought it. Instead of great adulation, she received minor amusement. There was no way of making a graceful exit to change, and she spent the evening seething with only dear Mr. Zukor separating her place at the table from me."[36]

Gloria always insisted she was innocent of such pranks. "I'm not a stupid woman and I hope I have common sense," she declared. "Someone wrote ... that Pola and I always tried to see who could make a later entrance to a party. What did I do, sit outside in an automobile until she went in first? Or be in cahoots with the butler who would call me up and say, 'She's arrived; now you can come over'? I never heard such nonsense in my life."[37]

However, Gloria did start to exercise her new power by riding from her dressing room to the set in a wheelchair pushed by a young lackey. She would later deny she had insisted on this treatment, claiming her costumes were just too elaborate and heavy for her to manipulate by herself. (There were no heavy costumes in her pictures at this time.) By the completion of *The Coast of Folly*, Gloria was being transported from the set to her bungalow and back by a sedan emblazoned with Henri's coat of arms and carried by four footmen, to avoid, she claimed, tripping over electrical cables. An orchestra, estimated to number seventy-five musicians, was instructed to play "The Marsellaise" periodically, and the cast and crew were requested to bow to her.

"But all the time we were pulling Hollywood's leg," Gloria would halfheartedly joke in her memoirs as explanation.[38] At the time, however, her behavior was very real, and the cost very expensive. Her lifelong friend Virginia Bowker said in 1950, "When she returned from France with Hank ... she was very much Madame la Marquise . . . That was the only time Gloria ever was guilty of bad manners."[39]

Still, for millions of fans Gloria represented the epitome of style and fashion, and that would keep her in the public eye no matter what. Women rushed to department stores to buy the "Poke," a cloche hat made of silk with a straw-edged brim, which Gloria was seen wearing. Many of her own hats were created by Viennese milliner Minna Glodenberg Lubin, who also designed bonnets for Norma Talmadge and Mary Pickford. And "the Beautiful and Smart" Gloria was featured in advertisements for hats sold by Martha Regnier's Hats in 1925. Gloria's short, boyish hairstyle, cut simply because her head had been shorn during her illness, became the rage. Gloria had a short body, thick waist, large head, and a slight slouch. Yet by standing as erect as possible, and by camouflaging her imperfections with fashion and dieting, she nevertheless managed to appear tall and stylish.

René Hubert contributed a study of Gloria to the *Los Angeles Times* at the end of May. In it he spoke about her views of fashion and her belief that women should know their clothes. "Miss Swanson designs all of her own clothes and all [her] costumes," he said. "In this I assist her . . . She makes a dress a part of herself, a part of her personality. She knows it thoroughly, wears it naturally and never with a hint of self-consciousness." Gloria by now would never have thought of purchasing anything off the rack, and thus all her clothes were made exclusively for her.[40]

As Gloria immersed herself in her work, her career, and her pleasures, Henri was often left to his own devices, when not called upon to escort his wife. Dedicated to Gloria and all that her money could buy, he acquired rights to a couple of properties he felt would make good screen vehicles for her. One was *Seventh Heaven,* based on the hit 1922 Broadway play, later filmed by Fox in 1927, and the other *The Love Call,* a turgid tale about a Paris streetwalker named Lucette Darbeil, "a beautiful eccentric woman" of about twenty-five, which he wanted to produce. Gloria herself purchased, on July 17, Leanore J. Coffee's book *Battalion of Death* for $1,750 as a possible property.

After three months in California, *The Coast of Folly* now completed, Gloria and Henri prepared to return to New York, but not before inviting Jesse Lasky over to the mansion to discuss business. United Artists treasurer Maurice Cleary had visited Gloria's bungalow on the Paramount lot during the last days of filming to advise her that his company was willing to do anything she wanted if she would sign with them, including negotiating the number of pictures she would make annually. UA would give her the full profit from her films after costs were recovered, plus preferred stock options and percentage deals from distribution profits. Besides still having three of the four founding artists still in the fold, Chaplin, Pickford, and Fairbanks, UA was about to add Valentino and Samuel Goldwyn, and feelers were out for Ronald Colman and Vilma Banky as well.

"[United Artists] assured Gloria she had too fine of a mind, was too brilliant a person and too great an executive to walk docilely through the golden years of her fame and not prospect a little on her own," wrote movie magazine writer Ruth Biery. Yet there were those who strongly suggested otherwise.

"There were a few friends who pointed out that if Gloria accepted the Paramount offer and lived parsimoniously on $5,000 a week she might have two million dollars in a trust fund at the end of two years. But, alas, their voices were lost in the din and the clamor."[41]

Lasky naturally caught word of the visit. Upon discussing the figures with Gloria, he said he would give her double what she was now earning. She told him what other offers had been made, and he upped it to $18,000 a week. He even offered Henri a position with the company, which, much to her dismay, Henri accepted. Gloria knew *she* could do business with Lasky and be a formidable opponent. However, Henri was too much a gentleman to do the same.

12

United Artists

On June 29 Jesse Lasky informed the East Coast studio chief, Adolph Zukor, that Gloria had engaged Maurice Cleary as her business manager and her personal representative and that he had been negotiating with them for the past two days:

> I HAVE FINALLY GIVEN THEM OUR BEST PROPOSITION . . .
> TWO HUNDRED THOUSAND DOLLARS ADVANCE AGAINST
> FIFTY PERCENT OF NET PROFITS OF EACH PICTURE WITH
> CONTRACT FOR TWO YEARS 3 PICTURES PER YEAR STOP . . .
> I HAVE TOLD HER OUR OFFER REPRESENTS BEST WE CARE TO
> GO BECAUSE HER FIFTY PERCENT INTEREST MAKES HER OUR
> EQUAL PARTNER AND WITH GUARANTY OF TWO HUNDRED
> THOUSAND SHE SHOULD BE WILLING [TO] GAMBLE FOR
> ADDITIONAL PROFITS OVER HER ADVANCES[1]

Gloria wrote that she met with Maurice Cleary in late June at her home before she and Henri headed east. Ironing out details of Gloria's commitment to his company over drinks, Cleary explained UA was basically a distribution company owned by its artists. As an independent artist, Gloria could buy $100,000 of preferred stock in UA and thereby profit from the company's complete output. Within days of the meeting, Allan Dwan met with her to inform her Lasky was willing to offer $22,000 a week if she would re-sign with Famous Players–Lasky. (Dwan later stated he was authorized to offer her up to $25,500 to sign.)

In a letter dated late Friday evening, July 3–4, 1925, Lasky advised Zukor:

> SWANSON AND CLEARY ... DO NOT SEEM TO KNOW
> WHAT THEY REALLY WANT ... I FINALLY INCREASED OUR
> PROPOSITION TO TWO HUNDRED FIFTY THOUSAND ADVANCE
> AGAINST HALF OF NET PROFITS ... NEXT PROPOSITION THEY
> WANT FROM US IS A STRAIGHT DISTRIBUTION CONTRACT WE
> TO ADVANCE COST OF NEGATIVES SHE TO MAKE HER OWN
> PICTURES SAME AS HAROLD LLOYD ... SHE FEELS SHE IS AS
> BIG AS ANY STAR IN BUSINESS ... SHE CANNOT UNDERSTAND
> WHY SHE CANNOT HAVE CONTRACT AS GOOD AS LLOYD STOP
> THEY KEEP MENTIONING LLOYD CONTRACT EVERY HALF
> HOUR AND THAT IS WHAT SEEMS TO BE WORRYING THEM ...
> I AM NOT IN FAVOR OF GIVING GLORIA A STRAIGHT DISTRIBU-
> TION CONTRACT IF YOU THINK DIFFERENTLY PLEASE WIRE
> ME WHAT YOU CONSIDER VERY BEST DISTRIBUTION
> CONTRACT I MIGHT OFFER THEM AND ALSO WHETHER YOU
> THINK I MIGHT AS LAST RESORT INCREASE OUR ADVANCE
> AGAINST FIFTY PERCENT OF PROFITS TO THREE
> HUNDRED THOUSAND PER PICTURE[2]

Though she professed uncertainty about producing her own films, Gloria relished the idea of being her own boss. She wrote that she signed with United Artists on July 15, 1925, agreeing to produce six motion pictures, at a salary of $200,000 each. She did not publicly announce the agreement, nor did she advise Lasky.

Three days later Gloria and Henri and Peggy Urson (the children were not mentioned in the press) boarded the *California Limited* bound for New York, arriving there late in the afternoon on June 26. That Thursday Gloria was at the Astoria Studio to discuss and approve costumes for her latest film, *Stage Struck*.[3] Based on a story by Frank R. Adams, with a screenplay again by Forrest Halsey, the film told of Jennie Hagen (Gloria), a diner waitress in love with the cook, Orme Wilson (Lawrence Gray). When the *Water Queen* showboat comes to town, Orme falls in love with its leading lady, Lillian Lyons (Gertrude Astor). Jennie enrolls in a correspondence acting course, to compete with Lillian, and auditions for the show's manager, Waldo Buck (Ford Sterling), who hires her. During a staged boxing fight with Lillian, Jenny falls off the side of the boat only to get snagged by the seat of her pants on a hook. Orme rescues her. They kiss and make up, and later open a lunch wagon. It was pure slapstick, with a two-tone Technicolor sequence (where Jennie imagines herself a great actress) at the beginning of the film and another at the fade-out.

Opening scenes for *Stage Struck* were filmed on location in Martinsville, West Virginia. Director Dwan, Gloria and Henri, René Hubert, and the film's cast and crew (forty in all plus sixty-five extras) arrived there on August 17. Half the town's 4,500 residents turned out to welcome the company. Gloria and Henri were put up at the Noll mansion on the Ohio River. The rest of the company was placed in private homes and the Riverview Hotel. Hundreds of locals were used in crowd scenes in the film.

Filming commenced the following day, with the *Water Queen,* an actual showboat, as background. Two local girls and a young man persuaded Gloria and Henri to allow them to be their house staff during the shoot, but they spent most of their time, wrote Gloria, gawking in awe at the famous couple. Henri and René Hubert would converse in French, ridiculing their behavior for Gloria's amusement. (Only later did they find out one of the girls was a French major at a local college.) By the end of the month, Gloria was back at the Astoria Studio filming interiors.

The week of August 30 saw the opening of *The Coast of Folly* at New York's Rivoli Theater. Mordaunt Hall of *The New York Times* was not impressed. "While viewing Gloria Swanson in her new film, 'The Coast of Folly,' a somewhat unconvincing and unimaginative effort, one is impressed by the lofty aspirations of the popular actress, who from allusions in one sequence obviously wishes to do her best to demonstrate that talent and not clothes make the player . . . [The picture's] entertainment value is chiefly due to Miss Swanson's appearances, and even she would do better to keep to those roles to which she was so well suited."[4]

Hall would later comment, "One does not see the changed Miss Swanson really acting as a seared old woman, but as a well made-up actress posing before the camera, apparently asking: 'Now aren't you all astonished? What do you think of me as an old woman?' "[5] Still, Gloria Swanson was box office, and tickets grossed $32,298.41 for the first week at the Rivoli alone, and nearly that same amount in distribution. "It wasn't a blockbuster," Dwan recalled, "but it was a good commercial picture."[6]

Harry Carr, of the *Los Angeles Times,* in the past a staunch advocate of La Swanson, said succinctly, "The illustrious Marquise de la Falaise de la Coudraye is not feeling so good . . . If Gloria had plotted against herself for a year, she couldn't have made a worse 'pick' of a play than 'The Coast of Folly' . . . Her attempt to act like Bernhardt was ridiculous and tragically absurd . . . When an actress finally gets a chance to play 'her life's ambition,' it is always and inevitably rotten. The reason for this is that when they get 'the great chance,' they always try to direct the picture themselves."[7]

On September 25, a subpoena was served to Gloria on the street outside her Park Chambers apartment building requesting her to appear in court on behalf of actress Janet Beecher in her ongoing divorce and custody battle with her husband, Dr. Richard H. Hoffmann, noted attorney on the Leopold-Loeb trial of 1924. Dr. Hoffman had been a friend of Gloria's during her "Sunday-salon days in New York."[8] It was reported that when Gloria was given the subpoena, she shrugged her shoulders and sighed, "I should worry."[9] She wrote in her memoirs she never read the document and promptly ignored the court order.

Paramount was still desperate to keep her in their fold. On September 23, Jesse Lasky sent a memo to Astoria Studio head Walter Wanger regarding a plan for the formation of an independent company. Gloria would receive $250,000 per picture, with a six-picture guarantee over two years, and 50 percent of net profits in installment payments per her convenience.

The more than generous proposal stated all her films would be shot at the Astoria Studio, she would receive sole star billing above the title, and she would be allotted star treatment and accommodations in travel, plus her picture wardrobe gratis. She would be provided a maid, and all her maid's travel expenses, as well as be handed quarterly statements of all accounting rendered and certified by Price, Waterhouse & Co. But still Gloria refused to, or could not now, sign with Paramount.

With *Stage Struck* completed, on Saturday, September 26, Gloria and her marquis boarded their beloved *Paris,* bound for Plymouth and Le Havre, for a three-week vacation. During their stay in Paris two scandals broke in the States, which Gloria brushed off in her book as merely "happy ending scandals."[10] One of the scandals questioned Henri's lineage. On October 6 at their Paris hotel suite, Gloria, dressed in a gold and yellow dressing gown, and Henri spoke with the press regarding the allegations. Furious at the doubt, she advised the papers that Henri could trace his ancestry back to 1271. She would later dismiss this whole episode as just a nuisance.

The other "embarrassment," as Gloria called it, was her being held in contempt of court and now facing jail time for ignoring the subpoena. Gloria recounted in her memoirs that the press supported her and praised her for her "good sense and fortitude."[11] Her history was less than accurate and the press never so humble. Actually, the case became more involved.

On October 24, Gloria was found guilty of contempt. She was ordered to pay a fine of $250 or spend time in the Ludlow Street Jail. Issued by Supreme Court Justice Robert McCurdy, the order was in regard to the battle between Beecher (who had appeared on stage in *A Bill of Divorcement*) and her estranged husband over their four-year-old son, Robert Wyndam Hoffmann. "My purpose," said Beecher's attorney, "in calling said Gloria Swanson as a witness in the petitioner's behalf was to show that the defendant [Mr. Hoffmann] was an unfit person to have custody and care of Richard Wyndham Hoffmann. The particular matter with respect to which I intended to examine her was the defendant's visiting the said Gloria Swanson at her home, awakening the child to be exhibited to her [Gloria], and taking her to restaurants, theatres and other places."[12]

That November, Gloria's attorney Richard J. Mackey filed an application for dismissal of the charge. It was denied. Then, adding injury to insult, another suit was filed against Gloria for $25,000 in damages by process server S. Alexander Cohen, who claimed she had slapped him when he handed her the subpoena, stating, "I should worry."[13] Cohen said he would institute another action against her for $100,000 for swearing he had not served her. She denied the allegations on December 1. On December 4 she paid the contempt-of-court fee of $250.

The $25,000 assault charge brought by Cohen was eventually dismissed in August after Gloria refreshed and revised her memory. In sworn testimony filed in the county clerk's office before the trial, she testified that though she was used to being accosted on the street by unknown persons because she was a public figure, on the day in question, September 25, she and Henri and a couple of gentlemen friends were entering her car in front of the Park Chambers on their way to dinner at the Colony Club when she was suddenly handed the subpoena. She did not recall saying anything, and she denied assaulting the process server. But the case did not go away. *The New York Times* later announced the $25,000 suit was settled on March 9, 1928. Possibly there was some truth in it.[14]

When Lasky at last was notified Gloria had signed with United Artists, he promptly fired Allan Dwan and washed his hands of Gloria Swanson. "When her contract came up for renewal she was offered one million dollars a year, plus half the profits of any film she appeared in," wrote Jesse L. Lasky Jr., "but it was not enough. Gloria's mind was set on forming her own company. Dad held an all-night conference with New York on the long-distance telephone . . . The final conclusion was the star had become too big for the company."[15]

Gloria and Henri, accompanied by René Hubert, returned to New York on the *Paris* on November 4. She wrote decisively in her memoirs, "When Henri and I returned to New York in October, we were heroes once again" after all the nasty publicity in the States.[16] That was the impression she wished to leave history.

By the end of the month, Gloria was at work on Paramount's *Tamed,* eventually called *The Untamed Lady,* directed by Frank Tuttle, with a screenplay by James Ashmore Creelman, based on a story by novelist Fannie Hurst. The ridiculously named St. Clair Van Tassel (Gloria) is a hot-tempered socialite who now wishes to retire to the countryside. Her car stalls on the way to the country, and handsome Larry Gastlen (Lawrence Gray again) stops to help her. They fall in love. Gastlen sails for Cuba on his yacht, asking St. Clair not to accompany him. She stows away anyway, and he steers the ship back to New York. St. Clair attempts to throw the boat off course when they encounter a gale. The vessel is battered, and she is forced to shovel coal in the stokehold. When they land safely, St. Clair heads to her Catskills hunting lodge with Larry in pursuit. He falls from his horse, and only then does St. Clair tame her temper, realizing she loves him. A ridiculous yarn, but apparently not foolish enough to keep Gloria from purchasing "Flood Tide," yet another story by James Ashmore Creelman, for possible development on November 21, for $6,000.

Some reports suggest Gloria, realizing at the start of filming that young director Frank Tuttle was unseasoned, redirected her scenes herself. She certainly told herself she was going to learn as much as possible about filmmaking on this picture and the next.

Filming on horseback in Pinehurst, North Carolina, for *The Untamed Lady*, Gloria mounted her steed briefly, then suddenly refused to complete the scene. She gave as a reason years later that she had a premonition of impending peril. Possibly. Or it could have been a display of Swanson temperament. At any rate, it was not missed by Tuttle, who displayed no love for his star and stated emphatically that the "lunatic had taken over the asylum and let the blood be on her."[17]

Stage Struck opened at New York's Rivoli Theater on November 15, unfortunately to tepid reviews. Mordaunt Hall for *The New York Times* wrote, "Miss Swanson is active and amusing, but this is hardly a worthy subject for her capabilities . . . The captions in this film are most tedious and at times they are not even grammatical."[18] "Sime" in *Variety* was disappointed as well: "As a Famous Players feature release it's a fine piece of hoke . . . The story is flat, flatter than the batter so important to the comedy . . . As her final picture under the direction of Mr. Dwan for F.P. [Famous Players] Miss Swanson may recall it as one of her worst, despite that her personal work in it is worthy of much more credit than it ever will receive from those who ever passed the fifth grade."[19]

However, film historian Jeanine Basinger disagreed, praising Gloria's work in the film: "In *Stage Struck,* Swanson is wonderful . . . Everything Swanson does is very precise, very small, very on the mark—she's a controlled pantomimist and a good mimic. She's a natural clown, a kind of Charlie Chaplin due to her small stature."[20] *Photoplay* magazine concurred, calling *Stage Struck* "a rip-snortin' comedy with Gloria Swanson juggling cups in a cheap restaurant and taking correspondence courses in acting."[21] Along with *Manhandled, Stage Struck* remains one of Swanson's best silent films.

As filming continued on *The Untamed Lady,* shortly before Thanksgiving Gloria was sent a two-page letter finalizing her obligations with Famous Players–Lasky, signed by Adolph Zukor on November 24, 1925. Zukor quickly cut to the chase with point one of the seven listed in the letter, advising Gloria she owed the company $35,000, which she had been paid for an additional unmade picture. This amount would be deducted incrementally from her hefty weekly paycheck, until the debt was paid off.

Gloria also owed the company $26,257.94, which had been loaned to her and included interest accrued. Other points in the letter dealt with release from all previous agreements plus Paramount's guarantee not to use her name in any future advertising. Zukor had built Paramount into the most important film studio in Hollywood by 1925, with an annual profit of $5 million plus, double that of Fox, triple that of Universal, and quintuple that of Warner Bros. And Paramount ran over six hundred theaters nationwide that exhibited its films by "block booking"—exhibitors receiving one star picture for every five or six programmers (B pictures), ensuring those theaters ran only Paramount product. Gloria's desertion caused but a brief disruption of Paramount's schedule and profits. In 1926 the studio would boast in its stable of stars such box-office giants as W. C. Fields, Wallace Beery, Clara Bow, and Louise Brooks.

The press at the time remarked, "Gloria Swanson has a quick mind and sweet manners, but she is not highly educated."[22] Perhaps so, but her instincts were still good. Gloria was now set to organize and produce her own films. That December she purchased another Creelman story, "Coral Blaze," as a possible property for her production company.[23] She filmed neither one of the Creelman's stories she bought.

In March Henri opened a bookstore to occupy his time, as Gloria began work on her twenty-seventh and final Paramount picture, *Fine Manners*, directed by Richard Rosson, brother of cinematographer Hal Rosson. With yet another story by James Ashmore Creelman and Frank Vreeland, *Fine Manners* cast Gloria in the role of Orchid Murphy, a New York chorus girl who lives in a cheap tenement with her brother Buddy (Roland Drew) and works in a crude burlesque theater. Buddy protectively guards her from wealthy older men who might corrupt her. Orchid meets Brian Alden (Eugene O'Brien) in Times Square on New Year's Eve. Buddy thinks Brian is an "uptown swell" and discourages Orchid's plans to become a lady. Brian's aunt Agatha (Helen Dunbar) molds Orchid into a refined young lady. Brian thereupon finds he misses the vivacious hoyden he had fallen in love with. ("Brian had sought his Orchid—and had found a pale white flower," bemoans the title card.) Orchid lets him know she has not changed her feelings for him.

The picture was originally begun with Tuttle at the helm, but Gloria did not like him. When he became ill and sailed to Nassau to recuperate, she had him replaced. She requested director Lewis Milestone, on loan from Warner Bros., but he told her he was not a free agent, and Richard Rosson was given the assignment at the beginning of May. Zukor had made it known that every department at the studio was to extend its highest courtesy to Gloria during the filming of her last picture for Paramount, and an amiable relationship existed throughout the production.

The film was produced on a "generous but by no means lavish scale in so far as sets go."[24] As production wound down on June 26, *Fine Manners* had cost Paramount $400,000, not including expenses for prints, etc., with another $50,000 expected before the final scene was in the can. Gloria suffered two bouts of influenza and was not at all well throughout the filming, often missing a day of work, or showing up in late afternoons to do her scenes. When talking to journalists, it was obvious she was fatigued, and she planned a long vacation before starting on her first United Artists picture.

In January of 1926, Edwin Schallert complained about Gloria's recent pictures, stating, "She needs a story of sweeping dramatic interest probably, at best."[25] Unfortunately her next film was not it. *The Untamed Lady* was sprung upon the public on March 15, premiering at the Rivoli Theater in New York.

Variety critic "Skig" was ruthless, "It's pretty awful—one of Miss Swanson's worst. She does nothing in the film other than to share a few closeups with Lawrence Gray, the hero, besides grabbing a few for her herself of course."[26] In advance of the film's West Coast premiere, Whitney Williams in the *Los Angeles Times* warned, "Gloria Swanson seems intent upon a grand 'flop.' Reports from the east declare her latest, 'The Untamed Lady,' one of the poorest pictures she has made in many moons. If it is anything like 'Stage-struck,' the least said the better. That production has rarely been equaled—in the vernacular, it was simply 'rotten' . . . At the rate she is going, 'Our Gloria' will soon be going to the bottom of the class, instead of leading it."[27]

James R. Quirk, editor of *Photoplay,* despite his adoration of Gloria could not censor his disapproval, calling *The Untamed Lady* "an awful disappointment," and "a total washout from beginning to end."[28] At home at the Park Chambers recovering from a bout of the "grippe," Gloria did not attend the New York premiere. In explaining away the poor reception of *The Untamed Lady,* she complained years later that Paramount was just trying to make money on her name alone. Perhaps so, but she had approved the script and made the picture.

As DeMille prepared to mount his epic *The King of Kings,* a telling of the story of Christ, he approached Gloria to appear in the role of Mary Magdelene. Gloria, recovering from her illness (frequently referred to in the press as a nervous breakdown), replied she could not start a new picture in mid-August. However, two weeks later, she changed her mind and wired DeMille she would like to talk about the schedule, the money, and the scope of her role. But as much as she needed a director like DeMille, she chose not to do the picture, possibly because she would not be its star (it was not called *The Queen of Queens,* after all) and the money was not substantial enough. (After being significantly altered and diminished, the part was given to Jacqueline Logan, who was paid $500 a week.)

On Thursday, May 6, 1926, *The New York Times* announced that the day before in Los Angeles Gloria Swanson had become a member of United Artists. The certificate of incorporation for the Gloria Swanson Corporation, Inc., was issued on June 8. The *Times* also announced that Gloria's first UA film would most likely be *Personality,* to be filmed in New York. (She had just turned down a chance to play with Adolphe Menjou in *The Last of Mrs. Cheyney,* which UA's Joseph Schenck had been badgering her to do.) In July, the press was stating Gloria's next film might be Lenore J. Coffee's *The Woman's Battalion of Death,* a true story of a modern Russian Joan of Arc.

When *Fine Manners* wrapped production, Gloria had three months to organize and begin her next picture. Immediately she clashed with Schenck. In her memoirs she vacillated between referring to Schenck as her benevolent former landlord to calling him "a squat, homely man who looked like a secondhand-furniture salesman."[29] Either Gloria did not read the fine print in her contract or she assumed she could just do as she pleased. What she discovered was that working within the UA organization was not going to be as easy as it had been at Paramount. At UA, everyone was the star. Gloria quickly learned she had to stand her own ground during long, tedious business meetings in New York with Joseph Schenck and his legal councils.[30]

Gloria had to undergo a physical examination to guarantee her health for a million-dollar life insurance bond from the Bank of America, which was financing United Artists through Art Finance Corporation (which would absorb Art Cinema by the end of the year). In creating a board of directors for the newly formed Gloria Swanson Productions, she bypassed Henri, as he was not a U.S. citizen, and elected to sign her mother instead.

She realized Henri could be of no support to her with film executives.[31] She relegated him to the foreign translations and distribution of her films. Henri also was serving on an aid committee headed by New York jeweler Pierre Cardin that organized and handled all American financial contributions to the stabilization of the French franc. Gloria set him up in his own suite of offices at 51 East Forty-second Street, complete with secretary. To keep himself active, he also wrote short stories and acted as a literary agent for French authors.

After putting her $175,000 Crescent Drive mansion and its contents up for auction on May 31, for whatever reasons, Gloria soon changed her mind and chose not to sell. She had originally placed the estate and its furnishings on the block in August 1925, asking $200,000. Confronted with the necessity of financing her first independent motion picture, and facing the reality of her own dwindling bank account, she had to take notice of what was happening within the motion picture industry as well.

Radio, a free form of entertainment, was making inroads into the consumer market. By 1925 Americans were spending millions of dollars on radio sets and accessories. The film industry, to combat the loss of movie theater ticket sales, decided it had to make better pictures. To draw audiences away from their homes, they needed to build bigger and better movie palaces. The industry and Gloria's professional life were in flux.

In July Gloria bought the rights to the 1917 play *The Eyes of Youth*, which had starred Marjorie Rambeau. The 1919 Albert Parker film version had starred Clara Kimball Young and Rudolph Valentino. (Gloria's deal required the Young film version negative be destroyed; fortunately copies of the film exist.) As director, Gloria wanted Allan Dwan but settled for Parker, whom she knew from her Triangle days. Parker required and was granted a two-picture deal at $100,000. Mary Pickford, said Gloria, had told her the formula for success as an independent producer was to find "the best people, pay them well, and keep them under contract."[32]

With Maurice Cleary now on the payroll for her Gloria Swanson Productions,

Gloria next contracted as her treasurer and business manager thirty-year-old Massachusetts-born Pierre Bedard, a prominent figure in French American cultural activities who had been a business manager for Paramount. She also appointed Thomas Alan Moore of Guaranty Trust as her New York business manager and her corporation's president, paying him $50,000 a year. Her important key corporate people in place, she next contracted René Hubert to design her fashions. His personal designs for her eliminated overdressing and stressed her personality.

In casting the picture, Gloria chose Spanish operatic basso Andrés de Segurola of the Metropolitan Opera for a leading role. After she spent many nights attending numerous plays on Broadway in search of just the right leading man, she selected thirty-year-old John Boles, who was appearing in the ill-fated musical *Kitty's Kisses*. She found Boles handsome and appealing "and more exciting [than] Milton Sills,"[33] and signed him to an exclusive contract on August 31 at $250 per week, five days after signing Richard Schable, an actor and director, to manage her production unit. Gloria took credit for "discovering" actor John Boles, and until the day he died in 1969, it seemed that every article, interview, or review that mentioned him would write that he was "discovered by Gloria Swanson." She then conveniently sent Henri back to Europe, explaining in her book that he needed to renew his visitor's visa.[34]

Gloria tearfully bid adieu to Henri at the French Line pier on Saturday, July 24, as "their" liner, the *Paris*, moved out of its slip. Among the other 1,143 other passengers on board was Rudolph Valentino's brother Alberto. Rudy was in town to promote his second United Artists film, *The Son of the Sheik*, and Gloria had a brief opportunity to visit with him at the dock. He was now romantically involved with Pola Negri, Natacha Rambova having ravaged his heart, and naturally Gloria wanted to hear all about it. Their conversation was brief, and they parted friends that afternoon.

13

Independence

On August 15 Rudolph Valentino collapsed at the Hotel Ambassador in New York, after a night of carousing with bandleader Harry Richman, Follies dancer Marion Benda, and journalist and war pilot Barclay Warburton Jr. Rudy was rushed to the hospital, diagnosed with appendicitis and gastric ulcers, and immediately operated upon. Gloria, like millions of other anxious citizens, read the reports coming from the hospital in the papers regarding his condition.

Late on August 17 Henri arrived back in New York on board the *Olympic*. Gloria and he were turned away at Valentino's hospital door, but Henri left behind a novel for Rudy to read. That afternoon Valentino complained of pain in the left side of his torso and his abdomen. Infection had set in, attacking the lining of his heart as peritonitis spread throughout his body. In the absence of antibiotics, the "Love God" was doomed.

Gloria and Henri phoned the hospital for news but were told nothing. As Valentino's condition deteriorated, his boss Joseph Schenck was allowed to enter his room as Norma Talmadge stood outside in the corridor weeping. Schenck quickly cabled Rudy's brother Alberto in Paris to advise him to catch the first boat to New York. Valentino's first wife, Jean Acker, arrived at the hospital with a box containing a ruffled white linen bedspread she had embroidered for him. After being administered the Last Rites, Rudy slipped into a coma. He died in the early morning hours of August 23. He was just thirty-one years-old.

Valentino's body was taken to Campbell's Funeral Home on Eighty-Second Street, where an estimated crowd of one hundred thousand mourners lined the streets to catch a view of their idol. His passing caused near-riots in the streets, and several windows of businesses near the funeral home were broken. Police were called in, and it was reported a couple of distraught female fans had committed suicide. Pola Negri, in the midst of filming *Hotel Imperial* for Paramount in Hollywood, claimed to be his fiancée and promptly left Los Angeles by train, arriving in New York on August 29. When taken to the Gold Room of Campbell's to view Rudy's body, Pola, draped in $3,000 worth of widow's weeds, wept, said a silent prayer, and promptly fainted. Now the funeral service could begin, but not before Pola obligingly repeated her dramatic faint for cameras.

Valentino's funeral was held on August 30 at St. Malachy's Roman Catholic Church on Forty-Ninth Street, between Broadway and Eighth Avenue. Honorary pallbearers included Douglas Fairbanks and Joseph Schenck. Five hundred mourners, by special invitation, filled the church as the solemn High Mass began. Attending were Ben Lyon and Richard Dix, serving as ushers, Marilyn Miller, Lois Wilson, Louise Brooks, and Henri and Gloria, "swathed in gray fur."[1] Conspicuously absent were the three revelers who were with Rudy the night of his attack, and Alberto Valentino, whose ship, the *Homeric,* did not arrive into New York until days later.[2]

After the funeral the body was sent to Hollywood by train for a second service at the Catholic Church of the Good Shepherd in Beverly Hills. Valentino's body is interred next to his discoverer, June Mathis, at the Hollywood Memorial Park Cemetery (now called the Hollywood Forever Cemetery). Gloria gave a statement to the press about her friend and former co-star, hailing Rudy as a leader in his profession and saying, "May the thoughts and prayers of the millions who loved Rudy help him on his journey to the unknown."[3] The permanence of film idols was proving to be fleeting, and in some ways Valentino's death marked the end of the silent film era.

Though not the juggernaut needed to end her slump, Gloria's last Paramount picture, *Fine Manners,* which opened in New York on August 29, did a lot to erase the memory of the two stinkers that preceded it. Mordaunt Hall of *The New York Times* compared its plot to George Bernard Shaw's *Pygmalion* before discussing Gloria's work: "Miss Swanson is attractive, but her boyish bob suits her better than the coiffure she has in this film."[4] Throughout the decade, film critics were caustic in their remarks about Gloria relying so heavily on hairstyles and wardrobe. Yet nearly every review commented on her appearance as more important than her performance.

Gloria critiqued *Fine Manners* many years later at a screening in New York. About her leading man Eugene O'Brien, she was none too keen, recalling he "had no sex appeal." "He was the most unlikely leading man . . . ," she said. "He's such a bad actor, bless his heart. Everyone thought he was handsome." Regarding her own work in the film, she admitted to the use of a double in a scene when Orchid gets excited and does cartwheels and jumps up and down on the bed. In a shot of Orchid crouching down and imitating Brian's walk, she chuckled, "You can be sure this was my nonsense. I used to amuse the director." About her appearance in the film, she swooned, "I'm such a baby here, pudgy and round-faced . . . I didn't have a fanny even in those days." And about a jarring, final close-up, she sneered, "Now, the cameraman wanted to raise his salary, so he did this."[5]

When the picture opened in Los Angeles on August 22, columnist Whitney Williams commented, "Gloria's cycle of atrocious pictures may be at an end. 'Fine Manners' may mark the beginning of a new era for her. If so, there should be many heavy sighs of relief."[6]

The film turned a tidy profit for Paramount, earning nearly $120,000 in foreign rentals alone. And *Fine Manners* is a delightful film. Though it lacked the production values of her past vehicles, it is one of Gloria's better post-DeMille pictures. Jesse Lasky liked the picture very much and sent Gloria a letter of congratulations, to which she responded in kind.

Though *Fine Manners* was relatively successful, it was hoped *The Eyes of Youth* would restore Gloria's marquee value. The project's title was changed to *The Love of Sunya*, meaning the love of "illusion" in Sanskrit, so publicity said. It was chosen by theater mogul S. L. Rothafel, known affectionately as "Roxy."

The plot is complicated: In the Mystic East, a young yogi (Hugh Miller, a Michael Rennie look-a-like) learns of a sin he committed in a past life in Egypt and sets out to atone for it. In the small fictitious town of Vanfield, Connecticut, he finds Sunya Ashling (Gloria) and Paul Judson (John Boles), the reincarnations of the two people he had wronged in a past life. Sunya has promised to marry Paul and live in South America with him. But she is also courted by millionaire Robert Goring (Anders Randolf) and opera impresario Paolo deSalvo

(Andrés de Segurola). When Sunya learns her father is in financial straits, she consults the yogi's crystal ball, and he advises her disaster and unhappiness will follow her regardless of whether she marries the millionaire or becomes an opera singer to save her father. After looking into the future, Sunya chooses to follow her heart and marry Paul.

Rothafel was the Sid Grauman of the East Coast. His movie palaces rivaled anything in Hollywood. He was then constructing the magnificent Roxy Theater at Seventh Avenue and Fiftieth Street. He asked Gloria for *The Love of Sunya* as his opening picture, promising her its premiere would be the biggest in film history. For the privilege Rothafel would give Gloria and United Artists $50,000, the largest single-week rental fee ever paid. A week later Gloria signed her name to the gold-leaf dome of the building, then under construction.

Filming began on *The Love of Sunya* on September 20 at the International Studios, formerly Hearst's Cosmopolitan Studio, located at 126th Street and Second Avenue in New York. (Henri was hoping to direct *The Paris Divorce* for Pathé around that same time, but it did not happen.) Though she was supposedly earning $20,000 a week according to her UA contract, Gloria's actual total salary for *The Love of Sunya* came to a mere $50,054.16. Other cast members were, as Sunya's siblings, young Raymond Hackett as Kenneth Ashling and Douglas Fairbanks's niece Florabell (billed as Flobelle) Fairbanks as "Rita Ashling." Gloria also cast Helen Eagles (family spelling), sister of stage actress Jeanne Eagels, in a small part.

She also discovered that producing a film gave her more worry than wonder. Because Boles and Fairbanks were novices, Gloria took additional time to help them with the scenes. The film was really four stories running parallel with each other, told through the use of the crystal ball as a plot device. Special effects and trick photography were important to the story. Camera operator Dudley Murphy, who in 1924 had created the landmark thirty-minute film *Ballet mécanique* with French artist Fernand Léger, was selected to work this out. But a feature-length melodrama was not as simple as an experimental film short.

Technically Murphy could not accomplish what he had intended, and he was not the same type of technician as Allan Dwan.[7] After Gloria consulted Russian refugee and industrial fan designer George de Bothezat on the development of mechanical props, the special effects started to fall into place.[8] The picture, however, was soon bogged down and over budget. The pressure built. Gloria had a lot to prove and immersed herself in every aspect of the production. *The Love of Sunya* eventually wrapped production in mid-December, at a cost of $545,048.36. With negative costs and prints, plus interest, its expenses eventually totaled $707,960.

With nothing much to do, as the year closed out Henri announced his entry into motion pictures after taking numerous screen tests and finding them satisfactory. He was hoping to star with Gloria in "high class comedies." Said Henri, "Just to show the public that I am independent of my wife's salary, I shall enter a producing company other than hers."[9] "I now plan to make one picture only," he also told *The New York Times.* "If it is very good, then I may appear in others."[10] For the time being the public bought it. Henri would not perform in front of the cameras until 1936, but in 1931 he did become a director.

On January 27 Gloria held an afternoon tea for the press at her $50,000 penthouse—which came complete with four doors costing $1,000 each, commissioned from a Spanish artist—atop the Park Chambers Hotel. Hers was also one of the only residences in New York that granted its star occupant a private and perfumed elevator (at Gloria's insistence).

From the moment she signed with United Artists, Joseph Schenck had encouraged Gloria to return to Hollywood and produce her films there. UA had just completed construction of a huge studio with a new office-bungalow just for her. Though she saw herself as a rebel in her East Cost stand against Hollywood, practicality won out. She realized that to compete in the industry she would need to work in California, and subsequently she had her Hollywood mansion prepared for occupancy.

The press announced Gloria's next picture would be written by actress Ouida Bergere (who married actor Basil Rathbone in April 1926) and directed by Albert Parker. Gloria purchased Bergere's original story *Desert Love* for $6,000 with $1,000 down on March 1, and John Boles was set to co-star. The title was changed to *The Goddess of the Sahara,* but it soon became lost in the sands of time.

On Friday, March 11, *The Love of Sunya* opened at the Roxy Theater in New York. The Roxy was billed as the largest motion picture theater in the world, and indeed it had no comparison at that time. Its architect was Walter W. Ahlschlager of Chicago, and it cost $10 million to build, seating 6,214.

With unique projection booths, four box offices, and a magnificent wrought-iron Roman–African–Spanish Renaissance (with a hint of Oriental) rotunda lit by a fifteen-foot crystal chandelier, the Roxy also boasted a tremendous Swedish-built pipe organ, with twenty-one chimes located 110 feet up inside the building that could be heard from the street. Rothafel also purchased the largest theater music library in the country, containing over ten thousand numbers and fifty thousand orchestrations housed in seventy-five asbestos-lined cabinets installed in the theater library.

The Roxy's opening was spectacular. Double rows of klieg lights mounted on motor trucks were focused on the theater, and its marquee was ablaze with lights. For the event René Hubert designed a gorgeous black evening gown for Gloria, who accentuated herself with art deco jewels. Her hair was slicked back in a bun at the nape of her neck in the same style she wore it in the picture. Crowds went wild at the sight of Mayor Jimmy Walker and his wife Janet, Charles Chaplin, Harold Lloyd and his wife Mildred Davis, Joseph Schenck and Norma Talmadge, Jesse L. Lasky, Walter Wanger, Sport Ward, Lois Wilson, Thomas Meighan, Will Hays, Irving Berlin, and the Shubert brothers, Lee, Sam, and Jacob. Gloria and Henri stood in a receiving line for twenty minutes before the screening. After a brief organ concert, there followed a solemn welcoming speech. Then the 110-piece Roxy Theater Orchestra played a tone poem as background for a pageant enactment of the creation of the Stars and Stripes. After another speech, the organ struck up, the lights dimmed, and *The Love of Sunya* began to unreel, starting not with opening titles but with a thin mist exuding from the sides of the stage, as the picture began in ancient times.

Despite all the remarkable hoopla, reviews of *The Love of Sunya* were mixed. *Variety* praised Gloria's performance but was bored with the picture. "This picture proves to be an extremely draggy affair, even though the star personally achieves a triumph in her characterization," said "Fred." "The part gives her every opportunity to make good, and she does so with a vengeance. But the picture is not what could be honestly termed a box office knockout."[11]

However, Harriette Underhill of the *New York Herald Tribune* was enraptured with the results, stating, "We never had any idea that she was so beautiful . . . So dazzling is Miss Swanson that words fail."[12] The following day, beginning with the 11:30 A.M. showing, tickets sold at up to a staggering $11.00

each. In New York, *The Love of Sunya* took in $125,927.40 its first week after having been seen by 157,602 filmgoers.

Gloria and Henri then left for the West Coast on March 17, in order to arrive in time for the Los Angeles opening of *The Love of Sunya*. Her United Artists contract was up for renewal as of June 1.

Little mention was made of Gloria's children during this frenetic period. She was intent that they never be commercially photographed. Indeed, she told the press after the birth of little Gloria that she hoped the public would forget she even had a child. "[Little] Gloria signed no contract with Mr. Lasky," she once told Adele Whitely Fletcher in a magazine piece. "I'm trying hard to remember, too, that she is an individual, and must not be hampered by anything I may or may not do. I must prepare her for the issues which will undoubtedly come to her, as well as I am able; be near if she wants me; talk things over with her without giving dogmatic advice, and brave enough to let her ultimately make her own decisions, whatever they may be."[13] Still, Gloria was much too busy to be around her children.

Gloria intended to stay in Hollywood at least a year. So the exodus began. She headed to California with her company people: Thomas Alan Moore and his wife, director Albert Parker, Mr. and Mrs. Irving Wyckoff, and Pierre Bedard. Both five-year-old Gloria and four-year-old Joseph traveled with the servants, accompanied by Katherine Nolen, Gloria's social secretary, and nanny Edith Simonson. Coming west later were Andrés de Segurola and John Boles (who landed in Hollywood on March 28, to be greeted at the train station by Gloria and Albert Parker), both under contract and scheduled to perform in Gloria's next production.

Arriving in Los Angeles the afternoon of March 21, Gloria and Henri were welcomed by a reception of some eight hundred enthusiastic onlookers, including Mary Pickford and Doug Fairbanks, John Barrymore, and Sid Grauman. Gloria was pleased to hear little Gloria's father Herbert was doing well, having established himself as a restaurateur, opening his first restaurant, the Brown Derby at the corner of Wilshire and Alexandria in Los Angeles, the year before. It was constructed in the shape of a brown derby hat and had become the "in" place to dine and see and be seen. Now that he was making money and able to support the upbringing of his child, Gloria was more than willing to allow him to see her, and father and daughter developed a close relationship.

Re-establishing her residency in California, Gloria set about refurnishing her home. She possessed an intelligent and quick mind, which made her a sponge for knowledge. She was enjoying her success, and one of her most valued possessions was her library. She collected first editions, including a copy of *The Prophet,* gifted to her in 1927 by its author Kahlil Gibran. (*The Prophet* would become a valuable tool in Gloria's later romances.) Along with keeping up the home disbursements, Henri had now become involved with the French automobile company Peugeot. He had ordered two crests for his Pony Peugeot, plus two new cars for himself and his wife. Henri as Peugeot's distributor was then commissioned to introduce the car to the American public.[14] Now settled, the couple awaited the release of Gloria's first independent production on the West Coast.

The Love of Sunya had its long-delayed opening in California on May 25 at a gala premiere at the Criterion Theater. By then word of mouth had dampened the enthusiasm of filmgoers. Gloria appeared on the stage with Boles and de Segurola to greet the audience. Not the huge moneymaker she assumed it would be, *The Love of Sunya* nevertheless eventually earned a respectable $630,370 in profits.

Viewing *The Love of Sunya* today is a real treat. It shows Gloria at her most glamorous. She is stunning to behold, quite interesting to study, and dressed in one lovely outfit after another. One particular gown of regal black velvet, bare in the back, with white fox and cloth of silver, was magnificent. The dress straps, necklace, earrings, and cuff bracelet were adorned with cabochon emeralds and diamonds, which were also shaped with the sharp points complementing the hem of the gown. Though the plot of the picture is contrived, Gloria's acting is remarkable. Whether dressed in stunning Hubert gowns, glimmering with art deco jewels, or garbed in rags in the rain, her performance rings true. And the special effects are stunning for the era.

On the Hollywood social scene, that May of 1927 would see the inauguration of ten stars' foot- and handprints, and their salutations to the owner himself, installed in the cement of the forecourt of Sid Grauman's new Chinese Theater. The first honoree was Mary Pickford, the other nine Norma Talmadge, Douglas

Fairbanks, Norma Shearer, Harold Lloyd, Constance Talmadge, William S. Hart, Colleen Moore, Tom Mix, and Gloria.

Cutting her expenses on the East Coast, on May 23 Gloria advised her real estate agent to place the Croton-on-Hudson estate on the market the next day, her asking price $75,000. The forty-acre estate was sold to Mr. and Mrs. George Biddle in June.

After losing out in a bidding battle for the film rights to the hit Broadway play *Dance Magic*, Gloria acquired Pierre Louys's 1898 novel *La Femme et le Pantin (The Woman and the Puppet)*. It was filmed once before in 1920 by Samuel Goldwyn, starring Geraldine Farrar, and was her least successful picture. Gloria considered it for her next vehicle, with a film adaptation by Hans Kraly. However, the press questioned the viability of the project considering the tepid results of *The Love of Sunya*, which also was a remake. (Gloria eventually passed on filming it; it was remade in 1935 by Josef von Sterberg as *The Devil Is a Woman*, starring Marlene Dietrich. It flopped.)

Perhaps all this press was camouflage for the real negotiations Gloria was handling at the time. Her goal was to make two films a year for UA. With her career in balance, Gloria suddenly made a deal that turned Hollywood and its film moguls on their ears.

Henri and Gloria had attended the premiere of *What Price Glory?* (Fox, 1926), considered one of the greatest of all pictures dealing with the First World War. It starred Edmund Lowe and Victor McLaglen. What Henri found most exciting about it was the straightforward, brilliant direction of Raoul Walsh. Gloria agreed with Henri and invited Walsh to breakfast.

After the meal the discussion eventually turned to what films like *What Price Glory?* Walsh might be interested in directing. He replied shyly, "Well, there's always *Rain*."[15] *Rain: A Play in Three Acts*, by John Colton and Clemence Randolph, was based on a short story entitled "Miss Thompson," by W. Somerset Maugham, that was published in *Smart Set* magazine in 1921. *Rain* was considered quite controversial when it was first staged because of its subject matter—a prostitute bringing about the moral downfall of a sadistic puritanical minister. With a brilliant performance by Jeanne Eagels, *Rain* was a sensation on the sophisticated New York stage. But the two elements that were censorable in film, the lechery of the minister and the fact that prostitute Sadie Thompson walked and talked like a sailor, made the project taboo. Most people believed it could not be made into a motion picture. Gloria and Walsh thought it could.

As adapted for Gloria, the story of *Sadie Thompson* told of a prostitute fleeing trouble in San Francisco and attempting to conceal her identity while traveling in the South Seas. In Pago Pago, she is stranded for ten days, her ship quarantined. There Sadie falls for Marine Sergeant Timothy "Handsome" O'Hara (Raoul Walsh) and promises to marry him. Alfred Davidson (Lionel Barrymore) is a maniacal reformer (no longer a minister) who recognizes Sadie for what she is. Obsessed with saving her soul, he chastises her incessantly, making her life miserable. He attempts to send her back to San Francisco, where she faces prison time for a crime she insists she did not commit. After Davidson "reforms" Sadie, he lustfully seduces her and then commits suicide. She and O'Hara are reunited, and they leave Pago Pago for a new life in Australia.

Not only did every actress worth her salt covet the role of Sadie, every studio in Hollywood was itching to buy the project but couldn't figure out how to work around the storyline. There loomed the specter of the Hays Office and "the Formula," a list of 150 books and plays that could not be adapted to film, which included *Rain*. Gloria set about working through the system securing the role for herself.

First she had to deal with "the Pinochle Club,"[16] a group of producers who had drawn up "the Formula," and then she had to present her case to Will Hays. Interestingly enough, nearly all the producers in the Pinochle Club had at one time or another expressed a desire to be the first to produce a film version of *Rain*. By placing *Rain* on its list of unfilmable stage projects, the Pinochle Club had more or less shot itself in the foot.

While the Hays Office's purpose was to ban selected books and plays from being made into films, its banned list did not include short stories such as "Miss Thompson." With this in mind, Gloria invited Hays and some other guests to an informal luncheon at her home. Sequestering him alone for a moment in the dining room as the others filtered out onto the terrace, Gloria told Hays she did not wish to offend the code, but she had a marvelous story about a sadistic missionary who punishes a social outcast, "Miss Thompson," by trying to rehabilitate her.

Gloria's dilemma was that if she kept the man a missionary in the screenplay she would run against the code and its strictures against the negative portrayal of clergy. If she didn't, she might not be able to secure the property from the story's famous British author. She asked if she might use Hays's name in an attempt to persuade Maugham to sell her the story and allow her to change the missionary to a reformer. Hays agreed she could.

Gloria then brought in Joseph Schenck, who understood the short-story gambit and agreed to offer $100,000, the same as the asking price for rights to the play. He also made sure no other studio would know of the deal until all was on paper, instructing a Los Angeles play broker to negotiate in secret with theater impresario Sam Harris on behalf of Maugham and the playwrights, referring to it as the Maugham-Colton-Randolph play, and not as *Rain*. The broker left for New York on May 10, sending a telegram to Maugham's agents advising them that an independent director was prepared to negotiate the film rights, and that he would meet with them on May 16.[17]

On May 25, five days after receiving encouraging news from the broker, Gloria was sent the following coded telegram:

VERY HAPPY TO ADVISE YOU ARE NOW OWNER OF THE TWO
MOLEHILLS OF NEBRASKA[18]

Meanwhile, Schenck acquired Raoul Walsh on loan from Fox and conferred with Gloria for a week before the broker returned with a contract for the rights to the play and the short story, which were quickly examined by legal advisers and reported valid. She then placed in the press the announcement that rights to Maugham's short story "Miss Thompson" (not "Rain") had been bought. The papers were at the time full of Charles Lindbergh's solo flight across the Atlantic, and perhaps naively Gloria thought nothing would be made of the notification. She could not have been more incorrect.

On May 27, it was announced that Raoul Walsh would direct Gloria's next United Artists photoplay, though the reports erroneously stated it would probably be *The Woman and the Puppet*. The following day, *The New York Times* announced, "Although the play 'Rain' is not to be filmed, Gloria Swanson has decided to appear in a screen transcription of W. Somerset Maugham's story 'Sadie Thompson,' on which the play was based."[19] The article also mentioned

Raoul Walsh, set to direct the picture on a five- to six-week schedule for release in November. On June 1, possibly in response to a request for an explanation, Joseph Schenck sent the following letter to Hays's office:

Dear Will:

I do not think I need to assure you that if any producer had any intention of producing "Rain," the United Artists would not distribute it.

Miss Swanson is producing "Sadie Thompson," based on a story by Somerset Maugham. Furthermore, she has assured me that there will be no preacher in the cast of characters in the screen vehicle of "Sadie Thompson," thus eliminating all possible objections on the part of the clergy as far as Sadie Thompson is concerned.

If there is anything else you wish to know about this story, please do not hesitate to either call me or write me and I shall give you all the facts.

Sincerely yours,
[signed] Joe Schenck[20]

Perhaps that pacified Hays, but the Pinochle Club went ballistic. Gloria had made several enemies in the film industry, chief among them these film executives. There were those who would have liked to take revenge on her for acquiring Sadie Thompson out from under them. However, there was one mogul in particular who was impressed with her victory. His name was Joseph P. Kennedy.

14

Joseph P. Kennedy

On June 10, 1927, Joseph Schenck received an official telegram of protest from the Pinochle Club demanding a halt to the production of *Sadie Thompson* and/or any variation of the story. Taking the high ground, the fifteen members had all agreed to not produce the play or book (though they individually had tried). In conclusion they wrote that their policy remained not to produce indecent plays or books, and to do so at that time would violate their public promises.[1]

Two of the members were William Fox and Winnie Sheehan, the heads of Fox Film, and Gloria faced losing her director and co-star. Schenck tried to pacify them with a telegram to Adolph Zukor, at his office in the Flatiron Building, which read in part:

> MISS SWANSON IS A STOCKHOLDER OF UNITED ARTISTS AND
> I WILL HAVE TO DISTRIBUTE HER PICTURE SHE HAS AT LEAST
> TWO HUNDRED THOUSAND INVESTED IN STORY DIRECTOR
> SCENARIO AND PRODUCTION OF SADIE UP TO THE PRESENT
> AND HER FINANCIAL CONDITION IS MOST PRECARIOUS WHICH
> YOU CAN EASILY ASCERTAIN . . . I WISH YOU WOULD TAKE A
> BROADMINDED GENEROUS VIEWPOINT OF THIS UNFORTUNATE
> CIRCUMSTANCE AND WITHDRAW YOUR PROTEST . . . THE
> PICTURE ITSELF WILL BE PRODUCED IN A VERY INNOCUOUS
> MANNER AND WILL NOT DO THE LEAST BIT OF HARM AND

IF NECESSARY I WOULD GET MISS SWANSON TO CHANGE
THE TITLE OF SADIE THOMPSON AND CALL IT SOMETHING
ELSE BEST REGARDS[2]

That same day Schenck received a copy, more or less, of the Pinochle Club letter. But this one was sent to him by William H. Hays, who now insisted on an explanation.

Gloria was furious that they were manipulating around her. She told Schenck and Walsh upon reading Hays's demand that she felt they, the Pinochle Club, were simply refusing to acknowledge her as a producer.[3]

On June 13 at midnight Gloria sent a Western Union telegram to all the producers listed on the official protest:

MR SCHENCK CALLED MY ATTENTION TO YOUR PROTEST
AGAINST MY PRODUCING SADIE THOMPSON . . . SADIE
THOMPSON IS A MAGAZINE STORY BY SOMERSET MAUGHAM
AND . . . I HAVE SINCE INVESTED OVER TWO HUNDRED
THOUSAND DOLLARS IN THIS PICTURE AND A GREAT DEAL OF
TIME AND THOUGHT OF MY OWN AND I AM IN NO FINANCIAL
CONDITION AT PRESENT TIME TO SACRIFICE THIS AMOUNT OF
MONEY I WILL ASK YOU TO BE GENEROUS AND BROADMINDED
AND WITHDRAW YOUR OBJECTION TO MY PRODUCING SADIE
THOMPSON . . . AS FAR AS THE STORY ITSELF IS CONCERNED IT
IS A GREAT LESSON IN TOLERANCE PLEASE DO NOT THINK I AM
USING THE LATTER WORD IN CONCLUSION TO POINT OUT TO
YOU THE NECESSITY OF YOUR BEING TOLERANT[4]

The first response to her letter, on June 14, was from Joe Kennedy's office, advising her Kennedy was out of town for two weeks. The second response was from possibly the most influential man of the pack, Marcus Loew, who empathized with Gloria's situation and agreed that if Hays had given his consent he would back it. She gave a sigh of relief. She was planning to request from MGM, a Loews company, the use of Lionel Barrymore for the role of the "reformer," formerly "Reverend," Alfred Davidson. Gloria sent Loew a letter of thanks. In his reply he apologized on behalf of the association for any disruption they might have caused. Taking that to mean he had called off the wolves, Gloria forged ahead with the production.

However, that was not the end of it. Will Hays then sent Schenck a letter from the MPPDA New York office. In part it read:

At the quarterly meeting of the Board of Directors yesterday the ... conclusion of the members was that I should advise you that the unanimous opinion of the members of the Association is that the integrity of the formula must be preserved ... The members are advised fully of the facts, including the fact that I told Miss Swanson that the magazine story which she called "Sadie Thompson" had not been through the formula and that therefore she had a right to produce it ... They understand, too, that the facts probably are, as you indicate, that at the time she had not purchased "Sadie Thompson" but that thereafter her agent bought the rights of "Rain," and that the representation that they had already bought the magazine story was probably false and probably for the purpose of deception ...

We are much distressed about the whole matter. This inevitable position is taken because of the realization of the absolute necessity for the preservation of the integrity of the agreements—agreements developed with great care and labor—under which we are making progress and on the preservation of which, as a matter of fact, the vital welfare of the industry depends.[5]

In short, Gloria was accused of deception by Hays. However, now Hays, Schenck, and the Pinochle Club realized that she could play hardball with the best of them.

When told Gloria Swanson was going to enact her signature stage role in a moving picture, the temperamental and emotionally fragile Jeanne Eagels became distraught. Wrote newspaper columnist Alma Whitaker shortly after Eagels's untimely death due to drugs and alcohol in 1929, "I think it broke Jeanne Eagels' heart. She resented with all her soul that there would be another Sadie Thompson ... 'She is mine, mine, mine,' she screamed at me when we discussed Gloria's venture. 'No one can do Sadie but me.'" Eagels was near hysteria. "I have lived and breathed Sadie for years," she told Whitaker. "I know her very soul. She's mine, only mine."[6] In fact, Gloria had watched Eagels perform Sadie in *Rain* twice on the Broadway stage.

After purchasing his story, Gloria contacted Maugham to ask if he would write a brief sequel to it, titled "The Life of Sadie Thompson," describing what happened to Sadie after she left Pago Pago. That would ensure, should the picture become a hit, that other studios could not immediately concoct a sequel. Maugham replied he had already been offered $25,000 to develop a sequel to *Rain* for Winfield R. Sheehan and William Fox (Walsh's bosses, hypocrites all) at Fox Film Co., and added that when he advised them he had sold the rights of *Rain* to Swanson, they backed out. "Hoist on their own petard," Walsh commented to Gloria when she showed him the letter.[7] She then sent a copy of Maugham's reply to Hays to show him just how deceitful his pious and "trusted" colleagues were in their desire to protect the industry and the moral fiber of the American public. She would have sent a copy to her one supporter, Marcus Loew, too, but he died on September 5.

With Walsh by her side, Gloria set about casting *Sadie Thompson*. According to Gloria's account, it was she who eventually talked Walsh into portraying Sadie's lover, Tim "Handsome" O'Hara, his first acting role in eight years. Walsh remembered it differently. He said, "I started testing Eddie Lowe and all those people to play the sergeant. She [Gloria] turned them all down. Two weeks go by, and Joe Schenck comes to me and says, 'You're never going to start this picture unless you play the part yourself. Don't you read her mind?'"[8]

In the integral part of Davidson (whose name changed from Oliver Hamilton to Alfred Atkinson to finally Alfred Davidson during production) was Lionel Barrymore, who advised Gloria he was not in the best of health and was taking painkillers. His personal hygiene was a bit questionable as well. He would not bathe or change his clothes throughout most of the filming. No matter how lethargic Barrymore appeared between scenes, however, his acting was electric.

Filming commenced in June. After location shots were completed on Catalina Island, interiors were lensed at the new United Artists studio facilities located at 7200 Santa Monica Boulevard, with art direction by William Cameron Menzies.

Handsome, six-foot-tall Raoul Walsh, born March 11, 1887, started in films in 1912 in Fort Lee, New Jersey. During his fifty-two-year career he worked as a cinematographer, director, and actor. In Griffith's *The Birth of a Nation* he was not only an assistant director and an editor, he also portrayed John Wilkes Booth. During the silent era Walsh directed (uncredited) Mary Pickford in *Rosita,* Douglas Fairbanks in *The Thief of Bagdad,* and Pola Negri in *East of Suez.* Unfortunately, his acting turn in *Sadie Thompson* would prove to be his last. Not only did Walsh direct and co-star in the picture, he also co-produced and wrote the scenario. Gloria and Walsh—recently divorced from his first wife, actress Miriam Cooper—held numerous meetings to discuss elements of the production; in actuality they were concealing an affair, which coincidentally ended when production wrapped.[9]

Walsh changed the intensity and dramatic feel of the picture and focused instead on the comedic and carefree life of the soldiers on the island, with Gloria in turn giving a much lighter performance than Eagels. Nowhere in the picture could the word "rain" be mentioned, though rain pelts the tin roofs of the buildings throughout. Some two hundred gallons of water were dumped on the set every day to simulate the monsoons of Pago Pago. "The artificial rain creates something out of the ordinary in stage annals, a scrim of water, which, illuminated with many colored lights, is said to give a spectacular effect," Edwin Schallert mentioned in the *Los Angeles Times.*[10]

For her cameraman, Gloria struck a deal with Samuel Goldwyn, also producing for UA, to use George Barnes. Barnes's work was highly praised in such UA pictures as *The Eagle* and *The Son of the Sheik,* both with Valentino, *The Winning of Barbara Worth,* and *The Magic Flame.* Unfortunately, once major photography got under way and the picture's mood was established, Goldwyn somewhat mean-spiritedly recalled Barnes for his Fred Niblo–directed misfire *The Devil Dancer.* Gloria was furious with the producer for reneging on his loan, though he legally had the right to do so.

Faced with locating a new cameraman who could match in shading and texture the extensive footage already shot by Barnes, Gloria was offered Mary Pickford's favorite cinematographer, Charles Roshner. His moody images, however, did not blend with Barnes's. Walsh then suggested Robert Kurlle, whose work was equivalent to Roshner's. He, too, did not work out. Finally Gloria secured

Oliver T. Marsh from MGM, whose photography matched superbly. Because of the cinematography issues, *Sadie Thompson* soon reached a cost of $650,000, $150,000 over the projected budget.

During the filming Gloria started to experience stomach pains. Believing her symptoms were most likely caused by ulcers due to stress, she sought out Dr. Henry G. Bieler in Pasadena, who diagnosed her problem. He asked her what she had been eating. When she told him her dinner the night before, he then asked her what was in each dish she consumed. By the end of the discussion she had figured out where he was going. After she eliminated rich, fatty, and spicy foods from her diet she started to feel better. He prescribed a new and simpler meal plan of steamed vegetables and vegetable broths (plus regular enemas) to rid her body of poisons. In fact, she credited Bieler with leading her to the macrobiotic lifestyle she would one day embrace. (Bieler also gave her a recipe of juices for a totally organic means to abort an unwanted pregnancy.)

In Hollywood Henri had developed several film projects, but they had all been rejected. Under the pseudonym Henri James Bailly, he had written *Antiques* and *Paris Luck,* both in 1927. Allan Dwan returned *Hearts and Clubs and Other Trumps* to Henri on March 29, saying it was very amusing but too short. *Coeur de Lilas* by "Tristan Bernard" was submitted to the William Fox Studios and also rejected by Harold B. Lipsitz, who wrote Henri, "I do not find this material suitable for our purposes, as it contains no novel situations or unique twists such as we desire."[11]

It was mandatory for Henri to make an annual trip to France to renew his visitor's permit and to conduct business, and each time Gloria and Henri denied to the press any marital rift. There were rumors that her affair with Walsh had something to do with Henri's coming departure to France. Though that may have been true, he *did* have to honor his immigration standing. Gloria advised the press, "If I were not engaged on a picture . . . I would be going with my husband instead of merely telling him good-by. However, we'll only be apart forty-five days and that doesn't sound nearly as long as six weeks."[12]

On August 15, Henri boarded the *California Limited* bound for New York, and Gloria was at the station platform to bid him a tearful farewell. Finding a secluded area away from the press, they shared a few moments of privacy. When the conductor announced boarding, it was apparent Gloria was upset. As the train pulled out, Henri thrust his hand from the window of his compartment, and she tearfully kissed it for photographers.

On August 20 he boarded the new luxury liner *Ile de France*, expecting to return six weeks later in time to catch a Dempsey-Tunney fight in Chicago. Gloria planned to meet him there. In New York, before departing, Henri said to the press asking about rumors of separation, "We are happy just like any other couple that is happy . . . and why the public should want us to be unhappy is more than I can understand."[13]

At the UA studio, Gloria was notified by Joseph Schenck's office that she was behind schedule and over budget. Words were exchanged, and Gloria excused herself to return to the set. She wrote in her memoirs that she told Pierre Bedard and Thomas Alan Moore to put her Park Chambers penthouse on the market, as well as property she owned in Malibu.

That, in fact would not be possible, since both were leased, not owned outright. The Park Chambers penthouse, which had remained unoccupied since March 17, was leased as of October 12 to Prince and Princess Levan Melikov de Somhetie for $1,000 a month. Gloria's original lease ran out on February 4, 1929, and on October 15 of that year she was faced with a balance due of $4,172.50 and still owing for the costs of a week of work done in alterations.

On August 30 Gloria had also leased a hundred feet of beachfront property at Rancho Malibu, as it was then called, planning to construct a seaside residence primarily for her children. She soon turned to Allan Dwan for suggestions on how to unload the property, which was valued at $130,025.23.[14] He suggested she talk to Robert Kane, a producer he knew at First National, who eventually rented the land from Gloria.

Furnishings of her recently sold Long Island summer home were auctioned off on July 19, bringing in "very little indeed[;] Samuel Marks, Inc., auctioneers dolefully admitted as much."[15] The house itself sold on July 14 for $55,337.18. On August 2, with a loan of $15,000, Gloria purchased lot 16, block 6 of the Beverly Trust on the west side of Canyon Drive between Brighton Way and Daytona Way in her mother's name. The grand concessions she boasted about in her memoirs were in exact opposition to her actual deeds.

The Crescent Drive estate was valued at $150,000, $125,000 for the land and $25,000 for the mansion and outlying buildings. When Irving Thalberg and his new bride, actress Norma Shearer, requested to lease Gloria's home for six months, December 20, 1927–June 19, 1928, at $1,200 a month, $2,400 in advance (for a total of $7,200), Bedard told Gloria to accept the offer and he would find another house for her nearby. He did, too, at 1735 Angelo Street at $700 a month.

Gloria was facing many financial catastrophes. For more than a year both Tom Moore and Bedard had made dedicated efforts to reel in her extravagant spending. She listened to no one. Albert Parker threatened to sue her for $60,000 she owed him per their two-picture contract, which she had no intention of fulfilling. (She had borrowed $20,000 from him, of which she had paid back about half the amount.) The Internal Revenue Service claimed back taxes stretching back to 1921 amounting to $100,000. She was cutting back the weekly cost of her New York office by $1,000, to $1,500, and there was just enough money for her secretary to pay that week's rent and telephone bill. She was down to her last dollar. It had been divulged in the papers that both John Barrymore and Gloria were insured for $750,000 by the Art Cinema Corporation, and about to be insured for $2 million by the Spectator Company, an insurance magazine publisher. In cold fact, Gloria was worth more dead than alive.

Speaking in confidence to producer Robert Kane, Gloria explained her plight and need to gather financing. Kane had a friend in New York who was savvy in the mechanisms of both banking and motion pictures. His name was familiar: Joseph P. Kennedy. Kane agreed to arrange a meeting between Gloria and Kennedy in New York.

"Gloria needs handling, needs being properly financed and having her organization placed in the proper hands," Kane advised Kennedy.[16] Perhaps he knew his friend very well, as Kane also told Kennedy that Gloria was the biggest star Famous Players had ever had and that both physically and mentally she was in the best shape ever.

Sadie Thompson completed production in mid-September. Its final cost totaled $931,761.04. Henri's return to the States was delayed, but he finally arrived in New York on board the *Paris* on September 21, greeting the press in a "'symphony of yellow,' wearing yellow leather shoes and socks, a shirt of the same color with blue stripes, a yellow tie with yellow double-breasted waistcoat, and a light tan suit with a diagonal silk stripe. The marquis said he had selected the suit in Paris to wear at the Dempsey-Tunney fight in Chicago that night, but would be unable to go."[17] Henri talked about his newest venture as a car sales-man. He was hoping to introduce the Bugatti automobile in America, explain-ing to the press that before he could sell his first automobile, the price of the chassis alone was $30,000.

Planning to stay in New York until September 25, Henri changed his mind and decided to linger a bit longer. As he returned to California, Gloria, ex-pressing her impatience, sent him a Western Union telegram, to car 306, com-partment C, westbound due at 11:45 A.M.[18]

Greeting her husband, Gloria clung to him for photographers.

More than eager to gain financing for her third film for United Artists, Glo-ria had *Sadie Thompson* previewed in San Bernardino the first week in Novem-ber. She was aware the picture would have to make at least $1 million to break even at the box office. She then decided she would head east on November 7. Arriving in Manhattan, she checked into the Barclay Hotel and arranged a luncheon with Kennedy on November 11 in the hotel's dining room. She told the maître d' that she would pay the bill, and should Kennedy make an offer to pick up the tab himself he was to advise him it was compliments of the house.

Gloria arrived armed with the facts and figures of her two United Artists pictures, plus two different financial proposals for her next film, one from Schenck and the other from Dr. Attilio Giannini, brother of Amadeo Giannini, who had helped set up the Bank of America. As Gloria entered the dining room she spotted Kennedy seated at a corner table. Kennedy noticed everyone in the room staring at her. She found Kennedy charming and liked his wit and humor. She was impressed by his six-foot stature, large biceps and muscular legs, and boyish enthusiasm. She ordered steamed vegetables for lunch, and he was curious about her diet. She was enchanted with his Boston accent. By the end of the luncheon she felt nothing had really been gained. Still, she wanted to see Kennedy again.

Joseph Patrick Kennedy was born in East Boston, Massachusetts, on Sep-tember 6, 1888, the elder son of P. J. and Mary Elizabeth Kennedy. Both his parents were first-generation American-born Irish. He had studied law at Harvard, Class of 1912, played on the baseball team, and was a member of the Delta Upsilon International Fraternity. His first job was as a state-employed bank examiner, where he learned about financing, his salary $1,500 a year. A young man with a lending ambition, he borrowed $45,000 in 1913, bought controlling interest in the Columbia Trust Bank, and was elected its president.

In 1919 Kennedy joined the Wall Street brokerage firm of Hayden, Stone & Co., where he trained in the stock market before leaving the company in 1923 to start up his own investment firm. Mastering the art of making money, he invested heavily throughout the 1920s. (Kennedy also knew when to sell, and did not suffer severely when Wall Street crashed in 1929. By then he had switched to dealing in real estate and motion pictures, substantially increasing his wealth.)

Turning his attention to Hollywood, Kennedy made huge amounts of money by financing and reorganizing motion picture studios. Purchasing sight unseen a small firm, FBO (Film Booking Offices of America, Inc.), for $1.5 million, Kennedy officially became a Hollywood film producer. FBO specialized in outdoor westerns, and their biggest star, Fred Thomson, was the first movie cowboy to co-star with his horse, Silver King.

Talkies arrived with the release of Warner Bros.' *The Jazz Singer* in October 1927, and Kennedy was shrewd enough to realize there would be a competitive scramble among sound equipment manufacturers to secure deals with the film studios. Radio Corporation of America (RCA) was setting up a market for its Photophone patents, attempting to combine movie producing with a chain of theaters to create an exclusive market. Kennedy would sell David Sarnoff of RCA an interest in FBO in late 1927 for $500,000. Then FBO bought 200,000 shares in the Keith-Albee vaudeville circuit from Edward F. Albee for $4.2 million, with Kennedy acquiring the stock at $21 a share; it more than doubled in value within three months. Albee believed Kennedy would keep him on as president, but shortly thereafter he was unceremoniously booted out.

Kennedy had set up offices in Hollywood in 1926. That same year he moved his growing family from Boston to Riverdale, New York. He had married Rose Elizabeth Fitzgerald, daughter of the Democratic mayor of Boston John Francis "Honey Fitz" Fitzgerald, on October 7, 1914. When he met Gloria, Kennedy was already the father of seven children, Joseph Jr., John, Rose Marie, Kathleen, Eunice, Patricia, and Robert. Rose was pregnant with their eighth child. Consumed with a religious view of devout and responsible motherhood, when asked once what exactly it was her husband did for a living, Rose Kennedy really did not know. She replied, "Business."[19]

Kennedy was mightily impressed with Gloria, but her finances were a disaster. Shortly after the luncheon, he wrote Kane. After telling Gloria not to be too choosy with her demands and to start another picture with UA, Kennedy stated, "I think the trouble is that she got herself all spread out with debts and one thing or another, and told too many people about it."[20]

Following the luncheon, Gloria returned to her hotel suite and conducted financial discussions with her United Artists sales and distribution people. Later that afternoon she was notified Kennedy had been calling for two hours, and now, at 5:00 P.M., he was in the lobby wanting to see her. She invited him up. Kennedy said he had called Sidney Kent, former head of Paramount distribution, regarding the foreign profits of her pictures, of which she could never get a true accounting. Kent would be glad to help her if possibly she could help him. Kent was in the process of divorcing, and his wife's attorney, Milton Cohen, who was also Gloria's legal eagle, was proving to be stubborn. Would Gloria call Cohen? She reluctantly did, and Cohen acquiesced to Kent's requests. This impressed Joe, who then promptly asked Gloria out for dinner.

Breaking her previous engagement with Sport Ward, Gloria dined with Kennedy. He picked her up at 6:30 P.M. and took her to a special place on Long Island. That evening he gave her a copy of his book *The Story of Films*, which was a series of speeches given by fourteen speakers at a Harvard symposium he had organized earlier that year. Among those speakers were Will Hays, Cecil B. DeMille, Adolph Zukor, Attillio Giannini, Jesse Lasky, William Fox, and himself. Gloria was impressed by Joe's ability to both convince Harvard of the importance of the film industry and get them to sponsor the program.

Gloria wrote in her memoirs they spent the remainder of the evening talking about pictures, the men who made them, and the process of acting. On the drive back into Manhattan, Joe excitedly told her about the "important" movies they could make together, movies made by great American directors, movies that would make them millionaires. He suggested she should be directed by Erich von Stroheim, whom Gloria had known as an associate of Herbert Somborn's back in 1919. The difficult but brilliant von Stroheim, who had not worked in three years after fighting bitterly with Paramount and MGM, wanted to direct again. Gloria was considering *Rock-a-Bye* as her next vehicle, but Kennedy told her it was not "important" enough. He insisted she trust him and let him take over her career. If she was willing to make some concessions, such as trading future film rights, he might be of some use.

Kennedy was fascinated with the glamorous Gloria, and he knew a gold mine when he saw one. He also sensed her growing attraction to him and his business acumen. Kennedy offered his coup de grace, suggesting he send a legal team to her New York office to review her files and finances. Gloria happily agreed. The next day her secretary Grace Crossman called to tell her that two men who looked like gangsters were at the office wanting to see the files. Gloria then extended her stay in New York for another two weeks.

Kennedy had written Milton Cohen and informed him that he was reluctant to guide Gloria's financial dealings. Having a change of thought, he then said he would put some of his people at her disposal to go over her financial affairs, but "if, at some later day, it looks like the services we might render have been of any value, we could at that time take up with you the consideration of any further deal."[21] Kennedy's services were soon called for. She agreed to trade the rights of *The Love of Sunya* and *Sadie Thompson* to Joseph Schenck in exchange for cancellation of all her debts owed to the studio, and Schenck in turn allowed her to use some of her UA stock to repay parts of her personal debts and taxes.

Sadie Thompson completed postproduction in October. Now Gloria needed to have the film made into prints, distributed, and properly publicized. She continued seeing Kennedy. But she did not curtail her spending, throwing lavish parties in her Barclay Hotel suite and insisting on chauffeur-driven limos.

Finally leaving New York on December 2, with a stopover in Chicago, Gloria arrived in California five days later. On December 20, Kennedy sent a letter to Cohen discussing Gloria's current affairs and reviewing the condition of the film industry. Repeating that he did not believe he would be able to do a trade with her to keep her out of bankruptcy, Kennedy wrote, "I would be very glad, after receiving word from you, to put myself and some of my people in my organization at her disposal to work out her problem as best we could without any cost to her until we found out whether it was really possible to work it out or not . . . I hesitate to make any suggestions at all; but if you desire, I will be very glad to cooperate to help work out some plan if in yours and Miss Swanson's mind this seems possible."[22]

Among the things Kennedy discovered was that Gloria had totally disregarded the IRS. "I cried all afternoon on [an IRS agent's] shoulder," wrote one of Kennedy's assistants.[23]

Gloria's production manager Pierre Bedard accommodated Joe's men as they took over Swanson's finances. He watched as both Cohen and Thomas Alan Moore were shown the door. Though Gloria repeatedly advised Bedard his job was secure, in the end he, too, was released. As Kennedy's accountant E. B. Derr reported, though "[Bedard] is a peach of a fellow, I know lots of peaches I can't pay $250.00 weekly."[24] Derr also told Kennedy he would take responsibility if Gloria opposed Kennedy's decision. She did not. The hairdresser and dressmaker she had on retainer were dismissed, and her household staff was severely reduced. Her New York secretary was given a desk job at the Pathé offices on Forty-fifth Street when Gloria's Fifth Avenue office was closed.

Gloria's last husband, William Dufty, once said about the relationship between her and Joe, "The idea that they were a great sexual match is a joke . . . Gloria was very intrepid sexually, but in terms of her relationship with men . . . She was very vulnerable."[25] Adela Rogers St. Johns agreed, stating Kennedy represented something more to Gloria. "She thought he would be her protector, that he would free her from all her financial worries, that he would always be there for her," said the journalist. "What she perceived at the time to be his strength of personality sealed her to him—for a time. She wanted to be safe; he represented just that, safety."[26]

Wrote one Kennedy biographer, "[Gloria] was free to believe she was pleasing Joe; she was taking care of him in one way and he was taking care of her in another . . . Joe, on the other hand, must have found the sex incredible. . . . Gloria was the antithesis of Rose. . . . As confident as Joe was, he must have been amazed he was actually waking up next to one of the world's most glamorous women."[27]

Over dinner one evening, Gloria entertained Kennedy and the controversial von Stroheim, director of such classic pictures as *Blind Husbands, Foolish Wives, Greed,* and *The Merry Widow,* whose last film, *The Wedding March,* had caused him to be "released" from Paramount. Von Stroheim's current project was called *The Swamp,* and his purpose that evening was to sell Kennedy and Swanson on his idea.

The story told of the Ruritanian kingdom of Kronberg, one of the states of Imperial Germany, where Queen Regina V (Seena Owens) plans to marry her

cousin Prince Wolfram von Hohenberg Falsenstein (Walter Byron). During military exercises, Wolfram meets convent schoolgirl Patricia "Kitty" Kelly (Gloria)
among a group of orphans. As the girls curtsey before the Prince, Kelly's panties
fall to her ankles. The Prince laughs, and she throws them at him. He is enchanted. To meet her again, he sets fire to the orphanage, kidnaps her, and takes
her to his palace, where the Queen chases her out with a lash.

Kitty attempts suicide by jumping into a river but survives and returns to
the orphanage. Her aunt (Sylvia Ashton) runs a dance hall in Dar-es-Salaam,
German East Africa, and summons Kelly there, where she is forced to marry
Jan Vooyheid (Tully Marshall), a crippled, drunken degenerate. Wolfram is
transferred into the Imperial German Schutztruppe in Africa where he meets
Kelly in her salon, after her husband's death. Queen Regina is assassinated and
Wolfram becomes ruler. He marries Kelly, and she becomes Queen.

Warning flags should have gone up immediately upon the telling of the tale.
Mythical Ruritanian kingdoms were a "specialty" for von Stroheim. In them
he could indulge his Hessian soul with expensive, detailed scenes of military
maneuverings, interlaced with social and sexual perversions of every kind.
Von Stroheim himself, as Gloria would find, was egotistical, arrogant, and pro-
foundly pleased with his every spoken word; yet he was brilliant and talented.

"Kennedy wanted to make an 'important' picture, having made nothing
but unimportant shit," said William Dufty. "Erich von Stroheim was a guarantee of importance, among other things."[28] Somehow Kennedy thought he could
control the maniacal spending and massive number of retakes von Stroheim
was noted for. "I have arranged to get von Stroheim to direct," Kennedy wrote
Louis B. Mayer at MGM on May 25. "I can already hear you saying: 'You have
had no troubles in the picture business yet—they have just started.'" Mayer
replied, "At least, if you weather the storm you will have something worth talking about."[29]

By the beginning of 1928, Kennedy had dissolved Gloria Swanson Productions, eliminated all of her former employees, and cut most of her personal staff.
Her new company was called Gloria Productions. From the first Gloria was
never referred to by name but simply as the "client." Gladly she signed over her
power of attorney to E. B. Derr, one of Kennedy's "Four Horsemen," as he called
them, the other three being Eddie Moore, Charles "Pat" Sullivan, and Ted
O'Leary. "I felt fortunate to have him taking charge of my finances," Gloria said.

"He was a Harvard graduate, he had shaken up Wall Street, and he wasn't a god-damned stuffed shirt like every other banker I'd ever met."[30]

Kennedy was headed to his Palm Beach, Florida, home at the end of January and asked Gloria and Henri to join him. Rose and the family remained up north. On January 24 Gloria and Henri boarded a train to Florida. That afternoon Kennedy received a telegram from Pat Sullivan saying that Gloria Productions had been incorporated.

Not everyone in her employ or involved in the now defunct Gloria Swanson Productions had been told of the takeover. When her train reached Yuma, Arizona, Gloria was handed a telegram from Milton Cohen, her bitter former friend and attorney, expressing his disappointment in Gloria's dismissal of his services.[31]

Smug and defiant, Gloria would not see she had done anything wrong. She jokingly sent Derr a telegram quoting Cohen's and asking him if she should cut her throat or not. Loyalty was not her strong suit.

Arriving in Palm Beach on January 29, Gloria and Henri were met at the station by Kennedy, O'Leary, and Moore, dressed in summer suits and sporting candy-striped straw hats. When Henri stepped off the train to arrange for the luggage, Joe bounded on board and entered Gloria's drawing room, kissing her twice and boldly stating, "I missed you. And I wanted you to know."[32] The electricity between them was palpable. Pointing out her husband on the platform, she took Joe by the hand and stepped off the train to introduce them. After the Horsemen attended to the luggage, they climbed into one car with Henri. Kennedy insisted she ride with him in the other.

On the drive to the Royal Poinciana Hotel, Gloria informed Joe that Cohen had resigned when he had found her company had been dissolved and he had not been notified. Joe let her know that most of the other "bunch of worthless passengers" she was carrying on her payroll had been permanently let go by Pat Sullivan.[33] At the hotel, the party awaited the arrival of Sullivan late that afternoon, at which time they put off discussions of business and dined in one of the establishment's large dining rooms.

The following day was prearranged by Kennedy himself. The party had agreed to go deep-sea fishing, as suggested by Eddie Moore. However, that morning Gloria conveniently convinced Henri she feared the water. "I'd much rather shop for presents for my children," she said she told them.[34] Then Kennedy backed out of the venture, complaining his stomach was giving him trouble. It was too late to cancel, as the boat had been secured, so the always trusting Henri and the boys bid adieu and left for the day. Gloria did go shopping, whether for her children or herself is not known, but when she returned to her hotel suite, she changed into a kimono and told her maid to leave.

Entering her suite as if on schedule as the maid departed, Joe, carrying an orchid corsage, rushed up to Gloria. With no protest, she allowed him to kiss her. "He stroked my body," her memoirs heatedly describe. According to Gloria, Joe Kennedy then quickly climaxed without even uttering anything meaningful.[35]

Theirs was no love affair by any stretch of the imagination. Gloria knew Kennedy was Catholic and would never entertain a divorce. And Gloria had no intention at this point of divorcing her titled, good-spirited, tolerant, and devoted husband. Yet she flirted with disaster. It was her nature.

Within two months, Kennedy was controlling Gloria's affairs.[36] Gloria was entering dark waters, becoming involved with a very powerful financial player. For the first time in her life, she alone would suffer the consequences.

15

Queen Kelly

After being proudly presented by Joe Kennedy at a series of parties and grand dinners, Gloria and Henri departed Palm Beach in the middle of February for New York to attend the premiere of *Sadie Thompson*. Henri then sailed to France to renew his visa. While her husband had been showing off his mistress and her marquis in Florida, Rose Kennedy had given birth to her eighth child, Jean Ann, in Boston. Gloria sent a large flower arrangement in congratulations.

Sadie Thompson had previewed already in San Francisco, the critics praising Gloria's performance, though they were not exactly thrilled with the picture. When it opened in New York on February 6, Mordaunt Hall wrote in *The New York Times*: "Notwithstanding the absence of sound and color, the film transcription of W. Somerset Maugham's story 'Sadie Thompson' . . . is a stirring pictorial drama, with a shrewd development of the plot and admirable characterizations . . . Sadie Thompson . . . comes to the screen as a brunette [Eagels was a blonde], in the person of Gloria Swanson, and while this actress may have given clever performances in some of her pictures, she displays more genuine ability and imagination in this present production."[1] In a subsequent, lengthy summarization of the picture, Hall was more generous, "Considering the obstacles that confronted Miss Swanson as a producer in tackling of the filming . . . [her] acting is an outstanding achievement."[2] But "Sid" in *Variety* was disappointed: "'Sadie Thompson' isn't great but it's big program material with the Swanson name and 'Rain' rep to help. They've let Sadie down and greatly."[3]

Film magazines, possibly more attuned to the taste of the general public, raved. *Screenland* said, "Gloria does one of the greatest come-backs in history. Give this girl a role she likes and she has a good time and gives everybody else the same."[4] *Motion Picture* magazine stated, "Despite censorial efforts at emasculation, La Marquise de la ETC., has packed the picture with TNT. Her characterization of the 'Frisco fill who takes the Apia-n way out far transcends any and all of her contributions to date . . . Gloria Swanson dominates the action throughout."[5]

Despite all the angst and turmoil of birthing *Sadie Thompson,* the picture earned $1 million in the United States, and another $7 million worldwide, netting Gloria's production company $776,539. However, by then it was in the ownership of Joseph Schenck and United Artists. Gloria did not share in the profits. On March 2, 1928, while en route by train to California, she signed over to Schenck and Art Cinema all the rights to *The Love of Sunya* and *Sadie Thompson.*

After its initial showings *Sadie Thompson* was lost for years. In 1955 Mary Pickford gave the only surviving print of the picture to the George Eastman House, minus its last reel, which had decomposed, losing approximately nine minutes. In 1987 archivist Dennis Doros reconstructed those minutes using an original script, film stills, intertitles, a brief silent clip from the 1932 sound remake, and a new musical score by Joseph Turrin.

In hindsight *Sadie Thompson* is considered one of the finest silent film dramatizations of the 1920s, if not for its social-historical significance, then for its ability to captivate and entertain. Gloria's character is quickly established in the opening scenes. Sadie is earthy and tantalizing yet vulnerable in Gloria's careful characterization, and there is keen chemistry between her and Walsh. Rivaling her performance is Lionel Barrymore, who was not yet crippled completely by arthritis. His characterization is magnificent and harrowing to behold. Sophisticated audiences enjoyed the film, while less discerning observers enjoyed more lucrative pastimes.

A new sport of moviegoers at this time was called the "cuss word puzzle," whereby audiences studied lip-reading to better enjoy the performances of actors in such pictures as *What Price Glory?, Beau Geste,* and *Sadie Thompson.* One could not censor what could not be heard, and many stars used choice profanity in these films, intercut with discreet titles to the contrary. In one scene Sadie clearly yells at Davidson, "You'd rip the wings off of a butterfly, you son-of-a-bitch!"[6]

In early March Kennedy returned to New York to advise Rose that he was headed for the West Coast indefinitely. By now he was running two film studios, Pathé Exchange and FBO, and was earning a personal income of $4,000 a week between them. He made an additional $2,000 at the recently merged Keith-Albee-Orpheum. That came to $312,000 a year, not including stock options. From June until August he would be an adviser to First National Pictures for a fee of $150,000, plus an offer to purchase twenty-five percent of the company's stock.[7]

Joe Kennedy's granddaughter Amanda Smith, in her book *Hostage of Fortune: The Letters of Joseph P. Kennedy*, wrote that Gloria's autobiography mentions her trysts with Kennedy and an alleged deepening of emotional attachment along with references to love and possible marriage. By contrast, the contemporaneous documentation relating to Gloria Swanson among the Joseph Kennedy papers addresses almost exclusively (if not clinically) the professional interactions between the star and the financier, and the legal and monetary arrangements that underpinned their working relationship. Their correspondence survives among his papers in the form of a number of curt and jovial (if businesslike) telegrams, often arranging for later telephone conversations of which no record survives.[8] So one must weigh carefully Gloria's history of their affair.

In her book Gloria wrote that Kennedy wanted to marry her. Over the years, she would adamantly and continually expand on how much Joe wanted a baby with her. He had eight children already, so this seems unlikely. Besides, "Joe approached sex like fast food," wrote one Kennedy family biographer, "bolting it down and then getting on with the day."[9] But by telling this story her way Gloria again made herself an object of romantic desire and a victim of love, thus minimizing her moral responsibilities.

In line with her upbringing, Rose believed the driving force of a wife and mother was to support her husband's work, care for the children, and understand that "lust from men was a chore for wives." Joe, on the other hand, was once heard to exclaim, "Now listen Rosie, this idea of yours that there is no romance outside of procreation is simply wrong . . . It was not part of our contract at the altar, the priest never said that and the books don't argue that."[10] After the birth of their ninth child, Edward, in 1932, Joseph and Rose ceased having sexual intimacy. For the rest of their married life they maintained separate bedrooms.

Joe appointed himself special adviser to Pathé in Hollywood to cancel their American holdings and to terminate their contract with DeMille. He made Henri European director of the Pathé Studios in Paris in January, conveniently eliminating Henri's having to renew his visitor's visa. And, of course, it kept Henri from interfering with Kennedy's and Gloria's affair. In Gloria's estimation, the devoted Henri could be easily manipulated, but she actually fooled herself. Henri more than likely knew exactly what was going on between his wife and Kennedy. Still, he sailed for Europe alone in late February to assume his new position.

"It is amazing to me how widespread and general has become the report that we are estranged," Gloria told the press in March. "I cannot understand where these reports originate, but it is the same old story every time he returns to Paris. I guess it is because we have been married three years that people think we ought to separate. We are still as happy as ever."[11]

For a week, Gloria disappeared to Palm Springs and checked into the El Mirador to await Joe. He was deep in discussions with DeMille about his Pathé contract; the director's spending and payroll, like Gloria's, were completely out of control. DeMille still had four more years to go on his contract, but Pathé wanted him out. In the end DeMille agreed to complete *The Godless Girl,* then in production, and depart.

In Paris Henri stayed at the Carlton Hotel while his passport papers were looked over in the United States. He told the press, "Oh, it's nothing serious . . . The papers had to be sent back to California for Gloria to go over, but I hate this delay. I already have missed a couple of boats."[12] The American consulate in Paris refused to grant Henri a visa because he had lived in America for a year already, but Henri was able to prove that he and Gloria had requested the extension in New York and that the papers had been sent to California in error. The whole affair cost him a lot of money, he said, and interfered with his business plans. He was free to depart as of March 26. (Gloria's new passport was issued in Paris, her presence not required, on March 16 under the name Madame la Marquise Le Bailly de la Falaise.) Yet Henri delayed his departure until April 11.

Catching the hundredth voyage of his beloved *Paris* from Le Havre, Henri arrived into New York after being away for six weeks. Denying rumors of divorce, he told the press he planned to stay in the States indefinitely and to remain in New York a week before journeying to California. He was traveling with his younger brother Alain, the Comte de la Falaise. Gloria met the two at the Santa Fe Station in California on April 28. Posing happily for photographers, Gloria laughingly told the press, "The trouble with these trips abroad is that they always end in business."[13]

In a strange moment of propriety, Kennedy found it irresponsible of Gloria that she had not yet baptized her son Joseph. It was only when her friend Lois Wilson, also a devout Catholic, agreed with Joe's concern for the child's soul that Gloria allowed the christening. Taking control now of "Brother's" future, Kennedy arranged for the christening party. According to Gloria he spoke more and more of combining families.[14]

Addie then surprised her daughter by suddenly marrying again without telling her. On May 17, she wed Charles C. Woodruff in Tijuana, Mexico. In a letter to Addie, Gloria wrote about having to run between the studio and the Ambassador Hotel, where she was posing for artist Leon Gordon, and her other activities. Then, offering her mother congratulations, she wrote, "After my surprise I felt as if it were my own child Gloria who had got married. Of course, I am still in a daze because I never suspected . . . I wonder why you seem like my baby to me."[15]

On the evening of Wednesday, June 6, Henri was at the Russian Eagle Café on Sunset Boulevard in the company of director Eddie Sutherland and actress Lili Damita. The café, owned by former Russian Major-General Theodore Lodijensky (who had appeared in Gloria's *Her Love Story*), had become the "in" place to be. Other celebrities at the club that evening were Charlie Chaplin and his manager Harry Crocker, John Monk Saunders, Colleen Moore and her husband John McCormick, and Estelle Taylor and her husband the boxer Jack Dempsey.

Throughout the evening Henri had noticed a wisp of smoke circling the room. The smoke, they discovered, was coming from a burning candle on top of a bunch of oil-soaked cloths in the attic. The café was evacuated. Authorities were called, but no one showed up for some time. When firemen did at last appear, there was a sudden explosion that blew the café's roof off and shook it from its foundation, and a fire followed. When Henri and Sutherland reentered the café, they found Lodijensky, a couple of patrons, and several fire officials seriously injured. Chaplin and Sutherland battled the blaze with a hose. The next day Henri was photographed by the papers among the ruins, smoking a pipe. Along with Chaplin, Moore, and others there that evening, Henri was subpoenaed to testify in court.

On June 13 Gloria was slapped with a lien of $18,889.93 on her 1923 earnings for taxes she had forgotten to pay. Thank goodness she had Joe Kennedy on this one. Rex Cole, a tax authority who founded the Equitable Investment Corporation in 1925, now represented her for these problems.

Earlier that month preproduction had begun on *The Swamp*. Casting was under way. On June 17 stage actor Bela Lugosi, recently arrived in Hollywood with the Broadway cast of *Dracula*, announced he had been tested in New York by the director for an important role in *The Swamp*, but he proved too tall alongside Gloria.

Von Stroheim was signed to direct *The Swamp* in May. He had been busy, contacting William Le Baron, vice president in charge of production at FBO, to suggest casting Edmund Lowe, under contract with Fox, for the male lead and to secure Gordon Pollock to photograph the picture. He then asked if he might finish filming his latest project, the second half of *The Wedding March* (called *The Honeymoon*), at FBO, though it was a Paramount film. Relations were strained between von Stroheim and Famous Players–Lasky. Said director Billy Wilder years later, "This obsession with foot fetishism, underwear fetishism, other sexual perversions which his pictures are filled with, was the *real* Stroheim."[16]

Jesse Lasky, who was von Stroheim's boss on *The Wedding March*, gave Kennedy fair warning. Kennedy laughed, "What the hell! J.L., nothing can go wrong. I've got two good men to police the Kraut."[17] Joe was referring to Benjamin Glazer and William Le Baron, who were assigned to watch von Stroheim's extravagances. Kennedy wrote von Stroheim that Fox's Winnie Sheehan would have an answer regarding the loan of Lowe within forty-eight hours (it was a resounding "No!"), that it would be advisable legally for him to complete *The Wedding March* at Famous Players, and that the idea of using Pollock looked sound. (Pollock was eventually contracted for *The Swamp*. However, after the first day of principal photography on November 1, he was unceremoniously replaced by Paul Ivano, whose costume test shots proved more satisfactory.)

Hollywood insiders were already placing their bets on the outcome of *The Swamp*. Said the acerbic Harry Carr, "Gloria Swanson is one of the few women on the screen with a sure touch for tragedy; and she will get her finishing touches in screen technique from Von [*sic*] Stroheim."[18] After von Stroheim made the selection of English actor Walter Byron to portray Prince Wolfram on July 27, construction of the royal palace and the convent were begun on the FBO back lot under the director's meticulous supervision.

Von Stroheim worked diligently on his script throughout the summer after it was passed by Hays's office. The FBO wardrobe department began its elaborate costumes for the extras in the crowd scenes, with von Stroheim observing every stitch. Revised to a twelve-week shooting schedule of 510 scenes, *The Swamp* had a budget of $228,000 and was to be filmed as a silent, with a synchronized music track to be added. Neither Gloria nor the director had much faith in sound, but Kennedy had Photophone available in any case. Because the title *The Swamp* was murky at best and likely to drive audiences away, on August 19 the press announced the name of the picture had been changed to *Queen Kelly*. (Other titles considered were *The Scarlet Saint, The Saint in Scarlet, The Orchid Lady,* and *The Orchid Woman.* Gloria would always claim she chose the title *Queen Kelly*.)

It was MGM studio head Louis B. Mayer's idea to start up an organization within the film community to honor films and performances annually and to call it the International Academy of Motion Picture Arts and Sciences. After inviting thirty-six leaders of the industry to a formal banquet at the Ambassador Hotel on January 11, 1927, Mayer saw his brainchild become official on May 4, with Douglas Fairbanks elected its president. Awards of merit and achievement were then designated, and in July 1928 nomination ballots were sent to the Academy members. Categories of recognition were specified and nominees chosen, selected from film productions released between August 1, 1927, and July 31, 1928.

The first year of the Academy Awards, in the category of Best Actress 1927–28, three were nominated: Louise Dresser, for *A Ship Comes In;* Janet Gaynor, for the three films *Seventh Heaven, Street Angel,* and *Sunrise: A Song of Two Humans;* and Gloria Swanson, for *Sadie Thompson.* George Barnes was also nominated for the Best Cinematography award for *Sadie Thompson.* Gloria didn't put much stock in award ceremonies, and she couldn't have cared less. She decided not to attend the ceremony, believing it might make Kennedy feel bad if she won, because *Sadie Thompson* was not his picture.[19]

In his August 26 *Los Angeles Times* column, Harry Carr forewarned Kennedy: "Life is tame when you are gone. You haven't bought a motion picture company for days and days. And another thing, Joe. This efficiency stuff [in reference to Kennedy's ruthless takeover of Keith-Albee-Orpheum]—you know. It is all very nice to go through a pay roll and cut off the uncles and cousins and other ornaments; and reduce the overhead by $20,000 per week; but the next thing is to make good pictures. It remains to be seen what kind of pictures you are going to make." And to Gloria, Carr warned: "Dear Gloria and Erich Von [*sic*] Stroheim: May the best man win."[20]

Henri quietly left for Europe again the third week in July. Gloria accompanied him to the train station and recalled later their good-bye felt like that of an old married couple. News of his departure was not mentioned in the press, but apparently Henri was "needed" by Kennedy in France to assume his position with French Pathé. That meant Gloria would be free to be with Joe at his Rodeo Drive home until late at night, when one of the Horsemen would drive her back to her house. Gloria meanwhile kept socially active that fall, contrary to her memoirs, where she stated she stayed home diligently with her children, who now attended the private Curtis School.

To slap her into shape, Gloria had Joe hire the tough, self-made Madame Sylvia Ulbeck, from Bremen, Germany, who was described in the press as "a tiny person magnetic and full of energy, spunky and saucy, able to hold her own."[21] Sylvia was the masseuse to the stars, paid $750 a week by such actresses as Marie Dressler and Norma Shearer. Kennedy built Madame a bungalow on the Pathé lot. "Madame Sylvia specialized in such excruciatingly painful massages," wrote one pair of Hollywood historians, "that it is said that her radio was equipped with a special amplification system in order to drown out the moans of her victims."[22] No pain, no gain. It was also whispered Madame Sylvia was capable of massaging away Kennedy's occasional impotency.

After his takeover of Pathé, Joe built up his roster of stars, which now included Ann Harding and Ina Claire. With Gloria's blessings, he signed a young actor named Joel McCrea, who had once been her newspaper boy. Also at her request, Kennedy pursued acquiring actress Constance Bennett, who was in Europe and recently estranged from her second husband, millionaire Philip Morgan Plant. Joe asked Henri to talk to the beautiful blonde about signing with him while he was in Europe.

Kennedy left for New York by rail on August 6. His father, seventy-year-old Patrick Joseph Kennedy, was dying of pancreatic cancer. For the remainder of the year, well into 1929, Joe would by necessity spend more and more time out east.

A telling display of Gloria's ego was recalled by Louise Brooks, by then an upcoming star at Paramount, who attended a party that summer at the five-acre, 110-room beach house of Marion Davies.[23] "[Gloria] decided to liven up a rather dull Sunday gathering with one of her favorite games. She took all the girls into a room off the big library, [and] sent the butler for a platter of strained honey which was set upon a table with her seated behind it. What the dodge was I forget, but one by one all the men were brought in blindfolded and led to the table. Some question which they could not answer was put to them, and then as a penalty Miss Swanson told them to bend over and pushed their faces into the honey. It was quite a sight, seeing the men rear back with honey dripping down their ascot ties and afternoon clothes." Gloria found the game hilarious, but the other women and Louise herself were totally baffled as to why Gloria would want to humiliate the gentlemen. It was spiteful, yet Gloria loved it, giving her an "apparently therapeutic exercise of power."[24]

After the premiere of FBO's first talkie, *The Perfect Crime,* on August 6, Kennedy and RCA's David Sarnoff met in New York, and in October FBO and Keith-Albee-Orpheum merged with RCA Photophone to form Radio-Keith-Orpheum (RKO), for which Kennedy was paid $150,000. RKO then traded its previously purchased stock in FBO for 20 percent of the newly created RKO stock, now worth $80 million, and won a market for Photophone equipment in some two hundred theaters. (Kennedy later sold his stock in FBO for more than $5 million.) That September Kennedy and his wife Rose celebrated his fortieth birthday vacationing in Cannes, in the company of Henri.

Gloria confided to the press in mid-September, over a month and a half before *Queen Kelly* began shooting, that she missed her husband. She was saddened to hear he was staying in Paris longer than expected. "It is possible that my husband may be delayed abroad or that he may prefer waiting for me to come over," she confessed. "In any case, I mean to go to France and meet him if my work will permit . . . We shall then remain abroad for a while, as I never wish to hurry when I am over there."[25] In truth, she was rushing out east because her lover Joe had called to say he missed her.

After spending several days in Manhattan, Gloria was asked by Kennedy to travel up to his Riverdale home and meet Rose and the children for a party. Gloria refused to go, but she did allow eight-year-old Gloria and six-year-old Joseph to attend with their nanny Miss Simonson. Eddie Moore drove them up, and they had a wonderful time playing with the energetic Kennedy brood.

Rose Kennedy incorrectly wrote in her memoirs that Gloria had come and had brought along "her small daughter, who was about the age of our Pat [Rose confused her daughters—Patricia was only four years old, while Kathleen was the same age as little Gloria], who was about ten. The two got along well together, and Pat [Kathleen] took her down to show her the Bronxville public school and meet her classmates and perhaps to show off a little, by introducing her as 'Gloria Swanson's daughter.' Nobody believed her . . . I can't recall the exact details but I do remember how completely indignant Pat [Kathleen] was when she and Gloria's little girl came home and told us."[26] Young Gloria would remember the costumes and all the Kennedy children. "It was fun going to that house," she recalled, "because no matter what age you were they had somebody to play with."[27] Young Jack Kennedy was impressed because little Gloria's father owned the Brown Derby restaurant where Tom Mix often dined.

Little Gloria had now grown to be a tall eight-year-old with beautiful green eyes, and blond streaks highlighting her hair. Her mouth was prettier than her mother's and she promised to be a beauty when she matured. Her relationship with her father was very good. They affectionately exchanged cards and letters. Her mother at least was civil to Herbert in discussions about their child. Young Joseph was an energetic six-year-old with large ears and handsome brown eyes. He loved all things mechanical, and was a very typical lad, though much to Gloria's dismay he became a little too attached to Miss Simonson, who had become somewhat of a mother figure to him.

As the papers speculated about the delays on *Queen Kelly*, which was to have begun filming on September 3, Gloria and her children arrived back in Hollywood the second week of October. *Queen Kelly* was now set to roll on November 1, though the reason for the delay was simple—Kennedy had to arrange the necessary finances. As the shooting date loomed on the horizon, Gloria became apprehensive. Kennedy reassured her he would put men in charge of watching von Stroheim and keeping him on schedule. He also sent a telegram telling Henri to not upset Gloria as she was expressing anxiety because the film was already three months behind.[28]

In 1925, when Gloria first arrived back in New York after marrying her marquis, she had made a second talking Phonofilm short at the Lee de Forest Studio, this time with Henri, Allan Dwan, and Thomas Meighan. She thought nothing more of it until April 1927, when it was widely distributed in theaters that had been equipped with sound. Now the pressure to talk on celluloid was serious.

Gloria finally gave in to sound in early September, agreeing to allow *Queen Kelly* to be that rare hybrid of pictures, a "part-talkie." Silent throughout until the final reel, the climactic scene with voices, music, and sound effects, *Queen Kelly* went into film production on Friday, November 1, 1928. Von Stroheim was in excellent humor, as every detail of his mythical kingdom seemed perfect. Even the playwright and editor of *Life* magazine Robert Sherwood declared the film would be a masterpiece.

Because most of the sets for the picture were still incomplete, the first day's shooting of *Queen Kelly* took place in Griffith Park. The opening sequence was with Gloria and the convent girls on Kambach Road as the handsome Prince Wolfram (Walter Byron) and his guard ride up over the crest on horseback and proceed down the road. As the girls bow at the sight of the Prince, Kitty Kelly's underpants fall down around her ankles as scripted. Then something shocking was added at the last minute. Von Stroheim had Gloria throw her panties at Byron in numerous takes, and in one the director obscenely instructed Byron to caress and sniff the undergarment momentarily before placing it inside his saddlebag. It had begun. Gloria recalled, "The experience of working with him [von Stroheim] was unlike any I had had in more than 50 pictures. He was so painstaking and slow that I would lose all sense of time, hypnotized by the man's relentless perfectionism."[29] That day she felt she would never finish the film.

In early November screenwriter Harvey Thew, who had contributed screen adaptations for FBO's lucrative "The Leatherpushers" film series (plus a few successes for Wallace Beery), announced to the press he had been assigned to do a screen story for Gloria under the direction of von Stroheim called *Clothes,* just in case *The Swamp* (aka *Queen Kelly*) became a misfire. Apparently FBO's Le Baron and Glazer were checking their backs. Thew was already working "at top speed" to complete an adaptation and have it ready as soon as *Queen Kelly* wrapped production in January.[30] (Gloria would buy the rights to *Clothes* from Pathé for $4,567.42 on June 26, 1929. For six months afterward the project remained in the works until she tired of it.)

When Gloria viewed the early rushes of *Queen Kelly* she was thrilled at the beauty and mesmerized by the artistic quality of the resulting footage. On November 16 the convent fire sequence was filmed. Edwin Schallert of the *Los Angeles Times* was on the set: "Gloria and Von [*sic*] Stroheim have formed a 'mutual admiration society' of which the two are the exclusive members, so great is the spirit of co-operation professionally between them. Gloria herself told me that she felt that she could rely on the executive ability of Stroheim completely—his faculty for military-like discipline, and that she was not worrying about her present picture."[31] Were it only to remain so.

Von Stroheim had arranged a six-day-a-week shooting schedule, beginning at 8:00 A.M. Then it was changed to 9:00 A.M., with daily filming running well into the night. On December 18 filming concluded at 5 A.M., the next day an hour later. On December 31, *Film Daily* commented, "Extras are swooning daily on the set from overwork, and the work goes on all night and continues through the day without a break."[32] Slowly the picture, not to mention the cast and crew, began to unravel, and run behind schedule. Still, Gloria was reassured by Joe in New York that von Stroheim was under scrutiny.

But when she began to see the project losing money, Gloria truly became concerned. So far just one-third of the picture, the palace section, and none of the African scenes, had been shot. Finally, right before Christmas the European sequences were completed, having taken forty-three days to film, plus an additional two days later on. At that pace the picture would take at least another four months to complete, and run far over budget. A break was called until after the New Year.

Attempting to justify the spiraling costs of the film, both Gloria and von Stroheim sent off New Year goodwill messages to the United Artists sales organization meeting in Chicago, expressing their regards for each other and optimistic hopes for the picture.[33]

Henri arrived from Europe the third week of December and immediately returned to California for the holidays. But the festive season was marred for Gloria and most of Hollywood when western film actor Fred Thomson, the handsome thirty-one-year-old husband of screenwriter Frances Marion, and father of two young boys, tragically stepped on a rusty nail in his stables and tetanus set in. He died of tetanus on Christmas Day 1928. A big name at FBO, Thomson had starred with Mary Pickford in *The Love Light*. Joe had boasted to Thomson about his affair with Gloria, at which time the actor said, "Joe, it won't work—[Joe's affair with actress] Evelyn Brent didn't work—none of it will *ever* work!" Joe countered that Rose's indifference to his sexual needs drove him to pursue other women. "But emotionally, Joe—emotionally, what are you feeling?" Fred had to ask.[34] Kennedy was without a clue.

With 1929 beginning with an air of gloom, *Queen Kelly* resumed filming, now with the African sequences, on January 2 on the Pathé lot. Joe built Gloria a marvelous art deco bungalow at the studio, complete with a grand piano. (In later years the structure would house the offices of David O. Selznick, and the bungalow's living room would become the publicity office for Carole Lombard. In the 1980s it was director Blake Edwards's office.) Then von Stroheim changed what in the script had been a dance hall and seedy hotel into an obvious brothel. The mood of the film turned dark, and Gloria became incensed. She knew von Stroheim had already shot more than ten hours of film, and at this pace he would film another ten. How was the picture ever going to play in cinemas, much less come in on budget? *Queen Kelly* was already a full month behind schedule.

Gloria reeled in revulsion at what she saw in the latest rushes. The African scenes were totally unrelated to the European episode in look and character. On January 6 she held a meeting to discuss costs and to secure a prognosis on the picture. Von Stroheim agreed to cut a lengthy and expensive sequence. Gloria's first African scenes were filmed the second week of January. She then called another meeting to discuss the addition of sound into certain sequences. Still the film's slow financial hemorrhage continued.

After the New Year Henri left suddenly for New York on his way to Europe again. Everything, it seemed, was unraveling. Gloria viewed some disturbing rushes on Sunday, January 20. The plots and subplots Hays's office had vetoed in the original script suddenly reappeared before her eyes. Von Stroheim was sinking into his own psychological dark, erotic hell, having the actors improvise scenes as they went along. The bordello sequences were bad enough, Gloria knew the Catholic Church would be displeased, and the execrable Ku Klux Klan riled, by the scene of an African priest giving last rites to Kelly's aunt (Sylvia Ashton).

The final straw came on January 21 with the lensing of the scene of Kelly's marriage to the lecherous and crippled Jan Vryheid over the deathbed of the dying aunt. The filming began at 9:00 A.M., on the seventeenth day of production of the African section, and by 7:00 P.M. over three hundred feet of film had been shot. Still von Stroheim was not satisfied with the sequence, which was horrifying in its depiction of darkness, decay, and filth. He instructed actor Tully Marshall to drool tobacco juice over Gloria's hand as he struggled to fit the wedding ring onto her finger. Sickened and exhausted by the terminal slowness of what she recognized as censorable, Gloria suddenly stopped the scene, said, "Excuse me," and quietly walked off the set, leaving actors and extras speechless.[35]

Gloria called Joe in Florida, where he was with his family. "Joseph, you'd better get out here fast. Our director is a madman . . . It's ruined!"[36] Kennedy remained in Palm Beach with his family but had E. B. Derr send Broadway playwright Eugene Walter to view the rushes and file a report. A six-page memo summarizing Walter's findings was sent to Kennedy, stating in part that Gloria was not being highlighted in the picture, and it was unclear whether her character was an innocent or a whore.[37] When Kennedy arrived in Hollywood, he sequestered himself, Derr, and Eddie Moore in a viewing room to witness von Stroheim's carnage. The production was shut down immediately and indefinitely, and von Stroheim was fired.

The director was vilified in the press. *Film Weekly* commented, "It is so sad about Erich von Stroheim. The kind hearted producers have done everything they could to help him turn over a new leaf. When by all rights, they could have spanked him and sent him home to mother in disgust, they found it in their hearts, time and again to forgive."[38] The article then proceeded to mention almost verbatim the exact contents of the Walter-Kennedy memo. It was apparent that revenge was sought.

But von Stroheim did have his supporters. Many industry insiders saw him for the artist he was, including actress Louise Brooks, who called the director "the one pure visual genius of film" and said that the true villains in the *Queen Kelly* saga were "those two vulgarians, Kennedy and Swanson, who really destroyed Erich."[39]

Kennedy was beside himself. Before Gloria, he had produced a series of successful yet indistinguishable programmers. She was his first big chance at the golden apple. At the age of forty, Kennedy had never had a failure. Now he was faced with what to do with *Queen Kelly*.

After the uncut footage was viewed, Joe seemed more incensed that Gloria's character had not been developed than that the picture was censorable. Though Derr tried to defuse the situation by telling his boss that rewrites were in the works, Kennedy nevertheless voiced his opinions, and possibly Gloria's demands, to Derr, who on January 25, sent a long, detailed telegram to Edward Moore, which read in part:

> MY OPINION IS THAT ORIGINAL DIRECTOR IN AN ATTEMPT
> TO BE BIZARRE AND UNSUSUAL HAS BEEN VULGAR GROSS
> AND FANTASICALLY IMPOSSIBLE . . . I SUGGEST NO ADDITIONAL
> MONEY OF REMAINING TWENTY THOUSAND BE PAID FORMER
> DIRECTOR . . . IN VIEW OF FLAGRANT VIOLATION CONTRACT
> TERMS STOP PLEASE BE CAREFUL LEGALLY NOT TO STATE ANY
> DISSATISFACTION IN STORY AND PICTURE AS YOU HAVE NO
> LEGAL GROUNDS ALONG THOSE LINES FOR TERMINATION
> STOP WILL DO EVERYTHING HUMANLY POSSIBLE TO START
> SHOOTING MONDAY OR TUESDAY[40]

Queen Kelly, it was determined after the January 6 meeting, was actually only about two or three weeks behind schedule, having cost $400,000 so far. Von Stroheim said at the time of his firing he could complete the film in an additional four to five weeks for an additional $400,000. He was prepared to cut the banquet scene (one day shooting, eight scenes at $10,331.06), the coronation scene (one day shooting, seven scenes at $8,844.36), and the swamp jungle, with Jan's hut (twelve days shooting at $22,899), a total savings of $71,595.95, which would have reduced filming by twenty-one days and brought the additional cost in at $300,000.

To the end of her days Gloria proclaimed the existing footage—twenty-two reels of over five and one-half hours, about one-third of the picture—had cost *her* $800,000. Kennedy would later insist to anyone who would listen that it had cost him $1 million of *his* money. No matter what the relationship Kennedy enjoyed with Gloria, his contract with her strictly offset the costs of *Queen Kelly* against the profits of her future films.

The picture was shut down but never meant to be abandoned. There are many factors that brought about the eventual demise of *Queen Kelly*. Von Stroheim, never one to even consider expenditures, put the blame solely on the coming of sound. Gloria herself is to blame in part, for she ignored until the last minute what was happening in sequences that did not include her character. When all the elements of pending disaster culminated in the tobacco juice oozing onto her hand, Gloria simply snapped.

The European sequences were to be but a prologue. What remains of them is a silly tale of a handsome, immoral prince who falls in love with an innocent schoolgirl. Gloria looks sixteen years old in these early scenes (if one can excuse the heavy mascara and lip rouge) due to von Stroheim's meticulous care in filming her.

The remaining story was the meat of the picture. The African scenes were meant to be dark, vulgar, and steamy, and these were approved in advance before von Stroheim became self-indulgent. His biographer Arthur Lennig wrote in defense, "Some criticism could also be leveled against Stroheim's producers, who knew that he had a fatal tendency toward long films and yet, somehow, approved gigantic shooting scripts. Everyone in power who read these scripts (did anyone really *read* them?) must have been carried away by Stroheim's imagination and detail, because no one had the strength or foresight to trim the excess before shooting began. Kennedy could be forgiven, as a novice, but not Swanson."[41] What remained of *Queen Kelly* was ten hours of innumerable retakes, and no one had a viable idea what to do with the footage.

Irving Thalberg at MGM suggested Kennedy try to salvage the film. After all, he had dealt with von Stroheim as well: "The New York critics loved *The Merry Widow* after I restored the Lehar frosting."[42] Under contract for $5,000 a week since February 4, director Edmund Goulding, somewhat obligingly, thought he could redeem the picture. He offered to come up with another project, which no doubt he had up his sleeve all along. When Richard Boleslavsky was brought in to direct, Kennedy was thoroughly dissatisfied. "This Polack, Boleslavski [sic], tells me a few songs, some dialogue, and a happy ending will work wonders," he told Gloria.[43]

One ponders why, with so much money spent, the sets and costumes made, and the cast on payroll, von Stroheim was not merely reprimanded and placed on probation. He could have reshot some of the African scenes, the section shortened, and the picture could still have been released in 1929, and possibly even recouped its cost. Benjamin Glazer was called in by Gloria to rewrite a workable script, using existing footage, and add a music soundtrack, but his script proved preposterously bad. Perhaps Gloria thought Goulding would take over and salvage the mess. But he had his own agenda. So Gloria had von Stroheim fired, and without von Stroheim *Queen Kelly* came to a halt. Until the time was right, it would remain on the shelf.

16

The Trespasser

Upon the halt of filming on *Queen Kelly,* the papers had a field day. Grace Kingsley broke the news on January 25 that Edmund Goulding was busy conferring with Gloria about sandwiching between *Queen Kelly* and *Clothes* a musical romance with John Boles, who was still under contract with her. On the twenty-seventh *The New York Times* reported Gloria was before the microphones recording songs and filming talking sequences for *Queen Kelly.* Von Stroheim himself apologized: "I have changed my attitude . . . One naturally does as one gets older. I am more philosophical about the making of pictures. I am, so to speak, aged in wood, mellower."[1] Mellower or not, he would never again direct another motion picture. With his firing from *Queen Kelly* von Stroheim became a pariah in Hollywood, his reputation shattered.

Meanwhile Gloria continued on her social rounds, her husband in Europe, and her lover handling her career. In Europe, Henri was pleasantly discovering Constance Bennett, whom Kennedy wanted to sign to Pathé. "Falaise's charms were not lost on Constance, and the affair blossomed as she took steps to extricate herself from her marriage," wrote Bennett's biographer.[2] Constance was leading the life of a social butterfly, fluttering about the Continent with her "adopted" (actually her very own) son Peter. Having given up her career during her two-year marriage to Plant, she was now weighing a return to the screen. When she met Henri, who offered her a film contract as well as consolation, Bennett was hooked. In mid-April she returned to Hollywood to begin her first

Pathé picture, *This Thing Called Love,* temporarily leaving her lover Henri in France.

Rumors had spread about town that Gloria was seeing someone else. Joe would stay in California at least until June. He planned to surprise Gloria by hosting a dinner party at his home on Rodeo Drive, inviting former aviator, adventurer, and documentarian Merian C. Cooper, who would become studio head of RKO in the 1930s and co-write and direct the classic *King Kong.* Kennedy "invited everybody that was 'in' in Hollywood to the dinner," recalled Cooper. As he related to film historian Kevin Brownlow years later, Cooper remembered the guests entering the long rectangular dining room, where Kennedy had placed life-sized blown-up photographs "of every man that was known to have slept with her [Gloria]" around. "In sweeps Gloria and she looked around at these pictures and said, 'Joe, I'm glad you remembered my former life.' She wasn't fazed at all. She wouldn't give a damn, you know."[3]

Gloria now focused on making a talking picture with Edmund Goulding as screenwriter/director. She took credit for suggesting Goulding to Joe, but that was not the case. The English-born Goulding had already been contracted by Joe to begin work on an original story for her next project. In record time, Goulding turned out a screen treatment for Gloria within a week. He then began making talking screen tests, shooting up to twenty-five a week, and was in the process of discussing the upcoming schedule with E. B. Derr and William Sistrom, former head of DeMille's productions, when *Queen Kelly* shut down.

Goulding had the foresight to recognize the possibilities of sound and music in motion pictures. (He had just completed writing the story for *The Broadway Melody* at MGM. It became the first successful movie musical, winning the 1927–28 Best Picture Academy Award.) His original screenplay for Pathé, *The Trespasser,* would prove to be one of the three very important films he would direct in 1929–30, the other two being *The Devil's Holiday* (Paramount) with Nancy Carroll and the musical comedy *Reaching for the Moon* (UA) with Douglas Fairbanks. Goulding was a cultured man, openly homosexual in an industry in which it was not always easy to be so, and was highly regarded as an actor, novelist, songwriter, singer, and playwright. His "flaws" could be overlooked if he was bankable.

After his tenure with MGM, Goulding contributed to a handful of pictures at Paramount such as *Paramount on Parade* (1930) just as the talkies were coming into vogue. He would continue to achieve acclaim as a director when he helmed such memorable classics as MGM's *Grand Hotel,* Warner Bros.' *Dark Victory* in 1939, and 20th Century–Fox's *The Razor's Edge* in 1946. His outline of *The Trespasser* was specifically designed to introduce Gloria in the most sympathetic light for her talkie debut. A strict soap opera, it would also feature her singing. Gloria, who was then quite fond of Goulding, knew the picture's story would work.

Kennedy, Derr, and Eddie Moore boarded a train headed east on March 7. Kennedy had now placed Goulding on the payroll as a director at $1,000 a week. Gloria and Eddie began to brainstorm the screenplay for *The Trespasser.* Over the next month, said Gloria in her memoirs, they spent their days in her breakfast room writing the original story. Actually it was Goulding who wrote the script, with Gloria adding bits of action she would like to do. He was assisted by Broadway character actress Laura Hope Crews, best remembered today as Aunt Pittypat in *Gone with the Wind,* whom Gloria had contracted at $1,000 a week to help her with her diction and speech.

"*The Trespasser* was totally Eddie's idea," Gloria's last husband, William Dufty, confessed. "He realized that the key to her [Gloria's] transition in sound was to go back to her roots. So he wrote her character as a little secretary from Chicago because that's where she was from. She was an excellent mimic so when she puts on airs in the movie, that's the character and Gloria's personality coming together."[4]

The story of *The Trespasser* told of stenographer Marion Donnell (Gloria), whose lawyer boss is Hector Ferguson (Purnell Pratt). She elopes with wealthy scion Jack Merrick (Robert Ames), son of John Merrick Sr. (William Holden, unrelated to the *Sunset Boulevard* co-star), who induces Jack to annul the marriage for a society wedding. Later Marion, destitute and caring for her infant son, returns to Ferguson's office. Ferguson provides her and her young son (Wally Albright Jr.) with a luxurious home. When Ferguson dies he bequeaths Marion $500,000. She sends for Jack, but his father finds out and attempts to gain custody of his grandson because Jack has remarried. When Jack's wife Catherine (Kay Hammond) agrees to divorce him, Marion surrenders the boy to his father. Then Catherine dies, and Jack and Marion are reunited.

Kennedy sent a letter to Henri in France, dated March 13, informing him about the collapse of *Queen Kelly*. He told the marquis Gloria was so distraught after closing down the picture, her weight had dropped severely and she had checked herself into a hospital. After viewing the rushes Kennedy wrote Henri that after working ten days he found director Goulding, and a handful of others, hopelessly inept with dealing with the picture.

That summer of 1929 the Austrian-born American film director Josef von Sternberg was in Berlin preparing for his first German talkie, *Der Blaue Engel (The Blue Angel)*, starring the first Best Actor Oscar winner, Emil Jannings, just returned from Hollywood. For the pivotal role of the temptress Lola Lola, who drives Professor Unrath (Jannings) to moral and mental destruction in the film, von Sternberg considered Phyllis Haver, Louise Brooks, and Gloria for the role. After testing Leni Riefenstahl, he settled on the enigmatic Marlene Dietrich, and the rest, as they say, is history.

On her birthday, March 27, the United States government filed a $24,880.82 tax lien against Gloria, for unpaid taxes for 1924 ($6,042.30), 1925 ($8,583.47), and 1926 ($10,225.05). She was not at all concerned, as Kennedy's men were working on it. Besides, she just did not have the time to think about it. Three weeks after Goulding and Gloria had begun their work on writing *The Trespasser*, the script was done. But Eddie felt the mood had not been set. When Kennedy advised Goulding Gloria possessed a beautiful soprano voice, he and Elsie Janis composed "Love, Your Spell Is Everywhere" for her character to sing in the framework of the film.

Screen tests for a leading man included one made of a new Pathé contract player named Clark Gable, dressed in white tie and tails. Gable was overtly uncomfortable in such fine duds. He photographed badly, his large ears sticking out underneath his top hat, and Gloria saw no future whatsoever in movies for him. Long in the industry without success, Gable had been a dance extra in von Stroheim's *The Merry Widow* in 1925. He was later featured in Pathé's 1931 western *The Painted Desert*, creating a huge impact with female filmgoers. He then signed with MGM the same year where he became a major star. Robert Ames, who would enjoy moderate success in the 1930s while also at Metro, was subsequently cast in the role of Jack Merrick.

* * *

A useless attempt was made to revive *Queen Kelly* before Gloria started *The Trespasser*. In a new rewrite of the script, it was decided the African scenes would begin the story, with Kelly's aunt running a dance hall. Kelly would be sent to a convent in Germany, allowing the incorporation of the early scenes and newly filmed ones. Kelly would not marry old Jan, either, but consummate her love with Prince Wolfram. New directors were considered—Mickey Neilan, Allan Dwan, and Raoul Walsh—but Gloria now favored Goulding. New sets were constructed, including the convent dormitory, chapel, music room, and hallways, among others.

Cameras rolled once more from April 2 until April 9 on *Queen Kelly*. Under the direction of Paul L. Stein, filming both silent and sound versions at an additional cost of $200,000, the whole thing bogged down when it was realized some days later that Stein's scenes had nothing in common with those shot already. The sound quality was poor, and the new sequences did not match the quality of the old. Gloria was also unhappy with the ending, which called for a fade-out of Kelly with tears in her eyes trying to decide whether to be with the Prince or return to the convent. It also became obvious Gloria had lost interest in the project. Again *Queen Kelly* was shut down.

Henri received a telegram from Joe Kennedy on April 15:

LOOKS VERY MUCH LIKE NEW FINISH UNSATISFACTORY TO
GLORIA AND PICTURE LIKELY [WILL] BE SHELVED . . . LOOKING
FORWARD TO CONSTANCES ARRIVAL[5]

On the evening of May 19, 1929, a banquet was held for the Academy members in the Blossom Room of the Hollywood Roosevelt Hotel, hosted by Academy president Douglas Fairbanks and chairman William C. deMille. The Golden Statuette for Best Actress was handed to twenty-three-year-old Janet Gaynor for her trilogy of work. Gloria, so the audience was told, was "out of the city," hoping "with the utmost sincerity" that Gaynor would win.[6]

Gloria had become quite unpopular within the Hollywood community. In her own fashion, when she received word she had lost, she chose to remind in-

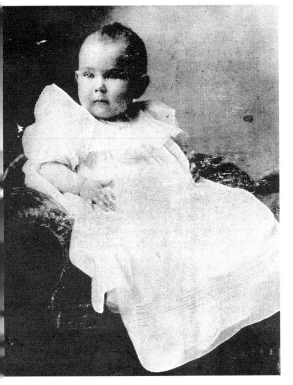

Gloria Josephine May Swanson, age nine months, 1900.

Ten-year-old Gloria sporting the mandatory large hat and bow, c. 1910.

With mother, Adelaide ("Addie"), at the Santa Fe train station in California, March 1928.

With father, Joseph Swanson, 1922.

At Essanay Studios, 1915.

Gloria as a bride in *Haystacks and Steeples*, Keystone, 1916.

At Keystone Studio, 1916.

With her first husband, Wallace Beery, 1916.

At Keystone Studio, 1917.

As a feature actress at Triangle Studio, 1917.
PHOTO BY WITZEL.

With Bobby Vernon and Keystone's Teddy, the Great Dane, Keystone, 1917.

Gloria greeting St. Louis Cardinal outfielder Jack Smith (left), with director Jack Conway (center) on the set of her first feature film, *You Can't Believe Everything*, Triangle, June 14, 1918.

With William Desmond in *Society for Sale*, Triangle, 1918.

With Ann Kroman in *Her Decision*, Triangle, 1918.

In *Station Content*, Triangle, 1918.

In *Secret Code*, Triangle, 1918.

With Tom Forman and Mae Giraci in DeMille's
For Better, For Worse, Paramount, 1919.

Gloria with Paramount hair stylist
Hattie Wilson Tabourne, c. 1920

As "The Lion's Bride" in DeMille's *Male and Female*, Paramount, 1919.

Herbert Somborn, Gloria's second husband, c. 1920.

The star in front of her Paramount dressing room, c. 1920.

With daughter, Gloria Swanson
Somborn, c. 1924.

TOP RIGHT: Milton Sills and
Gloria in *The Great Moment*,
Paramount, 1921.

MIDDLE: Wallace Reid, Gloria,
and Agnes Ayres in DeMille's
The Affairs of Anatol, Paramount, 1921.

On the set of *The
Affairs of Anatol*:
Cecil B. DeMille
(*seated*), Theodore
Kosloff, Gloria, Elliott
Dexter, Agnes Ayres,
Julia Faye, and
Wallace Reid
(*standing l to r*).

With Wallace Reid in *Don't Tell Everything,*
Paramount, 1921.

With Stuart Holmes in *Her Husband's
Trademark,* Paramount, 1921.

Gloria Glamour, 1921.

Madame Elinor Glyn, 1921.

With Rudolph Valentino (*top left*), Mme. Glyn, and director Sam Wood (*fourth and fifth, top right*) with cast and crew while filming *Beyond the Rocks*, Paramount, 1922.

With Rudolph Valentino in *Beyond the Rocks*.

With Rudolph Valentino, Mme. Glyn, and Sam Wood in gag photo early in the filming of *Beyond the Rocks*.

Marshall "Mickey" Neilan, c. 1922.

In *Prodigal Daughters*, Paramount, 1923.

ABOVE: In *Bluebeard's Eighth Wife*, Paramount, 1923.

LEFT: In *My American Wife*, Paramount, 1923.

With Rod LaRocque in *A Society Scandal*, Paramount, 1924.

Dressed as a boy in *The Humming Bird*, Paramount, 1924.

With Frank Morgan in *Manhandled*.

In *Manhandled*, Paramount, 1924.

As "Charlie Chaplin" with director Allan Dwan in *Manhandled*.

As "Charlie Chaplin" backstage at the Ziegfeld Theatre in New York for the ANTA Pantomime Benefit, May 1951.

As "Charlie Chaplin" on *The Carol Burnett Show*, 1973.

As "Charlie Chaplin" in *Sunset Boulevard*, Paramount, 1950.

In *Her Love Story*, Paramount, 1924.

Pola Negri, c. 1924.

Gloria *à la* Negri, c. 1924.

Posing as Peter Pan, 1924.

Departing onboard the *Berengaria*, bound for France to film *Madame Sans-Gêne*, September 3, 1924.

Gloria with Henri de La Bally, Marquis de la Falaise de La Coudraye, Paris, 1924.

A stunning portrait of Gloria as
Madame Sans-Gêne, 1924.

With Henri, her third husband, outside their
hotel in Paris on their wedding day, January 28,
1925.

With Warwick Ward and Charles De Roche in
Madame Sans-Gêne, Paramount, 1925.

Gloria and Henri arriving in New
York onboard their beloved *Paris*,
March 24, 1925.

Joseph Schenck (*left*) and Adolph Zukor (*right*) greet Gloria and Henri in New York, March 1925.

Mary Pickford, Douglas Fairbanks (*left*) and Joseph Schenck (*right*) greet Gloria and Henri in Los Angeles, April 25, 1925.

As the aged Countess Nadine in *The Coast of Folly*, Paramount, 1925.

dustry insiders that the awards business was like comparing apples and oranges. (*Sadie Thompson* cinematographer George Barnes lost as well, to Charles Rosher and Karl Struss for their work on *Sunrise: A Song of Two Humans*.) No one made much of that first ceremony at any rate, not knowing how long Mayer's idea would last.

After Cecil B. DeMille signed papers of separation from Pathé on April 18, he received $250,000 simply to disappear, leaving with the rights to *The King of Kings* and the first $500,000 gross for *The Godless Girl*, for which he would receive 40 percent thereafter. He then accepted another $200,000 as repayment for loans he had to make to produce his pictures for the studio.

With the constant starts and stops, no one really knew what to do with *Queen Kelly*. DeMille biographer Scott Eyman wrote, "Joe Kennedy had no particular interest in the movies beyond functioning as a quit-claim operator and sleeping with Gloria Swanson. But he had no shortage of gall."[7] In May, just a month after forcing DeMille out, Kennedy contacted the director to clean up the debacle of *Queen Kelly*. Possible projects were discussed. Business was business, as they say. DeMille could do nothing with *Queen Kelly*.

"Would you consider . . . directing Gloria in [a] picture to start as soon as possible? . . . Type picture similar to what you used to do with her," Kennedy wrote DeMille.[8] It is more than probable Gloria did not know about this correspondence. DeMille enthusiastically replied to Kennedy that he would do anything he could "in solving the Swanson problem." Suggesting she might star in either *The Cup* or *Silk*, directed by him and readied by Christmas, DeMille told Kennedy that for a million dollars "it would be fairly sure of two and one half million gross."[9] Negotiations apparently faltered at some point and Kennedy chose not to work with DeMille.

Instead, Goulding, working closely with Gloria from the start, began filming *The Trespasser* on June 3, after two weeks of tests and rehearsals. Shooting lasted nine hours each day, beginning usually at eleven in the morning, with a break for tea at four in the afternoon. Goulding literally invented techniques for shooting in sound. Sound cameras were in those days large and stationary. Because they made noise, they had to be wrapped in soundproofing materials, and thus were cocooned and outsized. Eddie devised ways the actors could talk into carefully concealed microphones placed throughout the set for *The Trespasser*, the photography was beautifully and tastefully handled by Gregg Toland, and three cameras were used at all times so that the actors could move from close-ups to medium shots to long shots, the action unimpaired.

Goulding gave a rare interview to the British *Picturegoer* magazine around this time, commenting on a particular sequence in the picture. "Gloria Swanson started in one room, walked into another, returned to the first room, crossed to her bedroom," he explained. "Each time, cameras picked her up. It was the longest actual non-stop scene ever taken."[10] Expressing pride in his work, Eddie had every reason to believe he would benefit professionally as well as financially from his revolutionary new techniques.

Still, it wasn't foolproof, and in the studio there were problems. Since the three bulky cameras could not move, the actors had to. This wasted a lot of film, but if one camera were to be shut off, the change in the level of electricity might affect another. Goulding was a stickler for time, and unlike von Stroheim, he watched the clock carefully. This challenged Gloria and the other actors to do their best, and in the process she lost weight and hovered near a nervous collapse. During the filming, exhaustion took its toll. Monte Westmore did the makeup on *The Trespasser,* and to save time he would make Gloria up at her home before she left for the studio. (She hated being seen anywhere without full makeup.) "Monte was a little afraid of Gloria because she was capable of changing moods right in the middle of a sentence—and often did," wrote his brother Frank.[11]

The Trespasser was completed on July 5 after twenty-one days of filming, coming in on time and under budget. From its start in Gloria's breakfast room until prints were made ready for distribution, the process took less than three months.

Goulding was paid a total of $45,000. According to an interoffice memo at Pathé, dated September 20, 1929, Gloria herself expected to earn $150,000 for *The Trespasser,* but that was raised to $175,000 after she said she helped create the screenplay. Budgeted at $654,604.11, *The Trespasser*'s costs were increased $25,000 to account for Gloria's salary increase, $48,369.03 for advertising and exploitation, and $341,792.80 for executive overhead, an ambiguous term meaning whatever the producers wanted it to, bringing the complete cost of the picture to $744,604.11. An additional executive overhead expense of $25,000 was added to the picture's budget on October 10, 1929, after the film's immense success.

After the filming Gloria advised the press she was traveling east. She would remain in New York for a few days before heading to France, to be with her husband, where she planned to stay for several months.

In actuality Kennedy had asked her to his new eleven-bedroom compound in Hyannis Port, Massachusetts, to spend a week with his family before her trip. He and Rose were also planning to sail to Europe. Derr had received an offer to premiere *The Trespasser* at the New Gallery Cinema on Regent Street in London in September, followed by scheduled openings in three other European capitals including Paris. In her memoirs, Gloria said she told Joe she would not sail on board the same ship as Rose, and did not mention visiting Hyannis Port.

Gloria departed Los Angeles by rail on July 17 and gave several interviews at stops along the way. As usual the children remained behind in Beverly Hills. She had not seen Virginia Bowker for some time, so when her train stopped in Chicago, Gloria invited Virginia to make the rest of the trip with her.

Arriving in New York on July 30, Gloria and Virginia checked into the Plaza and shopped in preparation for the voyage and the opening in London. That night there was a single preview of *The Trespasser,* and everyone who attended recognized it would be a hit. Gloria also traveled to Camden, New Jersey, and recorded the two songs from *The Trespasser,* "Love, Your Spell Is Everywhere" and Toselli's "Serenade," for the RCA record label. On the following day she flew up to Hyannis Port in a Sikorsky Curtiss amphibian plane and came to shore in a launch piloted by Joe himself.

A childhood friend of the Kennedy girls, Nancy Tenney Coleman, remembered Swanson's visit. "We didn't think of it as anything other than exciting, the big red Rolls and two dogs and the chauffeur jumping out," she recalled.[12] Rose welcomed Gloria as Joe's "closest and most important business client," exactly what he claimed she was.[13] Whether Rose knew the truth of her husband's relationship with Gloria at this point is uncertain. She treated Gloria as a sister. In fact, Joe publicly referred to Gloria as Rose's friend. "Was she a fool, or a saint," Gloria reflected. "Or just a better actress than I was?"[14]

For that week, the small seaside community followed Gloria's every move, even when she visited the garage clubhouse of Kathleen "Kick" Kennedy and her friends, decorated with movie posters and star photos. Gloria signed her name on the clubhouse wall, and the local press noted the event. (When Kick found out about her father's affair with Gloria, she did not remove the signature.

But she did become an avid fan of Constance Bennett.) Gloria's appearance at the Beach Club made front-page news in the community.

Joe could not wait to get Gloria alone. One afternoon, he finally had the opportunity, taking her out on the Kennedy yacht *Rose Elizabeth*. Once he anchored the craft in the bay, the two made love on the top deck. However, twelve-year-old son Jack had stowed away below, and upon catching his father and the actress having sex, he jumped off the side of the boat and began to swim for shore. "But Joe wasn't upset," Gloria recalled. "He just laughed, then he fished Jack out of the water. I was embarrassed, of course, and Jack was shaking, almost crying. He didn't really understand what we had been doing or how to react. Joe thought the whole episode was hilarious."[15]

After they returned from Europe a similar indiscretion occurred, when Gloria visited the other Kennedy home in Westchester County. She and Joe were in a heated embrace when suddenly they realized Jack was standing just feet away. "I automatically pushed myself away from Joe and tried to recoup," she said. "But Joe pulled me back to him and kissed me again, this time much more forcefully. He was doing it for Jack's benefit! I was ashamed, but here was Joe putting on a show for his little boy. Teaching him a lesson, perhaps. This time Jack just stood there with no emotion registering on his face at all, then wandered off as if nothing unusual had happened."[16] These displays of his father's infidelities made their impressions on the young Kennedy.[17]

Returning to Manhattan the day before sailing, Gloria and Virginia then boarded the *Olympic* shortly after midnight, August 10. Joe and Rose, with Joe's sister Margaret Burke, sailed on August 20 on board the *Ile de France*. The *Olympic* took Gloria and Virginia to Le Havre, and the *Ile de France* sailed to Southampton. The cost for Joe and Rose Kennedy to sail first class one-way on the luxurious, art deco French liner was $1,175, the bill charged to Gloria Productions.

In Gloria's memoirs she stated they all traveled to Europe together, when in fact they all traveled *back* from Europe together. She also completely left out the Paris opening and the dramatic events that occurred there.

When Gloria had settled in Paris, Kennedy cabled her on April 16 to advise her on the progress of *Queen Kelly*. Lance Heath, Gloria's publicist, had arrived in France a couple of days before her and arranged for waiting photographers to document her reunion with Henri. Settling in at the Plaza Athenée, once Virginia left them alone, both Gloria and Henri felt the strain of their shaky relationship. The Kennedys landed in London on August 31, and on September 3 Henri, Gloria, and Virginia crossed the channel to meet them. On September 5 Gloria sang on BBC Radio, and the broadcast was relayed to America.

On September 9, 1929, *The Trespasser* received its world premiere in London. Crowds were so large that Gloria feared somewhat irrationally they would break the windows of their slow-moving limo as it neared the theater and shards of glass would scar her face. Joe had Rose exit the car to clear a path for his paramour. Spectators asked Mrs. Kennedy who she was. The papers reported eight bobbies were swept off their feet by the masses gathered outside the theater. (Gloria later told the press it was seventy-five bobbies, and that it was *she* who was swept up by the crowd and carried into the theater, her dress being ripped in the process.)

"I will see her if I am killed for it," declared one stalwart female fan. Gloria, wearing a chinchilla wrap trimmed in blue, was heard to comment upon encountering the crowd, "I thought this only happened in America."[18]

The London *Daily Mail* critic wrote that the new medium of sound "brings us a more accomplished actress than we knew in the old days . . . Her performance can only be described as a personal triumph."[19] In *Variety*'s very first review from abroad for an American-made motion picture, reporter Frank Tilley, "Frat," commented, "On technical advance and story value, rated about the best talker seen here yet . . . It puts Gloria Swanson into the type of part in which she is seen acting, which her last two features have not done . . . Speaking and singing, she is okay, with a soft and clear diction which does not grate and with a singing voice of the kind audiences fall for . . . Framed to carry a sob at the end of every sequence and with a luscious part for Swanson to bring tears with, 'Trespasser' made a terrific hit at the premiere and will play all the houses wired in this country and those still to be wired."[20]

Yet another London film critic raved about Gloria, "Her first talking picture is not only a success in itself, and strangely satisfying since the use of words now enriches the hitherto purely pictorial drama, but a distinct score for herself as producer and Mr. Goulding as her director."[21] Gloria's singing voice was praised for its rich natural timbre, coupled with her precise, crisp diction.

In the film, when she sat down at the piano and began singing the haunting "Love, Your Spell Is Everywhere" (written by Goulding and Janis to fit her range), audiences were captivated.

Joe financed *The Trespasser,* though he dismissed it as a small and insignificant effort. The failure of *Queen Kelly* still festered in him. When Gloria and Goulding started reaping generous reviews and acclaim, Joe noticed it was they and not he who were praised. It galled him. Kennedy could not see that he was incapable of becoming a successful movie mogul. Lacking any artistic sensibility, he was simply out of his element.

Traveling to Paris on September 11, Joe and Henri talked business while the women enjoyed shopping at the leading couturiers of the day, including Lucien Lelong. Rose wrote in her memoirs that she developed an interest in fashion during this trip, as she watched Gloria draped and gowned in magnificent creations. She also liked Henri, and wrote, "Although 'Hank' (as his Hollywood friends called him) was very attractive, charming, witty, and [a] delightful man, a perfect consort for Gloria, he knew little about business, finance, or the complexities of film production."[22] Shopping done, and while waiting for their fittings, the four traveled to Deauville for a brief holiday before returning for the Paris opening.

Rose wrote, "At this point, unexpectedly, Gloria told Hank . . . and Joe, and all of us, that she was suing for divorce immediately and Hank could not escort her or be seen with her at the opening night in Paris—just a few evenings away— or any other opening."[23] She had discovered Henri's affair with Constance Bennett. Gloria had received a cable in their Paris suite, addressed to the feminine "Marquise" instead of the masculine "Marquis." It was a love letter from Constance in Hollywood. She was planning to come to France in a couple of weeks to finalize her own divorce. Gloria exploded in rage.

"When emotions had cooled enough, we began to take stock," Rose continued. "Joe . . . proposed that Hank and Gloria act out the relationship they had before the trouble began. Until the premieres were finished they were to appear in public as a devoted, happy, and glamorous couple. And that's what happened. Gloria of course was a wonderful actress, and Hank showed that he was quite an actor himself."[24] A lot of money was involved, and for long hours the party, including several of Joe's business associates, sat around and debated how best to handle the situation.

Gloria now had to live with a sham of a marriage, along with her surreal affair with Joe Kennedy. The Paris opening of *The Trespasser* was held on September 28. But instead of attending it as planned, Gloria and Virginia, Joe and Rose, and Joe's sister Margaret all departed from Le Havre on board the *Ile de France* bound for New York on September 18. Henri alone remained in Europe.

On board ship during the crossing, whenever Joe and Gloria appeared together, rumors of them having an affair spread. Rose would always say, "Poor Gloria," perhaps knowing her husband better than many thought. After arriving in New York on September 24, Gloria and her ten steamer trunks were escorted to the Plaza Hotel by Kennedy's aide Ted O'Leary. Rose journeyed up to the Kennedy home in Bronxville, and Joe checked into the Waldorf-Astoria Hotel to attend to Pathé business. He was thrilled over the success of *The Trespasser,* but he also continued to dismiss the film.

Gloria made an NBC radio broadcast on October 10, singing the songs from *The Trespasser.*[25] She then held a press conference in her suite. With the Victrola playing her records in the background, Gloria, garbed stylishly in black, was asked her opinion of the talkies. "I love the talking pictures," she replied. "I would like to make more. I would do Shakespeare in the films but would not modernize him." Did she take voice lessons? "No, I do not take voice culture lessons. I was once in musical comedy, you know [exaggerating her amateur hijinks]. Talking pictures are much harder than the silent kind. I shall make 'Queen Kelly' over again when I return to the coast. Not with von Stroheim."[26] Did she like being interviewed? "Well, we actresses feel that newspaper men always think of us as dull. But I really enjoy it." Did she ever think her public ever tired of her? "What, again? I certainly hope not." Then a question she could sink her teeth into: "What about musical productions?" "Of course I shall make one to be shown on an enlarged screen in color. I'll tell you a funny thing. In London when those crowds were hovering at the entrance of the theater where my picture was having its premiere, the manager of the cinema came to me and apologized for the great crowds. 'It has never happened before, I assure you, Miss Swanson,' he told me. And inside after the picture was over and they applauded long and loud, he came to me again and said, 'I am distressed at the noise, my dear Madam; I am really sorry.'"[27]

Continuing along that vein, Gloria spoke about making *The Trespasser:* "Films are such tiring work. You make a series of sequences and then you break them up and make insertions. Cutting is difficult, especially with a talking picture. I want to do everything myself . . . And on the sound stages. The hot electrical lights. Have you ever been in an electrical cabinet bath? Well, that's what it's like. All the costumes had to be made in duplicate because one was always spoiled in a short while. And the music and the photography and everything."[28] What a strenuous way to earn $8,000 a day!

On October 1, *Variety* reported a rift in the de la Falaise marriage. As understood from Paris, Gloria and Henri were "at odds . . . according to stories going around here." The report continued by stating the differences "came up before [Swanson's] sailing, aggravated by a telegram to the marquis from another celeb who is not named in the gossip, which peeved Gloria."[29] To save face, Kennedy was still writing Henri long newsy letters. On October 2, he sent one that read in part, "*Variety* today carries an article that there is a rift between you and Gloria. Can't imagine where they got this information, unless somebody in Paris talked."[30]

Prolific Broadway producer A. H. White had been after Gloria for some time to star in a stage production under his management. In fact, playwright Eugene Walter had begun writing a script. Unfortunately, Gloria was under contract with Kennedy for three more pictures and could not take the time to make her legit stage debut. However, when she returned to California she attended a performance of *Her Man,* the most recent play by Walter, at the Los Angeles Theater on November 10. She was invited as well to audition for legendary theatrical impresario Florenz Ziegfeld.

Wrote Norbert Lusk in the *Los Angeles Times,* "Of course, nothing will come of Florenz Ziegfeld's offer to star her in 'Ming Toy,' the musical version of Fay Bainter's old favorite 'East Is West.' Miss Swanson's chronic stage fright stands in the way. But Ziegfeld is understood to have made the offer in good faith after he heard her sing, and now that her voice has been heard by the public, no one wonders why."[31]

The stock market crashed on Black Thursday, October 31, with over $10 billion lost in one day. For the most part Kennedy and Gloria came out of it unscathed. On Friday, November 1, *The Trespasser* premiered in the United States at the Rialto Theater in New York. An agreement was arranged with Irving Berlin's music publishing house to produce copies of the "Love, Your Spell Is

Everywhere" sheet music, which were distributed about Times Square prior to the opening, as massive crowds surrounded the theater at Forty-Second Street and Seventh Avenue. Even though projectionists faltered in monitoring the sound levels and at times voices on the screen were muffled, the critics fell over themselves with praise.

Mordaunt Hall of *The New York Times* led them off: "Miss Swanson gives an even better performance than she did in 'Sadie Thompson,' for she is more of an actress than ever, speaking her lines naturally and without unnecessary pantomimic gestures. Her work is restrained, even in the emotional scenes . . . It is, as a matter of fact, no wonder London was bowled over by her sensitive interpretation." Later that month, he added, "Miss Swanson's singing, provided it meets with the proper sound reproduction in the theaters, is clear and appealing. It is charming to hear her humming and chanting as she glides from one corner to another of her apartment. Miss Swanson's speech is highly pleasing. She has an agreeable, unaffected style of talking and is mistress of the character she is acting."[32]

In his review, "Sime" Silverman, founder, editor, and publisher of *Variety,* raved, "Gloria Swanson is going to paralyze the picture goers with her singing voice. She sings like a prima [donna]. No wonder the Jos. P. Kennedy bunch decided it would be necessary for Miss Swanson's voice to go on the phonograph discs . . . Give Miss Swanson and her companion players all of the acknowledgment they should have, but a huge hunk must go to Goulding, the director and author."[33] Years later, Richard Barrios, in his exquisite book on early sound musicals, *A Song in the Dark,* pronounced Gloria had made "the most spectacular sound debut of any silent favorite except the white-hot Garbo."[34]

The Trespasser was a monstrous hit, bringing in $67,000 at the Rialto alone, where some 88,000 moviegoers saw it during its one-week run. Seen today, Gloria's performance is truly stunning. At the age of thirty, she never looked so appealing, and she radiates confidence throughout. Her talkie debut remains one of her most solid performances.

When Kennedy returned home with Rose to their children, John F. "Honey Fitz" Fitzgerald took Joe aside and expressed outrage over his illicit affair with Gloria. (Tellingly, Rose's own mother Mary Josephine, "Josie," had told her years before that "all men were alike, and Joe Kennedy was no different."[35] Rose's niece

Geraldine Hammon recalled overhearing a heated argument between Honey Fitz and Joe that summer. "Honey Fitz had confronted his son-in-law and told him that unless he stopped the affair with his movie star, he would tell Rose," wrote one biographer. "Undaunted, Joe threatened in turn that if Honey Fitz did tell his daughter, Joe would, goddammit, divorce Rose and marry Gloria Swanson."[36] The portly and equally faithless Honey Fitz himself had been involved years before with a showgirl, whom he called Toodles (Josie referred to her as "the wench"), a well-known affair most folks in polite society chose to ignore.

Even the future president of the United States Franklin Delano Roosevelt, himself involved in an affair with his aide Marguerite (Missy) Le Hand, suggested to Kennedy he give Gloria up. Roosevelt's son Elliott told the *New York Times* in 1973, "Father had urged the founding father of the Kennedy clan to end his long-term relationship with actress Gloria Swanson. Joe replied that he would be willing 'only if you give up Missy Le Hand.'"[37]

Perhaps Kennedy actually did try to end the affair. In Gloria's memoirs she details a questionable encounter that occurred upon her arrival back in New York. Shortly before her departure for the West Coast, Ted O'Leary called her at the Plaza and said Joe had arranged a meeting at another hotel for late in the afternoon. The man she was to meet was named O'Connell, a friend of Kennedy's. When O'Leary delivered Gloria to the hotel suite, they were greeted at the door by a young man wearing a clerical collar, who said, "His Eminence will be with you in a moment."[38] Avoiding Gloria's startled gaze, O'Leary looked uncomfortable and began to fidget. When "His Eminence" entered the room, he was introduced as Cardinal William Henry O'Connell of Boston, who had officiated at the marriage of Joe and Rose in 1914. O'Leary was excused, and Gloria and O'Connell sat down to talk.

What the cardinal said shocked Gloria. After preliminary conversation, His Eminence told her he wanted to talk about her relationship with Kennedy. She advised him they had a business partnership, to which O'Connell replied he wanted to discuss their personal relationship. Gloria, offended, suggested he address that issue with Joe. Standing up before her, the cardinal strongly advised Gloria to stop seeing Kennedy, as every time she did she opened an opportunity for Kennedy to sin.[39]

Stunned into anger, Gloria suggested that if Joe had revealed his affair in confession, the cardinal was overstepping his bounds in discussing it with her. He told her Joe had been denied divorce, after having discussed permission to live apart from Rose and the family. By being seen with him, Gloria was told, she was exposing Kennedy to scandal. Continued O'Connell, "As a Catholic, there is no way Joseph Kennedy can be at peace with his faith and continue his relationship with you. Please consider that very carefully."[40] Yet according to one Rose Kennedy biographer, "Joe was too greedy, too frightened of losing even a portion of his wealth, to consider divorce even if he had been a Protestant."[41]

When Gloria reached the lobby of the hotel, she demanded to know why O'Leary had not told her in advance who she was meeting. He replied that she would have refused to go and that he was under orders—but not from Joe; the cardinal had requested the meeting. If Swanson's story is true, perhaps the cardinal's source was actually Rose herself. "To save her marriage, it would not have been out of character for a devout Catholic woman of Rose's generation and upbringing to seek intercession, through her father or on her own, of the archbishop and family friend who fifteen years earlier had pronounced Joe and her man and wife," wrote biographer Axel Madsen.[42]

However, historian Doris Kearns Goodwin claims there are no records in the Boston Archdiocese archives that prove Cardinal O'Connell was in New York at that time, and adds that "the cardinal was a proud and imperious man who held himself aloof from the everyday problems of his parishioners—Joe would leave a substantial legacy to the archdiocese."[43] Most Kennedy biographers tend not to believe Gloria's account of meeting the cardinal. "It is doubtful that Joe would have gone to the Church to ask that he, Joseph P. Kennedy, honored Catholic layman and father of eight children, be allowed to become Gloria's fourth husband," wrote biographer Laurence Leamer.[44]

Years later, in July 1939, at the fortieth birthday party of a close embassy aide in London, Harvey Klemmer, Joe Kennedy was heard to remark, "Forty is a dangerous age. Look out, boy. Don't get in trouble. When I was forty, I went overboard for a certain lady in Hollywood of which you may have heard. It ruined my business. It ruined my health, and it damn near ruined my marriage."[45]

Throughout their three-year relationship Gloria never talked passionately or romantically about Kennedy. She wrote he was sexually aroused by her, he was excited by her success, and he wanted to have a child with her. But *never* did she write about him loving her or of her having a deep heartfelt passion for him. It was a relationship of convenience. And tellingly so, for why would she even allow the lecherous Kennedy, toward the end of their affair, to ask her if she would consider introducing his two oldest boys, fourteen-year-old Joe Jr. and twelve-year-old John, "Jack," to the pleasures of sex. "By then I can't say I was very surprised at anything Mr. Kennedy had to tell me," she said.[46]

Gloria left for the West Coast the day after the New York opening of *The Trespasser,* planning to spend twenty-four hours in Chicago with her mother. She attended the Chicago opening of *The Trespasser* on November 7, which was a huge success, and spoke from the stage of the theater. In an interview with writer Norbert Lusk, Gloria commented about her success in the film, "Fortunate, wasn't it, that in London the critics didn't take exception to the American accent in 'The Trespasser'? They accepted my speech as easily as if it were British and not Chicagoese toned down. I credit that to Edmund Goulding's direction, and, of course, Laura Hope Crews's coaching. But it was surprising."[47] She arrived in Los Angeles the second week of November.

The West Coast premiere of *The Trespasser* at the United Artists Theater had already been held on November 6. Again the critics were unanimous in their praise. The *Los Angeles Times* proclaimed, "It's a new Gloria Swanson you see and hear . . . with all the fire . . . the drama of the Gloria you love . . . You are amazed at her acting and stunned by the power of her portrayal . . . enchanted with the golden tones of her lovely voice . . . in this, the greatest of all talking pictures."[48] One film magazine raved, "Hats, and also gaiters, off to Gloria Swanson! After more than a year of heartbreak fighting the talking jinx, she has not only beaten it, but sat on its neck and made it say 'Uncle!' In *The Trespasser* her soft and vibrant voice and smooth and finished acting establish her as a dangerous competitor for screen honors of the future."[49]

Edwin Schallert of the *Los Angeles Times* wrote, "Yet another popular star achieves her transition from the silent to the talkies, and this time the march may be justly called triumphal. Gloria Swanson, in her first audible expedition, 'The Trespasser,' is an actress of both appeal and power. She will perhaps be even a greater success than she was as a personality and a player in the mute cinema . . . Gloria evinces a rare command over the feelings of her public."[50] By the end of the year, *The Trespasser* had grossed $562,886.09. A huge financial success, it would eventually reap over $1.2 million in U.S. rentals alone, allowing Gloria to repay the costs of *Queen Kelly* and break even.[51]

Gloria was advised on November 19 that her UA distribution contracts for *The Love of Sunya*, *Sadie Thompson*, and *The Trespasser* had now been canceled, allowing her one thousand shares of preferred UA stock to be available at her disposal. Her debts cleared, she still maintained a UA contract as of November 11 that yielded her $1,200 a week, escalating to $2,000 in six months.

After the success of *The Trespasser*, Kennedy was more determined than ever to rescue *Queen Kelly*. Filming resumed on December 2, 1929, under the direction of Richard Boleslavsky, contracted November 6, with a revised script by Laura Hope Crews. Kennedy, who told the press the picture just needed "a couple of dialogue sequences,"[52] had hired Vincent Youmans to deliver songs for Gloria to sing in it. Additional sets were constructed, and the cast was called back. Gloria agreed to accept as her salary the $50,000 that had already been paid to her for the original shooting. Walter Byron (his own salary raised from $300 to $800 a week) was loaned from Samuel Goldwyn as of November 10, and Seena Owens, who had remained on half salary since filming halted, was also available. New cast members included David Torrence, who portrayed a priest, and Sarah Padden, who played Mother Superior.

On December 4 voice tests were made under the direction of Dr. L. E. Clark, and five days later Gloria was filmed in dialogue with the chapel choir singing "Ave Maria." Optimism ran high, and the first rushes looked promising. The following day dialogue sequences along the road and in the dormitory were filmed. However, it soon became apparent that Boleslavsky's work paled in comparison with the artistic images von Stroheim had made. With a total of twelve minutes and forty-two seconds of sound on film, Boleslavsky still could possibly have finished *Queen Kelly* by the end of the nineteen-day shooting schedule. But, for whatever reasons, it was halted again.

After three days of starts and stops, Joe sent another telegram to Henri in Paris in December telling him that he was going to New York with the intention of asking Franz Lehar to compose a waltz for *Queen Kelly*, which would now become a musical operetta.[53] His effort went unacknowledged.

Determined not to be defeated, Joe sent Henri to Vienna to convince Lehar, who wrote the music for *The Merry Widow,* to compose "The Queen Kelly Waltz," which the composer did for $60,000. On January 6, 1930, from Berlin, it was announced Lehar would possibly travel to Hollywood to compose additional music for *Queen Kelly.* He did not. By then it was too late.

DeMille, encouraged by Mayer's enthusiasm for sound musicals, finally came through with an offer for Gloria in a cable he sent Kennedy on December 5 regarding his upcoming MGM film *Madam Satan:*

> THE PART OF MADAM SATAN IS PERHAPS THE BEST WOMAN'S PART THAT HAS EVER COME UNDER MY DIRECTION. IT IS THE TYPE OF STORY I USED TO MAKE WITH GLORIA, BUT DONE WITH SOME LIGHT MUSIC STOP I AM SPENDING ONE MILLION DOLLARS ON THE PRODUCTION AND IT IS ALL CENTERED AROUND THE ONE CHARACTER WHICH HAS THE BRILLIANCE AND DASH THAT SHE RESPONDS TO SO SPLENDIDLY AND NEEDS SO MUCH AT THIS PRESENT TIME STOP I SUGGEST YOU ADVISE ME BY WIRE OR PHONE WHAT THE FINANCIAL REQUIREMENTS WOULD BE[54]

DeMille apparently spoke with Gloria about the idea of reteaming, and she passed the word on to Kennedy. On December 29 Joe sent DeMille a telegram to advise the director that Gloria was still under contract with United Artists for three more pictures and that she should be finished with *Queen Kelly* by the end of February. However, Kennedy agreed with DeMille that the film would be a great idea and a tremendous boost to Gloria's career, and said he would work on it with her, thus building DeMille's enthusiasm for the project. Two days later, Joe killed it. Gloria did not make *Madam Satan.*

Kennedy's response regarding Gloria's participation in *Madam Satan,* dated December 31, was that "the money she might get out of picture would be so small in proportion to amount she could possibly get out of one made by herself I question whether it would be possible to get together on any terms."[55] Unfortunately for DeMille, *Madam Satan,* a rare musical comedy/drama/disaster film, the second of his three-picture MGM output, would come a cropper—a box-office disaster and one of the few times DeMille would listen to the advice of others in developing a film project.

Kennedy offered a $3,000-per-week contract to Goulding effective immediately until March 1930 if he would turn *Queen Kelly* into an operetta. Goulding was still smarting after being given his original contract to sign when in the middle of directing a scene. As a result, he didn't read it, and in effect he signed away to Kennedy and Gloria the rights for "Love, Your Spell Is Everywhere," which had become a huge popular success. Now Kennedy wanted him to rescue *Queen Kelly*. When Goulding adamantly refused the hopeless task, Kennedy was furious.

Observant actress Louise Brooks once wrote, "I watched Queen Swanson abuse Allan Dwan, her director, on the set, abuse Hank de la Falaise, her husband, at the dinner table, and abuse her secretary in her drawing room, so I was particularly anxious to learn what kind of abuse she would fire at Edmund Goulding."[56]

Pioneering female lawyer Fanny Holtzmann was asked by Goulding, one of her earliest clients, to approach Kennedy and iron out his financial share of profits from *The Trespasser,* now that it was a hit. Kennedy told her that he owed Goulding nothing. "I paid him a thousand a week while he was working; I can show you the vouchers!"

"But that was just expense money, Joe!" Fanny protested. "Something to tide him over. After all, Eddie provided you with a great story. And he put the whole project together. Why, he gets more money for that for—"

"Listen, I did the bum a favor," said Kennedy. "He was on the skids in Hollywood for running out on MGM. No other studio would touch him. I gave him a chance to get back on the screen."[57]

"I can't believe my ears, Joe," Holtzmann replied, stunned. "Eddie had a deal with you, a clear verbal contract. You were partners."

"'What contract?' Kennedy asked, with what one writer called "a steely smile."[58]

Kennedy then told Goulding when they met in person, "You have that Jew girl go after me and I guarantee you'll never be on a screen again. I'll tell a federal jury about some of those wild Goulding weekends and you'll be deported for moral turpitude."[59] For Kennedy to make that kind of statement indicates he indeed held a prejudice against the homosexual Goulding. His ruthlessness toward the man who salvaged his studio and his lover's career was deplorable.

"Gloria was peevish because I did not think it worth the cost to remake or repair *Queen Kelly*," Goulding said. "She had a big hit on her hands [with *The Trespasser*] and became generally hotsy-totsy."[60] Goulding even wrote a new story for her, which she showed little enthusiasm for. Gloria's nondefense of him during this period clearly showed her allegiance to Kennedy.

As a film producer, Kennedy was still an outsider in Hollywood, one apparently without the foresight, taste, or class to go farther in the business. When Pathé announced Goulding would not complete his work on *Queen Kelly* because he didn't wish to have "his individuality impaired," Goulding said to himself, "To hell with it,"[61] and contracted with Paramount, where in short order studio head Adolph Zukor gave him creative control.

With a total of twelve sound sequences filmed for *Queen Kelly,* there were still talking scenes in the Queen's study to be shot, Kelly's speech during the fire sequence, the Queen's speech during the whip lashing, a lengthy talking section at the tavern, and sound and talking sequences at the barracks, plus sound confrontations at the palace gate and on the street. Within three weeks Gloria could have salvaged *Queen Kelly* and made it into a partial success. Instead, the project died again. Wrote von Stroheim's biographer, "Unfortunately, those around Swanson had their own interests rather than hers at heart."[62]

By the Christmas holidays, Kennedy was back east with his family, and Rose took off by herself for Palm Beach. Both Joseph and little Gloria suffered strep throat, and Joseph had to be hospitalized; Gloria was embarrassed when several gifts arrived for the children from the Kennedys. She quickly ordered a puff billiards game sent to the Kennedy children, but her New York secretary cabled that she simply could not locate one in the city. Nevertheless, gifts were found and sent in Gloria's name. Her professional presents to friends and colleagues that season and for all the United Artists employees were gold pencils.

On Christmas Day, Gloria attended a party given by John Gilbert and his wife Ina Claire. Anita Loos and Cecil Beaton were also present. "It was a dull affair," wrote one biographer, "until someone knocked an aquarium into Gloria Swanson's lap. Beaton was thrilled; there was something almost surreal about a devilfish flapping about in Swanson's crotch."[63]

Henri wrote his wife that he thought he would stay in Europe during the coming year. That month, Constance Bennett divorced Philip Plant; she was awarded $25,000 and granted $700 a month support for life. With Joe on the East Coast and Henri in Europe, the holiday season proved to be depressingly gloomy for Gloria. The United States was entering the Great Depression, and she had no film projects ready for her. Over the next decade her career would spiral downward, and her personal life would become even more unsettling.

17

The Talkies

United Artists was a growing concern. As 1930 began, its roster included such performers as Charles Chaplin, Mary Pickford, Douglas Fairbanks, Lillian Gish, Ronald Colman, Eddie Cantor, Fanny Brice, Norma Talmadge, Conrad Nagel, Jeanette MacDonald, and Al Jolson. D. W. Griffith, Henry King, Irving Berlin, Rudolf Friml, Arthur Hammerstein, George M. Cohan, Sydney Franklin, Stephen Vincent Benét, Howard Hughes, Florenz Ziegfeld, and Samuel Goldwyn contributed on the other side of the camera.

Joe Kennedy wanted to be a major player in this milieu. Still attempting to salvage *Queen Kelly,* in December he accepted a new screen treatment for the film by Richard Boleslavsky, which dramatically changed the plot. It was decided that Sam Wood, now at MGM, would direct new scenes. MGM's Irving Thalberg agreed to allow Wood to work at Pathé in April if Gloria would come over to MGM for a film. Kennedy demanded $300,000 for her services. Nothing more was heard from Metro, so Kennedy chose Allan Dwan to resurrect *Queen Kelly.* Dwan replied he couldn't figure out if it was the story of a nun who becomes a whore, or a whore who becomes a nun. Either way, he thought it smelled.[1]

Now signed to the publicity firm of former humorist Ray Rice, a George Ade colleague, Gloria was eager to return to work. She was given a story submission by H. Taylor in early January entitled *The Littlest Rebel* (not the 1934 Shirley Temple vehicle of the same name). Nothing came of it. Then Kennedy gave her the script, bound in leather and hand delivered to her door, of *Purple and Fine Linen,* a musical comedy, having brought in Vincent Youmans to provide songs for the picture.

Gloria and Virginia Bowker, who was staying with her on Crescent Drive, eagerly began to read the screenplay and were disgusted. Scripted by James Gleason and James Seymour, and based on a story by Josephine Lovett (who wrote MGM's *Our Dancing Daughters* that year), *Purple and Fine Linen* told the story of recently widowed Tamarind "Tam" Brooks (Gloria), a young woman whose wealthy, much older husband has recently died. Sailing for Europe to experience life, she encounters various amorous suitors including lawyer Gerry Morgan (Owen Moore). Tam flirts with various men, but after numerous romantic interludes she finds it is Gerry who loves her. Pretty lame stuff, outdated, and completely worthless fare.

Gloria lost a night's sleep after reading it. Wrote biographer Axel Madsen, "[Kennedy] had no imagination and, worse, he had no knack for picking people who did. The point of making movies was not to defeat expectations but to outdo them." She sent the script to her trusted Allan Dwan for his opinion, and it was quick in coming. "It stinks," he replied in his customary fashion. When they met the next day in Gloria's studio bungalow, Dwan let Kennedy know what he thought of Lovett's "epic." He told Kennedy not to buy it. "It's already bought," Joe snapped. "I commissioned it."[2] The picture was already listed on Pathé's schedule and set to begin shooting in August, to be produced by Gloria Swanson Productions for United Artists.

Kennedy, however, did insist on a new title. Gloria invited several Hollywood literary sorts, including S. N. Behrman, Charles MacArthur, Sidney Howard, Elmer Rice, and Frances Marion (all Sam Goldwyn's main writers), to dinner, where they discussed the project and brainstormed a new title. As Gloria read the script aloud, one writer exclaimed, "What a widow!" Joe was galvanized. "Find out who said that and give him a Cadillac. I mean it."[3] Joe had his title. According to various accounts, Gloria's primarily, Pulitzer Prize–winning dramatist (for his play *They Knew What They Wanted*) Howard was awarded the car. (Interestingly, nowhere in the company records is there a charge for this expense.)[4]

Gloria caved in to Joe's desire to make *What a Widow!* Gloria later observed that Joseph Kennedy was a poster child of a man possessing ambition and intelligence, but little innate ability or artistry, thus echoing the opinions of others in Hollywood.⁵ This about the man she was sleeping with and allowing to control her career.

At the same time, Gloria received a not too unexpected letter from Henri, telling her their marriage was over:

> *Gloria, darling. We have come to it . . . that which should never, never have happened . . . has come to be!*
>
> *If you have kept some of my old letters, you may read them. Their only fault is that they did not, could not, express half of what I felt for you. That kind of feeling never dies, Gloria, but sometimes it is better to pretend to forget about it.*
>
> *I am going to seal this letter without reading it, because if I did I wouldn't send it—and I must.*
>
> *Good-bye, darling—it's all, all over now.*⁶

Gloria commented that it was so like Henri not to mention Joe Kennedy. Not at all sentimental, in her memoirs she then segues immediately into discussing *What a Widow!*

Constance Bennett arrived in New York on January 29 on board the German liner *Bremen*. The awaiting press asked about her alleged affair with Henri, who was observed on numerous nights out with her in Paris. When pressed, Henri said he had simply spoken several times with Bennett about songs for her new picture. (Bennett could not sing.) When she arrived by train in California on February 5, she said she was preparing for her new picture, *Lipstick*. The press was relentless, aware that she had been on several transatlantic telephone calls with Henri since her arrival in New York. When asked again about their alleged romance, she said it was "too ridiculous to even discuss," meaning obviously she had been found out. "That is all I've got to say," Bennett said, ending the conversation.⁷

Soon after, Gloria ran into Constance at Joe's Rodeo Drive house. When she entered the foyer Bennett was leaning against the stairway banister smoking a cigarette. Good timing? Gloria asked if she was staying for supper and excused herself to the library, not waiting for an answer. When Joe appeared nervous as a schoolboy, Gloria asked him what that Bennett woman was doing at his house, and his silly reply was, "She couldn't hook the boss, so she settled for one of the boys."[8] He just didn't tell Gloria that "one of the boys" was her Henri.

Gloria and Constance never were fans of each other. Wrote one Kennedy biographer, "Gloria's preeminence was not about to be seriously challenged. Constance might have quietly had the Marquis on a string [in Europe], but Gloria had the head of the studio and . . . he was in residence in California."[9]

When *What a Widow!* commenced production, Ian Keith was cast as Victor, but was soon dismissed. He photographed younger than Gloria. "This actress never surrounds herself with youths," wrote one columnist. "She wisely selects men of a vintage to render her juvenile by comparison. It's one of the cleverest moves made in Hollywood today."[10] Robert Montgomery was then considered, but his tests proved the same as Keith's. The venerable Lew Cody stepped into the role.

When six young men were requested for bit parts as Tamarind's suitors, Sam Wood sent over twenty-four-year-old Joel McCrea for consideration. Gloria liked what she saw; he was eye candy. She had actually been aware of the 6'3" hunk of beefcake as far back as October 1928, when Sam Wood first brought him to her attention.

Born Joel Albert McCrea in 1905, he had played numerous bit parts, including one in DeMille's first talkie, *Dynamite,* in 1929, before landing the lead in Pathé's *The Silver Horde* (1930) with Evelyn Brent and Blanche Sweet. Fox star Will Rogers liked the promising fellow and urged him to sign with Pathé. At some point before the 1930 casting call for *What a Widow!* Gloria and McCrea began an affair. She gifted him with a copy of her mandatory "aphrodisiac," Kahlil Gibran's *The Prophet.* Though she felt McCrea could never equal her in sophistication or intelligence, he was nevertheless good in bed, and for the time being that was all that mattered. On his part, after spending an evening with the enchanting Swanson reading "The Wind Bloweth" together,[11] McCrea fell hopelessly in love.

Gloria cast a spell over the young actor, and in his letters held in her archive in Texas they show he is tender, romantic, and terribly heartsick. There is a glowing decency about McCrea that comes through in this correspondence. He was full of charm, and yet touchingly, completely malleable. His last existing letter to her is telling. After he writes of his desperate love for her, and tells

Gloria God would never forgive her if she stopped seeing him, he then closes by promising her he would forever be her lover.[12]

Neither Gloria nor McCrea ever mentioned their affair in interviews. Though Gloria was still carrying on the charade of marriage with Henri she was also having interludes with other men, among them writer-producer Gene Markey (who in 1932 would marry Constance Bennett's sister Joan).

It is truly amazing how Gloria managed to fit McCrea into her busy amours. This affair was everything to young McCrea, but it was not worth the price of ink to Gloria in her "tell all" memoirs. Her only comment about the smitten young actor was that he was attractive and talented.[13]

In fact, Gloria did not have her boyish lover cast in *What a Widow!* after she discovered Constance Bennett wanted him professionally and personally as well. Bennett's *Sin Takes a Holiday* began filming at Pathé the same day as did *What a Widow!* In Bennett's following two pictures, *Born to Love* and *The Common Law* (both directed by Paul L. Stein for Pathé in 1931), McCrea was Constance's leading man.

Filming of *What a Widow!* was not without its difficulties. Director Dwan was from another era of filmmaking, and in *What a Widow!* the cast struggled with the required spontaneity and bouncy humor. Actor Owen Moore, Mary Pickford's first husband, was not well at the time. He was an alcoholic, as was Gloria's other co-star Lew Cody, in real and reel life. Neither man could remember his lines.

In the midst of *What a Widow!*, Joe Kennedy quietly announced filming on *Queen Kelly* would not be resumed. It was now permanently shelved, at an estimated loss of $800,000. Kennedy told the press the decision to make the film into an operetta was "too much music, too soon."[14] Filming continued on *What a Widow!* into early May. For the new comedy, Gloria wore twenty-one stunning outfits and costumes designed by René Hubert. *What a Widow!* was also filmed in its entirety in just three days in early March, as a lensed "dress rehearsal," while Ian Keith was still in the cast. The process cost between $10,000 and $12,000. Two cameras were used for the experiment.

"We made no preliminary announcement of our plan to take a dress rehearsal film of 'What a Widow,'" Joe Kennedy boasted. "Personally I wanted to make sure the experiment would prove successful . . . What we have secured is a rough draft of the entire picture. Instead of rehearsing and rehearsing without making any permanent record of what we did, we put it on the celluloid . . . The actor can see his own performance and correct details of his portrayal . . . The results of the lighting and action are really much better than you might anticipate . . . At all events, it is a visual map for whatever we do in the final picture, and will, I believe, shorten the time of actual shooting to an economical advantage."[15] The footage does not exist today.

When the picture was completed, Gloria wrote in her memoirs about what would be her final confrontation with Joe over dinner at his Rodeo Drive house, which she dates in November. When going over business records after the filming of *What a Widow!*, Gloria wrote, she allegedly discovered that the Cadillac given to Sidney Howard had been charged to Gloria Productions. He gave Howard the car, so he should pay for it, she told Kennedy. She wrote that she had told him that jokingly, which seems unlikely as Kennedy promptly choked on his food, then stood up and left the room without a word to her. After a half hour, Eddie Moore drove Gloria home. A few days later Gloria heard that Kennedy had left town without telling her good-bye.[16]

Kennedy and Moore actually had already departed Hollywood on April 11, 1930, a good seven months earlier, with no fanfare and with few knowing they were leaving town for good. Boarding a train east, Kennedy charged Pathé nearly $10,000 for his recent expenses. The lease on Kennedy's Rodeo Drive house then lapsed. E.B. Derr received a cable for Eddie Moore asking him to forward two suitcases and any other articles remaining in the house to them in New York.[17]

As soon as he was back east, the May 8 *New York Times* announced Kennedy's retirement from Gloria Productions. He then traveled to White Sulphur Springs, West Virginia, to regain his health and put on some weight, having lost thirty pounds. He was suffering from ulcers and smoking heavily. Kennedy would later check into Boston's Lahey Clinic, fearing he might have stomach cancer.

In hindsight Kennedy had ruined Gloria financially. His ruthlessness had destroyed the careers of several Hollywood professionals, and his name in Hollywood would always be associated with greed, ruthlessness, and professional failure.

Gloria was now, or so she preferred to be considered, the victim, this time of two men who had left her at very vulnerable points in her life. Her husband Henri was involved in a romance with the younger Bennett, and Joe had unceremoniously and ungentlemanly left her. What had prompted the end of her affair with Kennedy? "I questioned his judgment," Gloria would repeat over the years. "He did not like to be questioned."[18]

As the summer of 1930 waned, Gloria took stock of her financial position and realized Kennedy had indeed charged numerous "gifts" to her production company. Now she was responsible for the bills. Gloria Productions, Inc., continued to exist after Kennedy's departure, but slowly Gloria was learning how much her relationship with Kennedy, and her trust in him, had cost her. Rental fees for studio use had been jacked up over three times actual cost. The expenses of the making of each of her films were tagged on to her account. Her accountant Irving Wakoff had paid these invoices religiously, but now he began to question them as they continued to come in even after filming was completed.[19]

Kennedy had used Gloria Productions "as a sieve through which Pathé paid its personnel and covered its overhead when they had no productions of their own. Kennedy had loaned her money and then used it to pay expenses at his studio, leaving Gloria responsible for paying back those loans."[20] Along with $700,000 she borrowed from Kennedy, there was also a line of credit established through the Bank of America with a 65 percent interest rate. Her UA contract was the collateral.

Gloria was stunned and hurt. She had assumed theirs was a partnership, fighting the industry together, but Kennedy used her as a business deal. He provided the funding for her to make pictures, but she was responsible for paying back the costs. Of their three projects, *The Trespasser* alone was successful. But its proceeds repaid the investors, and she saw little financial reward. She would pay close attention to contractual details in the future. Her last husband, William Dufty, remarked that after Kennedy, "you should have seen that woman read a contract. She made sure she understood every word."[21]

While this professional drama played itself out, publicity regarding Gloria's children and her motherhood was generated to mask Gloria's humiliation. Adela Rogers St. Johns wrote, "I have never known as devoted and wise a mother as Gloria. She worshipped her children, she drove directors mad when she insisted on driving sixty miles home from location at night and sixty miles back in the morning to see them. At Malibu I lived two houses from her for several summers and even the other stars waited breathlessly each day in anticipation of Gloria's appearance, surrounded by her handsome offspring, followed by a maid with bags, robes and slippers, a houseman with surf mats and paraphernalia. But it was Gloria herself who built sand castles with her children and taught them to jump the waves."[22] Surely that was the image Gloria wanted the public to see. Her trips to and from location were possibly more for the sake of keeping secret romantic rendezvous. But Gloria was never one *not* to mention her children when covering up private indiscretions.

Henri arrived in New York on July 29 on board the *Ile de France*. When questioned about his pending divorce from Gloria, he feigned ignorance, stating he did not even know where she was. He returned to California the following week. On August 5, Gloria advised the press, "Henri and I have decided to continue living apart as we have lived for the last year and a half. He plans to remain at a hotel during his stay here, and I shall continue to live at the beach. We have found it possible to maintain separate establishments and still be the best of friends."[23]

After Kennedy's departure, Gloria was mentioned for a new film, appropriately entitled *A Paris Divorce*, if negotiations came through. They did not. Meanwhile, she and Henri were headed their separate ways. "We are faced with a very simple and natural problem," she told Muriel Babcock of the *Los Angeles Times*. Dressed in red-and-black lounging pajamas, over a breakfast of fruit, Gloria expounded on her situation: "The more it is discussed the more complex it seems to become. It isn't. My husband occupies a position of importance in his own country. In France I am his wife. In America, I am a motion-picture star with business and artistic problems to work on each day . . . What the future will bring us, I do not know."[24]

On Friday, September 12, 1930, *What a Widow!* premiered at the United Artists Theater in Los Angeles. Much was made of the innovative animated titles by William Dietz (creatively designed to prominently display "Joseph P. Kennedy Presents . . ."). One critic said, "There's no star on the screen who knows her clothes as Swanson does and can wear them with such grace. She knows her comedy touches, too—you'll find her completely charming. Her voice doesn't register as well as in 'The Trespasser,' however."[25]

When the ninety-minute feature opened at the Rialto Theater in New York in early October, critics liked moments of the film. But synchronization was off, and much of the picture's impact was lost. Mordaunt Hall of *The New York Times* wrote, "Gloria Swanson's second talking film, 'What a Widow!' ... is an unfortunate example of sound reproduction ... The utterances of the players were more often than not quite indistinct, and when Miss Swanson sang poor synchronization added to the faulty tonal quality ... It is a comedy of sorts, a farce that sinks to slapstick. Frequently the attempts to be funny are rather pathetic ... Sometimes the violent attempts to draw laughter cause one to think that Miss Swanson wished to emulate her early efforts in pictures under Mack Sennett, but the antics of the players, including Miss Swanson, invariably miss fire ... Miss Swanson takes advantage of the chance to array herself in a variety of costumes."[26]

"Sime" Silverman in his *Variety* review was generous: "Start of the picture with the titling is not the least attractive of the whole. It's Comedy and Tragedy in masks introducing the technical staff and quarreling over the story to come ... Dwan has given an unusually fast tempo to the entire direction. He weaves everything in and out. Miss Swanson ... has plenty of scope for airy playing. Often she is cute in her panto and sallies, greatly aided of course by the apt dialog, while her naturalness in the role is something to wonder at."[27] The picture did well in its first runs and made some money for UA.

Gloria's finances were just as much in shambles as they were before her careless ride with Kennedy. She approached Louis B. Mayer, who despised Kennedy as much as anyone in Hollywood, for a four-picture deal, at $250,000 a picture. Mayer countered the offer in August with $100,000 per picture payable thirty days after completion.[28] When the contract was drawn up, Mayer suggested she talk with Joseph Schenck regarding her situation with UA, as she still owed them two more pictures. (Mayer had longed to merge MGM with UA for some time.) Gloria interpreted that suggestion as a sign that the Pinochle Club was still in existence. The fact that she approached Mayer knowing her UA contract was still active was irrelevant.

Gloria wrote in her memoirs that she then made a much better deal with UA, signing a four-picture "million dollar contract."[29] That alleged contract is not found in her archives, and Gloria exaggerated. It is possible she agreed to receive a $10,000 guarantee per picture, payable at $2,500 per week for four weeks, as a flat salary.[30] There were rumors she would hit the concert stage, under the auspices of the National Broadcasting Company's Artists Bureau. But either her fear of live performance or her financial demands were too great. Nor was she planning to sign with A. H. Woods, Florenz Ziegfeld, or Lee Shubert for the legitimate stage. The same reasons applied.

At the end of September, the Academy of Motion Picture Arts and Sciences announced Academy Award nominees for the 1929–30 year. Along with Ruth Chatterton for *Sarah and Son* (Paramount, 1930), Norma Shearer for *The Divorcée* (MGM, 1930), Greta Garbo for both *Romance* and *Anna Christie* (both MGM, 1930), and Nancy Carroll in the Edmund Goulding–directed *The Devil's Holiday* (Paramount, 1930), Gloria was once again nominated in the Best Actress category for *The Trespasser*. (*The Devil's Holiday* was a picture Goulding had written especially for Gloria, who passed on it. It then went to Jeanne Eagels, whose sudden death gave the role to Carroll.) On November 5, 1930, at the Academy banquet, held at the Fiesta Room of the Ambassador Hotel, Norma Shearer was handed the award. Gloria did not attend.

A deal was struck on October 20 between Gloria Productions and Samuel Goldwyn Studios in connection with United Artists' forthcoming *The Prodigal*. The new picture, to be produced by Samuel Goldwyn for UA, would be written by the dependable B. G. DeSylva, Lew Brown, Ray Henderson, and Leo McCarey, and it would be a "bright comedy of modern life" with musical numbers.[31]

Gloria filed for divorce from Henri on October 16, acquiring the services of her former attorney Milton M. Cohen and C. O. Bacon. Because Henri resided at the Beverly Wilshire and not at the family home, charges of desertion were mentioned. On October 21, Gloria, ever the victim, charged Henri with willful and malicious abandonment—her third "abandonment." The bill stated Henri quit her on September 18, 1929.

Ever the gentleman, Henri did not contest the action. "Everything moves too swiftly here in Hollywood for a happy marriage," he sighed to the press.[32] To another reporter he said, "If Miss Swanson wants to put a legal stamp on a situation that has existed for some time it is all right with me."[33] There was no community property, and no children from the marriage. It wasn't hard for the general public to figure out what was really going on, despite the charges. Just the week before, Gloria, decked out in jewels and looking beautiful, and escorted by J.R.T. Ryan, attended the Mayfair Club Ball. Henri, in black tux and white tie, was also there with Constance. Neither party took notice of the other.

On November 6, Gloria was granted a divorce from Henri. It would be another year before it was final, however. Taking the stand a day earlier than planned, Gloria testified before Superior Judge Walter Guerin, who asked if she had requested Henri to come back to her: "Yes. I called him in Paris before I left for California, and he declined to accompany me. Later, when he came to New York, I asked him to come to Beverly Hills and live with us. He said no, he would live at the Beverly-Wilshire Hotel instead. He said he didn't care to live at our home."

Gloria's witness was Virginia Bowker. Under oath, Bowker stated, "I happened to be in Paris when Miss Swanson was there . . . I heard the defendant refuse Miss Swanson's invitation for him to come to her home." After the trial Gloria, with Virginia, fled to a taxi on Main Street telling the press, "Please excuse me from posing, boys . . . I was due back at the studio [she was not filming at the time] at 12 o'clock, and they are waiting on the set for me."[34]

Within forty-eight hours after the announcement of her divorce, Gloria was sued by her former agent Maurice Cleary, husband of actress May McAvoy, to the tune of $45,000 for agent's commissions due him after he had secured her original United Artists contract. Their agreement, dated July 15, 1925, gave Cleary $10,000 in cash and a note for $15,000. Cleary claimed he should have received an additional $7,500 for each of the six pictures Gloria was contracted for. The case dragged on for years. On February 25, 1933, a judgment in Cleary's favor was granted for $37,500.

On December 6, 1930, Hollywood learned the truth about Kennedy. Pathé was ending the year $2.6 million in the red, and Kennedy was selling it to the recently merged RKO Studio for $5 million. As a leading stockholder, crafty Joe made out like a bandit. Studio mogul Jesse L. Lasky's daughter Betty Lasky accurately commented years later that in the hundred-year history of the American film industry, "Kennedy was the first and only outsider to fleece Hollywood."[35]

Adela Rogers St. Johns best summed up Gloria's affair with Kennedy and her romantic inclinations when she wrote, "Swanson has always been a perfect idiot where her own interests are concerned. It is part of Hollywood tradition that the alluring Swanson has never been benefited by her love affairs. She never gets any particular advantage, financial or professional, from her beauty and her fascination."[36]

As the year closed out, Gloria's prospects were grim. She owned a script called *Rock-a-Bye,* which Kennedy had later strongly suggested she keep, but for the time being it was not developed. E. B. Derr, who had remained Gloria's accountant after Kennedy left Hollywood, then sent Gloria a letter with no greetings or salutations, dated December 31, 1930, stating he would no longer handle her books. (Appropriately by the end of January 1931, the last two of the Four Horsemen, Derr and Sullivan, would be booted out of their jobs—sacrificed at the altar of Joe Kennedy.)

18

Hollywood

Gloria Swanson was not the first female Hollywood star to earn over $1 million a year. That was Mary Pickford. Swanson was, however, the first actress to actually *spend* that amount in one year. Over the past decade she had made more than $8 million, and she spent almost twice that living the lifestyle she felt her fans demanded. The Depression changed that. Now, with a dwindling bank account of just $250,000, it was imperative she work.

Gloria's new agreement with United Artists required her to make two pictures a year—one of their choosing, and one of her own. For her own production, organized after the first of the year, she chose *Obey That Impulse*. It told of Geraldine "Gerry" Trent (Gloria), a dress designer who sends her boyfriend Jim Woodward (Monroe Owsley) away. Through her friend Buster Collins (Arthur Lake, later Dagwood in Columbia's popular *Blondie* series), Gerry meets Anthony "Tony" Blake (Ben Lyon), author of the advice book *Obey That Impulse*, who does just that and quickly proposes to her. Before she accepts, she wants to act out his book's theory.[1]

The plot gave Gloria ample opportunity to dress beautifully. And she was given two songs written by DeSylva, Brown, and Henderson: "If You Haven't Got Love" and "Come to Me." It was risky to add music to a film by 1931, as musicals had fallen out of favor after the first onrush of sound. However, Swanson was used to risks.

After a brief jaunt to Europe after the New Year, Gloria arrived back in New

York on February 3, 1931, on board the liner *Aquitania*. In California she reported to work at UA for her new picture, now entitled *Indiscreet*.

Filming was quickly completed, and Gloria prepared *Rockabye,* as it was now spelled, for sometime before September. As her relationship with Joseph Schenck improved considerably, her producer Samuel Goldwyn was pressuring her to make *Tonight or Never,* based on the then current, and last, play produced by David Belasco. (He died on May 14, 1931, and three days later Goldwyn acquired the property.) The stage production had opened on Broadway in November 1930 and had starred Helen Gahagan and her new husband Melvyn Douglas. It was a box-office success, and young Douglas, who completed his stage role in June, was signed for the picture.

Gloria claimed she had insisted Goldwyn buy the play for her. Then she decided to do *Rockabye* instead. But Goldwyn insisted on *Tonight or Never,* as he had contracted haute couturier Coco Chanel to fashion Gloria's costumes. Chanel, whom Hollywood fashion designer Irene Sharaff credited with laying "the foundation of present fashion,"[2] was currently on salary with Goldwyn at $1 million a year. When Gloria balked at Chanel, in a heated discussion the producer told her something to the effect that her own choices in fashion were not in good taste. Swanson was livid. Long considered *the* fashion trend-setter in Hollywood, Swanson was not prepared for such remarks. When she reminded Goldwyn who and what she was, his famous reply was, "If you are a fashion plate I am a Chinaman."[3] She refused to do *Tonight or Never,* and in a show of temperament dashed to New York for the premiere of *Indiscreet.* Just to distance herself even more from Hollywood, she then headed off to Europe.

Mlle. Coco Chanel didn't last a month in Hollywood. Departing France in late February on board the *Europa,* she arrived in New York on March 4. After two weeks in California, she told the press she was leaving and would never return to Hollywood, even though Goldwyn had just decorated a modernistic suite in beige and delft blue for her to use for two months out of the year. She had arrived an hour late for her studio reception, claiming the smell of new paint made her sick. Still, she was under contract. Declining to open Chanel of Hollywood, she chose to return to Paris and design her costumes for Goldwyn's upcoming film, *The Greeks Had a Word for Them* (1932), in her salon in France.

Returning to New York in late April and checking into the Mayfair House, Gloria was entertained about town by Sport Ward. She was eager to see the musical *Three's a Crowd*, which starred Fred Allen, Libby Holman, and her good friend Clifton Webb. One of the young nightclubbing friends of Ward's whom she met was bon vivant Jeff Cohen, who later rented his Paris home to her. Meanwhile, former advertising woman turned novelist Ursula Parrott was in California, commissioned to turn her latest book, *Love Goes Past,* into a film vehicle for Gloria. Parrott, soon disillusioned with all the wrangling, turmoil, and changes to her screenplay, had had her fill of both the interfering Goldwyn and the long-distance demands of Swanson, and by mid-May she asked for a release from her contract.

With advertising proclaiming, "Through one indiscretion—a woman with a future became a woman with a past," one would think the comedy *Indiscreet* was a melodrama.[4] When it opened May 6 at the Rialto, critics were somewhat kind. Wrote "Sime" Simonson in *Variety,* "About the biggest scene is Miss Swanson taking a shower bath, showing nearly everything through glass panel. Why she didn't show everything and kill the business of the stock burlesque at the Republic [Theater], around the corner of the Rialto, is likely one of those studio conservations . . . A pretty narrow margin left for Miss Swanson in this role on looks. The extreme youthfulness of Barbara Kent, as sister, helped or hurt, according to the way you see the Swanson role."[5]

Most critics remained unimpressed: "If you liked Gloria Swanson in 'What a Widow,' you'll undoubtedly like her in her latest. But if you prefer the Swanson you saw in 'The Trespasser,' you'll not like it . . . She is accumulating the solidity of the thirties, which makes her attempt at being a hoyden of twenty a trifle unbecoming and unreal. She sings two songs, but she introduces them in the 'Get ready, everybody—I'm going to do a song' style."[6] Another critic bashed: "Too free play has been given the famed Swansonian mannerisms, goo-goo-eyeing and curling her upper lip to show off her teeth."[7] *Indiscreet* has its moments, but very few. Most of the problems are due to dull pacing and the timing of lines. Gloria is far too cute, too coy for her age, and her waistline.

After her summer stay in New York, Gloria sailed into Cherbourg on August 31, settling herself and Virginia Bowker, and Joseph and little Gloria, and her staff into her new friend Jeff Cohen's residence in Paris. Henri, now working for French Pathé, was in France at the same time after having completed directing two pictures, *Nuit d'Espagne* and *Echec au roi,* the French versions of the Radio films *Transgression* and *The Royal Bed.* With the ever present Virginia in tow, Gloria quickly departed to London for the premiere of *Indiscreet*. Noël Coward met them at the London train station.

Indiscreet's premiere at the Dominion Theater was not as fabulous as that of *The Trespasser*. At an after-party at Claridge's, where ex-King Alfonso of Spain was honored, Gloria met twenty-six-year-old Lady Sylvia Ashley, a tall, mincing blond creature with a precious lisp. A former lingerie model and showgirl, she charmed into marriage Lord Anthony Ashley-Cooper in 1927. By the next year she had spent most of his fortune. He was the first of her five husbands.

Douglas Fairbanks was at the party as well, and without Mary Pickford. Gloria and Sylvia took to each other immediately, and just for fun Gloria introduced Sylvia to Doug. (Fast-forward to December of 1931. Gloria, back in London, was visiting Sylvia. Pictures of Fairbanks were everywhere. When Gloria feigned surprise, Sylvia reminded her, "But I thought you knew. After all you introduced us, remember."[8] Pickford never forgave Gloria.)[9]

In America, it was again announced Gloria would sign with Broadway impresario Edgar Selwyn to star on stage, now in *Defiance*. Perhaps that was just fluff placed by one of her publicists, Harry Reichenbach or Leland Hayward. *Defiance* at any rate did not pan out. In London, enjoying the town in the company of her two favorite British bon vivants, Eddie Goulding and Coward, Gloria partied unabashedly. She and Virginia then headed off to Paris, with the men joining them a few days later.

At a swank little nightclub off the Champs-Elysées, Gloria spied a tall, handsome young man at the bar with two dogs—one white, one black. Introduced by Coward as "a moody Irish playboy, . . . the 'adopted son' of a rich American woman," Michael Farmer ("I can't believe you've never heard of him," prattled Coward) wasted little time charming the interested Gloria.[10] When Farmer asked her and Virginia to join him and Goulding on his sailboat in the south of France, Gloria didn't hesitate to accept.

Her children secure with her staff at the Cohen house in Paris, Gloria took off with the attractive Farmer. She wrote that Cohen had returned to Paris and was insistent she spend time with him. (She also wrote she didn't like being compromised.) Farmer's invitation could not have come at a better time. Arriving in Cannes, the party sailed to Monte Carlo and spent a leisurely month sailing along the Riviera and staying at luxurious hotels, attending various parties in the south of France and at Eden Roc[11] in the company of Maurice Chevalier,

Sophie Tucker, Chaplin, and the Dolly Sisters. Painting a romantic portrait of their first night of lovemaking, Gloria told in her memoirs of a late night aboard the boat, the starlit ocean, and Michael setting aside his cognac long enough to slowly and passionately kiss her. "You're the only woman I'll ever marry," he pledged.[12] They then made love while anchored in the Baie des Anges off the coastline of Cannes. Fireworks and fade, just like in the movies.

On July 16 Gloria attended the wedding of American opera coloratura and film actress Grace Moore to Valentine Parara, a young Spanish movie actor, at the city hall in Cannes. That same day in Chicago, Constance Bennett stepped off the train on her way to New York. She was traveling in a private car with her maid, a nanny, two year-old son Peter Plant, and her lover Henri. The following day, upon arrival in New York, Constance told the press they were sailing on the *Bremen* on July 18 on their way to France. Immediately rumors swirled of their pending marriage.

According to Gloria, Michael followed her back to Paris, where he and Cohen were madly jealous of each other.[13] That early August she discovered a lump on one of her breasts and had it examined by Dr. Vodescal, the same physician who had saved her life in 1925. After examining her breast the doctor told her it was a common milk cyst, the kind that develops years after an abortion. Smiling knowingly at her, he joyfully added that she should not this time terminate her pregnancy. Gloria was with child.

In Paris for fittings with Mlle. Chanel for *Tonight or Never,* which she reluctantly had to do, and not disclosing the reason for her weight gain, Gloria somehow convinced the couturier to design a form-fitting undergarment to hold in her growing waistline. After a week of fittings with Chanel, Gloria had Eddie Goulding inform everyone the vacation was over and they were returning to New York.

Francis Michael Farmer was born to an impoverished family in Dublin, Ireland, on May 9, 1902. Arriving in London, young Francis became the "protégé" of a wealthy American named Wade Chance, who died in the late 1920s. Through his association with Chance, Michael met Mrs. Edmund Hubbard, who offered to "adopt" him. He declined because he wanted to be independent, yet she bankrolled him for years.

Mrs. Hubbard introduced Michael to another American, a Mr. Hogan, whom Michael professionally partnered, forming the insurance company of Hogan and Farmer. Michael was now "a man of affairs,"[14] writing up insurance, arranging for automobiles to be shipped from Europe to America, providing chauffeurs, and so on. He also inspected, bought, and sold motorcars through his firm Michael Farmer, Inc.

The strapping Michael Farmer had once had a romance with Mimi Brokaw (later wed to opera star Richard Tucker). After a brief romance with Mrs. Stanley Mortimer, Michael met the beautiful blond American stage actress Marilyn Miller, star of Ziegfeld's *Sally* and *Sunny,* in Paris in 1927 and fell in love. Miller, three years older than Michael, was just then filing for divorce from Mary Pickford's alcoholic brother, actor Jack Pickford.

Marilyn's friend Clifton Webb wasn't sure if she was serious or not over Farmer. Michael was undoubtedly virile and handsome, but he was also a social climber and considered nouveau riche. Farmer loved attention, and as far as Webb was concerned, "Michael Farmer didn't care how his name was used as long as it was spelled correctly."[15] On March 23, 1930, shortly after Michael ended a New York visit and sailed back to Europe on board the *Aquitania,* Marilyn announced their engagement.

Marilyn sailed from New York to Europe in the fall of 1930 aboard the *Bremen* with Fred Astaire and his sister Adele. She was reunited in Paris with Michael, who was jealous of rumors she was romantically involved with the fey Astaire. Michael was circulating with his bar buddies at the nightclub Bricktop's when news reached him that Marilyn and Adele were having drinks at the Ritz. Taking a cab to the hotel, Farmer rushed in like a madman, but the two women gave him the slip and took a plane to London despite a storm over the English Channel. Michael followed in pursuit aboard a boat and eventually caught up with them at a bar at the Savoy Hotel. The following week, he was back at Bricktop's in Paris boasting to Cole Porter that the engagement was still on after he and Marilyn had spent three days of lovemaking in London. Instead, Marilyn returned to New York in March 1931. Michael then met Gloria.

"Ascot in the royal enclosure to view the races, Dublin for the horse show, London for the polo and smart tennis gatherings, yachting on the Cowes, fast motors and yachts on the Mediterranean, riding to the hounds in shires of England," wrote one fan magazine piece, "all these come under the active sports this handsome young Irishman has been enjoying year after year . . . In Paris, as well as in London, Michael Farmer attends the most elegant 'parties,' held in the most magnificent homes in Paris or nearby Neuilly."[16] Farmer himself maintained an apartment in Paris at 52 Avenue Henri Martin.

With Virginia shuffling the children and staff back to the United States on another liner, Gloria and Michael set sail from Cherbourg to New York on board the *Aquitania* on August 8. Interviewed at the dock in New York on August 14, the press noticed Gloria had kept close company with the handsome young Farmer on the voyage and asked if she contemplated marriage when her divorce was final. "I would if it would make me happy . . . I wouldn't be surprised about anything," she toyed with them. "I wouldn't deny that, nor say yes, either."[17] Such cat-and-mouse games these people played.

After spending a weekend in Elmsford, New York, at the estate of her lawyer friend Dudley Field Malone, Gloria and Michael visited Clifton Webb and his houseguest Gary Cooper at Sands Point, Long Island. On the morning of August 16, at 11:00 A.M., Gloria and Michael were quietly wed in the town of Mount Pleasant by the mayor of Elmsford, John Murray. The witnesses were William Buckley, tax receiver for the township of Greenburgh, and Edward F. Hennessey. On the seventeenth they boarded the *Twentieth Century Limited*, along with Webb as a shield, and returned to Hollywood, arriving aboard the *Santa Fe Chief* into Pasadena the evening of August 20.

Greeting reporters at the station, Gloria, pleased with her New York pier remarks, repeated them and chastised the reporters, "Remember, my divorce is not yet final." Commenting on Farmer, she added, "He is a marvelous person and a wonderful friend, but please deny that we are engaged. I cannot understand why I am so misunderstood in New York."[18] When they arrived in Pasadena, Gloria was decked out in a new and fresh fashion ensemble, while Michael wore the very same pinstriped suit in which he'd disembarked the *Aquitania*, though he was sporting a different tie.

Once filming began on her new picture, Gloria wrote, Michael took to Hollywood very quickly; playing, dining, and weekending "with the smartest people in pictures."[19] He also sometimes embarrassed Gloria with his drinking, as evidenced in one press photo of them out on the town with Jeanette MacDonald and Lila Lee where Gloria attempted to stop Michael drinking a glass of champagne he had placed on top of two inverted empty champagne glasses, balanced on top of a champagne bottle, one of the more impressive drinking skills he had honed.

Directed by Mervyn LeRoy, *Tonight or Never* commenced filming in September. It told the story of Hungarian prima donna Nella Vago (Gloria), whose voice teacher Rudig (Ferdinand Gottschalk) tells her she will never sing properly until she experiences passion. She is distracted by a mysterious man (Melvyn Douglas) who walks in the courtyard below her balcony. She believes he is a gigolo. Eventually he confesses his love for her, pleading it is "tonight or never" to experience real passion. The following evening she sings *Tosca* with great emotion and depth.

Douglas recalled Gloria "was having things very much her own way at this stage of her career," with Goldwyn making excuses to his underlings: "We're overpaying her, but she's worth it."[20] Douglas would remember that as the film progressed Gloria's pregnancy began to show, and she had to have a completely new wardrobe designed for her by the end of filming.

"Performing opposite Gloria Swanson," he wrote, "a woman who had stirred hearts all over the world, was overwhelming. Nevertheless, having done *Tonight or Never* with Helen [Gahagan, his wife] for so long in New York, I could not help but wonder if certain scenes were coming off; for instance, where sequences depended for their wit upon the inflection in Helen's voice, Miss Swanson . . . didn't do anything at all—which worried me. When I saw the film later, however, there was something in her eyes, something in her approach that achieved the same thing."[21]

Chanel created beautiful outfits for Gloria for the film. One was particularly stunning. It was the "Tosca" gown, made of pale blue velvet trimmed in diamonds, mirrors, and steel beads, with a long train and puffy, embroidered sleeves. One of her evening gowns was white satin with a bodice encrusted with rhinestones. (Sadly, in 2011, it was confirmed by Samuel Goldwyn's granddaughter Liz that these magnificent creations, designed by one of the world's most renowned fashion couturiers and stored for seven decades, had been unceremoniously lost in a garbage bag.)

On November 9 the divorce of Henri and Gloria was final, the decree issued by Judge Charles E. Haas. Then it was officially announced Gloria and Michael had wed on August 16. Because that date was before the final decree, charges of bigamy were bandied about. Milton Cohen argued Gloria had committed no violation of California law, since she and Michael had not lived together in the state of California as man and wife (which was untrue). But then there was a law in New York regarding the validity of the union as the couple was married in a different township from which the license had been issued.

So Gloria and Michael wed again the afternoon of November 9, appearing at three o'clock at the Yuma County Courthouse in front of Justice of the Peace Earl A. Freeman, in Yuma, Arizona, their witnesses county clerks Donald E. Wisener and Opal McChesney. Gloria gave her age as thirty-one; Michael gave his as twenty-nine, his occupation as broker. Gloria, more than five months pregnant, was dressed in a tan sports suit, a brown and tan fox fur, a brown hat, and brown-and-white sports shoes. Michael wore a gray suit and a blue shirt.

When Gloria left Hollywood in late 1931, to avoid being tracked by the press, she and her New York secretary Grace Crossman developed an elaborate cable code complete with odd-even numbering. Gloria prided herself on her inventiveness in this scheme. She even included a two-page description of her code in her memoirs and was most pleased with her detailed deciphering cleverness. (To a lesser degree other stars of the era utilized the same deception in their travels to avoid the press.) However, Gloria's sense of international self-importance was perhaps a bit exaggerated. The press paid little attention.

Deliberately avoiding being photographed because of her condition, Gloria still made no announcement about her pending delivery. On November 20 the American liner *President McKinley* arrived in Los Angeles. Gloria and Michael were booked on board as "Mr. and Mrs. Martin Foster." During the ship's stop-over in California to disembark and load new passengers, the "elusive Gloria" and Michael posed briefly for photographers, Gloria in a wrap with dark fur cuffs and collar, and Michael looking dapper in a double-breasted light woolen overcoat and muffler. Her only comment was, "I have nothing to say."[22] Baffled by the intrigue, the newsmen could only speculate. The couple then sailed from Los Angeles to New York, via the Panama Canal, on Sunday, November 22.

That very day, after finalizing all the proper details, Henri and Constance Bennett, wearing a long blue dress with a hat and a string of pearls, and carrying a bouquet of orchids and lilies of the valley, were married by Lewis R. Work, residing civil appellate justice, at the home of director George Fitzmaurice in Beverly Hills. Bennett's father gave the bride away. Sister Joan was her matron of honor.[23] This was Bennett's third marriage. Henri's best man was Henri Didot, French consul in Los Angeles. Constance now was the top-salaried film star in the world, earning $30,000 a week. The couple then departed for Paris for their honeymoon. Ironically Constance would never truly become the second Marquise de la Falaise de la Coudray, due to a legal snag. France simply would not recognize her marriage to Henri.

Arriving in New York on December 5, Gloria and Michael sailed for Europe at midnight the next night on board the *Bremen*. She had packed a print of *Queen Kelly*, which she was determined to have shown in Paris. *Tonight or Never* was rushed into theaters on December 4, premiering in Los Angeles at the United Artists Theater. Critics failed to appreciate it.

Reviewer Philip K. Scheuer wrote, "Miss Swanson, as the singer with a lack, has been handsomely pictured in gowns by Chanel. Her portrait of Nella is, nevertheless, less complete than it might be. Neither girlish virtue nor artistic temperament comes within her present forte. Her flair for comedy—while considerably improved . . . is not yet developed to the point where it is especially deft or incisive, and the seducing scene, requiring the most delicate balancing between desire and modesty, finds her reverting once again to an earlier coyness."[24]

When the film opened at New York's Rialto Theater on December 17, the critics were a bit more enthusiastic. "Pictorially, the film . . . is an unusually striking production," wrote Mordaunt Hall, adding, "Miss Swanson's portrayal . . . falls short of Miss Gahagan's."[25] Norbert Lusk praised Gloria: "Miss Swanson's performance is recognized as among her best, poised, expert, adroit. True, she is not the Hungarian prima donna of the tale nor, in fact, does she suggest a singer at all except in the mechanics of projecting temperament, capriciousness or what have you. In this respect Miss Swanson again triumphs as an exceedingly clever comedienne."[26]

In Great Britain, the critic of *The Times* was brutal, calling the picture "a film that might have been designed to make us despise art and artists . . . Neither Miss Swanson nor Mr. Melvin [*sic*] Douglas, for all her practical abandon and his cunning restraint, is able to dispel our nausea."[27] Still, the picture did steady, if unremarkable, business. However, *Tonight or Never* scarcely earned back its cost at the box office. (A radio adaptation starring Douglas and Jeanette MacDonald was presented much more favorably on the sixty-minute *Lux Radio Theatre* on January 25, 1937.)

Gloria's edited version of *Queen Kelly* was given its long-awaited world premiere at the Théâtre Falguière in Paris shortly after she and Michael arrived. Audiences were not overly enthusiastic. Her children had sailed over on the *Ile de France* with their governess. After spending Christmas at the Hotel Princesse and visiting Sylvia Ashley, who was about to undergo plastic surgery (this was when Gloria discovered her affair with Fairbanks), the family took off for St. Moritz, where they took a complete floor of the Suvretta Hotel. Gloria then enrolled little Gloria and Joseph in private schools there.

After celebrating New Year's with actor Adolphe Menjou and his wife Kathryn Carver, Gloria and Michael began to fight continually, usually over his drinking. Michael also started acting irrationally, according to Gloria, sometimes pushing and poking her. Perhaps she instigated some of these arguments, as her feelings toward him were complicated. She insisted Michael's strange behavior was because of his manic jealousy, though she was seven months pregnant.

They then journeyed to London, where on February 12 Gloria finally announced her pregnancy. At that point she really couldn't keep it a secret any longer. The newspapers in America reported she was in Paris to open "a modiste's shop and perfumery . . . and [would have] a similar atelier in Hollywood."[28] Still considered a fashion maven, Gloria visited the salon of French fashion couturier Capt. Edward H. Molyneaux, who stated, "She is not only one of the best gowned women in the movies, but in the world."[29] All of this silly prattle, of course, kept Gloria's name in the papers.

Gloria's spending went unchallenged. She bought a harp worth over $350, which she used as a decoration in her salon. She shopped at Flato's and purchased a set of emerald and diamond earrings valued at $25,000–$30,000, and at Cartier's in Paris she purchased two of six newly designed, magnificent art deco diamond and rock crystal bracelets, which she would wear in countless professional and candid pictures over the next five decades. Fabricated in platinum, each bracelet had 25.35 carats of round- and baguette-cut diamonds set in half discs of opaque rock crystals, with an invisible coiled platinum spring to enable them to expand when placed on the wrist or upper arm.

In London, she was advised by Joseph Schenck and UA that she was, by leaving California without notice, in violation of several key paragraphs of her contract. Gloria wrote Schenck telling him she needed a year off to rest before she could make another picture, thinking Schenck would take a sentimental view of her condition, which she had kept from him. He didn't, and unceremoniously canceled her as his client. Foolishly she had overplayed her hand. Now she was without a producer once again and still owing United Artists another picture.

At the end of the month, while suffering bronchitis, Gloria was visited by Sylvia Ashley and Doug Fairbanks, who suggested she might consider producing her next United Artists picture herself in England. Doug put her in touch with the Hon. Capt. Richard Norton (he inherited the title of Lord Grantley in 1943), who in 1930 had been placed in charge of British quota films (pictures made by foreign investors) for UA. (Michael quickly became insanely jealous of Norton, or so Gloria wrote. Did it matter Norton was an elderly aristocrat who wore a monocle and walked with a permanent stoop caused by an old World War I wound?) Norton then set into motion the development of a screenplay.

Gloria and Michael stayed at London's Dorchester Hotel, as development proceeded on the production, before she found a house where she would deliver her baby. Her friend Lady Thelma Furness, aunt of Gloria Vanderbilt and great-aunt of Anderson Cooper, offered up a lovely townhouse at 10 Farm Street near Berkeley Square in the Mayfair district. It had just been vacated by Wallis Simpson and the future king of England, Edward, Prince of Wales. Sylvia met Gloria there with a royal midwife and two obstetricians. The following evening at 6:30, Tuesday, April 5, 1932, Gloria delivered a seven-pound two-ounce baby girl she named Michelle Brigitte Farmer.

19

Transition

According to Gloria, Michael's irrational jealousy never ceased, and it came to a head shortly after the birth of Michelle. Gloria had received a congratulatory telegram from actor Francis Lederer. Gloria wrote that Michael became enraged and made her touch a revolver he kept inside his coat pocket. She threatened him into docile submission. Gloria wrote in her memoirs she took total control of the situation, admonishing him, reminding Michael he was an adult and no longer a tempestuous child, and that if he didn't cease his irrational jealousies she would leave him. Gloria possibly liked dramatic scenes.

Throughout her life Gloria characterized men as one of three distinct types, either ruthless businessmen, the true enemy who threatened and challenged her, or one of two kinds of lovers—"daddies" to provide, pamper, and protect her, or mischievous boys whom *she* would control. There was never an acceptance of men's equality on Swanson's part, unless they were gay and/or shared her artistic and creative sensibilities.

Shortly after the birth of her baby Gloria received a telegram from Florenz Ziegfeld, dated April 26, requesting she play the lead in his Broadway revival of *Show Boat*. Ziegfeld, who had been in poor health since the Crash of 1929, had remained in contact with Gloria from the year before when he first asked her about his revival of the smash 1929 Jerome Kern–Oscar Hammerstein musical. Ziegfeld was willing to pay Gloria whatever she wished for an eight-week commitment. Her response to the ailing impresario was succinct, dated four days later:

> THANK YOU VERY MUCH FOR YOUR . . . OFFER STOP VERY
> SORRY MY PLANS FOR NEXT SIX MONTHS WILL NOT
> PERMIT ME TO ACCEPT[2]

In the end *Show Boat* was revived on Broadway in May 1932. Ziegfeld died two months later, on July 22.

For Gloria's British film, UA put up $75,000 of the cost to get it started, but she had to finance the rest. Edmund Goulding was originally requested to direct, but he suggested she contract Cyril Gardner, who had been the editor of *The Trespasser*. It was reported in the American press that Melvyn Douglas was denied a loan-out to appear in the film by Samuel Goldwyn. Then Laurence Olivier was mentioned. Gloria somewhat selfishly then petitioned to have Michael star as her leading man. From Cannes Gloria had wired Irving Wakoff at the Mayfair Hotel in London:

> WORRY NO MORE ABOUT FINDING LEADING MAN AS WE HAVE
> FOUND HIM AND RIGHT UNDER OUR NOSE STOP MICHAEL
> FARMER STOP JUST FOR FUN HE AND SOME OF HIS FRIENDS
> HELPED US OUT IN THE REGALLA AND HE ACTED AND LOOKED
> GREAT STOP . . . HAVE HOWARD MAKE EVERYTHING RIGHT
> WITH [MELVYN] DOUGLAS[3]

Gloria eventually took Noël Coward's advice, after Michael's tests proved amateurish, and cast young Olivier. But she took Sylvia's suggestion and cast Michael in the picture to keep him occupied. She then set up Gloria Swanson British Productions, Ltd., at 1 Frederick's Place, Old Jewry, London, and registered it in May 1932 as a private company. Thinking optimistically ahead, she also established a Gloria Swanson's Productions in Paris, at 118 Avenue des Champs-Elysées.

The script was by Michael Powell and Miles Malleson, from a story suggested by Powell himself. Called *Perfect Understanding*, it told of American

businesswoman Judy Rogers (Gloria), who is reluctant to marry her British lover
Nicholas Randall (Laurence Olivier). They both feel their marriage might be
stronger than their friends', George (Michael Farmer) and Kitty (Genevieve To-
bin) Drayton, and Sir John (Charles Collum) and Lady Stephanie (Nora Swin-
burne) Fitzmaurice. But Judy and Nick marry, signing a pact not to display
jealousy, to trust one another, and to maintain a "perfect understanding." After
some inevitable misunderstandings, they start to divorce but reconcile in the end.

Production began in May. Filming commenced ten miles out of London at
Ealing Studios. By the middle of the month the company moved to the south of
France for ten days of location shooting. The truly awful song "I Love You So
Much That I Hate You," music by Henry Sullivan, lyrics by Rowland Leigh, was
written for Gloria to warble to Olivier early in the film. After briefly nursing
Michelle, Gloria sent all three children and Edith Simonson to a flat at Maid-
enhead on the Thames for the duration of filming. When school started, little
Gloria and Joseph, as well as infant Michelle, were sent to the Chalet Marie-
Jose Home D'Enfants in Gstaad, Switzerland. Miss Simonson stayed near the
children in Gstaad, residing at the Hotel Rossli.

In later years Sir Laurence Olivier pronounced he had hated the film, calling it
"a disaster" and the title "a misnomer if ever there was one."[4] He would always
consider the picture the worst he ever made. Gloria had nothing so negative to say
about him and found his "looks positively blinding."[5] She wanted Italian fashion
designer Elsa Schiaparelli to design her gowns in Perfect Understanding, but René
Hubert eventually was assigned the task, and his work in this picture was superb.

With large amounts of money spent for the sake of "authenticity" on interior
scenes drenched in antiques, and exterior sequences filmed on location, Gloria
could not be bothered with rationalizing company expenditures. After two
weeks frolicking in the south of France, enjoying first-class accommodations
and luxury services at company expense, and filming only when necessary, Gloria gave no thought to her financial future, but the times had radically changed.
Humbly imploring Joseph Schenck again for funds, she was flatly denied. He
wrote her a letter on June 7, possibly jolting her to her senses, that read in part,

You will be wise if you limit the cost of your production to $500,000 or
as near $150,000 as you possibly can because returns on pictures today
are very small. Up to the present time, 'Tonight or Never' in the U.S. has

grossed about $125,000 and I don't think it will gross over $500,000 as business here is exceptionally bad and distributors pay but little money for pictures because they do not get it at the box office.[6]

Gloria eventually borrowed $200,000 from South African backers to complete the picture in late July at the RCA studios in Ealing. (Gloria had managed, however, to unload the screenplay of *Rock-a-Bye* by Horace Jackson. It was sold to RKO for $30,000. As *Rockabye* it was released in November 1932, starring Constance Bennett and Joel McCrea.) Her attorney Loyd Wright carefully explained to her in a letter what her financial obligations were in light of her extravagant spending.

Wright advised her that she was squandering the fortune he had helped her amass the year before by ignoring the program they had arranged the previous November. He told her too he would much rather see her bank her earnings and have them accrue interest than have her take what she already had, and could depend on, and spend it outright.[7] Wright further explained the situations existing with her various mortgages and outstanding debts, and carefully laid out the threat she was facing with her immense tax debt.

Wright's warnings came too late, and Gloria disregarded them in any case. On August 18, at Gloria's Crescent Drive estate, then under the watch of a lone caretaker, some one hundred pieces of rare furniture, appraised at $44,000, were seized by a writ of attachment from the sheriff's office. Its issuance was the result of a civil suit brought by the importing firm W. Jay Saylor Company to collect an unpaid balance due of $15,000 from when Gloria had had her home completely refurbished in 1931; at the time she paid $30,000 and promised the balance in a promissory note. The following day a temporary halt was issued. Wright secured a restraining order until August 26, and a security guard was placed at the mansion to guard Gloria's possessions until the Superior Court ruled on the matter.

Loyd Wright stated that in Gloria's business it was important she live as a star and that her elaborate lifestyle was necessary to maintain her status in the Hollywood community. On September 6 Superior Court Judge Wilson ruled in favor of Saylor. That same day Wright posted a surety bond of $7,000 to again prevent the seizure. On October 2 Judge Wilson dissolved that ruling, and Gloria's expensive belongings were saved. However, she was not in court as ordered on October 6 and was fined $7,340. The case continued in the courts for months.

Former actress and then Broadway producer Peggy Fears sought Gloria to star in a new play, and it was mentioned in the press Gloria would undertake the plum role in *The Worst Woman in Paris*.

Surprisingly, Joseph P. Kennedy arrogantly assumed he still had clout in the picture business. He was interested in dealing with Gloria on *Perfect Understanding*, writing her from his 485 Madison Avenue office on October 19 that, at the risk of seeming presumptuous, he had some ideas for her new picture which he felt might be helpful.[8]

She was wise not to respond. Or perhaps she did and the letter has been lost. In any event, she never worked with Kennedy again.

In a final attempt to earn back some of its costs, Gloria reedited the ill-fated *Queen Kelly* down from twenty-eight reels to a presentable length of ninety minutes, with a new ending, and released it commercially in South America and Europe in November 1932. (Von Stroheim owned a small piece of the picture and refused to allow its release in the States.) "It was ornate as promised, aglow with expensive costumes and sets, but it was a far cry from von Stroheim's original vision," wrote Goulding's biographer. "He repudiated the released version."[9] *Queen Kelly* would not be shown in America until a brief clip was inserted in *Sunset Boulevard* in 1950.[10]

Perfect Understanding stumbled ahead and was completed the first week of December. Gloria and Michael, accompanied by their terriers Mike and Pickles, arrived back in the United States on board the Italian superliner *Conte di Savoia* on February 16, 1933. According to Gloria, they argued throughout the crossing. Dressed in a dark pinstriped skirt and jacket, Gloria greeted the awaiting press in New York. Michael, sporting the very same suit he had worn when he first arrived in America with Gloria, was asked how he was doing and replied he was slightly staggered by "being married, a father and a movie actor all in one year."[11]

The seventy-nine-minute *Perfect Understanding* opened to dismal reviews at New York's Rivoli Theater on February 22. Advertised with "They Wanted to Be Free! She Wanted Him as a Lover . . . He Wanted Her as a Mistress,"[12] and heralded as Gloria's best picture since *The Trespasser*, the picture failed on all counts, and audiences issued a collective yawn.

Wrote Norbert Lusk for the *Los Angeles Times,* "Miss Swanson dominates the picture, which is what her public wants . . . If she has erred in overestimating the acting talent of her husband, Michael Farmer, she has at least satisfied curiosity in permitting the public a glimpse of him, which proves Miss Swanson is a showman first, last and always and Mr. Farmer is a lousy actor."[13]

Mordaunt Hall of *The New York Times* noticed, "Miss Swanson is undeniably good-looking, but she does not show any particular talent for acting in the film. She speaks her lines in a nervous manner, and this often destroys what value there might be in the episode."[14] "Rush" in his *Variety* column was dead on target: "Miss Swanson never once rises above the mediocre material with which she has supplied herself. Never does she suggest the vigor and comedy flair of her 'Mme. Sans-Gene.' Instead, there is the impression of a stock actress struggling with the futilities of an old-fashioned society drama."[15] *Perfect Understanding* brought in $23,000 its first week at the Rivoli and was grudgingly held over for another three while the theater waited for a replacement film.

With the failure of *Perfect Understanding* came the end of Gloria's agreement with United Artists. Because she opted to take a straight salary, waiving profit interests in her remaining UA pictures, it was estimated Gloria lost over $2.5 million in her United Artists deal. Because she needed money, Gloria readily sold her United Artists stock.

Arriving in California on board the *Chief* on April 3, Gloria, dressed sportily in a new Parisian traveling ensemble and hat, told reporters, "You don't know how it feels to be able to think of going home after living in hotels so long. After all there's no place like home and this is my home."[16] Immediately Gloria was mentioned in the running for Universal Pictures' *Glamour,* now in preparation, written by Sarah Mason, based on a short story by Edna Ferber.

Secretly Gloria had discovered yet another lump on her breast. With her physician Dr. Hal Bieler out of town, Gloria decided to return to Europe. On May 21 she and Michael boarded the *Chief* for New York, and then the *Ile de France* on May 27. In Paris they checked into the Hotel Crillon. Michael insisted Gloria see Dr. Marcel Der Martel, who at once removed the lump from Gloria's breast and pronounced it benign. In Switzerland they visited with the children. *Perfect Understanding* had opened to disastrous reviews in London, with gross receipts totaling just $5,875 by June. Gloria blamed the international economy for its demise.

Meanwhile, back on Crescent Drive, Gloria's furnishings were sold at auction on June 22, as ordered by the court the previous October, for $7,625.88 in favor of W. Jay Saylor. Civil deputy H. A. Llewellyn conducted the sale. Saved the humiliation of witnessing the sale, Gloria and Michael departed again from France on July 20 on board the *Olympic*.

Before leaving Europe, Gloria had signed a contract for three pictures over the next two years for Screen Plays, headed by J. I. Schnitzer, president, and Samuel Zierler, beginning in October, with a percentage agreement as a salary basis. Arriving back in New York on August 1, Gloria boasted to the press gathered on deck about a game she had learned from her children while in Switzerland, called "squat tag," which she had introduced to her fellow passengers, who "had a gay time scampering over the ship."[17]

Back in California on August 6, Gloria and Michael sublet the home of Dick Hargreaves. In September MGM began casting for the sound version remake of Franz Lehar's operetta *The Merry Widow,* with Maurice Chevalier. Among the actresses considered to star opposite him were Jeanette MacDonald, new to the Metro fold, Lily Pons, Grace Moore, Vivienne Segal, "the fading Gloria Swanson," and even Joan Crawford, who once sat in on a vocal rehearsal with MacDonald and proclaimed afterward, "You have only one teacher? I have two—one for my high voice and one for my low."[18] On February 15 Gloria was tested at MGM. The results were not promising.

Surprisingly, Gloria expressed a desire in late August to return to work with DeMille in his *Four Frightened People,* which starred forty-three-year-old British actor Herbert Marshall. Speculation naturally peaked because of her commitment with Screen Plays, but eventually her casting in *Four Frightened People,* and the Screen Plays contract, too, went the way of lost causes. Another property mentioned for Gloria was Paramount's *Miss Fane's Baby Is Stolen,* a baby abduction yarn based on a novel, with a screenplay by Adela Rogers St. Johns. It was to co-star the then popular infant Baby LeRoy. Gloria turned it down on October 5. She would not co-star with any scene-stealing infant.

In court regarding the Maurice Cleary lawsuit, Gloria arrived wearing a $2,000 diamond bracelet. She took the stand and testified she had "pledged everything she possessed to secure debts." Scrupulous eyes were more discerning. Cleary demanded the bracelet. Represented in court by Loyd Wright, Gloria stated the bracelet was a gift from her husband Michael and considered "wearing apparel," and thus exempt. Cleary's attorney Stephen Monteleone insisted the bracelet be turned over to his client. Superior Court Commissioner Kaufman ordered the gem-encrusted bracelet handed over.[19] On and on it dragged.

Quite unexpectedly Harry Cohn, head of Columbia Pictures, offered Gloria the role of Lily Garland in his film version of the Charles MacArthur–Ben Hecht hit Broadway play *Twentieth Century*. Preston Sturges was assigned to write the screenplay, with Gregory Ratoff set to portray the producer. Negotiations bogged down because of Gloria's exorbitant demands, and eventually the production, as directed by Howard Hawks, starred John Barrymore and Carole Lombard.

In early December Gloria and Michael attended the opening of the Mayfair Club social season. It would be the last public outing for them as husband and wife. On December 10 they separated, and Michael left for England. Perhaps Gloria had just tired of Michael's drinking, or possibly his indiscretions. One thing was for certain, she was totally bored with him.

While in New York, Michael, bunking at the Waldorf-Astoria, sent long passionate letters to Gloria. They were full of "Boy Loves Girl" enthusiasm and youthful pining, and yet also his playboy without-a-care attitude.[20] He wrote about seeing Irving Berlin's *As Thousands Cheer,* with a book by Moss Hart, at the Music Box Theater on Broadway. He wrote of their friends Clifton Webb, Marilyn Miller, and Helen Broderick, who starred in the revue, partying with him after the play. He rarely mentioned his child. Michael's fun-loving and youthful exuberance did not charm Gloria, and his letters for the most part went unanswered. Once back in Paris, at his flat at 9 Avenue Bugeaud, Kleiber, Michael continued to plead with his wife for reconciliation. On January 18, 1934, he sent her a fifty-page progressive letter begging for an explanation and expounding his love for her. Gloria focused on her career.

In late November Gloria spoke with MGM studio executive Irving Thalberg, a man of frail health who had been chronically ill for years. Gloria wrote Wright:

As you well know, I want to sign with Thalberg. But making a picture for him seems so far distant . . . It frightens me when I think that over three weeks have passed since the first time Thalberg called me. The first draft of the contract hasn't even been drawn, heaven knows how many weeks we shall be on that, and he, as he told me himself, does not believe

in indecision; that he prefers to make a mistake rather than be undecided about a thing.

In regard to my contract, I have had one disappointment already,
about the thirty-five thousand to forty, instead of seventy-five, which was
the figure Thalberg quoted to you. Really, I don't want any more disappointment.

So Loyd, please keep [in touch with] him. I realize he has worries
now, and is a very busy man, but if he really wants me, I should think he
would find time even if the evenings had to be devoted to it. I just cannot let all these things as well as time go by and then have something go
wrong—not even if it *is* "an act of God."[21]

On Christmas Day, Gloria attended a party at Colleen Moore's home, where
she ran into Henri, there by himself. He had recently been verbally attacked by
Murray W. Garsson, special immigration agent of the Labor Department, who
told him "in harsh terms that he was an alien and he had to get out or be deported."[22] Gloria and Henri sequestered themselves in a corner and shared a
quiet and lengthy talk.

On January 1, Edwin Schallert tantalized his readers in the *Los Angeles
Times* with "If Gloria Swanson joins the Irving Thalberg unit at MGM it's an
easy guess that it will be for the picture version of 'Biography.'"[23] Loyd Wright
was doing his job. And on a personal note, he notified Gloria that Herbert
Somborn was attempting to contact her. According to Gloria's memoirs,
Wright gave her Herbert's telephone number at the Cedars of Lebanon Hospital, where he was dying of cancer.

Gloria said of her final conversation with her second husband that they
discussed little Gloria. But the highlight of the visit, so Swanson wrote, was
him telling her she was the only woman he had ever loved or trusted. On January 2 Herbert Somborn died at the age of fifty-three of a kidney ailment. The
prosperous owner of three successful Brown Derby restaurants around Los
Angeles, he died a wealthy man. In his will he left the bulk of his estate to his
only child, twelve-year-old Gloria. "He was a very kind and gentle man and I
would see him on occasions," little Gloria said in later years. "He was always
good to me. But I know nothing of their [her parents'] life together."[24]

Warner Bros. considered Gloria for the role of Josephine in their projected

Napoleon, and at the same time Gloria was offered the lead in *I Loved an Actress,* an RKO property. She made neither picture. At the end of January, negotiations with Metro moved ahead on *Biography,* to be directed by Sam Wood, an almost sure bet. That month Gloria was advised Elinor Glyn's creaky "sex romance" *Three Weeks* was being dusted off by MGM's Irving Thalberg as a possible vehicle for her and either Clark Gable or Franchot Tone, with a new screen treatment by Frances Marion, who also was developing *Shantytown* for Gloria and Gable, about a woman's love for her man and her taming his gambling.

Another candidate for the male lead in the *Three Weeks* remake was Herbert Marshall, called "Bart" by his friends. A likable fellow, Herbert Brough Falcon Marshall was born in London on May 23, 1890, and made his stage debut in 1911. Trained as an accountant, he served valiantly in World War I with the London Scottish Regiment (which included actors Basil Rathbone, Ronald Colman, and Claude Rains). Marshall had lost his right leg and walked with a wooden one, a fact he ingeniously was able to disguise throughout his film career. He made his talking film debut opposite the doomed Jeanne Eagels in Paramount's *The Letter* in 1929, portraying her slain lover. (Marshall would portray Bette Davis's betrayed husband in the Warner Bros. 1940 remake.)

By 1934 Marshall had starred opposite some of Hollywood's most glamorous actresses, including Greta Garbo, Marlene Dietrich, and Norma Shearer. Married to British actress Edna Best, his second wife, Bart maintained a "modern" living arrangement with Best, who had remained in England to develop her career there. With his cultured, mellow baritone, Marshall was tremendously attractive to women and had already maneuvered affairs with such leading ladies as Kay Frances and Miriam Hopkins.

In January Gloria met Marshall at a dinner party at Edmund Goulding's. His charm and courtliness impressed and tantalized her. When he asked at the end of the evening if he might call her, she said yes. Gloria effusively and unashamedly wrote that within a week, she and Marshall were deeply in love, stating she could in no way have prevented it from happening.[25]

Marshall's problems with Edna, coupled with his excessive drinking, often created problems on the sets of his pictures. He could easily slip into dark moods. He complained constantly of "phantom pain" in his amputated right leg, and he suffered from depression. Gloria defined these deficiencies as vulnerability. On January 14 she and Marshall made one of their first public appearances together as a couple, attending radio crooner Russ Columbo's twenty-sixth birthday dinner party, which he threw for himself at the Beverly Wilshire Hotel's Gold Room.

A week later Gloria ran into Henri at the Screen Actors Guild Ball, and he discreetly kissed her on her brow. Returning to Europe soon after, Henri lived most of the rest of the decade at 20 Grosvenor Square, "shooting grouse in Scotland with Lord Throckmorton and chasing wealthy ladies in London . . . his hunting grounds, the aristocratic Club 400."[26] In Hollywood Marshall escorted Gloria to a performance at the Theater Mart, and one gossip commented, "There were four in the party, but Mr. Michael Farmer was not among them. He's in England."[27]

On February 17 it was official. Gloria was now to become a Thalberg star, an MGM contract player with a three-picture-a-year deal to prove it. However, the contract contained numerous conditions. After her initial picture (possibly *Three Weeks*), her second would probably be *The Merry Widow* at $100,000 plus an additional $100,000 upon its completion, and the third photoplay would land her $200,000, paid in twenty installments of $10,000 each. The problem was, no project was ready. Suggested were *As Husbands Go* and *Heavenly Sinners,* a story about Lola Montez. Neither was made. Robert Ritchie, Metro diva Jeanette MacDonald's current lover, was assigned to be Gloria's personal manager. (MacDonald would eventually play the female lead in *The Merry Widow.*)

As Metro weighed various projects, Constance Bennett arrived on the Culver City lot for *Outcast Lady,* which ironically starred her opposite Marshall. This galled Gloria considerably, first, because Bennett was beginning a class picture (which would turn out to be a moderate hit), and second, because she had demanded Marshall as her leading man. Was La Bennett playing games? Gloria did not have the clout she'd had a decade before, and she could do very little but complain. But she knew her Bart well enough to know he could see through the conniving wiles of Miss Bennett. And connive Constance did, which only amused Marshall and irritated Gloria the more.

Still the newspapers were guessing. "When Constance Bennett begins 'The Green Hat' [which *Outcast Lady* was based upon] she will have Herbert Marshall for the role of Napier . . . All Hollywood is watching this casting, since Constance Bennett is Gloria Swanson's romantic shadow," wrote columnist Mollie Merrick. "She it is who followed La Gloria in the affections of Henri La Falaise and she it is who gets Gloria's favorite leading man—Herbert Marshall— for her own lead of the moment."[28]

In London, on March 2 Michael was quizzed about divorce rumors by reporters, replying with a smile that Gloria "assured me that there was nothing to the story."[29] Perhaps he was just being noble, though it was not in his character. He probably did not know about Marshall. "But if there is no change of heart within the next four weeks don't be surprised if she goes to court to make permanent what is now described as a temporary separation, brought on by business demands from Farmer abroad," speculated one sly Hollywood reporter.[30] Whatever "demands" Farmer had in Europe had nothing to do with any form of "business."

In the meantime, Metro scrambled for a project for Swanson. Fans suggested Gloria star in the studio's projected film version of *David Copperfield*. (In which role was not mentioned.) At one point there was talk of casting her with her former husband Wallace Beery, now a major star on the MGM roster. He had just won the Best Actor Oscar (tied with Fredric March for his *Dr. Jekyll and Mr. Hyde*) for 1931's *The Champ*. The fan magazines were thrilled at the prospect: "Gloria means Glamour! Beery means Box-office! What a Combination!"[31] There was also talk that Gloria might star in Samuel Goldwyn's *Barbary Coast* with Gary Cooper, with production to begin June 1 following the filming of *Three Weeks*. (Cooper was replaced by Joel McCrea when *Barbary Coast* went into production, and Gloria's role went to Miriam Hopkins.)

The first week of April, Marshall left by train for New York. Daily he and Gloria, using the moniker "Mrs. Richardson," exchanged Western Union telegrams. In Chicago he dropped a brief message off to Gloria. Complaining of his misery at being separated from her, he wrote her of his growing passion for her at that very moment.[32]

Gloria then departed for the East Coast as well to begin a Metro-arranged tour to promote *Three Weeks*. Once settled into the Waldorf-Astoria, she received a long plaintive letter from Marshall. His letters were full of passionate and longing passages such as "Oh darling heart and wife of my eternal being."[33] She also received a letter from her husband Michael requesting a divorce. He had finally caught wind of her affair with Marshall. Judging by her response, Michael's letter must have been threatening. In part Gloria wrote:

> The inevitable divorce which we have often discussed, I want to get now—
>
> The sweetness in our lives is that we have a beautiful baby. I wanted her so much and you wanted a child before you were thirty-one. Our marriage served that purpose . . .
>
> Certainly our divorce will not be a surprise to the world. I intend to get it as quietly as possible on the grounds of incompatibility—There need be no unpleasantness about it . . .
>
> I am aware of the problem of the children, but it seems difficult to discuss this with you until my plans for the tour and my first picture date are set—that is, until I know exactly where I am going to be for the next six months or so, and whether and when I get a chance to go to Europe to see them during that time.
>
> Do let me know how Michelle and Miss Simonson are enjoying Paris.[34]

Michael's reaction to Gloria's letter could not have been pleasant. When she found he was preparing to sue her for divorce, she instructed an agent to write a letter to Seymour Berkson of Hearst newspapers in Paris, on April 10, begging for his cooperation:

> *My dear Mr. Berkson,*
> *This is an extremely confidential letter . . . Will you interview Mr. Farmer and tell him how very bad it would be for him to start action against Miss Swanson . . .*
>
> *Please do not indicate in any way that you have had a letter from me. Just act as a representative of the Hearst newspapers and let me know the result as soon as you have talked with him.*
>
> *We are trying to act secretly as his divorce suit might spoil Gloria Swanson's motion picture career. She is just starting a comeback . . . If he threatens to sue her then is the time to intimate that he might stir up a lot of animosity in America and most unfavorable publicity for himself.*[35]

From her London attorney, F. M. Guedalla, Gloria received a letter dated April 27 reporting Michael's latest response to her actions. He had just returned from a five-week cruise of Norwegian fjords on a friend's yacht:

> He spoke bitterly and regretfully that you should have come to such a decision . . . He also said that you had not written for a long time to the children or Miss Simonson. He then added that he knew very well why you wanted to divorce him. He said that Herbert Marshall was infatuated with you . . . He told me he got this information from his friends Lady Furness and Mrs. Reginald Vanderbilt [her twin sister and mother of Gloria Vanderbilt]. Edna Best apparently had been very bitter against you and Herbert Marshall. Michael evidently believed everything that his two lady friends had been telling him.[36]

Guedalla then advised Gloria she was still legally married to a British subject, and should she return to England with a new husband, she might very well be faced with bigamy charges.

In New York Gloria began preparation for her first vaudeville assignment. She also rendezvoused with Herbert Marshall. She had signed a vaudeville contract guaranteeing her $7,500 a week to appear in a live stage show, five times daily, beginning at New York's Paramount Theater on April 20. After her appearance there followed the news and trailers, an overture, and a feature film. Her act was produced by Edmund Goulding and written by stage producer George Haight. Gloria was introduced and brought out onto the stage, and then, following brief banter with actors Thurston Hall and Walter Greaza, she sang "Love, Your Spell Is Everywhere."

Showing obvious jitters throughout her first three performances, by midday Gloria was more relaxed. Critics for the most part were civil in their judgment of Gloria as a stage performer. "[Swanson] has a novel offering and gives an excellent account of herself, concluding her act with a song," wrote *Los Angeles Times* reporter Norbert Lusk on April 28.[37]

Audiences were thrilled to see Swanson live. Just that month she had appeared in the April 1934 issue of *Vanity Fair*. Gloria also performed over WEAF Radio's *Fleischmann's Yeast Hour* on April 19 at 8:00 P.M. in a scene from Rachel Crowther's play *Let Us Be Gay,* with actor Tom Powers. Afterward she sang "Love, Your Spell Is Everywhere." (She later took her vaudeville act on tour, making appearances at the Michigan Theater in Detroit and the Chicago Theatre in Chicago.) The evening of April 22, Gloria was spotted with Floyd Gibbons in the circular lounge at Manhattan's Hotel Ambassador during the cocktail hour and was cornered by the press. She felt it was time to announce her divorce from Michael. "I have thought about the matter for a long time," Miss Swanson said, "and I have decided our marriage was a mistake."[38] The following day it was made official.

20

Hollywood Redux

On the evening of April 23, through her lawyer Loyd Wright, Gloria officially announced her pending divorce. The following day in her dressing room backstage at the Paramount Theater, Gloria explained, "Michael belongs in one world and I belong in another. I have my work and I like to do what I am doing. He has just returned from a lovely yachting race in Norway, and I hear that he intends to take a trip around the world. How nice that Mr. Farmer has so much leisure. I am glad he is enjoying himself. For my part, I have obligations and it's up to me to take care of them. That is why I am here working."[1]

After confirming she was claiming incompatibility, Gloria denied any involvement with Herbert Marshall. She stated she would return to California around June 1 to film the Goldwyn picture *Barbary Coast,* then start her first film for Metro. That same day, April 24, Michael Farmer called his lawyer in London from Paris to ask if Gloria's statements were true and was told they did not know. "When you are away from Hollywood you never know whether you're being divorced or not," he joked to the press.[2]

As Michael continued to throw a series of large parties in Paris, it was announced Gloria might extend her stage appearances, as *Three Weeks* at MGM was delayed. Wright sensed Farmer was prepared to battle. After finally being notified of Gloria's actions by her attorney in London and advised of her blatant public relationship with Marshall, Michael made a statement the first week of May. He righteously told the press, "If Gloria really wants a divorce, I will give it to her if it makes her happy. But I feel at the moment if there is any truth in it, it may be just a whim and I would rather not give her a divorce." Asked why not, he pointed to the fact they had a two-year-old daughter, and for Gloria's sake he thought a divorce "would not be wise."[3]

Gloria wasn't taking chances. She had received an ominous letter dated May 8 from nanny Edith Simonson regarding Michael and his adopted "mother" Mrs. Edmund Hubbard and their desire to keep baby Michelle:

> I have made observations . . . Her [Mrs. Hubbard] mental condition is very bad. Will do all in my power to protect your baby and help you if it is necessary . . . She is crazy on the subject of Michelle. Every day she says my son has given me the baby nobody can take her away. She is mine I will go to the law about it . . . So much more, just the ravings of a woman whose mind is not all together normal. If she was normal she would realize you are her Mother and the one to have [Michelle].[4]

Michael, however, held the trump card in Paris. Gloria was much too busy to deal with the baby as she attempted to restart her floundering career and continue her involvement with Marshall. Gloria always insisted she be in charge of every situation as she plowed recklessly through uncharted seas, but she had obviously misjudged Michael. He was no pushover. Still, if it was a battle he wanted, a battle she would give him.

As her divorce raged on, Gloria, in Chicago, still saw Marshall. Returning by air to Los Angeles on May 21 (he took a separate flight), Gloria had little to say to the press other than "Mr. Farmer has acted in a gentlemanly manner in connection with the divorce."[5]

Gloria wrote that she met Edna Best the summer of 1934 when Herbert brought her and their baby daughter to Hollywood. At their meeting, Best wanted to set the matter straight. She asked if Gloria was in love with her husband. Gloria said yes. Edna asked if she knew about his drinking. Gloria said yes. Edna asked if Gloria understood there was a child involved, a young daughter. Gloria said yes. Bart drove Gloria home that evening.[6]

On May 31, 1934, Gloria was ordered to appear in court to explain why she still hadn't paid Maurice Cleary his $37,500. It was obvious. She didn't have the money. Negotiations for a settlement were begun on June 29. On August 3, after she started her next picture, the case was settled and taken off the calendar. The following week, Gloria's attorney Wright appeared before Judge Marshall F. McComb to obtain an order to return Gloria's valuable bracelet, which had been held in the custody of the clerk's office.

A new "morals code" was being called for, and MGM was now being bombarded by church groups and other religious organizations with demands to shelve *Three Weeks*. Gloria's professional outlook seemed bleak. It took the growing anti-Semitism in Europe and the immigration to California of displaced European Jews in the arts to actually kick-start her film career.

With Hitler's rise to power in Germany in 1933 came the migration of many of Europe's artists, actors, directors, and film craftsmen to Hollywood. Among those was former UFA Film Studio head Erich Pommer, edged out of his position by Germany's Reich Minister of Propaganda, Joseph Goebbels. The producer left for France, to produce *Music in the Air* for Fox-Europa, which Fox had purchased in June 1933 for $50,000, with lyrics by Oscar Hammerstein II and music by Jerome Kern (it had been some time since Kern agreed to be billed second). Pommer's contract enabled him to employ several of his fellow émigrés, including German director Ludwig Berger, who would direct simultaneously in English, German, and French, and Walter Reisch to create the screenplay. But with the unsettling political climate on the Continent and the devaluation of the U.S. dollar, it became unfeasible to film in Europe, and the project headed for Hollywood in the summer of 1934.

The Broadway musical *Music in the Air* had enjoyed an immensely successful 342-performance run at the Alvin Theater in New York in 1932. In Hollywood, with German exile director Joe May now set to direct,[7] Pommer suggested for the lead opera diva Grace Moore, whose early talkie experiences, *A Lady's Morals* and *New Moon* (both for MGM in 1930), were resounding duds. Studio chiefs Winfield Sheehan and Sidney Kent passed on her.[8]

Pommer's son John felt Irving Thalberg "had a commitment that he wanted to shove off to someone else."[9] Her name was Gloria Swanson. Still, Sheehan insisted on casting Gloria against Pommer's judgment. The producer found her too old, and so he was required to cast an older male lead. It was agreed MGM would announce that Gloria was "on loan" to Fox. (Gloria's version of these events in her memoirs differs considerably.) With the picture set to roll at the end of July, the rest of the cast was quickly signed.

The plot of the story is romantic and as lilting as its Alpine settings. In the Bavarian village of Abendorf where he teaches, Karl Roder (Douglass Montgomery) is in love with Sieglinde Lessing (nineteen-year-old June Lang). Karl writes songs for her father (Al Shean making his film debut, repeating his Broadway role). In Munich Karl meets the beautiful opera singer Frieda Hotzfelt (Gloria) and the librettist Bruno Mahler (John Boles). Frieda and Bruno are volatile and jealous lovers. Frieda flirts with Karl, and Bruno romances Sieglinde. In the end both couples are reunited.

Opposite Gloria was cast her former "discovery" John Boles. (Previously considered for the role were Phillips Holmes and Nelson Eddy.) Boles hoped that appearing opposite Gloria would reignite his faltering career, but his next Fox assignment would be portraying Shirley Temple's father in *Curly Top*, the death knell for a former matinee idol. Also in the cast were character actresses Marjorie Main, later to gain fame as Ma Kettle, who was also repeating her Broadway role as Anna (strangely, all her dialogue sequences were severely cut), and Sara Haden, later known as Aunt Polly in MGM's Andy Hardy series, who handed in an excellent turn as Martha.

The Broadway version of *Music in the Air* opened the same night Franklin D. Roosevelt was elected president, when the whole country was feeling an air of optimism after four years of the Depression. The lovely "I've Told Every Little Star" (the melody written by Kern after he heard the early morning warble of a bird outside his window) and "The Song Is You" were the two most popular songs to come out of the show. (Two other new songs were the title tune and "We Belong Together.") Walter Reisch was replaced by Billie (later Billy) Wilder, who co-wrote the screenplay—his first American screen credit—with Howard Irving and Robert Liebmann. Wilder recalled seeing Gloria on the Fox lot, "her pride and desperation wrapped around her like a tattered ermine."[10]

Having been "refreshed" in Europe, Gloria put herself through a strenuous health regime, lost weight, and looked absolutely stunning in the film. For her wardrobe in *Music in the Air,* Gloria secured René Hubert. His most stunning creation for her was an ivory silk crepe bugle-beaded, long-sleeved, high-necked, form-fitting gown with train, complemented by diamond clasps and emerald-green crystal beads, matching turban, and satin slippers, worn with an ostrich-feathered cape. It appeared on the screen for but one minute. Hats were an important Swanson accoutrement. One in particular protected her in a scene when Frieda pulls on a swing rope after an emotional outburst. An iron ring that held the rope accidentally fell on top of Gloria's head but did not cause her harm, the hat blocking the blow.

Gloria gave an interview to writer Frederick Russell during the filming. Sipping a glass of sherry, she prattled on about the blessings of motherhood. "I've learned a great deal from them [her children] . . . They help me keep simplicity in my point of view." Finished with that brief token of maternal information, Gloria quickly directed the conversation onto her favorite subject. "Clothes . . . are also vastly important to women. There is nothing like the comfort and assurance of knowing that you are well dressed."[11]

Most American women during the Depression were struggling to simply put food on the table for their families. Many stitched together their own clothing, as well as their children's, from flour and grain sacks. Gloria's gowns cost in the thousands of dollars. And for her to assume all women were even half as fortunate as she was a major error in her image promotion. Her indulgent lifestyle and behavior, as much as anything else, were probable reasons she had become passé, viewed as out of touch with reality.

Years later Gloria commented, "After I was through with the movies—or vice versa—I was so sore at my stupidity that I could've cut my throat. I woke up and discovered I was the all-time Hollywood dumb cluck who'd thrown away millions of dollars to put up a big front that fooled nobody but me."[12] Hindsight thought redeeming, perhaps.

Gloria was relieved to hear Thalberg and MGM were finally perparing a story for her Metro debut. The property was *Riff Raff,* a colorful romantic drama for Gloria and Clark Gable by Frances Marion, who had originally written it for her friend Mary Pickford in 1932. (Pickford then sold it to Metro.) The story is set on the New Orleans waterfront, and a riverboat is mentioned in the original publicity. Gloria was to play a wealthy woman and Gable a roughneck.

Because of censorship issues, however, the plot was altered from its original concept and now included a measure of comedy.

Sadly, on August 10, film director George W. Hill, Frances Marion's second husband, committed suicide, and Marion went into seclusion. On August 24 it was announced Thalberg had given James K. McGuinness the assignment to complete the screenplay of *Riff Raff.* The project was delayed further as Gloria's new debut Metro picture was announced to be *Women with Brains,* written by Edith M. Fitzgerald, who scripted *Riptide* and *Today We Live.* Confusion as to what would become of Gloria's Metro debut abounded.

Gloria could now at least afford to bring her children to California from Europe, and Joseph was enrolled in a military academy. With Marshall, Gloria attended Max Reinhardt's production of *A Midsummer's Night Dream,* elaborately staged at the Hollywood Bowl. She looked lovely though bored that evening, dressed in a long sleeveless velvet dress, a large dark satin hat, and her two Cartier crystal bracelets. Women clustered around Bart for autographs as Gloria was photographed patiently smoking a cigarette.

As the filming of *Music in the Air* wound down at the end the month, suddenly Gloria and Bart became the talk of Hollywood. After attending a party at the home of Ernst Lubitsch, around midnight Gloria invited John Monk Saunders, former Rhodes scholar and celebrated screenwriter of *Wings* and *The Dawn Patrol,* and his actress wife Fay Wray to her home for a game of Ping-Pong before the four ventured back to Lubitsch's. During the game, Saunders mentioned how the recent fan magazines had compared the looks of Gloria and Wray, noting their similarities. By now both men were well into their cups, and Marshall apparently resented the comment. Back at Lubitsch's soiree, seated in the game room, according to Saunders, "for some unexplained reason, Mr. Marshall began a tirade against me. I paid no attention, thinking it was a gag. Then he called me a name. When I saw he wasn't smiling I let him have one on the chin."[13]

Saunders claimed victory with a knockout. "If he [Bart] had read 'The Virginian' he never would have used that word without smiling," Saunders observed. Marshall denied the story: "I can say that Mr. Saunders' statement is the best proof that he is a writer of melodramatic fiction." Lubitsch was distraught, vainly attempting to cover the whole thing up, saying, "This is most regrettable. I can say only that it was nothing: just a little argument among friends and nothing at all to attract attention. As far as I know, it was an artistic argument."[14]

The fight produced no victors. "Any reconciliation at the moment was made impossible by Miss Swanson. She flew about in all directions in a furious display of hysterics and dramatics and generally took charge of the situation," Wray wrote in her autobiography.[15] "The very significant thing John omitted . . . is that, following the Ping-Pong, when he returned and sat at a table in the games room, John placed himself immediately next to Gloria and began exploring her décolletage . . . None of them seemed to notice . . . as John said, he [Bart] called him a bestial bastard, it was surely not with vitriol but, rather, kindly, a statement of fact . . . [Later that night] Gloria telephoned that Bart had a gun and was on his way to our house. But as she continued to talk and to lecture on the enormous difference in the drinking style of Europeans and Americans, I sensed that Bart was probably beside her. A man who could say what he said about John would not be out with a gun. He probably didn't have one."[16]

On November 7 Gloria's divorce from Michael was granted by default by Judge Clement Shinn. Appearing nervous on the stand, Gloria, dressed in a chic brown ensemble with slanted hat and matching brown gloves, and wearing a sable scarf (never a flattering color choice for Gloria, but brown always looked good in court), testified Michael had been quarrelsome throughout their marriage.

Lois Wilson, Gloria's devoted ally and now a bleached blonde, wearing a slanted feathered hat, testified she had witnessed Michael become verbally abusive at the very mention of American politics. "We were at the home of a mutual friend to hear one of President Roosevelt's speeches," Wilson related. "When we commenced to seriously discuss the president's talk, Mr. Farmer broke in with a long string of abuse against Miss Swanson, telling her she didn't know anything about politics and that she wasn't good at anything else."[17]

Gloria testified somewhat inaccurately that his cruel behavior started with *Perfect Understanding*. "He was going to do the lead and then he wasn't," she swore under oath. "Finally he was offered a small part and it hurt his pride and he wanted me to withdraw. He quarreled with me and it made me so ill I had to take ten days off to recover."[18] Perhaps she was referring to those days when she demanded that the film crew bask in the sun in the south of France, with the excuse of shooting some irrelevant yachting sequences off the coast of Cannes.

Judge Shinn granted Gloria a no-contest divorce, as Michael had failed to respond; his last given address was the Prince De Galles Hotel in Paris. Gloria was awarded custody of Michelle, and Michael was ordered to pay child support, including $1,125 which he was already in arrears on Miss Simonson's wages. After the ruling, Lois and Gloria were photographed outside the court looking very pleased.

"My mother's relations with men were mostly disastrous," Michelle would later say. "She wanted to be eternally in love. Her marriage to my father, Michael Farmer, an Irish playboy, an alcoholic, lasted over two years. Ultimately, she was looking for men to dominate her, which never really happened. Men came into her life like machos and they left like poodles sitting up for a biscuit."[19]

In New York, Gloria's film *Music in the Air* opened at the Radio City Music Hall on December 13. Critics were kind. Andre Sennwald in *The New York Times* liked the picture: "Mr. Kern's matchless songs are enough to insure 'Music in the Air' a position among the superior musical pictures . . . Joe May . . . tells this musical comedy story in a spirited style . . . Miss Swanson makes an agreeable return to the screen as the prima donna. The years have not scarred her loveliness; in addition she possesses a pleasing voice and a gift for light comedy."[20]

Variety's "Abel" was not so moved: "Apart from the basic shortcoming of a story that is never real there are also the cast deficiencies of the featured pair. Superficially, Gloria Swanson as the petulant prima [donna] sounds like a natural, and John Boles might even be acceptable as an equally temperamental librettist. But it doesn't work out that way . . . It's never believable . . . Photography is truly beautiful, but that's not enough."[21]

When *Music in the Air* opened at Graumann's Chinese Theater later that week, it drew raves. According to the *Los Angeles Times*'s Norbert Lusk, the picture featured the "dazzling return of Gloria Swanson to her rightful place on the screen . . . She is magnetic, compelling and enormously expert, her inspired pantomime placing her far ahead of those newer favorites whose training has been solely on the stage. Every least crook of Miss Swanson's little finger furthers the mood she happens to project with the unconsciousness of the keenly attuned and evocative actress."[22] *Music in the Air*, however, barely made back its costs, bringing in just $60,000 for the week at Radio City Music Hall.

Music in the Air marked the end of Continental-flavored musicals in American pictures. Perhaps because it was created by German exiles, *Music in the Air* relied on and exhibited what might have been too much sly humor. Certainly the actors performed exuberantly, leading one historian to say, "Gloria Swanson, singing and posturing with orotund, over-the-top intensity in her only full musical . . . enacts the tainted ingénue with hectic glamour."[23] But Broadway musicals historically translated poorly into cinematic outings, usually because the studio treated them so cavalierly. Between the somewhat heavy-handed direction of Joe May, who literally used a stopwatch to time scenes, and the "much-too-flamboyant, often whining performances by its stars,"[24] the film simply failed to make a profitable landing.

To view the eighty-five-minute *Music in the Air* today is a treat.[25] It opens with a scene somewhat similar to the one in *The Sound of Music* (20th Century–Fox, 1965), an aerial view of the Bavarian Alps. Immediately one is struck by the production values of the picture, the energetic, fast-paced line delivery, and the sharp editing, which contradicts a great many of the negative comments directed at the film when it was released. *Music in the Air* is charming, if prolonged. Its mood and the flavor are perfect. Characterizations are on point, from the surprisingly good Al Shean to Christian Rub as the stereotypical Tyrolean cobbler (his face and voice were later immortalized as Geppetto in Walt Disney's 1940 feature cartoon classic *Pinocchio*).

In 2011, noted film historian Leonard Maltin, viewing *Music in the Air* for the first time, wrote, "As much as I admired the ingredients of the picture, I found it too self-conscious in its cleverness and I'm afraid its charm wore thin after a while."[26] Perhaps he has a point. But it is a time capsule, a picture that should be looked at and reevaluated. Of all of Gloria's early talkies, *The Trespasser* aside, *Music in the Air*, her only true musical, represents possibly her best sound film work next to *Sunset Boulevard*.

In early March it was announced that actor Spencer Tracy was leaving Fox Films and taking a contract with MGM; his first picture slated was *Riff Raff*. Gloria was eventually off the picture, characters were altered, and the beautiful Jean Harlow stepped into the role intended for Gloria. As Metro fumbled about for a solid property, Gloria was approached to star in *Keystone Hotel* by another producer—a project that never got beyond the talk stage. And she was asked to do a radio show called *Norman's Court of the Air*, written by Vera Oldham and based on an idea by Dema Harshbarger. It never played.

When Herbert began filming *The Dark Angel* that spring of 1935 with Merle Oberon and David Niven for Goldwyn, Gloria was a constant visitor on the lot. Her devotion to Marshall was real, and the two would frequently spend their time off out of town, as they did in late April in Palm Springs.

On May 9 young British actor Niven made his theatrical debut on the American stage at the Pasadena Playhouse in a production called *Wedding*. Stumbling onto the stage obviously inebriated, Niven recalled the event. "I shielded my eyes from the footlights, an unforgivable thing to do, and [saw] that Bart Marshall had brought a party of about thirty people to witness my star debut. I caught a glimpse of Gloria Swanson and Charles Laughton."[27] He was fired after the curtain came down. Ernst Lubitsch, who found Niven's single performance somewhat relaxed but passable, then offered him a role in his upcoming Paramount remake of Gloria's *Bluebeard's Eighth Wife*.

In August Michael was involved in a car crash in Juan-les-pins, France. Traveling with a male companion and a Madame Delbarre, a wealthy woman to whom he said he was engaged, he drove his large touring car into the front door of the only American nightclub on the Riviera, curiously named Hollywood. No one was hurt, though the dancers in the club panicked. He said the accident was due to a defect in the steering gear, or perhaps it was caused by the unexplained "jostling by his man companion."[28] The incident didn't faze Gloria in the least.

Marshall left for the East Coast shortly after a preview of *The Dark Angel* to be with Edna and attend its New York premiere, while Gloria, dressed in a black lace sari, attended with Anderson Lawler the opening of Ina Claire's new play, *Ode to Liberty*, at the Belasco Theater. While Bart was out of town, Gloria could be spotted listening to Larry Lee's music at the Biltmore Wilshire. That month Edmund Goulding advised Gloria he had a chance to sell *The Trespasser* to Warner Bros. for a remake. She then contacted Joseph Kennedy, through Virginia Bowker as always. He was preparing to depart on board the French superliner *Normandie* to Europe, and Gloria wired him asking for the rights.

Kennedy cabled back the following day his consent to all the assets, advising her not to give the story away gratis as several other studios had wanted it.[29]

The remake became *That Certain Woman*, a Bette Davis vehicle. Kennedy must have been excited by this communication with his long-ago mistress, as throughout the month of November he kept up a litany of cable communications with her. In care of Ted O'Leary, Gloria sent a telegram on November 13 to Kennedy at his 230 Park Avenue address. He then sent Gloria a wire on November 15 requesting her telephone number, and advising her of his business address at 30 Rockefeller Plaza.[30]

Her response was quick in coming that afternoon.[31]

On Christmas Eve, Gloria and Bart Marshall were guests of Clifton Webb, currently under contract with MGM for the picture *Elegance* (it was never made), and his mother Maybelle at Webb's holiday soiree for wealthy New York dowager Lady Elsie Mendl. Revelers included Marlene Dietrich with John Gilbert, Merle Oberon and David Niven, and Cole Porter. They all sat around the Christmas tree waiting for "wassail and cakes . . . and Porter played the piano and sang."[32] Photographed with her good friend Rhea Gable, estranged wife of Clark, Gloria looked smart in a light-colored, floor-length, clinging gown and large fur cape.

On December 29 the still persistent Kennedy sent yet another cable to Gloria advising her he would be leaving the White House that evening and arrive in Palm Beach the next day. He wanted to know where she could be contacted at six o'clock Monday night.[33]

Careerwise, the New Year of 1936 did not look promising for Gloria. Nothing had developed yet with MGM, or any other studio, despite her hobnobbing with every film studio executive in town. Mercifully she still received her MGM weekly paycheck and attended one social event after another with and without Marshall.

Bart's drinking had escalated in the past year. He was moody by nature, and no doubt racked by some guilt over the separation from his daughter. Eventually he and Gloria split up. He left by train for New York, then sailed to England, where he announced he and Edna had reconciled. He arrived back in New York the third week of January and then reconciled with Gloria. It was ridiculous.

In Hollywood the children remained separated from their mother most of the time. In later years Michelle would fondly remember the Crescent Drive mansion, where Gloria still maintained four butlers, as well as two chauffeurs for her three Rolls-Royces, one white, one black, and one maroon. Michelle recalled playing in the house with her eleven-years-older sister and ten-years-older brother. "Our home, which all of us used to call the 'big house,' was a wonderful place with an enormous attic, a basement and an elevator and secret passageways," she said.[34] Of the moments Michelle spent with her mother, many years later she stated, "I was a little afraid of her but she was very dominating and had such a strong personality. But I did respect her!"[35]

Gloria still played the publicity game. About her career, she told one interviewer, "Yes I plan to make some more pictures, but first I must find the right story. I am looking for it now. I will never make another picture until I make a great one. It is no use making any other kind. I really shouldn't have made my last picture [*Music in the Air*], but I let them talk me into it. No more." Asked about New York publicity man Steve Hannagan, seen squiring her around Broadway, she said, "I'd rather not even discuss that."[36]

Gloria and Bart spent days between his picture assignments at La Quinta in Palm Springs. When he was shooting, she visited him at his studio, perhaps welcomed by producers as she would try to keep him sober. Marshall would star in over a dozen major, and a few minor, films for Paramount, RKO, 20th Century–Fox, and MGM during his years with Gloria. She made only *Music in the Air,* and then she was off the screen until 1941. Just to keep the public's appetite whetted for the frolics of the stars, Columbia Studios released a couple of "Screen Snapshots" film shorts that year featuring Gloria with and without Marshall at various Hollywood social functions.

Other than further discussions with MGM about film properties, Gloria and Marshall spent 1936 much as they had 1935, attending endless parties and industry functions, usually surrounded by the same crowd—Oberon and Niven, Evelyn Laye and her husband Frank Lawton, Goulding, the Ernst Lubitsches, the Rathbones, and on and on to distraction.

Michael arrived in New York on board the *Europa* in March along with the flamboyant, openly gay James "Jimmy" Donahue, cousin of millionairess Barbara Hutton. For the most part Michael had become a person to avoid, at least for the film crowd and some discerning folks in high society. He had completed a 12,000-mile, seven-month voyage on board Tony Duke's yacht the year before, traveling the Red Sea and on to China and Japan, crossing the Pacific to California, then continuing on to Europe. He did not visit with his daughter.

Michael merely pretended he was just vacationing away from Gloria. Rarely was he sober. On September 3 he wrote a newsy, chatty letter to Gloria from the Tower Hotel in Brinksome Park, Bournesmouth, letting her know all she was missing by not being with him in the social swirl of the Riviera. As Europe was facing inevitable political destruction, he was desperately trying to hold on to his carefree youth while being oblivious to what was happening before his very eyes. He wrote Gloria of having just come in from playing tennis and having but a few moments to write. He found Cannes "lousy" that year, so he was off to Deauville and Biarritz, then the Antibes for Elsa Maxwell's soiree for a couple of friends before they sailed. What a party—Beatrice Lillie sang and Noël Coward played the piano. And by the way, Lady Mandl was simply fading away.[37] All very decadent, and all very desperate.

In October, when Michael was in Hollywood staying at the Beverly Wilshire Hotel, Gloria sent him word regarding the cost of Michelle's nursery tuition and clothing. She asked if he was planning to visit his daughter. She then telephoned and was advised that he had spent all that afternoon with Clifton Webb at his 1005 North Rexford Drive address and could not be reached. Michael's pleasures held priority. She hung up in despair.

Tragedy hit the industry on September 14, 1936, which is remembered as one of the blackest days in the history of Hollywood. The thirty-seven-year-old "Boy Wonder" Irving Thalberg died of pneumonia. He was inurned in a private mausoleum at Forest Lawn Memorial Park. With him went Gloria's security at MGM. Thalberg might well have kept Gloria on contract out of loyalty, but Louis B. Mayer had never liked her and seldom, if ever, personally dealt with her. Even though properties were developed for her at MGM, they never met her demands. Her contract lapsed. In October rumors circulated that she might sign with the newly organized 20th Century–Fox.

On November 3 Gloria applied for complete legal guardianship of her daughter Gloria's estate. The child held a $7 million trust. The action, if she was successful, would allow Gloria to control her child's finances. (Norma Shearer applied that same day for guardianship of her two children by Thalberg as well.) On November 23 Gloria, darkly dressed with a fur stole and displaying a concerned scowl, answered questions put to her by Court Commissioner Bischoff. Most of those in the courtroom did not recognize her as she took the stand under the name Gloria Swanson Farmer. Her petition was granted by Superior Judge James Leslie Kincaid.

On December 8 Gloria, fashionably attired in a faux-fur-trimmed coat cinched at the waistline, with matching hat, arrived in New York on board the *Twentieth Century Limited* to discuss with Broadway producer Theron Bamberger the possibility of doing Gladys Hurlbut's stage play *Lovers Meeting.* "There was only one reporter present and less than a dozen persons in the crowded station recognized her," said the *New York Post.*[38] The play, which was quite a change from the old days, went unproduced. In Hollywood Frances Marion, out of loyalty to Gloria perhaps, began working on a new screenplay for her at MGM, and Adela Rogers St. Johns gave *G-Woman* (also called *Lady Eleven*) to Gloria, based on an idea suggested by Gloria herself. (Swanson cabled St. Johns at one point stating she did not understand the story.) Neither project materialized.

Back in California the first week of November, Gloria and Marshall were seen together at the Trocadero for a party hosted by Chester Morris and his wife. As 1937 wound down, gossip columnist Sheilah Graham (soon to inaugurate her own doomed love affair with married novelist F. Scott Fitzgerald) started off her inaugural *Los Angeles Times* column with "Hollywood is betting that Gloria Swanson will be Mrs. Herbert Marshall before the end of 1937."[39] However, the Swanson-Marshall affair had run its course. His drinking was ruining him, his career, and Gloria's love for him. Herbert left for Europe on November 16 on board the *Normandie.* And Graham soon changed to another newspaper.

21

New York Redux

In 1936, Gloria began a casual affair with the eccentric twenty-six-year-old Hungarian piano prodigy Ervin Nyiregyhazi, and that May she gifted "Neary" with a perfunctory copy of Kahlil Gibran's *The Prophet*. Nyiregyhazi was a brilliant pianist and, it was later disclosed, a clinically confirmed sex addict. After she sponsored a couple of his Hollywood concerts, by October 1938 their clandestine affair was over.

While staying at the Lombardy Hotel on Park Avenue in New York, Gloria was photographed about town with the handsome gay playboy millionaire Alex Tiers. After a brief relationship with New York Stock Exchange broker Jerry Gordon, Gloria returned to California, arriving February 4, 1937.

Meeting with reporters, she erroneously informed them she had been offered three plays in New York but had received an urgent telegram from MGM film producer Harry Rapf urging her "to forsake her stage ambitions and return to motion pictures."[1] The project at hand was the screenplay begun by Eugene Watts, which Frances Marion had diligently prepared for Gloria, called *The Infamous Maizie Kenyon,* from a play by Bayard Veiller, who was set to direct.

That same month it was reported Gloria would make her long-awaited Metro debut in *The Emperor's Candlesticks,* directed by George Fitzmaurice opposite William Powell. It would now precede *Maizie Kenyon,* a melodramatic programmer, spiced up with two songs for Gloria. "I can't afford to make an average picture," she grandly announced in the press after being "summoned" back to

Hollywood. "It must be a good picture. If I were just starting my career, it would be different, but when one has been a star, the public expects so much more."[2] Gloria's tests for *The Emperor's Candlesticks*, filmed in July with Powell, were not very good; in fact, they were embarrassing. Oscar winner Luise Rainer, who had originally been offered the role after newcomer Hedy Lamarr failed a test as well, finally took the part.

Eventually *Maizie Kenyon* did not work out either and was abandoned on March 10. The press reported, "Gloria Swanson has decided against playing a woman of 40 in 'Maizie Kenyon,' the film in which she was scheduled for a screen comeback, and is now searching for a story in which there is a younger heroine."[3] (Given the attention and encouragement she received from MGM, it is sad Gloria never worked on the Metro lot.)

Returning to New York that spring, Gloria obtained a new residence at 817 Fifth Avenue at Sixty-Third Street, a posh, third-floor, thirteen-room, four-bedroom apartment with a fifty-foot frontage on Central Park.

To Louella Parsons Gloria sent the following cable, dated April 16 :

AS YOU UNDOUBTEDLY KNOW MAIZIE KENYON DID NOT
TURN OUT TO BE THE PROPER VEHICLE FOR ME I THEREFORE
DID NOT SIGN WITH METRO STOP I AM SAILING FOR LONDON
ON THE QUEEN MARY WEDNESDAY TO CONFER ABOUT
DIRECTOR AND STORY WHICH IF I LIKE I WILL MAKE IN
ENGLAND WILL KEEP YOU ADVISED[4]

Accepting an invitation from a friend to attend the coronation of King George VI in London,[5] Gloria sailed off for Europe on April 21, with eight trunks in tow, on board the *Queen Mary*, dressed sportily in a light-colored coat, dark gloves, and a hat, waving happily to photographers. The papers suggested she was off to star in European films. On this voyage she did not take a deluxe suite as in days of yore but a more modest cabin, though still in first class.

In England, she checked into the Lansdowne House, Berkeley Square. While she had been in Hollywood Gloria had conferred with Harry Cohn, head of Columbia Pictures, which Cohn had founded in 1919. A studio once considered a "Poverty Row" outfit, Columbia now produced finely streamlined, fast-paced pictures. Gloria had apparently squeezed a sweet deal out of Cohn before sailing. She had remained on MGM's payroll at $1,000 a week for well over a year even after Thalberg died and before her contract lapsed, and she had not made a single picture for them, which irked Metro head Louis B. Mayer.

Gloria wrote Cohn before departure from New York on April 19, and true to form she quickly got down to her financial needs and demands:

> My sincerest wish is that you will never have any regrets on my account and that our first picture will be the best damn picture I have ever made . . . Of course we are going to have arguments . . .
>
> You told me not to ask for any money in London. This might be necessary, because out of the $2,500.00 received yesterday I must pay my hotel bill here, my telephone bill, which is going to be frightening, my passage, which is about $600.00 each way, without extras. Also I must send money to the Coast for Mr. Cole; my account there is $500.00 overdrawn, plus the bills of the first of the month and to avoid a scene in London, I must pay a $700.00 bill there . . . I hate to discuss these money matters, but they are worrysome.[6]

The European press picked up the news of Gloria's new contract, signed April 15, 1937, a one-picture deal for $15,000, at $1,000 a week for fifteen weeks, and announced her first vehicle would be a remake of the 1933 UFA picture *Brennenddes Geheimis (The Burning Secret),* by Frederick Kohner (based on the novel by Stefan Zweig).[7] The picture, however, was never made in Hollywood.

After vacationing with her unnamed friend in France and Switzerland, Gloria was beckoned back to Hollywood by Cohn, who announced her comeback film would be *The Second Mrs. Draper,* based on an upcoming novel by Noel Pierce and produced by Frances Marion, with filming set to begin July 1. Boarding the liner *Normandie* at Le Havre, Gloria arrived in New York on May 31. She later would tell reporters, "I might have spent the rest of my life quietly in Hollywood. But the minute I left I was missed."[8] Gloria took the train from New York, arriving in Los Angeles on June 10. By August she had been offered a role in *Manhattan Merry-Go-Round* with cowboy star Gene Autry and baseball legend Joe DiMaggio, for Republic Pictures for $50,000. At the moment, however, she was committed to Columbia.

Two treatments of *The Second Mrs. Draper* were submitted to Cohn, and he was dissatisfied with both. When Marion realized the project was not going to pan out, she dropped work on it. Cohn generously kept Gloria on salary while his lieutenants searched for another vehicle for her. They then announced she would star in a remake of the 1930 Pathé film *Holiday,* based on a play by Philip Barry. Columbia purchased the property for Gloria and retitled it *Vacation Bound,* to be produced by Sidney Bushman. Gloria didn't like it, but tested for it just the same.[9] She had sold Columbia one property she had owned since January 1937, titled *Ways and Means,* which they bought on December 20, possibly to pacify her and allow her more money. Nothing more was done with it.

Gloria eventually brought Cohn a property she really liked. "I'm not going to send it to you and let you use it as a prop to hide your phone to Santa Anita," she teasingly told him on the telephone. "I'm coming to your office and read it to you myself." When she finished reading the twenty-five-page treatment to Cohn, he told her he wanted to think about it.[10]

As Gloria recalled years later, "All of those movie producers you hear about in retrospect, most of them were cigar-chewing morons, dunked in luck . . . One day he [Cohn] called me up and asked me over to his private apartment. I said sure, but no funny tricks. He was famous for that. I told him I was very handy with a lamp. [Gloria would reference her femininity every chance she got.] I read him this wonderful, tender story and he said: 'Well, I'll tell you tomorrow.' Finally the phone rang and there I was twisted in 30 feet of telephone lines and he said: 'The story couldn't be any good because David O. Selznick wants to sell it.' I said: 'You're the stupidest man . . .' and used all the four letter words I knew."[11]

Telling the story on another occasion, she said, "I screamed and swore and called him everything I could think of. I only stopped when I realized that I had pulled the thirty-foot extension cord out of the wall."[12] The script was *Dark Victory,* and, Swanson said, "it made Bette Davis world famous."[13] (Davis was already "world famous," with a Best Actress Oscar on her mantel. After 1938's *Jezebel* [Warner Bros.] she would have another.) When the film opened in April 1939, Gloria sent Cohn a Los Angeles telephone book, in reference to his ability to read, along with a note that said, "Enjoy."[14]

On December 23, Cohn, remembering the generosity a young Gloria had shown him in 1919 by introducing him to industry giants, reluctantly dictated a letter to her:

Writing this letter is one of the toughest jobs I've had since I've been in the picture business. As you know, I had high hopes that we could work out something which would be to the advantage to both you and the studio.

I have given a great amount of time and thought in trying to secure a vehicle and setup which would start you off on another real success. As you know, I have bought several stories, intending them to be worked out for you. Despite the time, energy and the money used, nothing has worked out, and I have met with discouragement from those whose viewpoint I must consider in the making of a picture.

It is with deepest regret, therefore, that I have to tell you that I am letting our deal terminate and am closing our contract. I hope you will try to understand my position and the fact that I am trying to explain the very cold legal notice which is enclosed herewith.[15]

Gloria's balance sheet as of December 31 showed her total liabilities came to $4,075,359.41. At her Crescent Drive mansion, now but a "monument to a by-gone era," Gloria threw a huge cocktail party and announced to her friends gathered that evening that she was through with Hollywood because Hollywood was through with her. She put the house up for sale and prepared to sell its fur-nishings.[16] She then rented Bungalow 5, numbers 3–6, at the Beverly Hills Hotel for $575 a month.

The press then announced Gloria was contracting with Republic Studios, a definite B-studio that churned out John Wayne–Roy Rogers–Gene Autry west-erns. Signed by Moe J. Siegel, managing director of the studio, Gloria was com-mitted to star in three films, beginning within the month on *Ex-Love,* a story about the divorce racket, based on a novel by Mateel Howe Farnham. (Holly-wood also speculated that month about whether Gloria might appear in Uni-versal's *Mad About Music,* in support of teenage singing sensation Deanna Durbin.) In March Republic purchased another two film properties for Gloria: *Ladies in the News,* in which she would replace Frieda Inescort, with a story by Maurice A. Hanline, and *Two on the Aisle,* again by Hanline and Jerry O'Connor. Talks with Republic would continue throughout the next few months.

Young Gloria, now eighteen, was attending Beverly Hills High School on Moreno Drive and preparing for college. She was a member of the Methodist

Westwood Community Church. She rarely saw her mother. About their relationship she would admit several years later, "Michelle was much closer [to my
mother] and grew up really much closer than I had been as a child."[17] Sixteen-
year-old Joseph was still out east at a private school in Portsmouth.

Six-year-old Michelle, after having been first enrolled at Miss Luther's
Nursery and Kindergarten on North Canyon Drive, had just spent first grade
at the Hawthorne School on North Rexford Drive. Raised primarily by Edith
Simonson, Michelle was required to send little letters to her mother during
Gloria's travels.

After a cocktail party for American jeweler Paul Flato and his wife,[18] thrown
by Constance Collier on February 16, Gloria quit Hollywood. On the evening of
February 21, 1938, she stepped aboard a Union Pacific Streamliner bound for
New York. "I had stayed too long at the fair," she would later write.[19] Taking up
residency at 817 Fifth Avenue with her dog Pickles, and keeping her Beverly Hills
bungalow for another six months, Gloria began to prepare for the future. (Just to
keep her acting career alive, she signed with the Hawks-Volck Agency in Hollywood in April 1938 and renewed her SAG membership.)

Her New York apartment was a gift of Gustave "Gus" Schirmer, her lover.
Born in Boston in 1891, he was heir to the Schirmer music publishing firm,
founded by his grandfather Gustav in 1861. He had fallen in love with Gloria in
New York some time before. According to her memoirs he eventually professed
his feelings and offered her all his stock in the Schirmer music corporation,
which is doubtful.

Concerned about her finances, Schirmer insisted on helping her during this
transitional period at least until her California property sold. Gloria would
later call Gus "a restless soul."[20]

Adapting to living in New York, Gloria told friends she loved being domestic. In May she received approximately $250,000 when her Crescent Drive estate
sold. Gloria later wrote that unlike the fanciful plots of some of her movies, her
life now would not include fleets of expensive limousines or large, lavish dinner parties.[21] She now pondered how she would be able to support herself.

Gloria secretly sailed to Europe in late April, 1938, returning in Cabin Class
to New York on June 2 on board the *Europa*. Her purpose would be disclosed
later. Daughter Gloria's high school graduation was on June 15, so the trip
would be brief. She posed for the obligatory press photographers aboard ship,

looking every minute of her forty years and quite matronly, wearing a light-colored, spotted overcoat, dark gloves, and a veiled hat. When asked by reporters why the quick trip, she was vague. "It is something I have always wanted to do," she said. "It has nothing to do with the movies or anything theatrical."[22]

By the end of July 1938 the Republic Pictures deal was off. Again Gloria's many demands were too exhorbitant. Nothing pleased her, and she was tired of the battle. She sent a cable to Miss Simonson when she was advised by her child's pediatrician Dr. Bernard that Michelle was suffering with the mumps, and arranged for her daughter and Simonson to come to New York. Michelle was then enrolled at the private Lenox School at 53 East Seventy-Eighth Street.

Shuttled about throughout her much of her childhood, Michelle nevertheless maintained a healthy and stable attitude. "Mother had very definite ideas about bringing up her children, and even if she couldn't do it all alone, our governess had instructions never to bring Hollywood into our home," she said several years later. "There were no photographers, no movie magazines, no trace of studio life near the nursery."[23] And apparently none in the schoolroom either. Most children had no idea who Michelle's mother was.

Joseph, on the other hand, was becoming a handful. Gloria related in 1950 what happened in his seventeenth year. "I suddenly realized he was a shiftless, inconsiderate, spoiled brat," she said. "He wasn't to blame. The governess who raised him while I was batting around on a career made him utterly dependent on her, and she supplanted me in his affections. I had a terrible scene with Joseph, and finally ordered him out of the house to teach him self-respect and responsibility. I told him to expect five dollars a week from me, so that he wouldn't starve."[24] No "Mommie Dearest," still Gloria was a firm believer in discipline.

Gloria's mysterious European jaunt finally came to light. She had always been interested in science and what money could be made by inventions, dating back to the filming of *The Love of Sunya* and her involvement with George de Bothezat. Gloria was something of an inventor herself, sketching ideas for such things as dustless brooms. Contacting everyone she knew about patents, and buying up copies of *Popular Science,* she realized there was a need for a company to assist and bankroll the hundreds of primarily Jewish scientists now being forced out of Europe by the Fascist dictatorships of Adolf Hitler and Benito Mussolini.

Setting up business offices at Rockefeller Plaza, Gloria created Multiprises,

Inc., a profit-sharing enterprise that secured patents and markets for inventions. The endeavor cost her $200,000 of her own money to start up. With the help of Schirmer, who aided in selecting a board of directors, Gloria reinvented herself as the owner and CEO of her very own patent licensing firm.

On the West Coast, newspapers made mention of Gloria Somborn, a freshman at Stanford and member of the Gamma Gamma Sorority, and young Bob Anderson. They were an item. In late September, Hedda Hopper announced that a widowed friend of Gloria's, left with no money, had given her husband's inventions to Gloria to patent. After organizing Multiprises, Gloria was able to sell the first patent at a tidy sum and charter a yacht, the *Bidou,* for a brief cruise in the Caribbean. (Actually Schirmer chartered the boat.) Then, wrote Hopper, Gloria discovered a new type of button, and a device that could make letter copies without carbon paper. This was just the beginning.

Gloria's Multiprises office was located at 630 Fifth Avenue, high atop Rockefeller Plaza, where she would appear daily, her hair a natural deep brown, and her complexion still radiant through washing with just soap and water. She usually dressed in Valentina, who also whipped up for her a "Vesuvius" smokepot hat that sent out puffs of smoke. (Gloria had begun to wear veiled hats more frequently.) She employed at $155 a month a mysterious, dramatically masculine-looking woman with short-cropped blond hair named Iphigenia "Iffy" Engel, who was her private secretary. Iffy, who lived at the Hotel Rutledge at 161 Lexington Avenue, was well traveled and well versed in the world of music. Her brother was president of Schirmer's music company. On April 8, 1938, Schirmer handed Iffy a check for $450, for three months' salary and for traveling abroad "under a certain agreement between you and me."[25] It was through Engel's diligent efforts that a handful of inventors in Fascist Europe was able to come to the United States and survive the war.

Gloria would spend some $25,000 in just under nine months to spirit four inventors out of Europe and bring them to New York. Engel thus sailed to Europe to negotiate American distribution deals with German inventors and manufacturers. In the process she used Henri de la Falaise's Paris address as Multiprises's European base, calling it Swan Prizes, Inc. Gloria had originally been curious about developing a "luminous paint," which she was sure Hollywood would buy. Although available in the United States, it was only manufactured in Germany.

The inventor of this paint was Richard Kobler. Iffy located him, as well as Henri, who cabled Gloria requesting her to come to Paris.

Danger permeated the Continent. Kobler, whose father had incited the anger of the Nazis when they discovered he had refused to experiment with poison gas during the Great War, escaped to Switzerland after being arrested numerous times by the Gestapo. He was a Jew who headed a syndicate of other inventors. The twenty-nine-year-old Kobler was asked by Henri to come to Paris. He settled into the Hotel St. Louis on the Boulevard St. Michel, along with inventors Leopold Karniol, Anton Kratky, and Leopold Neumann, all on visitors' visas to France. All four could not leave Europe without sponsorship. With Henri's help in dealing with the French authorities, Gloria was able to bring them to the United States. She told one writer it was her way of doing something "constructive" with her money and to "justify my existence as a human being."[26]

Gloria sailed once more to Europe "on business" in mid-January on board the *Europa,* securing a suite in Paris at the Hotel Crillon. She was met at the port of St. Nazaire by the ever dutiful Henri.[27] Henri had filed papers of divorce from Constance on November 11, 1939. Through her patient attorney Milton M. Cohen, Gloria set about legalizing her divorce from Henri in France so that he could now marry the beautiful South American socialite Emmita "Emma" Rodriguez Restrepo de Roeder.

Gloria returned to New York on February 23 on one of the *Queen Mary*'s last peacetime voyages, then set sail to Europe *again* on March 15 on board the *Ile de France.* Also on board was theatrical impresario J. J. Shubert. "Now they're madly discussing a new play," wrote the then politically brainless Hedda Hopper in her column, not having a clue.[28] Gloria looked most chic, and younger, in a light knitted suit and a fur. (Possibly she went under the knife and had a rejuvenation lift in Switzerland on the previous trip to tide her over before the pending war.)

Gloria undertook a third quick, secret sailing, to Europe, arriving in Paris on April 6. She stayed two months, then departed on June 7.[29] On this journey inventor Anton Kratky was contracted and signed by Gloria in Paris on February 27, 1939. Trapped inside Germany since the *Anschluss* (the German takeover of Austria in 1938), the remaining refugee inventors had been hidden in Henri's house outside Paris until they were allowed to enter the United States under the immigration quota. Gloria paid for food and necessities, gave them salaries, and greased all sorts of political palms during that time. She also signed affidavits guaranteeing the men would not become public charges in the States. (Karniol had to wait it out in Cuba another ten months before gaining a visa.) Kobler, however, was stuck in France until Henri pulled strings to make him eligible for a Nansen passport (internationally recognized identity certificates originally issued by the League of Nations). Karniol and Leopold Neumann both arrived in New York aboard the *Europa* in January and February respectively. On June 19, 1939, Kobler arrived on board the *Ile de France*.[30]

In the summer of 1939 it was unsafe to sail on the Atlantic. By that fall it was deadly. On September 3 the German submarine U-30 sank the Anchor-Donaldson liner the *Athenia,* which carried 1,103 souls, off the coast of England. There were more than 300 Americans on board, and over 100 drowned. As Europe faced destruction, the United States edged further into the coming conflict.

"There is no question that Miss Swanson saved three lives," Kobler recalled in 1950, when he was a consultant for the Edison laboratories in California. "Nothing, probably, would have happened to Kratky, a gentile, had he remained in Austria, but the rest of us would have died in concentration camps like all our relatives. [K]arniol and I already had been arrested several times. Once more and we would have been *kaput*."[31]

In a letter to her shortly before her death, Kobler sentimentally wrote Gloria from his home in Switzerland about his memories of her introducing him to his attractive corner office on the twentieth floor of the International Building at Rockefeller Center, and how his first view of a circular working desk had reminded him of an ironic smile.[32]

Kobler invented the Televoice—a remote-controlled dictation device, an "endless band phonograph," based on a corkscrew theory. It became a dictating and amplification system, which was optioned by a manufacturer in 1938. He also proposed a Semi-Automatic Fingering Apparatus for possible submission. In 1941 he offered a new idea for sound recording, another for sound telegraphing, and yet another for multichannel transmission. Leopold Neumann, labeled a "citizen of the German Reich" on his contract with Gloria, took out patent 389311 in April 1941. His machine became the basis of a dictating attachment used by the Paramount Dictating Machine and Recording Company.[33]

By 1941 Kratky, a chemical engineer dealing with electro-chemistry and electro-metallurgy, had settled in midtown Manhattan, and Karniol was living in the Village. (Karniol's wife remained in Graenfeld, Vienna.) Gloria paid her main inventor, Kobler, and two key company personnel, Iffy and Gloria's personal secretary Anne R. Seiler, salaries of $99 a week. Neumann was paid $97.

In the course of its operation before filing for bankruptcy in 1942–43, Multiprises also contracted other inventors, in particular Alfred Bak (the Pestein-Drytex Patent) and John L. Berggren of Lusk, New York, whose "Auto-Eye" lamp and extension cord sold for $2.10 and became a somewhat popular item prior to America's entry into the war. (Gloria even sent one to Wallace Beery in October 1940.) A plastic-button-producing operation was located at the Lyndenhurst Manufacturing Company in New Jersey.

With Kobler in charge of management, Multiprises also diversified its research into metals, developing a hard metal alloy for machine tooling, buttons, and a new form of paper. Multiprises earned Gloria approximately $25,000 a year in royalties, with its biggest commercial success being the plastic-button operation patented by Karniol, which brought in about $3,000 a year. However, by June of 1941 the company's bank balance stood at a precarious $250. At the end of the month, thanks to a new picture contract with RKO, Gloria was able to deposit $7,400 into the company account. According to Gloria, she was set to make $250,000 for her interest in a steel-alloy cutting tool Kratky had brought to America when, for whatever reasons, she rejected his development, and a syndicate moved in and took it over.

In May 1939 Hollywood took brief notice of Gloria when newspapers mentioned she was up for the supporting role of Margit Brandt in David O. Selznick's remake of *Intermezzo,* produced by Leslie Howard and introducing Ingrid Bergman to American audiences. Gloria was not given the role. That stellar part instead went to Herbert Marshall's wife Edna Best. (The papers did note, however, that Gloria's first husband, Wallace Beery, was squiring around town the faded film queen Mae Murray.)

In California, Gloria's elder daughter was preparing for her upcoming wedding to Robert Anderson. Writing to young Gloria, Edith Simonson advised her that as the bride, she had to pay the organist, order the correct flowers, go over the music with the organist, make every detail perfect, and pay attention to the groom's family. The most telling recommendation Simonson offered was to have the press mention her father, neglected in print in the wedding announcements (perhaps by Gloria's dictate). She should say she was not just

Gloria Swanson's daughter, but also "the daughter of the late Herbert K. Somborn and Miss Gloria Swanson or vice versa."[34] To the end of her days, Gloria criticized Edith Simonson's concern and care for her children, telling one and all after young Gloria's wedding that Simonson had "poisoned [her] children's minds against" her.[35]

Now an impressive young woman, Gloria Somborn had her mother's eyes, though they were dark, and her father's gentle demeanor. Her fiancé was twenty-year-old Robert William Anderson, a University of Southern California student, son of wealthy Harold S. Anderson of Bel-Air, referred to in the press as both a caterer and building contractor, and Cynthia (née Hardy) Beal. The wedding was held at 4:00 P.M. on June 30 at the All Saints Episcopal Church in Beverly Hills, Dean William W. Fleetwood officiating. Gloria arrived from New York, and was fashionably photographed in a solid-colored blouse and wild print short skirt.

Young Gloria was escorted down the aisle by her father's business partner Robert Howard Cobb. Gloria kept a low profile throughout the service and was not part of the receiving line. For the wedding she wore a modest gown in several shades of green, sewn by Addie, now nearly sixty-one years old and happily married. The dutiful young Gloria saw to it her father was mentioned in the newspaper, which stated, "The bride's father was the late Herbert K. Somborn."[36]

Back on April 18, 1939, the luxury liner *Paris* caught fire while docked in Le Havre, temporarily blocking the French Line's flagship *Normandie* from exiting its dry dock. The *Paris* eventually capsized and sank at her berth, and remained there until after World War II. On September 20, 1939, Henri tenderly wrote a bittersweet letter to Gloria telling her of the memories that had drowned with the *Paris*'s sinking, of his deep love for the liner, and reminding Gloria of the tears he had wept as he stood years before on its deck for the first time watching his beloved France gliding away from him.[37]

The New York World's Fair, a symbol of progress and optimism for the future, which had so spectacularly opened in Flushing Meadows in 1939, was winding down in 1940. July 24 was proclaimed Gloria Swanson Day at the Fair, beginning with a luncheon at 4:30 in the afternoon at the Hall of Fashion.

The month before, on June 14, Germany marched into Paris and began its occupation of France. For most of 1940 Gloria lost track of Henri and his Emma. Then on October 21 came a much-welcomed letter. Because he had fought in the First World War, Henri was finding it dangerous, if not completely impossible, to apply for a passport from the Occupying German Command for himself. Emma was free to travel but told Henri she would stay with him. After numerous letters failed to reach Gloria—they had obviously been confiscated—one finally made it through detailing his plea for her to help him.[38] Though it took some time, Gloria made the effort.

While this drama played itself out on the international stage, Jimmy Fidler wrote in his *Los Angeles Times* column that the aging Wallace Beery, his film career waning, was attempting to have MGM cast Gloria as his wife in the upcoming picture *The Bad Man.* "It would be good showmanship and a good move for Gloria," Fidler quoted Beery.[39] Constance Bennett meanwhile quietly received her divorce from Henri, on grounds of desertion, in Reno on November 14. It was then announced Gloria would star in *Cue for Passion,* a Broadway-bound play written by Elmer Rice set to open in Princeton, New Jersey, on November 30. Two days later Gloria turned the role down.

She had taken Addie, visiting in New York, on a Caribbean cruise on board the liner *America,* which departed New York August 9 for the Virgin Islands, Puerto Rico, Haiti, and Havana, Cuba. Also on board were Irving Berlin and his wife. The seas were rough during the voyage, causing Captain Giles Stedman on November 12 to change a port of call from San Juan to St. Thomas. In December Gloria sailed again on board the *America* to the same ports of call, this time with her friends Anthony and Margaret Biddle, arriving back in New York on December 19, 1940. Within the year the United States would enter the war.

22

Theater

As the country geared up for entry into the war, Gloria knew her scientists would inevitably leave Multiprises. Because of the war effort, the government took over several private interests, Gloria noted in her memoirs. Both Anton Kratky and Leopold Neumann soon began work for the U.S. government, and Multiprises became a small concern.[1] The company would shut its doors after Pearl Harbor. Gloria began to look for other possible ways to supplement her income.

In January 1941 she started a new venture—importing dresses and garments created by Mrs. Edgar Carrillo of Cuba and making them available to the American public in New York. This enterprise would also give Gloria plenty of opportunities to sail to Havana for both business and pleasure.

An acting role reared its head in February when Gloria considered starring in the stage production *Tryout in Boston,* a play penned by the husband-and-wife team Ladislau and Mary Helen Fay Bus-Fekete, and to be directed by Eugene S. Bryden. The project never materialized. On March 7, Gloria and her mother boarded the liner *America* again in New York for its only World War II cruise to California via Colón, Cuba, and the Panama Canal. Arriving in Los Angeles on March 20, Gloria, appearing rested and chic, told the press she was merely on vacation and would be returning to New York in time to spend Easter with Michelle. Hedda Hopper, nose to the grindstone, announced Gloria was considering two motion picture deals.

Before leaving New York, Gloria had purchased a ground-floor garden apartment at 920 Fifth Avenue. (Actress Eleanor Boardman would later state Joseph P. Kennedy bought it for her.) Gloria and her secretary had been the only two residing at 817 Fifth Avenue, as Michelle was in boarding school at the Rose Haven School for Girls, run by Miss Ruth Van Strum in a lovely Dutch Colonial manor house located in Rockleigh, New Jersey.

While in California, Gloria read that Cecil B. DeMille was casting for *Reap the Wild Wind.* Dressed as a fashion plate, with a peacock feather decorating her stylish hat, Gloria visited her old mentor at his Paramount office. When he remarked, "Gloria, aren't you superstitious about wearing peacock feathers?" her reply was, "No . . . for when I started at Paramount they were lucky for me."[2] They weren't that day, however. The press then announced Gloria might star in Buddy DeSylva's forthcoming Paramount Technicolor musical *Louisana Purchase* with Bob Hope. She did not.

Gloria was then asked to test for a role at RKO, opposite her longtime friend Adolphe Menjou. She made the test on April 4 and was cast five days later. The picture was called *Father Takes a Wife,* with a screenplay by Dorothy and Herbert Fields. Gloria's RKO contract was signed April 17, guaranteeing her one picture for $25,000, five consecutive weeks at $5,000 per. Filming had already commenced on April 15. (Menjou would coincidentally co-star two years later with Pola Negri in UA's *Hi Diddle Diddle,* an embarrassing flop.)

Directed by the affable Jack Hively, *Father Takes a Wife* told of Frederick Osborne Sr. (Adolphe Menjou), a shipping magnate, who plans to marry actress Leslie Collier (Gloria) and turn his company over to his son "Junior" Osborne (John Howard). Junior and his wife (Florence Rice) are opposed to the wedding. At the farewell performance of Leslie's play *Practically Yours,* Frederick Sr. erupts in jealousy over Leslie's amorous embraces with her leading man Vincent Stewart (Neil Hamilton), but Leslie smoothes the moment over. Frederick Sr. and Leslie marry and take a honeymoon cruise to Mexico on board the SS *Leslie C.* A young stowaway, singer Carlos Bardez (Desi Arnaz), is discovered. Leslie decides to mentor him, making her husband very jealous in the process. Misunderstandings and confusion follow. By the end of the film everything is sorted out as Frederick and Leslie await the stork.

On her first day on the lot Gloria arrived at the former Pathé studio for makeup and hair at 6:45 A.M. Her costumes were created by René Hubert. Shortly after 9:00 A.M. director Hively escorted her to Stage 2. As she entered, accompanied by two maids, a hairdresser, and a wardrobe woman, the complete cast and crew of two hundred, including extras, greeted her with applause.

After completing her first scene, Gloria met the press. Disguising the fact she needed money, she told one reporter she had wanted to come out west via the Panama Canal for a rest with her mother and to see her married daughter, "But I couldn't get any rest . . . I could hardly even see my family. Too many people wanted to discuss movie making plans with me. This particular story looked like a good one . . . I figured that working in the movies would be easier than worrying about working in them. And more profitable, too."[3]

Asked about Multiprises, Gloria hedged, "We are doing some work for the government, in defense materials . . . but I am pledged not to talk about them . . . When I started my business of promoting inventions, I went to Europe and found several men who had perfected devices that interested me. Two of them are working with me now." Probably referring to Richard Kobler's father, Gloria dramatized her story: "A third is in a German concentration camp. He had invented a luminous paint for street signs. He signed up with me—and the poor man was imprisoned because he had not done business with the Nazis."[4] At the time, like most other Americans in 1941, Gloria believed that concentration camps were nothing more than enforced labor centers. Toward the end of the war, her own former brother-in-law Richard, Comte de la Falaise, would be betrayed by his mistress to the Gestapo for heading up a resistance group and eventually die of pneumonia at Buchenwald in Wilten, Germany.

As filming progressed on *Father Takes a Wife*, executives at RKO started to search for other properties for Gloria and Menjou. Both had long been considered among the best-dressed figures on the screen, and also the most difficult. The years had mellowed Menjou. But Gloria was "uppity" with fellow cast members, "and should know better after all those years of adversity," reported Jimmy Fidler in his column in May.[5] With the money she was making for *Father Takes a Wife*, Gloria was able to repay some personal loans. She sent a check for $2,500 to Gus Schirmer on May 15, thanking him: "I have waited so long for this day when I could start paying you back my indebtedness to you."[6]

Henri and his new wife Emma arrived in New York on board the Portuguese steamer *Guine* on April 15. Looking very smart and stylish in hat, vest, tie, and dapper suit, he told reporters when asked about conditions in France, "You know more about it than I do."[7] Throughout the early conflicts of World War II Henri had distinguished himself, attached as a liaison officer with the British 12th Royal Lancers. He had served in the tank regiment in the Battle of Dunkirk, was captured and escaped, and wrote about his experiences in *Through Hell to Dunkirk* (Military Services Publishing, 1943). For his bravery in World War II he was awarded a second Croix de Guerre. Through Gloria's contacts, he and his Emma were able to acquire proper papers and abandon Europe.

Rose Kennedy ran into Henri at a French restaurant shortly after their arrival in New York and met his third wife, "who looked very sweet in her French frocks," she told her children. "As he [de la Falaise] was never properly married before, he is now married to a Catholic so his mother is very happy, she piously added."[8] The couple eventually resettled in Europe after the war.

Michael Farmer made international news when he was arrested by French police in Nice on May 8. He had apparently violated some wartime regulation and was carrying no papers at the time. "He left his hotel in Cannes several weeks ago, moving to Monte Carlo, and was detained here after a hurried departure from Monaco," said the report.[9] No doubt Gloria was notified. But unlike with Henri, she did not, nor could she, intercede on his behalf. Michael was his own worst enemy. In December 1940 Gloria received a telegram he had sent her addressed to the El Morocco on East Fifty-fourth Street in New York. He had obviously been drinking.

After *Father Takes a Wife* wrapped on May 27, the papers announced that Cliff Reid was preparing a scenario for the second Swanson-Menjou teaming, and RKO was hoping to cast Gloria with Neil Hamilton for another picture as well. And if that didn't work out, said the press, Columbia Pictures was vying for her services. On July 7 RKO exercised Gloria's option. Hedda Hopper told her readers Gloria was being sought by DeMille, as well as MGM, and was wanted for a Bob Hope radio show. "Hedda, I feel as if I've never been away," Gloria told the gossip writer.[10]

In June Gloria returned east for Michelle's junior high school graduation. Gloria told the press that while in New York, she leased a new, more economical suite of offices at 501 Madison Avenue for Multiprises. RKO executive Daniel Winkler wrote Gloria that month inquiring if she had an option on *The*

Second Mrs. Draper, as one of his editors liked the first part of the story. It was being considered once again for her as an RKO vehicle. It never developed.

However, it then was announced that Gloria was a sure bet to portray Mother Goddam in Josef von Sternberg's *The Shanghai Gesture.* Bette Davis also coveted the role. Producer Arnold Pressburger was so set on Gloria for the part that costumes were created to fit her small size. Sadly, after the release of *Father Takes a Wife* in the first week of October, and its poor box-office returns, Gloria's comeback stopped dead in its tracks. Petite Ona Munson (Belle Watling in *Gone with the Wind*) was given the role after "von Sternberg was faced with a situation similar to that in *The Devil Is a Woman* [Paramount, 1935], when the departing Joel McCrea forced the casting of Cesar Romero on the basis of his shirt size."[11]

"There's Glamour on the Screen Again Because Gloria's Back!" and "You'll Suh-woon Over Her Trunkfuls of Stunning Fashions!" screamed the ads. One could surmise the studio had a dud on its hands. Wrote "Walt" in *Variety,* " 'Father Takes a Wife' emerges as good program entertainment . . . Miss Swanson shows her age to some extent in the face, but can only be tabbed as semi-matronly in that respect. Her figure is alluringly svelte, and she still carries that magnificent screen personality that made her a top attraction two decades ago."[12]

The *New York Times* was being generous when "T.M.P." cheered, "It is doubtful if Gloria Swanson could have hit upon a more complimentary vehicle . . . 'Father Takes a Wife' is the sort of thing which puts you in a good mood even though you realize that many of the situations are somewhat labored."[13] When the picture opened at the Hillstreet and Pantages Theaters in Los Angeles on October 3, columnist Richard Griffith raved, "Gloria Swanson's return to the screen is a modest triumph which may yet prove more substantial than many of the sensational debuts of recent years which have coruscated for a while, then fizzled. For what is offered is not merely a famous name or another glimpse of a magnetic personality but solid entertainment."[14]

Seen today, *Father Takes a Wife* is a pleasant enough picture, but forced. Gloria, sporting fifteen different Hubert outfits, is as good as expected, though she was not overly versatile in comedy. Actress Helen Broderick, just eight years older than Gloria, portrays her aunt Julie and is more than adept at delivering her comedic lines. The dialogue is clever (Frederick Jr. to his father: "Why do you want to get married?" "To avoid the draft!" he replies) but heavy-handed in

delivery. Menjou is always very good, as is Florence Rice. John Howard is a total bore, and Desi Arnaz is . . . well, Desi Arnaz. The sets are sumptuous, and
the photography and the musical score excellent. But the killing touches are
the labored and leaden direction by Jack Hively and the annoying coyness of
Gloria's performance.

Father Takes a Wife tanked, eventually losing $104,000, giving RKO great
consternation in their hopes of refloating Swanson. Gloria in later years dismissed the picture, taking no blame: "It could have been good, but the director
had never been out of Pomona."[15] Still, before the final vote was in Gloria was
summoned back to the Coast to discuss a new contract with RKO. Arriving in
Los Angeles on the Union Pacific Streamliner on September 23, Gloria, appearing stunning in a dark, wavy-print coat and a veiled hat, headed directly
to RKO.

At the same time, Warner Bros. had just successfully won from David O.
Selznick the film rights to Countess Elizabeth von Arnim's novel *Mr. Skeffington*. They were considering Norma Shearer, Tallulah Bankhead, or Gloria for the
pivotal female lead of Fanny Skeffington. Bette Davis took the part and received
another Oscar nod. (It is doubtful Gloria or Shearer would have accepted the
role, as Fannie, the mother of a grown daughter, aged considerably in the story.)
That October Gloria was considered for the female lead in *The Captain of Koe-
penick*, with Albert Basserman, to be produced for Fine Arts by John Hall and
directed by Richard Oswald. (It eventually saw the light of day in 1945 as *I Was a
Criminal*.)

In mid-November Hopper announced that Gloria's RKO option had not
been picked up. Gloria wrote despairingly to RKO executive Daniel Winkler
on November 21:

This letter is in strictest confidence and your reply will be treated as
such also. You know I have too much sense for you not to be perfectly
honest with your answer. I have been curious as to why RKO did not
take up my option. It could be only one of two things or perhaps both.
First—either RKO is in financial difficulty again and yet if they are going to continue to making pictures they need players or second—the
reason would be that my picture was not a financial success . . . Please, I
beg of you, answer this letter and not treat it as you did my telegrams

which, of course, were only kidding and under the circumstances didn't need a reply. When you find that you can't stand it any longer in that mad house out there and you feel a trip east coming on, I will never forgive you if you don't wire me so that I can be free to see you and entertain you.[16]

Winkler's response to her in the form of a letter came one week later:

First of all from all the facts and figures that I can gather the picture *did* make money [not completely true] . . . The order has been given out that we are to make all our so-called cheap pictures under $200,000 and on our upper budget pictures we are to spend more money. The decision, as I gather it, was that it was risky to try and pay you your money and come in under the lower budget and, as far as the upper budget pictures go, our entire schedule is laid out for the next nine months . . . The first flush of enthusiasm over the picture had died down by the time the contract was finally signed, which, in my opinion, had a great deal to do with the option not being exercised.

. . . Personally I still feel as I always have, that with the right story and the right cast and the proper exploitation, you should get money at the box-office.[17]

On December 7, 1941, Japan attacked and destroyed the American naval fleet at Pearl Harbor, Hawaii, and the United States was thrust into the war. Germany then declared war on the United States on December 11. With the world in conflict, Gloria's film career was not much of a concern to anyone but herself. The government was now claiming the services of her inventors, and Multiprises filed for bankruptcy and closed its doors on Madison Avenue. Gloria then actively pursued theatrical and radio work with her newly signed theatrical agent Bernie Foyer, who diligently scouted properties for her to consider. All he could come up with was an offer for a radio serial called *The House of Charm* in January. It did not pan out.

On February 15 Foyer officiously announced Gloria would star in, again, *Tryout in Boston,* set to begin rehearsals in three weeks with director Eugene S. Bryden. On March 8 producer Ben A. Boyer and Bryden decided to stage

Apples in Eden instead, by Frances Agnew, and Gloria was out. For the rest of the spring Foyer searched for a property for her.

In June it finally appeared Gloria would make her legitimate stage debut in *Reflected Glory,* a play by George Kelly (actress Grace Kelly's uncle) set to open in Scarsdale, New York, on June 22 with Leon Ames (soon replaced by Douglas Gregory) and director Harold J. Kennedy. *Reflected Glory* had opened at the Morosco Theater in New York starring Tallulah Bankhead in 1936 and enjoyed a modest 127-performance run. It tells of an emotional actress, Muriel Flood (Gloria), who wants to retire from the stage but finds she can't. For the revival Gloria signed an Equity contract for $700 a week, plus 50 percent gross of the house over $2,650.[18] After the Scarsdale tryout the play would open on June 30, 1942, at the Arlington Auditorium in Poughkeepsie, New York.

Recalling her first opening night on the "straw hat circuit," Gloria wrote:

As curtain time approached I was frozen with fright. I told the producer to keep the box office open so we could refund the money, since I was convinced when I opened my mouth not a single sound would come out. I also told him to sit in the fireplace onstage with the script.

When my cue came I sleep-walked onto the stage, I saw the lights, the other actors, the producer cross-legged in the fireplace, heard the welcoming applause, and then I saw the sea of faces out front. And suddenly, unaccountably, I was totally calm. I thought: "I have always been here. This is where I belong." And every word came out clean and crisp and clear. It remains even today one of the most rewarding experiences of my life.[19]

In her feigned modesty, once again Gloria was faced with insurmountable odds that, through her sheer talent and ability, she overcame. She enhanced her stage debut story later by adding, "I had to throw cues to three veteran troupers who blew up *their* lines."[20]

Gloria became a grandmother on September 23, when daughter Gloria gave birth to her first child, Christopher Hardy Anderson. (Two more children would follow—Lawrence Spurrier on February 16, 1944, and Gloria Brooke on April 10, 1948.) That same month, Gloria approached the prestigious Theatre Guild, at 245 West Fifty-Second Street, about the possibility of their producing on Broadway three-one act plays, under the title *Three Curtains*, in which she would star and portray three very different characters. The three short plays were George Bernard Shaw's "The Man of Destiny," Sir James Barrie's "The Old Lady Shows Her Medals," and Arthur Wing Pinero's "The Playgoers: A Domestic Episode." The Shaw piece was a comedy of egos, the Barrie play a dramatic tour de force, and the Pinero one-act a domestic comedy of manners. The Theatre Guild declined. But Gloria forged ahead.

Forming a stage company under the auspices of producer/director/actor Harold J. Kennedy (who at every opportunity he could made sure he cast *himself* in a showy role), Gloria secured as leading man her friend Czechoslovakian-born actor Francis Lederer. One of the company's backers was Gregory Ratoff. Rehearsals began in early November. Gloria was paid $2,500 a week, with 70 percent gross receipts of the house, unless it was under $15,000, when she would take 65 percent. Expenses exceeded $3,300 a week, so it was important the show play, even during inclement weather. (The cast and crew did get stranded in mid-December, and the scenery got lost in transit as well.)

The company opened *Three Curtains* in Hartford, Connecticut, on November 14, 1942, and toured with it throughout the harsh winter of 1942–43. When they performed in Wilmington, Delaware, the last week of that month, local theater critic William P. Frank wrote, "Miss Swanson . . . and Lederer . . . really cover themselves with laurels and glory. Their pace is marvelous, their sympathy and understanding, fairly flawless."[21]

Gloria turned in a magnificent portrait in the Barrie play. However, the weather remained an issue, and things got worse between the actors as well. Around Christmas, as they pulled into Boston, Gloria and her leading man came to a parting of the ways. According to Gloria, Clifton Webb had warned her before the tour that Lederer was temperamental. And in Boston, for no reason at all, so Gloria wrote, Lederer mocked her lines onstage. (He never exhibited that type of behavior onstage elsewhere.) Enraged by his unprofessionalism, Gloria closed the show on January 9, 1943. It is more likely she and Lederer had a failed romance. Gloria also probably knew *Three Curtains* just would never make it to New York.

That January Gloria joined the Author's League (annual cost $80), and submitted ideas for radio shows through her attorney L. Arnold Weissberger, including one suggestion for a quiz/variety show called *Charades*. In her 1943 daily diary, Gloria curiously wrote, "God's wisdom finds no solace, no satisfaction in sin, since God has sentenced sinners to suffer."[22] Perhaps that was just a reflection, or possibly an explanation.

Her good friend actor-director Gregory Ratoff wrote Gloria about the scripts *Tonight at Eight-Thirty* and *No Money in Her Purse,* which he wanted her to consider for Columbia Pictures. The latter would be "an ideal vehicle for you,"[23] he said, but she refused to make a film with Harry Cohn after the fiasco of *Dark Victory.* She also felt the current government cap of $25,000 for a star's salary per picture because of the war was below her status. She did ask Ratoff, however, if he would be interested in backing another one of her plays.

Gloria took a train down to Springfield, Massachusetts, with her dog Miranda on January 28, to begin rehearsals for her next production, *Let Us Be Gay,* a three-act comedy by Rachel Crowther that had opened on Broadway in 1929. It told of young, pretty Kitty Brown (Gloria, stretching credibility once again), who is invited to a stylish Westchester house party by the hostess to break up a romance. The play was set to open February 2 and run for a week. Arriving in town dressed in a sleek two-piece black suit trimmed with a pink crocheted jabot, Gloria refused to comment about the demise of *Three Curtains* and rumors of a backstage feud with Lederer, yet she grandly remarked, "I'm in love with the theatre. However, there's a great thrill in making a motion picture, too."[24]

When the play opened, one local critic raved, "Miss Swanson . . . breezed thru her part with just the right amount of skill for the type of character she portrayed . . . One of the features of the play was the glamorous display of gowns, which added much gorgeous color to the colorful setting and dialogue of the play."[25] However, reviewer Louise Mace was a bit more discerning: "Miss Swanson accepts the drift and floats through her character, seldom grasping it securely enough to provide the solidity even such a wraith deserves. There is obvious need of more rehearsing to integrate both action and performances—down the line."[26]

After a brief reprisal of "The Playgoers" at the National Theater in Washington, D.C., as part of the bill in *Priorities of 1943,* Gloria prepared to tour throughout the summer into the fall with *Let Us Be Gay.* When *Priorities of 1943* opened, the critic "Arke" in *Variety* said, "Strictly screwball, fun depends upon fast pace and timing. This it did not get opening night, but by latter part of the week was registering solidly. La Swanson looks tip-top, wears millinery that had ladies gasping and still has plenty of symmetry to fill gowns neatly. Women like to see how La Swanson has fared with Father Time and agree he has treated her nicely."[27] Meanwhile, Hedda Hopper erroneously announced in September that renowned novelist Erich Maria Remarque, author of *All Quiet on the Western Front,* was planning to write a play for Gloria. He did not.

Let Us Be Gay began its tour on June 1 at the Adams Theater in Newark, New Jersey. Gloria was joined in the cast by Kennedy, portraying Townley Town. She was paid $1,000 a week plus 10 percent of the gross receipts of the house over $6,000. The play set a house record for the season in Buffalo at the Erlanger Theater, where it brought in $7,200 during its one-week run. By the end of the tour in October, Gloria had done very well financially.

Kennedy then wrote *A Goose for the Gander,* a bit of Noël Coward-ish fluff, specifically for Gloria. Together they went about securing backers for the project. Kennedy, then twenty-nine years old, was born in Holyoke, Massachusetts, and was a student at Dartmouth and a graduate of the Yale Drama School. Having appeared in a small role on Broadway in Irving Berlin's *This Is the Army* in 1942, he industriously set about trying to establish himself.

The plot of *A Goose for the Gander* was sheer nonsense. Socialite Katherine (Gloria) comes home to find her husband David (Conrad Nagel) in the arms of another woman, Suzy (Maxine Stuart). Determined that what is good for her husband is good for his wife, Katherine invites masculine he-man Wally (David Tyrell), staid banker Jonathan (John Clubley), and social wit Tony (Kennedy) to a party where some guests drink too much champagne and jump into the pool with their clothes on. At the end of the evening, Katherine decides David is the one for her.

Backing was secured for the production by Rudolph Allen. (Gloria's son Joseph also invested $5,000 of his own money, possibly at her request.) Kennedy then arranged for some tryout dates at the Coliseum Theater in Evansville, Illinois, on April 20, with an eventual Broadway premiere set for early June. (Curiously, when the show opened at the Strand Theater in Stamford, Connecticut, it was produced and presented by Gus Schirmer Jr. The production that followed *Gander* into the Strand was *Without Love,* starring Constance Bennett.)

Michelle was offered a small role in *A Goose for the Gander,* and a chance to tour with her mother. One thing she took away from this experience was that "always—and whatever the demands of home and household—Mother had to be the Gloria Swanson of public legend. In that, as in all things else, she was a perfectionist."[28]

Joseph Swanson had been called up by the draft after his second year at Antioch College in Yellow Springs, Ohio. He sent his mother a long newsy letter dated May 28 while stationed at Camp Breckenridge in Morganfield, Kentucky. Telling her that his unit might be shipped overseas in five months, he asked her how his transfer request was coming. In her book Gloria says her son requested she contact Joseph P. Kennedy to expedite the request, but nowhere in the existing letter does he do that. Instead he suggested to his mother that it was the most appropriate time to ask for a transfer and said he would like to accept one to a different division so as to obtain a better job. Gloria's version of the story has Joseph then writing Kennedy to thank him personally. This was an obviously self-serving passage in her memoirs, perhaps to indicate she felt all men used her.

Ed Sullivan, in his April 3 New York *Daily News* column, ominously reported rumors that Gloria's former husband Michael Farmer had been tried by the French as a German collaborator and had been shot in a German concentration camp. However, while still seeking child support payments, in December 1944, through her attorney F. H. McRobert, Gloria discovered Michael had been reported as "flourishing considerably" at the Ritz Bar in Paris, putting on considerable weight after a "taste of concentration camp."[29]

Touring reviews of *A Goose for the Gander* were generous. Edwin Schallert in the *Los Angeles Times* reported, "Gloria Swanson has staged a spectacular comeback, both histrionically and sartorially, if not vocally."[30] When the comedy played a five-week run at the Blackstone Theater in Chicago, under the direction of Franklin M. Heller, critics were at least kind. The *Chicago Tribune* called Gloria "a piquant comedienne . . . a gift to the stage," and the *Chicago News* called the production "an amusing and witty play . . . Kept the audience laughing."[31] But despite the performances of the stars, the production was not bringing in the customers. Gloria, acting as attorney-in-fact on behalf of her son, attempted to close the play, which had cost $31,600.

A Goose for the Gander lost $4,000 at the box office during its run at the Blackstone. Said *The New York Times*, "In an effort to lower the overhead,

Mr. Allen had asked the author [Kennedy] and the star to take a cut. When they refused a closing notice was posted on Monday of last week."[32] Including Joseph's contribution, Gloria's own investment in the production had been $7,500. Rudolph Allen said Gloria had originally agreed to put up $15,000 as her share but then failed to do so. The play was temporarily shut down.

By the end of August, Jules Leventhal and Frank McCoy, who now owned the play, were taking over *A Goose for the Gander,* planning to bring it to the Bijou Theater in New York in late September. Allen promptly filed a complaint against author Kennedy and the Dramatists Guild, seeking to retain an interest in the production if and when it ever hit New York. The Bijou opening was canceled on September 14. Rehearsals began again on December 8 with a run scheduled in Detroit later that month. Hopes were for a January opening in New York. Business was good later in Washington, D.C., bringing in $21,000.

In October 1944 Gloria began seeing wealthy New Yorker William M. Davey. (Gus Schirmer and she were now just friends.)[33] Born in 1884,[34] William Melvin Davey made a fortune in California in the 1930s, purchasing the Equitable Building at Hollywood and Vine for an undeclared amount, and later the Bank of Hollywood Building, for $1.5 million. He also owned nine apartment buildings around Los Angeles.

The tall, blond-haired man had once been considered Hollywood's "No. 1 Catch."[35] Davey dated Rhea Gable after her separation from Clark Gable, and in New York he squired around the beautiful, multimarried Peggy Hopkins Joyce. In 1929 Davey wed twenty-year-old silent screen actress Alyce Mills. They divorced in Reno in February 1937.

On New Year's Eve, when she was performing in *A Goose for the Gander* in tryouts in Detroit, Davey sent Gloria a brief declaration of his affections, asking her to return to him in one piece.[36]

On January 23, 1945, the Broadway opening night of *A Goose for the Gander,* Gloria had supper with friends, but without Davey. Reviews were dreadful. The *New York Sun* lamented, "A dismaying trifle, an error for all concerned."[37] And *The New York Times'* reviewer Lewis Nichols called it simply a "Dead Duck":

As though the Playhouse were engaged in some macabre form of repertory, they opened up another one of those things last evening... Obviously Mr. Kennedy has been studying the works of Noel Coward, and he has written a play which probably seemed pretty funny in the middle of the last night he worked on it . . . Being the author, with all the privileges of royalty, Mr. Kennedy has written himself the best part . . . Miss Swanson is a victim of circumstance in that her role is silly, and last evening she seemed to be in a couple of moods about how to play it. Conrad Nagel's situation is downright desperate . . . With his eye on something, possibly the West Coast, Mr. Kennedy let it be known at the end that the husband hadn't been unfaithful after all. That completed it; no one had any fun.[38]

On January 27 Gloria and Davey together dined with friends who attended the theater that evening. After midnight, they had supper. According to her memoirs, in her brief four-paragraph allowance to Davey, she stated it was Michelle who had encouraged her to marry the man, because she liked Davey when she met him. Also, it didn't hurt that he was wealthy, which may have been Gloria's true motivation. At any rate, she would never assume complete responsibility for her mistakes. On January 29 Swanson took her fifth husband.

23

Sunset Boulevard

Giving her age honestly as forty-five, Gloria married William M. Davey, who incorrectly gave his as fifty-two, at the city hall of Union City, New Jersey; the wedding was officiated by acting city recorder Mervin Herzfeld and witnessed by Virginia B. Steebe and Lee O'Shea. Returning to Manhattan, Gloria resumed her work in *A Goose for the Gander*. It ran but thirteen more clumsy performances before it was hung out to dry on the Great White Way on February 3.

While plans were made to take the turkey, or rather "Goose," on the road Gloria and Davey quickly traveled to Hollywood. As an indication of how times had changed since Gloria's stardom, while in town she met child actress Margaret O'Brien, juvenile star of MGM's *Journey for Margaret* (1943) and *Meet Me in St. Louis* (1945). "You know, I used to be quite a movie star myself," Gloria haughtily told the youngster when they were introduced. "Did you?" replied O'Brien wide-eyed. "What happened?"[1] Gloria never particularly liked children.

Gloria's daily diary of 1945 succinctly detailed her marriage and described its quick collapse. On January 29 she wrote, "We were happily married [in] Union City, N.J.—and strangely enough—still happy." The following day Davey annotated in Gloria's diary, "Tried vainly to get my bride in the feathers, but still gave up (or in) 4 times." On February 3 he noted in it, "And I am very much in love with my brand new bride," to which Gloria added, "ditto." The couple then left for the West Coast, arriving in Los Angeles on March 1. They returned to

New York on March 16, and Davey became "sick" the following day and consulted a doctor. Gloria wrote "William still sick" on March 20.[2]

Michelle stayed at her mother's home, 920 Fifth Avenue, for a week. (Gloria and Davey maintained separate apartments.) Apparently Gloria had failed to recognize that Davey was a chronic alcoholic, though she noticed but largely ignored his drinking during the tryouts of *A Goose for the Gander*. With Michelle's help Gloria collected a handful of Alcoholics Anonymous pamphlets and placed them all around his apartment. They then went shopping all day at Saks Fifth Avenue. On March 23 William saw his lawyer. Davey's drinking was killing him and their marriage. Gloria's diary pretty much explained it all: March 25, "detectives called at 3 A.M."; March 30, Davey "still at office"; April 10–11, "William ill Dr. Seidlin"; April 14, William operated [on]"; April 17, "went to hospital"; April 23, "no word from William" (she hadn't heard a thing from him after Mother's Day). On April 30 he sent for his furniture and escaped to Martha's Vineyard. Becoming ill again, he was admitted to a hospital in May. May 16, "William left hospital"; May 28, "William called all day long" and arrived at her apartment at 8:00 P.M.; May 29 and 30, "William called two or three times"; June 2, she sent a letter to Davey, and he arrived at her apartment at 9:00 P.M. and left at 2:00 A.M., then called her when he arrived at his home.[3]

Davey basically walked out on Gloria. On July 9 she sued for separation after just six months of marriage. Claiming he had left her on April 19 "without just cause with the intention of never returning to me," Gloria charged him with abandonment, her usual alibi. Contacting her attorney William B. Jaffe at Rosenblatt and Jaffe Gloria filed suit. In the complaint she said, "My husband is worth over $10,000,000, enjoys an income of upwards of $200,000 annually, and lives in a style and manner appropriate to his great wealth."[4] She asked for $25,000 for counsel fees and $1,000 a week in alimony.

Davey's attorney Jacob M. Zinaman filed a cross-complaint in Superior Court charging his client did indeed leave Gloria's residence and returned on April 19, 1945, to his residence at 400 Park Avenue. Gloria had several times refused to live with Davey at his home, he said. More damaging to Gloria were claims that she had induced him into marriage by telling him she was in perfect health, though she regularly sought consultations with doctors, and fraudulently claimed she had certain obligations which could be fully satisfied and discharged for $12,000. Davey had believed her, but when he found she was in debt for over $67,000, he left. He was requesting the marriage be annulled and declared void.

In short order Gloria's immediate debts were paraded out in public. In reality they totaled approximately $14,200.[5] Gloria wrote Dr. William P. Healy, "My large medical bills (as he states) could not possibly touch [the] amounts he has spent for doctors and nurses for as he said unnecessary operations and drunkenness . . . We never quarreled after we were married except once when he threw *his* bills at me."[6] On April 19, when Davey left the hospital after his illness, he also left Gloria. The news hit the papers on August 31. On September 5 Gloria told the Supreme Court in New York City that Davey once ordered crepes suzettes when they were dining at the St. Regis. The waiter told him it was impossible to get butter because of wartime rationing. Davey then called his manservant, who brought half a pound of butter to the hotel. "War or no war, scarcity or no scarcity, when William M. Davey wants crepes suzettes, he gets it," she testified.[7]

Faced again with providing financial support of Michelle, Gloria sent a Capt. John Roberts on a mission to find Michael Farmer. In April it was reported Michael's benefactress Mrs. Edmunds Hubbard had died in New York in 1942, leaving behind a $9 million estate. From that she bequeathed Michael $150,000. Gloria was owed around $2,000 in back payments at that time, so she applied for $3,000 yearly child support for twelve years from Michael's inheritance. She also specified she would settle for $35,000. Through attorney John Krimsby, a contract was drafted and sent to Farmer.

To a friend, Michael wrote on April 21, 1945, care of the Ritz Hotel Bar in Paris, that he had been tossed out of Biarritz by the Germans at the end of August 1940, and had traveled to the Cannes Free Zone, where he refused to shake hands with a M. Giglioni (an Italian Consul hotshot there in 1940–41), who'd had Michael thrown out of Cannes. He then ended up in Marseille in 1941, where he ran into a couple of swags he knew. Michael then cabled pals Walter Riley and Woolie Donohue requesting they arrange passage on a clipper to America for him and a U.S. visa. They failed to do so. He then was involved in a fight at the bar at the Hotel Nouailles with a German officer in civilian clothes. Michael, it seemed, just could not avoid trouble.[8]

The German then had Michael jailed for a year, and interned a second year in a château from which he managed to escape. He ran into pals at the Ritz Bar, but the Gestapo caught up with him and placed him in prison. Managing to escape from there as well, he then ran into Bill Hearst, Edward Molyneux, and Marlene Dietrich, whom he wrote "looked swell," and was accompanied by Ernest Hemingway. He was in trouble because of an ex-girlfriend, and he still hoped to reach the United States. He wrote that Mrs. Hubbard had died in Grenoble in May 1942, and that he needed to take her remains to her mausoleum at Woodlawn Cemetery in New York.[9] Whether he did just that, or whether Gloria received any of his inheritance for Michelle, is not documented.

At that time, Gloria was looking over several radio scripts, such as one for an evening program to be called *Anything Can Happen,* to star her with Zasu Pitts. She also owned a story outline for *Marriage, Inc.* and a projected series called *A Date with Gloria Swanson,* plus a proposal for *Come Along with Me* (or *This is My Life*). Gloria signed a standard American Federation of Radio Artists (AFRA) exclusive agent contract for six months with agent Sheelagh Dille, who helped her acquire radio work.

On September 14 New York Supreme Court Justice Ferdinand Pecora awarded Gloria temporary alimony from Davey of $200 a week and $2,000 for counsel fees until a final settlement could be rendered within the coming month. Through attorney Wilfred C. Allen, she was able to settle various minor lawsuits, including one with Multiprises. Gloria then claimed in her separation statement from Davey she was penniless, which she was not. On November 28 Davey filed a formal protest of the $200 weekly payment to Gloria, stating she had paid her fourth husband, Michael Farmer, $25,000 plus an additional $24,000 at $3,000 a year in their settlement.

On January 10, 1946, a small article ran in a paper about Farmer, found living in near-poverty in a Georgian apartment in Dublin, Ireland. The paper reported, "At 44 he has a wallet full of newspaper clippings, a Christmas card from a princess, and a huge photograph of Gloria Swanson smiling from the writing desk of his hotel room."[10] Michael eventually sailed to New York on board the *Queen Mary* in February 1947. He ran into Clare Luce, who secured him a room at the Hotel LaSalle. Then he attempted to contact Gloria.[11]

That same week Gloria gave testimony in New York Supreme Court to Justice Morris Eder. She told the court several times she had tried to get Davey to attend Alcoholics Anonymous, but he would not listen, and "anyway her doctor told" her he was "a confirmed drunkard."[12] Under cross examination Gloria admitted she had "frequently and repeatedly separated from her first four husbands."[13] (And she did not remember how long she had lived with Herbert Somborn.) Gloria testified Davey promised her between $2,000 and $3,000 a month if he should die.[14] She said she found it difficult to get along on $200 weekly, the equivalent to almost $2,500 a week today.

When Davey took the stand, his attorney Zinamen asked if he had ever seen any other men at Gloria's apartment, and his reply was, "On two occasions two men, or it might have been the same man, climbed over the wall at 920 Fifth Avenue." As a result, Davey said, he had asked her to live with him at his ninth-floor, air-conditioned apartment on Park Avenue.[15] Gloria denied this. Davey also confessed he was vague about his wedding night. "I don't recall too clearly what happened that night," he said. He was then asked when it was he proposed, and he replied, "I think I proposed the day we got married." The attorney asked, "You mean you never mentioned it before that?" To which Davey admitted, "As a matter of fact, I can't remember discussing marriage at all."[16]

Gloria said her husband was worth $10 million; he said $350,000. She said his annual income was $200,000; he said it was more like $15,000. He said. She said. Justice Eder delayed his final decision on alimony until a referee could determine what was fair. At last, in March Gloria was awarded $300 a week for life or until she remarried. She had asked for $1,000 a week. In the end she told one reporter, "I have not seen a penny of it, yet. But I do have the satisfaction of knowing I won my case."[17]

Gloria's son Joseph, who before his war service had been studying to be an electronics engineer, was now invited by the University of Pennsylvania to work on its ENIAC project, a robot mathematical calculator. After his work with the U of P, and while employed at the Anaconda Wire and Cable Company later in 1948, Joseph reenrolled at Antioch College, where he met his future wife Susan. After entering into a business partnership with a fellow colleague and settling in Menlo Park, California, Joseph and Susan married on August 7, 1949.

After January, determined to make *A Goose for the Gander* pay off somehow, Kennedy and Gloria took it on the road again throughout the summer, beginning in June at the Roosevelt Theater in Beacon, New York. There was also some talk about Gloria appearing in a stage production of *Made in Heaven*. She did not do it. Hedda Hopper reported film producer Sam Bischoff, after viewing a test of Gloria, wanted her for his forthcoming United Artists picture *Intrigue*. The *Los Angeles Times*'s Edwin Schallert mentioned film producer Edward H. Griffith was also planning a picture for Gloria. Unfortunately, neither of these projects developed.

Sam Wood, at the time directing Universal's *Ivy* starring Herbert Marshall, wanted Gloria for the femme fatale role in his projected Russian Alaskan yarn *The World in His Arms*. It wasn't made until 1952, directed by Raoul Walsh. Motion pictures were very much a different business now than when Gloria had reigned supreme. In 1947 the U.S. government disbanded the studio-owned theaters in an antitrust decision. And a new form of free entertainment, television, began to make inroads into the profits of the industry.

In the late summer of 1947 Gloria visited her doctor in New York and discovered she had a tumor in her uterus. He advised surgery. She consulted two other physicians who concurred; the second advised her to undergo a complete hysterectomy. When the tour of *A Goose for the Gander* ended, Gloria consulted Dr. Bieler in California. After discussing possible alternatives, Gloria lit up a cigarette and chose to become a vegetarian, eliminating animal proteins from her diet in order to starve the tumor away. She wrote that she was successful, and remained somewhat of a vegetarian the rest of her life.

Curiously Gloria became a representative of the Haley Corporation Travel Bureau on East Forty-Fourth Street in New York, in 1947. One of fourteen employees, she was paid $100 a month, plus commission, for booking travel arrangements for preferred clientele. As a publicity junket, she flew via Colonial Airlines to Bermuda on September 19, 1947, and was feted for three days. The Haley Corporation provided her with income over the next two years. She booked vacations throughout the world for such friends as Zasu Pitts, René Hubert, Patsy Ruth Miller, and Pierre Bedard. However, her total commission during those two years came to less than $1,000.

Gloria did not write about her travel agent days in her memoirs. Perhaps the experience was too humiliating. These were particularly difficult years for her financially, though even during her leanest days she still spent an average of $7,000 annually on clothes. Her friend Virginia Bowker later commented about those dark days, "Nobody ever heard Gloria grouse about her comedown . . . If she was resentful that the parade had passed her by, she never showed it. She tried desperately to hang on when she realized she was on the downgrade, but that's only human nature. Once she knew she was through, she accepted it as gracefully as she had taken her enormous success."[18]

Scrambling at business ventures, Gloria failed to sell a daily and a weekly newspaper column called "Gloria's Day." Her facts were not always correct, for one thing, but mostly the rejections indicate that no one really cared. In 1939 she had tried to sell a column entitled "The Most Unusual For Ladies . . . by Gloria Swanson"/"The Most Unusual . . . For Women," which was rejected by the New York *Daily News* and United Features among other publications. In 1948 Gloria came up with "Memos and Memories," which was printed in some papers but failed to attract attention, as did "Gloria's Glories" the same year. In 1949 she pitched "Going Places" with her friend Robert Balzar. It, too, failed to gain attention.

In New York between 1947 and 1948 the sale of home television sets had risen from 17,000 to 300,000. The future *was* television, and on June 15, 1948, station WPIX-TV in New Jersey was launched. In early March 1948 Gloria had been approached by New York *Daily News* reporter Jimmy Jemail to appear on his television show *Man on the Street Interview,* his newspaper's latest venture. When Jemail asked Gloria on the air, "Gloria, what was your most exciting moment?" she replied somewhat coyly, "Why Jimmy, you mean—er—the most exciting moment? I couldn't say that in front of all these people!"[19]

Before she knew it Gloria was asked to host a sixty-minute show of her own, *The Gloria Swanson Hour.* The format combined interviews with segments devoted to fashion, cooking, and homemaking hints. For this Gloria was paid approximately $350 a week. She needed the work. Michelle's Dwight School fees for 1947–48 alone amounted to $1,700.

Immediately the publicity mill went to work promoting her debut on television. Jack Gould in *The New York Times* announced the deal on March 10. Then *Los Angeles Times* columnist Henry McLemore wrote, "Now it is not hard to imagine Miss Swanson discussing fashions, she has been one of the world's classiest dressers for a long time . . . However, who in his right mind, can picture Miss Swanson giving kitchen hints? I can't. She doesn't seem to be the mop, apron and broom type . . . She may open her program with how to make a delicious dish from leftover caviar and plover eggs."[20]

Gloria had accepted a limited stage engagement to pinch-hit for Ilka Chase, while she made a film, in the touring production of George Oppenheimer's *There*

Goes the Bride in Toledo, Ohio. To a reporter from the *Toledo Blade* on May 25, she spoke of another new business enterprise she was involved with, a modeling agency: "We register models or girls who would like to be models from all over the country. When photographers go out on location, we make it possible for them to hire a model in the locality in which they're going to work."[21]

After signing with WPIX, Gloria was spending money freely in Monte Carlo, Monaco, filming footage to use on her upcoming television program, when on May 13, 1948, Kathleen Kennedy was killed with her married lover, Peter Wentworth-Fitzwilliam, the 8th Earl Fitzwilliam, when their airplane crashed in the south of France. Gloria quickly dashed off a telegram to Rose and Joseph in Hyannis Port.

On June 15 a preview of *The Gloria Swanson Hour* was broadcast at 7:00 P.M. over WPIX Channel 11. Gloria's guests on that show included actor Neil Hamilton and designer Fira Benenson. Gloria handled all four segments, "Glamour on a Budget," "Chef's Holiday," "Design for Living," and "Trends," in a relaxed fashion. Her familiarity with the camera helped segment transitions, and the public loved it. Gloria settled in for a long run.

When *Variety*'s "Odec" reviewed the first show he commented, "Miss Swanson tees off on a new career, to sum up, with all the cards in her favor. Throughout the opening installment Miss Swanson maintained a relaxed air and elan that, along with a cute chuckle, imparted a sense of knowing what she was about and enjoying the job, which is no simple attribute on this type of assignment. Her ease and humor was reflected quite conspicuously in the minimum of nervousness and awkwardness prevailing among her guests and associates on the program."[22]

After the initial airing, handsome character actor Eric Rhodes was signed to the show to play her "butler" in a revised format to suggest Gloria was "at home." He and Gloria wrote many of the scripts for the show. "We worked like a charm together," Gloria later said.[23] (In production rehearsal notes on October 17 it was recorded that when Rhodes's butler said, "Miss Swanson is a sweet sugar plum," it was deemed not proper coming from a servant.)[24]

On October 8 Hedda Hopper ran a blind item called "Old Story": "Charlie Brackett and Billy Wilder's story on Hollywood may feature Gloria Swanson. It's about an aging actress who falls in love with a younger man. Heck, that's not a satire. It happens every day in Hollywood."[25] Journalist Thomas F. Brady, in *The New York Times*, then announced on October 26, "Charles Brackett and

Billy Wilder are writing a photoplay at Paramount about the history of Holly-wood and are discussing with Gloria Swanson the possibility of her appearance in the film."[26]

Something was afoot. Brackett flew to New York the first week of September and lunched with Gloria. In an unrelated trip in late October, Gloria flew to Paris for a shopping spree and was met at the airport by her former husband Henri. She returned to New York shortly thereafter. Then she flew to Hollywood in November to discuss the film project with Wilder and Brackett. They asked her to test for the part. She refused and flew back to New York on November 9. Screenwriter Michael Arlen was Gloria's featured guest on her December 16 show, and they likely in private discussed Gloria's trip to the Coast.

On December 20 Gloria underwent an emergency appendectomy at Doctors Hospital, a procedure she later wrote she didn't need, since she had correctly diagnosed and cured her internal medical problem on her own. While recuperating, so she said, she watched television and decided she didn't like what she saw. Within three weeks Gloria had her secretary send WPIX a letter of resignation. So she wrote.

Still, Gloria was appalled Wilder wanted her to test. "'Me? Test?'" she remembered saying to him. "I was revolted . . . Never made a test in my life [not true] . . . I was rude to him. I said what the hell do you have to test me for? You want to see if I'm still alive, do you? Or do you doubt that I can act?"[27] Gloria then had a long talk with George Cukor, who advised her Brackett and Wilder were the fair-haired wonder kids at Paramount at the moment and she should jump at the opportunity. In fact, Cukor helped Gloria prepare for it. If it took ten tests, her friends told her, she should do it.

A week later, on December 27, 1948, Gloria received her final divorce papers from Davey in Reno. Hedda Hopper wrote in her column, "I thought she had shed that guy years ago. After three months of marriage she knew it was a mistake."[28] Just days later Pola Negri was interviewed by Wilder, who was now calling his project *The Hollywood Story*. She found the plot depressingly shocking and threw the script at him. Wilder wanted the great Erich von Stroheim for a role, having directed him in *Five Graves to Cairo* for the studio in 1943; figuring one heavy accent was enough, he dismissed La Negri. Von Stroheim agreed to play in the film, then departed from Europe to Hollywood, humbly writing a friend, "This will amaze you. It has me. But this ugly face of mine is among the ten best drawing cards in all Europe."[29]

Thomas F. Brady of *The New York Times* announced the next day that Gloria Swanson, Erich von Stroheim, and young actor Montgomery Clift were all being considered for Wilder's upcoming film, "which involves a comparison of contemporary Hollywood with the town of two decades ago."[30] The title was now *The Sunset Strip* in some papers. Gloria and her mother Addie, who had been staying in New York with her, arrived in Los Angeles the third week of January 1949, taking a villa formerly occupied by William Faulkner near the junction of Watsonia Terrace and Milner Road.

On February 17 Gloria made her test. Asked to improvise dialogue as the character of a bitter, faded movie queen, Gloria let loose. "She exuded such savagery and madness from the screen that Brackett and Wilder shifted the story radically and now made [her] the central role in the film," wrote one Wilder biographer.[31] On February 23 Gloria was confirmed for the role and signed for $50,000 for a ten- to twelve-week shoot. "When she got the part she was thrilled," Michelle recalled.[32]

Society gossip Brandy Brent in his *Los Angeles Times* "Carousel" column wrote gushingly of his idol Gloria's return, "It was nothing short of heartwarming to see how friends of all ages rushed up to her and how everybody, strangers and all, watched her every graceful move. There is a woman who has been a great star and an incandescent personality for 30 years and has had more to do with bringing glamour to this town . . . than any dozen other actresses."[33] With Gloria, Brent attended a dinner at the Samuel Goldwyns' that month.

The picture was now called *Sunset Boulevard,* but was also referred to as *Sunset Blvd.* It was a project Wilder and Brackett had been kicking around for years, a dark and ominous tale of faded movie queen Norma Desmond and her doomed relationship with a young screenwriter, Dan Gillis (his first name changed later to Joe). Much has been written about the making of *Sunset Boulevard,* including a book explaining its definitive history. *Sunset Boulevard's* story was a revelation for its time. In 1949 Hollywood simply did not look at itself as ironically as did Wilder and Brackett and screenwriter D. M. Marshman Jr., a *Life* magazine reporter and film critic.

The casting history for *Sunset Boulevard* was quite eclectic. Originally Wilder and Brackett had envisioned a picture about an ex-burlesque queen, which Brackett thought would become "the laugh riot of 1950,"[34] and offered the role of Norma to Mae West. West, in her late fifties, did not like the script, and felt she was too young for the part of a silent screen actress anyway. Plus she felt no affinity for Hollywood. More important, she wrote her own scripts, and one shudders to think how she would have handled Wilder's lines. They then realized the story best fit an actual faded silent screen star. Mary Pickford, who hadn't made a picture since 1933, was approached next. Pickford, though slipping into alcoholism, was still a powerful force in the industry and a keen businesswoman.

Pickford had married film actor Charles "Buddy" Rogers, twelve years her junior, in 1936 after her divorce from Douglas Fairbanks. When Wilder first read and acted out the story for her, Mary liked it very much, and so did Buddy. She did not find the plot line of an older woman supporting a younger man, a gigolo, necessarily distasteful. But she did insist the man be completely subordinate to Norma so there would be no question who the star of the picture was.

On second thought, though, Mary said, "You don't want me . . . There are two actresses that could do this part better. One is Gloria Swanson—that's my first choice—and the next is Pola Negri."[35] Later, after viewing Gloria's powerful performance in the final film, Pickford commented in a different vein, "I wouldn't do that kind of picture; why, she kills a man." (As Pickford had done twice in her films.) Pickford then said Wilder's script was "too satirical. I don't approve of my people, of the picture industry, doing anything that would harm the reputation of motion pictures."[36] Sour grapes perhaps.

According to Wilder's biographer Ed Sikov, Swanson's name first came up over tea at the home of George Cukor. Wilder and Brackett then approached Gloria. "She had already been abandoned, she was a death knell," Wilder would say in later years. "She had lost a lot of money on the Paramount lot . . . But I insisted on her."[37] Her daughter Michelle agreed. "It was a real comeback for her . . . Before the film she was on the side of the road a little bit and had had to do summer stock [not to mention booking travel for friends] to earn a living."[38]

For the role of Gillis, Montgomery Clift was signed, and as of March he was still in the picture. However, just weeks before filming began, Clift reneged on his agreement. In Germany filming *The Big Lift,* Clift called his agent Herman

Citron and, over a bad transatlantic connection, shouted, "I can't do it, Herm. I'm not gonna do it!"[39] He would not listen to the pleadings of Wilder, but through his agent simply explained he felt he would not be convincing as a young man on the make with an older woman. The truth was it would always prove a struggle for the delicately handsome, homosexual Montgomery Clift to make love to a woman on the screen.[40]

Faced with disaster, Wilder and Brackett then approached Fred MacMurray, who had played the male lead in their 1944 noir classic *Double Indemnity* with Barbara Stanwyck. MacMurray had appreciated that break, but he was a now a major film star. He believed that if he played what amounted to a supporting role it would diminish his standing. (MacMurray also commented to Wilder in private that he found the role of a kept man morally objectionable.) Wilder and Brackett then briefly considered Marlon Brando but decided he was too much of an unknown at the time. They even offered the part to Gene Kelly, who had portrayed a "kept man" on Broadway in *Pal Joey* in 1940, but Metro would not loan him out. In the end, Brackett and Wilder chose the handsome thirty-year-old Paramount contract player William Holden. They were happy with him. And the front office, upon the withdrawal of Monty Clift, had saved $39,000.

"Holden was no baby," Gloria later said, "but I don't think it would have been good to have a very young person in it, it wouldn't have had the same desperation."[41] Holden signed on March 18. He truly did not want to play the role and risk losing his solid manly image to a woman who was a has-been; however, he was still not exactly a household name. While he was out shopping during the filming of *Sunset Boulevard,* an elderly woman approached him and said, "Young man, you ought to be in pictures; you look like Alan Ladd."[42]

Gloria commented about her test, "I looked about 30, 35, and I was pleased." However, when Holden was coerced to portray Joe, she had to test again and was made to look older. "So they took this test with this streak of white and they had nothing but top lighting. I came out looking absolutely drunk and dug up. I saw it and I said, 'now it will be a grueling picture for a young man to be in love with that.' 'Yes, but you've got to look older than Holden.' I said, 'Well, make him look younger!'"[43]

The story of *Sunset Boulevard* is now a classic. Norma Desmond (Gloria) lives in a fantasy world of her own imagination in a run-down Hollywood mansion[44] with her butler Max (von Stroheim), who deludes her into believing she is still a big film star, though she hasn't made a picture in decades. Along comes Joe Gillis (Holden), a desperate, out-of-work screenwriter, who helps her with a dreadful comeback screenplay based on the story of Salome. When Norma falls in love with the much younger Joe, tragedy ensues. The picture ends where it begins . . . on Sunset Boulevard.

"Originally her role in *Sunset Boulevard* was supposed to be much less important," recalled Michelle. "It sounds silly now when you see the film, but it's true. Every day Billy Wilder would rewrite the lines, so she'd have to learn them again. At night she would memorize her dialogue at home, then at the studio the next morning all the lines changed. They would bring new pages of script to her dressing room and she would sit there and memorize them."[45] Gloria herself might have told that story enough times to ingrain in her daughter's mind that it was true. Then again, Norma's role might very well have needed continuous altering as the story progressed. In contrast, Nancy Olson, who played Betty Schaefer in the picture, recalled. "We never deviated from the script . . . That was the tightest script I have ever worked on."[46]

Blending the fanciful with reality, Wilder and Brackett cast columnist Hedda Hopper as herself. Brackett had originally asked Hopper's rival Louella Parsons to appear, but she declined, and then didn't mention *Sunset Boulevard* in her column for months. And in a particularly jarring sequence, Norma invites "the Waxworks," old-time silent stars Buster Keaton, Anna Q. Nilsson, and H. B. Warner, for bridge.

Cecil B. DeMille portrayed himself in a somewhat surreal sequence, working on the picture for four days. After the shooting of his first scenes, DeMille said with a grin, "I don't suppose Paramount will pick up my option after this."[47] His sequence took place on the "set" of his own film *Samson and Delilah*. (Actually, it had already wrapped production, and the action DeMille is directing when Norma visits never appears in *Samson and Delilah*.) A. C. Lyles was present when DeMille enacted his scenes, and he recalled DeMille showed the utmost respect and affection to Gloria, being a gentleman with her throughout.

The most brilliant piece of casting, after Gloria's, was that of her former director, Erich von Stroheim, who arrived in California on the *Chief* on April 1. Having long ago made amends with the man, Gloria nonetheless felt compelled to comment later, "Mr. DeMille took direction like a pro . . . Erich von Stroheim on the other hand, kept adding things and suggesting things and asking if certain scenes might be reshot—very much in his grand manner of perfectionism regardless of schedule or cost."[48]

The acute irony of Wilder adding von Stroheim contributed to the baroque atmosphere of the film. Von Stroheim at first had declined his part, finding the role of the "God-damned butler" demeaning.[49] And he correctly feared it would become the role he would forever be remembered for.

With an estimated budget set at $1,765,000, principal photography on *Sunset Boulevard* commenced on April 11, 1949. (Four days later Gloria's first husband, Wallace Beery, died of a heart attack in Hollywood.) The story was shot in sequence. Wilder recalled later that *Sunset Boulevard* "was one of those pictures that started falling into place . . . After one weekend, we knew we had something."[50] And Nancy Olson agreed, "This was risky storytelling, risky in the sense that it was a little bizarre and it could have been farcical if it had not been played for ultimate reality . . . But this had a kind of purity of intent, right from the beginning."[51] Because *Sunset Boulevard* satirized Hollywood, there was little written about it in the press. The set was kept closed. Indeed, it was called *A Can of Beans* throughout its production just to ward off journalists. As Norma Desmond, Gloria would create her final iconic screen image.

24

Comeback

Likely pondering the possibility that *Sunset Boulevard* would become her crowning achievement, on her fiftieth birthday Gloria somewhat sadly told a reporter, "I never made an epic, a *Gone with the Wind*. I made program pictures. I was acclaimed more as a personality than as an actress."[1]

Edith Head was the costume designer on *Sunset Boulevard*, but Gloria of course took a lion's share of the credit for Norma's costumes. "Edith Head and I created perfect clothes for my character . . . I designed a hat with a single white peacock feather," she later maintained.[2] Gloria's immodesty aside, she was a true professional on the set. At the end of the last day's shooting, June 20, she was given an unusual honor, a silver cigarette case crafted by Allan Adler. The words inscribed read: "To Proclaim That Gloria Swanson Is the Greatest Star of Them All and the Idol of Cast, Staff and Crew of *Sunset Boulevard* June 20, 1949."[3]

Since 1936 Brackett and Wilder had teamed up on over a dozen motion pictures in a successful professional marriage. However, with *Sunset Boulevard* the honeymoon was over; the two fought bitterly. The most difficult clash came with the photo montage of Norma going through a battery of beauty regimens. Brackett hated it and thought it was degrading. Wilder believed it showed what Norma would do to keep her man. After a screening of the sequence, Brackett stormed out of the room. The sequence stayed in the film, and Wilder vowed he would never work with Brackett again.

One of the most significant moments in *Sunset Boulevard* is the scene of Joe and Norma watching her old movies, which features a clip from *Queen Kelly,* unseen by American audiences up until that time. As it unwinds, one is transported by the art, style, and beauty of the silent film and the youthful, classic Swanson/Desmond face. "Cast out this wicked dream that has seized my heart," reads the *Queen Kelly* title insertion. Norma, in the dark with Joe, explodes and leaps to her feet in the flickering projector light and cigarette smoke with her arm raised, her face contorted in frustration and anger: "Those idiot producers! Those imbeciles! Haven't they got any eyes? Have they forgotten what a star looks like? I'll show them. I'll be up there again, so help me." Reality and fiction clash at this precise moment, and it is a tribute to Swanson's brilliant portrayal that it is believable. It truly is "the lone buffer between a daring performance and cruel self-parody," wrote one film biographer.[4]

Filming of *Sunset Boulevard* officially wrapped on June 19, but on June 23 the stairway descent of Norma performing *Salome* for her director Max was reshot. The cast threw a party afterward. On June 25 additional rain and fog montage sequences were filmed. Gloria and Holden on July 9 reenacted their characters' initial meeting and the burial of the chimp. Wilder sensed something was just not right—the mood was off. In October they reopened the sets and reshot additional key sequences.

In December both Wilder and Brackett knew the final scene had to be reworked. By now the picture was over budget almost $180,000. On January 5, 1950, Gloria and minor cast members (minus von Stroheim and Holden) assembled for Norma's final walk down the stairway. Take after take was made, while Wilder asked Gloria to project different moods. "I had to do that scene barefoot," she recalled in 1971. "It was very hard, because it had to be done in rhythm to the music, with little dance steps. Hedda Hopper said she thought it wasn't so hard, but then she tried it, and almost broke her neck!"[5] For the last take, as the rehearsal track music of Richard Strauss's "Dance of the Seven Veils" from his opera *Salome* played (it was replaced by Franz Waxman's magnificent score in the film), and Swanson raised her arms in eerie and crazed gestures, Norma began her final descent.

"It went for thirteen weeks, *Sunset Boulevard,* and all of it full of love and excitement, the crew full of enthusiasm," Gloria said later. "I wept when it was over for I was so happy during the making of it. I was so unhappy when we finished, I wished we could have started all over again. The whole experience was magical."[6] Gloria knew she had been good.

"Before making the film, she had left Hollywood feeling angry with most of the studio heads and they in turn were still furious with her," Michelle Farmer related. "Although I had great respect for her professionalism and willpower, I have to admit that she was not an easy person." Michelle recalled her grandmother Addie sighing when Gloria would return home after filming night after night, "Oh, here comes Norma." "After each day's shooting, she carried on talking in the voice of Norma Desmond," said Michelle, "and she stayed in that personage for the duration of work on the movie." Finally, on the last day of filming Gloria announced to her mother and daughter when she entered the house that "there were only three of us in it now, meaning that Norma Desmond had taken her leave."[7]

Paramount's *Sunset Boulevard* has become *the* classic cautionary Hollywood tale. Its historic impact on the industry, and with fans and filmgoers, simply cannot be overstated. Swanson's riveting performance remains enormously intricate and shockingly mesmerizing. In November 2012, Paramount released a stunning transfer of the original film elements of *Sunset Boulevard* onto Blu-ray with more than two hours of extras, such as interviews and documentaries. It truly is the one film anyone fascinated with Hollywood and the lives of its immortals should view and study.

Was Norma Desmond based on fact? Though Wilder and Brackett never verified it, Norma Desmond could very well have been the once-beautiful and long-forgotten Mae Murray.[8] A former dancer who tangoed in clubs with Valentino, Murray signed with MGM in the mid-1920s. After she starred in von Stroheim's *The Merry Widow,* with John Gilbert, her temperament, ego, and self-enchantment ruined her in Hollywood, and her decline was rapid. In 1926 Murray wed penniless Georgian Prince David Mdivani, whose brother Serge married Pola Negri. Murray and David had a son.[9] She walked out of her Metro contract in 1927, following her husband's managerial demand, infuriating Metro boss Louis B. Mayer, who successfully blackballed Murray in Hollywood. Struggling to survive, she continued to dance, though now her matronly body was forced into short-skirted costumes with plunging necklines, her sagging face caked with makeup. Murray would never acknowledge her true age.[10]

Mae Murray years later saw *Sunset Boulevard* and allegedly was quoted as saying, "None of us floozies was *that* nuts!"[11] She then just faded away, sadly slipping into delusion and poverty. She was eventually discovered in 1964 wandering the streets of St. Louis, oblivious to her surroundings. Mae Murray lived the remaining months of her life at the Motion Picture House in Woodland Hills, passing away at the age of seventy-five in 1965.

In the 1970s Gloria was asked about her thoughts on Mae Murray and her association with Desmond. Was Murray crazy?

> Mae Murray used to board the Hollywood Boulevard bus and she'd sing strains from *The Merry Widow* just to make sure passengers knew who she was . . . And she'd go into the Academy Awards library and ask for her picture file and start shredding the photos she hated until she was asked to leave. But crazy? Well, Mae went into Larry Edmunds' bookshop and asked, *"Do you have any pictures of that fabulous actress Mae Murray."* And the clerk said, without batting an eye, *"Sorry, Miss Murray, we have nothing new from the last time you asked."* They were scared she'd start autographing them.[12]

Gloria's pity for Mae equaled that she had for her fourth husband Michael, who wrote her from Dublin, Ireland, on May 9, 1949, his birthday. In his plaintive letter, Michael asked Gloria for financial backing so that he could marry and get back on his feet again. He asked her to ask Michelle as well to come to his aid.[13]

That summer Gloria was mentioned to star in Warner Bros.' *Serenade,* a story about a young singer and an older woman, to be directed by Michael Curtiz, a role that had previously been announced for Joan Crawford, Ann Sheridan, and Jane Wyman; the film would eventually be made in 1956 starring Mario Lanza and Joan Fontaine. Sam Wood wanted Gloria for Columbia Pictures' *No Sad Songs for Me,* about a dying woman, similar to *Dark Victory.* (Rudolph Maté directed it, and Margaret Sullavan took the role.) Later that year Lloyd Bacon requested Gloria for *Glittering Hotel.* Producer Joe Kaufmann wanted her to co-star with Charles Boyer in an original screenplay by John Conrad called *Male and Female* (no connection to the DeMille film). None of these projects worked out for her. That year Gloria was in negotiations to pen a beauty book, *Beauty Hints After 50*. In 1953, she actually contracted with Prentice-Hall, but the book never came about.

On September 29, 1949, William M. Davey died in a Los Angeles hospital after a long illness. Most of his $350,000 estate was left to the University of Southern California, the Damon Runyon Fund, and the John Tracy Clinic (named after the hearing-impaired son of actor Spencer Tracy) for research in childhood deafness. No provision was made for Gloria in his will.

After her work in *Sunset Boulevard*, Gloria seemed to become more and more grandiose. She once attended a dinner party thrown by opera star Patrice Munsel and her husband Robert C. Schuler. "Gloria surprised us by arriving with her own boiled chicken dinner, which she handed to our butler, instructing him to serve it to her when we sat down to eat," wrote the late Shuler. "She was a bit overwhelming and announced, at dinner, that she had, personally, coined the name, 'Gloria,' and that, henceforth, all 'Glorias' in the world had been named after her. She was unswerving in her opinions and if you dared to disagree with her, she rolled over you like a Sherman tank. An aura of danger accompanied her, but she was also charming, amusing and uniquely beautiful, at an age when most other gorgeous woman had lost their allure."[14]

Gloria meanwhile had begun a self-serving affair, lasting until 1952, with attorney Joseph Sharfsin, whose law office was located in Philadelphia. He had been counsel to the city controller of Philadelphia from 1933 to 1936, become the city solicitor in 1936, and returned to general law in 1940. Sharfsin had represented Leopold Karniol in Canada and helped Gloria in securing a payment of $202.25 due her from the producers of *A Goose for the Gander*. By 1950 Sharfsin's letters to Gloria began with "My Precious One," "Dearest Beloved," and "Baby Dear."[15] In 1951 he would unsuccessfully run for mayor of Philadelphia on the Democratic ticket. The two would remain friends, with Sharfsin serving as her lawyer in several cases.

When Louella O. Parsons interviewed her in 1949, Gloria said, "Michele [*sic*] is like all the younger generation. She is 17 now, and she's had all kinds of offers for television and the stage, but she prefers to go to school and play basketball, hockey and to swim. She is so beautiful and she could have a great success. She has all the poise in the world, a voice like Tallulah Bankhead's and the grace of another Duse. But, not Michele [*sic*]! I have more vitality today than she has."[16] (Make no mistake, the interview was about Gloria.)

Michelle once admitted it was her mother who wanted her to have a movie career: "I wasn't that interested and after the experience of *Sunset Boulevard* I didn't want that crazy life."[17] Gloria had contacted Joseph Kennedy to secure her daughter a screen test and representation. He telephoned the reputable New York talent agent Charles Feldman, then in Hollywood, who put Michelle under a verbal contract for $200 a week for one year, ending on September 21, 1951.

In a letter to Joe Kennedy in Hyannis Port dated September 25, Feldman noted that so far that year he had paid Michelle $8,000. In August former David O. Selznick casting agent Henry Willson landed her a feature part in the touring company of Tennessee Williams's *Summer and Smoke*, which eventually played in La Jolla, California. Feldman advised Kennedy he had never asked for a commission on her earnings. He wrote she had done everything she had wanted to do, and that he had not hindered her.[18] He believed in Michelle and intended to test her for Paramount's Hal Wallis. Suddenly Gloria was pushing the envelope, requesting Joe become more aggressive with Feldman. Kennedy's contacting Feldman had no doubt been influenced by Gloria's decision now to place Michelle in other hands.

Michael was still in arrears in child support, and Gloria was adamant about securing money from him. He eventually settled a modest amount of his inheritance on his daughter. Gloria received another pathetic letter from him dated March 31. He was now living at 23 Birkenhead Road, Moels Cheshire, England. His letter stated he regrettably had suffered a nervous breakdown on Christmas Day and had had to give up drinking.

He wrote Gloria he had just paid $49,000 in legal debts, and again asked for money from Michelle. He pleaded in the letter for Michelle to help him acquire money so that he could remarry. Then, with an abrupt mood change, it was suddenly "Spring in Cannes!" Michael let Gloria know all about how Sylvia Ashley "had done well for herself" with a certain fellow she used to call Doug at the Dorchester in 1932.[19]

On and on . . . It was sadly apparent Michael could not deal with reality.

On April 30, Gloria wrote him, her frustration over his meaningless existence pouring out of her.

I am not going to help you financially for many reasons. You see, my obligations are to my mother and my family. You have never been a part of it—you made yourself a stranger . . . you relinquished your rights as a father—obligations go with parenthood—now you want your child to help you.

Imagine—help you finance a romance so that you can marry some unsuspecting woman . . . Michael, what has happened to you?—where is your soul?—how can you look at yourself?—have you ever thought of honest-to-God work? . . . Have you ever worked? No—you've been a "taker" not a "giver" . . .

Please help Michelle to have some respect for you—only you can do this.

I wish you well. [handwritten][20]

Settled back in New York in late 1949, Gloria acquired a new secretary, Jerri Roberts. She secured a new agent as well, Helen Ainsworth. Gloria then signed an exclusive $1,000-a-week "Good Will Ambassador" pact with Paramount for a year, remaining on the studio's payroll from October 1949 until August 1950. Gloria was used not only to represent a healthier and more wholesome view of the industry to the public, but also to promote *Sunset Boulevard* and the studio's *The Heiress,* with Olivia de Havilland and Montgomery Clift. Her tour took her to twenty-six cities, where she participated in citywide events, appearing on local television and radio shows, giving interviews, and showing up at charitable fund-raisers as well. In the end Gloria logged more than twenty thousand miles on the tour.

In Hollywood in April 1950, some three hundred industry insiders and selected members of the press were shown a preview of *Sunset Boulevard,* to qualify it for Academy Award consideration. After a dinner hosted by Louis B. Mayer for about twenty insiders, the group retired to a Paramount screening room where the audience, including Edith Head, Mickey Neilan, Mary Pickford and Charles "Buddy" Rogers, and Barbara Stanwyck, witnessed the unreeling. "As everyone watched the film, the screening room was silent," recalled Head. "The credits rolled, the screen went black, and still there was silence. Then there was thunderous applause. A few people walked out, murmuring that the film would be the ruination of Hollywood, but the rest swarmed around Swanson and Wilder. Stanwyck had tears streaming down her face as she pushed her way up to congratulate Gloria."[21]

A combination of horror and excitement permeated the room. Stanwyck knelt in front of Gloria, kissed the hem of her gold lamé dress, and wept, "I know where *my* place is—at your feet!" An unusually somber and stunned Groucho Marx was heard to say, "Here is the real place for that immortal line, 'What Happened?' I feel like I've been hit by an earthquake." Gloria asked where Mary Pickford was, and the reply was, "She can't show herself, Gloria . . . She's overcome. We all are."[22]

However, Louis B. Mayer vented rage at Wilder. The aging mogul was sadly out of step with the changing postwar attitudes of the public, though still full of self-importance. He had let his own life become a mess as he neglected his role as studio head to philander and lose money at the racetrack. Mayer attacked Wilder, hissing, "You bastard! You have disgraced the industry that made and fed you! You should be tarred and feathered and run out of the country!" Wilder's reply pulled no punches and showed no respect for the man whose time had passed. "Fuck you!" seethed Wilder. "Go shit in your hat!"[23] In less than two years, Mayer, much to his surprise, was unceremoniously fired from MGM and sent out to pasture.

Variety reviewer William Brogdon wrote in his evaluation of *Sunset Boulevard,* "Performances by the entire cast, and particularly William Holden and Gloria Swanson, are exceptionally fine . . . Miss Swanson, returning to the screen after a very long absence, socks hard with a silent-day technique to put over the decaying star she is called upon to portray."[24] Still, Gloria would feel it necessary during her tour to continuously defend herself: "It is *not* the story of my life."[25]

The Saturday Evening Post, probably more than any other publication at that time, put Gloria back into the public eye in July before the release of *Sunset Boulevard* with a two-part feature profile. Her agent Ainsworth, who represented such stars as Rhonda Fleming, Jane Powell, and Howard Keel, was also securing television work for her clients. When Gloria appeared briefly on Ed Sullivan's *Talk of the Town* (CBS) in September, looking stylish in an off-the-shoulder, long-sleeved dark satin gown, she was paid $3,500. When she appeared that same month on *Stop the Music* (ABC), her salary was $3,000.

On August 10, with ads confirming it "A Most Unusual Motion Picture," *Sunset Boulevard* officially premiered at Radio City Music Hall. It proved a winner. The critics raved. *Time* magazine said, "It is a story of Hollywood at its worst told by Hollywood at its best." *Look* magazine praised Gloria for "a brilliant, haunting performance . . . It will make one more generation of moviegoers aware of her as a vivid screen personality."[26]

Regarding Gloria's portrayal, James Agee in *Sight & Sound* commented, "There are plenty of good reasons why *Sunset Boulevard* (a beautiful title) is, I think, their [Brackett and Wilder] best movie yet. It is Hollywood craftsmanship at its smartest and at just about its best, and it is hard to find better craftsmanship than that, at this time, in any art or country . . . Miss Swanson, required to play a hundred percent grotesque, plays it not just to the hilt but right up to the armpit, by which I mean magnificently."[27] Kate Cameron in the New York *Daily News* exclaimed, "Brilliant, provocative, unforgettable! Gloria Swanson gives the performance of her career!"[28] Wrote Paramount Studio biographer John Douglas Eames, "For sheer audacity, *Sunset Boulevard* has rarely been equaled . . . The line between the real and the imaginary was continually blurred by writer-director Billy Wilder in his most diabolically clever mood."[29]

Still it continued. The reviewer from the *New York Journal-American* raved, "Gloria Swanson pulls you up to the edge of your seat . . . A great picture of a great story of a great star."[30] And "T.M.P." (Thomas M. Pryor) of *The New York Times* said, "It is such a clever compound of truth and legend—and is so richly redolent of the past, yet so contemporaneous—that it seemingly speaks with great authority . . . [It] is a rare blend of pungent writing, expert acting, masterly direction and unobtrusively artistic photography which quickly casts a spell over the audience and holds it enthralled to a shattering climax . . . It is inconceivable that anyone else might have been considered for the role as the wealthy, egotistical relic desperately yearning to hear again the plaudits of the crowd. Miss Swanson dominates the picture."[31]

Sunset Boulevard still packs a punch today. From its opening credits, with the shot of SUNSET BLVD stenciled on a concrete curb—Holden's billing is first, *then* Swanson's, followed by von Stroheim's—the film draws the viewer in. As film critic Richard Corliss keenly observed, *Sunset Boulevard* is "the definitive Hollywood horror movie."[32]

In its first four weeks at Radio City Music Hall alone, *Sunset Boulevard* took in $651,700 and was seen by 615,000 people. By the end of its seven-week run, the picture had grossed $1,020,000, the sixth-largest take for the Hall up to that time. *Sunset Boulevard* earned $2.25 million in domestic rentals, but never became a box-office smash, despite its favorable reviews. It would earn $5 million worldwide by 1960. Today *Sunset Boulevard* is considered one of the best films ever made about Hollywood, and a definite classic. In 1989 it was important enough to be placed on the list of the National Film Preservation Board.

Wilder never lost respect for Gloria. In 1963 he was asked if any of his films stood out as his favorites. His reply was interesting: "There are certain parts in a few of them which I remember with fondness; maybe parts of *Sunset Boulevard* and *Double Indemnity*; some of [*The*] *Lost Weekend* and [*Some Like It*] *Hot*. I also like the runt of my litter, *Ace in the Hole*." Asked which stars he enjoyed working with, Wilder was quick to respond, "Outstanding among them was Gloria Swanson. You must remember that this was a star who at one time was carried in a sedan chair from her dressing room to the soundstage. When she married the Marquis de la Falaise and came back from Europe to New York and by train from there to Hollywood people were strewing rose petals on the railroad tracks in her direction. She'd been one of the all-time stars, but when she returned to the screen in *Sunset* [*Boulevard*], she worked like a dog."[33]

In Dallas, Texas, on September 4–5, 1950, Gloria was awarded a Neiman Marcus Award for Distinguished Service in the Field of Fashion, after owner Stanley Marcus discovered she had designed in three days her personal wardrobe for the event. Her creations were then generously included in a scheduled fashion show along with those of Christian Dior and Balenciaga. Sharing the award with her were Pauline Trigere and Bonnie Cashin. To the ceremony Gloria wore a remarkable millinery creation with flowing veil and small birds called the "Hummingbird" hat.

Her film career back on track, suddenly movie offers poured in. One was from director William Dieterle and called *The Besieged Heart,* by screenwriter Robert Hill. It dealt with a woman dying of a mysterious disease and the attempts of her younger boyfriend to find a cure. It was eventually filmed with a highly altered plotline and called *Female on the Beach*, at Universal in 1955, starring Joan Crawford. Paramount wanted to test Gloria for *Darling, How Could You?*, an antiquated screen adaptation of Sir James Barrie's *Alice Sit-by-the-Fire*, which had been a stage success for Helen Hayes; Gloria would portray the mother of a teenaged daughter. But Gloria's ego surpassed her common sense. "Can you imagine!" she asked an astonished reporter referring to the test.[34] Proudly defiant, Gloria professed, "If they don't know what I can do by now, why bother?"[35] Joan Fontaine made the film.

Another realistic offer came from Hal Wallis. It was for *December Bride*, based on the Parke Levy novel, a comedy about a woman whose daughter and son-in-law conspire to get her married. Gloria declined. (In 1954 Levy created a popular television show out of his script, starring Spring Byington.) Hedda Hopper astutely remarked about Gloria, "Gloria Swanson is another who can't see straight today where her career as an actress is concerned . . . I suggested she might do a movie version, written by Frances Marion, of Frances Parkinson Keyes' *Dinner at Antoine's*. Not a chance. 'I couldn't possibly play the mother of an eighteen-year-old daughter,' she snapped. 'The part's too old for me.'"[36] Gloria at that time had an eighteen-year-old and was already the grandmother of three.

On October 4, 1950, Hopper let the cat out of the bag when she wrote, "I can't understand Gloria Swanson. She's had more publicity in the past year and a half than anybody except Harry S. Truman. She should have another picture ready for release now; and would have if she hadn't turned down a Paramount contract for seven films, with a salary starting at $75,000 per picture and working up to an astronomical figure. I hear she wants the astronomical figure now. I'm sorry to see Gloria miss the boat. I would have thought that by now she'd understand signs and figures."[37]

Furious at this disclosure, Gloria shot Hopper a scathing cable on October 5:

DEAR HEDDA I WISH TO INFORM YOU THAT AT NO TIME HAVE
I HAD A SEVEN PICTURE OFFER OR TWO PICTURES OFFER OR
ANY OTHER KIND OF OFFER FROM PARAMOUNT STUDIOS SO
HENCEFORTH WILL YOU PLEASE CONTACT ME DIRECT[LY] TO
PREVENT MISTAKES OF WHICH THERE HAVE BEEN SO MANY[38]

Gloria did not necessarily care who she offended. At this very crucial point in her career she might have done better to keep the still influential Hopper as a close ally. The industrious Hollywood gossip, much to her credit, would always revere Gloria as a true industry pioneer and film icon, though personally she never cared for her. The two would make amends in later years.

In New York at the end of October, Helen Ainsworth arranged for her to host a thirty-minute afternoon interview show, *The Gloria Swanson Show*, five times weekly over WOR Radio in the 2:30–3:30 P.M. slot. For this Gloria would be paid $1,000 a week, with the possibility of $10,000 a week if the show went into syndication. (It did not.) The deal also stipulated she would be able to record transcriptions onto discs (when she was abroad), and she was given a twenty-six-week option and 35 percent of the gross sales of those transcriptions, plus a $2,500 advance against her earnings. The contract was signed August 25, 1950. Gloria was also given return passage from England on board the *America* so she and Michelle could attend the upcoming Royal Command Performance.

Gloria, with her new male companion the columnist Brandy Brent, and Michelle sailed to Europe in style on board the Cunard liner *Queen Elizabeth* on October 17 for the premiere of *The Mudlark* (20th Century–Fox, 1950), starring Irene Dunne. Brent would become more or less Gloria's publicist, after her professional relationship with Ainsworth ended following her return from England. Ainsworth was very well liked and respected in the industry, but Gloria felt she knew more about handling her career than anyone else, which possibly explained why there were no major film projects lined up for her by year's end. Gloria eventually signed Wynn Rocamora as her agent.

In England Gloria, Michelle, and Brent stayed at the Savoy Hotel. On a rainy evening, September 30, at London's Princess Theater, after the screening of *The Mudlark*, Gloria May Josephine Swanson of Chicago, Illinois, was presented to King George VI, his Consort the Queen Mother Elizabeth, and the two princesses, Elizabeth and Margaret. Michelle accompanied her mother but was not included in the formal introduction line. As for Brent, who was definitely not invited to meet the royals, he no doubt was licking his wounds back at the Savoy. Gloria looked splendid in an off-the-shoulder dark organdy gown, wearing glittering diamond earrings, sparklettes in her hair, and a fur stole.

The international press announced Gloria had signed to make the murder drama *Another Man's Poison,* based on the play *Deadlock* by Leslie Sands, directed by Irving Rapper, and presented by Douglas Fairbanks Jr. for Eros Films in England. Once in London Gloria capriciously asked for a postponement of the filming while she accepted a play in New York. She was promptly released from her contract, and Bette Davis gladly stepped in. After the Command Performance, Michelle remained in Europe to study dramatics; she bid farewell to her tearful mother on November 13, when Gloria and Brent boarded the *America* in Southampton, arriving in New York on November 20.

During her absence the Academy Award nominations for 1950 had been announced, and *Sunset Boulevard* walked away with an amazing eleven, including Best Picture, Best Director (Wilder), Best Actor (Holden), Best Supporting Actor (von Stroheim), and Best Music (Franz Waxman). In the Best Actress category the nominees were Eleanor Parker *(Caged)*, Anne Baxter *(All About Eve)*, Bette Davis *(All About Eve)*, Judy Holliday *(Born Yesterday)*, and Gloria for *Sunset Boulevard*, her third Oscar nod.[39]

Recognition and awards started to appear for what was called the most celebrated film comeback in history. The Associated Press voted her one of the ten most outstanding women of the year. On December 21, the 25th Annual National Board of Review of Motion Pictures voted *Sunset Boulevard* as the Best American Film of the Year, with Gloria capturing its Best Actress award. At year's end *Sunset Boulevard* was accorded a spot on the Ten Best Pictures List of the New York Drama Critics as well.

Gloria appeared on numerous radio talk and variety shows upon her return to New York. On November 26 she starred in her first dramatic turn on radio as Julia Lambert in the two-hour "Theatre," broadcast on *The United States Steel Hour—Theatre Guild on the Air* (NBC). Based on a story by Guy Bolton and W. Somerset Maugham, the piece reunited her with Melvyn Douglas. She was paid $2,500 for the role. Gloria then decided to attempt a Broadway comeback as well.

25

Career

Gloria chose a revival of the Ben Hecht and Charles MacArthur comedy *Twentieth Century* as her next Broadway vehicle. Actor-director José Ferrer telephoned her on November 23, and by the end of their twenty-minute conversation she had agreed to do it. Ferrer had originally approached Lucille Ball to do the play, but she was unavailable. The role of Lily Garland had been portrayed on Broadway in 1932 by Eugenie Leontovich, and in the 1934 Columbia Pictures film by Carole Lombard, after Gloria proved too difficult. The new production was meant to run for just two weeks, December 24, 1950, to January 6, 1951, at the ANTA (American National Theatre and Academy) Playhouse. Rehearsals started on December 4.

On December 6 it was announced the play would open at the Fulton Theater on Broadway, with $110,000 in advance ticket sales, beginning Monday, January 8, after the ANTA run. Ferrer, who was directing the production, also took the male lead, with hopes of bringing it to Hollywood with Gloria for a new screen version. The plot told of egomaniacal theatrical producer Oscar Jaffe (Ferrer), in need of a new Broadway hit show, pursuing his former protégé and lover, the equally vain and temperamental Lily Garland (Gloria), to star in his new production. She has left him for a Hollywood career and is also on board the *Twentieth Century Limited* from Chicago to New York's Grand Central Terminal.

Twentieth Century was one of four revivals that would open on Broadway during Christmas week 1950. (One of the others was *Captain Brassbound's Conversion*, featuring Edna Best.) When *Twentieth Century* opened on December 24, the reviews could not have been better, wiping away all memory of Gloria's disastrous maiden Broadway effort. "Jose Ferrer and Gloria Swanson . . . make a very funny pair of cartoonists—broad in style and fast in pace; and *Twentieth Century*, which was hilarious when it was new, is still uproarious in the new version," wrote *New York Times* theater critic Brooks Atkinson. "Miss Swanson gives a vastly enjoyable performance as the Hollywood hellcat, darting swiftly around the set, tossing off the vernacular with snarling vitality and giving the vanity all its deliberate humor without burlesquing it. She plays with the relish and flavor of a good trouper who is having an uncommonly fine time."[1]

The *New York World-Telegram*'s William Hawkins commented, "Hilarious! It long since ceased to be startling that Gloria Swanson was amazing. It's only startling that she can go on being more amazing. Jose Ferrer has directed it with turbulent animation." Richard Watts of the *New York Post* agreed: "The indefinable thing called glamour is Gloria Swanson's in abundance . . . She is downright wonderful."[2] On December 31 Gloria and Ferrer enacted a scene from the play on Tallulah Bankhead's NBC radio show *The Big Show*.

The accolades continued. At the end of the year Gloria was placed by Mr. Blackwell and Celebrity Service, Inc., on the list of Top 1950 Celebrities.[3] Along with Faye Emerson and Sloan Simpson, on January 1 Gloria was added to the list of the Top Ten Best-Dressed Women, posted by New York's Dress Institute. She received the Hollywood Foreign Press Golden Globe Best Actress award for *Sunset Boulevard* on February 28, and the Best Actress Award from the first International Film Festival held in Punte del Este, Uruguay, on March 5. Gloria would later be given a New York's Page One Award in the field of entertainment, alongside Shirley Booth and Tallulah Bankhead, on April 13 at a ball at the Astor Hotel.

She also received a special Look Magazine Achievement Award for "making the greatest comeback in motion picture history," and her face graced *Look*'s February 30 cover. And if that was not enough, from New York's Fashion Academy, she received the 22nd Gold Medal Award for 1951's Best-Dressed Woman of the Stage.[4]

Due to laryngitis and a bad cold, Gloria had to drop out of *Twentieth*

Century for a week beginning February 5. The night before her return she appeared as a guest on Ed Sullivan's *Toast of the Town*. On February 18, she was heard in the dramatic radio play "The Promise" opposite Paul Lukas on another *United States Steel Hour,* for which she was again paid $2,500.

Gloria gave an insightful interview to the New York *Daily News* writer Ben Gross in February. One question he asked concerned her public popularity and Hollywood's apparent apathy toward her. "The fact is," Gloria rationalized, "that the most fascinating—and, yes, let's be honest, sexy, women in history have been older. Look at your leading actresses today; consider the women of the French court who were great charmers. Most of them were in their thirties, forties, fifties or even beyond that."[5] Gloria, her affinity for anything French notwithstanding, always prided herself on her great personal charm. She would use it to her benefit until the end of her days.

On the night of March 29 the Academy Awards were held at the RKO Pantages Theater in Hollywood, beginning at 8:00 P.M. Pacific Coast Time. Because so many of the nominees, including Gloria and Ferrer, up for Best Actor for *Cyrano de Bergerac,* Judy Holliday, Celeste Holm, Sam Jaffe, George Cukor, and Thelma Ritter, were in New York working, a radio hookup was installed for the winners' reactions. Gloria's birthday had been just two days prior, so a party was held at Café La Zamba on Fifty-Second Street with 280 guests. The press asked Gloria, Holliday, and Ferrer to pose for gag pictures with a fake Oscar statuette before the ceremonies. Gloria wrote that both she and Holliday were embarrassed to go along with the press.[6]

When Joan Crawford stepped to the podium at the Pantages auditorium to announce Best Actress, Gloria leaned across Ferrer and whispered to young Holliday, "One of us is about to be very happy." Holliday was named the winner, and as Gloria hugged her she said, "Darling, why couldn't you have waited for next year?"[7] The radio hookup did not pick up Judy's acceptance speech. The Best Picture Award went to *All About Eve.*

Gloria, dressed elegantly in a dark belted dress, white fur, and veiled dark hat with imposing dark egret feathers, and sporting her fabulous Cartier crystal bracelets, which she also wore in *Sunset Boulevard,* quietly kept up a front, telling the press, "Well, this just means the old workhorse has got to go back to work."[8] Many looked for some sign of disappointment, but she wouldn't give them the pleasure of an emotional display. She wrote, "They had been waiting, and rather hoping, to see the *Hindenburg* go up in flames."[9]

On April 19 Gloria announced she would next star in an adaptation of the French play *Nina,* a farce by André Roussin and adapted by Samuel Taylor in association with John C. Wilson. Gloria's old ally Gregory Ratoff would direct. In June 1951 it was announced at a party held at the Waldorf-Astoria that Gloria, who for years had purchased her clothing from such leading fashion houses as Scaasi, was now a vice president of Puritan Fashions' Puritan Dress Company of Waltham, Massachusetts. Spearheaded by Carl Rosen, Puritan Fashions, begun in 1912 by his father, had managed to sign European couturiers Pierre Balmain and Givenchy to design couture dresses that then were retailed under the Puritan banner for under $15. Rosen was not called "the King" in the fashion business for nothing.

Rosen gave Gloria a lifetime contract for such creations as the laughably entitled "Gloria Swanson's Mother's Day Dress." She nonetheless accepted the challenge and took over the original "Forever Young" line, adding her moniker. With designs specifically for short, stout women like herself, she made millions for the company. Her active role would begin after New Year's 1952 when she signed her contract.

Earlier that year Gloria met Detroit industrialist Lewis Bredin. He was vice chairman and CEO of a building materials corporation called Chamberlin Company of America, located in Detroit. It manufactured weather stripping, insulation, caulking, storm windows, and screen doors, and Bredin was worth millions. The four-time-married Lewis Leonard Bredin was born November 23, 1893, and attended Yale University, Class of 1920. He had served in World War I in the navy as a lieutenant, and in World War II earned the rank of colonel in the Army Air Force. His third wife was Dee Furey Mott, with whom he fathered a daughter named Denny. Lewis and Dee divorced in New Mexico in 1939.

His fourth marriage, in Las Vegas on July 24, 1945, was to forty-year-old Natalie Berthold. In 1951 he petitioned against her for divorce in St. Augustine, Florida, where he lived, on the grounds of incompatibility and mental cruelty. Natalie resided at their seventeen-room family home at 694 South Amalfi Drive in the Pacific Palisades. A sportsman and former head of the Michigan Gaming Commission, Bredin had also been the state racing commissioner under Governor Kim Sigler. He held several golfing trophies, was twice Michigan's amateur golf champion, in 1919 and 1921, and spent most of his time traveling from one international resort to another.

Upon meeting the glamorous Gloria, Bredin was smitten. She no doubt realized her opportunities as well. Here was an attractive man whose robust sexual appetite equaled hers, and the fact he was wealthy certainly was a plus. Over the following decade Lewis sent Gloria literally hundreds of romantic love letters from his travels. He would address them to "Gloria Darling," "Dearest Beloved," "Dearest Love," and "Pussy—My Beloved." The letters were passionate and endearing; he was a man truly in love.[10]

These letters were typical of his charming and sweet devotion to his lover Gloria. He would write her of his love and longing to obtain a divorce for her, how much happiness Gloria gave him, and his yearning for her to be patient.[11]

Because Bredin was married, his affair with Gloria had to remain secret. However, Walter Winchell broke that silence that summer in his "Along Broadway" column: "Gloria Swanson's new Big Secret is a Detroit tycoon."[12] Hedda Hopper caught up on September 8 and told her readers that the "tall, gray-haired gentleman who is constantly on her set at Republic," where Gloria was making a new picture, was Col. Lewis Bredin.[13] Very rarely the press would take note of their activities together, the public not being much interested.

That spring, Michelle, now nineteen and independent, was mentioned for a role in a film in Italy. Hoche Productions was producing *Monte Carlo Baby,* in which she had been cast. It would be Michelle's only film acting venture. While negotiating the project she met thirty-six-year-old Robert Amon, general manager for the film company.

On July 2 Gloria signed a contract with Brenco Pictures Corporation and producers Edward L. Alperson and Milton H. Bren, husband of actress Claire Trevor. Her new film was entitled *3 for Bedroom C* and was shot at Republic Studios in Monopak color, called Natural Color. It was unquestionably a B picture, costing a modest $550,000. Gloria's contract gave her $20,000, $5,000 a week for four weeks guaranteed. She also received an expense account of $5,000 for her wardrobe, which she designed herself, and a guarantee of an additional $50,000 after recoup of costs and worldwide gross.

For Hal Roach at MGM, Bren had produced the films *Topper* (1937) and *Merrily We Live* (1938), both with Constance Bennett, whose career was on the skids as well in the late 1930s. After *3 for Bedroom C,* Bren and his partner

Alperson planned two more pictures for Republic, *Snow Covered Wagons* and an ambitious remake of *A Star Is Born*. "That is one of the benefits in a small operation," he boasted to Thomas M. Pryor of *The New York Times*. "You don't have to rush a picture into production before you are satisfied that the script is right."[14] Unfortunately, Bren must not have had an eye for good scripts, as *3 for Bedroom C* ended his film producing career.

Gloria arrived in California on July 25. She was cast as film actress Ann Haven, who, with her young daughter Barbara (Janine Perreau), has sneaked aboard the *Santa Fe Super Chief* in Chicago bound for Pasadena to avoid her agent Johnny Pizer (Fred Clark). The train is full, and she and Barbara settle into compartment C, booked by Dr. Oliphant J. Thrumm (James Warren), a distinguished Harvard professor. Confusion and misunderstandings follow as Ann and the professor fall in love by fade-out. Filming began on August 14.

Gloria said she chose the property because all she had been offered after *Sunset Boulevard* were variations of Norma Desmond, and she wanted to do a comedy. This was not completely true. She had been offered numerous important roles in A pictures requiring her to be her age, and she had adamantly refused. After reading "some 50 movie scripts submitted to her since then," she complained heartily about roles offered to her. "I have felt the need of a film comedy following the heavy portrayal in *Sunset Boulevard*," she asserted. When asked what she thought pictures needed most, her reply was self-serving: "Adult romance . . . There is no reason why middle-aged actresses shouldn't have romantic roles on the screen—they do on the stage."[15]

In a more sensible mood, Gloria commented to Los Angeles reporter Bob Thomas about her follow-up film, "None of the majors came up with anything. There were a few offers from independents, but I didn't like the way the deals were set up." She resented accepting less money and control almost as much as she resented having to play her own age.[16]

In her first scene in the picture, fifty-two-year-old Gloria is shown in close-up holding a movie magazine in front of her face, with "Ann" on its cover. Made-up and lit very carefully, Swanson lowers the publication and delivers her lines in a high-pitched "younger" voice. Immediately she places her performance in parody. It is difficult to reconcile the shadowing of her jowls, and the spread of her decidedly middle-aged waistline, with the character of a young (granted, adoptive) mother of an eight-year-old. One cannot lose sight of this throughout the picture.

Bren originally planned the vehicle for his wife, Oscar-winning actress Claire Trevor, when he was associated with Fred MacMurray and William Seiter in Borderline Productions. Trevor told Edwin Schallert why she dropped out of the project. "I didn't feel that my name was strong enough to carry the picture along," she humbly confessed. "Gloria is ideal because of her tremendous success in *Sunset Boulevard,* and the complete contrast this role offers. I think securing her spells fine showmanship."[17] Perhaps Trevor was merely protecting her own career by rejecting the role in her husband's folly.

The Santa Fe Railroad allowed Republic to use an actual Pleasure Dome car, a Pullman sleeping car, and a dining car, disassembled on the lot, as sets. "Train travel in this country was extremely popular after the war and before the coming of the commercial jet age," confirmed rail historian Michael Sypult.[18] Americans by the thousands traveled the rails in comfort and luxury, and Pullman was eager to exploit its services. Gloria, as part of her contract, was featured in ads for the Pullman Company boarding, reading, and sleeping in a compartment and dining in the first class restaurant car (menu items included champagne, freshly caught trout, steaks, and lobster).

As her own costume designer for the film, Gloria was given free rein, creating four particular outfits. One was called the Tri-Travel Suit—a skirt, long-sleeved blouse, and cape; another was christened the Santa Anita, a checkered, snug-fitting skirt and matching long-sleeved top with a dark stole; the third, called the Mexican Border, was a kind of jumper with three-quarter-length pant legs and a cape; and the fourth one she called Happy Talk, which looked like a bunch of gathered towels around the waist extending to the floor. None was particularly becoming or exceptionally fashionable.

About her future on the stage, Gloria told writer Kevin Thomas her outlook on roles was optimistic. "They want me for all kinds of things—musicals, dramas, return engagements in *20th Century . . . ,*" she said. "But I'm starting rehearsals in September for *Nina . . .* It is a plum, but such a difficult play that it sometimes frightens me."[19]

When she was in Hollywood Gloria visited Mickey Neilan. Still battling alcoholism, he dreamed of forming a company between the two of them to be called Essanen (*S* for Swanson and *N* for Neilan) Productions; the first project would be a screenplay he wrote for her called *Millie.* Gloria must have sensed his desperation. She never signed the contract. Poor Mickey would inevitably call Gloria at all hours when in his cups, drowning no doubt in past memories.

She could only handle so much. He once called her in the middle of the night from the Lambs Club in New York on West Forty-fourth Street. Her sharp reply sent on July 11, 1952, said:

> THANKS FOR THE INCONVENIENCE
> NEXT TIME DON'T CALL ME WHEN YOU ARE INCAPABLE
> OF KNOWING WHAT YOU ARE TALKING ABOUT
> GLORIA[20]

In California Gloria was in talks with Bren and Alperson about another comedy, *Advance for Romance,* based on a story by Lloyd Shearer, about a fashion designer who makes her first million and then is romanced by a government income tax agent, to be filmed the following summer. Hedda Hopper announced in September the male lead would be Fred MacMurray. Gloria liked the story, but it never came about.

Filming completed in mid-September on *3 for Bedroom C,* and then Gloria flew back to New York to begin rehearsals of *Nina* on September 24. David Niven was cast as her lover. In the role of Nina's husband was British actor Alan Webb. Niven arrived in New York aboard the *Queen Mary* on September 19, and five days later director Gregory Ratoff disembarked off the *Liberté* from France. *Nina* was scheduled to open at the New Parsons Theater, run by Philip Langner, Charles Bowdon, and Nancy Stern, in Hartford, Connecticut, on Thursday, November 1, for three days. Then it would continue to Boston on November 5 and Philadelphia on November 10, before making its Broadway debut on December 5 at the Royale Theater.

"Opening night [in tryouts] we had a blue ribbon audience—the Alfred Lunts, Tallulah Bankhead, everyone," Niven told Hedda Hopper. "Gloria designed her own clothes. I was awaiting her on stage. As she made her entrance, the audience gasped with horror at her billowing taffeta dress. I smiled, couldn't get my lip back and had to play the entire scene looking like a mad gopher. When I took her in my arms, there was a loud report! Her stays burst and some 4½ in[ches] of whalebone came shooting up my nose."[21] He added, "I pushed it down but it kept coming back up. She couldn't see it, so I said 'Whalebone,' and she started to pull it and it stuck."[22]

Walter Kerr wrote in his pre-Broadway review the following day, "We understand from the program Miss Swanson designed her own clothes, which, like the play, fell apart in the first act." "After three weeks on the road, Gloria wasn't speaking to me," Niven recalled. "I've never known why."[23] After they opened in New York he vowed never to do Broadway again.

On November 22 Gloria sabatoged the production, claiming the play was poorly written. She then called a press conference in her dressing room in Philadelphia. "An artist is only as good as his or her lines," she wailed to the reporters. "I wanted them to get some fresh minds on the play and perhaps engage a play doctor to work on it. I even suggested more time on the road to iron the difficulties . . . The French are rather direct in what's fun and what's foolish. Some lines considered too risqué for American audiences have been cut out . . . Some of the critics on the road accused me of 'fluffing' lines. No scene in the play now is what we rehearsed in New York . . . There's been nothing but changes, changes, changes ever since we opened."[24]

This time Gloria's presumptions and the resultant publicity backfired on her. Tryouts were *supposed* to undergo changes, and her whining about it won her no sympathy. Unlike the movies, theater did not favor prima donnas. Whatever the reasons for her unprofessional behavior, she wasn't winning any friends, and her press conference threatened the future of *Nina*.

Actors Equity Association was furious with her. "I have no quarrel with Mr. Wilson, he's a wonderful person, but I have a responsibility to myself," Gloria announced grandly. "The happy solution would be to get somebody else for the role," she added. That, of course, was impossible and she knew it. In another useless attempt for sympathy, she rationalized, "It seems a pity that artists are compelled to come in with shows they do not particularly care for."[25] In reality Gloria saw she was not good in her role and that Niven would steal the reviews. She simply could not comprehend why her demands were not met. Meanwhile, despite the bad press ticket sales soared for the December 3 preview.

From the very same dressing room in Joinville, France, that her mother had used while filming *Madame Sans-Gêne* in 1924, Michelle announced her engagement to Robert Amon. She was in the middle of filming the role of

Jacqueline in *Monte Carlo Baby,* which starred Jules Munshin, Cara Williams, and twenty-two-year-old Audrey Hepburn. Directed by Jean Boyer and Lester Fuller, the comedy was shot simultaneously in English and French and released by Corona Pictures in Europe in 1952. It did only so-so business overseas, but it served to introduce young Hepburn to American movie audiences.

Growing up hadn't been easy for Michelle. Kept in baby bonnets way past her toddler years, she endured a series of nannies and nurses while being isolated from and neglected by her mother. "The only person she ever loved and respected was her [own] mother," Michelle said of Gloria. However, she did credit Gloria with grounding her with sound advice. "If you don't discipline yourself, life will," she had warned.[26]

Under the aegis of family friends, Michelle and the Turkish-born, thirty-six-year-old Robert Amon wed the evening of December 16, 1951, at the David Stuart Memorial Chapel of St. Paul's Episcopal Church in Paterson, New Jersey. There were fifteen guests present at the ceremony, presided over by the Rev. William L. Griffin. The nineteen-year-old bride looked radiant in a long-sleeved, knee-length satin dress. Gloria did not attend. She said she was ill and stayed home in New York writing gossipy letters to friends.

Nina made its Broadway debut on December 5. It was the first Roussin script to be produced in New York, and the fourth French transplantation of the season; the others were *Love and Let Love, Faithfully Yours,* and *Gigi* (which starred Audrey Hepburn). The critics played tag panning Gloria's farce. The New York *Daily News* said the comedy was "as out of tune as an attic harpsichord."[27] Brooks Atkinson in *The New York Times* agreed: "This is the play that Gloria Swanson said she would like to leave a fortnight ago. After the opening performance . . . it is easy to see why."[28]

However, veteran critic Walter Kerr best summed up Gloria's performance: "Miss Swanson is at sea in 'Nina.' She plays a . . . femme fatale who likes to think of herself as juggling husband and lover simultaneously. But she plays the part without any attack at all. She falls back on familiar mannerisms, she gives bittersweet readings through clenched teeth, she makes strong and abandoned gestures, she runs her voice up and down the scales in varied cadences, and everything she does is both meaningless and monotonous . . . She is obviously an actress who needs firm guidance, and since she has not got it in this instance, her best is just not good enough."[29] In her dressing room after opening night, Gloria was heard to say, "I will never, never act on the stage again."[30] On December 28 it was announced *Nina* would close on January 12, 1952, after only forty-five performances.

Though her professional career was in question, Gloria's personal life did not suffer. Despite her affair with Lewis, Gloria dated other men, including businessman Frank Chapman (he wore a cumberbund with his tuxedo, which impressed her). She also appeared frequently with the ever infatuated Brandy Brent.

In late December Louis C. Simmel, president of Simmel-Meservey, a film company, told the *Los Angeles Times* that Gloria would star in his television series *Better Grooming for More Gracious Living*. She didn't.

Gloria's Puritan contract paid her $25,000 a year, covering $20,000 she owed Puritan in advances the first year and leaving her $5,000. On March 17 Gloria made personal appearances at four different May Co. stores in Los Angeles. Three days later she picked up an Honorary Oscar for Joseph Schenck, who was recognized for his long years in the industry, at the 1952 Academy Awards ceremony.

Back in New York, on March 31 Gloria's "Forever Young" spring fashions were modeled at three different showings at the store Franklin Simon on Fifth Avenue. Gloria dressed in one of her own designs, a blue taffeta dress with a belling skirt that was embroidered slightly at the neckline and cuffs. Her small collection, all in navy blue and all priced under $20, was specifically designed in half-sizes. Bolero jackets were then favored. Gloria advised petite women not to clutter the throat and to keep the shoulders neat to emphasize height. A slight dip in the waistline in back would ensure a svelte line. The Puritan Fashions deal was a welcome and lucrative venture that Gloria would enjoy for years to come.

On March 22 she flew to Mexico City to sign a contract to star in a feature film and a series of television episodes with the TeleVox Company. Gloria had agreed to film prologues introducing twenty-six episodes, ranging from romance to drama to sophisticated comedies to mysteries, for her own television series, *Crown Theatre*, produced by Bing Crosby Enterprises. She would also perform in four of the half-hour episodes, three to be filmed in Mexico. They would take three days to shoot, and for her work Gloria was paid $3,000 for each.

In early March she again flew to Mexico, stepping off the plane in a tan vicuña coat and sporting a huge dark pearl on one finger. After posing for photographers, she said she was in Mexico visiting friends, adding, "I feel Mexico is in my blood," as she checked into the Colonia San Angel Inn at Villa Obregon.[31]

Gloria then stunned the public with her announcement that she would wed former society columnist Brandy Brent, who was now her personal manager. Born Brandon Brent in San Francisco on October 6, 1910, he had attended Kansas City University before graduating from UCLA and working for the *San Francisco News* until 1942, when he joined the wartime air force. After his discharge he worked as a writer and an assistant for film director Preston Sturges. In 1948 his first "Carousel" column appeared in the *Los Angeles Times*. To those in the know, and that meant nearly everyone in show business, Gloria's wedding announcement was a front. Brent was a closeted homosexual.

From August 1948 until April 1950, the good-looking, flamboyant Brent dazzled himself and a few others hobnobbing with the Hollywood social set, reporting in his "Carousel" column the latest society news. His bitchy snobbery became something of a laugh compared to the serious reporting by other more reputable columnists. Coming in contact with Brent in 1949 when he covered the surprise wedding of Tony Duquette and Elizabeth Johnstone at Pickfair, Gloria was drawn to his flashy handsomeness immediately.

After he met Gloria, items mentioning him with Swanson appeared in his "Carousel" columns: "Gloria Swanson (on the arm of your reporter!)"; "and, on the arm of your scribe, Gloria Swanson"; "on the arm . . . with your chronicler"; "with Gloria Swanson on his arm . . ." It was repetitive and obvious. He mentioned her every chance he got, until he finally lost his job with the *Times*. Becoming Gloria's unofficial escort and "personal manager," Brent subsequently ingratiated himself into her circle. In a day when a man was judged by the women he kept, Brent had succeeded in bluffing the unsuspecting public with his assumed heterosexual virility. In February 1952 he and Gloria dropped hints to the press of their upcoming nuptials.

Brent said he was married "once before—while in college."[32] Dorothy Kilgallen, in her "Voice of Broadway" column, told her readers the love of Gloria Swanson's life was not Brent but an older, wealthy man.[33] And Winchell spelled it out for his followers: "Gloria Swanson's No. 1 beau is the very social Detroiter Lewis Bredin, estranged from his wife."[34]

On the evening of March 20, Brent and Gloria departed the Mexico City

International Airport on board a Pan American Airways Clipper. The couple was unusually quiet and would answer no questions from the press. When asked to pose by photographers with one of the three men who had come to see them off, Brent was heard to say to Gloria, "You're not going to pose with anyone but me!"[35] So she posed alone. By the end of May, Earl Wilson told his readers Gloria's "romance with her secretary was a cover-up to fool the other side."[36] In the final outcome the affair would have tragic consequences.

On April 25 Gloria signed an agreement with the Farrar, Straus and Company to pen her autobiography, *Beyond the Star*. She was offered $2,500 plus 13 percent royalties and given twelve to twenty-four months to complete the manuscript. She would later change the title to *Glamour After Forty,* and still later to *The Other Side of Glamour.* As with her book contract a decade earlier, she never completed the manuscript.

Gloria was in talks with producer Albert Zugsmith for a role in *Crosstown* for American Pictures, based on George Zuckerman's prizewinning novelette. She was offered $5,000 upon signing, another $5,000 when filming commenced, and then another $10,000. She was also given the option to profit-share at 50 percent. Instead she asked for $80,000, sabotaging herself again, and the deal promptly fell through. She would also turn down lucrative offers from RKO, Columbia, and Universal.

Returning alone to Mexico City in late May, Gloria was particularly annoyed when there were no redcaps waiting for her at the airport to transport her abundance of luggage. She was equally irked when in June *3 for Bedroom C* opened to disastrous reviews. The official pressbook joyously announced: "The Star of 'Sunset Boulevard' is Spreading Sunshine now!" "She's uproarious in color that's glorious!" "It's all about a movie queen who hides out on a streamliner and it's a scream-lined delight!" Too bad such hype proved the opposite.

"Brog" in *Variety* categorically labeled *3 for Bedroom C* an undeniable, certified flop. "This is incredibly poor entertainment," he painfully wrote. "Miss Swanson['s] . . . trouping and Milton H. Bren's script and direction smack of the old silent Sennett days. She has mistakenly been given a free hand and attacks the passé techniques of yesteryear with enthusiasm but does nothing to prove that coy looks and fluttering eyelashes can successfully substitute for acting." Adding insult to injury, "Brog" concluded, "Also, Miss Swanson is unbecomingly gowned in her own fashions."[37]

When the picture opened at New York's Astor Theater on June 26, "H.H.T." of *The New York Times* wrote, "Whatever possessed the indefatigable Miss Swanson to toil anew in such a wretchedly inane flapdoodle is her own secret . . . The dismal absurdities of this comedy romp . . . come perilously close to suggesting that another such vehicle may find Miss Swanson switching professions."[38] And Edwin Schallert moaned in the *Los Angeles Times,* "*3 for Bedroom C* is Class C fare, and not even bedroom farce . . . The players seemed to be speaking into a vacuum—and that is the way my brain became after a while . . . Miss Swanson . . . tried hard to be amusing and once in a while I caught the old sparkle. But—and also—she still gritted her teeth as though under some kind of unseen unbearable tension, and soon I was gritting mine, too."[39]

Holiday magazine called the effort "a waste and a pity."[40] *3 for Bedroom C* slipped to the bottom of the bill in double-feature showings, and quickly disappeared. Gloria had only herself to blame. "I did [it] because nobody offered me anything else," she continued to moan. "My agent said that it would be a chance to do comedy, get away from the *Sunset Boulevard* image . . . I don't know where they got that leading man."[41] She chose to forget she had insisted on the casting of James Warren. She still had her television work.

Young film director Miguel Aleman was making quite a name for himself in Mexico at the time when Gloria began her series' filming. According to Hedda Hopper, things on set began to unravel quickly. "Miguel Aleman Jr., son of the ex-president [of Mexico], is a rare host," Hopper wrote in her December 4 column. "He is doing much for the film industry here. He started some TV films with Gloria Swanson, but after two [actually three] were made their business deal went kaput when she insisted on having the same attention as she did when a queen of the silent movie era in Hollywood."[42] To shed further light on what happened in Mexico after the three episodes had been lensed there, Hopper later added, "Gloria insisted on a leading man half her age and had her trunks sent by freight instead of taking them on the plane. They arrived after she'd finished her chore and was she furious."[43]

Thank goodness Gloria had the Puritan Fashions deal, and Lewis Bredin.

26

Fashion

Gloria presented her fall 1952 collection in New York at Franklin Simon on September 8. The *New York Times* fashion critic was delighted. "The fashions were budget-priced, yet had great chic whether for daytime or after-5," said the review. "Examples were a gray wool and nylon costume suit; a black faille coachman coat dress with black velvet collar, cuffs and large single pocket trim; a charcoal wool jersey afternoon dress with coral bib sparked with gunmetal nailheads and a classic wool gabardine dress with fly front and tortoise button trim. Dinner suits came in faille or barathea and cocktail dresses were shown in iridescent taffeta, lace over taffeta, or crepe."[1] "Gloria Swanson Originals" became quite popular in the 1950s, featuring her choices of colors, fabrics such as paper taffetas, and flourishes like "snag-proof" zippers.

On NBC on Monday, February 16, 1953, Gloria made her television acting debut in the live one-hour televised play "The Pattern" for *Hollywood Opening Night,* a drama by Ilene Prince taken from a W. Somerset Maugham story. It starred Gloria as a Broadway actress opposite Torin Thatcher and Virginia Gibson. Completing that, at the end of February she was in Hollywood, filming her last starring episode for *Crown Theatre* and renting Rudolph Valentino's former home, the majestic Falcon's Lair, during her stay.

While there Gloria was photographed by noted press photographer Nat Dallinger on April 3 with California governor Earl Warren at a Beverly Hills supper following the annual Academy Awards ceremony. She spoke with *Los Angeles Times* writer Walter Ames. "Every time I address a woman's meeting I give the girls a verbal spanking for chasing their past youth," she said. "They spend so much time trying to recapture it and worrying about it that it becomes strictly no-contest with age. Why, in Europe, a woman's not even considered interesting until she's 40."[2] She later told the paper, "Every time I make a film they cast me as an actress. I'm like the perennial Hollywood butler. But it pays off in greenbacks and that's important."[3]

Crown Theatre premiered over ABC on May 5 with an episode entitled "Up Ferguson Way." According to "Kap" in *Daily Variety,* the first show had its faults. The second episode, airing May 11, was "My Last Duchess," the first of four to star Gloria, and "Kap" was quite happy with it. "After a bad start, the *Crown Theatre* series moves into high gear with its second entry . . . Miss Swanson is fine in the key role, turning in an effectively shaded performance. She's still a little kittenish, though, in her role as emcee."[4] In the episode, about an aging actress desperately seeking an acting role (Gloria was allowed to play dress-up in a DeMille-ian Marie Antoinette sequence), she co-starred with Douglas Dumbrille and Denver Pyle.

Gloria's second acting episode, "If Speech Be Silvern," television writer Budd Lesser's story of a man who loses interest in life when his speech is taken from him, was filmed in Mexico and aired June 30. "Daku" in *Daily Variety* wrote, "Kevin Corbin contributes a good deal of sensitivity . . . Same can't be said for Miss Swanson, who over-emotes to the extent that she at all times appears to be Gloria Swanson, and not the character which she portrays. Director Edward G. Simmel holds to an evenly paced tempo, but evidently wasn't able to apply some restraint to Miss Swanson's histrionics."[5]

Gloria's third starring episode, airing August 18, was "Choice of Weapons," a romance about an adventuress falling in love with a stranger. It, too, was filmed in Mexico. Said "Helm" in *Daily Variety,* "Miss Swanson performs in a manner reminiscent of the star of silents and in a highly emotional scene she throws herself into a pother of excited frustration."[6] The fourth and last episode with Gloria was called "Short Story." A story within a story, again by Lesser, it told of a female novelist falling in love with an aging busboy and aired September 22. "Daku" noted, "Gloria Swanson in the lead is about as convincing as her screen name—Delphine Drake."[7]

Gloria's prologues for her show were also criticized. "Helm" said of one, "Gloria Swanson uses up running time to small avail," and "Gloria Swanson, whose gowns are billboarded as 'By Gloria Swanson' was giddy and smiling in front and back, contributing all the more to the dramatic letdown." "Kap" commented on another, "Sole carp still is that emcee Gloria Swanson is a trifle too kittenish" and "Those Gloria Swanson introductions are getting coyer by the week, and noticeably, no writer takes the blame for it."[8] Hedda Hopper, always one to get in the last kick, wrote of the first episode, "[Gloria] looked lovely, but to say she acted coy as a kitten would be the understatement of the week."[9] The show would be broadcast weekly until October 1953.

Gloria told writer Emily Belser, "I was very interested in playing the Joan Crawford role in *Sudden Fear*, but my studio read the script and decided it wasn't any good."[10] She embellished always—she was not under contract with *any* film studio. After Crawford earned a 1952 Oscar nomination for the film at RKO (she also co-produced), Gloria claimed in another interview, "I took *Sudden Fear* to Paramount. No one was interested. Now I'm not interested in Hollywood stardom."[11]

Continuing her work in fashion, for her spring 1953 line Gloria adapted styles in "Glamorous Cotton." Her creations included sleeveless sundresses, topped with bolero jackets, with geometric and floral prints on white backgrounds.

Lewis was having difficulty obtaining his divorce. Gloria decided to call her friend attorney Carlos Parraga in Havana, Cuba, on October 10 regarding Lewis possibly securing a divorce in Cuba. His written reply dated October 13 spelled it out: a) the grounds had to be the same as in American litigation; b) both parties had to appear in court, or have their respective attorneys appear; c) there could be no elements of collusion to invalidate the divorce, such as both parties being represented by the same attorney. The laws governing divorce in Cuba were the same as in the United States and, at that time, recognized as reciprocally valid. At this point, Lewis and Gloria were at an impasse. Natalie Bredin would not give Lewis a divorce.

In New York, on November 26, *Los Angeles Times* society writer James Copp mentioned in his popular "Skylarking" column that Gloria had recently held a cocktail party for Brandy Brent.[12] She received her invited guests dressed in bouffant leopard, and appeared disappointed when partygoers holding theater tickets couldn't stay for dessert. Back in Gloria's good graces, Brent did not realize time was running out for him.

Returning to his home on North Whitley Avenue in Los Angeles sometime in December, the handsome Brent struggled with his demons. On Tuesday afternoon, December 22, his lifeless body was discovered in a car parked on a lonely side road off Doheny Palisades near San Clemente. He had committed suicide sometime the night before or early that morning. The cause of death was carbon monoxide poisoning. The day before, he had been arrested on suspicion of a morals charge, taken to the city jail, and released on $500 bail. It had not been his first offense, as he had been charged in 1950 with the same public misconduct, fined $250, and given six months' probation. With public disclosure about to disgrace him, the forty-three-year-old Brent took his life. Gloria never mentioned him in her memoirs.

She was in Paris that following June; ostensibly there to view the latest fashions for ideas for her dress line, she also met her fourth grandchild, Michelle's son Guy Peter Amon, born on January 13. While there Gloria was photographed around the city promoting her work. She told the New York papers, "Wait till you see the French-flavored fashions I'm bringing back from the heart of Paris!"[13] By September Gloria was back in the swing of New York activities. When Lewis was in town the couple would dine frequently at their favorite eatery, the Mama Laura Restaurant at 230 East Fifty-eighth Street.

The "Gloria Swanson in Paris" collection was very successful. "Gloria Swanson went to Paris for inspiration, for flavor . . . but translated it for her newest collection right here in America for our way of life!" said the *Los Angeles Times*.[14] One design was a bell-skirted dress in acetate peau de soie with velvety bows and a rayon velvet collar trimmed with rhinestones. Another was a stunning rayon velvet, rhinestone-studded sheath. All her designs in this collection were in French blue.

In late 1954 Gloria began collaborating with singer-songwriter Dickson Hughes and actor Richard Stapley on a musical stage production. Hughes was born William Hucks Jr. in Akron, Ohio, on December 14, 1922. Stapley was born in Westcliff, Essex, England, on June 20, 1923. After the war Stapley came to Hollywood, married, and landed a contract with MGM, appearing in *The Three Musketeers* (1948) opposite June Allyson and *Little Women* (1949) with Elizabeth

Taylor. (He is best known for being menaced by Charles Laughton and Boris Karloff in Universal's 1951 *The Strange Door*.) Stapley had just completed a sizable role in 20th Century–Fox's *King of the Khyber Rifles* with Tyrone Power.

Soon after Stapley met Hughes in the early 1950s he divorced his wife and the two men became lovers, modestly residing in Malibu. In 1954 they collaborated on a revue, *About Time,* structured after *Time* magazine, that took humorous jabs at the day's headlines. That December they approached Gloria to star in their revue after Loretta Young and Luise Rainer turned them down. Gloria, staying at her friend Robert Balzar's Japanese-influenced Mulholland Drive home, invited the two over to play their music, and as Stapley recalled in his unpublished memoirs, "She was charming, friendly, and surprisingly down to earth." Gloria wrote in her diary, "At six pm I met these two young composers. Not knowing what to expect. Two hours later it was as though we'd known one another for most of our lives."[15]

Though she was impressed with their work, Gloria also had bitter memories of *Nina* and told them, "I just will not ever do another Broadway show. Well, not unless somebody writes a musical adaptation of *Sunset Boulevard*."[16] She had planted a seed. When the two men woke the next morning they played around with ideas and music for what would become their musical *Boulevard*. Their first song was "Those Wonderful People Out There in the Dark." Gloria liked it, and the three began to collaborate. She had Hughes and Stapley perform their work for D. A. Doran, a lawyer and executive at Paramount. Doran reluctantly said he would look into securing permissions. According to Hughes, "Paramount stipulated as one of the requirements that the studio would have the right to assess the material as it was created."[17]

Gloria wanted to have singer Gordon MacRae star opposite her and hoped that José Ferrer, who liked the music and the project and made numerous suggestions, would direct. After Hughes and Stapley performed the songs for young Paramount production assistant Alan J. Pakula, they were told, "Go ahead. Finish the project."[18] The studio, however, held all the cards. "Paramount seemed mildly interested in Swanson's project," wrote *Sunset Boulevard* historian Sam Staggs, "provided she [Gloria] take all the risks and make all the concessions."[19] Gloria, along with a "health nut" lady companion, and Stapley and Hughes, now on her payroll at $150 each a week, retired to the Casitas Del

Monte in Palm Springs, which Balzar (or possibly Lewis Bredin) rented for them. Little was accomplished in their "sessions," as Swanson called them, except that Gloria became infatuated with Stapley. He would write:

> All those years back—I had nearly succumbed to her ageless charm. On the citrus-perfumed terrace, seduced by the light of a full moon that exercised its magic over all persons and objects in its path. She was wearing a long white dinner dress and I swear to God she looked no more than in her twenties. Perhaps the reason I didn't grab hold of her was the fact I caught sight of that swimming pool . . . More and more I was aware my being was subjective to the characterization of Joe Gillis.[20]

After two months, in the first week of March, Gloria boarded the *Super Chief* back to New York and invited the boys to stay with her at her Fifth Avenue apartment. Gloria had Hughes play the *Boulevard* music for George Griskin of the William Morris Agency and television producer Joe Brandel and their wives. Brandel suggested *Boulevard* might work as an NBC television spectacular, and he offered to present it to William Morris to force Paramount's hand in releasing the rights.

Excited about the prospects of starring in a musical, Gloria contacted her old nemesis Erich von Stroheim in April at his home in France to discuss his possibly returning to America to reprise his role. Sailing to Europe, she and Lewis drove up the Champs-Elysées in *l'heure bleue* (the blue hour of twilight) to the Hotel George V, where von Stroheim and his mistress Denise Vernac were staying. Von Stroheim was frail and ill in 1956, with pains in his back. He was in the early stages of cancer, and was in no condition to work on the stage.

Gloria signed a new contract with the Puritan Dress Company on March 1; her compensation remained $25,000 a year plus $5,000 for expenses, effective until February 29, 1960. On May 7 she sailed again from New York, this time going to Naples in first class on the Italian Line's new flagship *Cristoforo Columbo* with Stapley and Hughes also in tow. At the farewell reception on board, champagne flowed and Gus Schirmer and the elderly Elinor Glyn bid them bon voyage. Lewis sent Gloria a cable when the ship reached Gibraltar on May 12 and then followed her to Italy later that month.

When the liner arrived in Naples, Captain Filipo Rando personally escorted Gloria down the gangplank, with Hughes and Stapley following respectfully behind them. Stapley wrote:

> The newspaper and magazine flash bulbs exclusively trained upon the classic beauty of Swanson's face, suddenly turned on me. "What the hell is going on?" she demanded of the Italian woman in charge of publicity.
>
> "I expect it's due to Mr. Stapley. The film he made with Tyrone Power opened last night all over the country."
>
> Gloria flashed a sort of tempestuous smile my way, hissed a seething "Why didn't you tell me," then turned her "it's the pictures that got small" contempt back to the press.[21]

Gloria had interested London theatrical producer Gerald Palmer in the musical project. It would cost $100,000, said Palmer, but he wanted the title changed to *Starring Norma Desmond*. "We've been offered the London Hippodrome by Mr. Bernard Delfont," she cooed to the boys.[22] But then Hughes overheard Gloria telling producer Palmer over the telephone her demands, effectively squelching the deal with "Well, if you think I'm being unreasonable then feel that way . . . Yes, then I guess we will just have to consider it cancelled, I'm sorry. Goodbye."[23] Gloria then casually advised Hughes and Stapley she was off on a brief holiday to France.

Once back in Italy, Gloria was photographed for her new "Gloria Swanson in Italy" collection. In Rome, Signore Rodi of the Banca d'America e d'Italia was ordered to set up a joint bank account for her with Bredin on August 10. Gloria then took a suite at the Residence Palace at 28 Via San Teodoro in Rome for the duration of filming a new picture.

On August 3 she signed with Titanus Films for the Italian comedy *Nero*, later *Mio Figlio Nerone* (also called *Nero's Big Weekend* or *Nero's Mistress*), co-starring Alberto Sordi, Vittorio De Sica, and Brigitte Bardot, and set to commence shooting the beginning of December for seven weeks. Gloria was to be paid 15 million liras, 2 million on date of signing, 1 million each in September and October, 500,000 on November 1, 1.4 million at the conclusion of filming, and the remaining 9.1 million in seven installments throughout, totaling

$10,969.54 by today's U.S. rate, or only about $2,000 per installment in 1955. Michelle's husband Robert Amon arranged the deal for his mother-in-law through her representative Raoul Levi.

The filming of *Mio Figlio Nerone* proved to be a disaster. In later years Gloria told the press she had only made it to co-star with the great Italian comedian Alberto Sordi, and he had done it to co-star with her. That made good copy, and Gloria felt it exonerated her from the film's eventual dreadful reviews. The picture's director was Stefano Vanzina, who went by the artistic nom de plume Steno. The lovely twenty-one-year-old French sexpot Brigitte Bardot, who had already appeared in over a dozen films, would be catapulted to fame later in the year in director Roger Vadim's . . . *And God Created Woman* (Cocinor, 1956).

The plot of *Mio Figlio Nerone* was simple. Nero (Sordi) prefers the company of his mistress Poppea (Bardot) and his adviser Seneca (De Sica), orgies, and music at his estate in Baia to military and political life. His domineering mother Agrippina (Gloria) tries to force him to behave like an emperor. He finally gives in to her, dresses like a soldier, and plays the lyre as Rome burns. It doesn't sound like much of a story, but somehow it was stretched out to a hundred minutes in gorgeous Eastman Color and CinemaScope.

Gloria understood absolutely no Italian, and De Sica was apparently the only one on the set who spoke English. Then there was the issue of Gloria's payments, which never seemed to be either on time or complete. The weather in Rome turned cold, and the massive sets at Cinecittà were like meat lockers. "Then they had snow for the first time in twenty years in Rome," Gloria said. "Five blizzards. There was no oil in the house and I had to go to the [Salvador Mundi] hospital to get warm and keep going on in the picture. I was never so embarrassed, never so miserable in my whole life."[24] Gloria was only exaggerating the truth, as she had started experiencing physical problems, such as her leg giving out and her collapsing on the set, which she attributed to psychosomatic incidents.

Hedda Hopper announced surprisingly in early September that Gloria was now a columnist for United Press International, contracted to file a series of newspaper reports in Europe, the first devoted to men. Gloria produced innumerable articles beginning in Paris, and later she worked for the Rome bureau, reporting on fashion and international events as she found them, including the upcoming nuptials of actress Grace Kelly and Prince Rainier of Monaco. UPI sent journalist Priscilla L. Buckley, sister of William F. Buckley, to Europe with 10,000 francs to have lunch with Gloria and offer her sound criticism on how to improve her column. According to Buckley, over lunch Gloria was more concerned about her omelet than about accepting any sage advice. Needless to say, her column was dreadful.

That fall Gloria and Michelle attended the 15th Annual Venice Film Festival with her friend celebrity party host Earl Blackwell. She continued to rent her Fifth Avenue apartment out for $800 a month, usually to Lewis. That fall Gloria was listed among the nineteen silent film pioneers, including Lillian Gish, Cecil B. DeMille, Mary Pickford, Henry King, Charles Chaplin, and Norma Talmadge, who were presented with the Georges Award by Jesse L. Lasky at the 1st Annual George Eastman House Festival of the Arts held November 19 in Rochester, New York. She was unable to attend as she was in Europe.

As the 1955 holidays came around, Gloria took pleasure knowing her mother Addie was living comfortably in Glendale, California, and that her own bank account at the moment was in the black. However, in Rome, she was lonely. At Christmastime Gloria received good wishes and gifts from friends in the States, including a 1956 desk calendar from Charles and Lillian Brackett.

On January 7 she wrote Michelle about her illnesses, "Your old Ma is cracking up at last. Lately, I have been unable to walk up or down stairs except like a crab, sidewise. I went to the hospital for some injections, God knows what, something like cortisone, so that I could get to the studio to work at seven at night . . . I just wish you could put yourself on a plane and fly over here shortly, or let's say the moment the finish of the picture is in view because it is a shame to have this beautiful apartment and no one to have fully enjoyed it . . . Oh, what a pleasure it would give me to see you."[25]

Completing *Mio Figlio Nerone* on January 20, 1956, Gloria made plans to travel to Florence and accepted an offer from Count Giorgini to attend a huge fashion ball on January 24. On January 22 she wrote Bredin, telling him she was suffering from bronchitis, that she had had two medical sound treatments (sound wave therapy) on her knees, and that she hoped she wouldn't have to have an operation. She then added, "Hope that if and when you fly off to Detroit [where he would periodically conduct business] you will just change planes on your way back and come in this direction."[26]

Feeling better, on March 1 Gloria landed in Monte Carlo, checked into the Hotel de Paris, and attended the April 19 royal wedding of Grace Kelly and Rainier III, which was covered by the world press. Gloria had a ringside seat for the pageantry accompanying the near-weeklong event. After the celebrations, Gloria traveled to Madrid in May and stayed at the Castellana Hotel.

Because she had found it so difficult to rent an apartment in New York while her own was leased, Gloria advised her secretary Gladys Griffith to ask Lewis for money for her expenses. Dated June 1, Griffith's letter to Lewis explained Gloria's plight, breaking down her financial requirements, which included state and government taxes, eyeglasses, and rent; her expenses for May totaled $1,000. "Miss Swanson's account is suffering from chronic financial anemia," wrote Griffith, "and a transfusion at this time would be so welcome . . . I have written Miss Swanson that her expenses here are $1000 monthly, and yet even that figure is not enough . . . This is a miserable bleating letter, but I must ask you for money, and nothing will make it sound any better."[27] On June 5 Lewis sent $2,000 to Griffith to deposit into Gloria's account. Gloria then settled briefly into an apartment located at 40 Avenue Foch in Paris. For several years thereafter she would maintain residency in Europe.

Gloria returned briefly to New York on board the *Cristoforo Columbo*, which departed Cannes on July 14, passing in mid-Atlantic her doomed sister ship the *Andrea Doria*, on her last eastbound voyage. (On her return to New York on July 26 the *Andrea Doria* collided with the Swedish American liner *Stockholm* off the coast of Nantucket and sank; fifty-two lives were lost.) In New York, Gloria rented an apartment for $1,000 a month after Puritan Fashions deposited a check for $6,250 into her bank account. She then returned to Paris.

Lewis arrived in Le Havre on board the *Liberté* in late July, bringing along Gloria's Rolls-Royce. From there they motored up to Eze, where the von Stroheims resided (her old co-star and director would die in 1957), on their way to Paris. Before he returned to the United States, Gloria showed Lewis the city, and they frequently spent nights out on the town, often in the company of Kay Thompson, who was in Paris filming *Funny Face* (Paramount, 1957) with Fred Astaire and Audrey Hepburn. In late September, after another brief visit to New York, Gloria returned to Europe aboard the *Independence*.

That fall Gloria was approached to appear in a television remake of *Sunset Boulevard* for the NBC anthology *Robert Montgomery Presents*. Instead, Mary

Astor stepped in to portray Norma for the one-hour broadcast on December 3. (*The Lux Video Theater* on the same network had also produced its one-hour "Sunset Boulevard" on January 6, 1955, starring Miriam Hopkins.)

Returning to Europe, Lewis joined Gloria for a brief spell in France. Hedda Hopper, sounding more like her rival Louella Parsons, reported in her column that Gloria was seen about Paris on the arm of "Colonel Sanders from Detroit" and that "everybody expects them to marry."[28]

When the hundred-minute *Mio Figlio Nerone* opened in Italy on September 13, reviews were bleak. "Hawk" in *Variety* wrote, "Lavishly mounted ancient Rome costumer . . . does not quite come off as consistently amusing . . . Sordi is also permitted to overact a basically hammy part . . . On the plus side are good performances by Gloria Swanson, as Nero's mother; Vittorio De Sica, as Seneca, and Brigitte Bardot, as a beauteous Poppea, in and out of the inevitable milkbath."[29]

Italian film scholar Giovanni Secchi, in a 2011 synopsis of the picture, wrote, "Basically it's a comedic look at young Nero and the three people in his life, his mother Agrippina, his lover Poppea, and his teacher Seneca. It often blinks its eye to Peter Ustinov's *Quo Vadis* [MGM, 1952] Nero and, for its time, was an expensive production for Italy; it was shot in color and CinemaScope (both of which were still expensive and relatively rare here, back then), directed by a famous comedy director, with an all-star international cast, for an important movie studio, Titanus . . .

"Today the movie is easily seen and easily forgotten . . . Swanson could easily have stolen the picture, and in some scenes she does just that, but of course Alberto Sordi and Vittorio De Sica are histrionics as much as her and so the competition is . . . tough . . . Gloria Swanson played it accordingly to the Italian screenplay."[30]

Mio Figlio Nerone was released in the United States in November 1962 under the title *Nero's Mistress*. "*Nero's Mistress,* a flapdoodle of a picture in splashy color, is not the kind of film to make an old movie buff wistful even though it is presided over by Gloria Swanson," commented Margaret Harford in her *Los Angeles Times* review. "The Italian import . . . is a source of embarrassment . . . Miss Swanson is more to be pitied than censured. Her make-up is ghastly and a coy, girlish dubbed voice makes her seem even more ridiculous. Ah, for the grandeur that was Rome—and Gloria Swanson!"[31]

In late fall 1956, Gloria's son Joseph and his wife Susan, living in their "dream home" in Menlo Park, California,[32] became parents for the first time. They named the child Christina and called her "Tina." Joseph was then working for the research company Radiation, Inc. On November 28, in Paris, Michelle gave birth to a baby daughter, Virginie Glory. That same month Gloria returned to New York. She received a telegram dated November 19 from Joe Kennedy from Hyannis Port addressed to her at the Hotel Crillon in Paris reprimanding her for not marrying Lewis yet.[33]

In early 1957 Gloria flew to California, where on January 23 she was the subject of a *This Is Your Life* episode, broadcast over NBC. Dressed in a black dress, hat, and a white coat, and wearing her famous crystal bracelets, she looked lovely. On hand were Robert Balzar, Rod La Rocque, Mack Sennett, Lois Wilson, Allan Dwan, Jesse L. Lasky, Wally Albright, and Walter O'Keefe. None of her children were present. Neither was her mother. Hedda Hopper called Mickey Neilan to ask why he had not appeared on the show, and he told her he had not been invited; nor was Billy Wilder or Charles Brackett. DeMille had been asked but conveniently found another engagement to attend.

That year Gloria's pent-up feelings against Joe Kennedy boiled over when he attempted to tamper with taxes based on the profits of the European limited release of *Queen Kelly*. Gloria had pursued the project at her own expense, as she assumed she held the rights to the film. Kennedy, however, refused to cooperate, insisting on a share of the minimal profits overseas. In a seething letter, Gloria gave old Joe the coup de grace:

My answer is long overdue, in fact, it is years late. It's about time (the last lap of our lives) that the truth concerning the most important matters in my life had God's spotlight turned on them, for it is possible that they have contributed to the fact that I have had to work instead of relaxing as you have so many times advised me to do, forgetting, of course, that one does not live on bread alone.

You know as well as you know your right name that every penny spent on *Kelly* was returned to you *out of the profits* of *The Trespasser*. All that I ever received from *Queen Kelly* or *The Trespasser* was what was given me as a salary during the making of these films. However, you did tell many persons that *you* stood the loss of *Queen Kelly.* This was, still is, and will be into eternity *a falsehood* (as a lady would say).

Moreover, you alone benefitted taxwise for I certainly did not . . . The second glaring matter (a bigger gall stone) I find hard to forget and surely you can't have forgotten either,—is the circumstances of my losing my valuable UNITED ARTISTS! *It was not I* who called for your help nor would I have lost my stock if I had *not believed you* . . . It was you who insisted upon helping me finish the picture so that I *would not* lose my stock. And then what happened, why you proceeded to evaporate into thin air— when every moment was so costly to me—leaving me with no alternative. Are you going to tell me you don't know who got my stock? . . . Unless you have greatly changed, your reaction to this letter will be one of anger, indignation—and self-righteousness which knows no bounds, but I beg of you to be kind enough to be equally frank with yourself so that such frankness on the part of both of us will erase all misunderstandings—

Life now is too short for any further—mistakes.

> P.S. Please believe me these pages carry no malice for I am blessed with forgiveness—and I pray you are blessed with the truth.[34]

It was an awful lot to ask of Joseph P. Kennedy. The truth was not his forte. Gloria was Mike Wallace's first guest on his new thirty-minute *The Mike Wallace Interview,* broadcast over ABC on Sunday, April 28, 1957. She was most candid in the interview, which touched upon some rather sensitive topics. Jack Gould in *The New York Times* wrote, "During the cross examination and close-ups she was responsive, cooperative and articulate."[35] Hedda Hopper commented to her readers, "I've never seen Gloria Swanson looking better. She tells me she loved the hour spent with Mike Wallace on TV 'because he was so kind.' And here I thought he'd grilled her like a district attorney!"[36]

On May 22 Gloria sailed to Europe aboard the *Queen Mary,* again to gather inspiration for Puritan Fashions. She also at the time coveted the Rosalind Russell role in London's West End production of *Auntie Mame* (Beatrice Lillie would take it). In France that July, she stayed at the Hotel Crillon before departing the next month for Cannes. Taking with her a new young lover, Gloria visited Joe Kennedy in Eze-sur-Mer, a small village between Nice and Monte

Carlo. Staying with him was his mistress and secretary of nine years Janet Des Rosiers Fontaine, who remembered Gloria incessantly complaining that the new crop of Hollywood stars had all gone to hell. "All she talked about was how inferior the actors and actresses of today were, and how none of them could act the way she did in her heyday."[37]

On September 16 Gloria's fall fashion line was shown on the third floor at Saks. Gloria arrived in New York on November 3 aboard the liner *Liberté*, "with trunkloads of the latest from Continental couturiers."[38]

In East Rochester, New York, along with actress Esther Ralston on September 26, Gloria helped curator James Card launch his new repertory theater Box 5, dedicated exclusively to silent film. A month later she was back to accept a special medal for her contribution to films from 1926 to 1930 at the George Eastman House at the 2nd Annual Festival of Film Arts. Among the other recipients, with presentations made by director Rouben Mamoulian, were Maurice Chevalier, James Wong Howe, Ramon Novarro, Mary Pickford, Janet Gaynor, Lillian Gish, Josef von Sternberg, Richard Barthelmess, and Frank Borzage.

In Manhattan, with Dickson Hughes by her side, Gloria rehearsed what would prove to be the culmination of years of dedicated work on the musical *Boulevard*. She performed an excerpt from the work on *The Steve Allen Plymouth Show* over NBC television. Both Hughes and Stapley in the intervening years had contracted with 20th Century–Fox, Hughes as a songwriter, Stapley as an actor. With a little financial aid from Gloria and her friend Gus Schirmer, Hughes was doing well. But Stapley's career had bottomed out and he was then working for Union Oil in Oklahoma.

On November 10, 1957, Gloria revisited Norma Desmond, with Hughes as the off-camera voice of Max (handing in a bad imitation of Bela Lugosi). Complete with full orchestration and a ballet troupe dancing in the shadows, Gloria sang the poignant number "Those Wonderful People Out There in the Dark." It was a startling moment. Few people had remembered Gloria could sing. Her voice was strong and assured, her performance uniquely her own. "Gros" of *Variety* disliked it, finding it "off and tedious . . . She sang something about 'Those Wonderful People in the Dark' who were probably getting a little dial-happy through it all."[39]

But the music was touching and theatrical, and when viewed today one can only ponder what Gloria Swanson might have done with *Boulevard*.

27

Television

In March 1958, while traveling the southern states in her Rolls with Dickson Hughes, Gloria vacationed in Key West, where she had made her singing "debut" in 1910 at the Odd Fellows Hall. Gloria and Hughes then sailed the Caribbean aboard the Puritan Dress Company's yacht *Minerva*, spending the Easter holiday with her friends the F. W. Magins and attending the Trinity-by-the-Cove Episcopal Church in Naples, Florida. Back in New York in May, musician Skitch Henderson belatedly came into the *Boulevard* project to do arrangements. Hughes played the score for the Theatre Guild's founder Lawrence Langner, and though Langner found the music entertaining, the Guild did not produce it.

Gloria then considered sponsoring Vitali Tea, "for Vim, Vigor, Vitality," for a lucrative stipend and told Lewis about it. Gladys Griffith, Gloria's secretary, wrote him on July 9, saying, "She has taken over all your old hobbies—painting, golfing, puzzles. Next will be 'whodunits.'"[1] On May 5 Gloria unveiled her "Gloria Swanson Goes to Paris" line of fashions in New York at Saks, exhibiting American versatility combined with French chic. That same day she chartered the *Kasidah* from yacht broker Jack Cheyne for $43,112 to sail the Caribbean that summer, possibly with Lewis. She became a grandmother again in July when Joseph and Susan welcomed a second daughter, Patricia.

On October 27, 1958, Gloria's onetime lover Marshall "Mickey" Neilan, largely forgotten and alone, succumbed to throat cancer at the Motion Picture

County Home and Hospital in Los Angeles. After divorcing Blanche Sweet in 1929, he never remarried. Many believed Gloria was the only love of his life.[2] Earlier that year, in February, seventy-seven-year-old Jesse L. Lasky had suffered a fatal heart attack at the Beverly Hills Hotel. It was becoming apparent the important men in Gloria's life were leaving her. Cecil B. DeMille would pass away on January 21, 1959. Strangely, Gloria made no comment to the press about his death, and she did not attend his funeral. That same month when Michael Farmer contacted Gloria from his home in Mold, Flintshire, North Wales, needing money, she sent him $200.

In February Paramount advised Gloria to cease her involvement with *Boulevard*. They were cutting her off.[3] She did not look back. Continuing with her fashion designing, on March 29 she was again at Saks on Thirty-fourth Street, introducing her "Forever Young" two-piece long coat or short jacket over a sheath dress with a gently indented waistline. As the newest craze, flower hats were introduced.

Gloria was by now an advocate of health foods, speaking out against the dangers of food additives. The Delaney Clause, named after Representative James Delaney of New York, was an amendment to the Food, Drugs, and Cosmetic Act of 1938, added in 1959, that allowed the government to regulate the use of pesticides and chemicals in everyday foods. Ten years later, on October 21, 1969, Delaney himself informed the press of Gloria's pioneering campaign for it, and her impact on the passing of several health amendments.

That spring of 1959 Gloria was asked by her old friend Harold J. Kennedy, now the managing director of the Grist Mill Playhouse in Andover, New Jersey, to appear on the straw hat circuit in the play *Red Letter Day* by Andrew Rosenthal, a three-act comedy-drama that had had a successful run at the Garrick in London in 1953. "He came to me," Gloria recalled, "and said, 'Wouldn't you like to find out if you like the theater—and if the theater liked you?'"[4] She said yes. The cast included Charles "Buddy" Rogers and Gloria's longtime pal Lois Wilson. Rehearsals began on June 16, and the play opened on June 27, 1959, at the Grist Mill, with hopes to tour it for eleven weeks. Gloria received $1,000 a week, plus a $1,000 expense account and 30 percent of the house gross.

Red Letter Day tells of the pending fiftieth birthday of Lora Sutherland (Gloria), bored with her husband Ned (Rogers) faced with becoming a grandmother, and having just learned her lover Manuel (Harry Kelkas) has lost interest in her.

Throughout the run of the play, Gloria prepared her own meals, had organic veg-etables delivered to her daily, and in one interview after another complained about pesticides, overeating, improper diet, juvenile delinquency, and taxes. Ken-nedy and Gloria wanted to bring *Red Letter Day* to Broadway. It opened at the Westport Country Playhouse to standing room only. Gloria's appearance at the Playhouse was cause for celebration. Critics thought otherwise about the play.

"It was . . . terrible," wrote the Playhouse's historian Richard Somerset-Ward. "With uncharacteristic acerbity, one critic reported: 'Miss Swanson, of course, is the main reason for the show and she gives quite a performance. It is doubtful any gesture she acquired in the history of motion pictures is not sandwiched into one fortunately short evening. She certainly does convince the audience she is amazingly well preserved for her 60 years and that her hair will not come out regardless of how hard she pulls and tugs. Outside of that, Miss Swanson conveys little . . . There were very few productions as bad as this one—most of them (be it said) were pretty good."[5] *Red Letter Day*, however, continued on tour. Gloria clashed on several occasions with the temperamen-tal Kennedy, especially toward the end of the run. Once *Red Letter Day* closed, Gloria signed for a couple of lucrative television appearances. In California as the new year of 1960 began, she was a guest on *Hedda Hopper's Hollywood*, a one-hour television special aired on January 10 over NBC.

In early 1960, young photographer Jack Mitchell, on assignment for *Dance Magazine*, met Gloria Swanson at the Roseland Ballroom, where her cousin and his partner, the dance team of Burns and Swanson, were to be given an award. After the shoot, Mitchell asked Gloria if she would allow him to photo-graph her. "Instead of 'why,' she said 'when,'" recalled Mitchell. "She never saw a camera she didn't like."[6] Throughout the decade he would take thousands of pictures of Swanson, many of which have become iconic.

Over the years, Mitchell would oftentimes have breakfast with tea and honey at her apartment, where he remembered the door from her bedroom to the garden was kept propped open by a heavy copy of the Kama Sutra. Gloria, with Mitchell in tow, would scour Manhattan in her Rolls-Royce in search of fertilized eggs and chemical-free meat. When he journeyed to Key West one time, he sent Gloria some Spanish limes, and she wired him two days later to exclaim that he had put her into her third childhood, bringing back long-forgotten memories.

Gloria's affair with Lewis had waned due to his inability to divorce his wife, coupled with his own failing health, and Gloria was seen often with film scholar and archivist Raymond Daum, whom she had met in 1956. He would become her confidant and the curator of her archive later in life. In California the attractive couple was photographed at a Trader Vic's party which Dickson Hughes threw on April 11. At the time Gloria was in negotiation with an agent for a television mystery-spy comedy series which never panned out.

Requiring a rest, Gloria and Bob Balzar boarded the liner *Matsonia* in California on August 20 and sailed to Hawaii.[7] In October she was back in New York, appearing on *The Today Show* with Dave Garroway to promote her fashion line. Gloria, perhaps influenced by her friend Kay Thompson's passion for Chanel-influenced cuts, did away with full skirts that fall, introducing slenderizing two-piece velvet suits and sheaths.

The fabulous Roxy Theater, where Gloria had triumphed in *The Love of Sunya* in 1927, closed its doors in March 1960, marking the end of an era for the great movie palaces. It was then demolished. Photographed by Eliot Elisofon on October 14, Gloria, wearing a strapless black Jean Louis gown with a flowing red boa, and decked out in $17,000 worth of diamonds, her hair wafting in the breeze, posed arms stretched out to heaven among its ruins. That color image appeared at the end of the month in *Life* magazine, and legend has it that it was this vision that was the impetus and inspiration for Stephen Sondheim's 1971 musical *Follies*.[8]

Before taking a TWA flight to Los Angeles on December 28 with her dachshund Max to spend the holidays with her mother, Gloria was asked to attend the inauguration of President-elect John F. Kennedy on January 20 in Washington, D.C. She declined. Her feelings for the Kennedys had definitely cooled. She wrote years later about her relationship with Joe, "I often wondered how all this [his behaviors with her] affected the children, especially Jack. And if in the White House he was doing the same thing to Jackie that his father did to Rose."[9]

Once when Joe Kennedy was showing his daughter-in-law Jacqueline a particular room at the Hyannis Port compound, he crudely boasted, "I used to bring Gloria Swanson to this doll room. She liked to make love here. Let me tell you, that woman was insatiable."[10] He did not spare Jackie any of the intimate details, graphically describing Gloria's genitals and gleefully boasting how many times she could climax in one night.[11]

Gloria was asked to star in *Pal Joey* for an ANTA New York City Center revival, but instead, she agreed with producer Daniel Blum to do another season of stock in a new play. After tryouts in Clinton, New Jersey, in July, the play *Between Seasons* by Malcolm Wells toured throughout August. Blum sent Gloria her contract dated June 17, which guaranteed her $1,000 a week plus a percentage of the house gross.

Between Seasons told of a middle-aged yet still glamorous married woman (Gloria) led to drink, who takes up with a handsome budding young actor (Ray Fulmer) to the chagrin of her noble husband (Charles Baxter). She gives up drinking, the young actor becomes her protégé and lover, and when the husband finds out he offers to give her up. But she sees her errors and returns to the bottle, and the actor leaves town. Strangely, Wells called *Between Seasons* a comedy. The critics called it a mess. When it opened at the Berkshire Playhouse in Stockbridge, Massachusetts, Kingsley R. Fall wrote, "Miss Swanson still can act and she still has glamor, but even she with all her talent and magnetism couldn't breathe anything fresh into this piece of hack writing . . . Anybody with sensitivity can sit through a bad play if it is honestly and deeply (sometimes even cleverly) meant, because something of integrity comes through. This is not one of those."[12]

After the tour of the play, Gloria took her mother to France to visit Michelle and her family, now residing in Neuilly-sur-Seine. They then stayed at the Hotel Crillon in Paris. While in Europe, Gloria paid a call on Dr. Paul Niehans's Clinique la Prairie in Vevey, Switzerland. Niehans had for years specialized in administering live cell therapy injections, taken from the placenta of pregnant sheep, into such patients as Cary Grant, Marlene Dietrich, the Duke of Windsor, and Merle Oberon, all of whom found the treatments rejuvenating. Gloria was no exception.

Arriving in London on October 2, Gloria and Addie checked into the Connaught Hotel, and Gloria appeared on a BBC Television interview program. The show's host kept asking about Norma Desmond and *Sunset Boulevard* and whether there were any similarities to her real life. Insulted, Gloria rebuffed him with "No, I don't have a body floating in my swimming pool. I don't even have a swimming pool. I don't live in the past. I am concerned only with the future."[13] Sir Alec Guinness, much to her pleasure, sent a note "congratulating me for standing up against the legend."[14]

In June the women returned to New York. On September 13 Gloria and actor Richard Arlen hosted the annual fall fashion show at the Saks dress shop, featuring Gloria's designs adapted from French and Italian designers. That season she emphasized petal-embroidered and pleated designs in Arnel jersey, full-skirted plaid dresses, and glamorous jacketed two-piece outfits. She also inaugurated Gloria Swanson Nylons (aka Gloria Swanson Hosiery), which was produced briefly, and unsuccessfully, in 1961 and 1962.

Gloria rented a mansion in Hollywood the following month during the filming of an episode of ABC's short-lived drama series *Straightaway*, an also-ran "*Route 66* with a T-bird"[15] that starred Brian Kelly and John Ashley, called "A Toast to Yesterday." She was paid $2,000 for her role as a silent film actress involved in a fatal hit-and-run accident. "Guess what I am playing," she complained to writer Bob Thomas, over vodka on the rocks. "That's right—an actress. Isn't it frightful, the type casting in this town? They got over it for a while, but now it's just as strong as ever. I can't fight it."[16] On the set, Gloria told one reporter, "I prepare myself thoroughly for a role, and I expect everybody else, including the man who makes coffee, to be equally well prepared."[17]

In her dressing room at Desilu Studios (once RKO), when asked if she found *Sunset Boulevard* biographical, Gloria jumped at the chance to neuter a *TV Guide* reporter. "Yes, dear, of course it was biographical. I live in the past. I really never got past 1935. And there's a man floating facedown in the bathtub upstairs. Would you like to see him?" The reporter was stunned, and actor Brian Kelly quickly intervened admiringly: "She is alert, talented, friendly, well-organized, [and] decisive—and still very much a queen."[18] When the word "glamour" was applied to her in another interview, she snapped defiantly, "I detest that word because it was applied to me so often. Say romanticism. It's dying out. I'm afraid it's dying out all over the world."[19]

Gloria was considered by Paramount producer Gant Gaither for the Broadway-bound drama *Hullabaloo*, with Robert Fryer and Lawrence Carr set to produce, Stella Stevens hoping for the role of the daughter, and José Ferrer scheduled to direct. It did not happen. So, reconnecting with Harold Kennedy in March, Gloria began rehearsals for a new play by him called *The Inkwell*, set to open at the Drury Lane Theater in Evergreen, Illinois, again with hopes of steering it to Broadway. Gloria was contracted for $1,500 a week.

Adding a compulsory showy role for himself, in *The Inkwell* Kennedy wrote about "a famous and fading film star, who returns to her home on a lecture tour to find her roots and pulls up everyone else's."[20] On opening night, March 20, critic Roger Dettmer penned, "Miss Swanson, vivacious to be sure, an authentic personality, and in flashes even an actress in a limited fashion, carries on heroically—to the extent of singing a couple of songs . . . If she does not exactly suggest the fountain of youth, she is a remarkable testimony to the rewards of self-care, and attendant preservation."[21] The Inkwell then played at the Cocoanut Grove Playhouse in Miami in February. Despite the effort, after a run at the Tappan Zee Playhouse in July, The Inkwell folded. It was obvious the play needed work.

Gloria was in Los Angeles that late fall, her new agent Allen Connor having lined up a teleplay called "Good Luck Charm" for the NBC drama series Dr. Kildare, which starred Richard Chamberlain and Raymond Massey. In it she portrayed a once famous actress, Julia Colton, who, though confined to a wheelchair, shows compassion for a sick girl. On October 31 filming began on the MGM lot. After her living expenses of $1,500 were paid, and her gross salary whittled away in taxes, Gloria's final net for the week's shooting was $128.11.

Said Gloria of the handsome leading man Chamberlain, "He's the most charming, unaffected young man I've met. He's what all young America should look like."[22] With a cigarette in a long holder, Gloria posed for photographers with him. Chamberlain recalled many years later, "She was terrific, but bizarre to work with. In television, time is of the essence, and our first morning's work she was in her [character's] hospital bed. Suddenly in between takes she said, 'Helen, Helen.' And her maid comes in with her breakfast. This elaborate breakfast on a big silver tray and everything stops because she is having her breakfast in bed. Nobody dared say anything because she was a real tigress and there she was and that happened every day."[23]

About her role on Dr. Kildare, Gloria said discreetly, "This Kildare part is the best aging actress I've found in some time."[24] One reviewer pragmatically noted, when the episode aired on February 7, 1963, "There is one really touching moment . . . In her tearful scene with the doomed girl, Miss Swanson mentions one of her plays. It was 'Peter Pan'—an uplifting deathbed plug for NBC-TV's repeat showing of that production [on the upcoming] Friday with Mary Martin. Kind of gets to you."[25]

Gloria then flew to Rome, checking into the Excelsior Hotel, on yet another trip to gather fashion tips for her next line of dresses. By March she was back in New York to begin a revival of Kennedy's jinxed *The Inkwell,* now renamed *Just for Tonight.* Set for a one-week run beginning March 19 at the Sombrero Playhouse in Phoenix, Arizona, the play was recast, except for Kennedy, who doggedly built up his showy role. Gloria's take had risen to $3,000 a week, plus 50 percent of the house gross. In April she was back in California at the Hotel Bel Air and filming a segment at MGM of *The World's Greatest Showman,* a TV documentary on Cecil B. DeMille that aired December 1 over NBC. Gloria was paid $3,500, which she quickly spent on a green chiffon dress created at Mrs. Barrett Regent Fashions and numerous beauty treatments. Gloria then hosted a television pilot, *Attention for Invention,* a science show for which she would make $3,000 an episode if it sold. It did not. In May Hermione Gingold told the *Los Angeles Times* that she, Gloria Swanson, Bette Davis, and another unnamed actress were set to star in a private-eye comedy film about four elderly ladies who rob a bank. Nothing came of it.

That same month actor George Hamilton, under contract with Metro, advised the press he had written an original treatment titled *The Brothers,* which he was planning to produce for his film company, Ash Productions, based on experiences he had shared with actor Errol Flynn's son Sean. Hamilton wanted David Niven to play the father's friend and Gloria to portray a contessa, a friend of the father's, but the project burned out. Hamilton then announced in May 1964 that Gloria would star as his mother in *Your Daddy Is Dead, Dear,* costarring Tuesday Weld. It, too, died. Undaunted, the persistent Hamilton then announced that *The Image and the Idol,* possibly a reworking of an earlier project, was to start production in January 1965. In the end, Hamilton and Gloria never worked together.

On September 12 Gloria introduced her fall line at Saks in New York. Her fashion output for 1963 was limited, no doubt because of her many acting roles and travels. One wonders why she went to Europe to get ideas as her spring dresses were common, very trendy, and ever more youthful, with no obvious Continental flair. "There is no age in clothes, that's ridiculous," Gloria proudly announced before the showing.[26] Gloria's fall line was chic and stylish, with two- and three-piece dresses giving way to straight lines and interesting fabrics. It was obvious, however, she was losing her focus on the line. And doggedly, Harold Kennedy and Gloria still traipsed *Just for Tonight* up and down the East

With Henri on the beach while filming *The Coast of Folly*. His look says it all.

In the Technicolor opening dream sequence of *Stage Struck*, Paramount, 1926.

In *Untamed*, Paramount, 1926.

With Henri during the filming of *The Love of Sunya*, 1926.

Henri and Gloria with S. L. "Roxy" Rothafel signing the contract to debut *The Love of Sunya* at his new Roxy Theatre, February 18, 1927.

John Boles and Gloria in *The Love of Sunya*, UA, 1927.

With Sid Grauman in the forecourt of Grauman's Chinese Theatre, May 1927.

As Sadie Thompson, 1928.

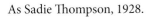

With Lionel Barrymore in *Sadie Thompson*. UA, 1928.

With Raoul Walsh in *Sadie Thompson*.

With Charles Chaplin and Marion Davies at the New York premiere of Chaplin's *The Circus*, January 6, 1928.

Gloria, 1929.

Joseph P. Kennedy, c. mid-1920s.

Erich von Stroheim, c. 1929.

In the unfinished African sequences of *Queen Kelly*, 1928.

Edward Thayer Monroe photo
inscribed to Morris Gershwin, father
of Ira and George Gershwin, c. 1928.

THE ARTHUR WHITELAW COLLECTION.

With Henri on the set of
Queen Kelly, 1929.

PHOTO BY BACHRACH.

As the virginal
Kelly with Walter
Byron in *Queen
Kelly*, UA, 1929.

Joel McCrea, c. 1929.

TOP RIGHT: Visitors on the set of *The Trespasser*, 1929. Gloria (*seated second from left*), director Edmund Goulding (*seated far right*).

MIDDLE RIGHT: The United Artists assembly in Hollywood: (*left to right*) Al Jolson, Mary Pickford, Ronald Colman, Gloria, Douglas Fairbanks, Joseph Schenck, Charles Chaplin, Samuel Goldwyn, and Eddie Cantor, November 8, 1930.

Gloria with the first William Holden in *The Trespasser*, UA, 1929.

In *What a Widow!*, UA, 1930.

On the set of *Indiscreet*, UA, 1931: B. G. (Buddy) DeSylva, Lew Brown, and Ray Henderson (*back row left to right*). Ben Lyon, Barbara Kent, Gloria, director Leo McCarey, Arthur Lake (*front row left to right*).

Melvyn Douglas, director Mervyn LeRoy, Michael Farmer, and Gloria (*left to right*) on the set of *Tonight or Never*, UA, 1931.

Michael displaying his talent in Hollywood with an embarrassed Gloria, Jeanette MacDonald (*center*) and Lila Lee (*right*) in attendance, 1931.

Wearing the fabulous Cartier crystal bracelets, *Perfect Understanding*, UA, 1933.

With John Boles in *Music in the Air*, Fox, 1934.

In Detroit while on her stage tour, May 8, 1934.

With producer Irving Thalberg at MGM, 1934.

Herbert "Bart" Marshall, c. 1936.

Gloria at MGM, 1934. Photo by Clarence Sinclair Bull

Gloria at Columbia, 1937.

Photo by Clarence Sinclair Bull.

With Edmund Goulding at the Santa Anita Handicap Ball, March 1, 1937.

With Herbert Marshall (*left*), and George Jessel in Hollywood, 1938.

With Adolphe Menjou in *Father Takes a Wife*, RKO, 1941.

Henri and his new bride, Emma (*left*), with Gloria and Leroy "Sport" Ward in New York at the premiere of Walt Disney's *Dumbo*, October 23, 1941.

With Allan Dwan (left) and René Hubert on the set of *Father Takes a Wife*.

Portrait for *Reflected Glory*, 1942.

With Harold J. Kennedy in tryouts for *A Goose for the Gander*, 1943.

With daughter, Michelle, and son, Michael, at the Stork Club, New York, 1944. PHOTO: THE STORK CLUB.

Gloria and husband number five, William Davey, c. 1945.

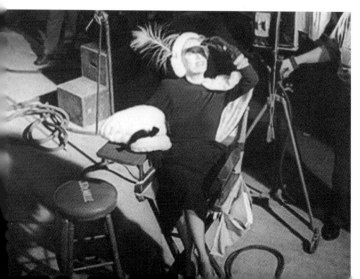

Norma Desmond under the microphone, *Sunset Boulevard*, 1950.

With Charles Brackett (*left*), and director Billy Wilder in talks for *Sunset Boulevard*, 1949.

Nancy Olson, the second William Holden, Gloria wearing the Cartier crystal bracelets, and Erich von Stroheim (*left to right*) in *Sunset Boulevard*, Paramount, 1950.

With James Warren in *3 for Bedroom C*, Warner Bros., 1952.

With Jose Ferrer in *Twentieth Century* on Broadway, 1951.

TOP LEFT: With Alan Webb, reclining, and David Niven in *Nina* on Broadway, 1952.

TOP RIGHT: With Brandon "Brandy" Brent, February 21, 1952. PHOTO: PHOTOFEST.

With Vittorio De Sica and Brigitte Bardot on the set of *Nero's Mistress*, Titanus, 1956.

TOP LEFT: In the foyer of her home in New York, August 7, 1960. PHOTO © JACK MITCHELL.

TOP RIGHT: Gloria with her mother, Addie; daughter, Gloria Anderson; and granddaughter, Brooke Anderson, on the set of *Dr. Kildare*, 1962.

With Gene Barry (*left*) and Gary Conway in the *Burke's Law* episode "Who Killed Purity Mather?" 1963.

With Dirk Benedict in *Butterflies Are Free* on Broadway, 1972. PHOTO: THE DIRK BENEDICT COLLECTION.

With Christa Venezia, October 1977. Photo: The Christa Venezia Collection.

William Dufty, "William the Sixth", with Gloria, c. mid–1970s. Photo courtesy of Photofest.

After the premiere of *Tempest* with Gena Rowlands, John Cassavetes, and director Paul Mazursky, New York, August 8, 1982.

Coast throughout the summer and early fall, performing in Boston in September. There was no hope for Broadway, and the play was put into mothballs.

Gloria reported to Four-Star Productions in Hollywood for the first of two appearances in ABC's groundbreaking crime comedy *Burke's Law,* produced by Aaron Spelling and starring Gene Barry and Gary Conway. Spelling, who originated the all-star sixty-minute television format, provided Gloria with a Rolls-Royce, caviar, flowers, and champagne, displaying a knack for seduction not lost on her. Her first appearance aired December 6, 1963, in an episode called "Who Killed Purity Mather?" Each episode of *Burke's Law* featured a handful of screen and show business stars who were given the opportunity to play against type. As a suspect in a murder, the deluded, eccentric, self-described "Goddess of Love" Venus Hekate Walsh, a character whimsically created by episode writer Harlan Ellison, Gloria wore a fright wig and handed out armfuls of mimeographed leaflets to Burke (Barry) and his partner Tim Tilson (Conway) to disperse advising her "disciples" she had returned to Earth. Paid $2,000 for her two days' work, Gloria delighted Spelling and the company with her turn as the crazy Venus.

"We had an actor a day on the show," Conway recalled. "There was a lot of downtime between setups on the set waiting, and we would talk with the stars . . . Gloria Swanson in my mind was tall, statuesque, and [yet] I remember towering over her doing our scene. I remember it [the show] was presented on a fun theory. She took [her role] in that spirit, and was always open and friendly."[27]

After filming another Steve Allen show, Gloria went over to Universal and Roncom Films for a *Kraft Suspense Theater* episode, "Who Is Jennifer?" costarring the talented Brenda Scott. (Gloria acquired a new agent, Ruth Webb, who she later declared was the best agent she ever had.) For "Who Is Jennifer?" Gloria was paid $5,000. It was during the weeklong filming of this show that President Kennedy was assassinated in Dallas on Friday, November 22. Gloria wasted little time in sending her condolences to Joe:

DEAR JOSEPH
I AM TRULY SORRY I HAVE TO WRITE YOU ON THIS OCCASION
STOP MY THOUGHTS ARE WITH YOU STOP PLEASE CALL
ON ME IF YOU NEED ANYTHING
—KELLY[28]

The *Kraft* episode aired January 16, 1964, and starred Gloria as Charlotte Heaton, who might be the wealthy mother of a runaway played by Scott. Though not scripted so, Gloria was heavy, almost fat, and looked overly made up and haggard throughout. However, she underplayed her role to perfection, and this dramatic turn is possibly her best television acting. Scott recalled of Gloria, "She was very nice, a funny woman, with a very funny, quick sense of humor. Very smart . . . She wasn't commanding, wasn't difficult."[29] Perhaps Gloria liked the young actress.

Renting costume designer Jean Louis's Pacific Palisades home while he was in Paris until after Christmas, Gloria began an *Alfred Hitchcock Presents* episode for CBS, entitled "Behind the Locked Door," which aired March 27, 1964, with James MacArthur. In it Gloria played another wealthy mother, Mrs. Daniels, whose daughter Bonnie (Lynn Loring) marries an unscrupulous young man (MacArthur) who plots to murder his young wife for her money. In typical Hitchcock fashion, the story takes a clever and unusual twist in the end.

Gloria continued work on her Puritan Fashions designs for 1964. In April she presented her spring line in person at Webb's Glendale in California, with two showings. Gloria's fashions were quite contemporary, including a three-piece Chanel-inspired two-tone costume and a "World's Fair" ensemble advertised as a four-in-one fashion.

That summer Gloria appeared on a slew of television variety and interview programs, including in June the syndicated *Steve Allen Playhouse,* doing a spoof of TV interviews, for which she was paid $265. For her appearance as Cleopatra on *The Hollywood Palace* in a spoof with Buster Keaton (as Marc Antony) she earned $3,000, plus $1,500 expenses (and $1,750 for first replay, $875 for each rerun afterward).

A Republican, Gloria backed Barry Goldwater in his unsuccessful 1964 presidential campaign. When he was defeated in November, Gloria gave up political stumping. (She had publicly and adamantly supported Wendell Willkie in 1940 and Thomas E. Dewey in 1944 in their unsuccessful presidential bids opposite Franklin D. Roosevelt.) Gloria was now almost sixty-six years old, and perhaps she realized that at that stage of her life she needed to pick her battles with a little more discretion.

On June 11 she flew to New York, and on the nineteenth departed for Paris. Taking a side trip to London and staying at the Connaught Hotel, Gloria was one of five showstoppers (the others being Jessie Matthews, Judy Garland, Merle Oberon, and Shirley Bassey) in the *Night of 100 Stars* held on July 19 at the London Palladium. Back in Los Angeles at the Desilu Studios once again on July 29–30, Gloria filmed an episode of ABC's comedy series *My Three Sons,* "The Fountain of Youth," starring Fred MacMurray, which aired March 11, 1965. Gloria portrayed Margaret McSterling, an old vaudeville friend of Uncle Charley O'Casey (William Demarest).

She then guested once more on *Burke's Law,* in "Who Killed Vaudeville?" with Gypsy Rose Lee, Gene Nelson (who also directed the episode), Phil Harris, and William Demarest, which aired September 23. Back in New York, on September 9, she attended the lighting of the 12 billion candlepower "Tower of Light" beam at the opening of the 1964 World's Fair. She was then off to Cleveland to co-host *The Mike Douglas Show* from September 16 to 21.

Gloria then filmed in California a dramatic episode, "Minus the Rusty Old Hacksaw," for the medical drama *Ben Casey,* which aired over ABC on March 15. She played Victoria Hoffman, the mother-in-law of County General Hospital resident Dr. Ted Hoffman (Harry Landers), who battles with Dr. Casey (Vincent Edwards). Gloria's performance was controlled and dramatically very measured. Of course, when vying for acting honors opposite the handsomely hirsute Edwards, it was always a hands-down victory for the other performer.

In 2010 Landers recalled meeting Gloria on the set. "First time I came on the set . . . she was probably there since five in the morning, being made up," he said. "When people introduced themselves, she would extend her hand. People would kiss her hand. I never kissed anybody's hand. So she extended her hand and I took it and said, 'How do you do?' I shook it.

"Slowly but surely, and I say this without any reservations, she fell madly in love with me . . . Last time I saw Gloria Swanson, she gave me a big hug and a kiss on the cheek, and she took my hand and squeezed it. I opened it and in it was a piece of paper, and she said, 'I suppose you can't be reached?' And I said no. She said, 'Here's my phone number. Call me. Please call me, Harry.' That was the end of Gloria Swanson. I wasn't very bright about those things."[30]

By May, back in New York, Gloria was bursting with news, as she had just completed a manic four-week marathon of developing a proposed picture to be shot in Italy called *Here, Kitty, Kitty.* Based on her own idea, it told of a philandering husband married to two women, one with boys (Gloria's role) and the other with girls, who know nothing of each other until after the man dies twenty years later. Gloria wanted to co-star with Marlene Dietrich, Charles Boyer or Maurice Chevalier, and Vittorio De Sica. She hoped to land Ross Hunter at Universal to produce the project, but he was just beginning his remake of *Madame X* with Lana Turner and Constance Bennett, the latter in her last film. Gloria then pursued George Cukor to direct and prepared to fly to Rome to arrange production there.

On May 1 and 2 she had recorded the music of the Stapley-Hughes *Boulevard*, "so now it can be heard in its entirety and I sing all my songs (something nice has happened to my voice)," she modestly boasted to Michelle in her letter.[31] She also asked Michelle to see if Boyer was at the Hotel Crillon and if René Hubert was in Paris, as he would *have* to design her gowns for *Here, Kitty, Kitty* and another film she was considering, *The Duchess and the Smugs,* a psychological thriller to be filmed in Argentina. Despite Gloria's immense enthusiasm for these projects, they both went unmade.

Even though she alleged Puritan had signed her for life, by the end of 1969 Gloria stopped lending her name to clothing. Her fashions were wildly appealing in the 1950s, her patterns selling well. But fashion itself had become more designer specific, women were not sewing as much as before and Gloria's home dress patterns had become obsolete, and the sexual revolution would eventually change couture completely by 1970. Still, in 1965, Gloria's sleekly designed chic and affordable dresses were selling in such stores as Bullock's and Gimbels.

As New Year's 1966 approached, Gloria was about to start a new venture, a line of cosmetics made exclusively from organic materials. "It should be ready next year, around my birthday," she told Angela Taylor of *The New York Times*. "The best cosmetics are in your own icebox—cucumbers, fruit, eggs. Papaya is good for bruises. Your grandmother used cornmeal on her face. It's just old-fashioned good sense." Gloria took her own food everywhere with her, half of which she used on her face, when she traveled for Puritan ("Death of a sales-woman, I call it," she would joke).[32]

In another interview at her Fifth Avenue apartment, a "maisonette" as actress Arlene Dahl recalled, a reporter noticed that Gloria's "chairs, sofas, even the has-sock in the living room [were] scaled down several inches."[33] Said Dahl in 2011, "Her furniture appeared scaled down because she collected seventeenth and eighteenth century fine furniture, and of course women were smaller then. Everything in proportion."[34] Gloria's bedroom contained two Japanese floor cushions. She would often sleep on the floor in the living room on Japanese quilts under a palm, claiming the circulation was better there. "I always sleep with my head to the north and my feet to the south," she explained, rationalizing, "Well, look at a compass. It faces north because of polarization."[35] Her living room was done in varying shades of green, dimly lit and cluttered with live flowerless green plants and numerous objects of art. "The chairs are upholstered in various shades of green or in off-white beiges executed in velveteen, satin, matelasses and other materials," commented the reporter.[36]

Gloria's parquet living room floor was painted antique white, as were the cupboards at either end of the space and the shutters covering a wall of windows. Her fireplace was framed in antique mirrored glass. She even had a green-colored piano. The walls of her home were covered with her favorite paintings; some with blue cornflowers and white carnations of her own creation. Granddaughter Brooke Anderson added, "Her apartment was filled with books . . . She didn't think the heating system was healthy, so she took it out."[37]

Beyond her library was a tiny garden, where she enjoyed dining. It had a satyr's mouth fountain that spouted water into a shallow basin. "A stone St. Francis and his birds [statue] stands against the ivy-colored brick walls," noticed writer Adele Whitely Fletcher. "There are scarlet geraniums and golden chrysanthemums, in season. A green and white-striped awning rolls up or down to suit the sun and the temperature. And on the inner wall are French doors which open to Gloria's bedroom with its low, wide-teak bed, Chinese chests and leopard rugs."[38] Gloria was at peace, and perhaps her happiest, here.

28

Finale

In early 1966 Gloria contracted with Vegetable Products in Syracuse, New York, and launched her all-natural cosmetic line Essence of Nature. The contract guaranteed her $7,500 the first year against 10 percent of gross income; her salary was set to increase to $10,000, with $5,000 increments every following year. Basic vegetables were used in her cosmetics such as safflower oil, lanolin, strawberries, cucumbers, almonds, and castor oil. Granddaughter Brooke Anderson said, "She wanted it so pure you could actually eat the ingredients."[1]

With Gloria designing the bottles and boxes, the thirteen packaged items offered in 1967 were Bath Oil, Body Silk, After Bath Crème Friction, Eye and Throat Oil, Eye Makeup Remover, Translucent Powder, Essential Moisturizer, Night Cream, Fluid Makeup, Cream Lipstick, Cleansing Lotion, Herbal Skin Freshener, and Hand Moisturizer Lotion. All were made from fresh, edible ingredients, but the line had virtually no shelf life, making it difficult to market. Gloria fumed unfairly when the endeavor failed to sell, stating "they" changed chemists without her approval, and so she withdrew. Essence of Nature did not last out 1968.

In January 1966 Herbert Marshall died of a heart attack, and surely Gloria felt the loss. Early that year she was pressuring British filmmaker and documentarian Kevin Brownlow and Michelle to help her with an American release of *Queen Kelly*. On March 28 Gloria's dream to see the film shown to American audiences finally came true when it aired over Public Broadcasting System networks on *A Million and One Nights of Film,* which Gloria hosted. Joseph Kennedy's name was not mentioned.

By March she was residing at her home called Casal da Sta. Adelaide on the Estrada do Rodizio near the beach in Colares, Portugal. Gloria advised Michelle it was cheaper for her to live there. Her annual income from residuals, acting turns, stocks and bonds, and union payouts was now fixed at $10,000 a year, and as she saw it, her New York address was for the time being a business investment. She had been advised she could rent her apartment, unfurnished, for $1,300 a month for five years. She eventually leased it to a young man in June at $250 a week.

Gloria returned to the States that March to start rehearsals for an all-star stage revival of Clare Boothe Luce's comedy *The Women,* for a tour that summer in the Bible Belt. She signed at $3,000 on July 19 to portray the Countess de Lage (a character loosely based on Gloria's old friend Countess Dorothy di Frasso). *The Women* opened at the Packard Music Hall in Warren, Ohio, on July 26. Cast with her were Marge Champion, Elaine Stritch, Marilyn Maxwell, the irrepressible Dagmar, and Sherry O'Neill.

Gloria's reviews were bad. "Miss Swanson, for all her remarkably well-preserved svelteness, was only going through the motions and added little luster to a performance that needed every whit of that quality it could muster," wrote one Dayton reporter.[2] Trouble brewed during rehearsals when Stritch and Gloria shared a scene; Stritch told the *New York Observer* in 2001, "She's the only actress I know of who critiqued the lunatic performance of a fellow actress when she was onstage with her at the time."[3] Suffice it to say, Stritch left the show in early August.

After the play's brief run, the tour was canceled, and Gloria agreed to appear on the hit CBS sitcom *The Beverly Hillbillies.* For the episode entitled "The Gloria Swanson Story," which aired November 30, she portrayed herself. The millionaire Clampett hillbillies (Buddy Ebsen, Irene Ryan, Max Baer Jr., and Donna Douglas) believe she is broke—her house is for sale (she was moving to New York) and her belongings are up for auction (for the Actors Relief Fund). Baer recalled Gloria was friendly throughout the week of rehearsal and shooting, yet she remained aloof and distant. "I don't think I had two words with her," he said in 2011.[4] There was little time for camaraderie. Baer recalled

Gloria was given her own dressing room and transportation. She was paid $2,500 for *The Beverly Hillbillies*.

About playing herself, she remarked, "When I got on the set I thought . . . how do I walk? . . . how do I talk? I don't know. I hadn't the slightest conception of what Gloria Swanson was like! It was the hardest thing I ever did because I found myself being very self-conscious. 'Is that the way I would do it? How silly!' It's strange."[5]

On Monday evening, October 26, 1966, Gloria's eighty-eight-year-old mother Addie passed away in her sleep. Gloria wrote that she had been a devoted daughter, sending Addie flowers on her birthday and calling her every weekend. Claiming Addie had suffered a stroke through a transfusion Gloria had not wanted her to have, Gloria sat by her mother's hospital bedside as she lay dying, gently coaxing her to let go.[6] Gloria owned two crypts at Forest Lawn Cemetery, which she had purchased for herself and Addie in 1937. Addie was laid to rest there.

As the year ended Gloria was set to begin a new film, *Blank Point,* producing the venture herself. Filming commenced in New York before Christmas, though she had no permanent director, final script, or co-stars. The first shot was lensed at Bergdorf Goodman on December 28. Gloria appeared at the store with her maid Margit Mikussey while traffic was held at bay outside on Fifty-Eighth Street.

In *Blank Point* Gloria was to play a fashion executive, a "typical American woman who wants her cake and eat it too," she told *The New York Times.*[7] Dressed in a white mink wrap and matching hat borrowed from Greenwood Furs, Gloria was accompanied to the shoot by her latest beau, writer William Dufty. After another week of starts and stops on the project, *Blank Point* folded.

Dufty would be the last man of significance in Gloria's life. They had first met in August 1965 in New York at a hearing for Dr. Andrew Ivy, later accused of fraud in his advocacy of the anticancer drug Krebiozen. Dufty had been involved as an organizer with the UAW (United Auto Workers) and wrote speeches for its former president Walter Reuther. He also edited Michigan's *CIO* (Congress of Industrial Organizations) *News* and was a publicist for Americans for Democratic Action. At the time they met, the six-foot-tall Dufty was overweight (220 pounds), had hemorrhoids and a hernia, and was suffering through a miserable divorce. He sat by Gloria at a luncheon; as he poured sugar into his coffee, she told him he was killing himself.

Born William Francis Dufty in Merrill, Michigan, on February 2, 1916, he was the oldest of three sons and two daughters; his father was a very Catholic banker. Considered a child piano prodigy, young Bill had his own local radio show at the age of eight. He attended Wayne State University, but dropped out, and served in the army during World War II in North Africa and Europe. As part of a newspaper contingent, Dufty was present in the Oval Office in 1940 as President Franklin D. Roosevelt "lied like a trooper about something (a long-shoremen's union matter) that transpired when I was on the scene and knew better."[8] According to the *Detroit News,* Dufty's first and most cherished cause was unionism.

A series of articles in the *New York Post* exposing J. Edgar Hoover's bungling leadership earned Dufty a name in journalism. Along with fellow *Post* reporters Fern Marja and Peter McElroy, in April 1956 he was awarded the 1955 George Polk Award in Journalism from Long Island University for metropolitan reporting. On April 25, 1946, Dufty married refugee Maely Daniele (1918–81), who had immigrated to the United States after the war and whose Jewish family perished in Nazi concentration camps. She was the former wife of child film star Freddie Bartholomew, who had been a film director at WPIX-TV when Gloria was hosting her pioneering talk show. Bartholomew was Maely's third husband. When she met Dufty, Maely was a Hallmark card writer. The couple had a son, born February 27, 1955, named Bevan (after British Labour Party politician Aneurin Bevan).[9] Maely and Bill later divorced, and after marrying once again, Maely moved and reared Bevan in California.

Bill was a lover of blues and jazz; he had met singer Billie Holiday in the 1950s, when she was deep into alcohol and drugs. The author of some forty books, many written under a pseudonym to avoid paying alimony to Maely, Dufty ghostwrote Holiday's 1956 autobiography, *Lady Sings the Blues.* It became a bestseller. In the book, one can almost hear Holiday's voice telling her story. Dufty was clever, said his partner for his last twenty years, Dennis Fairchild: "William was a journalist and a ventriloquist, and slipping into dialect, he could channel other people."[10]

In 1965 Dufty produced an English-language translation of Sakuazawa

Nuoiti's (Georges Ohsawa) groundbreaking tome *You Are All Sanpaku,* writing a remarkable introduction that was almost three times longer than the text of the book. The translation, advocating a wholesome spiritual and eating philosophy, introduced macrobiotics to Western culture. (*You Are All Sanpaku* was a favorite book of John Lennon and Yoko Ono.)

In 1966 Dufty reintroduced himself to Gloria, sending her a copy of *You Are All Sanpaku,* and she invited him over. "There was this trim, good-looking young man," Gloria told *People* magazine. "He told me that in a way I was responsible for changing his life. We wound up talking in the kitchen until 1 A.M., and we've been the best of friends since."[11] Before long they were dating. Gloria loved to dance, and Bill was a marvelous dancer. Significantly, she told him he reminded her of her father.

In January 1967 Gloria and Vincent Price were set to lens a Canadian thriller, *Graveside Story,* budgeted at $400,000, and to be directed by James Elliott. It never saw life. That March she and Dufty flew to Mexico City, where director-writer Dirk Wayne Summers (Gloria was his godmother) was filming *The Great Sex War* (Cinerama Releasing Corporation, 1969). Without being asked, she and Dufty completely rewrote the screenplay, much to Summers's dissatisfaction. They amicably parted ways.

Gloria was in Chicago in March for Harold Kennedy's third attempted resurrection of *The Inkwell,* now called *Reprise.* Kennedy was determined he and Gloria would take it to Broadway. Opening at the Ivanhoe Theater on North Clark Street in Chicago, *Reprise* ran four dismal weeks before continuing to Denver's Elitch Gardens Theater, where it quickly closed. It was still the same old play. When it reopened at the Huntington Hartford Theater in Los Angeles on October 3, critics were appalled. With its single set, *Reprise* showcased Gloria in the worst possible light. Gloria's appearance, wearing unbecoming fashions created by designer Daniel Werle, and donning a porkpie hat she had purchased in England in 1945, didn't help. Gloria and Kennedy paraded about the stage and even danced together, in a mishmash comedy-drama that audiences ended up wishing they had missed.

According to the *Los Angeles Times,* at the end of the play Gloria stepped before the curtain, saying, "'You're applauding my age, not my performance.' There were cries of 'No, no!' but the star was right. It was a pretty bad performance in a pretty bad play."[12] For the publication *Classic Film Collector,* Charles

Silver, now film curator at MoMA, wrote, "The whole thing is written like some exceptionally putrid soap opera one might regretfully stumble across on daytime television."[13] *Reprise* closed for good, and too late, on October 14, 1967.

In August Gloria had received the first draft of an episode of *The Lucy Show* with Lucille Ball over at Desilu for CBS. Entitled "Lucy and the Last Star," its storyline had Lucille Carmichael (Ball) and Vivian Bunson (Vivian Vance) stumbling upon the home of movie star Gloria Swanson, whom they find scrubbing her floor. Mistakenly assuming Swanson is broke, they attempt to rescue her from her "poverty." Ball thought the script hilarious. Swanson turned it down flat. It was eventually recast with Joan Crawford.[14]

In 1968 Gloria Somborn Anderson, then a widow, married Wilfrid Daly, vice president of Associated Aviation Underwriters in New York, and nephew of theatrical producer-manager Augustin Daly. Gloria did not attend the wedding. In April she signed with Puritan Fashions to continue her line under the moniker "Gloria Swanson Originals" until December 29, 1969. For her work she was now paid $1,538.46 every two weeks.

That spring of 1968 Gloria introduced her newest line of clothing. Mod fashions, so ingeniously marketed on London's Carnaby Street, had invaded the American market. As award-winning Broadway costume designer Tracy Christensen said of styles of the mid- to late 1960s, "Fashion was becoming more and more relaxed ever since the turn of the 20th Century."[15] By the end of the decade almost anything was acceptable in women's apparel, and the youth market reigned. Haute couture still existed for the privileged few, but Gloria's fashions were meant for the masses, so surely she felt out of touch with current trends.

Gloria and Bill flew to Russia in late 1968 to talk about Gloria's two favorite subjects—films and health foods. They returned to New York after the New Year, then in April headed to Portugal. Granddaughter Brooke, by then a graduate of the Westlake School for Girls in West Los Angeles, announced her engagement to James Robert Young on March 12. On August 23 the couple wed.[16] Gloria did not attend.

But she did appear live that year on David Susskind's talk show *Open End*, broadcast from New York. Appearing with her were Leatrice Joy, Lois Wilson, and Carmel Myers. When Gloria showed up at the last moment just before the show went on the air, she motioned to the two cameramen and said, "Listen, you darling fellows. I'm over sixty-five. I'm a grandmother. Please, make me look as good as you can."[17]

That spring of 1970 Gloria was offered an exciting opportunity to replace Katharine Hepburn on Broadway in the musical *Coco,* which had opened at the Hellinger Theater on December 18, 1969. The producer was Frederick Brisson, husband of Rosalind Russell. Based on the life of Gabrielle "Coco" Chanel, the book and libretto were by Alan Jay Lerner, second husband of Gloria's *Sunset Boulevard* co-star Nancy Olson. Music was by André Previn, the sets were designed by Cecil Beaton, and the choreography was by Michael Bennett.

For the role she was offered $3,000 a week plus 5 percent of the gross up to $75,000. According to Gloria, negotiations simply broke down, and French actress Danielle Darrieux was cast. The following year Gloria explained what happened: "I love Cecil Beaton's designs but I couldn't use Hepburn's clothes and *that's* how it started. They were getting chintzy. There was constant indecisiveness and they wanted to pay me less than Hepburn. So I said 'Forget it.' They didn't think I meant it . . . They wanted one preview only and then four nights of critics' shows. Once *that* was out of the way they were going to cut orchestra, singers, backstage staff—well, I didn't want to be a one-woman show. So I said 'Go ahead—get the little girl from France.'"[18]

On August 3, 1970, Gloria appeared on *The Dick Cavett Show,* an ABC talk show. One of Cavett's other guests was rock singer Janis Joplin, in what would sadly be her last television appearance. (She overdosed on drugs on October 4.) It is a difficult show to watch today, with obvious uneasiness among the participants; Cavett nonetheless appeared to be enjoying himself. Garbed in a blue plaid jacket and polyester flair-legged pants (and sporting lifts), Cavett, a shameless name dropper famous for knowing the famous, kept attempting to be clever and "with it" throughout the broadcast.

Joplin, braless in a silk blouse and jacket, wore crushed velvet pants, a boa, feathers in her hair, and beads everywhere. Annoyingly, she chain-smoked and repeatedly said "man" after every other word. Then out glided Gloria to the music of "Love, Your Spell Is Everywhere," in a blond wig, wearing a single-strap sheath, and holding a red carnation, which she had become accustomed to flipping about to make a point in her conversations. She posed shamelessly as the applause died down. Cavett's inane interview and both his and Gloria's futile attempts to drag Joplin into the conversation, specifically when talking about fashion, when viewed today make one's skin crawl.

Coco didn't happen for Gloria, but another stage offer did pan out. Young theatrical producer Arthur Whitelaw (*You're a Good Man, Charlie Brown*) approached Gloria to replace Eve Arden in a touring company of *Butterflies Are Free,* by Leonard Gershe, which had opened on Broadway in October 1969 and was still running, starring Eileen Heckart, Keir Dullea, and Blythe Danner. Arden was just not bringing in playgoers in Chicago with her portrayal of Mrs. Baker, the mother of a blind grown son. Gloria was offered either the tour or replacing Eileen Heckart, who was leaving the show to do the film version in Hollywood. She chose to tour first, then to replace Heckart.

Immediately over tea she told Whitelaw to call her Gloria. Before long she called him Junior. "She said she loved the play and would very much like to play the mother," Whitelaw wrote in his autobiography.[19] "I asked her who her agent was, and she said, 'You're talking to her!'" He asked her how much she wanted. "Equity minimum, $189 a week," she responded. Taken aback, Whitelaw replied, "I would be embarrassed to offer you that amount." To which she added, "Plus 10% of the house gross." Concluded Whitelaw after Gloria assumed the role, "She never walked out of that theater without less than $10,000 a week."[20]

"She was in my estimation absolutely terrible," Whitelaw recalled after opening night in Boston prior to her coming to Broadway. "She played it [the role] like a silent screen star . . . Her first entrance was at the end of the first act. On she comes wearing two big bracelets, one with 'G' on it, the other with an 'S,' a gold turban, leopard scarf around her neck, gold earrings dangling from her ears, a brocade pantsuit, and white rimmed dark sunglasses. She walks out and there was a hush from the audience before a big applause for her for two minutes. Well, they had never seen that before. Her [stage] son looks up and says, 'Hello, mother,' big laugh and the curtain comes down at the end of the act."[21]

Rushing backstage before the second act, Whitelaw knocked on Gloria's offstage-right dressing room door. Opening it, she said, "You hate it don't you?" He replied, "It's terrible! It's exactly wrong for the play because she's [Mrs. Baker] a lovely, sophisticated woman from Scarsdale, New York, who would never in a million years wear a pantsuit, let alone a turban and white sunglasses . . . and if you change one bit of it I will never talk to you again. You are so shrewd—that's exactly what the audience came to see. I don't know why I didn't think of it!"[22] During the rest of the tour the show averaged $38,000 gross a week.

When Gloria opened in the show on Broadway on September 17, her run was originally to last until Christmas. However, with Gloria in the role, the play was so successful it was extended until March 1972. Her co-stars then were David Huffman, who replaced Keir Dullea as her son, Pamela Bellwood, and Michael Shannon.

Walter Kerr of *The New York Times* gave Gloria a glowing review: "She is strong and freshly winning. She stylizes a few earlier comic responses a shade more than is necessary, freezing into stunned postures as though a playful animated-cartoon artist had pinned her to the drawing board . . . But that's shortly over with, and the moment the role begins to call for some complexity— yes, this is the nagging, overprotective, impossible Scarsdale mother . . . The actress promptly takes on stature . . . The grace is there always: Miss Swanson is something to see as she crosses her lithe legs in her tailored beige trousers, locks her hands over one knee, gets her chin to full mast and defies anyone to make her more of a villain than she actually is. But the intelligence is there, too. As she stands in a corner matter-of-factly folding a dish towel, grimly but quite coolly assaying the qualities of the rattle-brained girl who is making her son so happy, she does as much for the part and the play as when she is speaking her determined piece. It is excellent, non-nostalgic work."[23] Leo Mishkin of the *New York Morning Telegraph* wrote simply, "She is, after all, Gloria Swanson, and there's nobody quite like her anywhere, either on the stage or screen."[24]

William Dufty by now was Gloria's live-in companion and lover. She enjoyed sculpting busts, having completed one of little Gloria, Michelle, and one of Bill. To celebrate her opening in *Butterflies Are Free,* Gloria bought a new yellow Toyota Celica for $2,900 on September 13. One thing she truly enjoyed during the play's run was her drive to the theater every evening.

Handsome young Montana-born actor Dirk Benedict was asked to attend a performance of *Butterflies Are Free,* and then to replace David Huffman. "In early December I had had what was to be the final audition for the lead," Benedict wrote in his memoirs. "Everyone liked my reading of the part, but the producer, Arthur Whitelaw, was concerned that I was too All-American looking, too muscular to be believable . . . Miss Swanson explained to the producer that 'sightless' means without sight, not without muscles! I got the part."[25]

Benedict recalled recently, "She was terrified of having to do the role with someone new. She was very intimidating. Not a big woman . . . just scary. She wanted me to do it exactly the way David Huffman did it . . . About three or four days after my opening performance I made an attempt to apologize to her. And she said 'You do whatever you want.' About a couple of months later she invited me to dinner."[26] Leaving 920 Fifth Avenue that night with a pound bag of brown rice and a pamphlet on macrobiotics, twenty-six-year-old Benedict for the first time in his life felt he was on his way to discovering himself. "I knew she didn't do this for everyone," he added. After that he adopted the role of "son" in real life, as Swanson ("Oh, darling, just call me Gloria") took to him in a maternal and loving way.[27]

"I'll never forget the first time, though, when I saw her as a sexual woman," Benedict would write. "In her little garden, she was having a cigarette, and she was giggling like a little girl, flashing those piercing blue eyes, giggling and holding herself—and I got it! She was like an 18-year-old girl, laughing at some joke . . . She was the essence of femininity as she lifted up her leg and hugged it, twinkling and giggling . . . My heart skipped a beat. She was *so* sexy and sweet. The public didn't see that. She played that early in her career, but people forgot after *Sunset Boulevard*."[28]

During one performance, remembered Whitelaw, the electrician missed a light cue, one of only four during the show. Gloria was livid. When she found out he had missed it because he was listening to a ball game, "she let him have it," Whitelaw said: "How dare you miss that cue. I come into this show every day, I know every line, day after day, night after night. You have four lousy cues to remember, and you miss one! That is unprofessional!"[29]

On April 10, 1972, Gloria's beloved Henri died in a plane crash near Calvia on the island of Palma de Majorca, Spain. Over the past two decades Gloria had run into Henri and Emma in Europe at various fetes held by Aristotle Onassis, Gianni Agnelli (she'd had affairs with both), and the Duke of Atrante. Henri had recently restored his ancestral manor at St. Florent des Bois in Paris, installing electrical wiring and a telephone, and he and Emma also owned a home in Majorca. The de la Falaises were guests of Barbara Hutton once in Washington, D.C., in 1960 and ran into Joseph and Rose Kennedy. Emma was not impressed, feeling "Joe was a force of nature with the personality of a gangster and that Rose was smarter than anyone suspected. Young John had a way with women, Rose told the marquise during a *tete a tete,* but the presidency would keep him out of trouble."[30]

Gloria's run in *Butterflies Are Free* ended on July 2, 1972. Whitelaw recalled she never had stage fright. She was like Ethel Merman in that respect. "Why should I be afraid?" she told him. "The audience doesn't know what I am going to do. Maybe they should be afraid."[31] Gloria then continued with a limited run of *Butterflies Are Free* at the Painters Mill Music Fair in Baltimore, September 5–10, and at the Paper Mill Playhouse in Millburn, New Jersey, December 27–January 21, 1973. For this production, Whitelaw took over the staging.

On opening night, when the Act II curtain came up, Gloria's character was standing behind the sofa. After she delivered her first lines, Whitelaw saw her slip down behind the divan. Quickly rushing around to the wings, he saw her lying on the floor motioning them to continue as she slowly rose. The seventy-four-year-old Swanson had suffered a minor stroke, yet continued the play. Prompters hurriedly moved behind every flat to feed her a line if needed. She never dropped a cue. After seeing a doctor, Gloria completed her run at the Paper Mill. She realized she had to slow down.

In December 1973 Lewis Bredin died in France. Gloria was losing more of the men from her life. Yet she still had a healthy libido, and once shocked Benedict by telling a reporter in his presence, "I wish I had more sex." She was never lewd and never used foul language openly. Recalled the actor, "She was always very polite in a way when she referred to sex. It was wonderful to be around, the old school language she would use, which was never vulgar."[32]

Gloria hated mediocrity and avoided watching television as a general rule. When she heard comedienne Carol Burnett was doing a Norma Desmond ("Nora" Desmond) send-up on her hit CBS television variety show, Gloria tuned in. She became one of Burnett's biggest fans, and wrote her, "I sing—ask Sir Laurence Olivier or Alan Jay Lerner. I dance—ask Chuck Walters. I do pratfalls—ask Chaplin or Mack Sennett. I am in California—ask the FBI."[33]

When asked to appear on *The Carol Burnett Show,* Gloria jumped at the opportunity. "Don't be foolish, darling," Gloria told Burnett's husband Joe Hamilton, the show's producer. "Of course I will. That's why I wrote the letter."[34] Gloria appeared in three segments of the hour-long comedy show, taped on September 14 and broadcast on September 29. Dressed in a black-and-white single-shoulder gown, carrying a carnation, she joined Carol and regular Lyle

Waggoner in an introductory skit, flirting with the hunky Waggoner. She then sang and danced in a red-fringed outfit to a specialty number, "The New-Fangled Tango," with several male dancers. And finally she performed a long, elaborate silent skit as Charlie Chaplin with Burnett in her signature Charwoman garb. (This would be the fourth and last of Swanson's Chaplin impersonations.)

Gloria and Bill once attended a special screening at the executive screening room on the Paramount lot of *Fine Manners,* her final film under contract with the studio before her move to independence in 1926. "The most polite thing one could say about *Fine Manners* is that it is not a mind-gripper," wrote Kathleen Carroll in 1973. "But as weak a film as it is, it reveals the special qualities that made Miss Swanson one of the most unforgettable stars of the silent era." During the screening, Gloria was heard to comment, "I wonder what I'm thinking . . . You had to show then what you were thinking . . . I'm just a little gamin from the streets." (Sighed Dufty wryly, "With a Bergdorf dress.")[35] In another *Fine Manners* screening at MoMA the year before, she had said she couldn't remember making the film, yet she rhapsodized aloud over her image, "Why, she was *pretty,* wasn't she?"[36]

About her co-star in *Fine Manners,* Eugene O'Brien, Gloria commented during one sequence, "He's such a bad actor, bless his heart. Everyone thought he was handsome. He used to play a lot with Norma Talmadge." Back in the 1950s, the George Eastman House ran an hour of clips of Gloria's existing films dating back to 1914, in no particular order. That evening, she said, she couldn't sleep, as the disconnected scenes disturbed her. She admitted she didn't remember making some of the pictures. When asked about the tribute the following day, Gloria uncharacteristically broke down. "The dam burst," she said. "I started to cry. When you go to psychiatrists, and they take you back, at least they are kind enough to do it in chronological order. This was something weird and destructive."[37]

Bill spent a great deal of time flying back and forth to Portugal overseeing Gloria's property there, and the two together would travel to Europe frequently over the next few years. In New york, curator of film Charles Silver recalled that at a special tribute to Raoul Walsh at the Museum of Modern Art, Walsh, his ever-present eye patch in place, kept telling Gloria, who came to the event "with her little bags of fruits and nuts," that she was still the beautiful, sweet young girl he remembered from their days of lost youth. Sadly, Walsh was all but blind by this time. But Gloria ate it up, giggling like a little girl.[38]

Director Curtis Harrington approached Gloria in November to appear as a German wine-growing matriarch in ABC's "Movie of the Week," *The Killer Bees,* co-starring young Edward Albert and Craig Stevens. Harrington had already approached several other actresses to do the role, including Bette Davis, who was prepared to accept but declined because of one key sequence when the character was covered with swarming bees. She was guaranteed the bees would have their stingers clipped, but at the last moment she still canceled.[39]

"There are very few parts for a woman of my age," Gloria later told *Film Fan Monthly,* "and they always think in terms of glamour and I want strong characterization. I very much liked the German woman in *The Killer Bees . . .* who was, to me, a very amusing character that I had fun doing."[40] Gloria began filming her scenes in Napa Valley on December 13, rising at 6:00 A.M. every day to prepare for the day's shoot. Production ended four days later. During the filming she regaled the cast and crew with her dead-on impersonation of Katharine Hepburn.

When Gloria arrived in California, the producers told her they did not want a German accent for her character. "I said, 'Of course, I'll do the accent.'"[41] Gloria then went to work attempting to impress everyone with what sounded like the worst possible high school German accent, saying to an interviewer, "You vill forgive my accent. I try to stay in character for ze role. And ze clothes . . . you know, zis is ze first time I am playing a woman older than myself." (Not true.) When given no reaction, and regaining her senses, Gloria spoke more intelligently to the reporter. Asked what sort of men attracted her she replied, "Strong men. Physically strong and mentally strong. But I attract weak men, because I am a very strong woman. My husbands . . . I always ended up taking care of them. And then I'd want out. There was one man . . . he was different. I adored him. But he was married."[42] She was not referring to Joseph Kennedy; Gloria was thinking of Lewis.

The plot of *The Killer Bees* concerned the attacks of killer bees on the unsuspecting residents of a California wine valley community. In the climactic scene with actress Kate Jackson, the dormant, chilled bees were pasted and placed on Gloria's body. "I don't want them on my face," she demanded. The cameras ran, lights were turned on to stimulate the bees, and Jackson delivered her first offstage line, "Are you all right?" "Uff course," said Gloria's character. "I'm demonstratink for our visitors from out uff town how harmless are our little bees." Wrote *TV Guide*, "The bees were awake now, buzzing, crawling up toward her neck, taking to the air and flying about her face. [For the next take] She said the line again, more relaxed, cooing at the bees and beaming lovingly on them. A few crawled on her face. She cooed and she clucked, 'Fly little ones . . . liebchen . . . pretty bees . . .' Some flew near her eyes, but she didn't blink. Everyone watched spellbound. It was a remarkable performance. Finally 'Cut!' was called and the crew and bystanders broke into applause."[43] Once again DeMille would have been so very proud of her.

Extravagantly advertised in the media before it aired on February 26, 1974, *The Killer Bees* eventually became a minor cult film favorite. "Miss Swanson's grande dame is no mere gargoyle but a fascinating, at times even likably forthright woman with both dimensions of poignance and grandeur," wrote Kevin Thomas in the *Los Angeles Times*.[44]

After that, though, there would be no more major acting roles.

29

Legend

In 1974 twenty-nine-year-old Dirk Benedict was diagnosed with prostate cancer. When he told Bill Dufty about it, he and Gloria took action and introduced the young actor to macrobiotic expert Michio Kushi. Macrobiotics made sense to Benedict, and with the help of Dufty, he retreated to a secluded New Hampshire cabin and lived on whole grains and vegetables, seaweed, and Japanese miso soup for six weeks, dropping thirty-five pounds in the process. The tumor went away. He appeared on Gloria's Fifth Avenue doorstep afterward and lived briefly with Gloria and Bill, sleeping on their couch.[1]

A montage of Gloria's films was shown in Paris by film curator Henri Langlois at the Cinematèque Française on her seventy-fifth birthday on March 27. At the reception preceding the showing, Langlois presented Gloria, accompanied by daughter Michelle, with a birthday cake. In April Gloria flew to Washington, D.C., to begin her final film role as herself, in the disaster picture *Airport 1975* for Universal.

Actor Roy Thinnes remembered how the cast and crew were amazed at the amount of luggage Gloria brought with her when she arrived at Dulles International. The company soon found out most of it contained food and cooking utensils. In *Airport 1975,* the first sequel to Universal's hit 1970 film *Airport,* Gloria played herself in a cameo and needed but one outfit to wear, a simple hooded black-and-white Edith Head–designed number. Actress Linda Harrison, then using the acting name Augusta Summerland and married to former

20th Century–Fox head Richard Zanuck, played Gloria's secretary Winnie Griffith. "She took a special liking to me," recalled Harrison. "I knew when we met that I was going to learn something from her."[2]

Harrison and Gloria spent innumerable hours together between setups. One thing Gloria loved to talk about was her own sensuality. "She really went on about the sex she had with Joe Kennedy," Harrison added. "There wasn't anything she wouldn't say. Oh, God, he was going to marry her but he couldn't leave Rose and the children . . . he was a wonderful lover, and she'd detail it!"[3] Gloria always found her own history fascinating.

In *Airport 1975* a 747 jumbo jet collides in midair with a small aircraft, and the all-star cast must deal with their fears and emotions on board the damaged plane.

In the picture the midair collision kills most of the cockpit crew, and flight attendant Nancy Pryor (Karen Black) takes over the controls of the aircraft, with directions on flying it given to her over headphones, much to the horror of the passengers, coining the famous line "The stewardess is flying the plane!"

Directed by Jack Smight, it starred Charlton Heston, Karen Black, Myrna Loy (as a boilermaker-drinking alcoholic matron), George Kennedy (repeating his role of Joe Petrone from the original movie), Australian singer Helen Reddy (as, what else, a singing nun), and Linda Blair (fresh from *The Exorcist*, and now portraying a sickly young girl awaiting an organ transplant); Gloria's *Sunset Boulevard* co-star Nancy Olson portrayed Blair's mother. Though they shared no scenes, Olson told the press, "It intrigues me to be back with Gloria Swanson."[4] Gloria wrote in her book that it was suggested she play herself as "a normal human being dictating her memoirs into a tape recorder."[5]

Gloria was interviewed at the Beverly Hills Hotel on June 5 by writer Richard Lamparski, who was referred to by Dufty as the "man who writes about the unburied dead." When Lamparski's tall, good-looking Japanese cameraman entered the suite to set up, Gloria placed "one of her crimson-tipped fingers on his forearm and said, 'You and I need to be good friends. We don't want to disappoint those wonderful people out there in the dark, do we?'" After the interview, Lamparski said he wanted to share something with her.[6]

Flashing her ever-present red carnation about as if it were a magic wand, Gloria momentarily placed it in her lap as the young man told her about a recent incident when silent film actor George O'Brien, a huge star in the 1920s, took him to lunch at the Beverly Hills Club. O'Brien insisted the television at the bar be tuned on NBC and the sound turned up when Gloria appeared on *The Dinah Shore Show.* Then Lamparski recounted another time when silent screen actress Dorothy Revier told him that whenever Gloria's name was mentioned on TV, she would call former silent star Madge Bellamy, or vice versa. And the whole Motion Picture Country House and Hospital would almost shut down anytime Gloria was on TV. Gloria asked, "Why?" Lamparski told her, "To your generation you are the *stars' star.*"[7]

In Colorado, from August 30 to September 2, 1974, Gloria attended the first Telluride Film Festival, where she, legendary Third Reich actress and film director Leni Riefenstahl, and director Francis Ford Coppola were honored. DeMille's *Male and Female* was shown. On her last night at the festival, August 30, *Sadie Thompson* was screened before Gloria's award ceremony.

On August 27, 1974, Gloria had become a great-grandmother for the first time when Brooke Anderson Young gave birth to her first child, Ashley. (Two years later, on January 6, 1976, Brooke had a second baby girl, whom she named Courtland.) Gloria in the meanwhile told the press she planned to star in three "sexy-thrillings" (as she called them)—three movies to be filmed in Mexico, *Spasmo, Death Walks the Pavement in High Heels,* and *Sexual Revelations of a Maniac as Told to the Captain of the Mobile Squad.* Surely she must have been kidding!

In New York in the early 1970s Gloria befriended pop art guru Andy Warhol. The fortyish Warhol had already tapped Gloria's sanctified world when he embraced Henri's sister-in-law socialite Maxime Birley, former muse of Elsa Schiaparelli, and starred her in one of his films. Her daughter the late model Loulou de la Falaise became Yves St. Laurent's muse and was the mother of Alexis, Comte de la Falaise, who starred in Warhol's trashy short film *Tub Girls* in 1967. (His son Daniel, now a renowned chef, once appeared in a Madonna video.)

On October 18, 1974, *Airport 1975* premiered in New York at Loew's State on Broadway. It quickly crashed and burned at the box office. *The New York Times*'s Vincent Canby called it "a silly, jumbo-sized sequel" and noted young Linda Blair had "all of the naivety of a Vegas showgirl." Gloria's performance he called a "ferocious parody."[8] The film ranks—and reeks—as the least profitable and most unrealistic of the eventual four *Airport* disaster pictures, though it did make Universal some money. It received the dubious distinction of being honored as one of the "50 Worst Films of All Time" by film critics Harry Medved and Randy Dreyfuss.

In 1975 Michael Farmer died, though Gloria made little note of his passing. Brooke Anderson Young said about her grandmother, "She had a wonderful ability to shut out things that were uncomfortable to her."[9] But when her son Joseph, who made frequent trips out east as a consultant to MIT, was found dead on July 9 in a hotel bathroom in Danvers, Massachusetts, Gloria was devastated. He was just fifty-one years old, his death attributed to internal hemorrhaging. Ever optimistic, however, Gloria confessed to Bob Thomas, "Life is a constant surprise to me, and each morning I wake up and say, 'What now, God?' People grow old because they get bored—first with themselves, then with the world around them. They start getting ailments and they take something for the pain, so they're not all here much of the time. That's not my idea of living."[10] Not even the death of a child could sway Swanson's convictions.

Bill Dufty's book *Sugar Blues,* which warned of health dangers and addictions attributed to white sugar, was published in April 1975. In his dedication, he wrote:

> To Billie Holiday
> whose death changed my life
> To Gloria Swanson
> whose life changed my death.[11]

Gloria dutifully made television and radio rounds with Dufty, supporting him and his antisugar campaign, and talking at great lengths about nutrition and health foods. When they flew, she would sit in first class and Bill would be in coach. For the fifteen-city book tour, Gloria insisted she have a new wardrobe and approached costume designer David Graden, Arthur Whitelaw's partner, to design for her. Gloria specifically wanted pantsuits along the lines of long johns that would allow her easy access to the potty. Graden's tailors complained that Gloria insisted pieces of the clothing be made of different fabrics, which of course directly affected the pattern and construction of the outfit. They somehow were constructed.

Gloria then boldly told the *New York Post*'s Eugenia Shepard she had designed her wardrobe herself. "She took credit for everything she ever wore," Graden recalled. "Chanel, Head, [Norman] Norell, it didn't matter. She took the credit."[12] For the new year of 1976 Gloria intended to "open the windows and let the old air out and the fresh air in."[13] Taking a deep breath, she married William Dufty on his sixtieth birthday, in New York City, on Monday, February 2, 1976, in the chambers of Supreme Court Justice Allen Murray Myers. "We have all these mutual interests and have been traveling around promoting his book," Gloria rationalized to the press. "It just seemed silly not to get married."[14]

"It came as a shock," she told *Time* magazine. "After all, I haven't been married since the 1940s." Boasting about Bill, she added, "He's a convert of mine."[15] She advised *People* magazine they married rather suddenly and "completely forgot about all the blood tests and documents." Talking about proper diet, she added, "Why do people treat their bodies like garbage pails? . . . I sound like a broken record. Actually now I just tell people to go ahead and eat ground glass if they want. See if I care."[16] The couple then embarked on another three-week tour to promote *Sugar Blues.*

Young Bevan Dufty was then attending the University of California at Berkeley. He hadn't seen his father in years, and when he read of the marriage Bevan sent a Western Union cable to Bill's publisher, hoping to reach his father. Within two days he heard back. Bevan was scheduled to be in Washington, D.C., that summer of 1976 and came up to New York to meet Gloria. "She was very sweet, very nice, and into the 'drama' of the father-son reconnection," Bevan recalled. "But the house [920 Fifth Avenue] kind of tripped me out. She had a sculptured bust of my dad with a hat and scarf on it as if he was sitting there . . . And she probably had more roaches than you'd ever see on Fifth Avenue and 71st Street because she didn't believe in pesticides . . . I'd never seen so many roaches in my life!"[17]

The three attended a performance of the Broadway play *That Championship Season,* which primarily took place in a locker room. Seated between Bevan and his father, Gloria hissed and made negative comments throughout the performance. "She clearly didn't like it, finding it 'awful' and 'disgusting,'" Bevan recalled. When the lights came up, they did not move. Then the press and the actors came out, and Gloria stood and approached each cast member, taking his hands and saying something positive about each individual performance.

"What a life lesson," Bevan related. "She hated this play, but she knew what these people would remember from her and how it would mean to them."[18] Bevan made note of this when he entered the public arena of politics.

That summer Gloria was preparing a one-woman show she called *Look Back in Laughter,* which was scheduled to be presented on August 22 at the Westport Country Playhouse. She also recorded songs for nostalgia record producer Ben Bagley on Painted Smiles Records. They included "They're Either Too Young or Too Old," "We've Got Something," and "We Were So Young."

Talking freely at a taping of the talk show *Good Day* in New York, seventy-seven-year-old Gloria latched onto sex and aging. "Of course my sex life is very healthy," she said. The interviewer looked stunned, and Gloria added, "I'm a matriarch now, and I can say anything I want!"[19] When 1977 began, Gloria was interviewed at the historic Algonquin Hotel in New York for the thirteen-hour BBC Thames Television silent film documentary *Hollywood*, produced by Kevin Brownlow and David Gill, and narrated by James Mason. For that she was paid $1,500. That same year she posed in "What Becomes a Legend Most?" print ads draped in a Blackglama fur, sporting dark patent leather gloves, and holding a white carnation. That shot became an iconic symbol of the 1970s.

Gloria was now facing eighty, and her endeavors by necessity had to be carefully chosen. With Bill, she had companionship, as they traveled comfortably about the world, carrying their foods with them in Japanese lunch baskets. "Madame fixes the cold dishes, I do the cooked ones," Bill told a reporter.[20] Their favorite dishes were cooked rice and vegetables, paté, salads, and thermoses of pea and lentil soups.

One thing Gloria always found missing in her life was a man she could lean on. In talking with photographer Ellen Graham, she pointed out, "I want a man who is mentally and physically stronger than I am. I would like someone to say, 'Don't worry,' and take care of me just once. Someone with whom I can have mental intercourse on any subject. I've had everything in life but that."[21] To close friends she would always say Bill was the first man who actually took care of her.

In one interview that year, Gloria quite cleverly stated, "Sometimes it's better for a woman to add years, rather than subtract. That way, at least, someone is almost bound to say how good she looks for her age."[22] Said her friend, writer

Wayne Lawson, "Swanson had a sharp, clearly enunciated, cultivated voice and prided herself on being a grand lady. She was very careful how she presented herself, and was never off her guard."[23]

That October, back in New York, Gloria attended a dedication of the Astoria Studios as a New York Landmark. It was there Gloria had most enjoyed working in pictures, and that evening she was nostalgic and gracious. Young Eastern Airlines executive Christa Venezia and her escort, seated at a table with a major food critic, recalled Gloria: "She was so small, and I remember she was very nice and appreciative when we shook hands."[24] Gloria could now enjoy adulation. She loved the old studio and missed the glory days of the 1920s when she worked there.

Since she was young, Gloria had loved to play and sculpt with clay. Eventually she graduated to molding and bronze casting. In early 1978 she met former Argentine television writer Brian Degas, when he called her regarding her bust sculptures. Inquiring if she would consider giving a one-woman show at a gallery, Degas must have known he was flattering her ego. Her work was minimally artistic, yet when it was shown it sold for top dollar, more for Swanson's name than her creativity. Having attracted the attention of the tall, good-looking, and dangerously enigmatic Degas, Gloria wasted little time in cultivating his friendship.

Degas was quickly installed into the household. Born in October 1935, Degas, the father of two sons, had once been married. Gloria's file cabinets and office suite were sent to the top floor of her building when Degas moved in. Perhaps Degas's biggest draw for Gloria, indeed possibly with all his conquests, was his fading good looks, his accent, and his abundant charm.

One of Gloria's failures was her romanticizing, her need to be the center of her own sensual and commanding universe, which inevitably dimmed her reality. Degas, described as a darling or a demon, depending on whom one talked to, was quite able to romantically fulfill the needs of older women, said one of his former friends. Dirk Benedict was aware of Gloria's short-sightedness: "She could fall prey to people with ulterior motives simply because their manners were so elegant or they were multi-lingual; world travelled."[25]

In late November the sculptures, including a 1964 self-study and a statue of folded hands holding a paper, plus various paintings she had done, were placed on display at the Hamilton Galleries in London. Gloria paid for the exhibition, said Dufty's friend Timothy Rooks. He recalled, "Her sculptures were very nice. Her paintings not so."[26]

Gloria had grandly declared in 1969, "I am not going to write my memoirs. I want to become famous as the one and only who hasn't. Everyone writes their memoirs. I don't want an epitaph on my grave."[27] However, Random House offered her a contract in early 1979 for $500,000, signed on March 6 by Gloria and Random House president Robert L. Bernstein and editorial director Jason Epstein. The advance and all royalties were to be split between Bill and Gloria. To *The New York Times*, Gloria said, "Age, if nothing else, entitles me to set the record straight before I dissolve. I've given my memoirs far more thought than any of my marriages. You can't divorce a book."[28]

For years Gloria had nagged Dufty, "Bill, you must write my book." According to Dirk Benedict, he warned Gloria, "'You can either have the marriage or the book,' telling me he always had to drag the stories out of her and she didn't want to tell the truth."[29] Bill eventually buckled, however, and throughout the year worked on Gloria's memoirs. According to Dufty's later partner Dennis Fairchild, Bill "went to Spain for two weeks, and then when he came back agreed to do the book as a wedding present to her. Gloria then rented a crackerbox-sized apartment about four blocks down from 920 Fifth for Bill to work, and he wrote her book in twelve weeks."[30]

Virginie Glory, Michelle and Robert Amon's twenty-two-year-old daughter, died suddenly on July 7. "Much, much too soon. Much, much too young," wrote Gloria in her memoirs.[31] But Gloria never lingered on tragedy. With Bill down the street writing her life story, she spent hours alone with Degas, who contacted Wayne Lawson with the first hundred pages of Gloria's bio, which began with her birth. Lawson mentioned *Sunset Boulevard* as a possible highlight of her life to start the narrative. Gloria said no. It was the events surrounding her reception in America when *Madame Sans-Gêne* premiered that she recalled as her triumphant moment. And that's how her book began. Dufty would write a chapter a week, and then Lawson would edit the work, oftentimes rewriting whole chapters himself.

In early May 1980 Gloria secretly went to the publisher and added a codicil to the book contract, insisting now that one-third of the proceeds from the sales of the book be handed over to Degas, under an agreement with her new company, Gloria's Way, Inc. With $150,000 already paid out by Random House, the new contract stated that $125,000 would be advanced to Degas upon his signature, and $225,000 would be given to Gloria upon completion of the manuscript. When Dufty found out, he ended their marriage. A man of his word, he completed his writing of her story, then walked out of the apartment and out of the marriage in June.[32]

In January the papers announced the separation, not giving specifics but stating the marriage had "soured several months ago."[33] Many people assumed Dufty was in Gloria's employ or gay, or both, or that Gloria was unfulfilled physically. But that was not the case. "Bill was neither gay nor straight," said Dennis Fairchild. "He was very heterosexual until he fell in love with me."[34] There would be periodic moments of reconciliation between Gloria and Bill, mainly for the press, but the marriage was over.

When the superb documentary *Hollywood* aired in America on PBS, critics raved. Brownlow claimed the documentary was not a history but rather an homage. The history of Hollywood and the history of Gloria Swanson ran parallel. In the film, Adela Rogers St. Johns candidly observed, "Even today, when I think of a movie star I think of Gloria Swanson."[35]

Gloria at the same time told the press about her autobiography, *Swanson on Swanson,* set to be published that fall. "It's the manuscript that's finished and not me. It was a natural delivery," she said about the eighty-year-old act of labor. "Nobody can claim it was premature."[36]

With her marriage falling apart and her sights set on a younger man, Gloria was not in the mood to suffer fools. When *New York Post* columnist Cindy Adams attempted an interview with Gloria at her apartment she wrote candidly:

> It was straight out of a Hollywood scenario. Every single nook in every single room featured one to five fresh flowers.
>
> Strewn hither and yon were leopard rugs, leopard pillows, leopard throws, paintings, photos, mementoes. And whenever there weren't flowers or leopards, there were trophies.
>
> "Don't flatter yourself that my dog likes you," she said, flicking the daschund off my lap. "He likes everyone."
>
> "I'm looking for a Broadway play. Naturally, I'll okay the casting. And make sure you say it that way. Don't put words in my mouth."

"I'm a very direct person. Not temperamental, mind you, but direct.
I don't have time for flatteries. I don't need them. I know if I look well.
Nobody need waste my time telling me."[37]

In March Gloria was honored with a U.S. postage stamp of artwork she created for the United Nations "Decade for Women, 1976–1985," a portrait of the
earth, with a fetus as a continent, hurtling through space called *Woman, Like
Mother Earth, Has an Eternal Rendezvous with Spring*. Along with the stamp
issuance, 1,250 prints of her painting were made available to the buying public,
and Gloria signed every one.

Swanson on Swanson was published the first week of October 1980, and sales
took off. The whole world now knew about Gloria's affair with Joseph P. Kennedy. Random House promoted the book as "unashamedly direct,"[38] and reviews were generous. Malcolm Boyd of the *Los Angeles Times* felt it could have
been better: "Clearly, it needs better pacing, deeper self-examination and better
writing . . . The book is a social history of the first order, offering a phenomenal
panoramic view of Hollywood—place as well as state of mind."[39] But *The New
York Times* said, "Movie stars' memoirs don't get any better than 'Swanson on
Swanson,' a peppery account of a clever and headstrong individual . . . but it isn't
her story that makes her book so sparkling: It's the way that the story is told."[40]

Suddenly, Gloria was a cause célèbre, and the Kennedy family went into damage control mode. After a Barbara Walters *20/20* interview with Gloria, Kennedy's daughter Eunice Shriver, spokesperson for the family and most assuredly
her mother's daughter, openly challenged Gloria's claims. In a written rebuttal
to the network, Shriver proudly stated her mother's forty-five-year marriage
to Kennedy was the happiest part of her life. Rose had spent the time between
her eightieth and ninetieth birthdays writing her own autobiography, published
in 1974, and, said Shriver, "It inspired people everywhere." She added, "Gloria
Swanson's autobiography written at 80 may make her a popular figure. But what
lasting value has her life left us?"[41] Unlike Rose Kennedy, however, Gloria Swanson would not become a footnote in history.

"The Kennedy PR machine vilified her," said Bevan Dufty. "And that took
Gloria by surprise. She blamed Bill for that."[42]

Starting a ten-city book tour, first stop Chicago, Gloria departed New
York on November 10. Later in the year she was feted in England by Foyles

booksellers at a luncheon at the Dorchester Hotel, where she was photographed with actor Peter Sellers. For *Modern Maturity* magazine that year, Gloria spoke with writer Michael J. Bandler about her book and her life, telling him she longed not for her past stardom, but for a "romantic era when people didn't just stand around and take up space at a party without expressing their appreciation." About her youthful beaus, Gloria said:

> They sent you a flower or a note of thanks. There were pebbles at the window, notes of poetry slipped under the door. There was still a certain graciousness in life. The music was romantic. There were flirtations going on all the time across the room at dinner parties, but it wasn't 'Hiya, toots, how about it?' or women proposing to men.
>
> If we went to church, we dressed for it. If we went to a party, we dressed for it. We didn't go in blue jeans, we dressed for the occasion. It was another world. . . .

She finished the interview by telling Bandler, "I don't care how people remember me. I can't change their opinions—they either enjoyed my work or they didn't. And I don't even want a tombstone—people will remember me in their hearts or they won't."[43]

Gloria gave an interview in January to *New York Times* correspondent Carol Lawson, introducing Degas as "her business partner," the man who insisted she write her memoirs. "This is a very persuasive man," giggled Gloria. Degas told Lawson that after Gloria presented her artwork in London, "a few months later, I suggested the book." On and on Degas droned about his importance in Gloria's life and his involvement with her memoirs, stating he drew up the contract with Random House in February 1979. "It was magical. Gloria was not in town and wasn't aware of what was happening. Armed with the grand collage of her life, I gave a 45-minute pitch to Random House. There were no agents, no lawyers . . . I had no memo, not an outline. Nothing. The next day Random House made an official deal. They offered an advance with lots of numbers—in the big sixes. I typed out a letter of agreement, and then I called Gloria."[44]

"I structured it dramatically," Degas continued grandly. "I wanted it to read like a novel. Part of the deal was that Random House would not see the pages beforehand. There was no way to force Madame to write chronologically." He said Random House editor Jason Epstein made "judicious cuts" and yet gave him free rein. "Random House has been fantastic. They gave me the run of the departments. I worked with everything—photos, cover, publicity." However, Degas possibly gave himself away in closing when he remarked that he had the original manuscript and "it will be worth a great deal of money after Gloria dies."[45]

In early 1981 the *New York Post* noted, "Degas confides that the happy couple have a lot in common. Diet conscious Gloria watches over Degas' menu. And clothes conscious Degas takes a great interest in Gloria's wardrobe."[46] "Gloria married William Dufty out of loneliness," wrote one journalist. "Now she's back on talk shows . . . swept up in the thrill of celebrity life again, [and] there is no need for Dufty."[47]

Interviewed in Boston in February 1981, Bill said simply, "The last time I saw my wife was about a week ago. We have had loose arrangements for quite a while."[48] "When the lover [Degas] was traveling, he sent Gloria letters that fluttered her elderly heart," wrote one author. " 'Gloria, darling,' he wrote from a distant city, 'I am flying in a rush to New York and cannot get a moment to say good-bye, but you know how much I love you and how grateful I am for all your kindness.' "[49] Gloria and Degas then flew to Paris on the Concorde for a film festival in Spain on September 24, 1981.

As Gloria's life drew to a close, Michelle remembered, she concentrated more and more on her mortality. "I remember her saying very well that if she ever came back in a second life she would like to be a clinging vine, and one of those women who would say, 'Oh, darling, I don't know how to do anything. Would you mind doing this for me?' But she never would, you see. She was a very feminine woman with a masculine brain."[50]

As 1982 began, Gloria gave an insightful interview to one journalist. "Oh, no, I have no fear of dying: I'm going to have one eye opened," she contemplated. "I think you don't quite know when it's happened. I think you go through a period of limbo, and then—little by little—you can look back on your life . . . I'm very curious." About love and finding one's soul mate, she suggested, "It seems that it is a natural thing to want to find the other half. I think maybe at one time we were one, and we got separated."[51]

Of her six husbands, she said she loved only one desperately. When asked if Henri was her other half, Gloria quietly nodded. If she could go back in time so she and Henri could have stayed together, would she have done anything differently? "No," she replied. Gloria told the *New York Post* of her curious views on death, "We know *nothing!* . . . And I have this great craving to know how it happens, why we're here, what it's all about."[52]

That year Gloria's trusted friend Raymond Daum began archiving her career materials for a sale to the University of Texas at Austin's renowned archive the Harry Ransom Center. She said he had promised her he would archive the collection to give people "an impression of me, my life, and my career. Above all, let them remember me for being not only an actress but someone who had many interests and involvements. And don't let them think I was like Norma in *Sunset Boulevard*. Show them through my papers, pictures, and correspondences what I thought was important." As her memorabilia was leaving her Fifth Avenue apartment, she implored Daum, "My life is going out the door with these boxes. I want you to look after it." And Daum did just that, accompanying the archive to Austin and curating the collection for the next nine years.[53]

By now her lover Brian Degas was very much a part of Gloria's life. "She fell for Degas hook, line and sinker," said Raymond Daum. "She was like a little girl. She would sit on his lap and cuddle and coo and say to me, 'Look at that boy, he could play a leading man.' The whole situation was like a parallel to Norma Desmond, except in this case Degas made the schemer Joe Gillis in *Sunset Boulevard* look like an angel."[54] Daum would also recall, "In the early days Gloria would say to me, 'Look at him—he's gorgeous!' When he walked out of the room she'd say, 'Look at that tush!' . . . He'd call her darling. Oh, yes, you couldn't fool Gloria about many things, but you can fool the heart."[55]

Author Annette Tapert wrote, "Daum discovered that Degas was bilking Swanson out of almost all of the modest fortune she had left and had stolen valuable personal mementos and relevant documents to her career. But Swanson refused to believe Daum or her family when they came to New York to deal with the problem." Gloria told Daum, "This man will give me a new beginning, and a new career."[56] That August 8, Gloria and an unidentified escort attended the premiere of Paul Mazursky's *The Tempest* at Loew's Tower East in New York and the after-party held aboard the *Peking*, permanently docked at South Street Seaport in Lower Manhattan.

In July 1982 Gloria attended a performance by Charlie Chaplin imitator Tommy Breslin at Manhattan's cabaret/musical club Caroline's. Breslin coaxed her into starring in a musical play by him and his collaborator Michael Owen in hopes of presenting it on Broadway. There was also talk of turning *Queen Kelly* into an opera. (Gloria always longed to be an opera diva.) She also wanted to do the Broadway play *Rainbow Rider* (possibly the Breslin-Owen project), but it never got past the talk stage. In fact, Gloria was becoming more and more fatigued as 1983 began.

Bill and Gloria had a joint bank account in which they pooled their incomes from *Sugar Blues* and *Swanson on Swanson*. According to one source, Gloria signed away her account to a particular individual whom she trusted. He cleaned her out and disappeared within days. Another assertion said two gay men from Greenwich Village had approached Gloria to star her in a cabaret act they wanted to produce. She took dance lessons and sang their music and laughed with them, which apparently upset Degas, and there was a breakup.[57]

But the incident that most likely put an end to Gloria's relationship with Degas was the one that broke Gloria's heart. "The bubble burst when two producers who'd been negotiating with Degas for Swanson to star in a Broadway show taped their conversations with him in which he spoke disparagingly of her," wrote Tapert. Confirmed Daum, "When they played the tapes for Gloria, she finally realized she'd been betrayed."[58] Devastated, she wept to Daum, "You warned me. All along I was a fool."[59]

"She had just returned from Portugal," recalled Dirk Benedict. "Bill was upset with the people around her. People stole from her . . . Bill said she went nuts when these people took her place in Portugal. He pleaded with her to let it go. She simply could not accept her judgment was wrong about another man."[60] Afterward Gloria spent days in her apartment, alone with her thoughts. Her granddaughter Brooke said, "She'd stay up all night and read to ten, eleven, twelve in the morning and I know she would wander around her apartment and she just never would say 'I was really lonely last night, or will you come visit me?' She just always carried on as if life was really O.K."[61]

On March 20, 1983, Gloria complained of chest pains and was taken to the New York Hospital–Cornell Medical Center for treatment for what her friend Earl Blackwell advised the press was a minor heart attack. On March 21 she suffered another. Her attending physician was Walter Strauser. She then contracted what was thought to be pneumonia. Gloria had always feared doctors operating on her. "If they cut me, I'm going to die," she pleaded when alert.[62]

Degas had returned, telling the press he was Gloria's business manager. Jennings Parrott in the *Los Angeles Times*, in fact, referred to him as Gloria's "husband and business manager."[63]

Gloria's two daughters, alerted by Daum, insisted Degas be barred from entering their mother's room. Gloria then suffered a paralyzing stroke, and the doctors chose to operate to aid her breathing. Brooke arrived shortly before the procedure. Gloria was given the dreaded tracheotomy. When she came to after surgery, she found the tubes in her throat. She had been cut.

Gloria Swanson died of a fatal heart attack twenty minutes later at 4:45 A.M. on Monday, April 4, 1983.[64]

30

Epilogue

For some time Gloria had been fond of *Photoplay* magazine editor James Quirk's remark at the time of Mabel Normand's death in 1930: "She has gone home to the Great Heart that understands all." Gloria liked that phrase. "For some of the things I have done, that is what I shall need," she chuckled in private. "Understanding—laced with lots of compassion."[1] Yet publicly she preferred to say, "When I die, my epitaph should read: She Paid the Bills. That's the story of my life."

Gloria's obituaries were long and respectful, rehashing her lengthy life and career, her marriages and her affairs. *The New York Times* wrote upon her death, "Gloria Swanson . . . was young when the movies were young, and has to be mentioned in the same breath with Douglas Fairbanks, Charlie Chaplin, Mary Pickford, Rudolph Valentino. Unlike her peers, however, she eclipsed the successes of her youth with one remarkable performance in middle age." The article was titled "The Greatest Star of Them All."[2]

Her daughter Gloria remembered, "The one word my mother could not stand was 'glamour.' She used to say, 'What does that mean?' And yet, if ever there was a glamorous person it was her."[3] "Gloria Swanson was indisputably the epitome of the 1920s era," said former *Los Angeles Times* writer Kevin Thomas in 2011. "She was a legend during her lifetime and remained a legend until the day she died."[4]

"Ms. Swanson meant more to me, personally and professionally, than any other person I met in the business," wrote Dirk Benedict. "The degree and way in which she befriended this country boy from Montana, meant more to me than I was ever capable of telling her. Bill [Dufty], who outlived her by 20 years, understood. But he said she 'knew' how much she meant to me."[5]

Gloria's service was held at the E. Willis Scott Funeral Home in the Bronx. It was closed to the public. In her will she specified there be "no public funeral or display of any sort" and insisted the service be just for family members. A private family memorial was planned later. In lieu of flowers, the family requested financial contributions be made to the Salvation Army's Covenant House in New York. On April 5 Swanson's body was cremated and inurned at the Church of Heavenly Rest, in Manhattan. Her ashes lie in a columbarium in the basement of the church on the left side of the wall toward the back of the room. Her marker reads simply "Gloria May Josephine Swanson 1899–1983."

William Dufty avoided the aftermath of Gloria's death and had no involvement in settling her estate. He sequestered himself in his apartment a few blocks from Gloria's on Fifth Avenue until it was all over with. Dirk Benedict wrote, "Bill stayed away from Gloria's funeral. I know he was very upset as to how it went down . . . He told me the whole story of the funeral . . . It horrified me."[6] Benedict did not elaborate.

One report estimated her estate at just over $1,440,000, but in fact it came to just over $500,000. Her children and grandchildren were the benefactors. Columnist Shirley Eder quoted Dufty in May, "We started out with a premarital agreement. Considering her age . . . and other things, I insisted on that condition before we wed. It's been that way since 1975 . . . I've put all my life . . . [into] trying to get rid of things."[7] After Gloria's death Dufty had planned to move to Japan, but instead he returned to Michigan to care for his ailing mother until her death in the late 1980s. Dufty had met young Dennis Fairchild around 1976 in New York at one of his book signings. Dufty's mother lived right down the street from Fairchild's office in Michigan.

Dennis was an astrologist, and Bill would recall late in life, "Gloria was big into astrology. She would not make a move without consulting an astrologer in Beverly Hills. She wouldn't consider buying a house or signing a book contract."[8] Dennis recalled he personally spoke to Gloria perhaps three or four times over the telephone the last couple of years of her life. "She didn't like me. And I didn't like her."[9]

"I called him 'Poppa' and he called me 'Sonny Boy,' or 'my son the writer,'"
Benedict would later write about Dufty. "I thought I was maybe the kind of son
he never had . . . and of course was always, early on, aware that he was God's
Gift to me to be the Father-Mentor I lost."[10] In 1980, Dufty was diagnosed with
lung cancer and given a prognosis of only two years to live. He survived another twenty, passing away in Dennis's arms under hospice care at their home
on June 28, 2002. He was eighty-six years old. His ashes are buried atop his
grandfather's grave in Saginaw, Michigan.

Daughter Gloria Somborn Anderson Daly lived in New York for some time
after her mother's death. She was active in St. James Parish and was a chaplain's
assistant at Memorial-Sloane Kettering Hospital. She eventually returned to California, settling in Pebble Beach. In her later years she volunteered her time to aid
the Hospice of Carmel, California, and the Community Hospital of Monterey
Peninsula. She served on the board of trustees at All Saints Episcopal Day School
and was on the vestry of All Saints Church in Carmel. She died of brain cancer
on December 28, 2000, survived by her second husband of thirty-two years, Wilfrid Daly, three children, two grandchildren, and her sister Michelle.

Brian Degas disappeared from view in America after Gloria's death and lived
in England for some time before moving to South America. He had written an
unpublished piece of fiction under the pseudonym Cecelta Brown, called *Woman
Plus Woman*, which he had wanted Gloria to promote. Degas was but a moment
of Swanson's life, and represented the attributes that countless dozens of other
men had possessed and attracted Gloria. Had she been younger, healthier, and
stronger, his subsequent behavior would have excluded him from her life quicker
than most.

After her death there were several auctions of Gloria's personal belongings.
The first of five was held in September 1983 at the William Doyle Galleries in
New York, and consisted of primarily her household furnishings and decorations, including Venetian-style chairs and her Louis XV and XVI pieces—"much
of it custom-scaled to her diminutive 5-foot frame," erroneously reported the
Boston Globe.[11] Also in this auction were porcelain objects, including a Napole-
onic Capodimonte tea service, marked with an *N* in a wreath, and some of her
books (value realized, $35,000).

The "Important Estate Jewelry" auction took place on September 21 ($16,000
realized). The "Fashion Collection and Accessories" on September 22 included

150 outfits (Givenchy, Bill Blass, Adolfo, etc.), 150 hats, 44 pairs of size 6 shoes, 40 pairs of gloves, 50 handbags, and 40 scarves ($92,700 taken in). Later that day was the auction of "Cinematic, Theatrical and Personal Memorabilia" (final take $71,000); Gloria's scarf from the last scene of *Sunset Boulevard* sold for $5,750. "18th-Century English and Continental Furniture" were sold on October 19, and "Books, Manuscripts, Autographs and Prints" on December 8.

Gloria's sable coat brought in $3,900, and her black fox cape $2,600, barely achieving their estimated auction costs. Along with her own were, strangely, items of men's clothing. They were Bill's, which he had simply left behind when they separated, as well as items gifted him by John Lennon and Yoko Ono.[12] Her apartment, the maisonette with garden on Fifth Avenue, was placed on the block as well at $1.2 million (which would amount to over twice that at today's rate).

Gloria's large book collection was sold to the Gotham Book Mart in New York. Most of the volumes dealt with health and nutrition. On June 9–10, 1995, Manhattan's Sotheby's on York Avenue auctioned off another one of Gloria's chantilly scarves, which she had worn in *Sunset Boulevard*.[13] At Christie's at Rockefeller Plaza on August 27, 2004, Gloria's pair of diamond ear clips designed by Paul Flato was auctioned off at an estimated value of $25,000–$35,000.

In September 1985 a restored print of *Queen Kelly* was shown theatrically in New York. Snippets of footage had kept showing up over the years, including that of Kelly in the African bordello, discovered in 1963. Wrote historian Axel Madsen, "Gloria's print was in mint condition—perhaps the finest preserved film from the silent era." Shown for the first time in theaters in New York, Los Angeles, and Paris in the fall of 1985, it was painstakingly restored to ninety-six minutes, incorporating stills, explanations, and outtakes, and with Adolph Tandler's period score. The restoration "revealed all of von Stroheim's barbaric splendor and reckless flamboyance, his wry sexual fetishism, and his fascinations with aristocratic excess."[14] The print, now available on Kino DVD, removed Gloria's added 1931 sequences, and supplemented lost footage with production stills.

Wrote the magazine *Le Monde*, "Even incomplete, *Queen Kelly* can radically question today's movies. The point is not to go back fifty years, of course, but to measure what we have lost, even if it entails reinventing everything."[15] Stephen Harvey of the *New York Times* mused, "Viewed now, *Queen Kelly* is a poignant reminder of just what the screen was abandoning in the headlong rush toward sound . . . The resurrected *Queen Kelly* is tantalizing proof that the loony Norma Desmond of *Sunset Boulevard* had a point after all—in the end, the coming of sound may have been small compensation for the loss of all that magnificent fury."[16]

During the last years of her life Gloria expressed sadness and horror that there were no known existing prints of two of her most cherished pictures, *Beyond the Rocks* and *Madame Sans-Gêne*. A poorly preserved trailer of *Madame Sans-Gêne* does exist, but the complete picture seems to be lost, perhaps someday to emerge from some private collection. *Beyond the Rocks,* Swanson and Valentino together, was rescued from obscurity in 2005. Discovered by the Nederlands Filmmuseum, the new painstakingly restored print, spearheaded by Milestone Films head Dennis Doros, features a brilliant musical score by Dutch composer Henny Vrieten and is available on Milestone DVD.

In 1960 theatrical producer Harold Prince had imagined the perfect reincarnation of Norma Desmond for a musical version of *Sunset Boulevard*. "I had what I still think is a marvelous idea," he stated in 1991 as he reworked the property with Andrew Lloyd Webber. "And that was to star Jeanette MacDonald as Norma Desmond and Nelson Eddy as Max, her former co-star [*sic*] who had become her chauffeur." With his partner Robert Griffith, Prince met with MacDonald in December 1960 to discuss the project. Intrigued with the idea, and after performing a dead-on impression of Norma Desmond, MacDonald asked what the play would be called. "I replied," he said, "*The Iron Butterfly*. Rather coldly she replied, 'That is what *some* people in Hollywood call me.' "[17]

In the early 1960s Stephen Sondheim outlined a musical stage adaptation of *Sunset Boulevard* and actually wrote the opening sequence with librettist Burt Shevelove. At a party he met Billy Wilder and discussed the project with him. Wilder said *Sunset Boulevard* could not be developed as a musical but would have to be an opera, as Norma was a movie queen. Andrew Lloyd Webber saw the film *Sunset Boulevard* in the 1970s and wrote a title song for his vision, fragments of which were incorporated in the film *Gumshoe* (Columbia–Warner Bros., 1971). He spoke with Prince, who now owned the theatrical rights to the film, about a sequence of Norma returning to Paramount, but did no further work on his idea until after 1989 and the debut of his play *Aspects of Love*.

In 1991 Lloyd Webber asked Amy Powers to compose lyrics for his projected musical *Sunset Boulevard*. Don Black was brought in to work with Powers, and the two created a version that was performed at Lloyd Webber's Sydmonton Festival, with Ria Jones as Norma. A revised version, with libretto now by Black and Christopher Hampton, played at the 1992 Sydmonton Festival with Patti LuPone as Norma and was hugely successful. Incorporating several tunes he had written with Tim Rice for their short musical *Cricket* in 1986, Lloyd Webber opened *Sunset Boulevard* in London's West End at the Adelphi Theater, starring LuPone, on July 12, 1993. The Los Angeles version opened at Century City's Shubert Theater on December 9, 1993, with Glenn Close, and eventually bowed on Broadway at the Minskoff Theater on November 17, 1994, also with Close, where it ran 977 performances.

When *The New York Times* ran a full-page article by Ingrid Sischy on September 11, 1994, called "Welcome to 10086 Sunset Boulevard," few recalled Gloria's attempted *Boulevard*. Raymond Daum wrote the *Los Angeles Times* advising them Gloria had tried in vain to mount a musical production of the film in the 1950s. When she failed, Gloria told him, "When I go, my hope is that Norma will one day be played on stage as a musical by a Met opera diva, someone who is not only a high-voltage opera star but a great actress as well."[18]

Talent manager and press agent Alan Eichler contacted Dickson Hughes in the fall of 1993 about presenting a musical stage version of his and Stapley's aborted project *Boulevard*. Hughes was still working in musical theater after conducting five years at the Sacramento Civic Opera and touring South America and the United States. Eichler met with Hughes, hoping to get a jump on the Broadway opening of Lloyd Webber's *Sunset Boulevard*. What Hughes produced was *Swanson on Sunset*.

Swanson on Sunset was a retelling of the Swanson saga as seen through Hughes's eyes, incorporating the music from his and Stapley's collaboration. It opened in December 1994, in workshop, and ran a total of six weeks. Stapley, now an American citizen and author, was brought into the mix at the eleventh hour, his first connection with Hughes in decades. They remained amicable throughout the run.

Presented at the Hollywood Cinegrill in the historic Hollywood Roosevelt Hotel, site of the first Academy Awards dinner in May 1929, *Swanson on Sunset— A Musical Memoir* was a three-character play staged by director Luke Yankee, son of *Butterflies Are Free*'s original star Eileen Heckart. It featured the sixty-some-year-old Hughes narrating, playing music at a piano, and singing as himself *and* as himself as a young man in the 1950s. Stapley was portrayed by twenty-five-year-old Julliard School of Music graduate Richard Leibell. Swanson was played by actress Laurie Franks. *Swanson on Sunset* opened with the film clip of the famous "Those Wonderful People Out There in the Dark" number taped from *The Steve Allen Show* projected onto a screen. It enjoyed a brief run. Unfortunately, the Andrew Lloyd Webber *Sunset Boulevard* juggernaut totally overshadowed the small production. Hughes died on June 18, 2005. Stapley passed away in June 2010.

Gloria Swanson the woman is often difficult to define. Her family and friends give telling insights. "She wasn't sentimental," recalled granddaughter Brooke Anderson Young. "She was very current thinking . . . She was not remorseful . . . She was curious."[19] "She was incapable of being untrue to her beliefs about how one should live one's life," wrote Dirk Benedict. "From etiquette, to morals, to diet, to wardrobe, to romance, to language. Just completely uncompromising. She had a kind of . . . what's the word, not 'warrior' mentality; but perhaps 'rebel.' Though she was never difficult for the sake of being difficult, but simply because she could not stand, could not *stand* people who were lazy about life."[20]

With Swanson's passing came the end of an era. It is sad so few people alive today remember her from her glory days of the 1920s, and what an impact she made on not only moviegoers but on our very culture. "She lived for her fans and her public," recalled Raymond Daum. "Even in her later years she would never admit openly how much she cared about fans and the letters they sent. Up until her death, the fan mail continued to come in, diminished in numbers only slightly after sixty years and six generations of new fans."[21] As Norma Desmond said in *Sunset Boulevard*, "Stars are ageless. No one ever leaves a star."

Sunset Boulevard remains the cornerstone of Gloria Swanson's amazing career, so closely identified with it was she. Sadly, she knew why. "I had played the part too well," she sighed.[22] In the final analysis, Norma Desmond remains her most iconic film portrayal. Yet her long, diverse life was magical, mystical, and remarkably full. And she left an indelible impression on anyone and everyone she came in contact with. Truly, before Hollywood created stars, there were stars who created Hollywood. As Max Von Mayerling reminded Joe Gillis:

"Madame was the greatest star of them all."

Notes

ABBREVIATIONS

AMPAS The Academy of Motion Picture Arts and Sciences, Fairbanks Center for Motion Picture Study, Los Angeles, California
HRC The Harry Ransom Center, University of Texas at Austin
MOMA Museum of Modern Art, New York
NYPL The New York City Public Library, Library for the Performing Arts, Lincoln Center
WHS Wisconsin Historical Center, Madison, Wisconsin

INTRODUCTION

1. Colleen Moore, *Silent Star* (New York: Doubleday, 1968), 103–4, quoting Richard Whalen, *The Founding Father: The Story of Joseph P. Kennedy.*
2. Stuart Oderman, "Gloria Swanson," *Films in Review,* March 1988.
3. Moore, *Silent Star,* 104.
4. Carol Taylor, "Diet of Surprises Keeps Gloria Swanson Slim at 60," *New York World-Telegram,* December 7, 1960.
5. Richard Lamparski, *Manhattan Diary* (Albany, GA: BearManor Media, 2006), 153.
6. Hedda Hopper Collection, AMPAS.
7. Cecil B. DeMille, *A&E Biography,* "The Greatest Star," July 29, 1997.
8. Jeanine Basinger, *Silent Stars* (New York: Alfred A. Knopf, 1999), 237, quoting Richard Koszarski, *An Evening's Entertainment.*

9. Joe Franklin, *Classics of the Silent Screen* (New York: Citadel, 1959), 227.

10. David Chierichetti, "Gloria Swanson Today," *Film Fan Monthly*, February 1975.

11. Andrew Wilson, "Growing Up with Norma Desmond," *Observer* (U.K.), March 9, 2003.

12. Michelle Farmer (Amon), "The Swanson Story," *Los Angeles Times*, August 6, 1950.

13. Brooke Anderson Young, "Thoughts on Gloria Swanson," *Beyond the Rocks* DVD press-book, 2005.

14. Dirk Benedict, e-mail to author, September 23, 2011.

15. Wilson, "Growing Up with Norma Desmond," *Observer* (U.K.), March 9, 2003.

16. Cari Beauchamp, *Joseph P. Kennedy Presents: His Hollywood Years* (New York: Alfred A. Knopf, 2009), 277.

17. Young, "Thoughts on Gloria Swanson," *Beyond the Rocks* DVD pressbook.

1. CHICAGO

1. Dorothy B. Daniels, "An Ex-Secretary Tells on Gloria Swanson," incomplete article, n.d., WHS.

2. Gloria Swanson, *Swanson on Swanson* (New York: Random House, 1980), 12.

3. The family name is sometimes referenced Svensson, Svenson, or Swensson, which possibly is the original spelling. However, first and last names of immigrants were often Anglicized upon arrival in America. According to the 12th U.S. National Census Survey conducted in June 1900, Jons's name was recorded as John, last name spelled Swanson.

4. Her last name is spelled Klanowsky in the 1900 census.

5. Today a three-story corner brownstone located at 341 Grace Street is recognized as Gloria's birthplace. However, the 1900 census says otherwise. Gloria refers to it as her birthplace, probably because it was a much nicer dwelling than the one on Seminary Avenue. Addie and Gloria lived on Grace Street on the second floor in 1915.

6. There is no official birth record for Gloria Swanson. The Cook County Vital Records and the Illinois Vital Records offices were unable to supply the author with a valid birth certificate. However, the 1900 census sheds valuable light on the facts. The first twelve U.S. Censuses were fraught with minor spelling errors, and because they were written with pencil on rough parchment paper, they were often smudged. The 1900 census clearly gives the proper names and birth years for Joseph Swanson and his wife Adeline Klanowsky (with a *y*), and it lists their daughter "Glory" (which she was called) as "1 and ½" years old. The year written on the document *appears* to be 1897. Closer examination shows that the date is smudged. It is indeed 1899.

7. Michelle Farmer Amon, *A&E Biography*, "The Greatest Star," July 29, 1997.

8. Larry Carr, *Four Fabulous Faces* (New York: Galahad, 1970), 16.

9. "Little Glory's Copy Book," n.d., NYPL.

10. Gladys Hall, "Discoveries About Myself," as told to by Gloria Swanson, n.d., AMPAS.

11. Hall, "Discoveries About Myself."

12. Gloria Swanson, "There Is No Formula for Success," unknown publication, n.d., WHS.

13. Gloria Somborn Anderson Daly, *A&E Biography,* "The Greatest Star," July 29, 1997.

14. Tallmer, "As Gloria Was Saying," *New York Post,* September 11, 1971.

15. Carr, *Four Fabulous Faces,* 16.

16. "Gloria Swanson Wire Recording," 1955, *Beyond the Rocks* DVD (Milestone Cinematique, 2005).

17. Hall, "Discoveries About Myself."

2. ESSANAY

1. Swanson, *Swanson on Swanson,* 25.

2. Ibid., 28.

3. It is virtually impossible to completely compile Gloria Swanson's early film work with Essanay. In their Bushman biography, *Francis X. Bushman: A Biography and Filmography* (Jefferson, NC: MacFarland, 1998), Richard J. Maturi and Mary Buckingham Maturi state Gloria appeared in several Francis X. Bushman–Beverly Bayne pictures for the company from the summer of 1914 until June 1915. Those known Bushman-Bayne pictures were *The Countess, His Stolen Fortune, One Wonderful Night, The Masked Wrestler, Under Royal Patronage, The Private Officer, The Prince Party, Scars of Possession, Every Inch a King, The Fable of the Bush League Lover Who Failed to Qualify, Any Woman's Choice, Thirteen Down, The Accounting, Thirty, Graustark,* and *Providence and Mrs. Urmy.* Swanson also appeared as an extra or in bits in several other films at the studio during that period. These appearances are difficult to verify because most of these pictures are lost, the negatives destroyed in a studio fire in 1916. According to the *Los Angeles Times* (September 3, 1982), Gloria made her film debut in *Ladies' World* for Essanay. No picture of that era exists with that title. However, the Bushman-Bayne pictures *The Plum Tree* (September 1914) and *In the Glare of the Headlights* (October 1914) were adapted from short stories that appeared in *Ladies' World* magazine. Yet another Bushman-Bayne film, *The Great Silence* (March 20, 1915), was released "in conjunction with *The Ladies' World* as a prize mystery drama" (Maturi and Maturi, *Bushman,* 1998, 155). This is questionable as Swanson had already received her first screen billing in January. In her autobiography, Swanson is careful to make light of her early extra work, not offering up most film titles, avoiding emphasis of her status at the studio, and generally confusing her readers. She mentions she was paired with an older actor as extras in a lush party scene, directed by a "Mr. Webster." Essanay's resident director Harry (Henry) McRae Webster directed the following two films during Swanson's tenure with the studio: *The Devil's Signature,* starring Beverly Bayne, released September 11, 1914, and *Victory of Virtue,* with Gerda Holmes, released September 1915.

4. Swanson, *Swanson on Swanson,* 30. Gloria always claimed she never wanted to be a film actress. Her sights, she often repeated, were set on singing on the stage. "Probably the reason I wanted to be an opera star was because I heard Gallicuchi in the park, Lincoln Park," she said on page 49 of her unpublished 1951 autobiography transcripts (HRC). Whatever career she professed she yearned for, film acting nonetheless afforded her the attention she craved.

5. Lon Davis and Debra Davis, *King of the Movies: Francis X. Bushman* (Albany, GA: Bear-Manor Media, 2009), 65.

6. Swanson, *Swanson on Swanson,* 36.

7. Samantha Barbas, *The First Lady of Hollywood: A Biography of Louella Parsons* (Berkeley: University of California Press, 2005), 32.

8. Gilbert M. Anderson, as "Broncho Billy," had been a highly successful cowboy star since Edwin S. Porter's 1903 New Jersey–lensed western classic, *The Great Train Robbery.* He successfully ran the Los Angeles studio, grinding out a short western every week for 376 weeks. Also a brilliant businessman, it was he who introduced Bell to Howell.

9. Barbas, *The First Lady of Hollywood,* 36.

10. Barbas, *The First Lady of Hollywood,* 34.

11. Lawrence J. Quirk, *The Films of Gloria Swanson* (Secaucus, NJ: Citadel, 1984), 44.

12. Swanson, *Swanson on Swanson,* 36.

13. Swanson, *Swanson on Swanson,* 40.

14. Stanley Frank, "Grandma Gloria Swanson Comes Back," *Saturday Evening Post,* July 22, 1950.

15. Charles Chaplin, *My Autobiography* (New York: Simon & Schuster, 1964), 166.

16. Antoni Gronowicz, *Garbo: Her Story* (New York: Simon & Schuster, 1990), 164.

17. Gerald D. McDonald, Michael Conway, and Mark Ricci, *The Films of Charlie Chaplin* (New York: Bonanza, 1965), 82.

18. Swanson, *Swanson on Swanson,* 39.

19. Swanson, *Swanson on Swanson,* 50.

20. Swanson, *Swanson on Swanson,* 41.

21. Quirk, *The Films of Gloria Swanson,* 44.

3. SENNETT

1. James Robert Parish and John L. Bowers, *The Golden Era: MGM Stock Company* (New Rochelle, NY: Arlington House, 1975), 78.

2. Parish and Bowers, *The Golden Era: MGM Stock Company,* 79.

3. Parish and Bowers, *The Golden Era: MGM Stock Company,* 79.

4. Daniels, "An Ex-Secretary Tells on Gloria Swanson."

5. *Screen Book,* untitled article, n.d., WHS.

6. King Vidor, "Hollywood 1915: Reminiscence of a Simple Time," *Los Angeles Times*, August 31, 1980.

7. Adela Rogers St. Johns, "Madame la Marquise: The Saga of Hollywood's Hectic Cinderella," *Liberty*, November 30, 1929.

8. *Screen Book*, untitled article, n.d., WHS.

9. Swanson, *Swanson on Swanson*, 63.

10. Swanson, *Swanson on Swanson*, 11.

11. Simon Louvish, *Keystone: The Life and Clowns of Mack Sennett* (New York: Faber & Faber, 2003), 126.

12. Tony Bilbow and John Gau, *Lights! Camera! Action! A Century of Cinema* (Berkeley: University of California Press, 1995), 142.

13. Mack Sennett, *King of Comedy* (San Francisco: Mercury House, 1990), 171.

14. "Comedy King Was a Blacksmith," *New York Times*, April 25, 1926.

15. Daniels, "An Ex-Secretary Tells on Gloria Swanson."

16. Swanson, *Swanson on Swanson*, 66.

17. *A&E Biography*, "The Greatest Star."

18. Quirk, *The Films of Gloria Swanson*, 51.

19. Richard Hudson and Raymond Lee, *Gloria Swanson* (New York: Castle Books, 1970), 11.

20. Swanson, *Swanson on Swanson*, 51.

21. Barry Paris, *Louise Brooks* (New York: Alfred A. Knopf, 1989), 15.

22. Quirk, *The Films of Gloria Swanson*, 49.

23. Quirk, *The Films of Gloria Swanson*, 53.

24. Harry Carr, "The Changing of Gloria," *Motion Picture Classic*, n.d., WHS.

25. Swanson, *Swanson on Swanson*, 64.

26. In *The Films of Gloria Swanson*, Lawrence J. Quirk summarizes this film with a completely different synopsis, apparently to explain the set of "stills" used in this section that feature Gloria and Bobby in fencing clothes and situations, even mentioning how the film might have gotten its title, with an anecdote about Bobby Vernon's costume. In actuality the stills were from a newsreel promotional short made on the Sennett lot, with Gloria joining in mayhem with the Sennett Bathing Beauties. As for *The Nick of Time Baby*, it is unfortunately a lost film. Utilizing contemporary reviews from 1916, this author has given a proper synopsis.

27. *Manitoba Free Press*, Winnipeg, Canada, April 14, 1917.

28. *San Antonio Light*, San Antonio, Texas, April 8, 1917.

29. Grace Kingsley, "Studio," *Los Angeles Times*, February 11, 1917.

30. James Robert Parish and Gregory W. Mank, *Hollywood Reliables* (Westport, CT: Arlington House, 1980), 49.

31. Swanson, *Swanson on Swanson*, 66.

32. Oderman, "Gloria Swanson."

4. TRIANGLE

1. Louvish, *Keystone*, 163.

2. Sennett, *King of Comedy*, photo page.

3. Swanson, *Swanson on Swanson*, 78.

4. Swanson, *Swanson on Swanson*, 79.

5. Betty Harper Fussell, *Mabel: The Life of Mabel Normand* (Pompton Plains, NJ: Limelight, 1992), 92.

6. Sennett, *King of Comedy*, 173.

7. Quirk, *The Films of Gloria Swanson*, 64.

8. Kevin Brownlow, *The Parade's Gone By* (New York: Alfred A. Knopf, 1969), 372.

9. Swanson, *Swanson on Swanson*, 81.

10. In her autobiography, Gloria dates this as the day after America entered the war in Europe in April 1917. This is obviously incorrect. It was the fall of 1917.

11. Gloria wrote a rather fanciful tale in her autobiography about a hat she had once worn; Wally had given the same hat to one of his girlfriends, and the plot of the short film she was set to do with Bobby Vernon was about the same thing. Speaking to Kevin Brownlow in the early 1960s, Gloria said she had *wanted* the expensive green suit with the squirrel collar in the store window, but she could not afford it. By the early 1970s, the tale had changed—and now it was Sennett who had bribed her with the suit to get her to come back after her salary dispute. In her 1980 memoirs she had actually bought that green suit with her last dime. Such discrepancies abound in Swanson's autobiography, simply because they make for a better story or they shine a more favorable or sympathetic light in her direction. Early or original interviews are usually more truthful.

12. Jack Conway's greatest directorial fame would come in the 1930s after signing with MGM as silent films were dying out. He directed such motion picture classics as *Viva Villa!* (1934), starring Wallace Beery, *A Tale of Two Cities* (1935), and the more memorable pictures teaming Clark Gable and Jean Harlow. His second marriage, in 1926, was to Virginia Bushman, daughter of Francis X. Bushman. Conway died in 1952.

13. Swanson, *Swanson on Swanson*, 86.

14. Swanson, *Swanson on Swanson*, 86.

15. Gary Chapman, *The Delectable Dollies: The Dolly Sisters, Icons of the Jazz Age* (Gloucester, England: Sutton, 2006), 52.

16. A former film actor, as a director Frank Borzage specialized in romanticized films, such as *Seventh Heaven* (1927), for which he would win the first of two Best Director Oscars, *Street Angel* (1928), and *The River* (1929), all for Fox. His career would arguably peak after his second Best Director Oscar for *Bad Girl* (1931) and his brilliant *Three Comrades* (1938) and *The Mortal Storm* (1940), both for MGM and both starring Margaret Sullavan.

17. "Mark," *Variety*, April 26, 1918.

18. Carr, *Four Fabulous Faces*, 42.

19. Swanson, *Swanson on Swanson,* 91.

20. "Ibog," *Variety,* May 17, 1918.

21. Quirk, *The Films of Gloria Swanson,* 66.

22. *Nevada State Journal,* June 23, 1918.

23. "Old Film Days and New," *New York Times,* February 24, 1929.

24. Swanson, *Swanson on Swanson,* 93.

25. In a 1971 interview, Gloria professed mistakes she had made and recalled, "When I refused, at 17, to make a certain De Mille [*sic*] picture . . . I was made to go back to Triangle. I thought I would kill myself. What had I *done*?" Jerry Tallmer, "As Gloria Was Saying," *New York Post,* September 11, 1971.

26. "Screen," *Los Angeles Times,* June 23, 1918.

27. Quirk, *The Films of Gloria Swanson,* 70.

28. Quirk, *The Films of Gloria Swanson,* 68.

29. James Robert Parish, *The Paramount Pretties* (New Rochelle, NY: Arlington House, 1972), 19.

30. *Variety,* July 12, 1918.

31. *Variety,* July 12, 1918.

32. Swanson, *Swanson on Swanson,* 96.

33. *Variety,* August 30, 1918.

34. Swanson, *Swanson on Swanson,* 97.

35. St. Johns, "Madame la Marquise: The Saga of Hollywood's Hectic Cinderella," *Liberty,* November 30, 1929.

36. Parish, *The Paramount Pretties,* 19.

37. *Variety,* September 13, 1918.

38. Quirk, *The Films of Gloria Swanson,* 71.

39. *Variety,* January 10, 1919.

40. "Fred," *Variety,* December 27, 1918.

41. Swanson, *Swanson on Swanson,* 95.

42. Swanson, *Swanson on Swanson,* 52.

43. Henry Wales, "Gloria's Honeymoon Here," *Los Angeles Times,* January 29, 1925.

44. Parish, Mank, *The Hollywood Reliables,* 49.

45. Garson Kanin, *Together Again! Stories of the Great Hollywood Teams* (Garden City, NY: Doubleday, 1981), 100.

46. By the end of 1918, Triangle went up for sale and was eventually purchased by Samuel Goldwyn for his Goldwyn Pictures Corporation, which later became Metro-Goldwyn-Mayer.

47. Cecil B. DeMille, *The Autobiography of Cecil B. DeMille* (Englewood Cliffs, NJ: Prentice-Hall, 1959), 219–20.

48. Scott Eyman, *Empire of Dreams: The Epic Life of Cecil B. DeMille* (New York: Simon & Schuster, 2010), 150.

5. DEMILLE

1. The family name was originally spelled as two words, de Mille. But Cecil B. capitalized the *D* for his professional name and made it one word. His older brother, the director William C. deMille (1878–1955), also made one word out of the name. William's daughter, famed choreographer Agnes de Mille (1905–93), left it as it was.

2. Anne Edwards, *The DeMilles: An American Family* (New York: Harry N. Abrams, 1988), 93.

3. Swanson, *Swanson on Swanson*, 100.

4. Swanson, *Swanson on Swanson*, 100.

5. Swanson, *Swanson on Swanson*, 102.

6. Benjamin B. Hampton, *The History of the American Film Industry from Its Beginnings to 1931* (New York: Dover, 1970), 221.

7. Basinger, *Silent Stars*, 208–9.

8. Quirk, *The Films of Gloria Swanson*, 23.

9. *Variety*, February 7, 1919.

10. *Chicago Daily Tribune*, February 1, 1919.

11. *Motion Picture*, May 1919.

12. Swanson, *Swanson on Swanson*, 106.

13. "Jolo," *Variety*, May 2, 1919.

14. *New York Times*, April 28, 1919.

15. Quirk, *The Films of Gloria Swanson*, 78.

16. David Chierichetti, *Mitchell Leisen, Hollywood Director* (Los Angeles: Photoventures Press, 1995), 22.

17. Swanson, *Swanson on Swanson*, 120.

18. Swanson, *Swanson on Swanson*, 122.

19. DeMille, *The Autobiography of Cecil B. DeMille*, 222.

20. Gabe Essoe and Raymond Lee, *DeMille: The Man and His Pictures* (New York: Castle Books, 1970), 68.

21. David Chierichetti, *Edith Head: The Life and Times of Hollywood's Celebrated Costume Designer* (New York: HarperCollins, 2004), 14.

22. Chierichetti, *Edith Head*, 14.

23. Edwards, *The DeMilles*, 86.

24. Robert S. Birchard, *Cecil B. DeMille's Hollywood* (Lexington: University Press of Kentucky, 2004), 144.

25. *Motion Picture*, May 1920.

26. *New York Times*, November 24, 1919.

27. Mae Tinee, "Perhaps the Tail Is Too Long for the Peacock," *Chicago Daily News*, November 18, 1919.

28. Edwards, *The DeMilles: An American Family*, 93.

29. *Photoplay,* December 1919.

30. John Douglas Eames, *The Paramount Story* (New York: Crown, 1985), 19.

31. "Fred," *Variety,* November 28, 1919.

32. Elizabeth Leese, *Costume Design in the Movies* (New York: Frederick Ungar, 1983), 124.

33. Gavin Lambert, *Nazimova: A Biography* (New York: Alfred A. Knopf, 1997), 226.

34. Eyman, *Empire of Dreams* 155.

35. *Motion Picture,* July 1920.

36. Burns Mantle, *Photoplay,* May 1920.

37. Hampton, *History of the American Film Industry* 225.

38. *Theatre Magazine* 29, no. 5, 1919.

39. St. Johns, "Madame la Marquise: The Saga of Hollywood's Hectic Cinderella," *Liberty,* November 30, 1929.

40. Ibid.

41. Clara Kimball Young was a big star in her day. A native Chicagoan, like Gloria, Young began in pictures with Vitagraph, achieving her greatest success in the mid-teens for World Studios. Young's career suffered a slump after she divorced actor-director James Young on the grounds of her infidelity with producer Lewis J. Selznick. In 1916 she formed the Clara Kimball Young Film Corporation, with distribution through Selznick Productions. After four films, that partnership was dissolved. She began an affair with Harry Garson in 1917, and through his inept business acumen, her career took a dive. By 1919, when she met Gloria, Clara Kimball Young was attempting a comeback, but by 1925 her stardom had faded. In 1941 she retired; she died of a stroke at the Motion Picture House in Woodland Hills, California, in 1960.

42. Gloria Swanson interview on UK television show *Parkinson,* 1978, YouTube.

43. Swanson, *Swanson on Swanson*, 137.

6. FAMOUS PLAYERS-LASKY

1. *The Wanderer* was eventually filmed in 1925. It starred Greta Nissen, Tyrone Power Sr., and Wallace Beery, and it was directed by Raoul Walsh.

2. Grace Kingsley, "Flashes," *Los Angeles Times,* November 1, 1919.

3. Swanson, *Swanson on Swanson,* 142.

4. Swanson, *Swanson on Swanson,* 143. Strangely, there was a definite contempt *among* the Jews in Hollywood after World War I concerning their faith. "Of course, it was one thing for Jews to disparage themselves and another for gentiles to do it," wrote Hollywood film studios historian Neal Gabler. "The Hollywood Jews were never thick-skinned as far as anti-Semitism was concerned. For them it lurked everywhere, constantly menacing." Neal Gabler, *An Empire of Their Own: How the Jews Invented Hollywood* (New York: Crown, 1988), 279.

5. Dated January 11, 1920, HRC.

6. Swanson, *Swanson on Swanson*, 148.

7. Adela Rogers St. Johns, *Love, Laughter and Tears: My Hollywood Story* (New York: New American Library, 1979), 145.

8. Swanson, *Swanson on Swanson*, 150.

9. Eyman, *Empire of Dreams*, 182.

10. DeMille, *The Autobiography of Cecil B. DeMille*, 220.

11. Rui Nogueira, "I Am Not Going to Write My Memoirs," *Sight & Sound*, Spring 1969.

12. Eyman, *Empire of Dreams*, 168.

13. *New York Times*, July 11, 1920.

14. Parish, *The Paramount Pretties*, 22.

15. Swanson, *Swanson on Swanson*, 154.

16. "The Screen," *New York Times*, October 18, 1920.

17. "Rialto Still Keeps to the DeMille Play," *Los Angeles Times*, November 21, 1920.

18. Rosenberg and Silverstein, *The Real Tinsel*, 178.

19. Swanson, *Swanson on Swanson*, 155. Wallace Reid was a tragic figure indeed. Though his dependency on drugs and alcohol went unabated, he continued making films, Paramount pushing him into one picture after another relentlessly to cash in on his popularity. Sensitive and touchingly handsome, he starred in some of the studio's greatest box-office hits, his successes rivaling those made by Swanson, Valentino, and Meighan. After filming *Anatol*, Reid handed in possibly his finest screen moment in George DuMaurier's *Forever* (1922), portraying Peter Ibbetson. Reid's stamina and looks began to fail drastically after that. By the time he was shooting his last film, *Thirty Days*, in 1922, his weight had dropped from a muscular and healthy 170 pounds down to a skeletal 120 pounds. He looked like a zombie, said those who worked on the film. He had to literally be helped onto and off the set to enact his role. Henry Hathaway, assistant director on that picture, told film historian Kevin Brownlow about Reid's tragic final day on the set in the stunning 1980 documentary *Hollywood*. "He sort of fumbled about, and bumped into a chair, and then just sat down on the floor and started to cry. They put him in a chair, and he just keeled over. They sent for an ambulance and took him to the hospital." The end was at hand. By then his addiction was well known, and he bravely admitted the truth to the press. Reid was admitted into a sanitarium in December 1922; he contacted influenza and died in his wife's arms on January 18, 1923. His beloved Dorothy Davenport stood by Reid throughout his addiction and became a crusader against drugs. As Mrs. Wallace Reid, she produced and starred in two films, *Human Wreckage* (1923) and *Broken Laws* (1924), for the Thomas Ince Corporation. It was the tragic widow Dorothy Davenport who stepped before a radio microphone at a Hollywood awards banquet one evening not long after her husband's death and courageously announced, "Hello, everybody. This is Mrs. Wallace Reid." She never remarried and died in 1977.

20. Swanson, *Swanson on Swanson*, 156.

21. In April 1912 Lucy and her husband Lord Edmund Cosmo Duff-Gordon sparked a major controversy during the investigation of the *Titanic* disaster when it came to light that they had more or less "commandeered" Lifeboat No. 1, "the money boat" as it was referred to, which was built to hold forty people but was lowered from the doomed vessel with only twelve occupants, seven of whom were crew. As the *Titanic* slipped beneath the waves and over 1,500 souls died in the freezing waters in the early morning hours of April 15, 1912, Lady Cosmo Duff-Gordon was heard to remark casually to her maid Laura Mabel Francatelli, "There is your beautiful nightdress gone." Walter Lord, *A Night To Remember— Illustrated Edition* (New York: Bantam, 1978), 127.

22. Marjorie Rosen, *Popcorn Venus: Women, Movies, and the American Dream* (New York: Avon Books, 1973), 121.

23. Lasky, *Whatever Happened to Hollywood?* 56.

24. Quirk, *The Films of Gloria Swanson*, 95.

25. Chaplin, *My Autobiography*, 203.

26. Lasky, *Whatever Happened to Hollywood?* 56.

27. Ibid.

28. Swanson, *Swanson on Swanson*, 160.

29. St. Johns, "Madame la Marquise."

30. Swanson, *Swanson on Swanson*, 159.

31. Richard Griffith and Arthur Mayer, *The Movies* (New York: Simon & Schuster, 1957), 149.

32. Meredith Etherington-Smith and Jeremy Pilcher, *The "It" Girls: Elinor Glyn, Novelist and Her Sister Lucile, Couturiere* (New York: Harcourt Brace Jovanovich, 1986), 215.

33. Lasky, *Whatever Happened to Hollywood?*, 57.

34. "Divorces Gloria Swanson," *Los Angeles Times*, September 20, 1923.

35. Etherington-Smith and Pilcher, *The "It" Girls: Elinor Glyn, Novelist and Her Sister Lucile, Couturiere*, 220.

36. "The Screen," *New York Times*, July 25, 1921.

37. Edwin Schallert, "Radios," *Los Angeles Times*, August 17, 1921.

7. PARAMOUNT

1. *Los Angeles Times*, September 24, 1921.

2. Untitled article, n.d., AMPAS.

3. *New York Times*, September 12, 1921.

4. Eyman, *Empire of Dreams: The Epic Life of Cecil B. DeMille*, 170.

5. Ringgold and Bodeen, *The Films of Cecil B. DeMille*, 197.

6. *Motion Picture Classic*, September 1921.

7. With a little help from Johann Strauss's operetta *Die Fledermaus*, several aspects of *The Affairs of Anatol* can be found in DeMille's only screen musical, the spectacularly gaudy

Madam Satan (MGM, 1930) with Kay Johnson, Reginald Denny, and Lillian Roth. In April 1955 Paul Henreid and Bette Davis seriously discussed remaking *The Affairs of Anatol* as a vehicle for Davis and her husband Gary Merrill. Henreid owned the rights, which both Max Ophuls and Joseph Mankiewicz unsuccessfully attempted to acquire. By May of that year Henreid's attention turned to other projects.

8. Eyman, *Empire of Dreams: The Epic Life of Cecil B. DeMille,* 171.

9. "Fred," *Variety,* October 21, 1921.

10. Parish, *The Paramount Pretties,* 23.

11. "Sights & Sounds," *Photoplay,* September 1921, AMPAS.

12. Quirk, *The Films of Gloria Swanson,* 111.

13. Swanson, *Swanson on Swanson,* 165.

14. Moore, *Silent Star,* 101–2.

15. Ibid., 103.

16. St. Johns, "Madame la Marquise: The Saga of Hollywood's Hectic Cinderella," *Liberty,* November 30, 1929.

17. Swanson, *Swanson on Swanson,* 165.

18. *Toledo Blade,* March 31, 1922, NYPL.

19. Rosenberg and Silverstein, *The Real Tinsel,* 180.

20. Cari Beauchamp, *Without Lying Down: Frances Marion and the Powerful Women of Early Hollywood* (New York: Arcade, 2008), 141.

21. Noel Botham and Peter Donnelly, *Valentino: The Love God* (New York: Ace Books, 1976), 110.

22. "Smart Society," *New York Times,* November 24, 1906.

23. Swanson, *Swanson on Swanson,* 174.

24. Etherington-Smith and Pilcher, *The 'It' Girls: Elinor Glyn, Novelist and Her Sister Lucile, Couturiere,* 223–24. In the March issue of *Photoplay,* now that Gloria was the biggest star in Hollywood, Glyn would smugly state that Swanson and Thomas Meighan may have had "It" but not anymore. She instead bestowed her self-important endowment of "It" upon Clara Bow, Greta Garbo, and Gary Cooper, among others. And to add insult to injury, she surprisingly included on her list Wallace Beery and Pola Negri!

25. David Bret, *Valentino: A Dream of Desire* (New York: Carroll & Graf, 1998), 73; Brad Steiger and Chaw Mack, *Valentino: An Intimate and Shocking Exposé* (New York: Macfadden-Bartell, 1966), 115.

26. Michael Morris, *Madam Valentino: The Many Lives of Natacha Rambova* (New York: Abbeville Press, 1991), 106.

27. Bret, *Valentino: A Dream of Desire,* 74.

28. "Likes Glyn Story," *Los Angeles Times,* March 26, 1922.

29. Vincent Tajiri, *Valentino: The True Life Story* (New York: Bantam Books, 1977), 66.

30. Swanson, *Swanson on Swanson,* 175.

31. Axel Madsen, *The Sewing Circle* (New York: Birch Lane Press, 2005), 127. In 1979 former

William Randolph Hearst reporter Adela Rogers St. Johns told a television interviewer that there was never a doubt the murderer of William Desmond Taylor was Mary Miles Minter's mother Charlotte Shelby, who did the director in out of a fit of jealousy. Conducting his own investigation over the years, director King Vidor drew the same conclusion.

32. Quirk, *The Films of Gloria Swanson*, 115.

33. Ibid., 115.

34. The Jesse L. Lasky Collection, AMPAS.

35. Ibid.

36. Swanson, *Swanson on Swanson*, 176.

37. Paramount memo, n.d., AMPAS.

38. Ibid.

39. *Women's Wear Daily*, June 26, 1976, NYPL.

40. Swanson, *Swanson on Swanson*, 178.

41. Moore, *Silent Star*, 105.

42. "Gloria Swanson Abuses Hollywood," *Los Angeles Times*, June 3, 1922.

43. Moore, *Silent Star*, 105.

44. Gloria Stuart and Sylvia Thompson, *I Just Kept Hoping* (New York: Little, Brown, 1999), 61.

8. STARDOM

1. Emily W. Leider, *Dark Lover: The Life and Death of Rudolph Valentino* (New York: Faber and Faber, 2003), 190.

2. Grace Kingsley, "Flashes," *Los Angeles Times*, April 29, 1922.

3. "The Screen," *New York Times*, May 8, 1922.

4. Peter Kobel, *Silent Movies: The Birth of Film and the Triumph of Movie Culture* (New York: Little, Brown, 2007), xi. Today it is a shocking fact that 90 percent of silent films have disintegrated. Considered a lost film for over eighty years, a delicate nitrate print of *Beyond the Rocks* owned by a Dutch private collector was discovered by Elif Kaynakci Rongen and Giovanna Fossati of the Eye Film Instituut Nederland in 2003 in the Netherlands. Restored by the Nederlands Filmmuseum to six reels, instead of the original American version of seven, the picture was meticulously pieced back together with original color tints and English subtitles based on the original script held by the Academy of Motion Picture Arts and Sciences. *Beyond the Rocks* was subsequently released on DVD by Milestone Film & Video in 2005. "It's always cause for celebration whenever a lost film has been discovered," said Martin Scorsese upon *Beyond the Rocks*'s rediscovery (www .latos.org). He concluded with, "Every film found restores another piece of our collective memory, our sense of our past, and our history" (www.slantmagazine.com, June 27, 2006).

5. *New York Morning Telegraph*, June 25, 1922, AMPAS.

6. Quirk, *The Films of Gloria Swanson*, 125.

7. "'Her Gilded Cage' Not at All Wicked," *Los Angeles Times*, September 5, 1922.

8. Griffith and Mayer, *The Movies*, 218.

9. Grace Wilcox, "How Gloria Swanson Spent $10,000 in Paris," *Los Angeles Times*, August 27, 1922.

10. "A Long Film Career," *New York Times*, February 16, 1967.

11. Quirk, *The Films of Gloria Swanson*, 137.

12. *Motion Picture*, June 1923; Basinger, *Silent Stars*, 249.

13. Basinger, *Silent Stars*, 249.

14. Parish, *The Paramount Pretties*, 22.

15. Mick LaSalle, *Complicated Women: Sex and Power in Pre-Code Hollywood* (New York: Thomas Dunne, 2000), 20.

16. Quirk, *The Films of Gloria Swanson*, 134.

17. "Rush," *Variety*, October 27, 1922.

18. Rosenberg and Silverstein, *The Real Tinsel*, 179.

19. "Fred," *Variety*, January 5, 1923.

20. Quirk, *The Films of Gloria Swanson*, 137.

21. The furnishings included walnut appointments in the library, entrance hall chairs, tables, tapestries and carpets, dining room tables, sideboards, Oriental rugs, overstuffed furniture, rockers, and a Columbia gramophone player. The mansion also featured three bedrooms, a maid's room, a butler's room, a manservant room, a billiards room, three bathrooms, and the owner's suite.

22. Tapert, *The Power of Glamour: The Women Who Defined the Magic of Stardom*, 23.

23. Moore, *Silent Star*, 104.

24. For years skeptics theorized about the parental history of the boy, with many assuming in the early years that he must have been Mickey Neilan's son, and in later years, because Gloria named him Joseph Patrick, that he was the love child of Joseph P. Kennedy. Both of these assumptions are incorrect.

25. Somborn Daly, *A&E Biography*, "The Greatest Star," July 29, 1997.

26. Hedda Hopper, *The Whole Truth and Nothing But* (New York: Pyramid, 1963), 260.

27. Eyman, *Empire of Dreams: The Epic Life of Cecil B. DeMille*, 190.

28. Ibid.

29. Ibid.

30. Ibid.

31. Ibid.

32. Ibid.

33. Jackie Epstein, "Gossip Is Still Music to Jimmy Fidler's Ears," *Los Angeles Times*, April 30, 1978.

34. Dated January 2, 1923, NYPL.

35. *Los Angeles Times,* April 8, 1923.

36. "Rush," *Variety,* April 19, 1923.

37. Arnie Bernstein, ed., *"The Movies Are": Carl Sandburg's Film Reviews and Essays, 1920–1928* (Chicago: Lake Claremont Press, 2000), 166.

38. Swanson, *Swanson on Swanson,* 192. Film director Sam Wood (1883–1949) is largely forgotten today, although he helmed some of Hollywood's greatest motion pictures. He would later do a stint working for Gloria in futile attempts to get *Queen Kelly* off the ground. At MGM and the Selznick Corporation respectively he did damage control on such classics as *The Good Earth* (1936) and *Gone with the Wind* (1939). Other films of his include *Goodbye, Mr. Chips* (MGM, 1939), *Kings Row* (Warner Bros, 1941), *The Pride of the Yankees* (RKO, 1942), and *For Whom the Bell Tolls* (Paramount, 1943). Sam Wood was the favorite director of Metro star William Haines. DeMille and other right-wing Hollywood insiders called Wood a hero for naming names during the HUAC investigations. The Marx Brothers found Wood to be a humorless, pedestrian director, though he directed them in two of their best MGM motion pictures, *A Night at the Opera* (1935) and *A Day at the Races* (1937).

39. Parish, *The Paramount Pretties,* 35.

40. Swanson, *Swanson on Swanson,* 193.

41. "From Mummy to Bathing Girl," *Los Angeles Times,* July 18, 1923.

42. "Notes on People," *New York Times,* November 10, 1980.

9. NEW YORK

1. Dwan would make eight films with Gloria. While under contract with 20th Century–Fox in the 1930s, he directed his most important pictures, which included *Heidi* (1937) and *Rebecca of Sunnybrook Farm* (1938) with Shirley Temple and *Suez* (1938) with Loretta Young and Tyrone Power. In 1949 he helmed Republic Pictures' *The Sands of Iwo Jima* with John Wayne. Dwan suffered a stroke and died of heart failure in December 1981.

2. Cast as Zaza's maid Nathalie was the young Ziegfeld Follies beauty Yvonne Hughes, who would appear with Gloria the following year in *A Society Scandal.* Hughes also appeared in *The Sainted Devil* with Rudolph Valentino and film vamp Dagmar Godowsky, daughter of pianist Leopold Godowsky. Godowsky's brother Gordon met Yvonne during the filming, and they were briefly married. Falling on hard times and liquor in later years, Hughes met a gruesome end. In December 1950 she was strangled to death in her New York hotel room, murdered by a drunken lumberjack, Birger Nordkvist.

3. Peter Bogdanovich, *Allan Dwan: The Last Pioneer* (New York: Praeger, 1971), 65–66.

4. Leonard Maltin, *The Art of the Cinematographer* (New York: Dover, 1978), 96.

5. Matthew Bernstein, *Walter Wanger: Hollywood Independent* (Berkeley: University of California Press, 2004), 61.

6. Swanson, *Swanson on Swanson*, 196.

7. Ibid.

8. "The Screen," *New York Times*, August 7, 1923.

9. "Big Season for Films," *New York Times*, August 12, 1923.

10. Carr, *Four Fabulous Faces*, 21.

11. *Reading* (Pennsylvania) *Eagle*, September 23, 1923.

12. Sidney Olcott was born John Sidney Alcott in Canada on September 20, 1883, and began his career in theater in 1904 and in film in Fort Lee, New Jersey, in 1905, for Biograph. Hired by Kalem, Olcott directed 1907's *Ben-Hur* and later became the company president. In 1924, immediately after filming *The Humming Bird*, Olcott produced and directed Rudolph Valentino's first Astoria Studio–made picture *Monsieur Beaucaire*. Olcott retired in 1927 and died in Hollywood in 1949.

13. "The Screen," *New York Times*, September 17, 1923.

14. Edwin Schallert, "Right from the Front," *Los Angeles Times*, December 2, 1923.

15. Paris, *Louise Brooks*, 241.

16. Swanson, *Swanson on Swanson*, 200.

17. HRC.

18. "French Locales Dominate in Promising Picture," *New York Times*, February 17, 1924.

19. "National Notes," *New York Times*, August 22, 1971.

20. Helen Klumph, "Bible Episode Is the Best," *Los Angeles Times*, December 30, 1923.

21. Eyman, *Empire of Dreams: The Epic Life of Cecil B. DeMille*, 189.

22. Swanson, *Swanson on Swanson*, 212.

23. Rod La Rocque co-starred with Joan Crawford and Anita Page in *Our Modern Maidens* (MGM, 1929) and enjoyed a solid career in talkies, appearing in such films as *One Romantic Night* (United Artists, 1930) with Lillian Gish, *Let Us Be Gay* (MGM, 1930) with Norma Shearer and Hedda Hopper, the German-lensed *S.O.S. Iceberg* (UFA-Universal, 1933) with Leni Riefenstahl, and *Meet John Doe* (Warner Bros., 1941) with Gary Cooper and Barbara Stanwyck. In 1926 he married Hungarian film actress Vilma Banky, who had starred twice with Valentino, in *The Eagle* (United Artists, 1925) and his last film *The Son of the Sheik* (United Artists, 1926). After La Rocque's film career faded in the 1940s, he entered the world of real estate. Rod La Rocque died at his Beverly Hills home on October 16, 1969.

24. Among the cast was nineteen-year-old Thelma Converse, who played Mrs. Hamilton Pennfield. She was the identical twin sister of Gloria Morgan, the mother of Gloria Vanderbilt, who is the mother of today's television news journalist Anderson Cooper. Thelma enjoyed a passionate affair in the early 1930s with England's Prince of Wales, Edward, who became King Edward VIII before he abdicated in 1937 for the woman he loved, American born, twice-divorced Wallis Simpson. Thelma had introduced her friend Wallis to Edward. After his abdication Edward and Wallis became the Duke and Duchess of Windsor.

25. "Where Screen Gowns Go," *New York Times,* January 13, 1924.

26. "Fred," *Variety,* January 17, 1924. So popular was *The Humming Bird* in New York that in May a stage version of the film was produced at the Alhambra Theater, Knickerbocker Avenue and Halsey Street in Brooklyn, as a prologue to the picture's presentation.

27. "The Things They Say," *Motion Picture Classic,* n.d., WHS.

28. Helen Klumph, "Gloria Glows as an Apache," *Los Angeles Times,* January 20, 1924.

29. "The Screen," *New York Times,* March 10, 1924.

30. Quirk, *The Films of Gloria Swanson,* 158.

31. Edwin Schallert, "Playdom—Gloria in Duds," *Los Angeles Times,* April 14, 1924.

32. "Clare Eames Is Sensation," *Los Angeles Times,* May 11, 1924.

33. Grace Kingsley, "Stars Study Human Drama," *Los Angeles Times,* April 15, 1924.

34. Tallmer, "As Gloria Was Saying," *New York Post,* September 11, 1971.

35. The role of Peter Pan had been played on the stage by Maude Adams in 1902, and later by Marilyn Miller, Jean Arthur, Mary Martin, and Cathy Rigby. Other screen actresses coveting the 1924 film role in *Peter Pan* were Colleen Moore, May McAvoy, Madge Bellamy, Flora le Breton, Bessie Love, and Virginia Lee Corbin. Boy child star Jackie Coogan had even been approached to play Peter.

10. EUROPE

1. Edward Steichen, *Steichen: A Life in Photography* (New York: Harmony Books, 1985), n.p.

2. Which seems incongruous because as late as August American papers were still speculating on who might land the part. Bronson was announced the victor by the *New York Times* on August 16. Gloria's name was not mentioned on the list of over a hundred actresses considered for the part.

3. "Gloria and Heifetz Linked," *Los Angeles Times,* July 23, 1924.

4. Gloria in her book mistakenly calls the publication *L'Aurore,* a famous French liberal newspaper published by Prime Minister Georges Clemenceau, which closed in 1914. Its most famous headline was Emile Zola's "J'Accuse" concerning the Dreyfus Affair of 1898.

5. *The Internet Movie Database,* www.imdb.com.

6. When production commenced on the 1924 film version of *Madame Sans-Gêne,* Gloria touched the heart of the French when she, according to publicity, placed a wreath on the grave of Mme. Réjane, who died in Paris in 1920 and was buried at the Cimetière de Passy. The inscription on the wreath read, "I come very humbly to endeavor to place upon the screen the play which you immortalized upon the stage." *Rivoli Times,* April 17, 1925, NYPL.

7. According to papers in the NYPL, as late as 1931, Columbia University lecturer and vaudeville performer Dr. Louis Kaufman Anspacher, Kathryn Kidder's husband, of Ossining, New York, was still receiving pictorial residual rights. On January 15, 1916, Louis K.

Anspacher completed his manuscript of a novelization of *Madame Sans-Gêne,* which he later made into a one-act play by him called *The Washerwoman Duchess,* "based on a character created by Moreau and Sardou." It was published by Frederick A. Stokes Company, New York. Dr. Anspacher performed in the one-act play himself with his wife in 1937.

8. Swanson, *Swanson on Swanson,* 216.

9. Ibid., 217. Of her five days in Paris, Gloria was upset to learn that one was a French holiday, Monday, July 14, the day she and Jane trained down to Cherbourg. That only gave her Wednesday through Saturday to shop. Unfortunately, she could not confer with any dressmakers during that week. "I did manage to buy two dresses," Gloria told the New York customs agents. "I'm wearing one. Here's the other. You can't take much money away from me this time." Grace Kingsley, "Flashes," *Los Angeles Times,* August 2, 1924.

10. "Gloria and Heifetz Linked."

11. "The Screen," *New York Times,* July 29, 1924.

12. MoMA program notes; quote from Peter Bogdanovich, *Allan Dwan: The Last Pioneer* (New York: Praeger n.p. Film Library, 1971).

13. Paris, *Louise Brooks,* 241.

14. Edwin Schallert, *Los Angeles Times,* August 31, 1924.

15. Quirk, *The Films of Gloria Swanson,* 167.

16. "Fred," *Variety,* October 8, 1924.

17. "The Screen—Princess Swanson," *New York Times,* October 7, 1924.

18. Swanson, *Swanson on Swanson,* 221.

19. Ibid., 223.

20. Gloria wrote that Perret had once asked her to be in *Koenigsmark* years before, but that film was not made until 1935 in Britain.

21. In 1929 Paramount purchased the Joinville Studio outside Paris, equipped it with sound, and filmed foreign-language versions of most of its early talkie films, features and shorts, as well as producing several original productions. By 1933 Paramount-Joinville had made over three hundred films.

22. His Norman ancestors took part in two Crusades. Antoine de la Falaise was a gentleman-in-waiting to Monsigneur le Duc de Bourgogne, grandson of Louis XIV. In 1793 de la Falaise emigrated to London and married the daughter of the Fifth Marquis de la Coudraye. Henri's father Comte Gabriel-Louis Venant le Bailly de la Falaise married in 1892 Henriette-Lucie Frederique Hennessey, daughter of Richard Hennessy, of the Hennessey Cognac firm. Count Louis Gabriel was a three-time Olympic Gold Medalist in fencing and a former army officer. After their daughter Louise was born in 1894, Henriette-Lucie bore three sons in succession; Henri, the oldest and titled marquis, followed by Alain (1905–77) and Richard (1910–45), the latter both titled the Comte de la Falaise. Louis Gabriel also fathered their half sister, Henriette de Turcot, born in 1913.

Henri's brother Richard René Gabriel married Rayliane Gallineau, with whom he had a son in 1940. Richard was denounced to the Gestapo as a resistance fighter during World War II by his beautiful blond mistress Landette Legros, holder of the glider championship of France. He was sent to the concentration camp Buchenwald and died of pneumonia there in 1945. At Mlle. Legros's trial in 1946, Henri listened to his sister-in-law accuse Legros of betraying Richard de la Falaise. "I never betrayed Richard," she cried. "His wife is jealous because we loved each other and wants revenge." Legros was handed a sentence of five years of solitary confinement and, imprisoned, promptly slit her throat ("Convicted Betrayer of Count Cuts Throat," *Los Angeles Times*, December 5, 1946). Richard's only child, his son Gabriel Richard Antoine, was formally adopted by Henri and his last wife Emma after World War II.

Brother Alain would marry his first wife, Margaret Webb, "Miss Atlantic City 1929," in 1931. In 1946 he wed again to the beautiful Maxime Birley, daughter of eminent portrait painter Sir Oswald Birley. Maxime was a model, designer, and Elsa Schiaparelli's muse. She would later befriend pop artist Andy Warhol in New York in the 1960s, act under the name Maxime McKendry (her first husband's surname) in *Andy Warhol's Dracula* (Bryanston Distributing, 1974), and help design the menu for Andy's unrealized automat Andy-Mat. She died in 2009. Richard and Maxine had two children. Louise, born in 1947, became a fashion model in New York in the 1960s and under the professional name Loulou de la Falaise designed prints for Halston. She married Thadee Klossowski de Rola, son of the artist Balthus, in 1977, and the two became famous jet-setters of the era. She had one child, Anna. Loulou was the muse for Yves Saint Laurent and later created her own fashion and jewelry line for him until his death in 2002. In 2007 she designed jewelry for Oscar de la Renta. Loulou died in November 2011.

Alain's son Alexis became the Comte de la Falaise in 1977 until his death in 2004. Alexis acted in Andy Warhol's *Tub Girls* (Andy Warhol Films, 1967) with Brigid Berlin and Viva. Alexis married Louisa Ogilvy, and their daughter Lucie became the face of Yves Saint Laurent in the early 1990s, appearing on the cover of American *Vogue*. Lucie married Marlon Richards, son of the Rolling Stones guitarist Keith Richards and model-actress Anita Pallenberg. Alexis's son Daniel became an actor and appeared in the 1992 Madonna "Erotica" video. Today he is a renowned Parisian chef.

23. en.wikipedia.org/wiki/Henri_de_la_Falaise.

24. Somborn Daly, *A&E Biography*, "The Greatest Star," July 29, 1997.

25. Swanson, *Swanson on Swanson*, 227.

26. "Nobleman Woos Gloria," *Los Angeles Times*, October 27, 1924.

27. Tapert, *The Power of Glamour: The Women Who Defined the Magic of Stardom*, 21.

28. Basinger, *Silent Stars*, 223.

29. Swanson, *Swanson on Swanson*, 227.

30. Edwin Schallert, "Playdom—Gloria, O Gloria!" *Los Angeles Times*, November 10, 1924.

31. Mordaunt Hall, "The Screen," *New York Times*, November 24, 1924.

32. Harry Carr, "Harry Carr's Page," *Los Angeles Times*, December 3, 1924.

33. Swanson, *Swanson on Swanson*, 229.

34. Ibid., 230.

35. Ibid., 232.

36. Dennis Fairchild, conversation with author, February 28, 2011.

37. Swanson, *Swanson on Swanson*, 233.

38. Actress Patricia Neal would at least reference her own abortion of the child she carried by Gary Cooper as being *the* one regret of her lifetime.

39. Henry Wales, "Gloria's Honeymoon Here," *Los Angeles Times*, January 29, 1925.

40. "Gleanings from the Screen," *New York Times*, March 8, 1925.

41. Henry Wales, "Gloria and Henri Back on 'The Lot,'" *Los Angeles Times*, January 30, 1925.

42. Ibid.

43. "Titled Frenchman and GS Marry," *Evening Independent*, St. Petersburg, Florida, January 31, 1925.

11. LA GRANDE ILLUSION

1. Henry Wales, "Gloria's Honeymoon Here," *Los Angeles Times*, January 29, 1925.

2. Ibid.

3. Swanson, *Swanson on Swanson*, 244.

4. "Record Year in Filmdom; Warners Have Huge Program," *Los Angeles Times*, February 18, 1925.

5. "Gloria-Lasky Pact Unsigned," *Los Angeles Times*, April 8, 1925.

6. Eyman, *Empire of Dreams: The Epic Life of Cecil B. DeMille*, 216.

7. "Gloria, Marquis Sail Today for U.S.," *Los Angeles Times*, April 18, 1925.

8. Adolph Zukor papers, AMPAS.

9. "Gloria Swanson Brings New Mode," *New York Times*, March 25, 1925.

10. Carr, *Four Fabulous Faces*, 54.

11. Lawrence J. Quirk, *The Kennedys in Hollywood* (Dallas, TX: Taylor Publications, 1986), 68.

12. "The Silent Drama," *Life* magazine, n.d., WHS. *Madame Sans-Gêne* was remade in France in 1941 starring Arletty, in Argentina in 1945 with Nini Marshall, and in 1963 starring Sophia Loren. On December 14, 1936, it was condensed into a *Lux Radio Theater* presentation hosted by Cecil B. DeMille, starring Jean Harlow, Robert Taylor, C. Henry Gordon, and Claude Rains. Today, Paramount's 1924 *Madame Sans-Gêne* is a "lost" film, one of the two hundred most sought-after and elusive motion pictures in history. Prints are nowhere to be found, though clips are in existence. They show Gloria as radiantly beautiful in period costumes, though she may be perhaps a bit over made up. One can only speculate what the picture if viewed today would offer. It did rank as one of Swanson's most treasured experiences, and naturally she remembered it fondly. Try as she might until the day she died, Gloria sadly was never able to locate a copy.

13. "The Silent Drama," *Life* magazine, n.d., WHS.

14. Mordaunt Hall, "Block Street to See Gloria Swanson," *New York Times,* April 18, 1925.

15. Robin Karney, ed., *The Movie Stars Story* (New York: Crescent Books, 1984), 36.

16. "Gloria Pauses in Chicago," *Los Angeles Times,* April 22, 1925.

17. "Gloria Back in Triumph," *Los Angeles Times,* April 25, 1925.

18. Barbas, *The First Lady of Hollywood,* 99.

19. Hedda Hopper Papers, untitled article, c. 1950, AMPAS.

20. Swanson, *Swanson on Swanson,* 10.

21. Robert S. Sennett, *Hollywood Hoopla: Creating and Selling Movies in the Golden Age of Hollywood* (New York: Billboard Books, 1998), 45.

22. Charles Beardsley, *Hollywood's Master Showman: The Legendary Sid Grauman* (Cranbury, NJ: Cornwall Books, 1983), 49.

23. Carr, *Four Fabulous Faces,* 56.

24. "We shot in Fontainebleau, Malmaison, Compiègne, not just the garden, inside," Gloria would bemoan years later. "It was an absolute record of those rooms, and it's a crime that it is lost. I can't believe the French don't have a copy of it, because in those days we used to make 340–350 prints of each negative and a certain number were sent abroad. Now you know that when a picture finished its run, the prints were supposed to be returned to the exchange or destroyed. But nobody destroyed them." Nogueira, "I Am Not Going to Write My Memoirs," *Sight & Sound,* Spring 1969.

25. "Gloria, Versatile," *Los Angeles Times,* June 7, 1925.

26. Nogueira, "I Am Not Going to Write My Memoirs," *Sight & Sound,* Spring 1969.

27. Helena Huntington Smith, "Profiles: Ugly Duckling," *New Yorker,* January 18, 1930.

28. "We Lived as Royalty, Gloria Swanson Sighs," *New York Herald-Journal,* December 14, 1958.

29. Lita Grey Chaplin and Morton Cooper, *My Life with Chaplin: An Intimate Memoir* (New York: Bernard Geis Associates, 1966), 79.

30. Malcolm Oettinger, "Gloria, Ltd." (*Picture Play* magazine?), n.d., WHS.

31. Tapert, *The Power of Glamour: The Women Who Defined the Magic of Stardom,* 23.

32. "We Lived As Royalty, Gloria Swanson Sighs," *New York Herald-Journal,* December 14, 1958.

33. Richard Koszarski, *Hollywood on the Hudson: Film and Television in New York from Griffith to Sarnoff* (Piscataway, NJ: Rutgers University Press, 2008), 41.

34. Doug McClelland, *Hollywood on Hollywood: Tinseltown Talks* (Boston: Faber & Faber, 1985), 221.

35. Fred Lawrence Guiles, *Marion Davies* (New York: McGraw-Hill, 1972), 228.

36. Pola Negri, *Memoirs of a Star* (Garden City, NY: Doubleday, 1970), 228–29.

37. Jeanine Basinger, *Silent Stars* (New York: Alfred A. Knopf, 1999), 252.

38. Swanson, *Swanson on Swanson,* 267.

39. Stanley Frank, "Grandma Gloria Swanson Comes Back," *Saturday Evening Post,* July 22, 1950.

40. René Hubert, "Psychology of Gloria's Talent for Smart Frocks Is Simplicity," *Los Angeles Times*, May 31, 1925.

41. Ruth Biery, "The Troubles with Gloria," *Photoplay*, June 1931.

12. UNITED ARTISTS

1. Jesse Lasky Papers, AMPAS.
2. Ibid.
3. John Douglas Eames, *The Paramount Story* (New York: Crown, 1985), 34.
4. Mordaunt Hall, "The Screen," *New York Times*, August 31, 1925.
5. Mordaunt Hall, "Bright-Eyed Marquise Portrays Old Countess," *New York Times*, September 6, 1925.
6. Untitled article, WHS.
7. Harry Carr, "Harry Carr's Page," *Los Angeles Times*, November 1, 1925.
8. Swanson, *Swanson on Swanson*, 278.
9. "Contempt Fine for Gloria Swanson," *New York Times*, September 25, 1925.
10. Swanson, *Swanson on Swanson*, 278.
11. Ibid.
12. "Contempt Fine for Gloria Swanson," *New York Times*, September 25, 1925.
13. "Gloria Swanson's Contempt Penalty Upheld; She Is Also Sued for $25,000 for a Slap," *New York Times*, November 13, 1925.
14. "Gloria Swanson Suit Settled," *New York Times*, March 9, 1928. In June 1928 it went to a trial by jury, ending up in a hung vote. Gloria never appeared in court. (Twenty years later, S. Alexander Cohen, who made his living chasing other men's wives, was then head chief of detectives of the Supreme Detective Agency in New York. In 1948 he released a finding that stated that in his forty years of spying on unfaithful wives and husbands, women were in actuality less faithful than men.)
15. Lasky, *Whatever Happened to Hollywood?* 57.
16. Swanson, *Swanson on Swanson*, 278.
17. Quirk, *The Films of Gloria Swanson*, 198.
18. Mordaunt Hall, "The Screen," *New York Times*, November 16, 1925.
19. "Sime," *Variety*, November 25, 1925.
20. Basinger, *Silent Stars*, 226.
21. Quirk, *The Films of Gloria Swanson*, 192.
22. Alma Whitaker, "Metropolitan Features," *Los Angeles Times*, March 7, 1926.
23. James Ashmore Creelman would gain film immortality at RKO in the early 1930s with his story lines for *The Most Dangerous Game* (1932), which starred Joel McCrea, *The Last Days of Pompeii* (1935), and the classic *King Kong* (1933).
24. Norbert Lusk, "Warfield May Enter Pictures," *Los Angeles Times*, June 13, 1926.

25. Edwin Schallert, "Story Need Emphasized," *Los Angeles Times*, January 10, 1926.

26. "Skig," *Variety*, March 17, 1926.

27. Whitney Williams, "Under the Lights," *Los Angeles Times*, April 18, 1926.

28. Quirk, *The Films of Gloria Swanson*, 196.

29. Swanson, *Swanson on Swanson*, 281.

30. Ibid.

31. Ibid., 282.

32. Ibid., 284.

33. Ibid.

34. Ibid., 285.

13. INDEPENDENCE

1. Emily W. Leider, *Dark Lover: The Life and Death of Rudolph Valentino* (New York: Faber & Faber, 2003), 395.

2. Pola Negri's career in Hollywood did not last long. Paramount had given her dramatic vehicles equaling, if not surpassing, in scope those they handed Gloria. If there was indeed a feud between Pola and Gloria, it was Pola who lost. The more glamorized, coiffured, and beautifully photographed Pola was made, the more she became standardized. "Gloria's departure ended our ridiculous feud forever," Pola wrote in her memoirs. "It also left me the undisputed queen of the studio, a position with which I was not exactly displeased." Negri, *Memoirs of a Star*, 248.

   With Gloria gone, Negri's value at Paramount increased and she was paid $10,000 a week. The press dismissed her grief at the passing of Valentino as a publicity stunt, and her prolonged mourning was pronounced comical. In 1927 she married the impoverished Prince Serge Mdivani (brother of the equally impoverished David Mdivani, who had wed Mae Murray in 1926), which made Pola a princess and gave her an upper hand over Gloria's mere "marquise." By 1928 movie exhibitors were pleading for no more Negri films. When talkies arrived, Negri, who spoke with a heavy accent, was dead in the water in America.

   Returning to Germany, Negri became an immense star once again, reportedly one of Adolf Hitler's favorite actresses, in such pictures as *Mazurka* (Tobis, 1935) and *Tango Notturno* (UFA, 1937). Returning to the States in 1941, she attempted a futile comeback in *Hi Diddle Diddle* (UA, 1943), with Adolphe Menjou; her last film was Walt Disney's *The Moon-Spinners* (1963). She then retired to San Antonio, Texas, to live her final years with her female companion and benefactress Margaret West. Negri's autobiography, *Memoirs of a Star*, was published in 1970. She died of pneumonia at the age of ninety on August 1, 1987.

3. Leider, *Dark Lover: The Life and Death of Rudolph Valentino*, 395.

4. Mordaunt Hall, "The Screen," *New York Times,* August 30, 1926.

5. Kathleen Carroll, "Flashback of a Silent Superstar," New York *Daily News,* September 23, 1973.

6. Whitney Williams, "Under the Lights," *Los Angeles Times,* September 12, 1926.

7. As a director, however, Dudley Murphy was quite capable. He directed classic blues artist Bessie Smith in her only film appearance, the short *St. Louis Blues* (RKO-Radio, 1929), and the feature films *The Emperor Jones* (United Artists, 1933) with Paul Robeson, and *The Night Is Young* (MGM, 1935) with Ramon Novarro.

8. De Bothezat is credited with designing and pioneering helicopter flight. In Gloria's memoirs she concocted a story of planning some way to contact her servants when they were not within her immediate area. She says she talked to de Bothezat about her brilliant idea, and he had exclaimed to her she had created an invention. Gloria always liked to take credit for her brilliant thinking.

9. "Marquis Hunts Movie Job," *New York Times,* November 10, 1926.

10. *New York Times,* March 13, 1927.

11. "Fred," *Variety,* March 16, 1927.

12. Swanson, *Swanson on Swanson,* 291.

13. Adele Whitely Fletcher, untitled article, n.d., WHS.

14. Gloria later denied Henri sold cars, in her book stating he was much too busy handling her European affairs, which was not necessarily true.

15. Swanson, *Swanson on Swanson,* 297.

16. The Pinochle Club consisted of the producers of such studios as Chadwick Productions, Christie Film Company, Cecil B. DeMille Pictures Corporation, Educational Studios, FBO Studios, First National Pictures, Fox Film Corporation, Samuel Goldwyn, Harold Lloyd Corporation, Metro-Goldwyn-Mayer Corporation, Metropolitan Pictures Corporation, Paramount Famous Lasky Corporation, Hal Roach Studios, Mack Sennett Studio, United Artists Studio Corporation, Universal Pictures Corporation, and Warner Bros. Pictures. Those fifteen members of the Pinochle Club were William Fox, Winnie Sheehan, Abe Warner, J. J. Murdock, Marcus Loew, Robert Rubin, Robert Cochrane, Joe Kennedy, Sam Katz, John McGuirk, S. R. Kent, Adolph Zukor, Jesse L. Lasky, Sam Spring, and Richard Rowland. Swanson, *Swanson on Swanson,* 301.

17. Swanson, *Swanson on Swanson,* 303.

18. Ibid., 304.

19. "To Film 'Sadie Thompson,'" *New York Times,* May 28, 1927.

20. AMPAS.

14. JOSEPH P. KENNEDY

1. Swanson, *Swanson on Swanson,* 306.

2. AMPAS.

3. Swanson, *Swanson on Swanson*, 309.

4. AMPAS.

5. Ibid.

6. Alma Whitaker, "Old Memories Won't Fade Out," *Los Angeles Times*, December 15, 1929; Alma Whitaker, "Gamin Soul Is Set Free," *Los Angeles Times*, February 26, 1928.

7. Swanson, *Swanson on Swanson*, 324.

8. Kevin Thomas, "Movies—Raoul Walsh: From Silents to Talkies," *Los Angeles Times*, January 30, 1972.

9. Under contract with Fox, Walsh was scheduled to portray the Cisco Kid in 1928's *In Old Arizona* (Fox), billed as the first all-talkie filmed outdoors, but during production a jackrabbit jumped through the windshield of his car on an open road, and Walsh lost his right eye, requiring his wearing an eye patch the rest of his life. (Warner Baxter replaced him in the picture and won a Best Actor Oscar for it.) Walsh went on to become a renowned director of such "manly" pictures as *The Big Trail* (Fox, 1930), which introduced John Wayne to the screen, before hitting his stride at Warner Bros. later in the decade. In 1938 Walsh was one of but forty-five directors in Hollywood to earn more than $75,000 a year. (His income that year was $107,083.00.) Walsh's career was varied. He also directed a Marion Davies–Bing Crosby musical, *Going Hollywood* (MGM, 1933), and a Mae West comedy, *Klondike Annie* (Paramount, 1936). Walsh's last picture was in 1964. The thrice-married Walsh died of a heart attack on December 31, 1980.

10. Edwin Schallert, "Rain? Real Drops Fall in Prologue," *Los Angeles Times*, March 15, 1928.

11. HRC.

12. "Good by, My Love, I'll Miss You," *Los Angeles Times*, August 15, 1927.

13. "Gloria's Mate Denies Break," *Los Angeles Times*, August 21, 1927.

14. Allan Dwan was one of the first Malibu residents to actually build a house on his lease holdings.

15. "Gloria Swanson's Furniture Sold," *Los Angeles Times*, July 21, 1927.

16. Amanda Smith, ed., *Hostage of Fortune: The Letters of Joseph P. Kennedy* (New York: Viking, 2001), 61.

17. "De La Falaise Returns," *New York Times*, September 22, 1927.

18. HRC.

19. Axel Madsen, *Gloria and Joe* (New York: Berkeley Books, 1989), 70.

20. Smith, *Hostage to Fortune: The Letters of Joseph P. Kennedy*, 68.

21. Ibid., 61.

22. Ibid., 69.

23. Ibid., 60.

24. Beauchamp, *Joseph P. Kennedy Presents*, 153.

25. Ibid., 154–55.

26. Quirk, *The Kennedys in Hollywood*, 52.

27. Beauchamp, *Joseph P. Kennedy Presents*, 155.

28. Matthew Kennedy, *Edmund Goulding's Dark Victory* (Madison: University of Wisconsin Press, 2004), 76.

29. Smith, *Hostage to Fortune: The Letters of Joseph P. Kennedy*, 62.

30. Christopher Anderson, *Jack and Jackie: Portrait of an American Marriage* (New York: William Morrow, 1996), 28.

31. Swanson, *Swanson on Swanson*, 350.

32. Ibid., 351.

33. Ibid., 352.

34. Ibid., 356.

35. Ibid., 356–57.

36. Ibid., 357.

15. *QUEEN KELLY*

1. Mordaunt Hall, "The Screen," *New York Times*, February 6, 1928.

2. Mordaunt Hall, "Miss Thompson's Shadow," *New York Times*, February 12, 1928.

3. "Sid," *Variety*, February 8, 1928.

4. *Screenland*, May 1928.

5. *Motion Picture*, May 1928.

6. Joseph Schenck remade *Rain* for UA in 1932, borrowing Joan Crawford from MGM. Crawford had doubts about the role, and rightfully so. As directed by Lewis Milestone, her *Rain* bombed at the box office. Tallulah Bankhead took *Rain* back to the stage in 1935, and June Havoc did a musical called *Sadie Thompson* on Broadway in 1944. There was a blaxploitation film version called *Dirty Gertie from Harlem U.S.A.* (Sack Amusement, 1946). And Rita Hayworth starred in *Miss Sadie Thompson*, Columbia Pictures' 1953 Technicolor and 3-D production, with José Ferrer as Davidson. For years a television adaptation of the play was in the works, reaching a negotiation stage in 1961, when NBC announced its projected color production with Marilyn Monroe and Fredric March. (One ponders what *Rain* could have been with Monroe as Sadie Thompson.)

7. Beauchamp, *Without Lying Down: Frances Marion and the Powerful Women of Early Hollywood*, 229.

8. Smith, *Hostage to Fortune: The Letters of Joseph P. Kennedy*, 61.

9. Laurence Leamer, *The Kennedy Women: The Saga of an American Family* (New York: Villard Books, 1994), 175.

10. Thomas Maier, *The Kennedys: America's Emerald Kings* (New York: Basic Books, 2003), 87.

11. "Law Parts Gloria and 'Hank,'" *Los Angeles Times*, March 8, 1928.

12. "Marquis in Difficulty over Visa," *Los Angeles Times*, March 16, 1928.

13. "Comte's Joke Kicks Back," *Los Angeles Times*, April 29, 1928.

14. Swanson, *Swanson on Swanson*, 360.

15. HRC.

16. Arthur Lennig, *Stroheim* (Lexington: University Press of Kentucky, 2000), 90.

17. Betty Lasky, *RKO: The Biggest Little Major of Them All* (Englewood Cliffs, NJ: Prentice-Hall, 1984), 32.

18. Harry Carr, "The Lancer in Hollywood," *Los Angeles Times*, August 5, 1928.

19. Benjamin Glazer was the former head of the Famous Players–Lasky story department, and had, along with Erich von Stroheim, written the screenplay for *The Merry Widow* (1925). In 1928 he won the Academy Award for Best Screenplay for *Seventh Heaven* (Fox, 1927), the same year he became the head of production at Pathé.

20. Harry Carr, "The Lancer in Hollywood," *Los Angeles Times*, August 26, 1928.

21. "Sylvia Gossips About Filmdom," *Los Angeles Times*, November 1, 1931.

22. Christopher Finch and Linda Rosenkrantz, *Gone Hollywood: The Movie Colony in the Golden Age* (Garden City, NY: Doubleday, 1979), 160.

23. Marion Davies starred in *Show People* (MGM), a tremendously funny and highly successful film released in November 1928, directed by King Vidor and co-starring William Haines. In it Marion portrays an unpolished young woman who becomes a big movie star. There was no rancor between Marion and Gloria.

24. Paris, *Louise Brooks*, 241–42.

25. Grace Kingsley, "Lasky Fits Girl for Stardom," *Los Angeles Times*, September 18, 1928.

26. Patricia Seaton Lawford and Ted Schwartz, *The Peter Lawford Story: Life with the Kennedys, Monroe, and the Rat Pack* (New York: Carroll & Graf, 1988), 92.

27. Somborn Daly, *A&E Biography*, "The Greatest Star," July 29, 1997.

28. Smith, *Hostage to Fortune: The Letters of Joseph P. Kennedy*, 78.

29. David Shipman, *Movie Talk: Who Said What About Whom in the Movies* (New York: St. Martin's Press, 1988), 209.

30. "Harvey Thew to Prepare Swanson-Stroheim Story," *Los Angeles Times*, November 4, 1928.

31. Edwin Schallert, "Von Stroheim Hits New Tempo," *Los Angeles Times*, November 18, 1928.

32. Lennig, *Stroheim*, 277.

33. Swanson, *Swanson on Swanson*, 371.

34. Quirk, *The Kennedys in Hollywood*, 98.

35. Swanson, *Swanson on Swanson*, 373.

36. Ibid., 373.

37. Beauchamp, *Joseph P. Kennedy Presents: His Hollywood Years*, 247.

38. Ibid., 253.

39. Ibid.

40. Smith, *Hostage to Fortune: The Letters of Joseph P. Kennedy*, 78–81.

41. Lennig, *Stroheim*, 280.

42. Lasky, *RKO: The Biggest Little Major of Them All*, 50.

43. Ibid.

16. *THE TRESPASSER*

1. "Miss Swanson's New Role," *New York Times,* January 27, 1929.

2. Brian Kellow, *The Bennetts: An Acting Family* (Lexington: University Press of Kentucky, 2004), 126.

3. Beauchamp, *Joseph P. Kennedy Presents: His Hollywood Years,* 270.

4. Smith, *Hostage to Fortune: The Letters of Joseph P. Kennedy,* 82.

5. Ibid., 83.

6. Mason Wiley and Damien Bona, *Inside Oscar: The Unofficial History of the Academy Awards* (New York: Ballantine Books, 1987), 8; Anthony Holden, *Behind the Oscar: The Secret History of the Academy Awards* (New York: Simon & Schuster, 1993), 94.

7. Eyman, *Empire of Dreams: The Epic Life of Cecil B. DeMille,* 254.

8. Ibid., 254–55.

9. Ibid., 255. DeMille had been negotiating with United Artists, even going so far as to draw up contracts. But in the end neither the Pathé nor the UA deal worked out. Instead, he made his move to MGM, where he produced three early talkie duds in a row—*Dynamite* (1929), *Madam Satan* (1930), his only musical, and his third remake of *The Squaw Man* (1931).

10. Kennedy, *Edmund Goulding's Dark Victory,* 82.

11. Frank Westmore and Muriel Davidson, *The Westmores of Hollywood* (New York: Berkeley Medallion Books, 1978), 59.

12. Ronald Kessler, *Sins of the Father: Joseph P. Kennedy and the Dynasty He Founded* (New York: Warner Books, 1996), 74.

13. Peter Collier David Horowitz, *The Kennedys: An American Drama* (New York: Warner Books, 1985), 49.

14. Anderson, *Jack and Jackie: Portrait of an American Marriage,* 29.

15. Ibid., 30.

16. Ibid.

17. Before returning to the Canterbury School in New Milford, Connecticut, after the New Year, twelve-year-old John Fitzgerald Kennedy (at 294 Pondfield Road, Bronxville, New York) wrote Gloria a handwritten letter thanking her for the horse racing game she had sent him at Christmas.

18. HRC.

19. "London Women Fight to See Miss Swanson," *New York Times,* September 10, 1929.

20. "Frat," *Variety,* September 18, 1929.

21. Ernest Marshall, "Cinema Notes from London Town," *New York Times,* September 29, 1929.

22. Rose Fitzgerald Kennedy, *Times to Remember* (New York: Doubleday, 1974), 186.

23. Kennedy, *Times to Remember,* 188–89.

24. Ibid., 189.

25. The ownership rights to "Love, Your Spell Is Everywhere" lay in limbo for many years. In 1967 they reverted back to Gloria, but Edmund Goulding's sister Ivis finally laid claim in 1972.

26. "La Marquise Chez Elle," *New York Times*, September 29, 1929.

27. Ibid.

28. Ibid.

29. Smith, *Hostage to Fortune: The Letters of Joseph P. Kennedy*, 87.

30. Ibid., 86–87.

31. Norbert Lusk, "Altered Gloria Off for Coast," *Los Angeles Times*, November 3, 1929.

32. Mordaunt Hall, "The Screen," *New York Times*, November 2, 1929; Mordaunt Hall, "A Devil's Island Lover," *New York Times*, November 10, 1929.

33. "Sime," *Variety*, October 2, 1929.

34. Richard Barrios, *A Song in the Dark* (New York: Oxford University Press, 1995), 140.

35. Barbara Gibson and Ted Schwartz, *Rose Kennedy and Her Family: The Best and Worst of Their Lives and Times* (New York: Birch Lane Press, 1995), 92.

36. Madsen, *Gloria and Joe*, 293.

37. "A Roosevelt Son Defends His Book," *New York Times*, March 19, 1973.

38. Swanson, *Swanson on Swanson*, 393.

39. Ibid., 394.

40. Madsen, *Gloria and Joe*, 293.

41. Gibson and Ted Schwartz, *Rose Kennedy and Her Family: The Best and Worst of Their Lives and Times*, 94.

42. Madsen, *Gloria and Joe*, 294.

43. Ibid., 293.

44. Laurence Leamer, *The Kennedy Men, 1901–1963* (New York: William Morrow, 2001), 59.

45. Ibid., 60.

46. Anderson, *Jack and Jackie: Portrait of an American Marriage*, 28.

47. Norbert Lusk, "Altered Gloria Off for Coast," *Los Angeles Times*, November 3, 1929.

48. *Los Angeles Times*, November 7, 1929.

49. Untitled article, n.d., WHS.

50. Edwin Schallert, "Gloria Stirs . . . in New Medium," *Los Angeles Times*, November 7, 1929.

51. *The Trespasser* was remade at Warner Bros. in 1937 as *That Certain Woman*, with Bette Davis and Henry Fonda, and also directed by Edmund Goulding. In 1947 Republic Studios made *The Trespasser* with Dale Evans and Douglas Fowley. That film had nothing to do with its predecessors but the title. In it Evans sang "It's Not the First Love."

52. Beauchamp, *Joseph P. Kennedy Presents: His Hollywood Years*, 286.

53. Smith, *Hostage to Fortune: The Letters of Joseph P. Kennedy*, 88.

54. Cecil B. DeMille Papers, Brigham Young University, Provo, Utah.

55. Robert S. Birchard, *Cecil B. DeMille's Hollywood* (Lexington: University Press of Kentucky, 2004), 244.

56. Beauchamp, *Joseph P. Kennedy Presents: His Hollywood Years,* 283.

57. Kennedy, *Edmund Goulding's Dark Victory,* 85.

58. Beauchamp, *Joseph P. Kennedy Presents: His Hollywood Years,* 284.

59. Kennedy, *Edmund Goulding's Dark Victory,* 89–90.

60. Ibid., 90.

61. Beauchamp, *Joseph P. Kennedy Presents: His Hollywood Years,* 285.

62. Lennig, *Stroheim,* 288.

63. Gary Cary, *Anita Loos: A Biography* (New York: Alfred A. Knopf, 1988), 136.

17. THE TALKIES

1. Beauchamp, *Joseph P. Kennedy Presents: His Hollywood Years,* 291.

2. Madsen, *Gloria and Joe,* 299, 300, 302.

3. Ibid., 302.

4. Beauchamp, *Joseph P. Kennedy Presents: His Hollywood Years,* 454.

5. Swanson, *Swanson on Swanson,* 397.

6. Ibid., 399–400.

7. "Men of Church Held Messiahs," *Los Angeles Times,* February 6, 1930.

8. Beauchamp, *Joseph P. Kennedy Presents: His Hollywood Years,* 267.

9. Ibid.

10. Mollie Merrick, "Hollywood in Person," *Los Angeles Times,* March 23, 1930.

11. HRC.

12. Ibid.

13. Swanson, *Swanson on Swanson,* 400. Joel McCrea became a fine actor and attractive lead-ing man in motion pictures, starring in such classic films as *Come and Get It* (Goldwyn, 1936), *Dead End* (UA 1937), DeMille's *Union Pacific* (Paramount, 1939), Alfred Hitch-cock's *Foreign Correspondent* (UA, 1940), Preston Sturges's *Sullivan's Travels* (Paramount, 1941) and *The Palm Beach Story* (Paramount, 1942) before turning to western films, where he found his niche. In 1933 he married actress Frances Dee (*I Walked with a Zom-bie,* RKO 1943), and the couple had three sons. Jody McCrea became an actor as well and had a promising career in pictures in the 1960s. Joel McCrea died in 1990.

14. Beauchamp, *Joseph P. Kennedy Presents: His Hollywood Years,* 299.

15. "Film Innovation Revealed," *Los Angeles Times,* March 8, 1930.

16. Swanson, *Swanson on Swanson,* 403.

17. Beauchamp, *Joseph P. Kennedy Presents: His Hollywood Years,* 299.

18. David E. Koskoff, *Joseph P. Kennedy: A Life and Times* (Englewood Cliffs, NJ: Prentice-Hall, 1974), 36.

19. The most outrageous expenditure was for the cost and furnishing of Gloria's studio bun-galow, $19,000, which should have been a mandatory studio perk. It was *studio* property,

and not Gloria's to keep. An additional insult: In the mid-1930s when Gloria's bungalow was taken over by Russell Birdwell, publicity director for *Gone with the Wind*, a bugging device was discovered in the ceiling of the bedroom.

20. Collier and Horowitz, *The Kennedys: An American Drama*, 51.

21. Beauchamp, *Joseph P. Kennedy Presents: His Hollywood Years*, 308.

22. St. Johns, *Love, Laughter and Tears: My Hollywood Story*, 150.

23. "Decide to Remain Apart," *New York Times*, August 6, 1930.

24. Muriel Babcock, "Marquise or Film Star?" *Los Angeles Times*, September 14, 1930.

25. Untitled article, n.d., WHS.

26. Mordaunt Hall, "The Screen," *New York Times*, October 4, 1930.

27. "Sime," *Variety*, September 17, 1930.

28. HRC.

29. Swanson, *Swanson on Swanson*, 407.

30. HRC.

31. Grace Kingsley, "Fox Picks Youths for 'Yankee,'" *Los Angeles Times*, October 17, 1930.

32. "Gloria Swanson Sues for Divorce," *New York Times*, October 22, 1930.

33. "Miss Swanson Seeks Divorce," *Los Angeles Times*, October 22, 1930.

34. "Gloria Granted Divorce," *Los Angeles Times*, November 7, 1930.

35. *Vanity Fair*, April 2002.

36. Adela Rogers St. Johns, "Great Love Stories of Hollywood, No. 1—Gloria Swanson and the Marquis," *New Movie*, February 1931.

18. HOLLYWOOD

1. In 1934 a $1 million lawsuit and an injunction of further publication in book form of *Indiscreet*, filed by attorney Charles W. Dempster, was instigated by Ms. Arden Coombs, author and dramatist, against Gloria, United Artists, story editor Roland West, and B. G. DeSylva, Lew Brown, and Jay Henderson. Alleging she had submitted the story *Valiant Sinners* in October 1930 to UA by their request, it was returned to her in April 1931. Upon viewing *Indiscreet*, Coombs complained her story had been rearranged "with slight changes cunningly devised, and intended to conceal" her plotline. "Author Charges Film Piracy Asks $1,000,000," *Los Angeles Times*, April 22, 1934. The outcome of the suit is unknown.

2. HRC.

3. A. Scott Berg, *Goldwyn: A Biography* (New York: Alfred A. Knopf, 1989), 214.

4. *Photoplay*, July 1931.

5. "Sime," *Variety*, May 13, 1931.

6. Untitled article, n.d., WHS.

7. Parish, *The Paramount Pretties*, 36.

8. Swanson, *Swanson on Swanson*, 422.

9. Douglas Fairbanks and Mary Pickford had married in 1920. They were the Royal Couple of Hollywood for over a decade, their home Pickfair the town's official palace. If one was accepted at Pickfair, one was "in" in Hollywood. Doug reluctantly faced middle age. When he met Sylvia Ashley, he was smitten, and when he told Mary, she gave up her career (possibly it had ended before that) and took to drinking in private. Sylvia and Douglas married on March 7, 1936. He would die in December 1939, and Sylvia would eventually wed actor Clark Gable in 1949. Her fifth and final marriage, in 1954, lasting until her death in 1977, made her a princess when she wed Prince Dimitri Djordjadze of the country of Georgia.

10. Swanson, *Swanson on Swanson*, 411.

11. Ibid., 412.

12. Ibid.

13. Ibid.

14. Eulalia Wilson, "The Man That Gloria Married," *Photoplay,* February 1932.

15. Warren G. Harris, *The Other Marilyn: A Biography of Marilyn Miller* (New York: Arbor House, 1985), 168.

16. Wilson, "The Man That Gloria Married," *Photoplay,* February 1932.

17. "Gloria May Wed Again, She Admits," *Los Angeles Times,* August 15, 1931.

18. "Gloria Swanson Home; Michael Comes Along," *Los Angeles Times,* August 21, 1931.

19. Swanson, *Swanson on Swanson*, 419.

20. Melvyn Douglas and Tom Arthur, *See You at the Movies: The Autobiography of Melvyn Douglas* (Latham, MD: University Press of America, 1986), 86.

21. Douglas and Arthur, *See You at the Movies: The Autobiography of Melvyn Douglas,* 87.

22. "Miss Swanson Arrives; Pair to Sail for Europe," *Los Angeles Times,* November 21, 1931.

23. Sister Joan Bennett's first husband was John Fox, with whom she had a daughter named Diana, born in 1928. In 1948 Diana wed John Anderson, whose brother Robert wed Gloria's elder daughter, Gloria, in 1939.

24. Philip K. Scheuer, "Star's Film Shines," *Los Angeles Times,* December 7, 1931.

25. Mordaunt Hall, "The Screen," *New York Times,* December 18, 1931.

26. Norbert Lusk, "Entertaining Though Not Outstanding Pictures Comprise This Week's New York Offerings," *Los Angeles Times,* December 27, 1931.

27. James Robert Parish and Don E. Stanke, *The Debonairs* (New Rochelle, NY: Arlington House, 1975), 75.

28. Myrtle Gebhart, "Money Shrieks in Hollywood," *Los Angeles Times,* November 22, 1931.

29. Carr, *Four Fabulous Faces,* 44.

19. TRANSITION

1. Swanson, *Swanson on Swanson*, 425.

2. HRC.

3. Ibid.

4. Robert Tanitsch, *Olivier* (New York: Abbeville Press, 1985), 43.

5. Swanson, *Swanson on Swanson*, 427.

6. HRC.

7. Ibid.

8. Ibid.

9. Kennedy, *Edmund Goulding's Dark Victory*, 89.

10. A script entitled "New Story Version 'Queen Kelly'" by Harry Poppe, dated November 4, 1930, incorporating von Stroheim's scenes with a workable plot, was submitted to UA but not developed. The studio attempted to release the picture a year later, using a new, shorter ending filmed on November 24, 1931. Submitted for release in early 1932, *Queen Kelly* was three years too late. The company's distributor rejected it as an inferior product. As late as 1933 expenditures made on *Queen Kelly* were still in debate. Gloria's California attorney Loyd Wright sent Joseph Schenck a letter asking for an extension of a billing of $1,118.18 owed Consolidated Film Industries for work they had done on *Queen Kelly* until after the profits of *Perfect Understanding* came through. In 1939 independent film producer Walter Futter, who was in partnership with actor Leslie Howard at RKO, paid $10,000 for the negative and the script to *Queen Kelly* with plans to remake the picture, possibly including former cast members Seena Owen, Walter Byron, and Tully Marshall. His main interest in obtaining the negative was for the lavish banquet scene, which had allegedly cost $260,000. Nothing came of the Futter project.

11. "Gloria Swanson Felt Optimism on Liner's Deck," *New York Herald-Telegram*, February 16, 1933.

12. *Perfect Understanding* pressbook, United Artists.

13. Norbert Lusk, "News and Gossip of the Stage and Screen," *Los Angeles Times*, February 26, 1933.

14. Mordaunt Hall, "The Screen," *New York Times*, February 23, 1933.

15. "Rush," *Variety*, February 28, 1933.

16. "Gloria Back in Hollywood," *Los Angeles Times*, April 4, 1933.

17. "Stars Return," *St. Joseph* (Missouri) *Gazette*, August 1, 1933.

18. Edward Baron Turk, *Hollywood Diva: A Biography of Jeanette MacDonald* (Berkeley: University of California Press, 1998), 142.

19. "Gloria Will Lose Gems Seen in Suit," *Los Angeles Times*, September 11, 1933.

20. HRC.

21. Ibid.

22. Warren B. Francis, "Garsson Actions in Film Alien Cases Investigated by F.B.I. 13 Years Ago," *Los Angeles Times*, July 27, 1946.

23. Edwin Schallert, "Marx Bros. Due for Vacation from Movies; Jean Muir 'Autumn Crocus' Lead," *Los Angeles Times*, January 1, 1934.

24. Somborn Daly, *A&E Biography*, "The Greatest Star," July 29, 1997. Herbert Somborn

established himself as president of H. K. Somborn Enterprises in 1926 with the purchase of the original Brown Derby Restaurant at Wilshire Boulevard and Alexandria. His associates were Tom and Wilbur May, Joseph Schnitzer, Charles Rogers, Jack Warner, and Robert C. Cobb. The building itself was shaped like Al Smith's hat, symbolizing brashness and hope. The Brown Derby became a popular Hollywood eatery. When he died Herbert also left behind his mother and a sister. Per his wishes, his body was cremated on January 3, and his ashes sent to his mother for inurnment in New York.

25. Swanson, *Swanson on Swanson*, 437.
26. Madsen, *Gloria and Joe*, 344.
27. "Tip Poff," "That Certain Party," *Los Angeles Times*, February 11, 1934.
28. Mollie Merrick, "Star Plans Big Comeback," *Los Angeles Times*, April 24, 1934.
29. Read Kendall, "Around and About," *Los Angeles Times*, March 29, 1934.
30. "Gloria and Wally," incomplete article, Ben Maddox, n.d., MOMA.
31. HRC.
32. Ibid.
33. Ibid.
34. Ibid.
35. Ibid.
36. Ibid.
37. Norbert Lusk, "New Tarzan Film Highly Entertaining," *Los Angeles Times*, April 29, 1934.
38. Associated Press New York, "Gloria Swanson Will Seek Fourth Divorce," *Owosso* (Michigan) *Argus-Press*, April 24, 1934.

20. HOLLYWOOD REDUX

1. "Gloria, Hubby to Get Divorce," *Border Cities* (Ontario, Canada), April 24, 1934.
2. "Gloria's Mate Seeks News About Divorce," *Los Angeles Times*, April 25, 1934.
3. "Mate Hopes Star Will Stay Wed," *Los Angeles Times*, May 6, 1934.
4. HRC.
5. "Film Queen Says Little on Divorce," *Los Angeles Times*, May 22, 1934.
6. Swanson, *Swanson on Swanson*, 441.
7. Joe May, unlike many of his European exile associates, was unable to assimilate in Hollywood. In his native Austria he was a tremendous giant of the industry, rivaling von Stroheim or DeMille in his dictatorial approach to filmmaking. In Hollywood, he was assigned B pictures such as Warner Bros.' 1937 *Confession* (a scene-for-scene remake of the brilliant 1935 German Tonfilm *Mazurka*, which had starred Pola Negri) and *The Invisible Man Returns* for Universal in 1940. Except for these and *Music in the Air*, May directed nothing of merit. He and his wife, former silent screen actress Mia May, opened a

Viennese restaurant, which eventually failed. Quite unlike Billy Wilder, who *did* learn to adapt to American filmmaking and enjoyed tremendous success in the industry, Joe May sadly became but a footnote in film history. He died in obscurity in 1954.

8. Moore later slimmed down and signed with Columbia for *One Night of Love* that same year (1934), earning herself an Oscar nomination for Best Actress and a long-term contract with the studio in the process.

9. Ursula Hardt, *From Caligari to California: Erich Pommer's Life in the International Film Wars* (Providence, RI: Berghan Books, 1996), 146.

10. Maurice Zolotow, *Billy Wilder in Hollywood* (New York: G. P. Putnam's Sons, 1977), 57.

11. Russell, "Gloria Swanson's Guide to Happiness," *Film Pictorial*, July 7, 1934, NYPL.

12. Leonard Pitts Jr., *Glamour Girls of Hollywood* (Cresskill, NJ: Sharon Publications, 1984), 20.

13. "Film Writer Socks Actor in Row over Gloria Swanson; Foes Tell Different Versions of How It All Happened," *Pittsburgh Press*, September 25, 1934.

14. Ibid.

15. Fay Wray, *On the Other Hand: A Life Story* (New York: St. Martin's Press, 1989), 162.

16. Ibid., 164.

17. "Gloria Swanson Gets Divorce in Los Angeles Court," *Gettysburg Times*, November 8, 1934.

18. "Miss Swanson Free Again," *Los Angeles Times*, November 8, 1934.

19. Andrew Wilson, "Living with Norma Desmond," *Observer* (U.K.), March 9, 2003.

20. Andre Sennwald, "The Screen," *New York Times*, December 14, 1934.

21. "Abel," *Variety*, December 18, 1934.

22. Norbert Lusk, "News and Gossip of Stage and Screen," *Los Angeles Times*, December 23, 1934.

23. Richard Barrios, *A Song in the Dark* (New York: Oxford University Press, 1995), 422.

24. Roy Hemming, *The Melody Lingers On: The Great Songwriters and Their Movie Musicals* (New York: Newmarket Press, 1986), 93.

25. *Music in the Air* was considered for a remake by 20th Century–Fox in 1943 as a vehicle for Sonja Henie, and ridiculously years later for another remake to star Elvis Presley.

26. Leonard Maltin's *Movie Crazy* website, March 28, 2011.

27. David Niven, *The Moon's a Balloon* (New York: Dell, 1983), 200.

28. "Michael Farmer in Auto Crash," *Los Angeles Times*, August 20, 1935.

29. HRC.

30. Ibid.

31. Ibid.

32. Charles Higham and Roy Moseley, *Princess Merle: The Romantic Life of Merle Oberon* (New York: Coward & McCann, 1983), 84.

33. HRC.

34. Farmer (Amon), "The Swanson Story," *Los Angeles Times*, August 6, 1950.

35. Michelle Farmer Amon, *A&E Biography*, "The Greatest Star," July 29, 1997.

36. "Gloria Swanson Sees Plays, Tells of Her Own Career," *Milwaukee Sentinel*, January 25, 1936.
37. HRC.
38. *New York Post*, December 8, 1936.
39. Sheilah Graham, "A Gadabout's Notebook," *Los Angeles Times*, December 2, 1936.

21. NEW YORK REDUX

1. "Films Reclaim Gloria Swanson," *Los Angeles Times*, February 5, 1937.
2. Ibid.
3. Sheilah Graham, "A Gadabout's Notebook," *Los Angeles Times*, March 12, 1937. *Maizie Kenyon* was eventually retitled *Daisy Kenyon* (20th Century–Fox, 1947), and the screenplay heavily reworked for Joan Crawford and Henry Fonda, a strange teaming if ever there was one.
4. HRC.
5. Swanson, *Swanson on Swanson*, 449.
6. HRC.
7. Gloria was given an advance of $4,250 on March 16, another for $3,759 on May 3, another for $1,250 on May 8, and another for $1,000 on June 6, making a total advance payment between May 1 and June 19, 1937, of $7,666.67 against an amount already paid of $6,000. Another advance of $1,000 was given her on June 26, and from July 3 through December she was paid a straight $500 a week, a total of $24,166.67 against the advances made of $8,500.
8. Paul Harrison, "Acting Her Age," *New York World-Telegram*, n.d., NYPL.
9. Katharine Hepburn was handed the part after Gloria officially broke from Columbia in January 1938. The title reverted to *Holiday*.
10. William Raidy, "'Audiences Best Teachers,' Gloria Swanson Maintains," *Toledo Blade*, October 17, 1971.
11. Raidy, "'Audiences Best Teachers,' Gloria Swanson Maintains," *Toledo Blade*, October 17, 1971.
12. Otto Friedrich, *City of Nets* (New York: Perennial Books, 1987), 415.
13. Raidy, "'Audiences Best Teachers,' Gloria Swanson Maintains," *Toledo Blade*, October 17, 1971.
14. Tapert, *The Power of Glamour: The Women Who Defined the Magic of Stardom*, 33.
15. HRC.
16. Dewitt Bodeen, *More from Hollywood: The Careers of 15 Great American Stars* (Cranbury, NJ: A. S. Barnes, 1977), 116.
17. Somborn Daly, *A&E Biography*, "The Greatest Star," July 29, 1997.
18. Plato was considered one of America's foremost innovative designers of luxury jewelry.

19. Swanson, *Swanson on Swanson,* 450.

20. HRC.

21. Swanson, *Swanson on Swanson,* 451.

22. Frank Reil, "Line on Liners," n.d., NYPL.

23. Farmer (Amon), "The Swanson Story," *Los Angeles Times,* August 6, 1950.

24. Stanley Frank, "Grandma Gloria Swanson Comes Back," *Saturday Evening Post,* July 29, 1950.

25. HRC.

26. Pitts, *Glamour Girls of Hollywood,* 20.

27. After receiving the decoration Officer d'Academie in 1934, Henri, along with Constance Bennett, for Bennett Productions and DuWorld Films, produced two unique French documentaries in the mid-1930s—the two-tone Technicolor *Legong: Dance of the Virgins* (1935) and *Kliou the Tiger* (1936). Henri in 1939 was in the process of divorcing Constance Bennett.

28. Hedda Hopper, "Hedda Hopper's Hollywood," *Los Angeles Times,* March 27, 1939.

29. This final trip possibly could have been also for a meeting with film producer Oscar Futter, at the Hotel Queen Mary at 9 Rue Greffulhe in Paris, in regard to Gloria's insatiable desire to see *Queen Kelly* distributed internationally.

30. HRC.

31. Frank, "Grandma Gloria Swanson Comes Back," *Saturday Evening Post,* July 29, 1950.

32. Letter dated May 1, 1979, HRC.

33. HRC.

34. Ibid.

35. Ibid.

36. Douglas W. Churchill, "Screen News Here and in Hollywood," *New York Times,* July 1, 1939.

37. HRC.

38. Ibid.

39. Ibid. Henri's passionate letter of his war experiences up to that point was graphically included at length in Gloria's long autobiography, reprinted in complete accuracy. He told her of his urgent need to gain a diplomatic visa to leave Europe, as he found opposition to his departure daunting. Emma could leave Europe without any problem. But Henri was a French citizen and thus suspect.

Henri suggested to Gloria she contact Joseph Kennedy, whom he had spoken with in London after his heroic exploits at Dunkirk, to expedite his departure. With Emma's assistance Henri had been able escape a prisoner's camp in Brittany after the battle, and now he needed to come to America posthaste to allow Constance Bennett to divorce him (or the divorce would be invalid in France) so he could then wed Emma.

40. Jimmy Fidler, "Jimmy Fidler in Hollywood, "*Los Angeles Times,* October 18, 1940.

22. THEATER

1. Swanson, *Swanson on Swanson*, 467.

2. "Jean Gabin Given First Role," *Milwaukee Sentinel,* April 15, 1941.

3. Frederick C. Othman, "Ex-Siren Gloria Swanson Now a Big Business Gal, in New Film 'on Vacation,'" n.d., NYPL.

4. Othman, "Ex-Siren Gloria Swanson Now a Big Business Gal, in New Film 'on Vacation,'" n.d., NYPL.

5. Jimmy Fidler, "Jimmy Fidler's Hollywood," *Los Angeles Times,* May 16, 1941.

6. HRC.

7. "Ex-Mate of Two Film Stars Reaches America as Refugee," *Los Angeles Times,* April 16, 1941.

8. Maier, *The Kennedys: America's Emerald Kings,* 89.

9. "Michael Farmer Seized in France," *New York Times,* May 9, 1941.

10. Hedda Hopper, "Hedda Hopper's Hollywood," *Los Angeles Times,* May 12, 1941.

11. John Baxter, *Von Sternberg* (Lexington: University Press of Kentucky, 2010), 232.

12. "Walt," *Variety,* July 16, 1941.

13. "T.M.P.," "The Screen," *New York Times,* September 5, 1941.

14. Richard Griffith, "Swanson's Film Return Successful," *Los Angeles Times,* September 15, 1941.

15. David Chierichetti, "Gloria Swanson Today," *Film Fan Monthly,* February 1975.

16. HRC.

17. Ibid.

18. Each playhouse required a separate contract for summer theater. For example, for the run in Poughkeepsie, Gloria received $500 a week against 40 percent of the house over $2,100; for the Arlington Auditorium in Poughkeepsie, New York, the Garden Pier in Atlantic City, and Brattle Hall in Cambridge, Massachusetts, she received a flat $1,000 a week, etc.

19. Harold J. Kennedy, comp., "Highs and Lows of the Straw Hat Trail," *New York Times,* June 13, 1982.

20. "It's a New Kind of Screen for La Swanson," *Cue,* July 10, 1948.

21. William P. Frank, November 28, 1942, HRC.

22. HRC.

23. Ibid.

24. "Gloria Swanson Arrives Here to Rehearse for Play Next Week," *Holyoke* (Massachusetts) *Daily Transcript & Telegram,* January 29, 1943.

25. "Gloria Swanson and Fine Cast Score Big Hit in Comedy, 'Let Us Be Gay,'" n.d., NYPL.

26. Louise Mace, "News of the Theaters," *Springfield Daily Republican,* February 3, 1943.

27. "Arke, "New Acts," *Variety,* March 10, 1943.

28. Farmer (Amon), "The Swanson Story," *Los Angeles Times,* August 6, 1950.

29. HRC.

30. Edwin Schallert, "'Little House' Planned a George Pal Feature," *Los Angeles Times,* July 15, 1944.

31. HRC.

32. "Swanson Changes Her Mind," *New York Times,* August 15, 1944.

33. Gus Schirmer would eventually marry former Follies showgirl Mildred Boots, widow of songwriter Vincent Youmans, whom she had married in October 1935. She divorced him in January 1946, and Youmans died of tuberculosis in April of that year. Most of his estate was left to create the Vincent Youmans Tuberculosis Memorial, a public charity. Gustave Schirmer died in late May 1965, leaving behind his last wife Mildred and his son Gustave. At his death Schirmer was the president of the Boston Music Company. His son died at the age of seventy-three in 1992.

34. "Milestones," *Time,* January 10, 1949.

35. "Gloria, No. 5 Honeymoon," *Los Angeles Examiner,* January 31, 1945.

36. HRC.

37. Edwin J. Bronner, *The Encyclopedia of the American Theatre, 1900–1975* (New York: A. S. Barnes, 1978), 191.

38. Lewis Nichols, "The Play," *New York Times,* January 24, 1945.

23. SUNSET BOULEVARD

1. Allen Ellenberger, *Margaret O'Brien: A Career Chronicle and Biography* (Jefferson, NC: MacFarland, 2000), 9.

2. HRC.

3. Ibid.

4. "Gloria Swanson Sues Husband," *Los Angeles Times,* July 10, 1945.

5. HRC.

6. Ibid.

7. "Scarce Butter Figures in Swanson Suit," *New York Times,* September 5, 1945.

8. HRC.

9. Ibid.

10. "Playboy Who Set Europe Talking," HRC.

11. HRC.

12. "One Role Gloria Missed," n.d., MOMA.

13. Ibid.

14. "Gloria Swanson Tells Her Woes," *Los Angeles Times,* January 5, 1946.

15. "One Role Gloria Missed," n.d., MOMA.

16. Incomplete article, *New York World-Telegram,* January 4, 1946, NYPL.

17. "Alimony Satisfies Gloria Swanson," *Los Angeles Times,* April 3, 1946.

18. Frank, "Grandma Gloria Comes Back," *Saturday Evening Post,* July 22, 1950.

19. Gloria Swanson, "Return Engagement," n.d., NYPL.

20. Henry McLemore, "The Lighter Side," *Los Angeles Times,* March 15, 1948.

21. "Spring Arrives—But Gloria Swanson Can't See It—She's Memorizing Lines," *Toledo Blade,* May 25, 1948.

22. "Odec," *Variety,* June 23, 1948.

23. Richard Lamparski, *Whatever Became of . . . ? Ninth Series* (New York: Crown, 1985), 147.

24. HRC.

25. Hedda Hopper, "Hedda Hopper," *Los Angeles Times,* October 8, 1948.

26. Thomas F. Brady, "Ephrons Working in Film Musical," *New York Times,* October 26, 1948.

27. Andrew Wilson, "Living with Norma Desmond," *Observer* (U.K.), March 9, 2003.

28. Hedda Hopper, "Twentieth Will Get Lund for 'Bandwagon,'" *Los Angeles Times,* December 31, 1948.

29. Hedda Hopper, "Unique Zanuck Film Aimed at Star Trio," *Los Angeles Times,* December 30, 1948.

30. Thomas F. Brady, "Trio Considering Film on Industry," *New York Times,* December 31, 1948.

31. Zolotow, *Billy Wilder in Hollywood,* 163.

32. Wilson, "Living with Norma Desmond," *Observer* (U.K.), March 9, 2003.

33. Brandy Brent, "Carousel," *Los Angeles Times,* February 17, 1949.

34. Kevin Lally, *Wilder Times: The Life of Billy Wilder* (New York: Henry Holt, 1996), 187.

35. Eileen Whitfield, *Pickford: The Woman Who Made Hollywood* (Lexington: University Press of Kentucky, 1997), 338.

36. Whitfield, *Pickford: The Woman Who Made Hollywood,* 338.

37. Wilson, "Living with Norma Desmond," *Observer* (U.K.), March 9, 2003.

38. Ibid.

39. Patricia Bosworth, *Montgomery Clift: A Biography* (New York: Harcourt Brace Limelight Editions, 1992), 175.

40. At the same time, Monty Clift was involved with an older woman, the notorious torch singer Libby Holman (she had appeared with Clifton Webb in *The Little Show* in New York in 1929), who was accused of the accidental shooting death of her tobacco heir husband Zachary Smith Reynolds in 1932. She became an alcoholic and lived with Monty in Connecticut. Holman possibly persuaded Clift to reconsider the project. Monty would never regret his decision not to portray Joe Gillis, and he forever praised *Sunset Boulevard.*

41. Chierichetti, "Gloria Swanson Today," *Film Fan Monthly,* February 1975.

42. Lawrence J. Quirk, *The Films of William Holden* (Secaucus, NJ: Citadel Press, 1973), 22.

43. Chierichetti, "Gloria Swanson Today," *Film Fan Monthly,* February 1975.

44. The Renaissance-style mansion used in *Sunset Boulevard,* actually located at 3810 Wilshire Boulevard and Western, was then owned by the second Mrs. Jean Paul Getty, purchased by her husband for her in 1936 as part of her divorce settlement. Built in 1924

for $250,000 by William Jenkins, the twenty-five-room mansion, complete with an elaborate ballroom, was abandoned a year later when Jenkins moved to Mexico. Called the "Phantom House" in Hollywood, it stood vacant for over a decade. In lieu of a $50,000 rental fee for the place, Paramount agreed to install a workable swimming pool, and at great expense to replace the non-safety-regulated one they built for use in the movie. Stained-glass windows and a pipe organ were added, and palm trees placed in the conservatory. The swan-shaped bed in Norma's room had once belonged to entertainer Gaby de Lys, who died in 1920. It was also used in Universal's *The Phantom of the Opera* (1925). The first floor of the house can be seen in Technicolor in Paramount's *Fancy Pants* (1950) with Bob Hope and Lucille Ball. The mansion was also used in Warner Bros.' 1955 *Rebel Without a Cause*. It was torn down in 1957.

45. Sam Staggs, *Close-up on Sunset Boulevard* (New York: St. Martin's Press, 2002), 65.
46. Nancy Olson, in *Sunset Boulevard—"A Look Back,"* Paramount DVD documentary, 2002.
47. Simon Louvish, *Cecil B. DeMille: A Life in Art* (New York: Thomas Dunne Books, 2007), 391–92.
48. Robert Atwan and Bruce Forer, eds., *Bedside Hollywood: Great Scenes from Great Movie Memoirs* (New York: Moyer Bell, 1985), 267.
49. Lennig, *Stroheim*, 445.
50. Lally, *Wilder Times: The Life of Billy Wilder*, 199.
51. Ibid.

24. COMEBACK

1. Gene Handsaker, ("Gloria Swanson Retains Glamour," *St. Petersburg Times,* March 27, 1949.
2. Atwan and Forer, *Bedside Hollywood: Great Scenes from Great Movie Memoirs,* 267.
3. HRC.
4. Will Holtzman, *William Holden* (New York: Pyramid, 1976), 76.
5. Judy Klemesrud, "Name, Nose, Teeth, Bosom, Hair, Kidneys—Everything but Eyelashes—Is Real," *New York Times,* October 10, 1971.
6. Zolotow, *Billy Wilder in Hollywood*, 248–49.
7. Wilson, "Living with Norma Desmond," *Observer* (U.K.), March 9, 2003.
8. Murray, ten years older than Swanson, began her career as a dancer with Vernon Castle in 1906, and by 1915 she was a Ziegfeld Follies star. Mae became a quite successful film actress in the 1920s, after marrying first husband director Robert Z. Leonard, who helmed several of her Tiffany Pictures in New York.
9. The son, Koran Mdivani, was raised by others in New York. Murray won custody of the boy in 1940, but his adopted family continued his upbringing.
10. Deep in the archives of the Academy of Motion Pictures Arts and Sciences' Fairbanks

Library are hidden letters to columnist Hedda Hopper from the former screen queen. In one dated June 1947 Murray, who had not made a picture in over sixteen years, urged Hopper to ask the great German film producer Eric Pommer to contact her at her address at the Hotel des Artistes on West Sixty-Seventh Street in New York, *"so very important."* On June 28, 1947, the fifty-seven-year-old Mae wrote Hedda. Her words are chillingly similar to Norma Desmond's and one wonders if Hopper ever shared these comments with Wilder:

> *My dear Hedda,*
> *At this moment I am, with the help of B. Cohn at Universal, attempting to produce my own productions. I want to do* Mary Magdalene *I have written her as I know the truth to be. I feel her so strongly—always have—I can make it even greater than my "Merry Widow!" Thank God for imagination and inspiration.*
> *Fondly always*
> *Mae*

11. Quirk, *The Films of Gloria Swanson*, 36.
12. Jim Bawden, "She Was Still Big After the Pictures Grew Small," http://thecolumnists.com /bawden/bawden78.html.
13. HRC.
14. Robert C. Shuler, *The Diva & I: My Life with Metropolitan Opera Star Patrice Munsel* (Bloomington, IN: AuthorHouse, 2007), 217–18.
15. HRC.
16. Louella O. Parsons, "Louella O. Parsons in Hollywood," *Los Angeles Examiner,* April 3, 1949.
17. Wilson, "Living with Norma Desmond," *Observer* (U.K.), March 9, 2003.
18. HRC.
19. Ibid.
20. Ibid.
21. Edith Head and Paddy Calistro, *Edith Head's Hollywood* (New York: E. P. Dutton, 1983), 91.
22. Carr, *Four Fabulous Faces,* 110; Swanson, *Swanson on Swanson,* 485.
23. Lally, *Wilder Times: The Life of Billy Wilder,* 202.
24. William Brogdon, *Variety,* April 18, 1950.
25. *Time,* August 14, 1950.
26. Wiley and Bona, *Inside Oscar: The Unofficial History of the Academy Awards,* 202.
27. James Agee, *Sight & Sound,* November 1950.
28. *New York Times* ad, August 16, 1950.
29. Eames, *The Paramount Story,* 196.
30. *New York Times* ad, August 16, 1950.
31. "T.M.P.," "The Screen: Inner Workings of Filmdom," *New York Times,* August 11, 1950.

32. Danny Peary, *Cult Movies: The Classics, the Sleepers, the Weird, and the Wonderful* (New York: Dell, 1981), 327.

33. "Billy Wilder—June 1963," in Stephen Randall, ed., *The Playboy Interviews: The Directors* (Milwaukee, OR: M Press, 2006) 461.

34. Bawden, "She Was Still Big After the Pictures Grew Small," http://thecolumnists.com /bawden/bawden78.html.

35. Quirk, *The Films of Gloria Swanson*, 36.

36. Hedda Hopper, *The Whole Truth and Nothing But* (New York: Pyramid Books, 1963), 28–29.

37. Hedda Hopper, *Los Angeles Times*, October 4, 1950.

38. AMPAS.

39. *Sunset Boulevard* would win Oscars for Best Art/Set Decoration, Best Music, and Best Screenplay for Wilder, Brackett, and Marshman. It would also receive the Blue Ribbon Award for Best Foreign Language Film (1952); the WGA (Writers Guild of America) Award for Screenplay; the National Board of Review award for Best Film; the Italian National Syndicate of Film Journalists Silver Ribbon for Best Director; Golden Globe Awards for Best Picture, Best Director, and Best Musical Score and a nomination for Best Cinematography; the Directors Guild of America Award for Billy Wilder; and the Bodil Awards for Best American Film and Best Director, all in 1951, among many others.

25. CAREER

1. Brooks Atkinson, "At the Theatre," *New York Times*, December 25, 1950.

2. *New York Times* ad, December 31, 1950.

3. *Miami News*, January 25, 1951.

4. Hedda Hopper, "Drama," *Los Angeles Times*, February 26, 1951. Gloria continued to receive awards: On April 10 she was named "woman of the year in entertainment" at an annual luncheon of the Guild of the Home and Hospital of the Daughters of Jacob in the ballroom of the Waldorf-Astoria Hotel. On April 13 the Newspaper Guild of New York awarded Gloria, Shirley Booth, Tallulah Bankhead, Sid Caesar, and Imogene Coca awards in entertainment. Gloria was also honored with a Jussi Award for Best Foreign Actress with a Diploma of Merit; a Silver Ribbon Award from the Italian National Syndication of Film Journalists; and, of course, the National Board of Review and the Golden Globe Best Actress awards. A *Film Daily* poll honored Gloria as Best Actress of 1951; *Family Circle* magazine gave her the same acknowledgment; and the Associated Press said Gloria made more news as an actress than any other in 1950; she was voted Best Dramatic Actress of the Year by the New York Foreign Language Correspondents, given a Special Citation and Honorary Membership to the George Washington Carver Memorial Institute, and voted Outstanding Woman of the Year by the United Scandinavian Societies of New York.

5. Ben Gross, "Looking & Listening," New York *Daily News*, February 4, 1951.

6. Swanson, *Swanson on Swanson*, 257.

7. Wiley and Bona, *Inside Oscar: The Unofficial History of the Academy Awards*, 209; Sam Staggs, *All About All About Eve* (New York: St. Martin's Press, 2001), 214.

8. Staggs, *All About All About Eve*, 214.

9. Swanson, *Swanson on Swanson*, 259.

10. HRC. These letters, literally hundreds in all, were carefully preserved by Gloria, long held in restricted archives at the Harry Ransom Center, and finally released for research in 2011.

11. HRC.

12. Ibid.

13. Hedda Hopper, *Los Angeles Times*, September 8, 1951.

14. Thomas M. Pryor ("T.M.P."), "Hollywood Report," *New York Times*, August 5, 1951.

15. John L. Scott, "Swanson Swan Songs Turns to Hit Parade," *Los Angeles Times*, August 12, 1951.

16. Bob Thomas, "Less Problem Films, More Escapism Urged by Gloria," *Hollywood Citizen-News*, August 17, 1951.

17. Edwin Schallert, "'Sweet Girl' Role Desired by Trevor," *Los Angeles Times*, November 4, 1951.

18. Michael Sypult, correspondence with author, October 18, 2011.

19. Thomas, "Less Problem Films. More Escapism Urged by Gloria," *Hollywood Citizen-News*, August 17, 1951.

20. HRC.

21. Hedda Hopper, "Actors Have a Hand in Ruining Motion Picture Business—Niven," *Los Angeles Times*, January 6, 1963.

22. Earl Wilson, "On Gay Broadway: David Niven Explains H-h-h-ow to Stay Calm for Television Show," *Beaver Valley* (Ohio) *Times*, October 7, 1958.

23. Hopper, "Actors Have a Hand in Ruining Motion Picture Business—Niven," *Los Angeles Times*, January 6, 1963.

24. "French Comedy Not All Fun, So Gloria Tries to Exit," *Los Angeles Herald Examiner*, November 22, 1951.

25. Ibid.

26. Beauchamp, *Joseph P. Kennedy Presents: His Hollywood Years*, 389.

27. Bronner, *Encyclopedia of the American Theatre, 1900–1975*, 338.

28. Brooks Atkinson, "At the Theatre," *New York Times*, December 6, 1951.

29. Walter Kerr, *New York Herald Tribune*, December 6, 1951.

30. Radie Harris, "Drama," *Los Angeles Times*, December 16, 1951.

31. James Copp, "Skylarking," *Los Angeles Times*, March 25, 1952.

32. *The Deseret News*, February 22, 1952.

33. Dorothy Kilgallen, *New York Journal-American*, March 13, 1952.

34. Walter Winchell, untitled article, n.d., HRC.

35. "Gloria Swanson, Friend Fly Away; Mum on Nuptials," *Los Angeles Times*, March 22, 1952.

36. Earl Wilson, "It Happened Last Night," *Delta Democrat-Times* (Greenville, MS), May 28, 1952.

37. "Brog," *Variety*, June 4, 1952.

38. "H.H.T.," "Gloria Swanson in a Comedy," *New York Times*, June 27, 1952.

39. Edwin Schallert, "Gloria Swanson's Train Stationary—Like Movie," *Los Angeles Times*, June 16, 1952.

40. *Holiday* magazine, n.d. Not surprisingly, *3 for Bedroom C* would only earn back $390,706.37 by 1956. There would be no second feature for Gloria.

41. Chierichetti, "Gloria Swanson Today," *Film Fan Monthly*, February 1975.

42. Hedda Hopper, *Los Angeles Times*, December 4, 1952.

43. Hedda Hopper, *Los Angeles Times*, February 14, 1953.

26. FASHION

1. "Swanson Designs Shown," *New York Times*, September 9, 1952.

2. Walter Ames, "Atom Bomb Blast Telecast for March 17; Swanson Films Crown Theater TVers," *Los Angeles Times*, March 6, 1953.

3. *Los Angeles Times*, March 6, 1953, AMPAS.

4. "Kap," *Daily Variety*, May 14, 1953.

5. "Daku," *Daily Variety*, July 2, 1953.

6. "Helm," *Daily Variety*, August 20, 1953.

7. "Daku," *Daily Variety*, September 24, 1953.

8. Howard H. Prouty, comp., *Variety Television Reviews, Volume 15* (New York and London: Garland, 1991).

9. Hedda Hopper, *Los Angeles Times*, May 8, 1953.

10. Emily Belser, "Hey Gals—Blame It All on Gloria Swanson," *New York Journal-American*, February 19, 1953.

11. Erskine Johnson, "The Rise and Fall of an Illusion Known as Gloria Swanson," *Los Angeles Daily News*, March 5, 1953.

12. James Copp, "Skylarking," *Los Angeles Times*, November 26, 1953.

13. *New York Times*, July 11, 1954.

14. *Los Angeles Times*, September 12, 1954.

15. Richard Stapley, *To Slip and Fall in L.A.* (unpublished), 23.

16. Staggs, *Close-up on Sunset Boulevard*, 203.

17. Ibid.

18. Ibid., 206.

19. Ibid., 207.

20. Stapley, *To Slip and Fall in L.A.*, 25–26.

21. Ibid., 34.

22. Ibid., 35.

23. Dickson Hughes, *Swanson on Sunset* (play).

24. Nogueira, "I Am Not Going to Write My Memoirs," *Sight & Sound*, Spring 1969.

25. HRC.

26. Ibid.

27. Ibid.

28. Hedda Hopper, "Hedda Hopper," *Los Angeles Times*, September 21, 1956.

29. "Hawk," *Variety*, September 26, 1956.

30. Giovanni Secchi, correspondence with author, March 29, 2011.

31. Margaret Harford, "'Nero's Mistress' Inept Italian Film," *Los Angeles Times*, November 10, 1962.

32. HRC.

33. Ibid.

34. Ibid.

35. Jack Gould, "TV Mike Wallace Asks," *New York Times*, April 29, 1957.

36. Hedda Hopper, "Hedda Hopper," *Los Angeles Times*, May 3, 1957.

37. Kessler, *Sins of the Father: Joseph P. Kennedy and the Dynasty He Founded*, 326.

38. *New York Journal-American*, October 4, 1957.

39. "Gros," *Variety*, November 13, 1957.

27. TELEVISION

1. HRC.

2. On November 21, 1961, Gloria wrote about Neilan in a letter, "His charm was devastating. He played piano by ear and composed the song MY WONDERFUL ONE for me. He was a wonderful dancer. He had the sharp humor an Irish American blend produces. He was a wonderful host, and a most sentimental and romantic sweetheart. I saw him after his success had waned; I considered that he threw his career away . . . I . . . [am] blessed with affectionate memories of this dear friend." HRC.

3. The end of *Boulevard* proved the demise of Richard Stapley's dreams of a career and reconciliation with Hughes in America. In 1960 he returned to England, renamed himself Richard Wyler, and starred in the British television espionage series *The Man from Interpol* and enjoyed a moderately successful film and television career in Europe. In the 1960s he started racing sports cars and starred in several Italian made spaghetti westerns.

4. Stuart W. Little, "Old-Timers Warm Up for Broadway," *Los Angeles Times*, June 28, 1959.

5. Richard Somerset-Ward, *An American Theatre: The Story of the Westport Country Playhouse* (New Haven, CT: Yale University Press, 2005), 145.

6. Jack Mitchell interview with author, October 4, 2011.

7. Robert Balzar, along with being an eccentric grocer and wealthy businessman, was also a Buddhist monk. As president of his own corporation, Balzar built a meditation center in the San Jacinto Mountains in Idyllwild, California. The project became the Tirol Restaurant (1963), which won a 1965 *Holiday Magazine* Award. It had cost $150,000 and included a library, meditation building, and limited accommodation facilities. Along with Olivia de Havilland and Walt Disney, Gloria lent her name to the project. Credited with establishing the wine industry in California, Robert Lawrence Balzar died at his home in Orange, California, on December 2, 2011.

8. Stephen Sondheim, correspondence with author, July 12, 2011. Sondheim denied its validity.

9. Anderson, *Jack and Jackie: Portrait of An American Marriage,* 28.

10. Edward Klein, *All Too Human: The Love Story of Jack and Jackie Kennedy* (New York: Pocket Books, 1996), 126.

11. Joseph P. Kennedy had little time left to share with Jackie or anyone else his stories of romantic conquests and sexual peccadillos. On December 21, 1961, right before Christmas, he suffered a massive stroke and lost his ability to speak intelligently for the rest of his life. He died at the age of eighty-one on November 18, 1969. Rose survived him for another twenty-five years.

12. Kingsley R. Fall, "Premiere at Stockbridge," n.d., HRC.

13. Bob Thomas, "A Visit with Gloria Swanson," *Evening News* (Newburgh, NY), October 18, 1961.

14. Bob Thomas, "Gloria Swanson Not Thinking of Past," *Daytona Beach Morning Journal,* October 19, 1961.

15. *Los Angeles Times,* October 11, 1961.

16. Thomas, "Gloria Swanson Not Thinking of Past," *Daytona Beach Morning Journal,* October 19, 1961.

17. "Movie Queen's Comeback for a Night," *TV Guide,* December 9, 1961, NYPL.

18. Ibid.

19. Charles Denton, "No Swan Songs for La Swanson," *Los Angeles Examiner,* November 9, 1961.

20. Sam Zolotow, "'Inkwell' to Star Gloria Swanson," *New York Times,* January 16, 1962.

21. Roger Dettmer, "Pen Roams in 'Inkwell,'" HRC.

22. Hedda Hopper, *Los Angeles Times,* November 12, 1962.

23. Susan King, "Richard Chamberlain: Nervous in Paradise," *Chicago Tribune,* May 28, 2008.

24. Hal Humphrey, "No Swan Song for Gloria," *Los Angeles Times,* November 18, 1962.

25. Rick Du Brow, "Same Role Repeated by Gloria Swanson," *Eugene* (Oregon) *Register-Guard,* February 8, 1963.

26. Gloria Emery, "Tiny Star Stands High Among Lovely Women," *New York Times,* September 12, 1963.

27. Gary Conway, interview with author, August 10, 2011.

28. HRC; *A&E Biography,* "The Greatest Star," July 29, 1997.

29. Brenda Scott Hargrave, interview with author, February 4, 2011.

30. Stephen Bowie, "An Interview with Harry Landers," Sherman Oaks, CA, April 30, 2010, *The Classic TV History Blog,* http://classictvhistory.wordpress.com/2011/05/31/an-interview-with-harry-landers.

31. HRC.

32. Angela Taylor, "I've Never Had a Dull Moment . . . ," *New York Times,* November 8, 1965.

33. Agnes Murphy, "At Home with . . . Gloria Swanson," *New York Post,* November 28, 1965.

34. Arlene Dahl, interview with author, July 31, 2011.

35. Judy Klemesrud, "Doesn't Anybody Here Count Sheep Any More?" *New York Times,* November 3, 1971.

36. Murphy, "At Home with . . . Gloria Swanson," *New York Post,* November 28, 1965.

37. Brooke Anderson Young, "The Two Sides of Ms. Swanson," *Sunset Boulevard* DVD documentary, 2008.

38. Adele Whitely Fletcher, "Swanson, the Inimitable," *New York Journal-American,* December 12, 1965.

28. FINALE

1. Young, "The Two Sides of Ms. Swanson," *Sunset Boulevard* DVD documentary, 2008.

2. Gee Mitchell, "Kenley 'Stars' Shine Dimly," Dayton, Ohio, n.d., HRC.

3. John Heilpern, "Here's to the Lady Who Jumps: Elaine Stritch at the Public," *New York Observer,* December 2, 2001.

4. Max Baer Jr., interview with author, February 14, 2011.

5. Nogueira, "I Am Not Going to Write My Memoirs," *Sight & Sound,* Spring 1969.

6. Swanson, *Swanson on Swanson,* 518–19.

7. Enid Nemy, "For One Night Only: Bergdorf-Swanson," *New York Times,* December 31, 1966.

8. Jack Lessenberry, "The Many Lives of Mr. Dufty," *MetroTimes,* April 2001.

9. Bevan Dufty was a former member of the San Francisco Board of Supervisors from District 8. Raised in Harlem by his mother until he was sixteen, Bevan finished high school in Atherton, California. In 2006 he became a father with Rebecca Goldfader. They named their daughter Sidney Maely. A staunch Democrat, Dufty ran for mayor of San Francisco in 2011 but was beaten by Edwin M. Lee in November 2011.

10. Dennis Fairchild, interview with author, February 28, 2011.

11. Christopher Anderson, "At 76, Gloria Swanson Has a New Crusade—and a New Mate to Go with It," *People,* February 16, 1976.

12. Cecil Smith, "'Reprise' Playing on the Huntington Stage," *Los Angeles Times,* October 5, 1967.

13. Charles Silver, "17 Years Down the Boulevard," *Classic Film Collector,* Fall–Winter 1967.

14. Joan Crawford was not without her own vitriolic outbursts. Years later when she heard Gloria talking about sex, Crawford drunkenly lashed out, "'Gloria Swanson talks about her sex life.' Well, bully for her! But she was talking about the *past,* wasn't she? *She wasn't?* Well, I think it's shocking. I'd rather listen to a good poem." Patricia Bosworth, "I'm Still an Actress! I Want to Act!" *New York Times,* September 24, 1972.

15. Tracy Christensen, interview with author, November 16, 2011.

16. Herbert Somborn's partner and co-founder of the Brown Derby, Robert Howard Cobb, passed away on March 21, 1970. Gloria Somborn Anderson took over ownership of the original on Wilshire Boulevard in 1952, giving up her interest in the other three Derbies. Her husband Robert Anderson managed it, turning it into a Hollywood landmark. By 1960 the original Brown Derby had been remodeled, but it soon fell on hard times. In September 1980 it closed its doors and was set to be demolished, but preservation committees, the Los Angeles Conservancy, and Hollywood Heritage temporarily saved it. Completely gutted, it was eventually moved to a rooftop in a Los Angeles minimall.

17. Lamparski, *Manhattan Diary,* 146.

18. Michael T. Leech, "The High Point of Her Career is 'Now,'" *Show,* November 1971.

19. Arthur Whitelaw, *Working for Peanuts* (unpublished).

20. Arthur Whitelaw, interview with author, April 18, 2011.

21. Ibid.

22. Ibid.

23. Walter Kerr, "What Next for the Younger Generation?" *New York Times,* September 19, 1971.

24. Leo Mishkin, "Stage Review: GS in 'Butterflies,'" *New York Morning Telegraph,* September 16, 1971.

25. Dirk Benedict, *Confessions of a Kamikaze Cowboy* (Garden City Park, NY: Avery, 1991), 44.

26. Dirk Benedict, interview with author, June 18, 2011.

27. Ibid.

28. Ibid.

29. Arthur Whitelaw, interview with author, April 18, 2011.

30. Madsen, *Gloria and Joe,* 365.

31. Arthur Whitelaw, interview with author, April 18, 2011.

32. Dirk Benedict, interview with author, June 18, 2011.

33. Joyce Haber, "Gloria and Carol: Opposites Attract," *Los Angeles Times,* September 12, 1973.

34. Ibid.

35. Kathleen Carroll, "Flashback of a Silent Superstar," New York *Daily News,* September 22, 1973.

36. Joseph Gemis, "Only Gloria Could Forget Swanson film," *New York Newsday,* July 13, 1972.

37. Carroll, "Flashback of a Silent Superstar," New York *Daily News,* September 22, 1973.

38. Charles Silver, interview with author, April 11, 2011.

39. According to zoologist Jim Donaldson, bee handler for *The Killer Bees,* "The bees had to be out on Gloria Swanson and we had to be sure none could sting her or the other actors. We had to do it in the middle of winter, when no grown bees were available, so we had to de-sting 10,000 bees. We put them in a cooler in a motel bathroom near the location where we were shooting—a cooled down bee is immobile—and we couldn't pull out the stinger because that would kill the bee. We hired 10 girls for a solid week, 10 hours a day. They put the cooled-down bee in a shadow box and clipped off the end of the stinger with a sharp little knife. Then we took all 10,000 bees to the location and turned them loose in this room with Gloria Swanson and thank goodness not one strange bee got in from outside and no one was stung." John M. Wilson, "From Bees to Tarantulas," *Los Angeles Times,* September 12, 1977.

40. Chierichetti, "Gloria Swanson Today," *Film Fan Monthly,* February 1975.

41. Kevin Thomas, "Gloria Swanson: Between Glamor Puss, Old Shoe," *Los Angeles Times,* February 24, 1974.

42. Bob MacKenzie, "Queen Bee," *TV Guide,* February 23–March 1, 1974.

43. Ibid.

44. Kevin Thomas, "TV Movie Review," *Los Angeles Times,* February 26, 1974.

29. LEGEND

1. Gloria's friend Raymond Daum, whom she met in 1956 through Earl Blackwell, described Gloria's apartment: "You entered . . . from Seventy-third Street. You came into the foyer, and to the left was the dining room [which she later turned into an office] . . . Off the foyer you have this large—she called it 'the White Room.' It was almost a solarium. She turned it into a living room, with a piano. The other large room next to it was the library. Beautiful—very French with a plan of Paris hanging above the leather couch . . . and one of her portraits . . . Off that room was the bar and a tiny dining area.

"That led off to her little garden with a fountain. It had a wall around it, very well protected. You pass the guest bedroom on the left, then at the very end was Gloria's suite. She had a large bath whose windows looked out on the garden.

"Backtrack down the corridor and to the right is the kitchen, with her maid's quarters adjacent. Several small rooms for the maid." Staggs, *Close-up on Sunset Boulevard,* 58–59. There were also maids' rooms on different floors of her building, which Gloria rented periodically for her needs, including for her wardrobe storage—racks and racks of clothing.

2. Linda Harrison, interview with author, March 22, 2011.

3. Ibid.

4. Joyce Haber, "Frank Volunteers for Benefit on Green," *Los Angeles Times,* May 6, 1974.

5. Swanson, *Swanson on Swanson,* 503.

6. Lamparski, *Manhattan Diary,* 154.

7. Ibid.

8. Vincent Canby, "Screen," *New York Times*, October 19, 1974.

9. Brooke Anderson Young, *A&E Biography,* "The Greatest Star," July 29, 1997.

10. Bob Thomas, "Gloria Swanson Back Again," *Telegraph,* May 28, 1974.

11. William Dufty, *Sugar Blues* (New York: Warner Books, 1993), dedication.

12. David Graden, interview with author, April 18, 2011.

13. Judy Klemesrud, "Greeting the New Year, Some with a Bang, Some with a Whimper," *New York Times,* December 31, 1975.

14. "Notes on People," *New York Times,* February 6, 1976.

15. *Time*, February 16, 1976.

16. Christopher P. Anderson, "At 76, Gloria Swanson Has a New Crusade—and a New Mate to Go with It," *People,* February 16, 1976.

17. Bevan Dufty, interview with author, February 22, 2011.

18. Ibid.

19. *Time*, October 18, 1976.

20. Barbara Dubivsky, "How to Feast and Fast in Flight," *New York Times,* September 4, 1977.

21. Tapert, *The Power of Glamour: The Women Who Defined the Magic of Stardom,* 38.

22. Roderick Mann, "Gould—The Bad Times Are Over," *Los Angeles Times,* June 1, 1978.

23. Tapert, *The Power of Glamour: The Women Who Defined the Magic of Stardom,* 36.

24. Christa Venezia, interview with author, April 25, 2011.

25. Dirk Benedict, e-mail to author, September 22, 2011.

26. Timothy Rooks, interview with author, October 31, 2011.

27. Nogueira, "I Am Not Going to Write My Memoirs," *Sight & Sound,* Spring 1969.

28. "Notes on People," *New York Times,* March 10, 1979.

29. Dirk Benedict, interview with author, June 28, 2011.

30. Dennis Fairchild, interview with author, February 28, 2011.

31. Swanson, *Swanson on Swanson,* 518.

32. Timothy Rooks, interview with author, October 31, 2011.

33. Mike Hurwitz, "Gloria Calls It Quits with Hubby No. 6," n.d., MOMA.

34. Dennis Fairchild, interview with author, February 28, 2011.

35. Robert Musel, "Looking Back at the Silent Era," *Los Angeles Times,* February 3, 1980.

36. Jennings Parrott, "Newsmakers—Pope Speaks Out for Kidnap Victims," *Los Angeles Times,* March 31, 1980.

37. Cindy Adams, "Always the Superstar, Even in Her Own Home," *New York Post,* April 5, 1980.

38. *Los Angeles Times,* November 16, 1981.

39. Malcolm Boyd, "Inside View of Swanson's 'Glamorous Ghetto,'" *Los Angeles Times,* November 16, 1980.

40. Janet Maslin and Laurence Finberg, MD, "A Star Remembers," *Los Angeles Times,* November 9, 1980.

41. *A&E Biography,* "The Greatest Star," July 29, 1997. Gloria received several wretched letters vilifying her regarding her Kennedy claim. She kept these all in her archives, now resting at the HRC.

42. Bevan Dufty, interview with author, February 22, 2011.

43. Pitts, *Glamour Girls of Hollywood,* 21.

44. Carol Lawson, "Behind the Best Sellers," *New York Times,* January 25, 1981.

45. Lawson, "Behind the Best Sellers," *New York Times,* January 25, 1981.

46. "Headliners," *New York Post,* February 19, 1981.

47. Cherie Hart, "New Man in Life of 81-Year-Old Gloria Swanson Replaces Hubby No. 6," *Enquirer,* February 24, 1981.

48. Hart, "New Man in Life of 81-Year-Old Gloria Swanson Replaces Hubby No. 6," *Enquirer,* February 24, 1981.

49. Staggs, *Close-up on Sunset Boulevard,* 378.

50. Farmer (Amon), *A&E Biography,* "The Greatest Star," July 29, 1997.

51. "Gloria Swanson Still the Curious Rebel," January 1, 1982, NYPL.

52. "I Have No Fear of Dying," *New York Post,* April 5, 1983.

53. Tapert, *The Power of Glamour: The Women Who Defined the Magic of Stardom,* 39.

54. Ibid.

55. Staggs, *Close-up on Sunset Boulevard,* 379.

56. Tapert, *The Power of Glamour,* 39.

57. Staggs, *Close-up on Sunset Boulevard,* 378.

58. Tapert, *The Power of Glamour,* 39.

59. Staggs, *Close-up on Sunset Boulevard,* 379.

60. Dirk Benedict, interview with author, June 28, 2011.

61. Anderson Young, *A&E Biography,* "The Greatest Star," July 29, 1997.

62. Dennis Fairchild, interview with author, February 28, 2011.

63. Jennings Parrott, "Newsmakers," *Los Angeles Times,* March 24, 1983.

64. Dennis Fairchild, interview with author, February 28, 2011.

30. EPILOGUE

1. Quirk, *The Films of Gloria Swanson,* 38.

2. *New York Times,* April 6, 1983.

3. Tapert, *The Power of Glamour: The Women Who Defined the Magic of Stardom,* 39.

4. Kevin Thomas, interview with author, February 14, 2011.

5. Dirk Benedict, correspondence with author, September 21, 2011.

6. Dirk Benedict, correspondence with author, September 23, 2011.

7. Shirley Eder, "Gloria's Money? Bill Never Wanted It," *Detroit Free Press,* May 1, 1983.

8. Anderson Jones and David Fields, *Men Together: Portraits of Love, Commitment, and Life* (Philadelphia: Running Press, 1997), 21.

9. Dennis Fairchild, interview with author, February 28, 2011.

10. Dirk Benedict, correspondence with author, October 4, 2011.

11. Virginia Bohlin, "Movie Queen's Estate to Be Auctioned," *Boston Globe,* August 7, 1983.

12. Timothy Rooks, interview with author, November 16, 2011.

13. "Auctions at Southeby's," *New York Times,* June 4, 1995.

14. Madsen, *Gloria and Joe,* 364.

15. Ibid.

16. Stephen Harvey, " 'Queen Kelly' Opens—More than 50 Years Late," *New York Times,* September 22, 1985.

17. Turk, *Hollywood Diva: A Biography of Jeanette MacDonald,* 318.

18. "To the Editor," *New York Times,* December 18, 1994.

19. Anderson Young, "The Two Sides of Ms. Swanson," *Sunset Boulevard* DVD documentary, 2008.

20. Dirk Benedict, correspondence with author, September 22, 2011.

21. Tapert, *The Power of Glamour: The Women Who Defined the Magic of Stardom,* 36.

22. Wilson, "Living with Norma Desmond," *Observer* (U.K.), March 9, 2003.

Bibliography

Affron, Charles. *Lillian Gish: Her Legend, Her Life.* New York: Scribner, 2001.

Agee, James. *Agee on Film: Reviews and Comments by James Agee.* Boston: Beacon Press, 1958.

Alleman, Richard. *The Movie Lover's Guide to Hollywood.* New York: Harper & Row, 1985.

———. *The Movie Lover's Guide to New York.* New York: Harper & Row, 1988.

The American Film Institute Catalog of Motion Pictures, Feature Films 1911–1920. New York: R. R. Bowker, 1989.

The American Film Institute Catalog of Motion Pictures, Feature Films 1921–1930. New York: R. R. Bowker, 1971.

The American Film Institute Catalog of Motion Pictures, Feature Films 1931–1940. New York: R. R. Bowker, 1993.

The American Film Institute Catalog of Motion Pictures, Feature Films 1941–1950. New York: R. R. Bowker, 1999.

The American Film Institute Catalog of Motion Pictures, Feature Films 1961–1970. New York: R. R. Bowker, 1976.

Amory, Cleveland, editor-in-chief. *International Celebrity Register.* New York: Celebrity Register, 1959.

Anderson, Christopher. *The Day John Died.* New York: William Morrow, 2000.

———. *Jack and Jackie: Portrait of an American Marriage.* New York: William Morrow, 1996.

Anger, Kenneth. *Hollywood Babylon.* New York: Dell, 1975.

———. *Hollywood Babylon II.* New York: New American Library, 1984.

Ankerich, Michael G. *Dangerous Curves Atop Hollywood Heels.* Duncan, OK: BearManor Media, 2011.

Atwan, Robert and Bruce Forer, editors. *Bedside Hollywood: Great Scenes from Movie Memoirs.* New York: Moyer Bell, 1985.

Bach, Steven. *Marlene Dietrich: Life and Legend.* New York: William Morrow, 1992.

Bailey, Margaret J. *Those Glorious Glamour Years: Classic Hollywood Costume Design of the 1930s.* Secaucus, NJ: Citadel, 1982.

Balio, Tito. *United Artists: The Company Built By the Stars.* Madison: University of Wisconsin Press, 1976.

Barbas, Samantha. *The First Lady of Hollywood: A Biography of Louella Parsons.* Berkeley: University of California Press, 2005.

Barrios, Richard. *A Song in the Dark.* New York: Oxford University Press, 1995.

Basinger, Jeanine. *Silent Stars.* New York: Alfred A. Knopf, 1999.

———. *The Star Machine.* New York: Alfred A. Knopf, 2007.

Basten, Fred E. *Max Factor: The Man Who Changed the Faces of Hollywood.* New York: Arcade, 2008.

Baxter, John. *60 Years of Hollywood.* New York: A. S. Barnes, 1973.

———. *Von Sternberg.* Lexington: University Press of Kentucky, 2010.

Bazzana, Kevin. *Lost Genius: The Curious and Tragic Story of an Extraordinary Musical Prodigy.* Cambridge, MA: DaCapo, 2008.

Beardsley, Charles. *Hollywood's Master Showman: The Legendary Sid Grauman.* Cranbury, NJ: Cornwall Books, 1983.

Beauchamp, Cari. *Joseph P. Kennedy Presents: His Hollywood Years.* New York: Alfred A. Knopf, 2009.

———. *Without Lying Down: Frances Marion and the Powerful Women of Early Hollywood.* New York: Scribner, 1997.

Bego, Mark, editor. *The Best of Modern Screen.* New York: St. Martin's Press, 1986.

Behlmer, Rudy. *Henry Hathaway.* Lanham, MD: Scarecrow Press: 2001.

———, editor. *Memo From David O. Selznick.* New York: Modern Library, 2000.

Beijbom, Ulf. *Swedes in America: New Perspectives.* Vaxjo, Sweden: Davidsons Tryckeri AB, 1993.

Benedict, Dirk. *Confessions of a Kamikaze Cowboy.* Garden City, NY: Avery Publishing Group, 1991.

Berg, A. Scott. *Goldwyn: A Biography.* New York: Alfred A. Knopf, 1989.

Bergan, Ronald. *The United Artists Story.* New York: Crown, 1986.

Bernstein, Arnie, editor. *"The Movies Are": Carl Sandburg's Film Reviews and Essays, 1920–1928.* Chicago: Lake Claremont Press 2000.

Bernstein, Matthew. *Walter Wanger: Hollywood Independent.* Berkeley: University of California Press, 1994.

Bilbow, Tony and John Gau. *Lights Camera Action! A Century of the Cinema.* London: Little, Brown, 1995.

Birchard, Robert S. *Cecil B. DeMille's Hollywood.* Lexington: University Press of Kentucky, 2004.

Birmingham, Stephen. *Real Lace: America's Irish Rich.* New York: Harper & Row, 1973.

Blinn, Johna. *Celebrity Cookbook.* New York: Moby Books, 1981.

Blum, Daniel. *A New Pictorial History of the Talkies.* New York: Grosset & Dunlap, 1970.

———. *A Pictorial History of the American Theatre 1860–1970*. New York: Crown, 1970.

———. *A Pictorial History of the Silent Screen*. New York: Grosset & Dunlap, 1953.

Bodeen, DeWitt. *From Hollywood*. Cranbury, NJ: A. S. Barnes, 1976.

———. *More from Hollywood: The Careers of 15 Great American Stars*. Cranbury, NJ: A. S. Barnes, 1977.

Bogdanovich, Peter. *Allan Dwan: The Last Pioneer*. New York: Praeger, 1971.

Bojarski, Richard. *The Films of Boris Karloff*. Secaucus, NJ: Citadel, 1974.

Boller. Paul F. Jr. and Ronald L. Davis. *Hollywood Anecdotes*. New York: William Morrow, 1987.

Bordman, Gerald. *Jerome Kern: His Life and Music*. New York: Oxford University Press, 1980.

Bordman, Gerald and Thomas S. Hirschak. *The Oxford Companion to American Theatre*. New York: Oxford University Press, 2004.

Borradaile, Osmond and Anita Borradaile. *Life Through a Lens: Memoirs of a Cinematographer*. Quebec, Canada: McGill-Queen's University Press, 2001.

Bosworth, Patricia. *Montgomery Clift: A Biography*. New York: Harcourt Brace, 1992.

Botchkareva, Maria. *Yashka: My Life as Peasant, Officer and Exile*. New York: Frederick A. Stokes Co., 1919.

Botham, Noel and Peter Donnelly. *Valentino: The Love God*. New York: Ace, 1976.

Bradford, Sarah. *America's Queen: The Life of Jacqueline Kennedy Onassis*. New York: Penguin, 2000.

Bret, David. *Valentino: A Dream of Desire*. New York: Carroll & Graf, 1998.

Bronner, Edwin J. *The Encyclopedia of the American Theatre 1900–1975*. New York: A. S. Barnes, 1978.

Brooks, Tim and Earle Marsh. *The Complete Directory to Prime Time Network and Cable TV Shows 1946–Present*. New York: Ballantine, 1999.

Brownlow, Kevin. *The Parade's Gone By*. New York: Alfred A. Knopf, 1969.

Buckley, Priscilla L. *String of Pearls: On the News Beat in New York and Paris*. New York: Thomas Dunne Books, 2011.

Bull, Clarence and Raymond Lee. *The Faces of Hollywood*. New York: A. S. Barnes, 1968.

Burk, Margaret Tante. *Are the Stars Out Tonight: The Story of the Famous Ambassador and Cocoanut Grove*. Los Angeles: Round Table West, 1980.

Butler, Ivan. *Silent Magic*. New York: Unger, 1988.

Card, James. *Seductive Cinema: The Art of Silent Film*. New York: Alfred A. Knopf, 1994.

Carey, Gary. *Anita Loos: A Biography*. New York: Alfred A. Knopf, 1988.

———. *Doug and Mary: A Biography of Douglas Fairbanks and Mary Pickford*. New York: E. P. Dutton, 1977.

Carr, Larry. *Four Fabulous Faces*. New York: Galahad, 1970.

Chaplin, Charles. *My Autobiography*. New York: Simon & Schuster, 1964.

Chaplin, Lita Grey with Morton Cooper. *My Life with Chaplin: An Intimate Memoir*. New York: Bernard Geis Associates, 1966.

Chapman, Gary. *The Delectable Dollies: The Dolly Sisters, Icons of the Jazz Age*. Gloucestershire, UK: Sutton Publishing, Ltd.: 2006.

Chierichetti, David. *Edith Head: The Life and Times of Hollywood's Celebrated Costume Designer*. New York: HarperCollins, 2004.

———. *Mitchell Leisen: Hollywood Director*. Los Angeles, CA: Photoventures Press, 1995.

Coleman, Terry. *Olivier*. New York: Henry Holt, 2005.

Collier, Peter and David Horowitz. *The Kennedys: An American Drama*. New York: Warner Books, 1985.

Corliss, Richard. *Talking Pictures: Screenwriters in American Cinema*. Woodstock, NY: Overlook Press, 1974.

Cut! New York: Barron's Educational Series, 2005.

Dallek, Robert. *An Unfinished Life: John F. Kennedy 1917–1963*. New York: Little, Brown, 2003.

Dallinger, Nat. *Unforgettable Hollywood*. New York: William Morrow, 1983.

Daniels, Bebe. *Life with the Lyons: The Autobiography of Bebe Daniels and Ben Lyon*. London: Odhams Press, 1953.

Davis, John H. *The Kennedys: Dynasty and Disaster 1848–1984*. New York: McGraw-Hill, 1985.

Davis, Lon and Debra Davis. *King of the Movies: Francis X. Bushman*. Albany, GA: BearManor Media, 2009.

de Acosta, Mercedes. *Here Lies the Heart*. New York: Reynal & Company, 1960.

DeMille, Cecil B. and Donald Hayne, editor. *The Autobiography of Cecil B. DeMille*. Englewood Cliffs, NJ: Prentice-Hall, 1959.

Dmytryk, Edward. *Hollywood's Golden Age as Told by One Who Lived It All*. Albany, GA: BearManor Media, 2003.

Doherty, Edward. *The Rain Girl: The Tragic Story of Jeanne Eagels*. Philadelphia: Macrae Smith Company, 1930.

Dooley, Roger B. *From Scarface to Scarlett: American Films in the 1930s*. New York: Harcourt Brace Jovanovich, 1984.

Douglas, Melvyn and Tom Arthur. *See You at the Movies: The Autobiography of Melvyn Douglas*. Latham, MD: University Press of America, Inc., 1986.

Drew, William M. *Speaking of Silents: First Ladies of the Screen*. Vestal, NY: Vestal Press Ltd., 1989.

Druxman, Michael B. *Charlton Heston*. New York: Pyramid, 1976.

———. *Make It Again, Sam: A Survey of Movie Remakes*. New York: A. S. Barnes, 1975.

Dufty, William. *Sugar Blues*. New York: Warner Books, 1993.

Eames, John Douglas. *The Paramount Story*. New York: Crown, 1985.

———. *The MGM Story*. New York: Crown, 1976.

Edmonds, Andy. *Frame Up! The Untold Story of Rosco "Fatty" Arbuckle*. New York: William Morrow, 1991.

———. *Hot Toddy: The True Story of Hollywood's Most Shocking Crime—The Murder of Thelma Todd*. New York: Avon, 1990.

Edwards, Anne. *The DeMilles: An American Family*. New York: Harry N. Abrams, 1988.

Eells, George. *Hedda and Louella*. New York: Warner Paperback Library, 1972.

Ellenberger, Allan R. *Margaret O'Brien: A Career Chronicle and Biography.* Jefferson, NC: McFarland, 2000.

Essoe, Gabe and Raymond Lee. *DeMille: The Man and His Pictures.* New York: Castle Books, 1970.

Etherington-Smith, Meredith and Jeremy Pilcher. *The "It" Girls: Elinor Glyn, Novelist and Her Sister Lucile, Couturiere.* New York: Harcourt Brace Jovanovich, 1986.

Evans, Peter. *Nemesis: The True Story.* New York: HarperCollins, 2004.

Everson, William K. *Claudette Colbert.* New York: Pyramid, 1976.

Eyman, Scott. *Empire of Dreams: The Epic Life of Cecil B. DeMille.* New York: Simon & Schuster, 2010.

———. *Ernst Lubitsch: Laughter in Paradise.* New York: Simon & Schuster, 1993.

———. *Mary Pickford: America's Sweetheart.* New York: Donald I. Fine, 1990.

Finch, Christopher. *Rainbow: The Stormy Life of Judy Garland.* New York: Grosset & Dunlap, 1975.

Finch, Christopher and Linda Rosenkrantz. *Gone Hollywood: The Movie Colony in the Golden Age.* Garden City, NY: Doubleday, 1979.

Finler, Joel W. *The Movie Directors Story.* New York: Crescent Books, 1985.

———. *The Hollywood Story.* New York: Crown, 1988.

Fleming, E. J. *Wallace Reid: The Life and Death of A Hollywood Idol.* Jefferson, NC: McFarland, 2007.

Fowler, Karin F. *David Niven: A Bio-Bibliography.* Westport, CT: Greenwood Press, 1995.

Franklin, Joe. *Classics of the Silent Screen.* New York: Citadel, 1959.

Freedland, Michael. *Jerome Kern: A Biography.* New York: Stein & Day, 1978.

Friedrich, Otto. *City of Nets.* New York: Perennial, 1987.

Frischauer, Willi. *Behind the Scenes of Otto Preminger.* New York: William Morrow, 1974.

Fussell, Betty Harper. *Mabel: The Life of Mabel Normand.* Pompton Plains, NJ: Limelight Editions, 1992.

Gabler, Neal. *An Empire of Their Own: How the Jews Invented Hollywood.* New York: Crown, 1988.

Gavin, James. *Stormy Weather: The Life of Lena Home.* New York: Simon & Schuster, 2009.

Gelman, Barbara, editor. *Photoplay Treasury.* New York: Bonanza, 1972.

Gerhing, Wes D. *McCarey" From Marx to McCarthy.* Lanham, MD: Scarecrow Press, 2005.

Gibson, Barbara and Ted Schwarz. *Rose Kennedy and Her Family: The Best and Worst of Their Lives and Times.* New York: Birch Lane Press, 1995.

Gish, Lillian. *Dorothy and Lillian Gish.* New York: Charles Scribner's Sons, 1973.

Glyn, Anthony. *Elinor Glyn.* Garden City, NY: Doubleday, 1955.

Golden, Eve. *Platinum Girl: The Life and Legends of Jean Harlow.* New York: Abbeville Press, 1991.

Goldschneider, Gene and Aron Goldschneider, editor. *The Secret Language of Birthdays.* New York: Viking, 1994.

Goodwin, Doris Kearns. *The Fitzgeralds and the Kennedys: An American Saga.* New York: Simon & Schuster, 1987.

Granger, Farley and Robert Calhoun. *Include Me Out: My Life from Goldwyn to Broadway.* New York: St. Martin's, 2008.

Greer, Howard. *Designing Male.* New York: G. P. Putnam's Sons, 1951.

Griffith, Richard and Arthur Mayer. *The Movies.* New York: Simon & Schuster, 1957.

Grobel, Lawrence. *The Hustons.* New York: Charles Scribner's Sons, 1989.

Gronowicz, Antoni. *Garbo: Her Story.* New York: Simon & Schuster, 1990.

Guiles, Fred Lawrence. *Marion Davies.* New York: McGraw-Hill, 1972.

Hamilton, Nigel. *JFK: Reckless Youth.* New York: Random House, 1992.

Hampton, Benjamin B. *The History of the American Film Industry From Its Beginnings to 1931.* New York: Dover, 1970.

Hardt, Ursula. *From Caligari to California: Erich Pommer's Life in the International Film Wars.* Providence, RI: Berghahn Books, 1996.

Harris, Warren G. *The Other Marilyn: A Biography of Marilyn Miller.* New York: Arbor House, 1985.

Haskell, Molly. *From Reverence to Rape: The Treatment of Women in Movies.* New York: Holt, Rinehart, and Winston, 1974.

Head, Edith and Paddy Calistro. *Edith Head's Hollywood.* New York: E. P. Dutton, 1983.

Heide, Robert and John Gilman. *Stardust: The Wonderful World of Movie Memorabilia.* Garden City, NY: Doubleday, 1986.

Hemming, Roy. *The Melody Lingers On: The Great Songwriters and Their Movie Musicals.* New York: Newmarket Press, 1986.

Heymann, C. David. *A Woman Named Jackie.* New York: Lyle Stuart, 1989.

Higham, Charles. *Bette: The Life of Bette Davis.* New York: Macmillan, 1981.

———. *Cecil B. DeMille.* New York: Scribner, 1973.

———. *Merchant of Dreams: Louis B. Mayer, MGM, and the Secret Hollywood.* New York: Bantam Doubleday Dell, 1993.

———. *Orson Welles: The Rise and Fall of An American Genius.* New York: St. Martin's Press, 1985.

———. *Sisters: The Story of Olivia de Havilland and Joan Fontaine.* New York: Dell, 1986.

———. *Ziegfeld.* Chicago: Henry Regnery, 1972.

Higham, Charles and Roy Moseley. *Princess Merle: The Romantic Life of Merle Oberon.* New York: Coward, McCann, 1983.

Hirschhorn, Clive. *The Columbia Story.* New York: Crown, 1990.

———. *The Hollywood Musical.* New York: Crown, 1981.

———. *The Universal Story.* New York: Crown, 1983.

———. *The Warner Bros. Story.* New York: Crown, 1979.

Holden, Anthony. *Behind the Oscar: The Secret History of the Academy Awards.* New York: Simon & Schuster, 1993.

Holtzman, Will. *William Holden.* New York: Pyramid, 1976.

Hopper, Hedda. *From Under My Hat.* Garden City, NY: Doubleday, 1952.

———. *The Whole Truth and Nothing But.* New York: Pyramid, 1963.

Hudson, Richard and Raymond Lee. *Gloria Swanson.* New York: Castle Books, 1970.

Hunter, Tab and Eddie Muller. *Tab Hunter Confidential: The Making of a Movie Star.* Chapel Hill, NC: Algonquin Books, 2005.

Hutchinson, Tom. *Niven's Hollywood.* Salem, NH: Salem House, 1984.

Irvin, Sam. *Kay Thompson: From Funny Face to Eloise.* New York: Simon & Schuster, 2010.

Jacobson, Laurie. *Hollywood Heartbreak.* New York: Simon & Schuster, 1984.

Jewell, Richard B. and Vernon Harbin. *The RKO Story.* New York: Arlington House, 1982.

Jones, Anderson and David Fields (photographs). *Men Together: Portraits of Love, Commitment, and Life.* Philadelphia: Running Press, 1997.

Jorgensen, Jay. *Edith Head: The Fifty-Year Career of Hollywood's Greatest Costume Designer.* New York: Running Press, 2010.

Kael, Pauline. *Kiss Kiss Bang Bang.* New York: Bantam, 1969.

Kanin, Garson. *Together Again! Stories of the Great Hollywood Teams.* Garden City, NY: Doubleday, 1981.

Karney, Robyn, editor. *The Movie Stars Story.* New York: Crescent Books, 1984.

Kass, Judith M. *The Films of Montgomery Clift.* Secaucus, NJ: Citadel, 1979.

Kay, Karyn. *Myrna Loy.* New York: Pyramid, 1977.

Kellow, Brian. *The Bennetts: An Acting Family.* Lexington: University Press of Kentucky, 2004.

Kennedy, Harold J. *No Pickle, No Performance.* New York: Berkley, 1979.

Kennedy, Matthew. *Edmund Goulding's Dark Victory.* Madison: University of Wisconsin Press, 2004.

Kennedy, Rose Fitzgerald. *Times to Remember.* New York: Doubleday, 1974.

Kessler, Ronald. *Sins of the Father: Joseph P. Kennedy and the Dynasty He Founded.* New York: Warner Books, 1996.

Kidd, Charles. *Debrett Goes to Hollywood.* New York: St. Martin's Press, 1986.

Kinn, Gail and Jim Piazza. *The Academy Awards.* New York: Barnes & Noble Books, 2002.

Klein, Edward. *All Too Human: The Love Story of Jack and Jackie Kennedy.* New York: Pocket Books, 1996.

Klepper, Robert K. *Silent Films 1877–1996: A Critical Guide to 646 Movies.* Jefferson, NC: McFarland, 1999.

Kobal, John. *People Will Talk.* New York: Alfred A. Knopf, 1985.

Kobal, John and V. A. Wilson. *Foyer Pleasure: The Golden Age of Cinema Lobby Cards.* London: Aurum Press, 1982.

Kobel, Peter and The Library of Congress. *Silent Movies: The Birth of Film and the Triumph of Movie Culture.* New York: Little, Brown, 2007.

Koskoff, David E. *Joseph P. Kennedy: A Life and Times.* Englewood Cliffs, NJ: Prentice-Hall, Inc., 1974.

Koszarski, Richard. *The Astoria Studio and Its Fabulous Films.* New York: Dover, 1983.

———. *Hollywood on the Hudson: Film and Television in New York from Griffith to Sarnoff.* Piscataway, NJ: Rutgers University Press: 2008.

———. *Von: The Life and Films of Erich von Stroheim.* New York: Limelight/Proscenium, 2001.

Koszarski, Richard, editor. *Great American Film Directors in Photographs.* New York: Dover, 1984.

Koszarski, Richard, introduction. *The Men with the Movie Cameras.* Brookline, MA: Film Comment, 1972.

Kreuger, Miles, editor. *The Movie Musical From Vitaphone to 42nd Street.* New York: Dover, 1975.

Lacey, Madison S. and Don Morgan. *Hollywood Cheesecake: 60 Years of Leg Art.* Secaucus, NJ: Citadel, 1981.

LaGuardia, Robert. *Monty: A Biography of Montgomery Clift.* New York: Arbor House, 1977.

Lally, Kevin. *Wilder Times: The Life of Billy Wilder.* New York: Henry Holt, 1996.

Lambert, Gavin. *Nazimova: A Biography.* New York: Alfred A. Knopf, 1997.

———. *Norma Shearer.* New York: Alfred A. Knopf, 1990.

Lamparski, Richard. *Lamparski's Hidden Hollywood: Where the Stars Lived, Loved and Died.* New York: Simon & Schuster, 1981.

———. *Manhattan Diary.* Albany, GA: BearManor Media, 2006.

———. *Whatever Became of . . . ?* New York: Ace, 1970.

———. *Whatever Became of . . . ? (Fourth Series).* New York: Bantam, 1975.

———. *Whatever Became of . . . ? (Eighth Series).* New York: Crown, 1982.

———. *Whatever Became of . . . ? (Ninth Series).* New York: Crown, 1985.

LaSalle, Mick. *Complicated Women: Sex and Power and Pre-Code Hollywood.* New York: Thomas Dunne Books, 2000.

Lasky, Betty. *RKO: The Biggest Little Major of Them All.* Englewood Cliffs, NJ: Prentice-Hall, 1984.

Lasky, Jesse L. *Whatever Happened to Hollywood?* New York: Funk & Wagnall, 1973.

Lawford, Patricia Seaton and Ted Schwarz. *The Peter Lawford Story: Life with the Kennedys, Monroe, and the Rat Pack.* New York: Carroll & Graf, 1988.

Lawton, Richard. *Grand Illusions.* New York: Bonanza, 1994.

Learner, Laurence. *The Kennedy Men 1901–1963.* New York: William Morrow, 2001

———. *The Kennedy Women: The Saga of an American Family.* New York: Faber and Faber, 2003.

Leese, Elizabeth. *Costume Design in the Movies.* New York: Frederick Ungar, 1983.

Leider, Emily W. *Dark Lover: The Life and Death of Rudolph Valentino.* New York: Faber and Faber, 2003.

Lennig, Arthur. *Stroheim.* Lexington: University Press of Kentucky, 2000.

Leonard, Maurice. *Mae West: Empress of Sex.* New York: Birch Lane Press, 1991.

LeRoy, Mervyn and Dick Kleiner. *Mervyn LeRoy: Take One.* New York: Hawthorne, 1980.

Levin, Martin, editor. *Hollywood and the Great Fan Magazines.* New York. Arbor House, 1970.

Linet, Beverly. *Ladd: A Hollywood Tragedy.* New York: Berkley, 1978.

Lloyd, Ann. *Movies of the Forties.* London: Orbis, 1982.

Loew, Rachel. *Film Making in the 1930s Britain.* London: Allen & Unwin, 1985.

Loos, Anita. *Kiss Hollywood Good-bye.* New York: Viking, 1974.

———. *The Talmadge Girls: A Memoir.* New York: Viking, 1978.

Lord, Walter. *A Night to Remember—Illustrated Edition.* New York: Bantam, 1978.

Louvish, Simon. *Cecil B. DeMille: A Life in Art.* New York: Thomas Dunne Books, 2007.

———. *Keystone: The Life and Clowns of Mack Sennett.* New York: Faber and Faber, 2003.

Macpherson, Don and Julie Welch, Louise Brody. *Stars of the Screen.* London: Octopus, 1989.

Madsen, Axel. *Gloria and Joe.* New York: Berkley, 1989.

———. *The Sewing Circle.* New York: Birch Lane Press, 2005.

Mahar, Karen Ward. *Women Filmmakers in Early Hollywood.* Baltimore, MD: John Hopkins University Press, 2006.

Maier, Thomas. *The Kennedys: America's Emerald Kings.* New York: Basic Books, 2003.

Maltin, Leonard. *The Art of the Cinematographer.* New York: Dover, 1978.

———. *Carole Lombard.* New York: Pyramid, 1976.

———. *The Real Stars.* New York: Curtis, 1973.

Mann, William C. *Behind the Screen: How Gays and Lesbians Shaped Hollywood 1910–1969.* New York: Viking, 2001.

———. *Kate: The Woman Who Was Hepburn.* New York: Henry Holt, 2006.

———. *Wisecracker: The Life and Times of William Haines, Hollywood's First Openly Gay Star.* New York: Viking, 1998.

Marshall, Peter and Adrienne Armstrong. *Backstage with the Original Hollywood Squares.* Nashville, TN: Rutledge Hill Press, 2002.

Maturi, Richard J. and Mary Buckingham Maturi. *Francis X. Bushman: A Biography and Filmography.* Jefferson, NC: McFarland, 1998.

McClelland, Doug. *Hollywood on Hollywood: Tinseltown Talks.* Boston: Faber and Faber, 1985.

———. *Hollywood Talks Turkey: The Screen's Greatest Flops.* Boston: Faber and Faber, 1989.

McDonald, Gerald D. and Michael Conway, Mark Ricci. *The Films of Charlie Chaplin.* New York: Bonanza, 1965.

Medved, Harry and Randy Dreyfuss. *The Fifty Worst Films of All Time.* New York: Popular Library, 1978.

Meyer, John. *Heartbreaker: My Life with Judy Garland.* London: W. A. Allen, 1987.

Michael, Paul, editor-in-chief. *The American Movies Reference Book: The Sound Era.* Englewood Cliffs, NJ: Prentice-Hall, Inc., 1969.

Moore, Colleen. *Silent Star.* Garden City, NY: Doubleday, 1968.

Mordden, Ethan. *The Hollywood Studios: House Style in the Golden Age of the Movies.* New York: Alfred A. Knopf, 1988.

———. *Movie Star: A Look at the Women Who Made Hollywood.* New York: St. Martin's Press, 1983.

Morehouse, Ward and Ward Morehouse III. *Broadway After Dark.* Albany, GA: BearManor Media, 2007.

Morella, Joe, Edward Z. Epstein, and John Griggs. *The Films of World War II.* Secaucus, NJ: Citadel, 1973.

Morley, Margaret. *The Films of Laurence Olivier.* Secaucus, NJ: Citadel, 1977.

Morley, Sheridan. *The Other Side of the Moon: A Biography of David Niven.* New York: Harper & Row, 1985.

Morris, Michael. *Madam Valentino: The Many Lives of Natacha Rambova.* New York: Abbeville Press, 1991.

Moss, Marilyn Ann. *Raoul Walsh: The True Adventures of Hollywood's Legendary Director.* Lexington: University Press of Kentucky, 2011.

Negri, Pola. *Memoirs of a Star.* Garden City, NY: Doubleday, 1970.

Nelson, Al P. and Mel R. Jones. *A Silent Siren Song: The Aitken Brothers' Hollywood Odyssey, 1905–1926.* New York: Cooper Square Press, 2000.

Niven, David. *The Moon's a Balloon.* New York: Dell, 1983

Oberfirst, Robert. *Rudolph Valentino: The Man Behind the Myth.* New York: Citadel, 1962.

Osborne, Robert. *80 Years of the Oscar: The Official History of the Academy Awards.* New York: Abbeville Press, 2008.

Osborne, Robert, foreword, and Molly Haskell, introduction. *Leading Ladies: The 50 Most Unforgettable Actresses of the Studio Era.* San Francisco: Chronicle Books, 2006.

Paris, Barry. *Louise Brooks.* New York: Alfred A. Knopf, 1989.

Parish, James Robert. *The Best of MGM: The Golden Years: 1928–1959.* Westport, CT: Arlington House, 1981.

———. *The Debonairs.* New Rochelle, NY: Arlington House, 1975.

———. *The Golden Era: The MGM Stock Company.* New Rochelle, NY: Arlington House, 1975.

———. *Hollywood Divas: The Good, the Bad, and the Fabulous.* New York: Contemporary, 2003.

———. *Hollywood Players: The Thirties.* New Rochelle, NY: Arlington House, 1991.

———. *The Hollywood Reliables.* Westport, CT: Arlington House, 1980.

———. *The Hollywood Songsters: A Biographical Dictionary.* New York: Garland, 1991.

———. *The Paramount Pretties.* New Rochelle, NY: Arlington House, 1972.

———. *The RKO Gals.* New Rochelle, NY: Arlington House, 1974.

———. *The Tough Guys.* New Rochelle, NY: Arlington House, 1976.

———. *The Slapstick Queens.* New York: A. S. Barnes, 1973.

Pasternak, Joe as told to David Chandler. *Easy the Hard Way.* New York: G. P. Putnam's Sons, 1956.

Peary, Danny. *Cult Movies: The Classics, the Sleepers, the Weird, and the Wonderful.* New York: Dell, 1981.

Peary, Danny, editor. *Close-Ups: The Movie Star Book.* New York: Workman, 1978.

Peters, Margot. *The House of Barrymore.* New York: Simon & Schuster, 1990.

Petro, Patrice. *Idols of Modernity: Movie Stars of the 1920s.* Piscataway, NJ: Rutgers University Press, 2010.

Philips, Baxter. *Cut: The Unseen Cinema.* New York: Bounty Books, 1975.

Pitts Jr., Leonard. *Glamour Girls of Hollywood.* Cresskill, NJ: Sharon Publications Inc., 1984.

Prouty, Howard H., compiler. *Variety Television Reviews Volume 1 Daily Variety 1946–1956 and Variety 1923–1988.* New York: Garland, 1989.

———. *Variety Television Reviews Volume 2 Daily Variety 1957–1960 and Variety 1923–1988.* New York: Garland, 1989.

———. *Variety Television Reviews Volume 3 Daily Variety 1923–1950 and Variety 1923–1988.* New York: Garland, 1989.

———. *Variety Television Reviews Volume 4 Daily Variety 1951–1953 and Variety 1923–1988.* New York: Garland, 1989.

———. *Variety Television Reviews Volume 6 Daily Variety 1957–1959 and Variety 1923–1988.* New York: Garland, 1989.

———. *Variety Television Reviews Volume 8 Daily Variety 1963–1965 and Variety 1923–1988.* New York: Garland, 1989.

———. *Variety Television Reviews Volume 10 Daily Variety 1970–1973 and Variety 1923–1988.* New York: Garland, 1989.

———. *Variety Television Reviews Volume 15 Daily Variety 1946–1960 and Variety 1923–1988.* New York: Garland, 1991.

Quirk, Lawrence J. *Fasten Your Seatbelts: The Passionate Life of Bette Davis.* New York: Signet, 1990.

———. *The Films of Gloria Swanson.* Secaucus, NJ: Citadel, 1973.

———. *The Films of William Holden.* Secaucus, NJ: Citadel, 1973.

———. *The Kennedys in Hollywood.* Dallas, TX: Taylor, 1996.

———. *Norma: The Story of Norma Shearer.* New York: St. Martin's Press, 1988.

Ramer, Jan. *The Naked Truth About Hollywood: Hottest Secrets.* New York: Award Books, 1974.

Randall, Stephen, editor, and the editors of Playboy. *The Playboy Interviews—The Directors.* Milwaukee, OR: M Press, 2006.

Ringgold, Gene and DeWitt Bodeen. *The Films of Cecil B. DeMille.* New York: Cadillac, 1969.

Robinson, David. *Hollywood in the Twenties.* New York: Paperback Library, 1970.

Robinson, David and Ann Lloyd, editors. *Movies of the Silent Years.* London: Orbis, 1984.

Rogers St. Johns, Adela. *Love, Laughter and Tears: My Hollywood Story.* New York: Signet, 1979.

Rogers, Ginger. *Ginger: My Story.* New York: HarperCollins, 1991.

Rosen, Marjorie. *Popcorn Venus: Women, Movies and the American Dream.* New York: Avon, 1973.

Rosenberg, Bernard and Harry Silverstein. *The Real Tinsel.* New York: Macmillan, 1970.

Roston, Leo C. *Hollywood the Movie Colony: The Movie Makers.* New York: Harcourt, Brace, 1941.

Russell, Rosalind and Chris Chase. *Life is a Banquet.* New York: Ace, 1979.

Sarris, Andrew. *The American Cinema: Directors and Directions 1929–1968.* New York: E. P. Dutton, 1968.

Schanke, Robert A. *Shattered Applause: The Eva Le Gallienne Story.* New York: Barricade, 1992.

Scherman, David E., editor. *Life Goes to the Movies.* New York: Time-Life Books, 1975.

Schessler, Kenneth. *This Is Hollywood: An Unusual Movieland Guide.* La Verne, CA: Gresha Publications, 1979.

Schickel, Richard. *The Men Who Made the Movies.* New York: Atheneum, 1975.

———. *The Stars: The Personalities Who Made the Movies.* New York: Bonanza, 1962.

Schulberg, Budd. *Moving Pictures: Memoirs of a Hollywood Prince.* New York: Stein & Day, 1982.

Schuler, Robert C. *The Diva and I: My Life with Metropolitan Opera Star Patrice Munsel.* Bloomington, IN: AuthorHouse, 2007.

Sennett, Mack, as told to Cameron Shipp. *King of Comedy.* San Francisco: Mercury House, 990.

Sennett, Robert S. *Hollywood Hoopla: Creating and Selling Movies in the Golden Age of Hollywood.* New York: Billboard, 1998.

Shearer, Stephen Michael. *Beautiful: The Life of Hedy Lamarr.* New York: Thomas Dunne Books, 2010.

———. *Patricia Neal: An Unquiet Life.* Lexington: University Press of Kentucky, 2006.

Shipman, David. *The Great Movie Stars: The Golden Years.* New York: Bonanza, 1970.

———. *Movie Talk: Who Said What About Whom in the Movies.* New York: St. Martin's Press, 1988.

Shorris, Sylvia and Marion Abbott Bundy. *Talking Pictures with the People Who Made Them.* New York: New Press, 1994.

Shulman, Irving. *On Sunset Boulevard: The Life and Times of Billy Wilder.* New York: Hyperion, 1998.

———. *Valentino.* New York: Pocket Books, 1968.

Sikov, Ed. *Dark Victory: The Life of Bette Davis.* New York: Henry Holt, 2007.

Silver, Alain and Elizabeth Ward, editors. *Film Noir: An Encyclopedic Reference to the American Style.* Woodstock, NY: Overlook, 1979.

Slide, Anthony and Edward Wagenknecht. *Fifty Great American Silent Films 1912–1920: A Pictorial Survey.* New York: Dover, 1980.

Smith, Amanda, editor. *Hostage to Fortune: The Letters of Joseph P. Kennedy.* New York: Viking, 2001.

Somerset-Ward, Richard. *An American Theatre: The Story of Westport Country Playhouse.* New Haven, CT: Yale University Press, 2005.

Spada, James. *Peter Lawford: The Man Who Kept the Secrets.* New York: Bantam, 1992.

Springer, John and Jack Hamilton. *They Had Faces Then.* Secaucus, NJ: Citadel, 1978.

Staggs, Sam. *All About All About Eve.* New York: St. Martin's Press, 2001.

———. *Close-Up on Sunset Boulevard.* New York: St. Martin's Press, 2002.

Stallings, Penny and Howard Mandelbaum. *Flesh and Fantasy.* New York: St. Martin's Press, 1978.

Stapley, Richard. *The Slip and Fall in L.A.* Unpublished manuscript, 2004.

Steichen, Edward. *Steichen: A Life in Photography.* New York: Harmony, 1985.

Steiger, Brad and Chaw Mack. *Valentino: An Intimate and Shocking Expose.* New York: Macfadden, 1966.

Stenn, David. *Clara Bow: Running Wild.* Garden City, NY: Doubleday, 1988.

Sterling, Bryan B. and Frances N. Sterling. *Will Rogers in Hollywood.* New York: Crown, 1984.

Stevens Jr., George, editor. *Conversations with the Great Moviemakers of Hollywood's Golden Age.* New York: Alfred A. Knopf, 2006.

Stine, Whitney. *Stars and Their Handlers: The Business of Show.* Santa Monica, CA: Roundtable Publishing, Inc., 1985.

Stine, Whitney and Bette Davis. *Mother Goddam.* New York: Berkley, 1975.

Strick, Philip. *Great Movie Actresses.* New York: William Morrow, 1984.

Stuart, Gloria and Sylvia Thompson. *I Just Kept Hoping.* New York: Little, Brown, 1999.

Stuart, Ray. *Immortals of the Screen.* New York: Bonanza, 1965.

Stuart, Sandra Lee and John Prince. *The Pink Palace: Behind Closed Doors at the Beverly Hills Hotel.* Fort Lee, NJ: Barricade, 1993.

Swanson, Gloria. *Swanson on Swanson.* New York: Random House, 1980.

Swindell, Larry. *Screwball: The Life of Carole Lombard.* New York: William Morrow, 1975.

Tajiri, Vincent. *Valentino: The True Life Story.* New York: Bantam, 1977.

Tanitch, Robert. *Olivier.* New York: Abbeville Press, 1985.

Tapert, Annette. *The Power of Glamour: The Women Who Defined the Magic of Stardom.* New York: Crown, 1998.

Taraborrelli, J. Randy. *The Secret Life of Marilyn Monroe.* New York: Grand Central, 2009.

Taylor, Deems and Marcelene Peterson and Bryant Hale. *A Pictorial History of the Movies.* New York: Simon & Schuster, 1943.

Thomas, Bob. *Golden Boy: The Untold Story of William Holden.* New York: St. Martin's Press, 1983.

———. *Joan Crawford: A Biography.* New York: Simon & Schuster, 1978.

———. *King Cohn: The Life and Times of Harry Cohn.* New York: G. P. Putnam's Sons, 1967.

Thornton, Michael. *Jessie Matthews.* St. Albans, UK: Granada, 1974.

Tornabene, Lyn. *Long Live the King: A Biography of Clark Gable.* New York: G. P. Putnam's Sons, 1976.

Turk, Edward Baron. *Hollywood Diva: A Biography of Jeanette MacDonald.* Berkeley: University of California Press, 1998.

Tuttle, Frank and John Charles Franceschina. *They Started Talking.* Albany, GA: BearManor Media, 2004.

TV Guide 25 Years Index. New York: Triangle Publications, 1979.

Vallee, Eleanor and Jill Amadio. *My Vagabond Lover: An Intimate Biography of Rudy Vallee.* Dallas, TX: Taylor, 1996

Vance, Jeffrey. *Douglas Fairbanks.* Berkeley: University of California Press, 2008.

Ventavoli, Bruno. *Al diavolo la celebrita (To Hell With the Celebrities).* Torino, Italy: Lindau Publishers, 1999.

Vermilye, Jerry. *The Complete Films of Audrey Hepburn: Her Life and Her Career.* New York: Citadel, 1995.

———. *The Complete Films of Laurence Olivier.* New York: Carol Publishing Group, 1992.

———. *The Films of the Twenties.* Secaucus, NJ: Citadel, 1985.

Vieira, Mark A. *Hollywood Dreams Made Real: Irving Thalberg and the Rise of M-G-M.* New York: Harry N. Abrams, 2008.

———. *Hurrell's Hollywood Portraits.* New York: Harry N. Abrams, 1997.

———. *Irving Thalberg: Boy Wonder to Producer Prince.* Berkeley: University of California Press, 2010.

Vieira, Mark A. and Darrell Rooney. *Harlow in Hollywood: The Blonde Bombshell in the Glamour Capital 1928–1937.* Santa Monica, CA: Angel City Press, 2011.

Vogel, Michelle. *Marjorie Main: The Life and Films of Hollywood's "Ma Kettle."* Jefferson, NC: McFarland, 2006.

Wallace, David. *Exiles in Hollywood.* Pompton Plains, NJ: Limelight, 2006.

Wanamaker, Marc, editor. *The Hollywood Reporter Star Profiles.* New York: Gallery Books, 1984.

Watkins, Mel. *Stepin Fetchit: The Life and Times of Lincoln Perry.* New York: Pantheon, 2005.

Watson. Coy Jr. *The Keystone Kid: Tales of Early Hollywood.* Santa Monica, CA: Santa Monica Press, 2001.

Wayne, Jane Ellen. *Crawford's Men.* New York: Prentice-Hall, 1988.

———. *Gable's Women.* New York: Prentice-Hall, 1987.

Webb, Michael, editor. *Hollywood: Legend and Reality.* Boston: Little, Brown, 1986.

Weinberg, Herman G. *Stroheim: A Pictorial Record of His Nine Films.* New York: Dover, 1975.

Westmore, Frank and Muriel Davidson. *The Westmores of Hollywood.* New York: Berkley, 1978.

Whalen, Richard J. *The Founding Father: The Story of Joseph P. Kennedy.* New York: New American Library, 1964.

Whitelaw, Arthur. *Working for Peanuts.* Unpublished manuscript, 2011.

Whitfield, Eileen. *Pickford: The Woman Who Made Hollywood.* Lexington: University Press of Kentucky, 1997.

Wiley, Mason and Damien Bona. *Inside Oscar: The Unofficial History of the Academy Awards.* New York: Ballantine, 1987.

Wilkerson, Tichi and Marcia Borie. *The Hollywood Reporter: The Golden Years.* New York: Arlington House, 1984.

Williams, Iain Cameron. *Underneath a Harlem Moon: The Harlem to Paris Years of Adelaide Hall.* New York: Continuum, 2002.

Wilson, Arthur. *The Warner Bros. Golden Anniversary Book.* New York: Dell, 1973.

Windeler, Robert. *Sweetheart: The Story of Mary Pickford.* New York: Praeger, 1974.

Wray, Fay. *On the Other Hand: A Life Story.* New York: St. Martin's Press, 1989.

Ziegfeld, Richard and Paulette Ziegfeld. *The Ziegfeld Touch: The Life and Times of Florenz Ziegfeld Jr.* New York: Harry N. Abrams, 1993.

Zierold, Norman. *The Moguls.* New York: Avon, 1972.

Zolotow, Maurice. *Billy Wilder in Hollywood.* New York: G. P. Putnam's Sons, 1977.

Zukor, Adolph and Dale Kramer. *The Public Is Never Wrong.* New York: G. P. Putnam's Sons, 1953.

Acknowledgments

A biography is the final work of many. For their assistance, knowledge, generosity, efforts, and consideration I would like to thank the following:

First and foremost, my deepest appreciation to Steve Wilson and his staff, including Kristin Ware, Debbie Smith, Albert Palacios, Lynne McPhies, Emilio Banda, Moses Lira, Richard Mikel, and Ms. Carlos King, at the Harry Ransom Center at the University of Texas at Austin. This is where I spent untold hours wading through the some 600 boxes which comprise the Gloria Swanson Collection so meticulously archived by her close friend, the late curator Raymond Daum. Mr. Wilson and his generous staff have made a researcher's work a dream and a pleasure.

I approached Jeanine Basinger, Crown-Fuller Professor of Film Studies, and founder and curator of the Cinema Archives at Wesleyan University, Middletown, Connecticut, to write the Foreword to this book after she had written a positive and much appreciated review in *The Wall Street Journal* of my book *Beautiful: The Life of Hedy Lamarr*. Ms. Basinger, whose work I have long admired, is a brilliant film historian. To her and Lea Carlson, associate director, Center for Film Studies at Wesleyan University, I give my sincere and humble thanks.

I am indebted to all those individuals who knew and loved Gloria Swanson, and to members of her family, Michelle Farmer Amon, Gloria's daughter, and

Brooke Anderson Young, Gloria's granddaughter. Their recent interviews offered up telling and loving memories.

Most certainly I wish to express my gratitude to Dirk Benedict, whose professional and personal relationship with Swanson goes beyond fact. Gloria and her last husband William Dufty became Benedict's "stage parents," people who loved and cared for his well-being. Swanson and Dufty generously took the young actor under their wing in the early 1970s, nurtured him, and gave him a life-altering knowledge of wholesome health and living, literally transforming his mental and physical being, inspiring him to become a survivor. Dirk Benedict's introspective memories of Swanson and Dufty, as painful and cleansing as they were in his sharing, are sincerely appreciated.

For their personal memories of William Dufty, I would like to thank his son Bevan Dufty, whose stories about his father were kind and considerate; Dennis Fairchild, who shared the last twenty years of Dufty's life—his memories were especially tender and protective; and to Timothy Rooks, whose love and appreciation of William Dufty echo the words and thoughts of everyone who knew the man.

I would like to thank those people who worked professionally with Gloria Swanson and graciously allowed me their time to reminisce about a glamorous and exciting, glittering era of film and television: Roy Thinnes, Gary Conway, Arlene Dahl, Arthur Whitelaw, David Braden, Max Baer Jr., Mike Connors, the late Phyllis Diller, Barbara Eden, Brenda Scott Hargrove, Linda Harrison, Jayne Meadows Allen, Patrice Munsel, Rex Reed, Regis Philbin, Robert Vaughn, Barbara Walters, Carl Reiner, Nancy Olson, Tony Lovello, Julius LaRosa, Carol Burnett, the late Marvin Hamlisch, Larry Flynt, Jackie De Shannon, Richard Chamberlain, Pat Boone, and Phyllis McGuire.

My research has been conducted at various archives and libraries listed below. I am beholding to the following individuals and institutions:

In New York and New Jersey: Jeremy McGraw, John Calhoun, Reference Librarian, and the staff of the New York City Public Library of the Performing Arts, Lincoln Center, New York; Tad Nadan, Lee Spilberg, and Thomas Lannon, the New York Public Library, Manuscripts and Archives Division; Charles Silver, film curator, and the staff at the Museum of Modern Art film archive; Howard and Ronald Mandelbaum of Photofest; Jerry Ohlinger's Movie Memorabilia Store; Julia Strohmeyer, Bill Gaiton, and the staff of the Fort Lee Public Library, Fort Lee, New Jersey; the reference staff of the Little Ferry, New Jersey, Public Library; Dennis Doros and Amy Heller at Milestone Films, Harrington Park, New Jersey; Eve Golden at the Everett Collection; Edmund Rosenkrantz of Migdal, Pollack, Rosenkrantz and Sherman (Swanson Collection/Gloria Swanson Inc.); and the following individuals: Mark Monteverdi for his research on Swanson's home on Long Island, Christa Venezia, Julie Wilson, Robert Osborne, the late Mike Wallace, Tracy Christensen, Molly Haskell, Joe Franklin, Stephen Sondheim for his background on the history of *Follies*, and Wayne Lawson.

In California: First and foremost, the brilliant Ned Comstock at the University of Southern California (USC) Cinema-TV Library, who is *the* curator of film history, a diligent, knowledgeable, and persistent friend to any serious film scholar; Sandra Aquilar, curator, and Jonathon Auxier at the University of Southern California (USC) Warner Bros. Archives; Barbara Hall, Christine Kreuger, and Jenny Romero, and the staff of Margaret Herrick Library of the Academy of Motion Picture Arts and Sciences, Fairbanks Library; B. Caroline Sisneros and the staff of the Louis B. Mayer Library at the American Film Institute; Mark Quigley at the University of California Los Angeles Media Lab; Mark Echeverria, owner and proprietor of the Musso and Frank Grill; Jonathon Foerstel of the *LA Time Machine*; Jeffrey Mantor, Mike Hawks, and Flash at Larry Edmunds Bookshop; the ultimate bookstore proprietor Dennis Wills of D. G. Wills Books, La Jolla; and the following individuals: Leonard Maltin, Derrik Lewis, Richard Leibell, Luke Yankee, Alan Eichler, Margaret O'Brien, Rhonda Fleming, A. C. Lyles, Betty Lasky, Betty White, Tab Hunter, and Rose Marie Guy.

In Nevada: Corinne Entratter Sidney, David Stevenson, Beverly Washburn, and Esther Lynn.

In Great Britain: Kathleen Dickson, Jose de Esteban, and Natasha Fairbaim at the British Film Institute, London; and Kevin Brownlow.

In Italy: the staff of the Biblioteca Centrale-Palazzo Sormani di Milano, Milan.

In France: Brigitte Bardot.

In Minnesota and Wisconsin: Maxine Ducey, Dorinda Hartman, Lee Grady,

Spencer Brayton, and the staff of the Wisconsin Center for Film and Theater Research, Film and Theater Archive, at the Wisconsin Historical Society, Madison, Wisconsin (the Daniel Blum Collection and the William P. Philips Collection); and the following individuals: Janet Waller, manager of Barnes and Noble Booksellers, Har-Mar Mall, Roseville, Minnesota; and Tom Letness, owner of the Heights Theater, Columbia Heights, Minnesota.

In Utah: James D'Arc, Russ Taylor, and the staff of the special collections holdings (the DeMille Archives) of the L. Tom Perry Special Collections at the Brigham Young University, Provo, Utah.

In Washington State: Randall and Loretta Hucks.

For their help and assistance in translation, I wish to give sincere thanks to Tony Morris, my oldest and dearest friend for more years than one can count, for translating the French; Italian film historian Giovanni Secchi for not only researching Swanson's work in Italy, but also for translating the Italian; and for his knowledge of Spanish, Jack Cagle.

Special thanks and appreciation to my brother, Michael Dean Sypult, pastor, educator, railroad historian, and webmaster of the Arkansas Boston Mountains Chapter of the National Railway Historical Society in Springdale, Arkansas; Sylvia and Chris Mackey, owners, and Roseanne Steele, innkeeper, of the Austin Folk House, Austin, Texas; Mariusz Kotowski and Naomi Emmerson at Bright Shining City, Austin, Texas; Michael Ankerich; RLN; Scott O'Brien; Lon and Deb Davis; Mark Lynch at WICN Radio; and Trudy Collins and Anthony Macchio for their generosity, hospitality and friendship. To those I may have failed to mention I offer my apologies and gratitude.

My sincere thanks to my literary agent, Deborah Ritchken, and to Julie Castiglia of the Castiglia Literary Agency in Del Mar, California. At Thomas Dunne/St. Martin's Press, I would like to thank my publisher, Thomas Dunne, for understanding what dedicated biography is about. To my editor, Peter Joseph, my undying gratitude for his patience and understanding of my passion for Gloria Swanson. To Margaret Sutherland Brown, his assistant and editor, who never ceases to be helpful, and to art director Steve Snider, for his brilliant cover design, my nod of appreciation. Also, I would like to give my sincere thanks to my publicist, John Karle, for helping get the word out.

My special thanks to my extended church families of Saint Peter's Lutheran Church in New York, Grace in the Desert Episcopal Church in Las Vegas, and Central Lutheran Church in Minneapolis.

As always, I thank my family for their unlimited support. To my partner, Michael Wickman, and Maxwell and Madeleine for your patience, love and understanding, I give you my heart. And to the late Charlene Wickman, we miss you.

Index